Conversos, Inquisition, and the Expulsion of the Jews from Spain

T0295031

Publication of this volume has been made possible in part
by a grant from the Program for Cultural Cooperation Between
Spain's Ministry of Culture and United States' Universities

Conversos, Inquisition, and the Expulsion of the Jews from Spain

Norman Roth

The University of Wisconsin Press

The University of Wisconsin Press
1930 Monroe Street
Madison, Wisconsin 53711

www.wisc.edu/wisconsinpress/

3 Henrietta Street
London WC2E 8LU, England

Printed in the United States of America

Library of Congress Cataloging-in-Publication Data
Roth, Norman, 1938–
    Conversos, Inquisition, and the expulsion of the Jews from Spain / Norman Roth.
    446 p.   cm.
    Includes bibliographical references and index.
    ISBN 0-299-14230-2 (cloth)
    ISBN 0-299-14234-5 (pbk.)
    1. Jews—Spain—History. 2. Inquisition—Spain. 3. Marranos—Spain—
History. 4. Spain—History—711–1516. 5. Spain—Ethnic relations. I. Title.
DS135.S7R675   1995
946'.004924—dc20   94-23486

If there were an Inquisition in Castile many "Judaizers" would enter the flames and thus be saved from eternal fire

—Alonso del Espina

For the fire is lighted . . . it will burn until it reaches the extremes of the driest wood

—Andrés Bernáldez

Punishment should be reserved for the few conversos who have relapsed, but not for the many who have not; otherwise there would not be sufficient wood for the burning

—Fernando de Pulgar

And now in our time their smoke has ascended to the heavens in all the kingdoms of Spain and the isles; a third has been burned in fire, a third fled hither and thither, and the remainder lives in great fear and awesome timorousness from the dread of their hearts and vision of their eyes

—Isaac ʿArama

Contents

Contents

Acknowledgments

The great debt which any scholar of the Jewish civilization of medieval Spain owes to the many hundreds of Spanish scholars, living and dead, who have written so extensively on the subject is obvious.

Nevertheless, I should like to record my particular gratitude to at least some of the contemporary scholars, in Spain and in this country, who have so graciously assisted me with their friendship and support. These include Luis Suárez Fernández, Emilio Mitre, Miguel Ángel Ladero Quesada, Carlos del Valle, José Ramón Magdalena Nom de Déu, Miguel Ángel Motis Dolader, and my friends Antonio Collantes de Terán Sánchez and Isabel Montes Romero-Camacho who gave me so generously of their time in Seville, and many others.

Among scholars in America who deserve particular thanks are Brian Dutton, who constantly and generously assisted in the work on converso poets, and Robert I. Burns, S.J., and Thomas Glick for their reading of the manuscript and helpful suggestions.

A scholar who is able to work in an institution with an outstanding library is fortunate, indeed, and my gratitude to the University of Wisconsin Libraries in general, and to the interlibrary loan personnel in particular, is great. I am, however, particularly indebted to the gracious cooperation and generous help of a great many Spanish libraries and archives. I would particularly like to single out the entire staff of the famous Biblioteca Nacional in Madrid, but especially the rare book and manuscript department, as well as the libraries of the Universidad de Barcelona, the rare book and manuscript room of the Universidad de Salamanca, the libraries of the Consejo Superior de Investigaciones Científicas in Madrid, the courteous and always helpful staff of the private Ateneo library of Madrid, and especially the courtesy and efficiency of numerous local archivists (especially those of Burgos and Huesca), as well as even public municipal libraries such as Tarragona.

Generous grants from the famous Comité Conjunto and from the Consejo Superior de Investigaciones Científicas, although not limited specifically to the research for the present work, are gratefully acknowledged.

Finally, my sincere thanks to the University of Wisconsin Press for being willing to publish a work that other publishers refused even to consider, simply because of its length.

Introduction

The history of the Jews of Spain is a long and colorful one. It is perhaps not generally realized that Jews lived in Spain longer than they have lived in any other country, including their homeland (ancient Israel). For well over a thousand years Jews played a major role in the cultural and socioeconomic evolution of the Iberian Peninsula, first under the Visigoths, then the Muslims, and finally in "reconquered" Christian Spain. More Jews lived in Spain than in all of the countries of medieval Europe combined. In marked contrast to those lands, however, Spain's Jews were not concentrated primarily in a few major towns and cities, but lived in every village and town throughout the land, sometimes in dense populations and sometimes as few as two or three families in a town.

Culturally, of course, Jews achieved levels in Spain never before and never again attained. Here biblical commentary and the scientific study of the text were born; here, too, was the miraculous "renaissance" of the Hebrew language made possible by the creation of Hebrew grammar, which in turn gave birth to Hebrew secular poetry and literature on the Arabic model.[1]

Original Jewish contributions in the area of philosophy also came into being first in Muslim Spain, and continued in the later Christian period, with works in Arabic, Hebrew, Castilian and Catalan. Jews, indeed, apparently made the first contributions to written Spanish, certainly in the earliest biblical translations, and in other less complete forms.

Except for a relatively brief period of persecution (although greatly exaggerated in most accounts) when the Almohads invaded in the twelfth century, Jews lived generally in quite harmonious relations with their Muslim and Christian neighbors.

This cooperation in the cultural sphere may also be seen in the realms of science and medicine, where Jews soon played a major role. Virtually all of the most significant Jewish writers in the fields of astronomy, mathematics, geography, medicine, and other sciences in the medieval period were from Spain. Their importance was not merely as "transmitters" of Arabic knowledge, but also as original authors, for example of the majority of the scientific treatises of the so-called Alfonsine corpus (Alfonso X of Castile, who was merely the patron of these and other works ascribed to him).[2]

Jews were equally at home in the "secular" and "religious" spheres of study in Spain (a distinction most would not then have made), and it is important to realize that also the most renowned medieval Talmudic scholars, commentators, codifiers of law, etc., were Spanish Jews.

Precisely because of the harmonious relations and the general lack of discrimination, and certainly of persecution, it was also possible for Jews to attain positions of power and authority in the government at all levels, from tax officials and administrators of dukes and local overlords or ecclesiastical properties to the highest level of running the affairs of the kingdom. There was no distinction in this regard between the medieval kingdoms of Castile-León and of Aragón-Catalonia.

All of this remarkable history and culture came to an abrupt end in 1492 with the astonishing order expelling the Jews from all the (now united) Spanish kingdoms.

How this could have taken place is a topic of complex dimensions, the full consideration of which would involve nothing less than the study of the entire history of the Jews in medieval Spain. Indeed, the time has not yet arrived when such a comprehensive history can be written; meanwhile, I have set for myself the task, on which I have been occupied now for many years, of eventually dealing with the topic of intergroup relations among Jews, Muslims, and Christians in Spain. Until that study is completed, the present book provides a partial exposition of certain aspects of that problem, namely the issues of conversion, the Inquisition, and the expulsion of the Jews in the latter part of the medieval period.

The first topic to be considered is the nature of Jewish conversion to Christianity, beginning the fourteenth century. It will become apparent why, although there were certainly instances of conversion before that time, the role of the convert was entirely different then, and entirely different from what it had been in other lands. There still is enormous confusion, not only among laymen but also among scholars, about the conversos (Jewish converts) of medieval Spain. According to the romantic myth of "crypto-Judaism," it is apparently inconceivable that a Jew could willingly abandon his "faith" and become a Christian, under no pressure or duress whatever. Therefore, it is argued, such conversos certainly were forced, and in any case could not have believed in the Christian religion and so must have lived a life as "crypto," or secret, Jews. Their former coreligionists, furthermore, are presumed to have been in great sympathy with the plight of the conversos, and patiently waited (for centuries) for their "return" to the fold.

The facts present quite a different picture, however. Far from being sympathetic, the Jewish authorities knew that these conversos had deliberately and of their own free will abandoned not merely their faith but their people, as they said. That is, they had become complete Gentiles, and were no longer to be considered part of the Jewish people in any way. We shall see that this was not only true in the fifteenth century but was already the case with regard to the conversions of the fourteenth century.

The role of the conversos in Spanish society will also be examined here for the first time in detail. The rejection by Jews certainly did not disturb the conversos, for they considered themselves in fact to be true Christians and totally separated from Jewish society, for the most part. However, the increasing jealousy and then open persecution of the conversos by "old Christians," i.e., Christians by birth, became a major problem. At last, in the mid-fifteenth century, this gave rise to actual open warfare between the "old" and the "new" Christians. Kings were involved; armies fought; certain modern weapons of war were used for the first time; cities were besieged; and finally the conversos concocted a scheme to have their own state, a scheme which is stranger than any modern novel (or novels passing as history) could invent.

However, the conversos are not only important as a subtopic of the history of the Jews of Spain; they also played a major role, if not *the* major role, in the development of Spanish poetry and literature in what has been termed the "Golden Age" of that literature, already beginning with the fifteenth century. (How ironic it is, perhaps, that the greatest period of Jewish cultural achievement is popularly called the "Golden Age" of Spanish Jewry, while the "Golden Age" of Spanish literature is chiefly the product of the converso enemies of Jewish culture!)

Not only literature and poetry, however, but also anti-Jewish polemical works, historical chronicles, philosophical writing, etc., were produced by conversos. Each of these subjects, as well as the nature of "humanism" in converso thought, is dealt with all too briefly and inadequately in the pages of this book, since each deserves a book by itself. Surprisingly, however, no attempt has hitherto been made to undertake this task at all, and it is hoped that this book will at least point the way for future research in these areas.

Much of the converso literature has great merit in itself as literature (the first modern play in any language, the *Celestina,* was a product of conversos, for example). However, equally important for our purposes, much of that literature, particularly the poetry, reveals the tensions of the world of the conversos and the polemics which they generated. Virtually none of this has been previously discussed, and attention is called to some of these poems for the first time.

The Inquisition is a subject about which, of course, a good deal has been written, but not always in a very enlightening way. The problem with most, if not all, of the work done since the last century is that each book attempts to deal with the entire history of the Inquisition, whether for a town or a region, from what the author assumes was its origin until the modern period (the Inquisition in Spain continued down to the nineteenth century). The result, predictably, is rather like undertaking to write the history of the world in two hundred pages.

My treatment of the Inquisition here is more narrowly focused. It does, in the first place, what no other study so far has done, and that is to connect the later-fifteenth-century Inquisition with its predecessor in Aragón-

Catalonia. Second, the focus is on the relation of Jews to the Inquisition and on the testimony concerning conversos in the period prior to the Expulsion only. Sources which, for one reason or another, have hitherto been ignored in other studies are therefore taken into consideration. Nevertheless, obviously this cannot pretend to anything like a complete treatment. Again, it may help open the way to further investigation.

If myth and even bias have distorted the understanding of the situation of the conversos and the Inquisition, this is certainly also the case with regard to the Expulsion. There is no correct or unbiased account of it in any language. Baer failed to present the facts and evidence completely and accurately. This has, in turn, led his disciples (Netanyahu, Beinart, and others) to label one or both of the Catholic Monarchs "bigot," "fanatic," etc. The cold evidence simply does not support any such characterization, and in fact totally contradicts such judgments. It is hardly surprising, however, that once again the general public operates under the assumption that Fernando and Isabel secretly contrived a plot to eliminate the Jews from Spain.

It is unfortunate, again, that the confines of space do not permit here the full and complete presentation of the true story of the attitudes and actions of the Catholic Monarchs with regard to the Jews, details of which must again be reserved for my future book. Nevertheless, it is possible to present enough of that part of the story strictly dealing with the period just before the Expulsion and the event itself, to demonstrate how completely false previous understanding of the question has generally been.

An important, and hitherto little-emphasized, characteristic of fifteenth-century Spanish Jewry was the almost complete lack of leadership. Here again, myth and romanticization have stepped in to create what in reality never was. We shall see men like Isaac Abravanel, in fact by his *own admission* solely concerned with his own power and wealth (and this is, indeed, supported by the documents which all who have written on him have ignored), being portrayed as "champions" of the Jews making noble efforts to annul the edict of expulsion. Even worse, Alfonso de la Caballería, the *grandson* of a converso, is falsely portrayed as a "hero" of the Jewish people on the basis of a mere rumor that he likewise tried to obtain the nullification of the decree—and this in the face of the testimony of a member of his own family (if we did not already know this from other sources as well) that he was an enemy of the Jews who, in fact, urged their expulsion.

The tragic lack of Jewish leadership in the fifteenth century was in marked contrast to the earlier period. It was a foreboding, indeed, of the centuries to come after the Expulsion. Never again did the Jewish people recover its effective and foresighted leadership until, possibly, the nineteenth century. In the horrendous period of the Khemilniki massacres in Poland and the Ukraine in 1648, no leadership whatever was to be found in the Jewish world. Refugees wandered through Europe despised and rejected by their "coreligionists," and relief was given them primarily at the hands of the Baptist clergy of England. The fiasco of Shabetai Ṣevi, the false messiah who ultimately converted to Islam, found the majority of European rabbis, as well as nearly all the Sefardim, blindly supporting him.

The more immediate response to the Exile was no less ineffective. There really was no "Jewish Renaissance." Quite rightly did Cecil Roth (no relation to the present author) entitle his popularized study of the Jews in Italy in the sixteenth century *The Jews in the Renaissance,* and not "the Jewish Renaissance." For the most part, Jews prospered in Italy during those years, and yet their prosperity was essentially that of assimilated Jews. The exiles from Spain, and later still from Portugal, brought with them all the aristocracy and pretensions of the wealthy class of Spanish Jews of the fifteenth century, with little or nothing of the culture.

Nor can it be claimed, again, contrary to popular myth, that Jewish culture flourished either in North Africa or in the Ottoman Empire, the main centers to which the exiles fled. One or two Hebrew chronicles were written, and some rabbinic responsa, but for the most part they contented themselves with reprinting the standard Hebrew classics already produced in Italy and in Spain; and, indeed, with translating those works into Spanish since the majority of the Jews no longer could read Hebrew at all. Modern students of Spanish language and literature are enthralled with the Ladino ballads and *romanceros* of the Sefardic Jews of these lands, but the deplorable decline of Hebrew culture goes unmourned.

Mysticism and *qabalah* had won the hearts and minds of even some of the best intellectuals of the late medieval period in Spain, and although there is considerable evidence that this in itself had been a contributing factor to the massive conversion of Jews (hardly philosophy, as Baer and his followers claimed; in fact, not one single philosopher ever converted), it continued its hold on the exiles. Almost the entire history of the rabbinate of the centuries following the Expulsion is caught up in wild fantasies of messianic speculation, "practical" (magic) *qabalah,* etc.

The Expulsion truly marked the end of an epoch in the history of Jewish civilization.

Information for the Reader

Some important information on such matters as Jewish and converso population in the fifteenth century, names of important converso families, and a critical survey of previous literature on some of the subjects dealt with in this book will be found in the appendices. Some may wish to read the survey of literature before turning to the text itself.

The notes to each chapter contain not only bibliographical references but also additional material, and should be consulted. I have decided to limit the bibliography at the end of the book only to those works which are cited repeatedly in the text or Notes. Full bibliographical citations for all other items will be given in the Notes.

A note on transliteration of Hebrew: there is no practical reason for the traditional "doubling" of certain Hebrew letters, and such doubling therefore has been avoided except in the case of common and familiar Hebrew names or holidays, etc. There is a glossary of foreign terms (Hebrew, Spanish, etc.) at the end of the book.

"Castilian" forms of names are used for rulers of Aragón-Catalonia, etc., because these are the forms which they themselves used (e.g., Juan instead of Joan), at least until the fifteenth century. Generally, all forms of names are as found in the sources. Where the Hebrew (Arabic) *Ibn* represents a family name, it is capitalized.

Preface to the Paperback Edition

The welcome success of the hardcover edition of this book, and the decision to reissue it in a new paperback edition, provides an opportunity for necessary updating of some issues in light of new publications, which is done in the new Afterword. The text of the book, and pagination, remain unchanged from the first edition, but some errors have been corrected in the text and the index.

The introduction to the hardcover edition, as well as the Critical Survey of Literature, noted the inadequacy and incomplete nature of many books on the Inquisition, as well as the lack of work on the conversos and the Expulsion. In the years since, I had hoped that situation would improve. There has, indeed, been a proliferation of new books, at least on the Inquisition and some on the conversos, but few have made any significant new contribution. Obviously the most important, not only because it is by far the largest (1172 pages of text and another 212 of notes) but because it is the result of years of research and reflection by an important scholar, is Benzion Netanyahu's *The Origins of the Inquisition in Fifteenth-century Spain,* which appeared in the same year as my book. To my dismay, I found that the book not only lacks much important information but is marred with errors and is distorted by a view of Spanish "racism" that is very far from my own (all of this is dealt with in the Afterword here). Far more sound is Henry Kamen's new book on the Inquisition; this and other literature are discussed also in the Afterword. To aid the reader, perhaps it is useful to highlight what is particularly new and important in *Conversos, Inquisition, and the Expulsion of the Jews from Spain.*

It is the first, and still the only, complete discussion of conversion of Jews in the fourteenth, as well as the fifteenth, centuries. Further details have, of course, come to light in various articles, but no such overall analysis has otherwise been done. Along with this is an explanation of the "missionary" campaign of those centuries that resulted in such massive conversions. There is also important new information relating to the Tortosa disputation and conversions resulting from it.

That the conversos were not "crypto-Jews" and not members of the Jewish people at all was long ago established by Netanyahu (although now he appears to have withdrawn somewhat from that position), but here is new and irrefutable evidence of this, not just from rabbinical sources (some of which were overlooked by Netanyahu) but from the record of daily relations with Jews.

There is detailed information, most of it presented for the first time, on converso statesmen, church officials and writers, including new information on Pablo de Santa María and members of his family. Conversos were among the most powerful government officials of the fifteenth century, particularly in Aragón-Catalonia where they virtually controlled the government, and were chroniclers and secretaries to the king and queen. Most of this information was ignored by Netanyahu, and also by most previous writers. Some of these are surely of interest for students of general history, such as Pedrarias Dávila, who aided in the conquest of Granada and was governor of Nicaragua and founder of Panama, and one of whose daughters married the famous explorer de Soto.

There were also many important converso writers and poets, and while attention has been given to some of these, a complete record of all of them and their writing is nowhere else to be found. This includes an analysis of the satire against other conversos and other elements of this poetry that should pave the way for future detailed research. Most reviewers have ignored this aspect of the book, with the result that students of Spanish literature remain largely unaware of the important new information here. Similarly, the section on conversos and humanism should at least be suggestive for future research (183–86). As noted, nationalism, also found in the converso chronicles, as well as humanism emerged not in the fifteenth century but already in the fourteenth (160–61). The issue of so-called "converso mentality" in the writers and poets is also discussed and shown, hopefully, to be a misconception (particularly 158, 188; see also the index).

The Jewish ancestry of King Fernando, as well as possible converso connections with other royals, is of interest. While this has been casually alluded to by other writers, the sources had not previously been mentioned (reference to a new article on the same subject by David Romano will be found in the Afterword).

Most importantly, perhaps, there is new information on the origins of the Inquisition, not only that of Castile in the fifteenth century but the earlier one in Aragón-Catalonia in the thirteenth and fourteenth centuries, utilizing sources hitherto (and still) completely ignored by other writers. With regard to the fifteenth-century Inquisition, the myth that it was "controlled" by the rulers is shown to be false. Once unleashed, it became a powerful and independent force serving its own ends and which led ultimately to the expulsion of the Jews.

The hostility not only of "old Christians" but of Jews to the conversos and descendants of conversos is one of the most important themes in medieval Spanish history. If the myth, still widely believed, of the conversos as "crypto-Jews" were true, then they surely would have been supported by their "coreligionists," secretly or openly, in anticipation of their full return to the Jewish fold. Indeed, as I point out, they could have left Spain at any time, not even facing the perils of a journey to foreign lands but simply by crossing the border into Muslim Granada (as some few did, and also some Christians who converted to Islam or Judaism). They did not do so, nor, of course, did Jews support and encourage them, as they had for example with the true forced converts in Germany following the First Crusade. On the contrary, Jews testified falsely against conversos to the Inquisition, knowing that this would result at least in the imprisonment and probably the death of the hated apostates. The truth is that the Jews converted of their own free will, for a variety of reasons. They, and in the fifteenth century already descendants of conversos, were very devout Christians, and the Inquisition made them even more so. Even if it is conceivable, which it is not, that the conversos would have risked their lives and confiscation of property in order to "observe" such trivial things as they were accused of, the question remains why they did not simply leave the country and become fully practicing Jews (as many of those converted in 1391 in fact did). On the contrary, they became priests, monks (whole religious orders were "infested" with conversos), bishops, and archbishops. As I have observed (see 115), if the many important "old Christians" who wrote defenses of the conversos had not known for certain that the overwhelming majority were sincere Christians they would not have risked their own reputations in such ardent defense of .hem.

If the conversos were such good Christians, why was there so much animosity against them among certain "old Christians," and why was the Inquisition initiated (or, more correctly, reinitiated)? Not all "old Christians," of course, hated the conversos, yet a powerful minority did hate them and were ready literally to go to war against them. The reasons for this had to do with jealousy of their power, wealth, and influence. When the rebellion and the battles against the conversos failed, a new and pernicious doctrine of "racial impurity" was invented that sought to discriminate against them on the grounds of their Jewish racial heritage. While this was firmly rejected by the popes, and although the actual discriminatory laws were restricted in number, it unleashed for the first time in medieval history racial anti-Semitism—directed not at Jews, but at conversos. Netanyahu sees it differently; according to him, the entire history of Spanish-Jewish relations was marred by "anti-Semitism." This is, of course, completely false, and is contradicted by the response of many important Spanish Christian theologians and others who wrote strong defenses of the conversos and rejected outright the implicit and explicit condemnation of Jews in the new racist theory. For further discussion of Netanyahu's theory of Spanish anti-Semitism and other comparisons of the Inquisition and the Expulsion to Nazi Germany, see the Afterword here.

The tragic end of the Jewish civilization in medieval Spain was the greatest calamity that befell the Jews since the loss of their homeland in the war against the Romans (69–70 C. E.). The conversion of the overwhelming majority of Spanish Jews and the resultant decline in rabbinic and lay leadership and cultural development was to prove a disaster of lasting consequences for those Jews who left in 1492, and for their descendants, in the numerous lands of the Sefardic dispersion.

Conversos, Inquisition, and the Expulsion of the Jews from Spain

1

Marranos and Conversos

The first specific mention of the term "*Marrano*" is found in the records of the *Cortes* (parliament) of Soria, convened by Juan I of Castile in 1380. The significance of the text, reflecting already the ecclesiastical objection to discrimination against conversos which was to cause a major conflict in the fifteenth century, is such that it is best to translate the text in its entirety:

> An offense and great harm and insult to the holy Catholic faith is that Jews or Muslims, recognizing that they live in mortal sin and [then] receiving the sacrament of baptism, should be insulted by Jews or by Christians or others because they convert to the holy faith. And Jews or infidel Muslims excuse themselves because of these injuries from not becoming Christians, even though they know our faith to be holy and true. Therefore we order and command that no one shall call any convert *Marrano, Tornadizo* [renegade], nor any other injurious term. Anyone who, on the contrary, does this shall pay 300 *mrs.* each time he so calls him, or says this about a person to insult him; and if he has no property with which to pay, he shall spend fifteen days in prison.[1]

As a precedent for this, we may note that already the *Fuero* (local law) of Brihuega, ca. 1239–42, punished with a fine of 2 *mrs.* anyone who called a Christian "*tornadizo.*" In 1242, Jaime I of Aragón-Catalonia enacted a similar law, imposing unspecified "penalties" on anyone who called a converted Jew or Muslim "*tornadiço,*" and we find the same thing in the *Fuero real* and the *Siete Partidas* of Jaime's son-in-law Alfonso X of Castile.[2]

We must state emphatically that we have absolutely no clear idea as to what the term "Marrano" means in Spanish, or, indeed, if it is a Spanish word at all. Numerous guesses have been made as to the meaning, and it has become more or less popularly understood that the word means "pig." However, there is no evidence whatever to support this.

As I have suggested elsewhere, it is possible that the term is related to the Aramic expression *maran atha*, "Our Lord has come" (1 Cor. 16.22). This phrase is itself the subject of some debate in contemporary New Testament scholarship, and the consensus is to divide it as *maran tha,* possibly an imperative: Lord, come!" However, both the Vulgate (medieval Latin translation) and the medieval Spanish translations of the New Testament understood it as I have here explained.[3] This possibility is not some farfetched fancy, as are the other suggested etymologies, but rather is expressly said to be the origin of the term in an anonymous reply rebuking Fernando de Pulgar's extremely important letter in defense of the conversos (to which we shall return).[4]

Yet another, perhaps more remote, possibility is that "Marrano" is derived from the Arabic *marana,* "to be flexible, pliant" (n. *marāna,* "pliancy").

Whatever the origin of the word, the essentially insulting and derogatory meaning was clearly understood, and is eloquently expressed by the early-sixteenth-century writer Antonio de Guevara:

> To call a dog a Moor, or a Jew an infidel [these are] words of great temerity and even little Christianity [but] calling a converted Moor a dog or [converted] Jew a Marrano is to call him a perjurer, false, heretic.[5]

Terms which appear in Jewish legal sources, however, have a very precise meaning which it is essential to understand in order to comprehend the change in attitude which took place in Spain with regard to Jewish conversion to another religion. The first of these is the term *min,* usually translated as "heretic." Whatever the possibility, indeed, probability, that this term was applied also to Christians in the Talmudic period, medieval Jewish authorities generally agreed that it applied only to Jewish heretics or sectaries like the Qaraites. Menaḥem ha-Meiri, an important fourteenth-century scholar of Provence who spent some time elsewhere in Spain as well and was familiar with the general situation, already maintained that an "apostate to idolatry," i.e., a convert to Christianity, is to be considered a *min:*

> everyone who goes out of the general category of the Jewish law and enters into that of another law is considered by us as a member of that [other] law in everything except for divorce and marriage.[6]

That is, marriage contracted by a converso (or conversa; female) with a Jewish spouse is considered a legal marriage in that the spouse may not remarry without a bill of divorce from the converted partner; also, a converso may grant a valid bill of divorce. What is of interest in Menaḥem's statement is that his language already comes very close to the startling legal innovation we shall discuss according to which the converso is considered to have left the Jewish people altogether.

The *mumar,* on the other hand, is an apostate; i.e., one who has abandoned religious belief or practice in whole or in part, but has not converted
to another religion. Such apostates are divided into two categories: "apostate with regard to the entire Torah" (*mumar le-kol ha-Torah*), and "apostate with regard to idolatry" (*mumar la-ʿavodah zarah*). These two together
comprise the first category of *mumar,* and both of these are nevertheless still
considered as Jews. Maimonides (Moses b. Maimon), however, considers
one who willfully denies the Torah to be a complete heretic and Gentile. He
also explains that an "apostate with regard to idolatry" is, in fact, one who
converts to another religion *at a time of persecution.* Abraham b. David, in
his strictures on Maimonides, objected that such a one is a *min,* according
to Maimonides' own definition; and, indeed, Maimonides elsewhere did
designate a convert to another religion as a *min.* However, as noted, here
he speaks of conversion at a time of persecution.[7]

Maimonides' position becomes clearer when we examine what he wrote
elsewhere:

> An Israelite who worships idolatry is like an idolator in all things, and is not
> like an Israelite who transgressed a commandment [for which the punishment
> is] stoning

which would appear to mean that an "idolatrous Jew" is not to be considered a Jew at all. Similarly, he stated elsewhere that one who denies even the
"oral Torah" (the Talmud) and its divine authority is like other heretics and
informers and apostates, "that all of these are not in the general category of
Israelite" at all and may be killed by anyone at any time.[8] These statements,
too, therefore become a precedent for the above-mentioned ruling we shall
encounter that a converso has left the Jewish people.

The second category of the apostate is *mumar la-ʿaveirah aḥat,* or *mumar
le-oto davar,* who is an apostate with regard to a particular law which he
does not observe. Furthermore, this type of apostate is also divided into two
categories: "defiant apostate" (*mumar le-hakhʿis*) who acts out of spite and
willfully violates the law, and "appetitive" or "lascivious apostate" (*mumar
le-teʾavon*) who merely violates a law because of his desire for something
forbidden and his inability to control his urge. The "defiant apostate" is
among those of whom it was said that they have no portion in the world to
come (should they die without repenting), whereas the "lascivious" apostate is called the "normal sinner." In neither case is such an apostate considered a convert, of course, and he remains in the category of complete Jew,
although a transgressor. (Netanyahu, who discusses these and the other
terms, somewhat incorrectly uses the word "convert" to refer to persons in
all these categories. It should be clearly understood, on the contrary, that
they were never considered converts in any sense at all in our sources.)[9]

The true convert is designated by the term *meshumad,* which means one who completely and willfully abandons the Jewish people and is generally not to be considered any longer a Jew, but rather a complete Gentile.

The "forced convert," or *anus,* is one who converts under duress and is assumed to be a "secret Jew"; i.e., one desiring to return as soon as feasible to the practice of Judaism and who meanwhile is admonished to observe in private as much of Jewish law as is possible. (It should be pointed out that this is not, of course, what Maimonides meant about one who converts at a time of persecution; rather, he meant that such a one *willingly* converts when the Jewish people are generally under pressure to do so and when he certainly should have resisted.)

Nor is it correct, again as Netanyahu thought, that the concept "Israelite even though he sins remains an Israelite" (to be discussed below, p. 11 and see n. 9 here) was applied "only to cases of *real* conversion" (i.e., *mumar*) and not to an *anūs* prior to the Spanish period. The fact is that there was not always a clear distinction made between *mumar* and *anūs* in the French and German Jewish legal sources.[10]

With regard to the term *meshumad,* the medieval authorities took it for granted that the word derives from *shemad* (destruction; thus, persecution), and this is indeed the accepted view of modern authorities. Nevertheless, there was another, very widely held opinion. Solomon Ibn Farḥūn (the correct form of the name, not "Farḥon" or "Parḥon"), a twelfth century grammarian, who lived in Calatayud and then in Salerno, cites Haya *Gaon* that *meshumad* is actually *meshuʿmad,* but because of the "trouble" (of pronouncing it, especially the proper pronunciation of the letter ʿ*ayin*), the ʿ*ayin* was dropped, resulting in *meshumad.* He adds that the word refers to immersion in water in the "Edomite" language (Syriac, ʿ*a-m-d*).[11]

The original source of this interpretation, at least for the Jews in early Muslim Spain, appears to be the Talmud, in relation to the Christians and Joshua b. Peraḥyah, reputed to have been the teacher of Jesus, as cited by Moses Ibn ʿEzra(h).[12] Judah ha-Levy appears to have borrowed or learned it from him, and wrote that Jesus and his followers were *meshuʿmadim* (note the spelling) associated with the sect of the "immersers" in the Jordan River.[13]

The tradition persisted among the Jews also in the Christian period in Spain. Abraham Zacut (fifteenth century) discusses the whole topic of Yanai and the sages and Joshua b. Peraḥyah in a manner which indicates that he utilized the "*Kuzary*" of Judah ha-Levy as well as the original Talmudic sources, and adds that the tradition that Jesus was a student of Joshua is true "and this [Christianity] is the third sect of heretics, the sect of the disciples of Jesus the Nazarene, *meshuʿmadim* who observed the laws of immersion." However, he cites Naḥmanides (Moses b. Naḥman) that the term *meshumad* means one whose deeds estrange him from God, etc., and so also Rashi (*Shabat* 87a), but mentions also Haya *Gaon*'s explanation in a somewhat offhand manner.[14]

Simon b. Ṣemaḥ Duran, who fled Majorca in the persecution of 1391 and went to North Africa, also repeats the enumeration of the three sects, with the third being the *meshuʿmadim,* but he combines elements of the discussion in Moses Ibn ʿEzra(h) and the *Kuzary* with Naḥmanides, saying that the *meshuʿmadim* are different from *meshumadim,* for the latter are idolators who have estranged themselves from God.[15]

The issue of Jewish conversion to other religions was, of course, a very old one which predated the period of the Jews in Spain. We may never be in a position to know with any degree of certainty the extent of conversion to the new Christian religion in ancient Palestine, for example, and although the actual numbers appear to be small, this phenomenon must have had a demoralizing effect on the Jewish community. Even in "pagan" times, many Jews must have converted to those religions, throughout the Hellenistic and Roman empires, for example. If the high estimate of Jewish population in the Roman period, as much as eight million or more according to some authorities, is accurate, then it is obvious that the overwhelming majority of these Jews had disappeared through either assimilation or conversion by the early Middle Ages. Never until the modern period was the total world population of Jews to approach anything like such a figure.

In "Babylon" (Iraq and the Persian Empire), where the majority of the Jews in the Diaspora lived in the Talmudic period, Christianity was hardly a threat, of course. Quite otherwise was the situation in the Byzantine Empire, and here, too, there must have been widespread conversion.

It was the rise of Islam, however, which appears to have presented the greatest challenge. Not only did the Muslim conquest of the whole of the Persian Empire, Palestine, Syria, Egypt, and later North Africa and Spain bring under the dominance of the Muslims the majority of the Jewish population of the world, but their generally tolerant attitude and the close affinity of the Hebrew and Arabic languages and of the two cultures, with the uncompromising monotheism of Islam, served to encourage conversion.

The early rabbinical authorities, the *geonim* who headed the Talmudic academies situated in the heart of Muslim Iraq (near the caliphal capital of Baghdad), dealt with several questions related to such conversions. These, in turn, while not exactly binding upon medieval Jewish communities, became precedent for attitudes toward conversion in Christian Spain. One such question dealt with whether a convert to another faith who then repented and returned to the Jewish fold requires immersion in a ritual bath (like a proselyte), and the ruling was that he does not.[16] This was to become a more or less frequent topic of discussion in the later period when it became clear to the Spanish Jewish authorities, at least, that the conversos were by no means to be considered as *anusim,* that is, forced converts, but as having willfully abandoned their people. Their decision, not surprisingly then, was that any who might desire to return to the Jewish people certainly did require immersion.

Earlier we referred to the "romantic" view of certain rabbis of the post-Expulsion period, in Turkey and elsewhere, who appear to have eagerly expected a significant "return" of descendants of these Spanish conversos (Marranos). Thus, Yom Ṭov Ṣahalon maintained that "*anusim*" (again, he is talking about *descendants* of the original conversos) who desire to return to Judaism do not require circumcision or immersion like proselytes, for they are *no worse* than a *ger toshav* (a Gentile, such as a slave, who observes certain specified commandments) who does not practice idolatry. Such "*anusim*," therefore, although he admits that they will ultimately have to be circumcised, also do not cause "libatious wine" (a Gentile who touches wine makes it unfit for Jewish use because of the fear that he intended it for idolatrous libations). Nevertheless, he concludes that this applies only to those "*anusim*" who leave their land, but those who remain are to be investigated carefully with regard to their intentions and practices, as Isaac b. Sheshet (whom he cites) had earlier ruled (we shall come back to that opinion).

It should be pointed out that Ṣahalon's views here were excessively lenient, and not shared by other rabbis even in his generation. Also with regard to women, descendants of converts, he ruled that immersion is not required if they desire to return, since they, too, are "of Jewish seed" and like the men have repented. Especially is this true of Portuguese women, for, he says, "the faith of Israel is implanted in their hearts and they teach the men and bring them close to the faith of Israel, as we have heard and even seen." [17]

This is important testimony as to what, indeed, may have been fact concerning the surviving loyalty to certain Jewish traditions among the Marranos of Portugal. This loyalty is also demonstrated by the fact that descendants of these Marranos did leave Portugal in the seventeenth and eighteenth centuries and go to Italy, Turkey, and the Netherlands, as well as southern France and some other countries, where they converted to Judaism. It is easy to explain why there was this difference between the converted Jews of Spain and those of Portugal. In the former case, as we shall see, none or almost none of the conversions had anything to do with duress or persecution. Rather, they were the willing decision of Jews, acting entirely on their own, to abandon their people and become Christians.

The already pitiful and harassed Jews who were expelled from Spain and made their way into Portugal, however, were soon faced with real compulsion when they were rounded up and ordered to convert or leave the country. Those who chose conversion under such conditions may, in a sense, be considered to have acted under duress and thus to be in the category of *anusim* (not, of course, according to the previously cited ruling of Maimo-

nides). In any case, they had been of those Jews who had courageously chosen to cling to their traditions and to their people and leave Spain rather
than take the relatively easy road of conversion then, in 1492. This means
that such Jews were more likely to have had some degree of Jewish education
and respect for traditions, and when in a state of despair they chose conversion in Portugal rather than again face the bitter road of exile, it is likely
that they made reluctant Christians at best and that they preserved a stub-
born loyalty to Jewish traditions.

The situation of the Jews in medieval Spain must be clearly understood
by any who wish to understand the converso problem. In the confines of the
present book it is, of course, impossible to present that history. Several factors are important, however. First of all, it is necessary to realize that Jews
lived in medieval Spain longer than they had in any other country in the
world, including Israel. Whether or not Jews were present in the biblical
period, as their tradition maintained, or in the time of Saint Paul, as some
modern writers assert, we know for a fact that there was a significant Jewish
population already by 300 c.e. This gives us approximately twelve centuries
of continuous Jewish presence in Spain, therefore. Second, more Jews lived
in medieval Spain than in *all* the other countries of Europe combined. They
were by far the most important Jewish community of the world. Finally, and
this is not generally realized, unlike other countries the Jews in Spain lived
scattered throughout the length and breadth of the land, in the tiniest villages and in the major cities. Most, indeed, were rural rather than urban
dwellers. This could be possible only in a situation where Christians generally were not only tolerant but friendly toward Jews, and where Jews felt
entirely safe in living, sometimes only two or three families, in a remote
Christian village.

The special situation of the symbiotic relationship between Jews, Muslims, and Christians in Spain is given a special term, untranslatable into
English: *convivencia*. To call this "living together," or coexistence, as is
sometimes done, is wide of the mark, for people may live together and yet
not like each other. There was, in fact, an *interdependence* of the three
peoples in medieval Spain; a phenomenon that survived the Christian "Reconquest" of Muslim Spain which was completed in the thirteenth century.
Muslims, too, then lived intermingled with Christians, though to a less extensive degree than the Jews. The Christians found themselves heavily indebted, culturally and in daily life, to Muslims and Jews.

Aside, perhaps, from Sicily under Frederick II, Spain was the only truly
pluralistic medieval society. It was also, to a large degree, a "democratic"
one in that it was the earliest one to have representative government, which
evolved into the national *Cortes,* or parliamentary system. Each town was
governed by its local custom and laws, and from the very earliest period
these took cognizance of the Jews and their special importance. Full equal-

ity was mandated for Jews in these local laws, and therefore no matter what the theoretical intent of those (largely clergy, and those who had spent most of their adult lives outside of Spain) who sought to draft discriminatory legislation on a kingdom-wide scale for Castile and later for Aragón-Catalonia, in reality they could not overcome the opposition of the towns who refused to relinquish their cherished rights.

Nor did the kings, especially such powerful and basically fair-minded rulers as Alfonso X of Castile and Jaime I of Aragón-Catalonia (under whose auspices these attempts at unified legislation were made), fail to realize the importance of the Jews. This was not, as Baer suggested, because the Jews were used as a "sponge to be squeezed" for taxes. Taxes were fair and fairly apportioned, and at no time did Jews pay any unwarranted share of them. However, Jews literally by the hundreds rose to positions of great power and influence at the courts of the kings. Popular knowledge of a few of the most important and famous of such men obscures awareness of the very many who served as local officials throughout Spain. An aristocratic upper-class elite was thus produced in the Jewish community from the early thirteenth century.

On the level of daily life, friendly and cordial relations between ordinary Christians and Jews were the norm rather than the exception. Even though this was true also of medieval Europe in general, contrary to what we are led to believe in uninformed "histories" of Jews, it was not on so large or significant a scale as was the case in Spain. This aspect of *convivencia* included also the clergy: archbishops and bishops, monasteries and convents, local priests—all were constantly involved in business and social relations with Jews. Skeptics will perhaps immediately conclude that what we are talking about here is borrowing money from Jews. Yes, that did take place, but almost equally there were cases of Jews borrowing from Christians, including from these ecclesiastical authorities. Church property was administered, church taxes collected by Jews. Bishops had such close personal social relationships with Jews that it is the rare exception to find one who was not friendly. One of the great archbishops of Toledo (prelate of Spain), Pedro Tenorio, prized among his possessions two gilt cups engraved with his seal which were a Christmas present from one of his Jewish friends.

All of this evidence, and more, is to be carefully set forth in my work on the theme of *convivencia*, and cannot be detailed here. The important point is to show the atmosphere of trust and friendship which was created in Christian Spain. While we may, indeed, stand in awed admiration of this situation, it had its negative as well as positive side: it led to complacency on the part of the Jews, who believed that this situation would continue indefinitely, and it also encouraged many to consider that their position might be even better were they to convert to Christianity.

Another factor which stimulated the massive conversions witnessed as early as the end of the fourteenth century was purely internal. Baer, as we have commented, sought to blame what he called "Averroism," or the supposedly corrupting influence of philosophy. However, the fact is, as previously noted, that *not one single philosopher* is known to have ever converted, whereas a great many rabbis and their disciples did. How is one to explain this curious phenomenon?

There is strong evidence that "messianic speculation" was rampant in medieval Spain, from the time of Maimonides on. Nearly every important Jewish writer and rabbi had calculated the exact year for the "redemption" and the coming of the messiah. As each predicted date came and passed unfulfilled, great despair must have set in among many Jews. The interminable length of the exile was something for which no easy explanation was possible.[18]

Christian polemic quickly took advantage of this, and Jews were increasingly challenged to explain this delay in the fulfillment of their hopes, particularly in the wake of the new "missionary" zeal of the Dominican and Franciscan orders of the latter half of the thirteenth century.[19] The first disputation ever held in Spain was convened in Barcelona (actually, there were two of them, both involving a French or Provençal Jewish convert). Naḥmanides, commanded to respond to the Christian charges, certainly did not "win" this debate, as the probably forged Hebrew account would suggest. He was, in fact, denounced and forced to flee the kingdom, going to Palestine, where he died. This situation must have had an even greater demoralizing effect on the Jewish community, challenged at the core of its beliefs and deprived now of the leadership of one of its greatest authorities (though not a rabbi, Naḥmanides was the acknowledged leader of Catalan Jews).

Finally, the fanatical preaching and rabble-rousing activities of an obscure archdeacon, Ferrant Martínez, in Seville culminated in the summer of 1391 in a series of attacks on Jews throughout Castile, and soon spread to Aragón, Catalonia, Majorca, and Valencia. Much robbing and looting took place, and some Jews were killed. It is not true that whole Jewish communities (including even, supposedly, Barcelona) were "wiped out," as Baer and other writers have stated. As we shall see, the kings and local authorities acted promptly and energetically in ending the riots and punishing the perpetrators, but the damage was done.

Certainly many Jews converted in the wake of these attacks, or before them in an effort to save themselves. While we have no evidence of a "wave of despair" sweeping the Jewish communities, as some have claimed, the decline in Jewish population in many towns (including Barcelona, although the Jewish community did not "disappear") can be explained only on the basis of such conversions.

However, as we shall see, the conversion of Solomon ha-Levy, a rabbi of Burgos, and with him his entire family, took place some time *before* the events of 1391. This is an example of conversion motivated not by fear but by sincere belief. His example inspired others, such as his former disciple Joshua al-Lorqi, also to convert. What such conversions meant to the larger Jewish community can well be imagined.

Undaunted by the relative failure of their early missionizing activities, the Dominicans and Franciscans renewed their efforts at the beginning of the next century. Vicente Ferrer, probably the greatest Christian preacher of the Middle Ages, went the length and breadth of the land stirring up Christian penitence and emotionalism to a fevered pitch, and incidentally bringing about the massive conversion of Jews, sometimes of entire communities, wherever he went.

Vicente Ferrer did not content himself merely with preaching, however. He played an active, perhaps even decisive, role in instigating the drafting of legislation at Valladolid in 1412 (following a fervent sermon preached to the queen mother Catalina, regent for Juan II) which would have severely restricted Jewish economic and political activity and virtually brought an end to the aspects of *convivencia* which we have described. Although Baer claimed among other things that this was a plot of the "Church Militant" and the "Estates," and that the commercial restrictions were a result of "the monkish policy" to virtually enslave the Jews," they were, in fact, *specifically restricted* to the city of Valladolid alone, and were never actually enforced even there. That there was then "no king in Castile," as Baer claimed, would very much have surprised the young but hardly incapacitated Juan II, who even then was acting to undo the harmful results of these very laws.[20]

In Murcia, where Ferrer's activities were especially fruitful, and also brought great danger to the Jews, his preaching resulted yet again in the conversion of some rabbis, who then were put on the payroll of the city council; one was even given money for a trip to visit the pope. Francis Oakley has observed that Ferrer's preoccupation with the coming end and the last judgment (he was himself already an old man), which his letter to Pope Benedict XIII in 1412 demonstrates, also explains in part his concern for the conversion of Jews, which would be a precursor of the final events.[21]

One of the most notoriously anti-Jewish of the medieval popes was the Spaniard Benedict XIII, the "antipope" of Avignon whose jurisdiction was recognized by all of Spain. In 1413 he instituted yet another disputation, in Tortosa in Catalonia, in which major Jewish rabbis and thinkers were "invited" to participate. The primary spokesman for the Christians was none other than Joshua al-Lorqi, who upon his conversion had taken the name Jerónimo de Santa Fe and who became, in fact, a leading Christian theologian. The result of this disputation, which lasted well into the following year, was again the conversion of large numbers of Jews, including many rabbis and prominent leaders, among whom were some of those who took part in the disputation itself.

To this dreary picture, we must add the information that the foremost Jewish rabbis, such as Isaac b. Sheshet, who served in Zaragoza and then in Valencia, and Simon Duran of Majorca, and others, fled the country owing to the persecutions of 1391. Thus, from the beginning of the fifteenth century, Spain's Jewish community was virtually devoid of informed and effective rabbinical leadership. Also in Castile few leaders remained, and after the end of the fourteenth century, with the family of Asher b. Yehiel (whose sons were also famous scholars), we find that almost no more rabbis of sufficient learning or stature to make any impression on Jewish life. The yeshivot closed, not to be renewed again until, on a very small scale, the last few years before the Expulsion. There were certainly no longer Jewish leaders with the vision or authority of a Naḥmanides, an Ibn Adret, or an Isaac b. Sheshet.

There is, therefore, no question but that the fifteenth century saw a complete breakdown and virtual collapse of the high level of Jewish learning which had characterized Spanish Jewry from the earliest days. The vacuum was filled, to the extent that it was, not by Baer's nemesis, philosophy, but by its opponent, *qabalah*. Speculative mysticism was rampant, and the wild allegorization of the Bible, and with it of the commandments themselves, further contributed to the deterioration of Jewish life and adherence to tradition. We shall have occasion to examine some of these things in detail. All of these factors paved the way for the final chapter, which saw the conversion of undoubtedly the *majority* of the Jews of Spain before the Expulsion was decreed.

To conclude once again with a consideration of terminology, we can see from the sources the difference which existed for Christians as well as Jews between the early Jewish converts and those of the fifteenth century. The early sources continuously refer to Jewish converts by the term *tornadizo*, "renegade," which is a very strange expression indeed, since one would expect Christian sources to refer approvingly to such converts. No doubt this reflects the Jewish attitude, which saw such converts already as those who were abandoning their people. (It has been suggested that the earliest such reference may be in a law of Fernando III in 1180, stipulating that the residents of Zorita inherit the possessions of *tornadizos* who have died without children; however, it is more likely that this refers to Muslim converts than to Jewish converts.) [22]

In one of the first acts of his reign, Jaime II of Aragón-Catalonia in 1296 issued a decree for all his kingdoms that any Jew or Muslim who wished to convert to the "orthodox" faith was to be guaranteed possession of all his property and absolute freedom and equality with all Christians. Severe pen-

alties were to be imposed on anyone who dared call such a convert "renegade" (tornadizo).[23]

In the fifteenth century, as we have seen, it was not that such converts
were contemptuously called, by Christians as well as Jews, "renegades" for
having abandoned their faith, but that the conversos were being insulted
with the derogatory and illegal name of Marrano. Thus, Hernando de Talavera, himself of converso origin (possibly), wrote in 1481: "It is complained that the newly converted are named among the Christians *marranos*
and *marrandíes*. . . . In this manner, not without grave offense to Jesus
Christ, are insulted and reproached sometimes the new Christians and their
descendants."[24]

If the campaign of the Franciscan and Dominican orders, with the blessing of the pope, to convert Jews on a large scale to Christianity had been
successful well beyond their expectations, something certainly had gone
sadly amiss when we find that these new converts were not welcomed with
rejoicing in the Christian faith, but instead were reviled and ridiculed.

The reasons for this, and the implications also for the Jews, remain to be
unfolded later in this book.

Early Phase of Conversions:
Thirteenth and Fourteenth Centuries

As we have noted in the previous chapter, the evidence of Christian legal sources demonstrates that there was already a sufficient number of cases of conversion of Jews in the thirteenth century to cause the converts to become the subject of legal protection. In the ruling of Jaime II referred to (1296), besides forbidding that they be called *tornadizos* and protecting their property rights, he also decreed that Dominican preachers be allowed to debate with Muslims and Jews and that the latter must respond. Jews were also often compelled to attend sermons preached to them in an effort to get them to convert. Nevertheless, when the Jews of Majorca complained of the "danger" to them from having to attend such sermons in the churches because of the "great multitude" of people there, the king saw the justice of their complaint and ordered that no more than ten Christian men of the better class be allowed at such sermons.[1]

In this he was merely following the precedent of Pedro III, who in 1279 noted that when the Dominicans of Huesca and Zaragoza compelled Jews to listen to their sermons they were accompanied by large groups of Christians whose presence might cause danger to the Jews, and ordered that neither Christian laymen nor priests be allowed at such preaching. Similar letters were sent to the majority of the justices of the realm, and the king wrote the Jewish communities that he had prohibited Christian laity from going into the synagogues at all (where the sermons were then preached) and ordered the friars not to preach "contumely" and things which could cause scandal. (Such letters were indeed sent by him to various monasteries.)[2]

The very real danger from this preaching may be seen in a letter of the same year (1279) from the king to an official in Huesca ordering him to investigate an incident where a scroll of the Torah was "baptized," the Jews were insulted with "derisive songs," and their religion was treated with contempt, concluding with the mock choosing of a "Jewish king." At the same time, he also ordered that in Calatayud Dominican and Franciscan preachers not be accompanied by more than fifteen or twenty people, and that the gates to the Jewish quarter be closed before the sermons were preached in the synagogue, for the protection of the Jews. Nevertheless, only a few months later the king was informed that numbers of Christians were attending the sermons and insulting and injuring Jews. Therefore, the king ordered penalties (fines, probably) imposed on Christians who attended such sermons, "except for three or four honorable men." This order went to Barcelona, Gerona, Vich, Manresa, Villafranca, Tarragona, Cervera, Tárrega, Montblanch, Huesca, Zaragoza, Tarazona, Jaca, Borja, Egea, Barbastro, Calatayud, Daroca, Teruel, Valencia, and Játiva. This list shows the extent of these compulsory sermons.[3]

In 1297 the Jews of Zaragoza complained to Jaime II about *converted Jews* preaching and exciting the people against the Jews, resulting in "scandal" and damage to them. The king ordered local officials to prevent such preaching, but permitted conversos and other preachers (Dominicans) to dispute with Jews in their synagogues concerning the Christian faith.[4] Apparently a number of Muslims and Jews in the kingdom of Valencia converted, for in that same year the king issued a series of laws concerning them, essentially the same as his previous rulings but with the added provision that converts who did not follow the advice of the Dominicans (who were given direct supervision of converts) might be compelled to do so by the *bailes* or other officials. In 1299 the king gave permission for the famous Ramon Lull to preach to the Jews, and in 1306 also for the converso Jaime Pérez of Valencia. The last that we hear of such compulsory sermons in the reign of Jaime II was the ruling of the *Corts* (parliament) of Barcelona in 1311 that Jews and Muslims must attend them.[5]

In the fourteenth century, Pedro IV granted permission to one Romeu de Pal, described simply as "master of the sacred scriptures" and as having a thorough knowledge of Hebrew and Latin (both Franciscans and Dominicans had begun learning Hebrew in the thirteenth century), to publicly dispute with Jews wherever he wished and to compel them to attend, with the aid of Dominican and Franciscan officials. Nevertheless, in 1346 the king responded vigorously to the complaints of the Jews of Cervera against Pedro dez Quo, a Franciscan, who for some time had been inciting people against the Jews by his sermons. The king noted that it was not his intention to cause danger or harm to the Jews, "whom we sustain and defend," and therefore ordered the friar transferred to another monastery.[6]

Such complaints were less frequent in the fifteenth century, but we do find some, as when in 1411 the Jews of the city of Murcia complained to Juan II about Dominican preachers there who incited the people to riot and to rob and kill the Jews. The Castilian ruler also protested this behavior in vigorous terms to the officials of the city, noting that it was causing some Jews to convert against their will. All Jews were to be protected and have freedom to move about as they wished, and so that no one could claim ignorance of this order he commanded that it be posted in public plazas and markets. In 1450, the Jews of Seville complained to the same king about Franciscans preaching "scandalous sermons" there to incite the people against them.[7]

There can be no doubt, therefore, that whatever the sincere intentions of the more noble of religious leaders or men like Ramon Lull, for example, who was genuinely tolerant, the majority of the Franciscan and Dominican friars who took it upon themselves to "preach" to the Jews and to the Christians *against* the Jews were guilty of inciting riot and causing considerable harm to the Jews.

The above-mentioned order of Jaime II to Valencia in 1297 makes reference to the law as prescribed in the *Usatges de Barcelona,* and we find, indeed, in that code a law that any Jew or Muslim who aids a convert to return to his former faith, or calls a convert "renegade," etc., shall be fined "20 ounces of Valencian gold" (the *Usatges* date from the mid-twelfth century, but obviously this law could not have been written then; rather, it was one of the later additions made at the time of Jaime II).[8] This, therefore, added another dimension to the question of relations between Jews and conversos; namely, that Jews, even if they wished to do so, were prohibited from aiding or encouraging conversos to "repent" and return to their former faith. It is also of interest to note that this law, for the first time, specifies that *Jews* (and Muslims) may not call a converso "renegade," whereas we recall that other such laws refer to the use of such an insult essentially by other Christians.

In 1315 Jaime II granted safe-conduct to one Abraham, a Jew of Morocco, and his family who had come to live in Aragón. The king noted that the two minor sons of Abraham had been taken by Christians to a church and baptized, but the king recognized that because of their tender age they could not be said truly to have consented and so he permitted them to be restored to their parents, at which time they conducted themselves as Jews and were allowed to follow the Jewish law.[9]

This is also extremely important, as revealing, once again, the typical "commonsense" approach of the Christian rulers in dealing with such matters. For reasons which are not altogether clear to me, Aragón-Catalonia, possibly influenced by the proximity to the papal court at Avignon and to "pious" France, was more receptive to reactionary religious forces than was Castile. Thus, the Dominicans and Franciscans were able to establish a strong position there earlier, whereas it was not really until the fifteenth century that their program began to be seriously carried out in Castile. It is for this reason, too, as we shall see, that the Inquisition was established in Aragón-Catalonia long before Castile.

What this meant in practical terms was that the Dominicans, particularly, exercised a certain moral authority over the rulers (Jaime I and Jaime II, especially, were very religious men), who were willing to support their missionary activities and even their "right" to dispute with Jews on religion. However, the rulers were also both personally friendly to Jews and realistic about the benefit which accrued to them and their kingdom from the Jews, and thus would brook no outright acts of hostility. More than this, they were basically men of good will with a strong sense of justice and therefore always responded positively and vigorously to complaints by individual Jews or Jewish communities. This was an important factor which no doubt did much to prevent even more widespread conversion of Jews. The truth is that there was never any reason for a "wave of despair" to engulf the Jewish community and compel the conversion of Jews, and with rare exceptions those who did convert chose to do so of their own free will.

The thirteenth century in Spain, as elsewhere in Europe (most notably France), was marked by what has been more than once called a "new missionizing" activity with regard to the Jews.[10] Unquestionably, this campaign was initiated by the Dominican and Franciscan orders. While it may have had papal blessing and support, there is no evidence that the popes directed or ordered such a campaign. Officially, the Christian attitude toward the Jews had not changed from what it had always been. The Jews were considered to be heretics, in that they "knew" the truth of Christ and yet deliberately rejected him (as such, Jews are dealt with under the rubric of "heretics" in canon law). Nevertheless, they were seen as "witnesses" to the truth of the Christian faith in that they preserved the original scriptures, the Hebrew Bible which alone was divine revelation and upon the authority of which the entire "New Testament" depended.[11] Second, they served as "witnesses" in the sense that in Christian scripture they were the people of Christ according to the flesh and had rejected him (rejected, it should be stressed, and not "crucified"; contrary to popular opinion, the overwhelming majority of Church authorities never entertained the notion that the Jews were responsible for the crucifixion, an opinion held by only a handful of writers throughout Christian history).

In this, they were seen in a very different light from the Muslims, who were also viewed as heretics but of a much worse degree. Further, the Muslims were seen as "enemies of the faith" (*enemigos de la fe*), a term rarely if ever applied to Jews. In fact, the Muslims were true enemies of Christianity, of course. Not only is the *Qur'ān* itself full of polemic almost as violently anti-Christian as it is anti-Jewish, but the Muslim concept of conquest viewed the world at large as divided between two spheres: *dar al-Islam* (the "house of Islam," countries already dominated by Muslims) and *dar al-ḥarb* ("house of the sword," countries ripe for conquest). The concept of *dhimmī,* so-called "protected minority," which extended to the *ahl al-kitāb,* or "people of the scripture," certain rights in return for heavy taxation, applied to Jews, of course, but only to those Christians who did not resist the manifest destiny of Muslim expansion and conquest. In those lands which did resist, a state of *jihad,* or "holy war," existed.

In response, the Christians declared their own "holy war," the Crusade, and in Spain this became the Crusade of the "Reconquest" of the land held by the infidel. In practice, of course, at least in Spain, there was a good deal of toleration and mutual interdependence between Christians and Muslims, and at least until the fifteenth century there was no serious effort to drive the remaining independent Muslims from the Peninsula. Nevertheless, in theological terms the Muslims remained "enemies of the faith."

None of this, of course, applied to the Jews at all. The Jews were no less polemical against Christianity than were the Muslims (a fact which may not yet have been fully known to the Christians, since the Jews concealed these views in Judeo-Arabic or Hebrew writings), but they were not engaged in outright warfare against the Christians. Indeed, more than that, the Jews had achieved a position of privileged status everywhere in Europe, and not just Spain, owing in large measure to their economic importance to the Christians. This was an important factor, which meant that even if the attitude of "the Church" had been as hostile as many wrongly believe it to have been, the Jews could rely on the certainty of royal protection.

Nowhere was this more apparent than at the time of the First Crusade (1095), when several Jewish communities of Germany were in fact attacked, and many Jews were killed and many more forcibly baptized. We should note, again contrary to the popular misconception, that "the Church" had nothing whatever to do with these events, which were rather perpetrated by gangs of criminals and lower-class "soldiers" on their way to join the crusading armies. The important point, however, is that when the Holy Roman Emperor, Henry IV, and William II of England heard of the events, both permitted the Jews who had been forcibly baptized to return to their religion—a decision which, *contrary* to canon law, was supported also by the pope.[12]

In Spain during the early stages of the "Reconquest," while it is true that in some cases Jews fought by the side of Muslims against Christian invading forces (also augmented by Jewish soldiers), there appears to have been no bitterness against them on the part of the victorious Christians.

The Jews thus enjoyed a considerable advantage over the Muslims in Christian attitudes and in the reality of their treatment. From a practical perspective, this was due less to the theories of theology, which rarely if ever played any real role in the thoughts or deeds of ordinary people, than to the fact that Jews in Spain possessed an ability which most Muslims did not:

they were fluent in Romance, as well as in Arabic and Hebrew. From the earliest period of Muslim dominance of Spain and following the Reconquest, few Muslims were ever able to acquire more than a superficial knowledge of the Christian languages. This ability, or perhaps rather desire, of the Jews to master both Castilian and Catalan, as well as Arabic in many cases, enabled them not only to play a pivotal role as "transmitters of culture" but to integrate themselves quickly and effectively into the general society.

To what, then, are we to attribute the "new" missionary campaign of the mendicant orders in the thirteenth century, and how to explain this deviation from the long-standing Christian policy of permitting the Jews the free exercise of their religion until the expected Second Coming of Christ when they were supposed finally to convert? I believe the answer must lie in the repeated failure of the Crusades. Only in Spain, and there only to a degree, had the Christians been successful in routing Muslims and retaking land held to be "Christian" by a venerable tradition, half mingled with legend and folklore. Repeated attempts in the Holy Land, while resulting in an ill-fated and short-lived "Christian Kingdom," had failed to wrest Jerusalem completely from the hands of the "infidels." In light of this failure, it would appear, the friars now decided to turn their attentions to efforts at converting the Muslims, first in Christian Spain and second in Muslim-held territory both in Spain and in North Africa. Together with this, it seemed perhaps natural to mount a campaign also to convert the Jews.

Two other factors played a major role in this decision. The first was the threat of the Albigensian (elsewhere Cathar, Waldensian) heresy among the Christians, and the second was the propaganda of Jewish converts.

The Albigensian heresy emerged as early as the twelfth century; it was denounced at the councils of Toulouse (1119) and Tours (1163) and was already the subject of a decree issued in 1194 by Alfonso I in Catalonia, the first official act of the Catalan Inquisition (long before the Inquisition was officially established in Toulouse in 1229). Coincidentally, the center of this heresy was in Provence, then part of the kingdom of Aragón-Catalonia, and precisely in the areas where there was a large concentration of Jews, and circumstantial evidence seems to suggest a connection between Jews and the heretics. Yet, as I have elsewhere demonstrated, there is no proof whatever for the conjectured "Jewish influence" on this heresy. Recently advanced notions of the influence of the *Sefer ha-bahir* and other qabalistic ideas are also totally without foundation.[13]

However, there was a long-standing Christian tendency to connect heresy of any kind with "Jews," even to the point of labeling Christians suspect of heresy as "Jews." When the Albigensians infiltrated León in the early thirteenth century, Lucas of Túy (later the bishop there, but at the time a deacon) wrote a diatribe against these heretics, attempting to connect them

with the Jews, whom he despised. In the study just mentioned, I also demonstrated the similarities between some of the anti-Jewish charges made by
Lucas and those found in the work of his near contemporary Caesarius of
Hesiterbach; and, most important, I suggested the possibility of the influence of Lucas's ideas on Bernard Gui's famous Manual for Inquisitors.

There was, therefore, a direct relationship which can be established between the attempt of a Lucas of Túy to connect the Albigensian heresy with
Jews and the emphasis of the original Inquisition of Provence on "Jewish
heresy" and practice among Christian heretics. However false in reality such
charges were, they nevertheless made a strong and lasting impression on the
Dominican Inquisition.

The second factor mentioned above, the propaganda campaign conducted by willing and eager Jewish converts to Christianity, has been frequently discussed by a number of scholars, unlike the Albigensian issue. The
instigator of this new campaign of anti-Jewish propaganda was the convert
Nicholas Donin, in Paris in the 1230s and 1240s. His efforts were directed
primarily against the Talmud, and he succeeded in convincing the Dominicans, and through them also the pope, of the "blasphemies" contained in
that work, which led to the wholesale condemnation and burning of the
Talmud in Paris. Although the pope, Gregory IX, condemned the Talmud
in the strongest terms in 1239 in letters sent to the kings of France, England, Aragón-Catalonia, Castile, and Portugal, in 1247 the next pope, Innocent IV, responding to the pleas of the Jews of France that they could not
observe their religion without the Talmud, rescinded the order (a fact virtually overlooked by scholars who have written on this issue).[14]

The damage was nevertheless considerable, for the Dominicans now had
testimony from the mouths of apostate Jews to something which perhaps
they had long suspected but could not prove, that the Talmud contained
"blasphemies" against the Christian faith. This charge was further supported by the claims of the convert Paul Christiani, and his testimony, added
to the advice of Ramón de Peñafort, certainly the most anti-Jewish friar in
thirteenth-century Spain, convinced Jaime I of Aragón-Catalonia in 1263 to
order Jews to remove all "blasphemies" from their books on penalty of a
fine of 1,000 mrs. That this was generally connected to the plans of the
Dominicans for the conversion of the Jews may be seen in the fact that at
the same time the king prohibited the use of violence to force the Jews to
leave the call (Jewish quarter) to hear sermons by the Dominicans.[15]

The following year, in clarification of the decree, the king allowed the
Jews the right to defend their books against charges of blasphemy within
one month's time before a special tribunal composed of the bishop of Barcelona (Arnau de Gurb), Ramón de Peñafort, Arnau de Segarra, Ramón
Martí, and Pere de Genoa. Except for the bishop, all these were Dominican

friars and all were virulently anti-Jewish, especially the two "Ramons."
Later that same year, however, the king relented further and promised the
Jews they should no longer have to account for their books or respond to
the demands of the Dominicans for censorship, or receive from them any
writing of any kind, a promise he repeated in 1268 (which must indicate
that such charges nevertheless continued).[16]

Obviously, something changed the king's mind from his initial support
of the Dominican program to his permission a year later allowing the Jews
to defend their books and then his cancellation of the entire censorship
plan. What had convinced him was no doubt the combined effect of the
two disputations involving Paul Christiani at Barcelona, one with Bona-
strug de Porta (probably in 1241) and the second with Moses b. Naḥman
(Naḥmaides) in 1263 (These were not, as Baer mistakenly wrote, the same
people.). Neither of these had succeeded in establishing that the Talmud,
in fact, contained "blasphemous" material. Second, it would appear that
the Dominicans had overplayed their hand. Not content with having van-
quished Naḥmanides, the most important spokesman for the Jewish community, they had attempted to compel Jews to attend their missionizing sermons. This repeated interference with the Jews of his realm was something
which the king, normally a tolerant and beneficent ruler as far as they were
concerned, simply could not permit to continue.

Nevertheless, the Dominicans, and especially Ramón de Peñafort, were
powerful enough so that they were able to press their program and repeatedly challenge the good will of the king. Ramón, too, was responsible for
the introduction of a whole series of restrictive measures on Jews which
were written into the *Fueros* of Aragón, similar to those he had previously
tried to have enacted in the *Siete partidas* in Castile (a law code which had
only advisory status in that kingdom, however).

Nevertheless, although we may never have any reliable information on
this, it would appear from what has already been presented here that the
missionary activities of the Franciscans and Dominicans in the thirteenth
century in the kingdom of Aragón-Catalonia had only a limited degree of
success. It was to be entirely otherwise in the subsequent centuries.

The Fourteenth Century: Jewish Sources

The chief legal authority, not only for the kingdom of Aragón-Catalonia but
for all the Jews of Spain and to some extent throughout Europe, in the latter
thirteenth and early fourteenth centuries, was Solomon Ibn Adret of Barcelona. Personal friend and counselor of kings, he was, unlike his teacher Naḥmanides, actually a rabbi (Naḥmanides proudly asserted that he was never

a rabbi), and head of the Jewish community of Barcelona. There are extant from his pen close to three thousand responsa, filling eight large volumes (actually nine, for the first published collection was not included in later editions). Writers such as Epstein and Baer by no means adequately realized the importance of these as a source for the history of this period, and hardly began to do them justice. The difficulty of the technical language employed and the lack of systematic indices have perhaps served to keep scholars from approaching them. Several of these responsa, or legal decisions rendered in reply to direct questions from other rabbis or communities, deal with conversos. It is to be noted that these are all from a period long before the persecutions of 1391, and have been for the most part hitherto entirely ignored.

One of these concerns a Jew (apparently in Monzón) who deliberately violated all the Jewish laws and finally went to live in the house of some Christians. When other Jews tried to convince him to abandon his evil ways, he replied that he no longer believed in the God of Israel, and that indeed even while living among Jews he had only made himself appear to be a Jew, but in his heart he was a Christian.

Here, then, is an early example of exactly the *opposite* of the so-called crypto-Jew: a Jew who was secretly a believing Christian and could hardly wait to escape the Jewish community so that he might live his new faith openly. In his reply, Ibn Adret approved the ruling of the local rabbi that no Jew was to have any dealings with the man, and he added that since the man in fact was an apostate (*mumar*) with regard to the entire Torah, he was *not to be considered a Jew at all*. In this, he clearly followed the exact ruling of Maimonides; namely, that such a one is no longer a Jew but a complete Gentile.[17] Elsewhere, Ibn Adret ruled that one who separates himself entirely from the community (a *min, meshumad, apiqoros* [heretic], despiser of the holidays, or denier of resurrection) may not be given funeral rites or have mourning observed for him when he dies.[18]

In his early responsa, apparently, Ibn Adret was not yet altogether clear himself as to the meaning of these various terms. Thus, in a question from Lérida, he was consulted about a quarrel between two Jews, one of whom called the other a *meshumad,* which resulted in the insulted party's bringing charges. The complaint stated that *meshumad* means "heretic," which the Gentiles call "renegade" in their language (i.e., *tornadizo*). Ibn Adret was asked to explain the meaning of the Hebrew term, and replied that it refers to anyone who is accustomed to commit even a single transgression (i.e., repeatedly), and not even "defiantly" (*le-hakh'is*) but only "lasciviously" (*le-te'avon*), but who still remains a Jew. He cited several Talmudic sources to substantiate this, and concluded that it appears that *meshumad* does not mean "renegade" but one who "breaches the fence" (transgresses) because of desire—to eat what is prohibited, etc.[19]

Clearly, this contradicts his opinion in the previously cited case (which may, in fact, have been written later), where he ruled that such a one is not to be considered a Jew at all. In that case, however, he dealt with one who may be said to have abandoned the entire Torah, whereas perhaps in general Ibn Adret considered a *meshumad* to be a transgressor only of specific laws. Yet one is inclined rather to assume that it is a question of the different periods of time when the two responsa were written, and that as the problem of willful converts increased in frequency, he came to the conclusion that a *meshumad* is a complete Gentile.

In any event, this last-cited opinion of Ibn Adret on the meaning of the term *meshumad* does not coincide with the language of the *geonim* in several of their responsa, as we have seen already, nor with the use of the term by other Spanish authorities. Indeed, in the Christian polemical anti-converso work known as *Alborayco,* written in 1488, the Hebrew term *meshumad* is defined precisely as "rebel" (just as in the question to Ibn Adret), or one who voluntarily converts to Christianity, as opposed to *anūs,* defined as a "Christian by force," that is, converted under duress:

> tomaron ellos [i.e., conversos] entre sy un sobrenombre en ebrayco *anuzim* que quiere dezir forçados. Ca sy alguno se torna Xpistiano, llamanle *mesumad,* que quiere dezir en ebrayco rreboluedor.[20]

There is also a problematic responsum attributed to Ibn Adret in which it is stated that a convert who returns to Judaism requires lashes for his transgressions of the law (while he was a Christian) but does not require immersion like a Gentile proselyte. Nevertheless, the same responsum is already found in some of the collections of responsa of the *geonim,* where it is attributed to Natronai *Gaon.* Still, a difficulty remains, in that Natronai elsewhere ruled that a convert does not inherit from his father, for his conversion, "removes him from the sanctity of Israel," which would directly contradict the statement here that he remains a Jew even after having converted.[21] Either the responsum does not belong in Ibn Adret's collection at all, since it is apparently by Natronai, or else we may assume that Ibn Adret was asked a similar question and merely copied the earlier opinion of the *gaon* (unlikely).

Whether or not Ibn Adret wrote this decision is finally irrelevant, for the original decision of Natronai was certainly known in Spain, and indeed is cited (though simply as "a responsum of a *gaon*") in the fourteenth century by the chief legal authority of Castile, Jacob b. Asher (*Tur, Yoreh de'ah,* no. 267.20).

Similarly, in the responsa of Ibn Adret ascribed to Naḥmanides (most are actually by Ibn Adret, with some few by Naḥmanides) there appears a "question to Rabenu Moses *Gaon*" concerning a Jew who converted and then returned to Judaism. The problem concerns wine which he touched after returning to Jewish observance, and whether it is considered "libatious wine." The reply was that if he went to a place where he was not known and there observed the Sabbath "in the market" (in his business, kept closed on the Sabbath) and kept all the other commandments, he would be accepted *as a complete Jew* and his wine permitted.[22]

The problem is, who wrote this decision? Müller did not hesitate to attribute it to Moses *Gaon* of Sura (Moses Kahana b. Jacob, head of the Sura academy, in Iraq, from 825 to 836).[23] But the text as we have it in the collection of Ibn Adret cannot be by this Moses, for it cites the opinions of "R"Y b. Abraham, of blessed memory," who is, of course, Rabbi Yonah (Jonah) b. Abraham Gerundi, another teacher of Ibn Adret. The clear proof that this responsum is, in fact, by Moses B. Naḥman (Naḥmanides) and not Moses *Gaon* is the citation of Elʿazar (erroneously, in the printed text, Eliʿezer) b. Judah of Worms (thirteenth century). It so happens that Naḥmanides elsewhere also mentions him, and says that a portion of this book had come to him.[24]

It is also important to observe that the responsum states that even after the returned convert has gone to a place where he is not known, he is not then required to return to his former place of residence (where he was known as a convert), "for if he returned there they would kill him." Had this, in fact, been written by a *gaon* it would also be correct, and would refer to the Muslim law which generally required the death penalty for all Muslims or converts to Islam who abandoned their faith.[25] However, since we have seen that it is actually written by Naḥmanides, this is important testimony to the fact that Christians in Aragón-Catalonia actually punished by death a convert to Christianity who returned to Judaism, as required by canon law.

The matter of incorrect identification of an authority again arises in connection with a very important decision which has previously received attention. In one of the cases in a collection of responsa of the *geonim* appears the statement that "*ha-R"IF*" (Isaac al-Fāsī of Muslim Spain) said in the name of his teachers that a "defiant apostate" who has eaten forbidden foods may be charged interest on a loan, like a Gentile, but a "lascivious apostate" may not. The implication is clear: even the defiant apostate, like a complete convert, is not considered a Jew according to this opinion.[26]

However, the responsum is not by al-Fāsī at all, but rather by "*ha-R"I*," in this case, Isaac b. Samuel of Dampierre in France, the nephew of Rabenu Tam, and in its original form it deals not with an apostate at all but with the son of a converted woman (*ben ha-meshumedet*). It was reported that Rashi, the famous commentator of the Bible and Talmud, had said that it was forbidden to lend money on interest to the son of a convert.[27] However, Isaac reports the tradition of his uncle, Rabenu Tam (Rashi's son-in-law), that it was permitted, and adds that the important statement that such a one is a follower of idolatry, and that converts of this time are under the influence of Gentiles with *no hope* that their children may return to Jewish practices (this was in France and Germany). Such a one "who is attached to the ways of the peoples of the world and is considered one of them and is polluted by them and worships idolatry, abandoning the Torah of Israel completely, *is a complete Gentile in all respects.*" [28]

The case about which Rashi was consulted is cited also by Nissim b. Reuben Gerundi of Spain, with the opinion of "students of Rashi who said in his name" that it is forbidden to lend money on interest to the son of a converted woman (*woman* here is important, for Jewish descent goes after the mother, i.e., in this case, such a one is still considered a Jew) and also Rabenu Tam's opinion permitting it. Nissim, however, merely cited Naḥmanides in his novellae on the Talmud, who also ruled that it is permitted, and noted elsewhere that a convert remains a Jew with regard to such laws as impurity of the corpse, marriage, and divorce (but not with regard to such matters as lending money on interest). In his novellae, he cites the case of Rashi, without apparently being aware of the decision of Isaac of Dampierre, and independently reaches the same conclusion as had Isaac (permitting lending money on interest to the son of a converted woman) and for the same reasons. There, however, he states that a convert is not considered in the category of "your brother" (i.e., a Jew, to whom it is biblically forbidden to lend on interest). This seems to contradict his previously mentioned responsum where he says that a convert remains a Jew with regard to certain laws, where he also discusses the permissibility of lending money on interest. In the end, it is somewhat unclear whether he considered a convert still a Jew or not. [29]

Meir Ibn Abī Sarwī, a student of Jonah Gerundi, cites Rabbi Shemayah (the son of Rashi's daughter) in the name of Rashi that it is prohibited to lend money on interest to a convert, and mentions also the reasoning of Isaac of Dampierre, finally adding a further explanation which he heard from his teacher (Jonah). [30]

Yet another area of concern relating to converts was the question of marriage. Rashi had also been asked about a girl who married and whose husband was forcibly converted. He replied that she requires a bill of divorce, "for even a willful convert [*meshumad la-raṣono*] who contracted marriage, the act is valid, as it is said 'a Jew even though he transgresses is still a Jew,' and certainly forced converts [*anusim*] whose hearts are directed to heaven," for they will certainly return to Judaism when able. The importance of this decision did not escape the attention of later Spanish rabbis, several of whom cite it. [31] Nevertheless, it soon became apparent that the situation in Spain with regard to converts was altogether different, and the term "forced convert" (*anūs*) was no longer used to apply to converts there, for they did not for the most part act under any duress at all, but were willful converts; i.e., they chose to become Christians. It could hardly be said of them that "their hearts are directed to heaven" and that they desired to return to Judaism. Furthermore, it should be mentioned that Rashi's legal reasoning, with all due respect to the great authority, was incorrect. Marriage in Jewish law is not some kind of "sacrament" but merely a contractual obligation like any in civil law. What is important is not the status of those who enter into the contractual act, but the nature of the contract itself and whether it is in accord with Jewish law.

This becomes clear in a case about the validity of marriage between a convert and a Jew which was brought to the attention of Ibn Adret for a decision. At issue was the concern that the Jewish wife be left a legal widow ('agunah; cf. Giṭin 26b), because her converted husband could not be forced to give her a bill of divorce. Ibn Adret correctly explained that only the nature of the contractual act is considered, and even though "this [convert] has gone out of the category of the law of Moses and Israel, the act [of marriage] itself is according to the law of Moses and Israel." He adds, however,

> In truth, as long as the wife is unable to flee from [avoid] him and not be intimate with him, lest a violent [or oppressive] son [ben-poriṣ; i.e., a Christian, who might grow up to oppress the Jews] be born, she is obligated to flee from him as from a serpent.[32]

Nothing could more clearly demonstrate the radical difference between the attitude of Spanish rabbinical authorities and that of the authorities of France and Germany with regard to converts. In fact, obviously Rashi understood very well the nature of marriage in Jewish law as a civil contract, but took the position he did in an effort to be as lenient as possible with the converts whom he understood to be "forced converts," following the persecutions of the Crusades, in the hope that they would soon return to the Jewish fold. This, too, was the attitude of other Franco-German rabbis. Ibn Adret already knew that, in Spain, this was unlikely if not impossible.

Interestingly, Maimonides had already ruled that a convert, even a willful one, may contract a valid marriage with a Jew even after converting. In the period after the mass conversions in Spain in the fifteenth century, however, rabbinical opinion was inclined to be strict in dealing with *descendants* of converts, to whom the laws of Jewish marriage were no longer considered to apply. Since these were clearly and without question no longer Jews at all, it was impossible for them to contract a valid obligation according to Jewish law.[33]

Sometimes, even the king was willing to intervene to aid Jews in preventing one of their community from being converted, as happened in the case of a certain converso who went to his house on the Sabbath and forcibly took his wife away in order that she should also be converted. The community decided to send messengers to inform the woman's father in another town, and also messengers to bring a document from the king to save her.[34]

Rabbi Judah Ibn Crespa (or Crisp) of Toledo addressed several questions to Ibn Adret of Barcelona, and one of these dealt with a man who came from Seville with a woman; witnesses testified that he had taken her away from her husband by adultery and that both of them had converted to Christianity, but she had received a bill of divorce from her husband. Now the man and woman appeared in Toledo acting as Jews and as husband and wife. Ibn Crespa said he had the power to turn them over to the government for punishment, and asked what he should do. Ibn Adret replied that an adulterous wife must be divorced from her husband, even against his will, and is also forbidden to the man who had sexual relations with her. That man also is under a kind of ban, and no one may live with him, "but to hand him over to the government to kill him [apparently since he was a renegade convert], this is not for me; it is for you, if you see that the testimony of the witnesses is true and that he converted and also took the woman adulterously, and you see a 'fence' [to prevent others] in the thing by handing him to the government, I have already written to you" (that it may be done); if not, then lashes should be administered and both of them exiled to different places.

Isaac b. Sheshet, after he left Spain in 1391 and went to North Africa, responded to a question by the rabbi of Majorca, Moses Ibn ʿAmar, in 1392, concerning a bill of divorce received by a conversa from her Jewish husband. The question involved the use of both a Jewish and Gentile (Arabic) name for the husband in the document, as it was common in Spain to have two such names. In his reply, Isaac also mentions that "the government is strict not to allow a converso [*mumar*] to be mentioned by his Jewish name but only by the Gentile name, and they punish [violators] on this; and because of our sins converts have increased there [Majorca] and among them are informers and 'speakers in darkness' against the Jews," because of whom the Jewish scribes possibly fear to write a Jewish name in a document concerning a converso.[35]

Yom Ṭov Ishbīlī replied to a question from Valencia (corrupt in the text) which contained a document written "in the Gentile language" (possibly Arabic) involving a case where the trustee appointed to administer the property of children whose father had died was attempting to nullify the marriage contract of the parents (and thus the benefits of property to the widow). One of the charges was that she had "transgressed the Mosaic and Jewish religion" and was thus "rebellious." He replied, with respect to this charge, that there was no evidence to sustain it, and in such a case witnesses are required and also a prior warning to her, in accord with Jewish law.[36]

While this deals with a charge of supposed transgression, and not actual conversion, the legal principle of testimony and warning sheds some light also on views concerning actual conversion.

In this regard it is important to clarify that being Jewish is not a matter of "religion," a concept which did not exist in Jewish thought (or in the Hebrew language) until contact with Christianity necessitated the creation of a new term in Hebrew to refer to the phenomenon of "religion." (Throughout this book the term "Judaism" is used, but this is done for convenience of understanding. In fact, it is a complete anachronism, for the term did not exist until modern times. No medieval Jew would have understood what "Judaism" is.) The point is that Jews defined themselves as a *people,* not followers of a religion.[37]

This being true, it was extremely difficult to envision a situation in which an individual could legally cease being a member of this people, rather like the difficulty of expelling someone (or voluntarily withdrawing) from a family. This explains the adherence of the French and German rabbinical authorities to the concept that "an Israelite [Jew] even though he transgresses remains an Israelite."

In other words, even though a Jew was seen to have become an adherent of another faith, the important thing was that he or she was considered to remain technically a Jew and part of the Jewish people. True, a distinction was made as to whether such a convert, presumed to have acted under duress, observed at least in private as much of Jewish law as possible. This had nothing to do with "religion" (contrary to the modern distinction between "religious" and "secular" spheres of life, Jewish law embraces *all* of life), but with demonstrating individual commitment to maintaining a relationship with the Jewish people and eventually returning to it.

In medieval Spain, therefore, it was not an easy thing to come to the almost novel conclusion that a convert was no longer a Jew at all, but had left the Jewish people and become completely a Gentile. "Almost" novel, because, as we have seen, there was already some precedent for such a view in decisions of the *geonim* and in the opinion of Maimonides. Nevertheless, this was a difficult conclusion to reach, and one which deliberately set aside the prevailing precedent of the Franco-German rule of "Israelite even though he transgresses."

As we have seen, two necessary conditions were requisite for such a conclusion: the conversion had to be *willful,* and there had to be conclusive evidence of a deliberate and total rejection of Jewish law and of Jewish peoplehood on the part of the convert. Without these two conditions, no rabbinical authority in medieval Spain would have dared to reach so bold a decision which *irreversibly* and *categorically* removed the convert from the ranks of the Jewish people. It is impossible to overemphasize the importance of grasping this point.

Yet another issue concerning the ability of a convert to inherit from his Jewish father. Maimonides already ruled that a convert does inherit from a Jewish relative, but added: "and if the Jewish court saw fit to forfeit his money and punish him that he not inherit in order to strengthen their hands [discourage conversion], they have permission." In such an instance, if the convert has Jewish children (who were born before his conversion and who remain Jews), the inheritance which should have gone to the convert would go to them, "and so is the custom always in the Maghrib" (Spain and North Africa).[38]

Ibn Adret cited the responsum of Haya (Hai) *Gaon* that a convert does not inherit, since he as "gone out of the sanctity of [the people] Israel," for a convert "goes from people to people, and this is not done."[39]

Similarly, the *geonim* ruled that the property of a woman who converted and then died could not be inherited by her Jewish husband. Netanyahu correctly observed, therefore, that the *geonic* opinion thus was that a convert changed not only his or her "religion," but also "peoplehood," going completely from one people to another.[40] This is correct, but only with regard to this one issue of inheritance; however, it is likely that this ruling influenced the attitude of the Spanish Jewish authorities with regard to converts in general, as noted above. Maimonides' contrary position must be explained in that he most probably was considering Jewish conversion to Islam, which he did not consider idolatry. He took a very strict position with regard to conversion to "idolatry" (Christianity, in his view). The essential underlying Talmudic text which provides us with the distinctions in terminology which we have previously discussed appears to be 'A.Z. 26b, where the distinction is made between an "appetitive" or "lascivious" and a "defiant" apostate. One opinion holds the "defiant" apostate to be a *min* (in the context, one who eats ritually unfit meat; obviously a Jewish heretic is meant). According to the other opinion, however, a *min* is one who worships idols; i.e., not a heretic but a complete Gentile. Maimonides ruled:

> *minim,* and they are idolaters, or one who commits transgressions defiantly . . . and *apiqorsin,* Jews who deny the Torah and prophecy, it is an obligation to kill them if one has it in his power, with a sword in public; and if not, let him initiate actions which will cause their death

such as placing them in a situation of danger and not helping them. But Gentiles (idolators) with whom Jews are not at war must not be dealt with in such a manner; yet nevertheless it is forbidden to actively save them from danger. Even a Jew who is habituated in committing transgressions falls into this latter category, and is no longer considered "your brother" who must be saved; but a Jew who commits transgressions only for his own pleasure (an appetitive apostate) must be saved—i.e., is still considered a Jew.[41]

Jacob b. Asher, son of the renowned rabbi of Toledo and author of the *Tur*, was more circumspect with regard to Gentiles, and interpreted all rulings not to save them as applying to "Canaanites" at the time the Jews had their own land. Nevertheless, he included in his definitive legal code that *minim*, informers, defiant apostates, and *apiqorsim* are to be "killed with the hands."[42]

Ibn Abī Sarwī had apparently yet another text of the Talmudic passage, which stated that a *lascivious* apostate is a convert (*meshumad*) and a defiant apostate is a *min*, and also that *even* a defiant apostate is a *meshumad*, and a *min* is an idolater. Although this is a patently absurd reading, it was also the text which Menahem ha-Meiri had (*Beit ha-behirah, ad loc*). Indeed, Ibn Abī Sarwī himself was puzzled by the reading of the text as he had it, and noted that there is no difference between a *meshumad* and a *min* in this case. (This, of course, is much less a difficulty than why it should occur to anyone that a lascivious apostate would be considered a *meshumad*. No such opinion had ever been recorded or even suggested by any legal authority.) He offers the explanation of his teacher, Jonah Gerundi (did he also have the same incorrect text?) that if a *meshumad* in the time of the Temple brought an offering, it was received, but not that of a *min*. The difference "in this time" (after the Temple) would be that if a *meshumad* slaughtered an animal, and Jews supervised the slaughter, the meat is permitted. All of this is due, however, to the error in the Talmudic text he had, for the text should read (as it does in the present versions) *mumar*, and not *meshumad*. Indeed, it is astonishing that Ibn Abī Sarwī, and if we are to rely upon his testimony also his teacher Rabbi Jonah, could have forgotten here the important and lengthy discussion of precisely these laws in *Hulin*, or the discussion of them by authorities like Ibn Adret.[43]

The law is unmistakably that neither a *mumar* with respect to idolatry, nor a *meshumad*, may bring a sacrifice, nor is their slaughter acceptable. Students are rarely to be relied upon in reporting what their teachers said, however; and as for Ibn Abī Sarwī himself, obviously he needed to learn considerably more before writing anything. These are not phenomena with which we are unfamiliar in modern times as well.

Yom Ṭov Ishbīlī is also reported to have said that a convert to Christianity, or a proselyte who reverted to his former religion, is considered with regard to purchasing and selling or contracting financial obligations to be still a Jew, unless the law of the kingdom is that he buy and sell in accord with Gentile law, in which case "the law of the kingdom is the law." Furthermore, a Jew who transgressed the Jewish law, and then repented, does not require immersion according to the letter of the law (as a proselyte would); nevertheless, he should be immersed from the viewpoint of rabbinical law.[44] If we examine this reliably reported opinion carefully, we see that it does not permit us to conclude that Ishbīlī considered a convert to be still a Jew from the point of view of full and complete status, but only with regard to certain contractual obligations. This is in accord with the previous rulings on marriage which we have discussed. The *contractual obligation* still falls under the category of Jewish law, while the *status* of the person is, in fact, no longer that of a Jew. This explains why he requires immersion for a repentant *meshumad*. What this means, in fact, is that a returning *meshumad* is viewed exactly as a Gentile, and must therefore undergo complete conversion (thus immersion is required in such a case, for he would already have been circumcised, of course; later Marranos, after the Expulsion, who left Portugal or in rare cases Spain also had to be circumcised as part of their conversion to Judaism).

Thus, the position which was unquestionably held by such fifteenth-century theorists as Isaac ʿArama, and by the overwhelming majority of rabbis after the Expulsion—namely, that the Marranos were *complete Gentiles* and that the minority of "returners" among them were to be considered "not as penitents, but as proselytes," i.e., converts to Judaism—is found already firmly established in legal opinion in the fourteenth century.[45] The conclusion is thus inescapable: the Jewish authorities of Spain already considered the conversos to be not *anusim* but *meshumadim*, not "forced" converts acting under duress but complete and willful converts who were no longer part of the Jewish people, and this in the *fourteenth* century, not just in the fifteenth.

One might suppose that the attacks on Jewish communities in the summer of 1391 resulted in massive conversions due to fear, like those of the First Crusade in Germany. Indeed, there is considerable evidence of mass conversion, but given the forceful reaction of the kings there was clearly no reason for "fear," nor did the rabbinic authorities treat those conversions as happening under "duress" but, again, as complete *willful* conversion. Furthermore, those who had the opportunity to leave the country and return to Judaism did not do so.

The Historical Record

Turning from the Hebrew sources to the few historical records we have concerning conversos in the early fourteenth century, we hear, for example, of three Jews in La Almunia (a small town near Calatayud) who in 1342 paid 10,000 *sous* to Pedro IV to be pardoned for having aided and encouraged certain conversos to return to Judaism. The accused Jews had been seized by the Inquisition for this crime (they were Gento [Yom Ṭov] Almuli, his wife Gemila [Jamila], and their son Jucef, who certainly was the Jucef Almuli who was physician to the *infant* Alfonso in 1324 and after).[46]

As we shall see, it was only in such rare cases that the Inquisition was allowed to touch Jews at all; otherwise, they were strictly forbidden to investigate Jews.

The Black Death, or plague, in 1348 which decimated much of Europe also affected Spain, although perhaps to a lesser degree (certainly less in Castile). Jews were also blamed in some communities, particularly in Aragón-Catalonia, and attacked, and some were killed, in spite of the strong efforts of the king to prevent this. We hear, however, nothing about conversions, except in Perpignan (in Provence) where several Jews apparently converted. A question was addressed to Nissim Gerundi concerning a woman whose husband died some four years before the plague and who had a brother who had converted and now lived in the village of Gaillac (near Albi). This man's Jewish name had been En Samuel de Castres, and after his conversion it was changed to maestre Benedit (which would indicate, probably, that he was a physician). Other conversos at the time of the plague in Perpignan are also mentioned there.[47]

It was, however, the unprecedented attacks on Jewish communities throughout Spain in the summer of 1391 which constituted the worst episode in Spanish Jewish history up to that point. This is not the place to detail all the many important facts and new information concerning these tragic events. What is of importance for our present purposes, however, is information concerning the conversion of Jews at that time. In Castile, where the attacks began at the incitement of the fanatic archdeacon Ferrant Martínez in Seville, the young king (twelve at the time), Enrique III, left Madrid in May and went to Segovia, where messengers came and informed him of the attack on the Jews in Seville, the robbery of the Jewish *aljama* there, and the conversion of "most" of the Jews, and similarly in Córdoba, Toledo, and elsewhere. The king acted promptly, sending not only messengers with orders that such attacks be stopped, but also archers to other towns to defend the Jews.

Pedro López de Ayala, the chancellor and chronicler of the king, notes that the attacks were due more to greed than to devotion, and that people wished also to attack the Muslims (a fact totally ignored by historians) but refrained because of fear of what might happen to Christians in Granada and North Africa. He concludes that Martínez was able to incite the attacks because no one feared the boy king.[48]

The king wrote a letter to the council and justices of Burgos which basically confirms López de Ayala's judgment of the situation, concluding that he and his council had decided to arrest anyone involved in such offenses, for the Jews were always guarded and protected by "the kings, my ancestors, and the Church [read *eglesia*] itself by law" guarded and defended them. In a subsequent letter, the king said that some persons of the lower class and of little understanding had attacked the *judería* also in Burgos and forced some Jews to convert, against both his law and that of the Church, and he took the Jews under his protection. Nevertheless, in 1392 the king again wrote that the Jews were being robbed and many had fled to take refuge in the homes of "good men" (Christians) in the city. Some desired to convert, others already had, while others wished to return to the *judería*. In a second letter that summer the king noted that conversos were molesting the Jews and ordered this stopped, nor should conversos be allowed to compel Jews to convert. "Our law neither orders nor consents that any should turn to the Catholic faith by force and against his will. The Jews who by their own will desire to become Christians, it is well to receive them, but not to force those who of their own will do not [wish to] convert." Nor should they be compelled to listen to sermons of conversos or (old) Christians.[49]

Our most important Jewish source is the letter of Ḥasdai Crescas, the renowned philosopher and also rabbinic leader of Aragón-Catalonia. He states that many Jews in Toledo were killed, and many converted, unable to save themselves (but see p. 372 below). So also in Valencia and Majorca. As for Barcelona, he notes that the Jews took refuge in the king's castle and that the governor of the city worked to save them; nevertheless, many died (including either a son, or more probably, a son-in-law, of Crescas himself) and others converted. A statement of Reuben, son of Nissim Gerundi, confirms Crescas' letter, and estimates that a total of 140,000 Jews converted (in the kingdom of Aragón-Catalonia alone). He blames the disaster on the preaching of the friars, but adds that "many of the governors of the cities and the ministers and nobility defended us, and many of our brethren took refuge in castles, where they provided us with food."[50]

Juan I of Aragón-Catalonia ordered measures taken to protect the Jews, just as Enrique had done in Castile. In Perpignan, for example, he later also prohibited the forced conversion of Jews, and gave orders for the protection of Jews in Zaragoza, Tortosa, Barcelona, and other cities. When a Jew of Zaragoza was forcibly detained in a castle of the bishop of Osma, the queen wrote not one but two letters protesting this abuse. She stated that she would be pleased if all the "infidels" of the world would convert, but not through force, "for any act which is not voluntary is without merit."[51]

Even allowing for the great exaggerations in the letter of Crescas (the "destruction" of the community of Toledo, which we know to be false; that no Jews were left in the whole kingdom of Valencia, etc.), these attacks were a catastrophe for the entire Jewish population of Spain. Nevertheless, given the absolutely undeniable fact that both in Castile and in Aragón-Catalonia the kings and nobles acted promptly and effectively to stop the attacks and severely punish the perpetrators, and at least in the latter kingdom also to prohibit the forced conversion of Jews and permit any thus converted to return to their faith, the inescapable conclusion is that the overwhelming majority of the conversions were voluntary. Certainly, the converted Jews who remained Christians in spite of the permission to return to their own people did so voluntarily. This, as we shall see, was a fact well known to the rabbinical authorities of the period.

Other facts also confirm it. Thus, in Barcelona the synagogue of the *call* En Sanahuja, one of several in the city, was transformed by five conversos into a church of the Holy Trinity. Another synagogue eventually became the present Church of San Jaime, near the street called *Tres Llits* (three beds), which actually was *Tressallits,* or "renegades" (conversos).[52] Even given the opportunity to resume their Jewish status, the conversos of Barcelona only too willingly chose to remain Christian.

Hitherto overlooked by scholars (Baer, Netanyahu, Beinart, etc.) is the important document, available in a book published in 1941 and reviewed by Cantera in 1944, from the Christian judges of Valencia (1403) to certain conversos who had fled to Argel in North Africa and there returned to Judaism. However, "recognizing their error," they had now reverted to Christianity and severed all connections with Jews there and desired to return to the Church (and to Spain). The judges expressed their great pleasure at this.[53]

In July of 1391, Isaac b. Sheshet (Perfet), rabbi of Valencia and chief legal authority of the Jews of the kingdom of Aragón-Catalonia, was compelled to convert, after having been accused of "a crime" for which he was sentenced to death (possibly, although there is no evidence, he may in fact already have been compelled to convert and then "relapsed" to Judaism, for which he was now condemned). After the intercession of officials of the *infant* Martin and because his conversion was seen to "do much good" (i.e., influence the rest of the Jews to convert), a pardon was granted to him.

When the aged Isaac b. Sheshet left Valencia in 1391 and went to North Africa, he replied to a question from a rabbi there, previously a rabbi in Majorca, concerning a Jewish will that had been made in a Christian court. He stated that the doubts concerning it would be proper if it had been made by Jews in a place where they were allowed to act according to Jewish law, "but this testator was living in Majorca in the presumptive state of being an *idolator,* and so his widow who seeks to inherit from him was also there in the presumptive state of a Christian, and so [also] these who are relatives seeking to inherit; and even when they were yet Jews they had to judge everything according to Christian laws, for thus the community of Majorca always did by its own choice." (He gives a Hebrew summary of the text of the document of the *baile* of Majorca addressed to the *consuls* and *qadis* [Muslim judges] concerning the converso Joan From, whose Jewish name had been Abraham Yaḥyun, and of his will in favor of his wife, Bonietta, previously Esther, dated 30 December 1401.)[54]

Thus we see that in the opinion of the foremost legal authority of the age such conversos were to be considered "idolaters," and also that the Jewish community of Majorca had voluntarily decided to judge all such matters in accord with Christian, rather than Jewish, law already long before the persecutions of 1391. This may be an important clue to a growing tendency toward assimilation which made it all the easier for the majority of the Jews of Majorca to willingly convert in 1391.

Interestingly, it happens that Simon b. Ṣemaḥ Duran, who himself fled Majorca in 1391 and became a rabbi also in North Africa, dealt with this same case in his responsa, but his version is slightly different. First, he indicates that it was the intention of Abraham Yaḥyun and his wife to *leave* Majorca and come to North Africa. Second, whereas Isaac b. Sheshet spoke in hostile terms about their being "idolaters," and referred to them as "apostates," Duran talks about "compulsion" and the "land of persecution." He indeed cites the decision of Isaac, with which he disagrees sharply (as usual), and contrary to what Baer understood, he decided against Isaac's ruling.[55]

Isaac again mentions the practice of the Jews of Majorca of bringing all matters before Christian courts in yet another responsum: "When we came to this land [North Africa], we did not see any custom in [the matter under discussion there], for the inhabitants of the land did not go according to the laws of our Torah but rather all disputes are brought before the Muslim judge. Also the community of Majorca, from which the *majority* of our community [in North Africa] comes, only followed there the law of the Muslims [*sic;* apparently a slip of the pen for 'Christians']." However, Duran again sheds a different light on this when in his letter of 1435 to Majorca he writes: "You are in a place where they *do not permit* you to judge civil matters" by Jewish law. There is some evidence from Christian sources to support this even for the fourteenth century.[56]

One apparent exception to this general attitude toward conversos was that of Profiat Duran, who also had converted to Christianity and then returned to Judaism. In his letter of condolence to En Joseph Abraham of Gerona on the death of his father, Abraham b. Isaac ha-Levy, he wrote that the most important and ancient of the commandments was circumcision, which alone sufficed for the redemption of the people, and continued:

> And I say that [the tribulations of the Babylonian exile] are a hint to the portion of the seed of Abraham *compelled* to neglect the Torah openly and upon whom have passed decrees of apostasy in this great region [Aragón-Catalonia] [but] he [Abraham b. Isaac ha-Levy] saw the reluctance of part of the people to repent . . . it is possible already to consider from this that that portion [of the people] has gone out of the generality of the people which God has chosen as His inheritance, [therefore] he tore his clothing and cried and said, "Perhaps, heaven forbid, they have no remedy" . . . and the situation in this exile is like that in other exiles and as in the exile of Egypt when the people

stumbled in idolatry willingly [but] not for this were they excluded from the generality of the seed of Abraham [i.e., they were still considered Jews] and [God] did not refrain from bringing them out of Egypt. . . . In the Babylonian exile, although all of them stumbled in idolatry and under compulsion . . . not for this were they excluded from the seed of Abraham, and in His love of them and His compassion [God] redeemed them. So is it proper that it continue in this great exile, for although a portion of the people has stumbled in like manner [idolatry] due to *complete compulsion* from fear of the decrees, not for this have they been excluded from the people of God.[57]

It is clear from this that, shortly after 1391, Duran believed that the majority of the converts had acted under duress and because of their fear of what might happen. However, his reference to the *reluctance* of some to repent after the persecutions ended, and to the possibility therefore that they had *withdrawn completely* from the Jewish people, already indicates his conviction that those who remained as converts were no longer Jews at all.

Isaac b. Sheshet was asked in another case about a woman, described as an *anusah* (convert under duress), who was divorced from her husband who had also converted, where the bill of divorce was signed by *anusim* (as witnesses). The woman succeeded in fleeing Spain and went to North Africa, where she could "serve God at ease and without fear," and the witnesses were known to be Jews at heart but unable to leave Spain. However, there was some suspicion that they remained in Spain only because of their possessions there, and thus might in fact be considered "completely wicked." The rabbi replied that in the case of duress, where there is fear for life, even if one violates one of the commandments under which it is required to die rather than transgress (idolatry, adultery, or murder), he is exempt from any punishment, and thus they were acceptable witnesses. He also cited the previously mentioned responsum of Ibn Adret. But all of this, he makes clear, is only in the case of a true *anūs,* whereas in the case of an apostate, even an "appetitive" or "lascivious" apostate, such a one is unfit for testimony. He concludes by warning that converts who remain for some time in the land where they converted, and do not flee to another land, must be investigated carefully:

> for some of them could have left that land [Spain] and saved themselves from persecution, but even though the beginning of their apostasy was in compulsion, afterward they rejected the yoke of heaven and severed the tradition of the Torah from themselves and *willingly* walk in the law of idolaters, transgressing all the commandments of the Torah. Not only this, they pursue [persecute] the unfortunate Jews among them to accuse them and annihilate them as a people, that the name of Israel should no longer be mentioned. Also the *anusim* whose hearts are toward heaven and endeavor to leave the persecution, these evil ones [converts] inform on them to the government—as we have heard concerning some in Valencia and in Barcelona.[58]

Nothing could be more eloquent than the language of this important responsum. This is not 1492, but a whole century earlier, and we already hear of *willful* converts who abandon the entire Torah and the commandments and become such zealous Christians that they persecute their fellow converts who are wavering, and even inform on them to government authorities. All of this was to be exactly repeated following the Expulsion, and even before, in the fifteenth century, when "new Christians" became the worst enemies of those of their brothers who clung to any extent to some vestiges of Jewish identity, informing on them to the Inquisition in order to prove their own zeal as faithful Christians.

As we shall see, the Christian authorities were willing to allow any conversos who wished to leave Spain after 1391 to do so, even though they knew that their intention was to go to Muslim lands and there return to Judaism. In plain point of fact, very few of these who were able to leave Spain did so.

Isaac b. Sheshet, writing from Algiers about 1395, related that a certain would-be sage came to the city and wanted to take over and drive Isaac from the community, but was prevented from doing so by the community leaders. They wanted also to excommunicate the man, who, in Majorca had also insulted scholars, but Isaac intervened, saying that "after what happened to him" (apparently in the persecution) they should not deal harshly with him. He then continues, "one day a ship arrived here from Majorca with 45 'souls' of *anusim* from Majorca, Valencia, and Barcelona, and the [Muslim] governor wanted to bring them into the city" because of the great benefit financially they would bring. Previously, Jews were allowed free entry, and the judge of the city became angry at some Muslim merchants who wanted to impose an entry tax because they feared competition, to which he replied that God could take care of the whole world, including these Jews and these merchants. When the governor also wanted to impose a tax, in the hope that many would return to Majorca, he was supported by some of the local Jews who apparently also feared competition. Isaac became angered at this and imposed excommunication on any Jew who caused any of these *anusim* to return to Majorca (nevertheless, two rabbis of Algiers nullified his decree, and it was only through the intervention of the Muslim ruler that he was able to reinstate it).[59]

Simon Duran, also in Algiers, was asked about wine that had been sent by a *meshumad* in Majorca, and whether it could be used by Jews. His lengthy reply states that it is certainly prohibited, citing Maimonides that one who does not flee a land of persecution when he is able is like an idolater, "and it is obvious that these *anusim* were able to save themselves and flee, as many of them did," he concludes. On the other hand, he was willing to be lenient with them and say that either they were not able to obtain money to leave, for the expense was great, or they did not leave because of fear of being caught and punished, or they indeed tried to flee and were somehow prevented from doing so. In short, he judged even those who remained as true *anusim* (under duress) until it was revealed that they transgressed commandments of the Torah without any danger of coercion. Although they might have remained only because of fear of financial loss should they leave, they were not yet to be considered idolaters (see *Pesaḥim* 25a). As to the wine itself, he came finally to the conclusion that these *anusim* (as long as they did not violate the Torah) were not suspect, and especially with regard to wine which they claimed to have made for consumption by observant Jews and according to Jewish law. Not only was this directly contrary to the position of his colleague Isaac b. Sheshet, and indeed to the majority of Jewish authorities of the fourteenth century, but Duran himself changed his position and apparently reversed himself in another responsum written shortly after this (1404–5).[60]

Nevertheless, those authors who have dealt with these two responsa have somewhat exaggerated the extent to which Duran in fact changed his position. In the second responsum, Duran is discussing a particular convert and whether his testimony that wine left for safekeeping with a Gentile is still pure, against the testimony of an observant Jew that it has become defiled. Duran says: "And with regard to the trustworthiness of an *anūs* against [testimony] of another [a Jew], certainly if he worships idolatry not under duress or coercion, or desecrates the Sabbath publicly without coercion, he is not believed at all." There is no "change of position" here at all, for of course this is the law, and he stated exactly that in his previous responsum. He goes on to say, however, that if the person does *not* serve idolatry when there is no coercion and *does* keep the Sabbath in public, he is to be believed when he says that the wine involved is permitted. Then he adds:

> And there is in the matter of their trustworthiness and their touch [of wine] a thing very difficult. I shall not explain all the reasons concerning this, but I shall write for you the language of Maimonides who wrote [*M. T. Madaʿ*: "Yesodey ha-Torah" 5.4]: "but if he is able to flee and save himself from the hand of the evil king and does not do so, he is like a dog who returns to its vomit [Prov. 26.11], and he is called a willful worshipper of idolatry and is denied the future world and descends to the lowest level of hell."

It is obvious that Duran is merely summarizing here briefly what he discussed at great length in his earlier responsum. It was not necessary to go again into a long analysis of Maimonides' statement because it did not apply if this particular *anūs* was not of the category discussed.

The heart of Duran's opinion is in the following paragraph where he tells his correspondent from Majorca that they are there in a position to decide if this *anūs* is observing the customs of a Gentile and is considered a true Christian by the Gentiles. Since this appears to be the case, he concludes that *this* wine is prohibited for several reasons. Again, this is a particular case, completely unlike the previous one, and so the law dictated clearly that such wine is prohibited. We do not learn from this of any "change" or "reversal" in Duran's views.

However, at the end of the responsum Duran discusses the general practice among the Jews of Majorca of believing *anusim* when they say they bought wine from a Jew or made it for a Jew, but not relying on them when they say the wine was in the possession of Gentiles. He says that they have not made it clear whether all *anusim* are alike, "for we see those who come here [North Africa], that some are complete idolaters [Christians], and therefore who can determine who is fit and who is not?" Further, they do not consider that "the majority; close to all" of the converts profane the Sabbath publicly, and that they did not leave Spain even when government permission to do so was given to them. Many, indeed, built houses and married off their sons and daughters (thus revealing their intentions not to leave at all). Some of the converts who fled to North Africa even returned to live in Spain.

He complains that it seems the Jews of Majorca consider that Maimonides wrote only about severe persecutions, where the king constantly persecutes the Jews and does not allow them to leave at all,

> but in these decrees [of 1391], and particularly in that place [Majorca], they are lenient with the *anusim* and allow them to do as they will and do not coerce them to worship idolatry, and they are almost in a presumptive state of being Jews as far as they [the Christians] are concerned, so that they give them permission to leave as they desire. But if a true Gentile [convert] were to leave there to return to the faith of Moses, even were he to give all the money in the world, they would not permit him; on the contrary, they would kill him. From this [that *anusim* are allowed to leave] it appears that they are in a presumptive state of complete Jews as far as they [Christians] are concerned; but [= for] in the requirement of their religion, one who has converted even under duress cannot return to the religion of Israel. Therefore, they close their eyes at [these converts], and there is nothing in their conversion except that their names are Gentile names . . . and since the *anusim* see this, they consider their remaining there completely permissible.

He concludes that the leniency of the Jews in considering them trustworthy has encouraged them to remain, and it is of *this* that he says, "and this is not my opinion"; i.e., it is not that Duran did not believe that the *anusim* were good Jews, for he says that he does not know and that the local Jewish community must decide that, but that in his opinion the true *anusim* should be encouraged to leave (see further discussion in the note).[61]

Nothing in Duran's opinion has "changed." In 1404, as in 1391, he regarded the true *anūs* leniently, as possibly willing to return to Judaism; but the complete and actual convert (whom he correctly calls *meshumad*) was, of course, another matter.

In a responsum referring, apparently, to new converts in the persecutions in Majorca in 1435 ("these last *anusim* who as yet do not have a reputation of profaning the Sabbath publicly"), and whether wine which they made and sent to North Africa should be permitted, Duran ruled that it should not, especially since "without doubt" they did not themselves refrain from drinking Gentile wine and thus were suspect with regard to their own wine.[62]

Note that he distinguishes here among the "first *anusim*" (those of 1391), between those who really were compelled by the sword to convert, and "those that were not compelled by complete compulsion," i.e., who willfully converted.

However, there is yet another responsum by Duran, overlooked by Netanyahu, on the same issue. This was written to Mordecai Najār in Tenes, sometime in the period after 1404 but before 1435. The case concerned wine sent to Najār by an *anūs* of Majorca with an accompanying letter indicating that it had been made by an observant Jew in "Murbiter" (Murviedro, presently Sagunto, on the coast north of Valencia). Duran wrote that certainly *anusim* are not to be relied upon in this, but in this case the wine obviously was not made by the *anūs* nor did it even come from Majorca, "and everyone can recognize by its taste and its fragrance that it is from the kingdom of Valencia," and furthermore it is "obvious" that *anusim* do not engage in the sale of forbidden wine to Jews since they know this must not be done, and this alone is sufficient to permit the use of all the wine which comes from Murviedro to "these lands" (North Africa) which is sent by *anusim*.[63]

More important still is another responsum, also neglected by Netanyahu, written to his senior colleague Isaac b. Sheshet concerning the permissibility of eating cheese obtained from an *anūs* who is suspected of not observing the relevant dietary laws. Isaac wanted to rely on the reasoning of Aaron ha-Levy of Barcelona that it is permitted to eat such food if the *anūs* is suspected only of eating forbidden foods but not of giving (or selling) them to Jews. Duran countered with the contrary argument of Ibn Adret, and wrote that the opinion of Aaron ha-Levy on this was not to be accepted at all.[64]

Yet another overlooked ruling concerns a bill of divorce written by a *meshumad* in Majorca and sent to his Jewish wife in Tenes. Duran wrote that the document was null and void, like that of a Gentile who is not legally fit to write a bill of divorce, "and such is the law with regard to a *meshumad* with respect to idolatry or public desecration of the Sabbath, who is like a *meshumad* with respect to the entire Torah." Yet another question from Tenes concerned such a bill of divorce "written in Majorca by one of those *called anusim,* and *without doubt* they bow down to idolatry and desecrate the Sabbath publicly." Yet this person was said to have lived like a Jew, and when he died the Christian authorities did not want to bury him until they were bribed by his former wife. Here, Duran expressed doubt about the previous ruling, and wrote that just as an act of marriage by a *meshumad* is valid, so should a divorce be (an obviously fallacious argument, since divorce requires a document whereas marriage does not necessarily).[65]

One of the most famous of these opinions concerns two *anusim* who married women of the same category: whether such marriage is valid according to Jewish law, and if there should be any distinction between those born before the persecutions of 1391 and those born afterward and raised as converts (Christians). Duran replied that by law even a *meshumad* may contract a valid marriage, from the rule "Israelite even though he transgresses," and by analogy with a proselyte to Judaism who returns to his former religion, whose marriage remains valid (again, a faulty argument). After a lengthy discussion, Duran makes an important observation: all that he has so far said about the validity of the marriage applies only to a *meshumad* with respect to *one* transgression of the commandments, but one who is completely contaminated by idolatry (in other words, a willing convert to Christianity) is like a *min* and may be killed; and since this is so, he is not in the category of "brother" (i.e., a Jew) with regard to the validity of any such contract.

Duran then raises the question of witnesses, noting that marriage requires valid witnesses, and thus if the marriage of *anusim* was before observant Jews it would be valid, but if before *anusim* it would not be valid, for they are like a Jew who commits transgressions and thus not suitable as a witness. It is thus not all the converts about whom Duran is speaking, but specifically those who remained in Spain after 1391 of their own free will and willfully violated the Torah even in private and worshiped "idolatry."[66]

Nor are the above by any means the only responsa of Duran overlooked by scholars. Duran wrote to Maimon (Maimūn) Najār, the Jewish judge of Constantine, concerning the question of mourning the death of the son of a *meshumad.* He ruled that if the son died while still a minor (under thirteen), certainly he is to be mourned, for in any case he is not obligated to observe commandments. However, if he had grown up and still continued his nonobservance, and in fact was himself a *meshumad* (Christian) without any duress, then he may not be mourned, "for one does not mourn an enemy of God, nor does [a priest who is a relative] become defiled for him, and thus it is written in *Sifra* [apparently the reference is to "Parshat Emor" 1.1.16], and it is forbidden to assist him to live, and permitted to lend him money on interest [like a Gentile]." He concludes that he is a complete *meshumad* who lives by the laws of idolatry, and his relative not only must not mourn his death but should put on white clothes to celebrate the death of an enemy of God. "*But if he holds to the religion of Moses and Judaism* [Mosaic and Jewish law] *in secret,*" he is not of this category, and it is an obligation to mourn him, "for there is no greater duress than this."[67]

We see that Duran still thought it theoretically possible for a convert to practice Judaism, but that in the overwhelming majority of cases converts did not, and were thus complete Gentiles.

All of this introduces another important consideration. As Isaac b. Sheshet rightly pointed out, there are three commandments which are considered so basic that the Talmud warns that one must die rather than transgress them. One of these is idolatry. While it is technically correct that there is no punishment if one violates this injunction and transgresses, this means that there is no punishment at the hands of man (a Jewish court), but there is from God. No Jew could possibly have thought that he was permitted to convert to Christianity and willfully remain a convert. Even the rabbis of France and Germany were lenient in dealing with converts only because they assumed they were under duress and would return to Judaism. Failing that, it is quite clear the convert is no longer regarded as a Jew, but as a complete Gentile. Not only this, but the Jews had an alternative: namely, they could flee the land of "persecution" and go elsewhere. Many, we know, did just that in 1391 (besides fleeing himself, Isaac b. Sheshet provides testimony to it in several of his responsa, and there are numerous references to it throughout the responsa of Simon b. Ṣemaḥ Duran; many Jews also went to Palestine). Already Maimonides, in response to the Almohad persecution of the twelfth century, and in spite of the fact that he did not consider Islam to be idolatry at all, warned that Jews must flee the country if there is no other way to escape the necessity of conversion.

Thus, even if we were to assume (in my opinion, an absolutely incorrect assumption) that the situation in 1391 was such that Jews were under duress and were in fear for their lives, Jewish law was extremely clear as to how they were expected to act. They must die rather than transgress the commandments (indeed, according to the Talmud, in a time of religious persecution Jews must die rather than transgress even a minor custom), and they must flee the land if they think that there is no other way out. In fact, of course, none of this was the case. The relatively few Jews who were actually forcibly baptized no doubt could have easily returned to the Jewish community once the riots of the summer were over. The kings acted promptly and vigorously to stop the persecution and to punish all involved. There is absolutely no evidence to suggest that the officials would have stood in the way of any Jews who wanted to leave and go to North Africa or any other country, as many did. Nor, as Duran proves, did these officials even stand in the way of those converts who later wished to leave. This same thing remains true of the entire fifteenth century as well, and leaves us with the inescapable question which so far not one single scholar has attempted to address: if Jews were being "coerced" into converting in Spain, why did they not simply leave the country? The answer, of course, is that they were not so coerced, but that they freely *chose* to become Christians.

It thus became necessary early on to have some clear criterion by which to judge the intent of a converso. That criterion was to be the actions, and not merely the words, of the person in question. This is clearly seen not only in Duran, but even much earlier in a decision of Jonah Gerundi, cited by his student Ibn Adret. He was asked about a man, an apparent convert to Christianity, who went from city to city. He said that he believed in Christianity when he was with Christians, and he entered the synagogue and claimed to be a Jew when he was among Jews. Rabbi Jonah answered that he is to be believed when he says he is a Jew, because it is likely that he lies about "idolatry," and when he says he believes in it, it is only due to "the pleasures of his evil inclination, and he does not believe in his heart"; but his belief in Judaism (not the term used) is "an upright faith, and good, proper, and true, and a thing which is likely." *Nevertheless,* an apostate who profanes the Sabbath in public is a *min,* considered a complete Gentile. The same presumption applies to one who "worships idolatry" three times, and thus establishes that he is truly a convert.[68] Thus we see, in spite of the sentimental view about one's good intentions with regard to Judaism, that what is of decisive importance is action, and not mere words: if one commits an act which establishes that he or she is a sincere convert, there is no longer any presumption of Jewishness.

Naḥmanides explained that a convert is like a Jew with regard to obligations of the Torah; i.e, he may contract a valid marriage, divorce, etc., just as even a Gentile may (because we are concerned he may be from the "lost tribes" and thus possibly a Jew!). However, he argued that a convert may also inherit, and from this it is clear that the law of a Jew still applies, in his view, to a convert. This was, as we have seen, a minority position.

Even with regard to the laws of sales and damages, converts have the full status of Jews, and only with regard to such things as returning lost objects to them are they to be treated as non-Jews (indeed, worse, for lost articles must be returned to non-Jews). He concludes by admitting, strangely, that he has not seen the rulings of the *geonim* or of the rabbis of previous generations on this issue, and specifically asks his correspondent to investigate the writings of Judah b. Barzilay on this.[69] Note that this entire ruling completely contradicts the position taken in his novellae on the Talmud, previously discussed. We must therefore conclude that this responsum (indeed, probably all of them) was written in his youth, before the novellae, and that he changed his view in later years. One is also forced to this conclusion by the incredible statement that he has not seen the opinions of the *geonim* or of the previous rabbis, and that he has not even seen the work of Judah b. Barzilay, who had been a rabbi in Barcelona.

Further indication that a convert was *not* considered a Jew is found in the comment of Joseph Ibn Ḥabib on the statement (*Sanhedrin* 60a) that at this time one who hears the cursing of God or profane utterance of God's name by an idolater need not tear his clothing (as a sign of mourning), since it is so frequent that if this were required one's clothing would be full of rips. Ibn Ḥabib observes that in his time the same applies to a convert to "idolatry," but if a Jew were so heretical as to use God's name in such a way one must still tear the clothing. Thus we see that a Jew who converts was considered to have no respect for the God of Israel at all.[70]

Two cases involving Ishbīlī are instructive. In the year 1314 in the town of Daroca, two Jews were caught late at night in the synagogue, where they broke open the doors of the ark where the Torah scrolls were kept in order to steal the silver ornaments on them. They were placed in a kind of community jail but managed to escape. The mother of one of them came to the Jewish court with the plea that she feared her son would convert because he had been banished from the town, as four other Jews and their mother (the widow of one of the Jewish thieves) who had previously been banished had all converted. The mother further explained that her husband had voluntarily washed all the Jewish corpses for the community (to prepare them for burial), and that she herself acted as midwife to all the Jewish women; thus, the accused man certainly did not come from a nonobservant home. In his reply, Ishbīlī ruled that if the community truly feared that the man would convert, and if he appeared repentant and would accept suitable chastisement as atonement, the banishment could be lifted.[71]

In the second case, two Jewish men and their wives, who were neighbors, quarreled constantly, until one of the men struck the other with a knife, also striking the man's wife. The community leaders imposed certain decrees (unspecified) on all four of them. However, some of the local Christians interceded on behalf of one of the men, both in groups and individually, until the governor of the city himself investigated the case. He ordered the decrees lifted, and any fine due to the government nullified. However, the Jewish leaders said they did not have the authority for this. Then the *alcaide* (military official), son-in-law of the governor, came to the synagogue on the Sabbath to entreat the entire congregation to show mercy on this Jew. They agreed to consult Ishbīlī, the leading rabbinical authority of the time. They feared, as they explained to him, that the man might convert if they did nothing. Ishbīlī found a means by which he could permit them to annul the decrees they had imposed.[72]

Not only in the legal sources and responsa literature, but also in some of the homiletic literature of the fourteenth century (just as in the fifteenth century), we find confirmation of the sincerity of the conversos' commitment to Christianity. Commenting on the biblical passage (Deut. 4.27–28) which warns the Israelites that they will be dispersed among the nations, and there serve idols of wood and stone "which neither see nor hear nor eat nor smell," Nissim Gerundi said in a sermon that this was a warning to the Israelites that if they worshiped idols in their own land, because of the great artifice (*hithokhmut*) of that idolatry which caused them to do great evil in the sight of God without considering it, their punishment would be exile from their land and dispersion among the Gentiles and the loss of their wisdom (*hokhmah*):

> And because the custom of [their] fathers was in [their] hands, therefore [they] worship images of which no aspect of wisdom or spirituality is seen in them; not like those which [they] worshiped in their land because of that artifice, rather [they worship these] because of absolute folly, for they see no sign from [these idols] at all. That is why [scripture] expands upon it saying: "They do not see and hear," that is, they do not see in them that same strange thing that was seen in those they worshiped in their own land—for there is no doubt that they saw in those [idols] very strange things.[73]

Clearly all of this alludes to those Jews who have *willfully* converted to Christianity in Spain, and who worshiped the statues of saints, etc. This he blames on the sins of their ancestors, who nevertheless at least worshiped idols in the land of Israel because of some "artifice" which made them believe those idols had actual powers (Maimonides had made a similar observation). Now, however, the Jews have lost their "wisdom and understanding," and deliberately follow idols which show no signs of powers at all. There is no sympathy here whatsoever for the Jews who have converted, and there is not one word about any kind of compulsion or any expectation for their return.

Finally, mention must be made of the most important document which so far has been almost entirely ignored, probably because of its extremely difficult Hebrew. Although Baer, for example, discussed this document, which he himself had published, neither he nor anyone else has drawn attention to the important testimony it contains concerning conversions. This is the document of enactments, or ordinances, of the union of Jewish communities of Aragón-Catalonia and Valencia in 1354 (which Baer incorrectly assumed had to do with the Black Plague). The relevant portion of the introduction reads:

> And many faint-hearted [and] weak of nature who are [as if] in fetters [2 Sam. 3.34] when they see the wheels of the chariot [i.e., of Christianity] cutting off its branch [Israel; the Jews who have converted] have no strength to stand in the hall of the trial and have gone over—being in distress—the pass [Isa. 10.29; here with the meaning of "converted," cf. Isa. 24.5, Dan. 9.11]. Fire and sulphur and a scorching wind is the portion of their cup [Ps. 11.6]; to shoot the upright in heart [the loyal Jews] they bend the bow and make ready

according to their desire their arrows [Ps. 11.2]. . . . Many noble communities
that dwelt securely were brought in a moment to desolation [Ps. 73.19]. . . .
All the hardships which befell us we saw with our own eyes, and we are silent,
and we were destroyed, and we waited.

Therefore, children of transgression [conversos; Isa. 57.4] have become
great and grown rich [Jer. 5.27], and those who are borne from birth [Isa.
46.3] have changed their glory and that which they promised [Deut. 26.17]
for shame [Hos. 4.7; i.e., they have converted].

There is no doubt whatever as to the meaning of this text. Both the reference
to "going over the pass," and even more, that to "changing their glory for
shame," are clearly understood Hebrew metaphors for conversion. Here,
too, is an apparent reference to the same thing mentioned by Isaac b.
Sheshet, the persecution of fellow converts and even of Jews by the zealous
conversos. This activity, clearly, has put the entire Jewish community into
real or potential danger. It was largely in response to this situation, then,
that the leaders of the communities decided to enact these ordinances.
"What shall be done for it [Israel]?" they ask, alluding to Song of Songs 8.8
(and cf. Ibn 'Aknin's commentary on this),[74] "put on the garment of vengeance [Isa. 59.17] as the clothing of the remnant [the faithful], and let those
who sustain the work, who rule the people, be united; let them speed, haste
[1 Sam. 20.38], all of them holy, the entire assembly" to enact the necessary
measures.[75]

The Jews of León and Castile did not participate in this extraordinary
union of Jewish communities, undoubtedly because the phenomenon of Jewish conversion had not yet reached anywhere near the alarming proportions
it had in Aragón-Catalonia. Indeed, this conclusion is supported not only
by an argument *ex silencio*, the fact that we hear hardly anything of conversion in the Jewish sources of Castile prior to 1391, but also in the observation made by Joseph Ibn Naḥmias, religious judge of Toledo and a student
of the great Asher b. Yeḥiel, who discussed the sin of idolatry at length, and
commented matter-of-factly, "but all of us are free of that sin."[76] By the end
of the century, and throughout the fifteenth century, of course, such a statement could no longer be made. Then, vast numbers of Jews in southern
Spain were converting as well (it is significant, for example, that in a recently
published summary of documents relating to the Jews of Toledo, the only
instances of conversos recorded appear after 1394).[77]

Conversos and Crisis:
The Fifteenth Century

The fifteenth century, especially in the kingdom of Castile (Castile and León and the entire southern region called Andalucía, excluding only the last remaining Muslim stronghold, the kingdom of Granada), began as a period of turmoil, wars, plagues, and general upheaval.

The "boy king" Enrique III, who began his reign the year before the attacks on the Jews, died in 1406, leaving his minor son, Juan II, to inherit the throne. The queen mother, Catalina, served as regent together with Fernando de Antequera, brother of the late king, who became king of Aragón-Catalonia in 1412 while continuing to act as regent of Castile (until 1416).

Fernando vacillated in his policy with regard to the Jews. As regent of Castile, in 1408 he issued, in the name of the child king, a decree noting that the *Siete partidas* (an encyclopedia of law composed in the reign of Alfonso X, largely the work of the anti-Jewish Dominican whom we already have encountered, Ramón de Peñafort) had proclaimed it a "sacrilege" for Jews to have power over Christians in any way. The regent concluded, therefore, that "great harm and disservice" had resulted to the Crown from failure to enforce these laws (which had never been intended to be enforced). Jews were henceforth forbidden to hold any office, serve as tax collectors, etc., not only for the Crown but for archbishops, bishops, military orders, etc.[1] Clearly, this law was never enforced in practice, but it is revealing as to the attitude of the regent. Nevertheless, in the previous year Fernando intervened in Murcia to order the council to protect the Jews there from some who threatened to attack them.[2]

Not only did the famous "compromise of Caspe" in 1412, which granted the throne of Aragón to Fernando, still leave him as coregent of Castile, but through his children he maintained tight control over much of the latter kingdom, and in effect had personal overlordship of a good deal of it. The potential danger of this power in the hands of those who were now the *infants* of Aragón was realized by the powerful Castilian chancellor Álvaro de Luna, and although we must not accept at face value the judgment of Fernan Pérez de Guzmán and other contemporaries who sought to portray Juan II as a totally ineffective ruler interested only in hunting, and Álvaro as a tyrant with hypnotic control over the young king, his own desire for advancement was perhaps as strong a factor as his sincere concern for the future of the kingdom. It was this ambition, as well perhaps as his very real concern, which was to have tragic consequences.[3]

Another important factor, particularly as it was to affect both Jews and conversos, was that during his regency Fernando cultivated the friendship and support both of Benedict XIII, the notoriously anti-Jewish pope, and Vicente Ferrer. Torres Fontes has described Fernando as a "faithful devotee" of Ferrer's doctrines.

A sixteenth-century Catholic chronicler claimed that under the influence of Ferrer, Juan II ordered the expulsion of all Jews from his kingdom, unless they wished to convert, which many did. However, that author must have confused Juan II of Castile with João II of Portugal (1493).[4]

In 1413 Fernando, then already king of Aragón-Catalonia, wrote to Ferrer concerning some Jews in Tortosa who, with "hearts inspired by the holy spirit," had converted and were in need of instruction. The king urged the preacher to go there, and thence to Zaragoza for the coronation, where he could also preach to the Jews of the city.

Apparently as a result of Ferrer's preaching, the entire Jewish population of Tortosa, except for six houses (families), converted, according to a document of 1416 written when the conversos Jerónimo de Santa Fe and Francesch Clement went to the city to seize for the king the community buildings and goods which had formerly belonged to the Jews.[5]

In Castile, the Ordinances of Valladolid of 1412 were apparently the direct result of a fervent sermon by Ferrer, who implored the queen mother to act against the Jews. The resultant restrictions included a requirement that Jews and Muslims live separated from Christians in every town and city, in an enclosed quarter with only one gate; that the Jews be restricted from engaging in certain occupations (including grocers, apothecaries, physicians, etc.); that those who wished to convert "not be hindered" in doing so; the imposition of clothing restrictions; etc.[6] In reality, very few (if any) of these laws were enforced, and most of them were intended to apply only to Valladolid itself. We know that Jews continued in all these occupations, and continued also to serve as government officials. (Baer exaggerated greatly in claiming that the "communities of León" were affected when "the government of Castile" [as if these were separate entities; in any case, Valladolid is not "León"] made these laws, a plot of "the Church Militant and the Estates" and a "monkish policy" to "enslave the Jews.")

The fifteenth-century Jewish chronicles of Spain, usually not of much interest or reliability, this time provide some interesting insights. Joseph Ibn Ṣadiq of Arévalo, for example, wrote that Ferrer, at the instigation or with the permission of Queen Catalina and Fernando, converted more than two hundred thousand Jews in 1412. Many of these, he continues, went to Portugal:

> The king don Juan [João II, 1481–1495] of Portugal, by the merit of the *anusim* he received [from Spain], even though they scorned his faith (and even though the Christians informed on him, this king went) to the city of Ceuta which lies on the coast of the sea and found there a stone on which was written that Ceuta was built by Shem, son of Noah.

The words in parentheses are added from the text of Abraham b. Solomon, another chronicler who generally copied from Ibn Ṣadiq. They are somewhat enigmatic: the "Christians" informed on the Portuguese king—to whom? Possibly the Inquisition. What this would appear to mean is that the king knowingly received, and permitted to remain in his kingdom, some conversos from Spain who relapsed to Judaism there (in Portugal).[7]

There can be no doubt that all of these factors had a demoralizing effect upon the Jewish population throughout Spain from as early as the beginning of the century. Other factors played a significant role in the changed situation of the Jews. In an otherwise not very enlightening article, MacKay analyzed the tax records for some of the Jewish communities of Castile for the years 1450, 1453, 1464, and 1474. The conclusion he reached was that the "greatest density of population and wealth" was in the northern diocese of Palencia, which indeed contributed a larger percentage (14.03) of the total assessment in 1464, for example, than did the diocese of Toledo (13.46). However, this does not necessarily prove more *wealth* among the Jews of Palencia, though it probably does demonstrate a greater population (not density) there. In any case, in 1474 their share of the assessment decreased to only 12.1 percent, a change not commented upon by MacKay.[8]

What is interesting, if it actually reflects the reality of the situation (reliance on tax registers, already a major problem in Baer, is very risky), is the apparent decline of the Jewish population in major cities such as Burgos, Toledo, and Córdoba, and the tremendous increase of Jewish population in small towns and villages.

What does this mean? Certainly there were massive conversions of Jews in the cities after 1391, and again after the Tortosa disputation, but these tax records from a much later period can hardly be used, as MacKay does, to argue a drastic decline due to those incidents (he does not mention Tortosa). It may be more likely that Jews left the cities in increasing numbers in the latter part of the fifteenth century because of the famines, plagues and other crises, or indeed because of their desire simply to escape the cities which had now become the major centers of the converso population, demonstrably hostile to the Jews. (See Appendix B.)

There can be little doubt, too, that a major factor in the changed attitude toward the Jews and, especially, the conversos, was the "new nobility" of the cities, and particularly the minor nobility of the *caballeros* and *hidalgos*. Nor were all of these of Spanish origin; in Seville, the powerful Bocanegras were descendants of Genoese admirals, and the Pachecos and others were Portuguese. In Seville and other cities, the *caballeros* virtually ran the city government. Besides nobility of foreign origin, there was, at least in Seville, another group no doubt particularly hostile to Jews, the conversos themselves (this includes Jewish converts but also Muslims, or *Mudejares*).[9]

Throughout the fifteenth century the nobility was taking control of the cities—legally where possible, by force if necessary. Obviously, the conversos were the single most powerful element standing in their way. Members of that group were already solidly entrenched in government positions precisely in the cities.

Whether the plot to overthrow the conversos in Toledo in 1449 (discussed later in detail) began with Sarmiento acting on his own (unlikely), or was already the result of the animus of certain members of the noble class there, in the end it certainly served their purpose. The success achieved in Toledo encouraged the nobility to expand their operations, in Villa Real, Córdoba, and numerous other cities.

During the rebellion of certain of the nobility against Enrique IV, an attempt was made by Juan Pacheco and other rebel leaders (the Sentence of Medina del Campo in 1465) to impose certain restrictions. They insisted on putting an end to inherited offices, for example, and at the same time (as they had the previous year) on the establishment of the Inquisition in Castile. The aim of all this was not so much to establish "constitutional checks" on the power of the monarchy, or even to "control" the monarchy, as has been recently suggested (both interpretations somewhat anachronistic), but to limit or rather eradicate the converso opposition and power.[10]

An example of the conflict between the minor nobility and the Jews in this period (and it is only one of many which could be cited) concerns Joseph Ibn Shem Tov, an important Jewish figure (died ca. 1480), author of a commentary on Profiat Duran's famous letter and the translator into Hebrew of Hasdai Crescas' anti-Christian polemical treatise. He was, probably, also the *contador mayor* of Enrique IV. As an author, he is most famous for his qabalistic and antiphilosophical work *Kevod Elohim*. However, what was not known until recently was that he was also a preacher, and among his (unpublished) sermons is one which refers to attacks on Jews in Segovia during Holy Week of 1452: "in the year 1452 . . . when the *principe* don Enrique [IV], may God bless him, had come to the cities of Andalusia, the community of Segovia sent to him two distinguished Jews." These complained about the libels against the Jews on Good Friday, and the *infante* ordered Joseph to go to the governor of the city with letters concerning this. Joseph "berated" the nobles of the city for not protecting the Jews, and the next day (Sabbath) he preached a sermon in the "Great Synagogue."[11]

If the situation for both Jews and conversos was precarious at best in Castile, it was much better in Aragón-Catalonia, where little changed even under Fernando I, whose brief reign was not marked by any particularly anti-Jewish policy (although Hillgarth's claim that he "prevented" the anti-Jewish laws "promulated by the queen," Catalina of Castile, from taking effect in his own kingdom is without justification).[12] Queen María of Castile, wife of Fernando's son Alfonso V, played a particularly valiant role in protecting the Jews, as had so many of the Aragonese queens and other females of the royal families before her. In 1422, for instance, she wrote a strong protest to the Dominican friar Pedro Cerda about his preaching to Jews and against Jews, inciting people to riot against them. She objected that she had already written many times that he must not do this, but he had disregarded these warnings and now was telling Christians to neither buy from nor sell to Jews. She concluded that while it was pleasing to her and the Lord that he should preach sermons, it was not pleasing that he should do so against the law and the rights of Jews or use compulsion and force, for one does not become a good Christian by force. The Jews were to be preserved from insults and attacks.[13] In 1438, the queen also gave permission to the Jews of Cervera to open the gates both to the *judería* and to the Christian quarter, thereby ending their isolation.

In 1437 the conversos of the kingdom, including Valencia, petitioned Pope Eugenius IV (who only four years earlier had issued a special bull protecting the Jews), complaining that the "old Christians" in many cities had insulted them and that some conversos had even left the country. Now, they said, most of the first-generation conversos (surely from before 1391) were dead and the majority of those remaining "are born and nurtured in the Catholic faith, and live according to its rites." They alluded to the disputations of Jews and Christians before the "antipope" Benedict XIII (to whom, incidentally, Spain owed obedience, and not Eugenius), at which time many Jews were baptized who now also lived as good Christians. However, these and the children of the earlier conversos continued to be persecuted by "old Christians" who refused to allow them to hold public offices or enter universities, etc., nor would they marry with them. The result was that their status was "worse than if they had remained in Judaism."

However, the pope apparently did not respond favorably to this petition. It was shortly afterward that, influenced by the converso bishop Alonso de Cartagena, he issued the strongest condemnation of Jews and Judaism that any pope had done in centuries (totally contradicting his earlier bull). Later, he responded more favorably to the plight of both Jews and conversos. His bull protecting the Jews (1447) does not belong to this discussion, but in 1449 he issued the bull *Humani generis* against the abuse of conversos in Castile, and ordered that any persons suspected of harming them be judged and punished by the secular authorities. The pope specifically mentioned discrimination in secular and ecclesiastical offices, etc. Nevertheless, it is strange that there is no reference to the conversos of the kingdom of Aragón-Catalonia, who had been the ones who complained to him. Indeed, this lack of response may have encouraged the widespread attempts in 1437 (e.g., Lérida, Seville), discussed further below, to restrict conversos.[14]

Another element of importance in the crisis of the fifteenth century, already discussed in the last chapter, was the decline in Jewish scholarship and rabbinical leadership throughout Spain. Baer claimed that there were, in fact, a great many rabbis and scholars, among whom he lists the "intellectually inclined" preachers Isaac ʿArama, Shem Ṭov Ibn Shem Ṭov, and Isaac Abravanel. With respect to ʿArama and Ibn Shem Ṭov, preachers though they may have been, they were hardly great scholars. As for Abravanel, he was no "preacher," and in fact wrote almost none of his works until he had left Spain (some few were begun earlier in Portugal). Baer then mentions, without naming them, "talmudists and cabalists" (the error in spelling is the translator's). Among the latter, he includes Abraham b. Solomon Ardutiel. His work is, indeed, entitled *Sefer ha-qabalah,* but it is a chronicle, which Baer appears never to have consulted.

Indicative of the severity of the decline in learning which in fact took place is the case of an important scholar, Rabbi Yeshuʿah ha-Levy, who because of Muslim persecution of the Jews in Tlemcen (North Africa) in 1467 fled to Toledo. There, he met one of the leaders of the community, don Vidal Ibn Labī (otherwise unknown; certainly a member of the famous Benveniste-Ibn Labī family, primarily of Aragón-Catalonia, though with branches in Soria and Guadalajara). Vidal asked the rabbi to compose a book as a guide for the study of the Talmud, since there was then a complete lack of such works (the resultant book, *Halikhot ʿolam,* became a classic).[15] The very need for such a work, however, indicates the drastic decline in scholarship in the city of Asher b. Yeḥiel and his family.

Most of the important rabbis who had not converted in 1391 fled to North Africa, we recall. Only one of those, Amram Marwās Efrati, later returned to Spain, settling in Muslim Granada.

Isaac de León was one of the few important scholars of Castile in the fifteenth century. He was head of a yeshivah in Salamanca in 1463 and died in 1490 (there is no evidence he ever also had a yeshivah in Toledo, although he is said to have died there). Whether his uncle, Yuçaf Bienveniste of Toledo, had any scholarly reputation is unknown. Segovia was another center where Jewish learning was revived and continued at least until 1491, in

which year we have a manuscript of Averroes' commentary on Aristotle's
De anima (in Hebrew), copied in the yeshivah of Shem Ṭov Ibn Shem Ṭov,
author of an important philosophical work, who was head of the yeshivah
until his death in 1430. The Hebrew manuscript of Averroes' commentary
on Aristotle's *De generatione et corruptione,* begun in 1316 by Qalonymos
b. Qalonymos, was also completed in the yeshivah of Shem Ṭov. (Joseph
Yaʿaveṣ, one of the 1492 exiles, indeed wrote that there were more yeshivot
than ever at the time of the Expulsion, but this was hyperbolic background
to his attack on them precisely for this interest in philosophy.)[16]

Samuel Valanci of Zamora, who died in 1487, was also head of a yeshivah, according to Abraham Zacut, who said that he was a relative of his
mother.[17] Isaac Canpanton was certainly one of the most famous scholars
of the latter part of the century, author also of an introductory guide to the
study of the Talmud. Abraham Ibn Megash, a sixteenth-century author in
Constantinople, who undoubtedly was a descendant of exiles from Spain,
reported a tradition he had heard that Canpanton had several outstanding
students and that when they were studying a difficult law he would give
them various opinions and instruct them to consider these carefully. When
the students "came with the book" before him (i.e., when they investigated
the actual Talmudic text), they recalled perfectly his instruction and worked
until they were able to understand the text and the various opinions themselves. One of these students, in fact, was no less a figure than Isaac Aboab
(sometimes called the "last *gaon,*" or great rabbi, of Castile). According to
Zacut, his pupil, Aboab died in Portugal in 1493, seven months after the
Expulsion from Spain (Zacut preached a sermon at his funeral) at the age
of sixty. Jacob Fasi of Toledo (born ca. 1462) was perhaps the "chief student" of Aboab. He wrote no surviving works, but later in Salonica he was
the teacher of many students.[18]

Salamanca, indeed, hosted three important scholars: Isaac de León (who
lived also in Toledo), Jacob Ibn Ḥabib, and Meir ʿArama (son of Isaac, a
young man at the time; he died in Naples in 1556). The only other city in
Castile which could claim any Jewish scholars of note in the fifteenth century was Zamora: Moses Alashqar; the above-mentioned Samuel Valanci;
Jacob Ibn Ḥabib (born in Zamora) and his son Levy; and Joseph Taitachek
(who spent twenty-five years studying there with Levy); and, finally, Isaac
ʿArama. This is an apparently impressive list, especially for a relatively small
community, but we must remember that most of these men achieved their
real fame as scholars only after the Expulsion and in other lands.

Nor was the situation better in Aragón-Catalonia. Many rabbis converted as a result of the Tortosa disputation. Tiny Monzón, still today a
quaint medieval town, was home to ʿElī (or ʿAlī) Ḥabillo, an important
translator and philosopher who died sometime in the 1470s, and also to the
famous scholar and rabbi Zeraḥyah ha-Levy (Ferrer Saladin), who earlier

had lived in Zaragoza and Tolosa. Aside from this, there was not a single important scholar.

Lacking leadership, scholars, schools, books (Ibn Ḥabib complained that only fragmentary copies of the works of the great French rabbis were available in Spain), Jewish scholarship and adherence to the "faith" fell off disastrously. This was certainly another major cause for the massive conversions of the later fifteenth century.

The Tortosa Disputation

The conversion of Joshua al-Lorqi, an important Jewish scholar (to be discussed in further detail below), was perhaps the close of the "final chapter" in the long process of conversion dating back to the events of 1391 and before. From another perspective, it marked the beginning of a new wave of even more conversions.

It is unclear whether Vicente Ferrer was responsible for his conversion or whether, more probably, he received a reply to his famous letter to Pablo de Santa María (the converted rabbi of Burgos) which convinced him. In his own letter to Pablo he already spoke of his "doubts" about certain matters of faith. In any event, he was baptized at the hands of that fanatic missionary, Ferrer, and shortly thereafter he began his own missionary campaign, and wrote what was to be the first in a series of anti-Jewish polemics under his new Christian name, Jerónimo de Santa Fe.[19]

This treatise, and his meeting with Benedict XIII, strengthened the pope's resolve to move forward with the conversion of the Jews. The pope sent letters to various Jewish communities throughout Aragón-Catalonia, ordering them to attend a public disputation with Jerónimo, over which the pope presided, at Tortosa.[20] The disputation began in 1413, in February, after a delay from the original opening date set for January. With some minor errors, Baer has given a generally adequate summary of the actual disputation itself.[21] In spite of the able defense provided, this time not merely by one scholar as in the Barcelona disputations, but by several, the result of the lengthy disputation (lasting nearly a year, on and off) was that many Jews, and especially rabbis and community leaders, converted.

The poet Solomon de Piera, one of the last great Hebrew poets of Spain, also is supposed to have converted, or so it is frequently claimed. Evidence for this is based on two sources: a poem by Solomon Bonafed and an epigram attributed to de Piera himself.[22] According to the epigram, he was seventy years old when he supposedly converted, and yet Baer insisted that he converted at the disputation or shortly thereafter. Not only is this impossible in terms of what is known of the dates of his life, but as Bernstein had already correctly objected, it ignores the fact that he was still writing Hebrew poetry in 1417, several years after the disputation.[23]

The heading of Bonafed's poem indicates that it was written to Solomon de Piera and "the sage don Vidal Ibn Labī." On the basis of this, it has also been accepted without question that not only de Piera but also his one-time student and later companion Vidal Joseph, son of Benvenist Ibn Labī de la Cavalleria of Zaragoza (a minor official in the service of both Pedro IV and Martin I), also converted.[24] Baer, particularly, was certain that Bonafed's poem refers to this Vidal. Possibly this is so, but it remains to be proven.

The de la Cavalleria family (related to the Ibn Labī and Benvenist families) was an extremely prominent one for centuries in Zaragoza and elsewhere. Although much has been written about part of this family, chiefly the de la Cavallerias, much remains to be done.[25]

The facts concerning the conversion of Vidal Joseph are difficult to establish with certainty. Apparently the poet de Piera was hired as tutor for the sons (three, of whom one died as a child) of the aforementioned Benvenist, and *apparently* it was one of these sons, Vidal Joseph, who became his chief pupil and also a poet, with whom de Piera exchanged poems for years. To add to the confusion, there are several "Vidals" in the extended de la Cavalleria family. There is also another Vidal, of a related family, Vidal b. Labī Benveniste, who is known to have converted to Christianity.[26] It was this Vidal who was one of the participants in the Tortosa disputation and author of a polemic (still in manuscript) against Jerónimo de Santa Fe, the converso. He was also the author, before his conversion, of a Hebrew *maqamah* (rhymed prose fiction), the printed editions of which (sixteenth century) bore a poem by the printer, "*Mumar marrano*," condemning the author because of his conversion.[27]

While Bernstein, in fact, did a very fine job in his time in discussing the historical background and identifying, or attempting to identify, the various figures involved in de Piera's life and poetry, his conclusion that Vidal Joseph b. Benvenist Ibn Labī de la Cavalleria (de Piera's student) did not convert was incorrect. What probably is correct is his further suggestion that, at least if Vidal Joseph *did* convert, it was sometime after the Tortosa disputation, since he and de Piera continued to exchange Hebrew poems after that date.

Baer was thus correct, but for the wrong reasons. The proof that Vidal Joseph converted comes from only one source, the testament of his mother (who remained Jewish), doña Tolosana, who left money to her two converted sons, Gonzalo (formerly Vidal Joseph) and Juan (who must have been Samuel, mentioned by Bernstein as a third "possible" son of Benvenist).[28] We shall have more to say about these and other converso members of the family.

To return to the supposed conversion of de Piera himself, there is no evidence from either of the sources Baer cited, the heading to Bonafed's poem or the epigram attributed to de Piera. In the first place, it is known to scholars of Hebrew poetry that the headings, or introductory notes, to such poems were written usually many years (even centuries) after the poems, by copyists or editors of the manuscripts. Without other supporting evidence, it is unwise to rely on these as a source.

However, this is irrelevant in light of the fact that Bernstein long ago showed that by no means all of the manuscripts contain the words in question in the heading to that poem.[29] Given this fact, the "evidence" of the heading is totally worthless. Furthermore, nothing either in Bonafed's poem or in the epigram supports the conclusion that de Piera converted. Bonafed addressed his poem to "the musicians [singers] of the time and kings of song [poetry] who have changed [*ḥalfu;* not "undone"] the law of language, have broken [*heferu;* not "renounced"] the covenant of eloquence." This is merely a way of reproving them, apparently for not having written poetry for several years (which is a fact, at least for de Piera himself). The rest of the poem is one of friendship and mild rebuke for having neglected Bonafed. Similarly, de Piera's own epigram is only a rebuke to Vidal Joseph for neglecting him. Nothing in either poem suggests even the possibility of conversion. Furthermore, Vidal replied to de Piera (why Baer chose to ignore this reply is a mystery), chastising him strongly ("so your soul has whored against God," etc.). If Vidal had already converted, incidentally, how could he possibly rebuke de Piera for the same thing? Rather, it obviously refers to a personal quarrel between them, common in poetry.[30]

Baer asserted that Bernstein "ignored" Bonafed's poem, and appeared to believe that only he, Baer, was aware of its implications for the supposed conversion of de Piera. But this is not so, for Graetz and Luzzatto had already discussed this matter, and Bernstein was certainly aware of the poem in question. Baer, however, failed to examine carefully either Bernstein's earlier article (in a journal to which Baer had easy access) or what he wrote in his introduction to the *Divan.*[31]

It has been necessary to elaborate on this debate because Bernstein's interpretations, and even his editing, of some poems through his long career have sometimes rightly been criticized, whereas Baer's authority is unchallenged. Nevertheless, this does not mean Bernstein was *never* correct in his interpretation. Certainly in this case there can be little doubt as to the validity of his position regarding de Piera (this was recognized also by the perceptive Spanish scholar of Hebrew poetry Millás Vallicrosa, and has been accepted also, as mentioned, by Schirmann, the greatest authority on Hebrew poetry).[32]

Equally erroneous was Baer's attempt to argue that the letter of de Piera to Astruc Cresques (Crescas) of Solsona did not refer to the plague of 1412, as Brody had believed, but to the "pogrom" of 1391 in Zaragoza. This certainly is not the case, as the opening of the letter proves: de Piera had left Zaragoza for some (unspecified) place, probably Monzón,[33] where he informed Astruc that he had found respite "in the shade of complete health at this season and time; so may it be always. However, the city of Zaragoza and its environs have not yet been purified from the contamination of the *ḥaldat* [slaughter? cf. *Ḥulin* 9a] of the plague which came suddenly" (for this meaning of *mitragesh*, cf. *B.Q.* 80b, etc.). Clearly, Brody was right about his interpretation of the letter and Baer wrong.[34] Baer, being convinced that de Piera converted at or as an immediate result of the Tortosa disputation, could not believe that he wrote a Hebrew letter as Jew in 1412. However, both Brody and Bernstein have already shown that he wrote Hebrew poetry long *after* that date, and that, in fact, he never converted.

The real converts to whom Baer refers, who converted as a result of the disputation, Fernando de la Cavalleria, "the former Bonafos," and Vidal b. Labī Benveniste, were fairly influential officials in the service of the king. (We shall have more to say about the conversos of the important de la Cavalleria family.)

Solomon Bonafed of Zaragosa was another important Jewish poet of this period.[35] Several of his poems deal with the crisis of the Tortosa disputation. The heading of one of these is of particular interest:

> When I was in Tortosa at the time of the disputation, the spirit of poetry there was like flowing water, for the majority of the [Hebrew] poets in the kingdom were there with the rest of the scholars.

Among these, he says, was don Vidal (b.) Labī, the same mentioned above, who later converted, and to whom Bonafed addressed this poem.[36]

After the disputation, many of the Jews of Zaragoza (and elsewhere, of course) also converted, and Bonafed sent a poetic lament to his relative Astruc Bonafed about this.[37]

He also sent a letter, together with some of his poems, to one of his friends in Fraga who had converted. Fraga was the town where Astruc Rimokh (who also converted, taking the name Francesch de Sant Jordi) lived, and we know that Bonafed wrote a sharp letter of rebuke to this zealous convert who attempted to influence others to convert. However, there were several Jews in Fraga who converted, and it is impossible to guess the recipient of Bonafed's letter. It begins in a very friendly and even respectful tone, but hidden in his words lies a distinct sarcasm which at last bursts into a flame of indignation:

> and may the Eternal Overseer [error in the text: read -ḥ instead of -h], whose strength will never change and who never intended but one eternal Torah, and it is given to us and to you to return the souls of the entire congregation of

Israel to the source of life to be a remnant from all the nations, watch from
the abode of his dwelling to benefit you at your end from his "beginning" [the
Torah] . . . and souls which are separated shall be restored to their former
state.

The "benefit," of course, which he wishes upon the recipient refers to the
curses contained in the Torah.[38] We see, once again, from such sentiments
exactly what the faithful Jews felt about the conversos.

Bonafed also wrote a lengthy poem to his relative Profiat Duran, who
had converted and then boldly returned to the Jewish fold, in which he
stated that after the death of Ḥasdai Crescas the generation was left like a
flock without a shepherd, but that his books (he refers therefore not only to
the philosophical *Or Adonay,* but also to Crescas' anti-Christian polemical
work) remain to guide his disciples, Astruc ha-Levy, Matityahu ha-Yiṣhariy,
and Joseph Albo. These, together with other scholars, remain as a refuge
for the Jews of Aragón.[39]

Nonetheless, if these scholars, participants also in the disputation, were
a "refuge," they were a pretty poor one. Matityahu composed a commentary on Psalm 119, which he used as a basis for urging the study of the
Torah, knowledge of Jewish law, and "reasons for the commandments," but
he also urged the study of secular sciences.[40] It certainly is not the bold
attack on the conversos, or polemic against Christianity, which the times
demanded. Nor was Albo's pedantic and rather boring treatise on the "principles of faith" likely to stem the tide of conversion. The truth is that the
"leaders" of the generation were thoroughly demoralized and ill equipped
to tackle the challenge.

Baer's claim that the Tortosa and San Mateo disputations were the work
of "a Church bent on destroying its few remaining Jewish opponents" may
be discounted as polemic, but his further assertion that the conversion of
the Jewish scholars, thoroughly trained in Bible, Talmud, philosophy, etc.,
was hardly due to any sudden conviction on their part of the truth of Christianity, and that "both before and after their conversion they remained
Averroists, unaware of any uniqueness in their [Jewish] national tradition,"
deserves comment.[41] This claim is based entirely on one letter by Bonafed,
the opening part of which appears in the English translation of Baer's book
(although very selectively; the important passage was left out by Baer in his
original Hebrew text as well). It is significant enough so that the complete
passage should be translated:

When I saw that the hand of faith is weakened, and the feet of many of the
sons of the exile falter for want of hope, and that they bring alien counsels to
extirpate the roots of religion, and the pious of the generation believe that
[philosophical] contemplation is the essence and deeds unessential, to the

point where their ignorance has brought them to believe that the Torah is necessary only for the masses raised on the knees of faith and tradition, and that contemplation, which is the knowledge of God and his providence—from which alone results human welfare and which is knowledge of the books of natural science and metaphysics of Aristotle, and they have hung [this view] on a great tree, namely Maimonides, who filled his books from beginning to end with the providence of God and knowledge of him by way of contemplation . . . but the profit in the practical portion [observance of the commandments] which God created to make for us a house in his paradise almost is left without mention in his speculative books. Perhaps the paucity of their understanding of the opinions of the rabbi [Maimonides] brought them to this [view], for it is not correct that he was of this opinion.[42]

The passages omitted by Baer are of great importance, for in them Bonafed acknowledges that true philosophical contemplation focuses on the knowledge of God and God's providence, and that Maimonides in fact "filled" his speculative writings with these things. At fault is not Maimonides but those ignorant men who do not properly understand what he wrote. There is not one mention of "Averroes" in all of this, nor is there any evidence whatever to support Baer's claim that the Jewish leaders who converted were "Averroists" both before and after their conversion. Indeed, what benefit would conversion have been to them, supposedly motivated only by philosophy, if they retained the same position after their conversion that they held before it?

At the end of his letter, Bonafed says that he particularly was aroused to his task by, or depended upon, En Shaltiel Gracian, whom he knew to be "perfect in his Torah." (The letter and accompanying poem are, in fact, addressed to him.) Baer nowhere mentions him, but he was rabbi of Barcelona (Ḥen being the Hebrew name of which Gracian is the Spanish form), and son-in-law of Joseph Rimokh of Fraga, probably the father of the previously mentioned Astruc who converted in 1414. In 1369, Shaltiel left Fraga to become rabbi in Alcolea de Cinca, who had gone to Toledo, and in approximately 1376 he was chosen rabbi in Barcelona to replace Nissim Gerundi.[43]

Astruc Rimokh, a physician in Fraga, who in 1391 had written a letter of consolation and support to a certain Jew whose relatives had converted, himself converted in 1414 and took the name of Francesch de Sant Jordi (Saint George being the patron saint of Catalonia), together with his son Andreas, also a physician. Prior to his conversion, Astruc had also been a poet, highly regarded by Solomon de Piera, who exchanged poems with him. Francesch now wrote a letter, in Hebrew, to his friend Shaltiel Bonafos, attempting to convince him also to convert. But his efforts were not successful, and furthermore friends of Bonafos worked to persuade him not to convert. Bonafos replied to Francesch (the letter has not survived), but the poet Solomon Bonafed was not satisfied with this reply and so wrote his own much stronger rebuke to Francesch in which he attacked the very fundamental principles of Christianity.[44] The whole correspondence has been adequately summarized by Baer, who nevertheless insisted on his incorrect interpretation of "Averroism" as the cause of the conversion.

Philosophy and Its Opponents

As remarked previously, the fact remains, in spite of Baer's efforts to blame "Averroism," that not one single philosopher is known to have converted, whereas a great many rabbis did. This was the case both before and after 1391, as well as after the Tortosa disputation and throughout the fifteenth century. Along with the more famous rabbis who converted, mention may be made of one, described as "master of Hebrew or Chaldean [Aramaic] letters," who took the name Pau de Bona at Tortosa in 1416.[45]

Baer built much of his case on a work by Solomon Ibn Laḥmis (or Laḥmias), also called Alʿami, who probably lived in Portugal and who in 1415 wrote a small ethical treatise inspired by the events of 1391 and subsequently. While most of it contains the usual moral platitudes, some parts are of interest as reflecting at least the author's understanding of conditions of the Jews at the time. Thus, he warns: "Do not send [a son] to commerce and craft in his youth; also keep him from the opinions and words of the Greeks." It would be as foolish to conclude from this that "Averroism" corrupted the Jews as to conclude that commerce did. Baer cites a part of the text, but tampers with the text at one crucial point, making it read that, deprived of their usual role of tax-farming, the majority of the Jews "left their religion" and many artisans, too, "left the fold." In fact, the text actually says that "the majority of the oppressive tax collectors *left there*" (i.e., Spain), and also that some of the craftsmen "went out," i.e., left the country—*not* that they left their religion.[46]

Baer also ignored the fact that this writer blamed not the philosophers but the rabbis for the depressed state of the Jewish condition. Alʿami criticizes them for their arguments and quarrels with each other, because they have multiplied books of commentaries on the Talmud but have neglected the "righteousness" of its ways, and, indeed, some have tried to interpret the Torah in accord with philosophy. Worse than these, however, are some of the "evil" people who pursue a little knowledge of philosophy and distort the meaning of the Torah according to their incorrect understanding. Finally, he takes to task the leaders of the community, "their scholars and 'shepherds' who stand before the kings." These communal leaders, he says, are given charge of the kingdom, and the kings give the keys of their treasury to them, and all obey their orders, but they "exult in their wealth and great-ness and forget the humble and poor Jews," forgetting also God, "and they take large mules for their carriages and wear clothing of the court, the cloaks and mantles, and dress their wives and children in finery of nobility and ornaments of gold and silver and precious jewels."[47]

While there is no doubt much pious exaggeration in his charges, there certainly is also some truth, for otherwise he would not have dared to say such things. It also should be stated that the situation he describes, and his words in general, appear to apply more to Castile than to Aragón-Catalonia; yet the situation was not really all that different in the latter kingdom.

Profiat Duran, whom we shall discuss in detail later, who himself had converted to Christianity and then returned to the practice of Judaism, wrote in 1403 his important work on Hebrew grammar, and in the intro-duction to that work (ignored by Baer) he criticized the excesses of three groups: the "Talmudists," who insist that only the study of the Talmud is permitted, excluding not only secular studies but also even the Bible; the "philosophers" who mistakenly place philosophical study above Talmudic study and who misinterpret Maimonides in allegorizing laws, etc.; and the qabalists who adhere to a secret learning and even "practical *qabalah*" (magic) which seeks to change nature.[48] His objection to all these positions is not that they are absolutely and completely wrong, but rather that each represents an excess (he admits, for instance, that of the three that of the qabalists is closer to the "true Torah" position, but because there is much disagreement about their views and teachings it is better to be cautious). He definitely was not opposed to philosophy, which his other writings (chiefly in manuscript) demonstrate that he was expert in, and most certainly was not opposed to secular studies (science, etc.), in which he was also an expert. Rather, he opposed the *misinterpretation* of philosophical teaching by those not properly trained in the essentials. He himself not only was not against Averroes, but even made commentaries on and translated the writings of that great Muslim philosopher.

To conclude, therefore—and we could muster even more evidence, but that this is not the place for such details—it was not "Averroism," i.e., phi-losophy itself, which the pietists attacked, but rather the ignorance of some of the masses who used their limited knowledge of philosophy to allegorize and otherwise misinterpret the Torah and the commandments. Nor was this the only, or even the chief, cause of the degenerated state of Spain's Jews in the fifteenth century. As Al'ami (Ibn Laḥmis) stated, and other sources con-firm, the decline in rabbinic leadership and in the quality of rabbis was at least as much to blame, as well as the emphasis on luxury and personal advancement of the Jewish courtiers.

Duran saw yet another cause, which he considered the most serious of all, and that was lack of knowledge of the Hebrew language and study of the Bible. The neglect not only of the Torah but of the entire Bible, he says, led to the disastrous expulsions and conversions of Jews in other lands (i.e., as a punishment by God), "and now in our time this disease [conversion] has spread to Spain also" for the same reason; "because they sinned against the Torah of God and the words of prophecy that are compared to water, He poured upon them like water because of it," clearly an allusion to baptism, "and who knows but that the salvation of the communities of Aragón—which were the principal ones that were saved of the Spanish diaspora," apparently in 1391, when few Aragonese communities were affected in comparison to those of Catalonia, "was due to their great diligence in prayer and rising in the night watches to entreat God with supplications, the foundations of which are the words of scripture and the Psalms." (The reference is to the extremely pious practice of getting up at midnight to recite psalms and prayers.) Later on in the text of the work itself, in his interesting discussion of the use (and neglect) of Hebrew, he adds that this neglect has caused destruction and disaster to come upon the Jews, because their ignorance of Hebrew has caused them to misinterpret the Bible, "and there happened what happened, as you already know"; referring, certainly, to the events of 1391 and the conversions.[49]

Netanyahu also devoted many pages to a discussion of the attack on "philosophy" as the supposed cause of conversion, and seemed in general inclined to agree with Baer on this. Nevertheless, he listed the names of only a few very minor philosophers who "were most faithful and devoted Jews," without noting that, in fact, *every* philosopher known to us was, and remained, a "most faithful and devoted Jew." More correct is his statement, unfortunately buried in a note, that Jewish philosophy in most cases led to "the bolstering of Jewish faith rather than to skepticism and denial." Some important aspects of the discussion of criticism of philosophy were also overlooked by Netanyahu; for instance, Hasdai Crescas' hostile attitude to Maimonides; (shared also by Joseph Albo) and his statement of "principles of faith" by which to combat philosophical heresy were severely attacked by Isaac Abravanel (of whom Netanyahu himself is the chief biographer).[50]

Major critiques of "philosophy" were presented by two important, but generally neglected, fifteenth-century figures, Shem Tov b. Joseph Ibn Shem Tov (d. ca. 1430) and his son Joseph (d. ca. 1480), both of whom were severe critics of Aristotelian philosophy, the father only somewhat more than the son. Both are discussed briefly by Netanyahu, but somewhat misrepresenting the position especially of Joseph, nor is the most important passage in his book discussed. Joseph there states that the study of natural sciences is permissible and even necessary, but that philosophy *can be* dangerous. Experience shows that such danger can result, as it has in this time when the "endeavors to acquire this knowledge" were the "reason for the loss of the congregation of Jacob [conversion] in the majority of Castile and Aragón[-Catalonia], and the most illustrious of them left the fold and converted when they saw that they were strengthened by scholars who knew this wisdom"; i.e., after their conversion they were enabled to study.

He continues: "Almost for this reason they turned quickly from the path which God commanded them, believing that they are wise in seeing the opinions of masters of this knowledge, for whom religion is not important in their eyes, but [only] speculative knowledge is considered the ultimate goal of man." Then follow the words which Netanyahu misinterpreted completely: "We see from experience that in every nation and kingdom which never heard of philosophy many thousands were killed and burned," and he cites Levy b. Gershon (the reference is to his commentary on Lev. 26.33–34) to the effect that in France many thousands were killed; whereas in Spain nothing of this happened. (This is the passage alluded to also by Abraham Zacut: "And Levy b. Gershon testified [read ha'id] in his commentary on the Torah on their destruction by the Gentiles [in France, 1306] that concerning them was fulfilled [that "prophecy"]; for double [the number of] those who left Egypt [in the exodus] were lost.")

This clearly refers not only to the expulsion of the Jews from France in 1306, however, but more particularly to the "Black Death" of 1348, when Jews in France and other lands were blamed for the plague and many were killed. He does *not* say, as Netanyahu mistranslated, that in lands where philosophy was not "widespread" many thousands "laid down their lives for their faith," as though the meaning was that Jews who knew nothing of philosophy were more ready to "sanctify" themselves and die a martyr's death than those who knew philosophy.

This was far from his mind and from his intention. Rather, he seems to have intended the exact *opposite*, that philosophy itself cannot be blamed for the evils which have befallen the Jewish communities, and what happened in France and other lands where philosophy was not known is proof of this.

He then continues to cite the opinions of scholars (Asher b. Yeḥiel and others) against the *excesses* of philosophy, which led to the ban imposed in the fourteenth century. "And these *maestres* [Sp., teachers, scholars] did not decree against the knowledge of natural science" nor deny its utility and truth, but rather the danger of the works of the "philosophizers" (*mitfalsafim*) which led to heresy. He concludes that he believes he has found a *triaca* for this disease (the word is Spanish, derived from Greek *thēriakē*, and means "a remedy against venom"), which is that young students should study Torah properly in yeshivot with scholars who can properly guide them until they are able to investigate such philosophical knowledge in a manner consistent with their religious training.[51]

Note that he does not oppose philosophy completely, nor does he ultimately believe that philosophy itself has corrupted the people and caused conversion. He opposes only the misinterpretation of those ignorant ones whom he, like others before him, contemptuously terms "philosophizers."

Indeed, it should be noted that both Joseph and his father demonstrate their own profound knowledge of Greek, Muslim, and Jewish philosophers, and that Joseph's two sons, Shem Ṭov and Isaac, both wrote commentaries on Maimonides' *Guide* (the former is published, while the latter is still in manuscript).[52]

Conversos in Castile: Some Specifics

Because of the abundance of documentation for the Jews of Toledo, and to a much lesser extent Seville and some other cities of Castile, it is possible to gather a much clearer picture of the extent of conversion, position of the conversos, etc., there than for the rest of Spain.

With regard to Toledo, for example, it is obvious that although the riots of 1391, which resulted mostly in robbery in the various Jewish quarters of the city, affected the Jews, there was very little resultant conversion. Only in 1394 and 1395 do we hear of the names of one or two conversos: Juan Ferrández, previously don Çag Abzaradiel (Abzardiel), a member of a prominent Jewish family, who lived in Torrijos where he owned some property, and Alfon Pérez of Seville, who had been don Yuçaf Aben Sabad (Abenxabat), also from a prominent Jewish family.[53] In 1401, the names of a few more conversos appear in the Toledo records (Ferrand Rodríguez Israel, Gudiel Alonso Izrael, Pero Alonso, Manuel Fernández, Ferrand Pérez). After this date, there is virtually no mention of conversos in the documents of Toledo until after the Expulsion.[54]

By contrast, in Seville (where, we recall, the events of 1391 began) it appears that the *majority* of the Jews converted, and while the statements as to the population of Jews in Seville in the fifteenth century range from the absurdly high (thirty thousand or more) to the equally improbably low (seventy families, or five hundred individuals), it is clear that the decline of Jews was significant.[55]

The few documents which have come to light concerning the conversos in Seville in the fifteenth century unfortunately do not permit us much of an understanding of their social situation or their relations with Jews. In one case, a converso rented a house to a Jew in 1473, just as conversos in Toledo sometimes rented or sold property to Jews.[56] This fact in itself does not, of course, signify that there were friendly relations between the two groups. The chief justice, Diego López de Estúñiga (a converso family) in his will in 1407 left to his son houses and gardens which had belonged to the Jew

Yuçaf Picho, treasurer of Enrique III, and which Diego had purchased from Juan Sánchez, who before his conversion was Samuel Abravanel, ancestor of the famous Isaac (about both of whom we shall have more to say). By the middle of the century, the descendants of don Diego owned some seventy-four houses in the *judería*.[57]

Relations between Jews and Christians remained extremely cordial throughout the century in Seville, as in Toledo and elsewhere (full details on this await my previously mentioned book, and include such things as Jews and Christians apprenticing their children to live with each other for periods of years). Nevertheless, if this was the case on a local scale, there were certain discriminatory measures being imposed by the kings which already forecast a change in official attitude. One of these was the decree of 1412, according to which both Muslims and Jews were to be concentrated in special *barrios* in the city. According to the converso chronicler Alvar García de Santa María, the Jews were made to live near the Puerta de Córdoba, and some converted rather than give up their old homes. The Jews protested this decree to Fernando de Antequera and it was finally revoked.[58]

But in 1437, Juan II complained to the city council that certain measures concerning Jews were not being enforced, and again ordered that Jews live in separate *barrios*. The Jews protested this new decree to the archbishop of Seville, arguing that they were poor and could not afford to buy new houses, which the Christians (who owned the houses in the proposed new *barrio*) would sell at exorbitant prices to them. Instead, they proposed that they be allowed to live in the *barrios* of Santa Cruz and Santa María la Blanca, a sector of some sixty-five houses, and the calle Verde near the Church of Santa María la Blanca (some fifty-six houses) in the old *judería*. However, the Christians (many of whom were conversos) who lived in these neighborhoods protested bitterly, objecting to the "dangers" of living mixed with Jews, and especially the "great danger" involved in contact between Jews and conversos ("en mesclamiento e conversación con los conversos"), who were the majority of the inhabitants of Santa Cruz. Whatever may have been the official resolution of the dispute, in fact by 1450 Jews were again found scattered throughout the city, concentrated chiefly in the old *judería*.[59]

In that year, 1450, the Jews of Seville also complained to the king about Franciscan friars preaching "scandalous sermons" to incite the people against them.[60]

Our information concerning the Jews of Córdoba in this period is virtually nonexistent, owing perhaps to the paucity of sources, or the failure of scholars to look for them. In any case, it has been said that the old *judería* virtually disappeared after 1391 because of the massive conversions there.[61] As we shall see later, the number of fifteenth-century conversos must have been in the thousands.

There has been almost the same neglect of research with regard to Jaén;

apparently there, too, most of the Jews converted in 1391. However, either not all of them did so, or else new Jews moved into the city, for in 1480 the Catholic Monarchs (Fernando and Isabel) specifically ordered the enforcement of their law on separation of the *juderías* from Christian quarters for the towns of Jaén, Baeza, Úbeda, Andújar, and others.[62]

In Salamanca apparently the majority of the Jews of the city converted in 1411 as a result of the preaching of Vicente Ferrer. The perhaps legendary account of this "miracle" and the inscription indicating the very gate of the synagogue through which Ferrer entered to preach are preserved in a seventeenth-century source. However, the synagogue, converted into the Church of Vera Cruz (true cross), is still there today. In 1413 Juan II granted the houses of the former *midras* (i.e., *bet ha-midrash*, school or synagogue) of the Jewish community to the university to be converted into a hospital for the care of sick students, inasmuch as "the Jews of the said city have converted to the holy Catholic faith, so that only a few Jews remain."[63]

We shall return later to the political events of the second part of the century, and how these affected the conversos in Toledo and Seville and elsewhere. However, at this point it is interesting to look again at the above-cited complaint of the Christians of Seville about the "dangers" of contact between Jews and conversos. This again relates to the central question of the attitudes of Jews toward conversos and the sincerity of their conversion (or, to put it more correctly, the sincerity of their adherence to Christianity after their conversion).

In the latter part of the century, after the enormous success of Ferrer in converting thousands of Jews, it apparently became more difficult to continue the missionary activity among the Jews who remained loyal to their identity in spite of all the difficulties. This may, indeed, explain the virtual lack of references to conversos in Toledo and the surrounding towns, for instance. This difficulty in converting Jews was a phenomenon well known to the Christians. Thus, Alonso Díaz de Montalvo, an important jurist and editor of legal texts in the reigns of Juan II and Enrique IV, wrote that Jews are difficult to convert and must be more skillfully opposed than (pagan) Gentiles ("& peritiores ad subvertendum quam Gentiles") because they have the Law and the prophets. Preachers must be sent to the places where Jews live to explain the Catholic faith to them and to "compel" them to listen to this preaching.[64]

Another factor which no doubt strengthened the resolve of the Jews not to submit to such missionary activity was the increasing anti-Jewish polemic of the conversos themselves. The *Censura et confutatio libri Talmud*, a polemic against the Talmud which we shall discuss later, written by the converso Antonio de Ávila for the Inquisitor General Tomás de Torquemada sometime in or after 1483, for example, states that descendants of conversos are known as "*anuzes*" (*anusim*) and that Jews believe they are obligated to cause such persons to return to the practice of Judaism. Nevertheless, he argues that the testimony of Jews against these *anusim* should be accepted by the Inquisition, "contrary to those who instigate before the most serene monarchs [Fernando and Isabel] saying that Jews should not be accepted as witnesses," etc.[65] The significance of this willingness of Jews to testify against conversos before the Inquisition is something we shall discuss in detail in the chapter on the Inquisition.

Yet another example of such anti-Jewish polemic is the previously mentioned work, perhaps written by an "old Christian," *Alborayco*. Netanyahu (*Origins*, 848) argued that it was written "about 1467" (not 1488 as Loeb thought) and cites a statement about Jews coming to Spain some fourteen hundred years earlier (i.e., 70), which would result in a date of 1470 for the writing. There is also reference to a "war in all of Spain" sixty (not seventy, as in Netanyahu) years before, which must refer to the wars of Castile and Aragón and the Castilian civil war (1356–66), not the "pogroms" of 1391 as Loeb, and Netanyahu, surmised. Thus, Netanyahu's conclusion that the work was written "a few years after 1461" is incorrect. The author refers to the "destruction" of the Jewish *aljamas* in that war, destruction which nevertheless appears to be a figment of his imagination, adding, "and those who remained alive for the most part were baptized by force [untrue, of course] and took among themselves the surname [!] Hebrew *anuzim*, which is to say 'forced.' When one becomes a Christian he is called *mesumad*, which means in Hebrew 'rebel,' for he rebels with the Christians [joins them]. And if one of this lineage arrives at a place where these evil people [Jews] are, they ask him, 'Are you an *anuz*, Christian by force, or a *mesumad*, Christian voluntarily?' If he responds '*Anuz*,' they give him assistance and honor him; and if he says 'I am a *mesumad*,' they do not speak more [with him]."[66]

While, of course, it was absolutely untrue that there were any "forced" converts to Christianity in Spain (except possibly some in 1391), such damaging testimony in the hands of Christians aroused the fear of Jewish authorities, and is at least in part an explanation for their insistence that conversos are not *anusim* but *meshumadim*, complete Gentiles who have abandoned the Jewish people.

A chronicler of Murcia, Diego Rodríguez de Almela, writing shortly before 1490, distinguished between the recent conversos who had converted from fear, "and therefore many of them never were good Christians, nor those who descended from them, as is now recently apparent," and those who had been converted by the preaching of Vicente Ferrer, who became "good Christians, better than those who were converted by force and fear."[67] Of course, we must not draw hasty conclusions from such testimony, which may reflect only the situation in Murcia (where, indeed, attacks against the Jews and the existence of discriminatory laws may have compelled some to convert at the end of the century), or even more likely, the subjective judgment of a Christian probably hostile to all the new conversos. Nevertheless, his statement that those who converted as a result of the preaching of Ferrer became "good Christians" is important evidence.

As we shall see, Fernando de Pulgar, the converso secretary of Isabel and chronicler of the Catholic Monarchs, in relating the beginning of the Inquisition in Toledo, stated that many conversos "observed neither the one nor the other law"; i.e., they were neither Christians nor Jews.

This ambiguity and religious indifference (hardly "Averroism") of many of the conversos early in the century is noted especially also in the *Alborayco,* which observed that some kept the Sabbath and other Jewish "ceremonies," were circumcised "like Muslims" (!) but observed the Sabbath like Jews, "and only in name are Christians, and are neither Muslims, Jews, nor Christians, although by volition they are Jews but they do not keep the Talmud nor all the ceremonies of the Jews, nor even less the Christian law [religion]." Therefore, in some places such conversos are called *alboraycos,* which refers to the legendary beast of Muḥammad which was neither horse nor mule (*al-burāq*).[68]

One of the charges against the "*alboraycos*" is that, like the legendary beast, they do not work, nor do they make war on their enemies (Muslims, enemies of Spain) or engage in difficult labor like agriculture, but only promenade on the streets of "Christians." Among Jews they claim to be Jews, and among Christians they say they are Christians. They eat the food of Christians and Muslims (except pork), but they eat the *adafina* (stew kept warm on the Sabbath) of the Jews. Just as the *burāq* was part horse, part woman, the conversos "invented sodomy" (as we shall see, the charge of sodomy was one frequently found in fifteenth-century poetic satires against conversos, usually written by other conversos).

On the other hand, the author hastens to add that all this is not to condemn the "good conversos" of Castile who are mixed among those of Andalucía and Toledo, or to say that conversos should all be condemned as heretics. Just as in "Old Castile"—Burgos, Palencia, Valls (!Loeb incorrectly suggested this was "Valderas"), León, Zamora, etc.—many conversos are not heretics, so also in Toledo, Murcia, all of Andalucía, and the Estremadura there are many who are "faithful Christians."[69] Some Jewish sources support this picture of a certain vacillating element among the conversos; e.g., Isaac ʿArama, a philosopher and religious commentator, who also condemned this "halting between two opinions." Even more significant are the observations of Isaac Caro (born in Toledo, ca. 1440, he lived in Portugal at the end of the century): "the Gentiles say, 'These [conversos] did not change their religion because they believe in our faith, but so that we should not kill them, and they do not keep either our religion or theirs'; and this is 'a proverb and byword' [Deut. 28.37]."[70]

There is also sufficient testimony that at least some conversos of the fifteenth century were secretly practicing Jewish marriage customs. Thus,
Simon b. Solomon Duran (grandson of Simon b. Ṣemaḥ Duran who fled
Majorca in 1391) of North Africa wrote concerning conversos in Valencia
who were said to bring two Jews to their homes as witnesses to a marriage,
and before them "the husband gives *qidushin*" to the wife (a strange expression, since according to Jewish law all that is required is the giving of a
token object, and surely in the case of conversos no document was written)
and then recites the betrothal blessing, after which they go to a church and
are married by a priest.[71]

In the previously discussed responsum of his grandfather concerning the
marriage of conversos, mention is made of those who entered into a marriage according to Jewish law but before converso (not Jewish) witnesses,
"*as is their custom.*" Even if it could be said that such witnesses were totally
unfit, if Jewish witnesses in the town knew that the couple cohabited afterward, this in itself might establish the validity of the marriage according to
Jewish law and reveal their intent to make such a valid marriage. "The reason they do not marry before valid [Jewish] witnesses is that they say that
anusim are more valid in their eyes than Jews," because the heart of an *anūs*
is directed "towards heaven"; i.e., they secretly desire to be Jews. However,
only in such a case was Simon b. Ṣemaḥ willing to consider that the marriage
was valid (to require afterward a bill of divorce should one of the partners
"repent" and return to Judaism)—when intercourse had occurred or when
the act of marriage was performed before two Jewish witnesses—but if the
witnesses were themselves conversos the act was not valid and the "wife"
was like a concubine.[72]

This preference of conversos for their "own kind" is attested in another
responsum of his grandson Simon about a conversa in Valencia who "left
her infant son and her husband and climbed out of the window and went to
a place which today is Jewish, and said that she wished to marry a penitent
Jew like herself." Very significant also is his statement, written shortly after
the Expulsion: "there is an established presumption that *none* of the *anusim*
marry Gentile women, and this is known to be their practice generation
after generation from the time of the 'decree' [Expulsion] until today . . .
every *anūs* who comes to repent, just as we presume that his father was a
Jew so we presume about his mother that she is not a Gentile . . . and even
though some of them have been intermingled with Gentiles and take wives
of their daughters, only a *very few* do so."[73]

Nevertheless, we should not be too impressed with all this, remote as it
is in time and place from the realities of medieval Spain. As Netanyahu has
shown, after the establishment of the Inquisition for the unified kingdom
(1480, not 1481), there was an increase in the number of conversos who left
the country (to call this a "movement" is too strong). It is also obvious,

from the need to tell the rabbis in the Muslim lands to which the conversos were going the whole history of the conversions in Spain, that few conversos had gone to those countries "in decades," and therefore these rabbis had little experience with them. They tended to take, perhaps not a "favorable," but a conciliatory stand toward these repentant conversos (repentant, in many cases, because they feared the Inquisition).

Similarly, the Jewish community of Málaga enquired of Saʿadyah Ibn Danan, a rabbi of Granada, concerning "one of these *anusim* who came from the land of Castile to repent, and they are those whose fathers were compelled and converted to go out of the general [category of Israel] some ninety years ago." Since it is impossible to know precisely when this was written (certainly before 1492, when Ibn Danan left Spain, and since it appears to refer to the Inquisition, after 1481), it is difficult say whether the reference is to conversions of 1391 or later. In any case, this particular descendant of conversos had married in Málaga in accord with Jewish law and then had died without children. However, he had brothers, *mumarim* who did not "repent." The question involved the possible obligation of the widow to perform the necessary levirate marriage with one of these brothers, and whether they were to be considered "wicked" Jews or complete Gentiles. If "wicked Jews," are they to be considered *anusim* or *meshumadim?*

Ibn Danan replied that those of the first generation who were compelled to convert are considered *anusim,* but their descendants, as long as they are known and recognized to be of Jewish ancestry, are considered "wicked Jews" and not complete *meshumadim* (for they themselves had not converted and an "aspect of compulsion" clings to them), "even though they are able to flee from the government which compels them [to remain Christian] and repent" and become Jews. Not only that, but even complete *meshumadim* may contract legal marriage according to Jewish law with a Jewish woman, and may also write a bill of divorce in their names ("let their names be whatever they are," he says, in evident disapproval of the use of Christian names).

He adds that this law is known to all scholars and that none disagrees with it, for great sages have already discussed it. Nonetheless, a certain man, whom he denigrates, wrote that the *anusim* are complete Gentiles and worse than *meshumadim.* With respect to this specific case of the man who died, Ibn Danan says a strange thing: that in his opinion he was a proselyte (*ger ṣedeq*), because he had repented and lived as a Jew. This would seem entirely to contradict his previously expressed opinion that such descendants of *anusim* are "wicked Jews," for if so, why would the term "proselyte" apply to one who had repented, instead of "repentant Jew" (*baʿal teshuvah*)? If he is a "proselyte," then this can only mean that previously he was to be considered a complete Gentile.

With regard to the famous opinion of Maimonides that a Jew who wor-ships idolatry is a complete Gentile, he agrees that "we behave with the *meshumadim*, as we behave with complete Gentiles," in order to separate from them and not learn from their evil ways "and in order that they will remember and return to God." Further, he adds that there is a great distinc-tion between *meshumadim* and *anusim*, "who are compelled to convert, and who confess [Christianity] in their mouths and with their lips because of the stretched-out sword and drawn bow and because of the burden of war [i.e., compulsion; or, perhaps, a reference to the heavy taxes Jews paid for the war against Granada]; but they [in truth] do not conceive this and in their hearts do not think thus, for the unity and love of God is in their hearts and many of them perform the commandments in secret and at dan-ger to themselves. Even the wicked among them, inclined to heresy [disbelief in Jewish teachings], the Gentile 'emptiness' [*hevel*] is considered as nothing in their eyes and their hearts are not able to believe that there is anything of substance in it, and they are separated and rejected in the eyes of the Gen-tiles and they reproach and revile them all day and call them Jews and hate them because of their inclination to the law of Judaism." Many even have died a martyr's death (no doubt this means the Inquisition), and should these be called *meshumadim* and "complete Gentiles"?[74]

Important as this responsum is for revealing that some of the conversos, at least, were thought to observe Jewish law and be lukewarm in their Chris-tianity, it must be remembered that this rabbi was also living in a Muslim land, Granada, where he had little actual experience with conversos. Also, it is clear that he hoped to encourage the "return" of many of the conversos by adopting a lenient attitude. The rabbis of Christian Spain, who had long experience and firsthand knowledge of conversos, shared no such hopes, however.

Also, as a question to Simon b. Solomon Duran (and others already pre-viously discussed) stated, these conversos could have fled to a nearby land of the Muslims but did not; rather, they and their descendants remained in a state of *complete Gentilehood*. Yet Duran himself was also willing to be lenient even with regard to the immediate descendants of conversos of 1391, just as Ibn Danan was.

The reason for this leniency was, as we have said, to encourage their return to Judaism and perhaps even more (in the case of Duran, for instance) to encourage the flight of conversos from Spain and their settlement in Mus-lim lands.[75]

By contrast, Isaac Caro, who was born in Spain ca. 1440 and left Spain in the Expulsion and went to Portugal, wrote that the Jews of the Diaspora commit a great sin in "worshiping idolatry," whether by force or willfully, "for even force is willful, since they are obligated to sanctify God's name," and therefore were it not for the mercy of God they would not be worthy to have their repentance accepted. A definite distinction, therefore, must be made between the "propagandistic" stance of sixteenth-century rabbis outside of Spain and that of earlier Spanish Jewish authorities. Of the latter, Netanyahu correctly stated (and here we have added further proof) that they considered the conversos "not as crypto-Jews, but as gentiles, and, consequently, they considered the returners not as penitents, but as proselytes."[76]

Even in faraway Palestine, where Jews from Spain had settled at least from 1391 on, it was understood that Spanish conversos and their descendants were Gentiles who had to convert to Judaism if they wished to return. Rabbi David b. Netanel Carcassonni of Constantinople was asked about a Jew, "one of the *anusim* in Spain," who married a non-Jew and had sons by her. After he died, one of these sons decided to go to Palestine and become a Jew with the full and sincere intent of keeping the commandments. He converted and became a fully observant Jew, and the question was whether he could act as a rabbi to judge civil law, or a trustee of public charity funds. The rabbi replied at length, citing Talmudic precedent, that certainly it is permitted to a proselyte to judge civil cases and all the more to serve as a trustee.[77]

Nevertheless, it may be argued that the facts in the various cases here discussed are not in dispute, and thus it would appear that there were at least some conversos and their descendants who were secretly observing Jewish practices. What does this do to our contention (and it was also the contention of Netanyahu) that the conversos were neither *anusim* nor "crypto-Jews," but complete and willing Gentiles?

Many of them, of course, never having been "good Jews," had no real desire to become "good Christians" either. Their conversions were neither forced nor sincere, but rather motivated simply by a desire to improve their social standing and avoid the increasing difficulties associated with being Jewish. They would have been perfectly content to continue living their secularist existence, but as we shall see, the "old Christians" would not let them, and therefore the farce of the Inquisition was created. The possibility that a small minority of conversos and their descendants, at least prior to the Inquisition, were secretly loyal to Judaism does not negate the fact that the vast majority, nearly all, were complete Gentiles, whether "good" Christians or not.

In 1465 the powerful council of nobles, in which a place of chief importance was occupied by Alonso de Oropesa, general of the Order of San Jerónimo and notorious for his anti-Jewish bias, presented Enrique IV with a lengthy list of demands. Among these was the order that he immediately rid himself of his Muslim guards, who "scandalize" the people and the Christian faith, that he proceed with the war against Muslim Granada, and third—and here the voice of Oropesa may certainly be heard—since there are "many bad Christians and suspect in the faith" who cause great "damage," that the king take measures to imprison and punish them. Their goods should be seized for the royal treasury, or used for the war against Granada. Those who are found *not* to be guilty of heresy or observance of Jewish customs should not be insulted or defamed or mistreated in any way, however. Furthermore, if any Jew or Muslim should attempt to convert a Christian to his faith, or circumcise a Christian, the "secular judges" (again, not Church officials) should punish all involved, in accord with justice and royal laws (such a measure, it should be noted, would directly go against the decretal of Boniface VIII).[78]

This demand must be seen as a reaction against the king's request (undoubtedly at the insistence of anti-converso forces) to the pope for the establishment of an Inquisition in Castile in 1462. Alonso emphasized that "all the archbishops and bishops of the kingdom" should be responsible for punishing this heresy (a position consistent with that expressed also in his book, to which we shall return), since it is "principally their responsibility." Although his intention, therefore, was to ensure local and ecclesiastical control (rather than Dominican) over any Inquisition, there is no doubt that such demands paved the way for the actual establishment of the Inquisition in Castile twenty years later.

Relations between Jews and Conversos

What is the reality of relations as they existed between Jews and conversos in medieval Spain prior to the Expulsion? The details are important evidence for the question of the status of conversos and Jewish attitudes toward them.

Already in 1284 the Jews of Barcelona complained to the king, Pedro III, that the officials and justices of the city were permitting the Dominicans to investigate them on charges of hiding and maintaining conversos in their houses, charges which the Jews denied. The king replied that the Jews were his subjects and he had to protect them, and ordered all such investigations against them stopped. If any were guilty of such a deed, it should be left to the king himself to investigate the matter. In 1296, Jaime II prohibited any converted Jew from having any relations with Jews, speaking with them, entering the Jewish quarter, etc.[79]

These early examples already indicate several constants throughout the medieval period in regard to the converso issue: suspicion on the part of some that Jews are secretly encouraging converts to return to their former faith, and resentment on the part of Jews of such charges, a resentment which easily transferred to a resentment of the conversos in general.

Negative aspects of relations between Jews and conversos emerged as conversion increased in the fourteenth century in Aragón-Catalonia. In Tortosa in 1314, for example, Jaime II was informed that many Jews and Muslims converted to Christianity were still being taxed by their former *aljamas*, and he ordered the *bailes* to see that they were relieved from their "ancient servitudes" (religions) since they now enjoyed equal rights with other Christians. A law of Barcelona required that no baptized Jew, just as no Christian woman (only; not man), could enter the Jewish quarter whether by day or by night (apparently there was special "danger" presumed to exist of contamination of women and converts with Jews).[80]

Pedro IV in 1383 received demands from the Jews of Majorca, among which was that no converso be allowed to enter the Jewish quarter or speak with any Jew on pain of a fine of 100 *sous* or a hundred days in prison. The king agreed to this, and also sent a letter to all of the Jewish *aljamas* ordering that no converso be allowed to enter any one of them anywhere in the kingdom. Obviously this was done, at the request of the Jews, to protect them from the missionary efforts of the conversos.[81]

In 1311 in Zaragoza, a report of the Christian judges to Jaime II mentioned among other things a certain Jew (Salamon Abenbeli) who was baptized and subsequently disowned ("renounced") by his brother and several of his Jewish relatives (the report merely states the facts and does not offer or request any action to be taken). It was precisely this practice, required by Jewish law, of disinheriting a willful convert to Christianity which caused various laws to be enacted to ensure the rights of inheritance of such converts. Thus in Castile in 1302 the church council of Peñafiel, presided over by "Gonzalo archbishop of Toledo" (actually there were two "Gonzalos" in that year in the see of Toledo, Gonzalo Díaz Palomeque y Gudiel and Gonzalo García, both nephews of the previous archbishop), ordered that if Jews or Muslims converted to the Catholic faith "they should not for this reason lose any of the goods they had before."[82]

Juan I of Aragón-Catalonia, having been informed (1393) that conversos continued to have contact with Jews and that Jews and conversos dressed alike so that sometimes they could not be distinguished, ordered that no converso could live in the same house with a Jew or eat and drink with a Jew, nor could conversos participate in Jewish services. The penalty for violation was public whipping. In order that "Christians by nature" should not be deceived as to who was a Jew and who a converso, every Jew was required to wear a scarlet gown (in Castile, worn only by judges) or other "dark, honest cloak" down to the feet, with a circle of cloth of yellow "like the Jews wear at present in the city of Valencia" (an attempt to reintroduce the infamous "badge," mostly ignored in Spain). The Jews soon convinced the queen to annul the decree of the badge, which she noted had not been the custom of Jews in Valencia previously, because it brought upon them much "derision and scorn" from Christians. However, this was not the end of the matter, for in 1433 Queen Maria, wife of Martin I "the Humanist," issued a decree to the *cofradía* of conversos in Barcelona, apparently at the instigation of the bishop and others, which quoted in its entirety the text of the earlier decree of Juan I, including the badge and the complete separation of Jews and conversos.[83]

In 1339 Pedro IV issued orders that Jews be compelled to listen to the sermons of, and dispute with, mestre Pedro de la Merce, a convert from Judaism "to the light of Christ," from the village of Berga (near Manresa), who had abandoned his wife and children and "all worldly goods" for the sake of Christ and now sought to convince other Jews of the truth of the Christian faith. One might be skeptical of the great learning, to say nothing of the sacrifice of "worldly goods," of this convert from so obscure a village, but such zealous missionary conversos were more dangerous to the Jews than were the Franciscan and Dominican friars to whom they were normally compelled to listen.[84]

A Jew in Tarragona converted to Christianity and then returned to his former faith. All his goods were confiscated to the Crown (however, it should be noted that he was neither imprisoned nor killed, as canon law demanded). When he died in 1315, the king granted the petition of his Jewish widow and children for relief.[85]

Isaac Necim (Nissim) of Valls was condemned to death in 1323 for hiding in his house a Jew who had similarly converted and then relapsed. Furthermore, the stipulations the sentence included that his possessions be seized and his houses (more than one) burned. However, his goods having been confiscated for the archbishop of Tarragona and the king, it was decided that the burning of the houses would be a waste, and the king (Jaime II) granted the rights to them to an official of his son Alfonso.[86]

The motives of converts who suddenly found the "true faith" were not, of course, always pure. The example of a Jew who murdered another Jew and then became a refugee for twenty years before he converted and convinced Jaime II in 1326 to pardon him "for the honor of God and the holy Catholic faith" was probably not unique.[87]

Juan de la Cavalleria (royal purchasing agent and member of the distinguished Jewish family of Zaragoza) and his brother Gonzalo, both conversos who did not bother to change the family name, rented to Jews some houses they owned in Zaragoza in 1414 (Fernando, another converso member of the family, was then treasurer and counselor of the king). Gonzalo and Fernando were mentioned above in connection with the Tortosa disputation. Juan de la Cavalleria was one of the alleged conspirators in the assassination of the Inquisitor Pedro Arbués, to be discussed. He was imprisoned and died in 1490.[88] In that same year, 1414, Gonzalo and Juan borrowed 9,400 *sous* from a Jew of Castile. Also in that year the Jews of Zaragoza paid Gonzalo 2,000 *sous* (*sueldos*) to serve as their ambassador to John XXIII in Rome (Serrano correctly concluded that, due to the anti-Jewish policy of the recognized pope, Benedict XIII, the Jews sought protection from the Roman pope). They were successful in this, and in 1419 the apostolic nuncio annulled the anti-Jewish decrees of "anti-pope" Benedict.[89]

Yet another converso member of the family, Gaspar, entered into a *commenda* partnership (whereby one partner invests money and the other does the actual work of selling) with the widow of Todroz Constantin, a Jew of Calatayud (probably the physician of that name known from other sources), and their daughter Astruga entered into a similar arrangement with Juan de la Cavalleria. Luis de la Cavalleria, later to become treasurer of Juan II of Aragón, in 1416 was lending money to Jews in Zaragoza. The combined *confradías* of the Jewish community of that city sold certain houses to Gonzalo de la Cavalleria because they were desperate for money to meet expenses, and in 1423 the Jews of Jaca borrowed 100 gold *florins* from Gonzalo.[90]

Yet there is also evidence of hostility between conversos and Jews even in this early period, as when in 1416 Alfonso V had to instruct the "official" of the church of Zaragoza to release a Jew held in prison for a year by some conversos, who claimed that he had converted and then relapsed, at which the king "marveled" (not at the charge, apparently, but at their holding him in prison). He ordered that in the future no Jews be harmed in person or property on similar pretexts by accusations of conversos. In the following year, however, because of certain conversos (such as Florente Vidal and Jaime Trigo, also of an important Jewish family) the church of San Andrés in Zaragoza became a center of missionary activity against the Jews. The conversos were again preaching sermons. When the Jews complained to the king that this was stirring up "rumor and tumult" against them, he ordered the activity stopped.[91]

In 1459 the notorious anti-Jewish son of a converso, Pedro de la Caballería, requested Pope Pius II to dissolve his marriage to Blanca Palau of Valencia, claiming that her mother was of Jewish birth and that Blanca practiced Judaism. The pope ordered an investigation, and he promised, if the charge was found to be true, to grant an annulment or a divorce.[92] Such charges, of course, could be easily fabricated and just as easily "proved."

Martin Pastor, *neofito* (converso) of Huesca, in 1423 renounced all claims or actions against the widow of a Jewish shepherd of Zaragoza. In 1434 the Jewish wife of three different conversos (apparently all dead or divorced) testified that another converso was not guilty of the murder of her brother, also a converso. In the same year, a Jewish woman received 75 gold *florins* from her daughter, a conversa, for some houses "in the *carnicería*" (butchery) of the Jews; i.e., apparently in the street where the butcher shop was located. Also in that year Lope de Heredia, a converso, absolved a Jew of his debts to him.

The Christian community of Fraga granted an annuity of 500 *sous* a year to the Jew David Abnaxech of Alcolea and his son, a converso ("agora a la fe tornado") called Johan Díaz Daux (de Aux), who later appointed a Jewish representative to receive 333 *sous* for him from the city council of Sos. Gonzalo de la Cavalleria continued to grant an annuity to the Jewish burial society (*confraria de Cabarim*) in 1443.[93]

In Lérida (Lleida) in 1403 the city council enacted a law that no converso could enter the *judería* for any reason. We have already seen that in Seville later in the century conversos protested bitterly about the "danger" of living among Jews, but in Lérida it was the opposite: the conversos protested this law barring them from entering the Jewish quarter, claiming that it was based on an old law *requested by the Jews themselves* that no "Christian" (converso, surely) be allowed in the *judería*. The council listened to the protest and annulled the law.[94]

In 1435 the council of Lérida enacted a new measure that no Jew could live in houses outside the *judería*, nor could any Christian (including, of course, conversos) permit a Jew, secretly or openly, to live in a Christian-owned house or employ a Jew. This was at the particular instigation of the Inquisitor Francisco Nadal, who noted that Jews and Muslims were living in various parts of the city among Christians and "even among conversos." Throughout 1437 there was a bitter fight over a new law attempting to prohibit conversos from holding certain brokerage offices (*corredor*) in the city, which privilege was to be restricted to Christians of the fourth generation or more. Even the intervention of the bishop failed to have any effect, and finally the conversos appealed to the queen, who succeeded in getting the law annulled.[95]

Thus we see that in Aragón-Catalonia, particularly in the fourteenth and early part of the fifteenth centuries, more or less normal relations continued to exist between many Jews and conversos, and yet there were also increasing signs of suspicion which led finally to laws prohibiting contact between them.

In Castile there is some evidence for such "normal" relations also in the fourteenth century, as in Toledo, where we find some conversos after 1394 still maintaining houses in Jewish neighborhoods and having other contact with Jews.[96] In the early fifteenth century, prominent conversos received tax-farming rights on such items as the public oven and "store of soap" in the Jewish quarter.

In some families, one member would convert and others remain Jewish. An example is don Mosé Marimuchel, "Jew of Maqueda" (near Toledo), son of Pedro González, and his Jewish wife doña Ceti, who in 1454 sold some olive orchards to the church of Santo Domingo.[97] In other cases, wives remained Jewish when their husbands converted. Presumably, in all such cases more or less natural relations continued to exist between the Jewish and the converso members of the family. An interesting example is the case of Gonzalo Rodríguez de San Pedro, the converso nephew of López Fernández Cota, also a converso and member of an important Jewish family of Toledo. Both uncle and nephew were public officials of some importance in the city in the fifteenth century. The cathedral chapter of Toledo, on at least two occasions, willingly conceded "perpetually for 54 years" (something of a contradiction in terms) certain of Gonzalo's lands in Figueruela to his Jewish sons, who did not convert, Yuda and Santo Aruque. A similar case can be cited with the converso Juan Rodríguez de Ocaña, father of Moses, Sisa (Ziza), and Yuçaf, all members of the important Abravalla family. The sons did not convert and they retained farmland which had belonged to their father.[98] It is worth noting that the numerous instances of such conversions of a member of the family while others remained Jews are further proof of how little these conversions had to do with fear of persecution.

What does such evidence tell us about the relations between Jews and their converso relatives? Admittedly, our sources are limited, as previously mentioned. However, it is apparent from the examples at least of Toledo, which seem to be confirmed by several also in Aragón-Catalonia, that relationships were very strained. Individual conversos usually moved from their previous residences in the Jewish neighborhoods, as we have seen also in Murcia. The fact that Jewish members of a family where one had converted, even sons acting against their fathers, took legal action or otherwise intervened with various authorities (as with the cathedral chapter in Toledo) to retain rights to land and property which previously had belonged to the converso is another indication of this.

On the other hand, the very fact that cities were small (as they still are in Spain; one can easily walk through the entire city of Toledo, or the medieval part of any other city, in less than a whole day), to say nothing of the tiny villages where so many Jews lived, made it virtually impossible not to have some contact between conversos and Jews. We find a few cases, for instance in the Toledo documents, where a converso moved entirely out of the city to another town presumably to avoid just such contact. However, for the most part Jews would have come into almost daily contact with conversos who were former relatives or friends.

The converso Franciscan theologian fray Diego de Valencia (Valencia de don Juan in León), one of the poets whose poems are found in the *Cancionero de Baena* compiled during the reign of Juan II, wrote a poem to a Jew whom he called don Samuel Dios Ayuda, a Jew of Astorga, praising his noble character and generosity in lending him money, "reales nin dobles," i.e., more than he asked for, apparently. This "great courtesy," he says, is "contrary to the nature of the *judería*." He adds that if he continues in this way, which is not that of his ancestors, truly he will be like the biblical Samuel, or like "Fanec" (Paneaḥ), called Joseph (Gen. 41.45). This Samuel also later converted, taking the name Garcí Alvarez de León (the Spanish name Dios Ayuda probably originally was Azariah).[99]

While we have examples of positive relations between conversos and Jews, there are, of course, many of the opposite kind. An important instance occurred when Abraham Seneor, the chief judge of the Jewish *aljamas* of Castile under the Catholic Monarchs (who himself converted rather than leave Spain in 1492), and other Jewish leaders, including Jaco Cachopo, *procurador* of all the Jewish *aljamas,* refused to accept maestre Juan de Talavera as tax official of the Jews because he was a converso. In 1485 there was an investigation at Segovia, and finally two royal officials were appointed to deal with the case. The Jews of Segovia also objected to his owning certain houses and property.[100]

As we shall see, the Inquisition records are full of testimony, most of it false in nature, against conversos by Jews. Before the Inquisition, however, cordial relations between the two groups appear to have been normal.

It was precisely this kind of contact which the Christian fanatics, men like Oropesa, had begun to fear and which motivated the fifteenth-century legislation which sought to restrict Jews to their own quarters, the official *judería,* and prohibit them from living in "Christian" neighborhoods. As we have seen, Oropesa felt that the danger was not that Jews would convert faithful Christians or conversos, but that they would contaminate them through their false doctrines. He wrote:

> Therefore, we arrive at the conclusion that those who are called Jews, but are not, as the Apocalypse says, are the synagogue of Satan [Rev. 3.2, 2.9], and therefore *must be avoided with the greatest care* by the faithful and conversed with only with great caution as we would do with servants and sons of Satan, to whom they are subject.

Further, he warns strongly against the danger of Jewish contact with conversos, who freely mingle—as is natural, being of the same "origin of race"—with Jews. Therefore, he insists that the clergy do everything in their power to discourage this contact by severe penalties (on the conversos).[101]

That there was some real danger of association of this kind there can be no doubt. For instance, when the entire Jewish population of Orihuela (in Valencia) converted in 1391, the Jews of nearby Murcia in later years were accused by one of the conversos of sending "agents" to work in Orihuela as craftsmen in order to "pervert" the conversos there. He demanded that Jews be prohibited from working with conversos; that instead they be permitted to work only with "old Christians." How much of this complaint reflects reality and how much perhaps fear of economic competition is, of course, another question. In the city of Murcia itself in 1392 the council objected that some conversos were living in the *judería* and mingling with Jews "day and night, and it is well-known that they [conversos] eat meat on Fridays and Saturdays" (i.e., in apparent honor of the Sabbath), and therefore they were ordered no longer to live in the Jewish quarter.[102]

An even earlier example of contact between the Jewish community and a converso on an official level involved the donation of some property for a school to the Jewish *aljama* of Écija by its most important native, Yuçaf de Écija, an official of Alfonso XI, in 1332. The Hebrew document was translated for him into Spanish by a converso, Manuel Ferrandes, who had been a rabbi (Meir) in Seville. (This was certainly not because Yuçaf did not know Spanish, of course, but because of the technical legal formulaic language necessary for such documents.)[103]

Many, if not indeed *most,* of the conversos turned against their former "coreligionists" with a ferocity not calculated to win any feelings of pity or goodwill from the Jews. In Seville, for instance, as early as 1386 a converso was paid 500 *mrs.* to preach sermons in the Jewish *aljama* to convert other Jews. There were other examples of this kind.[104] We have already seen the danger of such sermons when preached by zealous conversos, whether they became friars or not.

Another such danger from conversos, that had already begun with the two Barcelona disputations involving Paul Christiani in the fourteenth century, was that they brought with them to their new faith a sometimes considerable knowledge of Jewish sources and practices. Centuries of attempting to convince the Jews from the Bible of the truth of the claims of Christianity had failed, but now the missionizing forces (essentially the Dominicans and Franciscans) had at their disposal an undreamed-of resource: the Talmudic and midrashic literature. Such texts, even more than the Bible, could be twisted and forced to mean almost anything that a skilled preacher might wish. There is little doubt that the more gullible and less educated among the Jews were sometimes convinced by such sermons.

Andrés Bernáldez, chaplain of Cardinal Mendoza and chronicler of the Catholic Monarchs, complained that the "heresy" of the conversos was due to the "continuous conversation" between them and Jews, and the converso custom of eating Jewish foods, such as *manjerejos* (?), or *olletas* (small pots?) of *adafina* (a sort of stew, discussed below, Chapter 7), *manjarejos* of onions and garlic fried with oil, and meat cooked with oil (instead of butter)—all of which causes a very bad odor in their houses. The same odor is that of the Jews themselves, because of their food and their not being baptized! This, of course, is the old medieval myth of the "evil smell" of the Jew, and while the testimony of this notorious anti-Semite with regard to contact between conversos and Jews is not to be trusted, there may be some truth in it.[105]

The small town of Molina de Aragón, in the province of Guadalajara, had numerous conversos by the end of the fifteenth century, and some

120 Inquisition processes against them have survived. While, as usual, it is necessary to be skeptical of the charges that these conversos, after the Expulsion, engaged in openly Jewish practices, such as fasting on Yom Kippur, etc., it is possible that the testimony in one case is true. According to this, some conversos (by then deceased) in 1476 had asked a Jew of the town the date of Yom Kippur. When that Jew left the town, these conversos then asked another converso, who is said to have had "many books in Hebrew" in his house.[106]

In Huete, which had a fairly substantial Jewish community, the Inquisition records of 1491–92 indicate that Jews and Christians, including conversos, regularly used to exchange gifts of food at Passover and Christmas (this is somewhat believable, since Jews and Christians normally did so in Spain throughout the medieval period). On the other hand, the same sources refer in a contradictory manner to the "profound enmity" which existed between Jews and conversos.[107] This is yet another indication of the extreme caution which is necessary in dealing with Inquisition sources.

Occupations of Conversos

We have already seen that part of the polemic of bigoted "old Christians" against the conversos in the fifteenth century was that they were all rich aristocrats, seeking only public office and other honors, and that none of them worked in manual trades or agriculture, etc. Bernáldez, the aforementioned anti-Semitic cleric and chronicler of the Catholic Monarchs, was particularly vicious in his denunciations in this regard, claiming that "all" of the conversos were merchants or collectors of taxes, officials, etc., and that "none" worked the land or was a laborer, carpenter, etc. Surprisingly, perhaps, we seldom if ever find similar charges made against the Jews, probably because the Christians knew that this was not true. A certain rabbi, with scholarly pretensions, once complained that Baer listed virtually every conceivable trade and occupation of the Jews, and that this was unnecessary. On the contrary, not only is it necessary but there are far more occupations which Baer should have noted but did not.

Whereas we have an overwhelming abundance of sources for the variety of trades, crafts, and agricultural and other occupations of Jews in Spain, there is an equal paucity of sources concerning the conversos. The truth of the matter is, that perhaps because of the tremendous "heat" that has been generated over theories about "crypto-Judaism," there has been very little if any solid research done on the conversos. One problem, of course, is that it is often extremely difficult to identify a converso name in the sources unless the person is specifically identified as such (as is the case with some of the

Toledo documents; some, however, refer to people who can be identified from other sources as conversos, a fact not known to León Tello, who accordingly did not identify several of them).

The extremely limited data currently available do not, therefore, permit us to draw any sound conclusions. Nevertheless, for Toledo (and the surrounding towns which belonged to the province) we have the following information (from León Tello):

1396   Alfon Pérez de Sevilla—*arrendador mayor* (1391)
1401   Pero Alonso—bakery
1401   Manuel Fernández—soap store
        Ferrand Pérez—tailor
1408   Ferrand González de Alcalá—shoemaker
1421   Francisco Fernández Cohen—scribe of the city
1422   Lope Fernández Cota—scribe of the king
1424   Alfonso González de San Pedro and Gonzalo Rodríguez de San Pedro (he was the nephew of Lope Fernández Cota, and Alfonso was perhaps his brother)—owned a farm

Also, in the previously mentioned conversion of the Jews of Orihuela in 1391, when the Jews of Murcia were accused of sending "agents" to work among those conversos, the occupations mentioned included shoemakers, tailors, and drapers.

It should be noted that these were the more "traditional" occupations of the middle-class Jews in Spain. In only one case, that of the San Pedros, do we find specific mention of conversos who owned a farm, and this was an inheritance. However, many Jews in the Toledo province and elsewhere continued to engage in farming, and particularly viticulture (wine) and olive growing, throughout the fifteenth century.

Bookbinding and Book Selling

Another interesting example of a trade largely in the control of Jews and conversos (in Barcelona, Jews had a monopoly until 1391, and conversos nearly so after that date) was bookbinding and book selling. Before printing began, chiefly through the agency of German craftsmen who came to Barcelona and who also worked with conversos, bookbinders bound handwritten individual paper or vellum copies. In the fifteenth century, however, we find bookbinders or dealers who are also ordering the printing of books.

Among the converso bookbinders and sellers are Salvador Suyol and Luis Estrus (or Estruch) in Gerona, already in 1392 and after.[108] The most important name for the fourteenth century, however, is maestre Alfonso in Burgos, who was a scribe and bookbinder for the *infanta* doña Blanca, granddaughter of Alfonso X, *señora* of the famous Monasterio (convent) de las Huelgas in Burgos. He is, of course, none other than Rabbi Abner of Burgos, who converted and took the name Alfonso de Valladolid (discussed in Chapter 6). The implication of this, thus far unknown to historians, is obvious; like most medieval rabbis he was not salaried and earned his living in another way, in this case as a scribe and bookbinder, an occupation which he continued after his conversion (since both forms of his name, Hebrew and Christian, are found).

Important fifteenth-century converso bookbinders include Guillermo Ça-Coma of Barcelona, who in 1482 also edited a (printed) edition of Josephus; Antonio Çalom of Barcelona, son of a doctor (Pedro), whose wife, Blanquina, was condemned by the Inquisition after he died; Lorenzo Costa, also of Barcelona, who in 1414 also sold books in partnership with another converso, Francisco Ça-Calm (whether or not he is the same Lorenzo Costa condemned to death by the Inquisition in 1487, together with his wife, Narcissa, is unclear).[109] It would seem probable that En Johan Çacoma, who in 1480 edited the *Regiment de princeps* and thus is the first known editor of a printed book in Barcelona, was also a converso and related to Guillermo Ça-Coma.[110]

Book dealers in Barcelona had their shops chiefly in the Plaza de San Jaime (so popular with tourists today), or the calle dels Especiers near the Jewish quarter. One of the most important of these was the converso Antoni Ramon Corró, an important figure from 1440 on. He and his wife were burned by the Inquisition in 1489, as were his son Joan Ramon Corró (also a book dealer) and his wife.[111] The converso book dealer Gureau Sastre in 1483 was given an exemption of debts, whether to Christians, Jews, or Muslims, because of "poverty." Bartholomew (Bartolomé) "Sartre," a book dealer whose wife, Isabel, was burned in 1489, is probably an error for Sastre, and thus related to Gureau. A certain Rafael Dauder married Beatriz, the daughter of Bartolomé Sastre, in 1467.[112] Finally, another book dealer of our period was Pere Far, who in 1488 had his store seized by the Inquisition (was he condemned?). Apparently the majority of the bookbinders in Majorca in the fifteenth century were also conversos, and no doubt other examples may come to light.[113]

Medicine

Medicine was simply one of the many "sciences," or areas of knowledge, which the educated Muslim or Jew was required to master. Not surprisingly, therefore, a disproportionate number of physicians in medieval Spain were Jews. Every one of the kings, both in Castile-León and Aragón-Catalonia, had more than one Jewish physician and surgeon serving him personally. From the mid-fifteenth century, however, Christians increasingly moved into these professions, and we also begin to encounter the names of conversos who are identified as such; no doubt there were many more whom we are at present unable to identify.

Enrique IV of Castile had several Jewish physicians in his service, and possibly one converso surgeon (1464), Pedro de Ávila (not to be confused with Pedro Arias Dávila, definitely a converso, who was *contador mayor* of the king). This Pedro de Ávila in 1468 concluded an agreement with Rabbi Çag Brudo of Toledo to repair a wall between their houses in the *judería*. While this does not prove Pedro's converso origin, it indicates that it is likely.[114]

In Murcia at the beginning of the fifteenth century two Jewish doctors, at least, converted and experienced difficulty with the Jewish community. One, an eye doctor, complained that before his conversion he received from the city council an annual salary of 400 *mrs.*, but after his conversion the Jews would have nothing to do with him and he lost his annual salary. He was granted a new stipend by the city council. Another converso doctor could not afford a house in the Christian part of the city and continued to live among the Jews, but was not welcome there and was finally granted 600 *mrs.* by the city council to buy a house. (Being the *only* Christian doctor then in the city, he was able to make new demands by threatening to leave, and in 1413 was granted an annual salary of 1,000 *mrs.* However, in 1416 another Christian doctor came to the city and the converso left.)

Alonso Yáñez Cohen, a converso, became the only Christian pharmacist in the city, but in 1417 he gave up his practice to become a collector of taxes.[115] Before his conversion he had been the only pharmacist of any kind in the city. In 1391, not because of the persecutions, which did not affect Murcia, but apparently simply to enhance his financial position, he had gone to nearby Orihuela in Valencia; news of the pogroms soon reached that city, however, and he fled at night to return to Murcia, leaving all his possessions behind. When the few Jews of Orihuela who did not convert then also fled to Murcia, his goods were seized by the officials of Orihuela, and even the council of Murcia was unable to obtain their return. Increasing hostility to the Jews in Murcia, however, and preaching of Vicente Ferrer in 1411 led to his conversion. A chief factor was certainly the new law, no doubt enacted at the instigation of Ferrer, prohibiting Jews from acting as pharmacists or physicians in Murcia.[116]

Seville also had some converso physicians on the city payroll. Manuel Romi was one who was possibly a converso.[117] Moses b. Samuel *ha-Sefaiy* (de Roquemaure, in France) converted at Seville in 1358, taking the name Juan de Aviñon. He translated Gordon's *Lilium medicinae* into Hebrew (MS) and composed in Spanish the famous work *Sevillana medicina,* published in 1545 (reprinted 1885). Diego Aboacar (of the famous Ibn Waqār dynasty, most of whom were physicians) is another probable converso, who together with Romi was *alcade* (*alcalde*), or "examiner," of doctors and surgeons in the city in 1452. In 1455 that position was held by Juan Levi.

Alonso de Chirino (d. ca. 1429), father of the renowned Diego de Valera, was another converso physician who was named *alcalde* of all physicians and surgeons of the kingdom by Juan II of Castile. He was also the author of two works on medicine.[118]

Fernando and Isabel themselves had various converso physicians in their service. Lorenzo Badoç, personal physician of Fernando in the 1470s, whose skilled care of Isabel the king credited for the successful conception and birth of a male heir (the *infante* Juan), was one of these. By 1487 he was deceased, and one of the first acts of the Inquisitor Alonso del Espina in Barcelona in that year was to seize the goods of his condemned widow and children. Fernando and Isabel had bestowed considerable sums of money on the physician and his family, and in 1493 Fernando finally intervened personally to release money from the estate for the marriage of Lorenzo's daughter. Gabriel Miró, physician of Fernando's father, Juan II, was burned by the Inquisition in 1490 (as we shall see). "Rabbi Samuel," a famous preacher, was physician to the duque de Cuéllar in the 1490s. He later converted and was known as maestre Fabricio; he was also condemned by the Inquisition.[119]

Américo Castro wrote that Álvaro de Castro was a converso, but the converso origin of this family has been challenged, and Millás Vallicrosa has shown that some Hebrew notes are found in certain manuscripts of his work, but there is no proof that they are de Castro's own notes. However, Francisco López de Villalobos, physician to the duque de Alba as well as to Fernando, was a very important converso (discussed further in Chapter 6).

In 1492 Pedro González de Mendoza, cardinal of Spain, had a Jewish physician, "Rabbi Abraham," who converted. The cardinal, along with the papal nuncio, served as his sponsor (perhaps he is to be identified as Rabbi Abraham Aven Bueno, a physician of Segovia in 1492).[120]

Elsewhere, we hear of other conversos who were physicians, as in Majorca in 1480, where two of the three "most prestigious" physicians were conversos, mestre Garriga and Juan Alejandro Adret (the name "Adret" was fairly common, and there is no reason to assume he was related to the famous Solomon Ibn Adret). The first was "reconciled" (i.e., made to do penance) by the Inquisition, and the second fled to Naples. In addition, there were at least eight converso "surgeon-barbers" (minor surgical providers).[121]

In Aragón-Catalonia in 1307 Jaime II, after examining papal letters and writings of cardinals, concluded that one Vincent Esteban, a "Spanish physician" (thus, perhaps, from Castile), had converted from Judaism and so took him under royal protection. Astruc Rimokh, the previously mentioned physician of Fraga, converted after the Tortosa disputation, and under his new name of Francesch de Sant Jordi continued his practice, as did another converso, Tomás García of Zaragoza. Another was Berenguer Cabra, whose home was sacked by a group of Jews after his conversion.[122]

The relative paucity of converso physicians in Spain, in contrast to the large number of Jewish ones, perhaps is further testimony to the fact that secular learning hardly contributed to conversion.

4

Conversos and Political Upheaval

The crisis of the fifteenth century in Spain begins with the turmoil of the reign of Juan II, a weak and ineffective ruler. Pedro López de Ayala, a powerful noble of Toledo, vacillated in his "loyalty" to the king and finally in 1440 entered into an alliance with the *infante* Enrique in open warfare against his father.

Many of the other nobles of Castile joined in a confederation against Ayala. The king himself, unfortunately, did nothing, and the rebellion soon spread throughout the land. It took some months before the king was able to regain control of the cities. In 1444, he pardoned his son and Ayala, but the continued rebellion led him finally to depose Ayala of his powers and castles. Two years later, however, as part of the compromise which was an attempt to end the conflict, the king was forced to restore Ayala to power.

It is against this background that the anti-converso hostility must be understood. Although one writer has it that animosity against conversos played no special part in the violence of the era, adding a warning against being "hypnotized by the purely anti-Semitic [*sic*] aspects" of this violence, in fact *all* of the instances of violence and popular unrest which he enumerates involved either Jews or conversos or both.[1]

The truth is that the increasing hostility against Jews, and more especially against conversos, was able to erupt into actual violence and riots because of the general state of anarchy which prevailed. The anti-Jewish nature of these riots was not a mere manifestation of the general social unrest, however, but was a separate and very real issue.[2]

In 1448 there was yet another plot by some rebellious nobles against the king. Many were arrested, and some, like the admiral don Fadrique Enríquez, escaped across the border. Badly in need of money for the war against the Muslims of Granada, Juan asked for financial aid from the cities. In Toledo the following year Álvaro de Luna entrusted a wealthy converso merchant, Alonso Cota (member of the famous Jewish and converso Cota family), with the responsibility of raising the required sum.

Álvaro de Luna, *condestable* of the king and Master of the Order of Santiago, was himself of a converso family, though perhaps distantly, as was probably his treasurer and chronicler Gonzalo Chacón, later *contador mayor* of Fernando and Isabel.[3]

In 1441 serious charges had already been brought against de Luna, some possibly true (illicit alliances and political intrigues) and others no doubt exaggerated (murder, homosexuality, black magic). In 1443 he was a sponsor of legislation, the *pragmática* of Arévalo, in favor of the Jews. This, of course, does not mean that he had a particularly "pro-Jewish" policy, as some have claimed.[4]

In 1453, when an angry mob attacked de Luna accusing him of treason while he was staying at the palace of Pedro de Cartagena, brother of the converso bishop Pablo de Santa María, in Burgos, he sought to protect Álvaro, Pedro's son, from the mob, which was also attacking conversos in general. However, in the end de Luna's own followers convinced him that Cartagena could save *him*, since he knew secret ways out of the palace and the city. Together, they barely escaped with their lives. Chacón later invented a speech in which de Luna supposedly complained of the evil which conversos sought to do him, though he treated them better than anyone in the realm. This is unlikely, for it contradicts not only his previous statement that he wished to save Álvaro de Cartagena from the mob that was attacking conversos, but also the fact that many conversos later supported him in the 1449 riots.[5]

Meanwhile in Toledo in 1449 suspicion fell on the conversos that they were somehow the instigators of the special tax imposed by the king, perhaps in order to "humiliate" the "old Christians" who clearly could not afford to pay such a sum, reportedly 1,000,000 *mrs.*

The *alcalde mayor*, Pero Sarmiento, and his assessor, Marcos García de Mazarambrós, urged resistance to the tax and also sought the intercession of the *infante* Enrique with his father.

A riot broke out in the city, which began with a mob in the Church of Santa María (a former synagogue, now a national monument). The house of the converso Alonso Cota was burned, although he survived the attack and was to retain his post under Enrique IV. Houses of other conversos were also attacked.[6]

The result was actual war, culminating in a siege of the city by Álvaro de Luna (a papal letter condemning Sarmiento refers to the use of "machines of war" in the conflict).[7] This was the first time in Spanish history that any such attack on conversos erupted into real war.

Less fortunate than Cota was another tax collector, also a converso, Juan de Ciudad, who was killed and whose body was dragged to the plaza de Zocodover. Chacón says that some of his descendants later went to other lands and became Jews.[8]

The illegitimate son of the king of Navarre, Alonso, attacked Cuenca, but the city was ably defended by its bishop, Lope de Barrientos, who later would write a profound defense of the conversos (discussed below).

When Juan II came to Toledo in May of 1449 he was presented with a defense and demands by Sarmiento and other rebels of the city, among which were charges against Álvaro de Luna, including the claim that he gave offices to "infidels and heretics, enemies of our sacred law." Furthermore, Sarmiento accused him of "publicly defending and receiving conversos of Jewish lineage, who for the most part are found to be infidels and heretics who have 'Judaized' and continue to do so and observe most of the Jewish rites and ceremonies."[9] A contemporary, Pedro de Escavias, also refers to the uprising, caused by the "great division" between Christians (!) and conversos, led respectively by Sarmiento and Juan de Ciudad. The "old Christians" (this time, at least, he has it right) cried, "Death to the heretics," and the conversos, "Death to those who are against the king."[10]

As Benito Ruano correctly understood, it was in large part due to Sarmiento and the other rebels' need to find a justification for their treason (in spite of having been pardoned by the king) that they blamed the conversos. On the other hand, it is doubtful, as he suggested, that in light of Nicholas V's bull declaring discrimination against conversos heretical, an organized tribunal like that of the later Inquisition could have prevented persecution of the conversos.[11] It was precisely the Inquisition which hypocritically persecuted and burned thousands of conversos, whom its officials knew to be good Christians, totally ignoring papal bulls and objections to the Inquisition itself.

Continuing with his program, Sarmiento assembled various officials in the city in June and issued the "*sentencia-estatuto*" prohibiting conversos and their descendants from holding any public office. One of the first statements in the statute refers to a privilege granted the city of Toledo by "don Alfonso, king of Castile and León," affirming that no public office in that city be given to a convert of Jewish descent "because of [such converts] being suspect in the faith."[12]

Amador de los Ríos (an important nineteenth-century historian of the Jews of Spain) and Benito Ruano have argued that (although which king "don Alfonso" is not stated) no such privilege exists nor is there any mention of it. However, Netanyahu correctly pointed out that the gloss of Alonso Díaz de Montalvo (to be discussed later) does refer to it; more important, he discovered that in three different manuscripts (which Benito Ruano had not used) of the *Memorial* of Marcos García de Mora (also called "Marquillos") defending the *sentencia* there is an important section, missing in the edited text, which clearly refers to laws given as a "special city enactment" to Toledo by the "king don Alfonso" prohibiting baptized

Jews from holding public office. Furthermore, whereas one might assume that the privilege of "don Alfonso" referred to is none other than the *fuero* of Alfonso VII given to Toledo in 1118 which prohibited Jews and those "recently converted" from holding office, Netanyahu argued that this cannot be the document referred to, for a variety of reasons (especially because it said "*recent* converts," whereas in the text cited in the statute *all* converts and their descendants are mentioned).[13]

However, his conclusion that sometime after the *fuero* of 1118 ("say, in 1145") the Christians of Toledo petitioned the king for yet a new law prohibiting not only the "recent converts" of 1118 but even their descendants from holding public office is not convincing. There may have been some Jews who converted in the 1108 riots in Toledo; on the other hand, the *fuero* seems to be speaking in theological generalities, "no Jew or one recently converted," which may well simply reflect canon law and not refer to the 1108 incident at all.[14] In any event, there is no evidence of any large number of converts at that date, and certainly not later. More particularly, there is no evidence at all to support the contention that "old Christians" already resented Jews' holding public office in Toledo in the twelfth and thirteenth centuries. On the contrary, Jews often held offices of great importance in Toledo. Thus, if the alleged privilege of "don Alfonso" has any reality, it most *probably* refers to the *fuero* of 1118, which the supporters of the statute misinterpreted, accidentally or deliberately, as barring descendants of conversos from holding public office.

The statute complained that, nevertheless, "most" of the offices such as public scribes, etc., were held by conversos. Therefore, they were henceforth to be prohibited from holding any office, as this caused harm "to old Christians of pure lineage" (*a los christianos viejos lindos* [193]; possibly the first use of this term of "purity").

In spite of the absurd charges against the conversos, the real cause of Sarmiento's hatred is revealed a few lines further on: some conversos of Toledo supported Álvaro de Luna, his old enemy. The robbery and killing which took place he blames not only on the conversos themselves, but on Jews generally, "enemies of our holy Catholic faith." This loaded term, frequently used against Muslims, was rarely applied to Jews in Spain, and this proves the anti-Semitism of Sarmiento.

Like other anti-Jewish polemicists before him (e.g., Lucas of Túy), he goes back to the ancient legend that Jews betrayed Toledo to the Muslims at the time of the conquest in 711 (a totally false story). So the "descendants" of those Jews, the conversos, continue to rob and deceive the people. Not only that, they have robbed and destroyed "the majority" of the houses of old Christians in the city and throughout the realm (194).[15]

Certain public officials known to be conversos are named: López Fernández Cota,* Juan Fernández Cota, Gonzalo Rodríguez de San Pedro (nephew of López Fernández Cota),** Juan Nuñez and his brothers Pero† and Diego, Juan López del Arroyo, Juan González de Illescas, Pero Ortíz, Diego Rodríguez *el Alba,*‡ Diego Martínez de Herrera, the *alcalde* Diego González Jarada and his son Pero González (195).

Some of these family names—Cota, Nuñez, González de Illescas, Ortíz—appear in the list of most commonly occurring names of conversos in Toledo in 1485, 1495, and 1497.[16] No doubt this is only a partial list of converso officials in Toledo, and perhaps represents those whom Sarmiento particularly hated.

In response to the infamous "statute," many outstanding Christian authorities wrote stinging rebuttals in defense of the conversos. Among those which have come to light (there were no doubt others), those of Fernan Díaz de Toledo, Alonso Díaz de Montalvo, Alonso de Cartagena, Juan de Torquemada, and, especially, Lope de Barrientos are the most important.

Not all of these were themselves conversos, as has been erroneously claimed. Lope de Barrientos certainly was not (although many writers have said he was), nor was Alonso Días de Montalvo, and Torquemada was at most of possible remote converso origin.[17] Another treatise was apparently written by Francisco de Toledo, dean of the cathedral, and was directed to Torquemada and also to the pope, but it has not survived (unless it is the base of Torquemada's own work). This Francisco later became bishop of Coria, and was of converso descent.[18]

Lope de Barrientos (born 1395, not 1382; died 1469), Dominican master and bishop of Segovia, Ávila, and Cuenca, had been confessor of Juan II and then his *chancellor mayor*. His defense, *Contra algunos zizañadores de la nación de los convertidos del pueblo de Israel,* was addressed to the king. Barrientos condemned Sarmiento's henchman Marquillos as "another Haman," but noted that whereas Haman had attacked Jews, Marquillos attacked Christians (conversos).[19]

He raises the obvious objection that this persecution discourages others from converting and leads to "blasphemy" among those already converted, who say that it would have been better not to become Christians. Indeed, he admits, conversos are persecuted much more than Jews are (183). From

---

* In 1422 he was *escribano del rey* (royal scribe) and farmed the tithes of the Jewish community for the cathedral chapter (León Tello, *Judíos de Toledo* 2:224, etc.)

** Ibid., nos. 759, 902, 922, 934, 942, 965, 1011. As noted previously, his sons Yuda and Santo Aruque are described as Jews (339).

† He may be the *regidor*, deceased, named in the Inquisition proceedings of 1494; ibid., no. 1692.

‡ Could this be the doctor Diego Rodríguez of Valladolid, of the royal council (frequent mention in *Crónica de halconero,* etc.)?

a moral-historical viewpoint, Barrientos argues (as does Torquemada) that the prophets and apostles were all Jews, and logically the latter would have been persecuted as conversos according to Marquillos' position. Later, he mentions Saint Julian, the Visigothic bishop of Toledo, a converso, and also a bishop of Barcelona, born in Valencia, in his own time, whom Barrientos met and spoke with, who was of Jewish descent (we shall later attempt to identify this person). Not only that, it would be a great dishonor to Christ himself to insult and abuse those of "that line of his holy humanity" (Jewish converts) by denying them offices and benefices within the Church. According to canon law, the *Siete partidas,* and the agreement of all *Cortes,* indeed, not only must Jewish converts not be "disdained," they must even be favored (184–86).

He refers also to questions to Enrique II in the *Cortes* concerning the conversos, and calls those who already then sought to persecute them so many "perverse Hamans." That king issued decrees in favor of conversos, he says. Barrientos says he himself also saw a papal bull addressed to Enrique against the persecution of conversos.

He notes that hundreds of Christians have become Muslims, recently even the brother of the bishop of Zamora. (This refers to fray Alonso de Mella, a Franciscan and brother of Juan de Mella, bishop of Zamora and later a cardinal. Fray Alonso was the founder of the Durango heresy and leader of that movement, many followers of which were imprisoned and burned by order of the king. Alonso fled to Granada, where according to Pére de Guzmán, he was condemned to death).[20] He further notes that many Christians are heretics; among the Basques and in Bohemia, for instance. Yet no one persecutes these because some are heretics, nor robs and kills the Andalusians because every day many of them go to Granada and become Muslims (195–96) (the *Cancionero de Baena* already contains poems attacking a certain Christian who went from Málaga to Granada and converted).[21]

Remarkable also is another insight: since virtually all of the Jews in Visigothic Spain converted to Christianity, who among the Christians of Spain could be certain that he is not a descendant of those conversos (197)?

Of great significance is the list he gives of prominent Christian families who have converso members or are of converso descent. This reads like a veritable "Who's Who" of Spanish nobility: the Manriques, Mendozas, Rojas, Sarabias, Pimenteles, Lujanes, Solis, Mirandas, Osorios, Saucedos (Salcedos), and others, including relatives of Juan Hurtado de Mendoza, *mayordomo* of the king, and the *mariscal* Diego Fernández of Córdoba. Also on the list is Francisco Fernández Marmolejo, who was *contador* of the "king don Alonso" (this is an error for Pedro I, however), whose descendants include many *regidores* and *caballeros* in Seville (198–200). Of course he also mentions Juan Sánchez of Seville (Isaac Abravanel's grandfather), the *contador mayor* of Enrique III, as well as the Lunas, Stúñigas (later Estúñigas), and others.[22]

Particularly important is his statement that the admiral of Castile, don Alonso Enríquez, on one side was descended from Alfonso XI and Enrique II, and on the other from Jews (that Fernando, king of Spain, was thus descended from Jews will be discussed in detail in the next chapter).[23] Not only the royal line of Castile, but also that of Navarre contained descendants of conversos, for the king don Carlos (Carlos de Viana) is descended by his mother from "pure Israelites" (i.e., apparently, Jews and not conversos [202]).

Fernan Díaz de Toledo, a converso counsellor and secretary of the king, prepared an "Instrucción," or background paper, for Barrientos (possibly in October of 1449).[24] He sought the bishop's favor on behalf of "all this poor persecuted nation of the lineage of our Lord Jesus Christ according to the flesh, which above all things is blessed of God." They will surely be rewarded, he claims, for all their merits and "laudable works" which they have done and do.

He warned that such persecution may prevent other Jews "outside the faith" from converting, and observed that many conversos leave Toledo every day for the land of the Muslims or other kingdoms to become Jews, saying that their (Christian) faith is of no benefit nor does it protect them against such evils. As we have seen, Barrientos utilized these arguments and even expanded upon them. Díaz further condemns the prohibition against conversos holding office as contrary to canon and civil laws, noting the opinion of many canonists that the Visigothic prohibition applied only to apostates who returned to Judaism, not to those converts who remain in the Christian faith.

Furthermore, both the *Partidas* and other laws of the kings, and especially a privilege granted by Enrique III when many Jews in Toledo converted, specifically prohibit this discrimination (this refers, of course, to the conversions of 1391; unfortunately, however, the text of this privilege, referred to also by Barrientos, apparently has not survived).

Of great interest is Díaz's statement that "D. Juan Gomez," archbishop of Toledo, was a converso and son of a Jew (*judío;* read perhaps *judía?*) of Toledo (246). No such name appears in any list of the bishops of the city, and the only possibility seems to be the archbishop Gutierre Gómez (1310–19), who in fact was the son of Gome Pérez, *alguacil mayor* of Toledo, and his wife Horabuena (Ora Buena).[25] That name is so exclusively Jewish in medieval Spain, and particularly Toledo, that there can be little doubt as to her background. The archbishop's brother, interestingly, was Fernand Gómez, chancellor of Fernando IV and frequently involved with the Jew Samuel who was in the service of that king. It happens that Fernán

Alvarez de Toledo (d. ca. 1460), the conde de Alba, was a nephew of Gutierre Gómez and also of Iñigo López de Mendoza, which further supports the possibility of the converso background of the archbishop (of course, the archbishop Juan de Cerezuela, brother of Álvaro de Luna, was thus also of converso origin, but somewhat remote; although he can hardly be described as the "son of a Jew," he was considered a converso).

However, immediately following this, Díaz quotes from Rodrigo Jiménez de Rada (himself an archbishop of Toledo and a famous chronicler) a statement which is supposedly about this converso archbishop, but in fact is about Julian of Toledo. We must assume a lacuna in the text here, and the name of "Julianus Pomerius" (a common confusion of the name of Julian of Toledo, found also in the text of Alonso Díaz de Montalvo discussed below, and in other writers) should be here added as yet another converso mentioned by the author. It is to him, i.e., Julian of Toledo, that Rodrigo refers (he could hardly have talked about a converso archbishop who lived after himself). Nevertheless, there can be no doubt that Fernán Díaz mentions this "Juan Gomez." [26]

No less important is the statement that there have been, and are, many other prelates of converso origin in Spain. He also mentions among these the bishop of Barcelona, a master of theology and almoner of Benedict XIII, whom Díaz says he saw in Morilla some thirty-six years ago (about 1413). We recall that Barrientos repeated this information essentially, adding that he personally knew this converso bishop (see Chapter 5 on him).

Christians ought to treat the conversos graciously, Díaz says, and with all possible "good," help, sustain, and honor them, treat them "fraternally and charitably and even with all manner of love."

"Thanks be to God," he adds, many noble families in Spain are of converso origin. (He names all of them, as found in Barrientos' list, but adds—a shocker—Cervantes. Juan de Cervantes was cardinal of San Pedro, and, of course, the converso origin of the famous author of *Don Quijote* is still debated; however, there was more than one Cervantes family.) Also the royal houses of Castile, Navarre, Aragón, and Portugal have converso "descendants."

Even though a certain amount of bragging and self-aggrandizement is evident in all this, he would not dare make such statements (nor would the more renowned and sober Barrientos repeat them) were they not true. As *relator* and secretary to the king, Fernan Díaz was "always with him," as Barrientos says in his *Crónica*, and personally knew all the nobility. A descendant of one of the converso families named, Salcedo, later archbishop of Seville, was indeed the one who preserved the manuscript of this document. [27]

A response to Fernan Díaz, in the form of a "memorial" or treatise, by bachiller Marcos García de Mora ("Marquillos") prompted the reply of

Barrientos which we have previously discussed.[28] The memorial is a fanatical diatribe, marred not only by anti-Semitism but by vile attacks on Álvaro de Luna. Making no distinction between Jews and conversos, he claimed that the whole kingdom was tyrannized and destroyed by "Jews."

Most of the tirade is a defense of his and Sarmiento's actions in Toledo, but he unleashes a series of patently false charges against all (or most) of the conversos of the city: they kept Jewish holidays and Sabbaths, worked on Sundays, maintained lamps in the synagogue, went there to pray every day, etc. Therefore, he says, those who were burned deserved their death, for heretics must be burned in accord with canon law.[29]

Against the charge of virtual treason, in that Sarmiento and his followers refused to receive the king in the city, he replies that they sought to "save" the king from slavery to Álvaro de Luna and the "Jewish counsel" of the infidels (conversos). Personal jealousy and spite were no doubt the key motives of his attack on the conversos, for he complains that "Mose Hamomo" (his derisive name for Fernan Díaz) not only was a notorious "Jew" but that, although a doctor (of law), "he knows no letters at all except Jewish and heretical ones," where he (García) though only a *bachiller* is a "famous legist and canonist." How far from the truth this charge is can be seen in the aforementioned fact that Alonso Díaz de Montalvo himself was a pupil of Fernan Díaz.

Unnoticed by all who have written on this subject is the manuscript of a treatise by bachiller Alfonso González de Toledo, also addressed to Barrientos.[30] In it, he refers to the decree of IV Toledo (the Visigothic council) against Jews holding public office, but says that he has seen the glosses of those decretals and that one of them specifically states that the prohibition is against Jews but not descendants of Jews ("aquellos que son de la fe de los judíos mas non de los quen son de la gente de los judíos" [fol. 129r]).

Another argument which he uses against the discriminatory treatment of conversos is of great interest: the "fame" of the archbishop-elect, who he observes will no doubt be honored throughout the world (fol. 129v). This can only refer to Alonso Carrillo de Acuña (1447–82). He was born in Cuenca, the son of don Lope Vázquez de Acuña and doña Teresa Carrillo del Albornoz, sister of the deceased cardinal of San Eustaquio, and in 1435 he became bishop of Sigüenza. In view of such a background, one might wonder what possible reason our author could have for claiming that he was a "converso." He himself was not, of course, but much suspicion attaches to the family ties. In the first place, he was nephew of Pedro González de Mendoza, who succeeded him as archbishop, and the converso connections of that family have already been stated. The countess of Alba, doña Mencía, was also a Carrillo, and there were converso "intrusions" into the Alba dynasty as well (interestingly, her Jewish *mayordomo* was Jacob Abengato of Toledo, of a family which included many conversos). Finally, it should be noted that there were Jews in Toledo with the family name Carrillo, contemporaneous with the archbishop.[31]

The same manuscript contains also the lengthy reply of Lope de Barrientos, but there is nothing new there not already known from his previously cited work (fols. 132v–154r).

Alonso de Cartagena, a converso and son of the converso Pablo de Santa María, succeeded his father as bishop of Burgos, after serving first as bishop of Cartagena. It was at that time that he wrote a lengthy Latin defense of conversos, particularly seeking to refute the arguments of "Marquillos" (Marcos García Moro). Following a lengthy introduction, much of it anti-Jewish polemic, he argues for unity of Christians, both "old" and converts, drawing support from such sources as Augustine, canon law (particularly the Council of Basel, in which he himself played a leading role, as we shall see later), the *Siete partidas,* and laws of Enrique III.[32]

Turning directly to his refutation of "Marquillos," we find that Alonso refers to a nearly complete copy of the canons of the Visigothic Toledo councils which he was able to see at Basel, since no perfect copy existed in Spain (a very important piece of evidence as to the lack of influence of this anti-Jewish legislation in later medieval Spanish law; in fact, Rodrigo Jiménez de Rada, thirteenth-century archbishop of Toledo, had a copy in his library, which he presented to the Monastery of Santa María de Huerta, but either it was not complete or Alonso did not know of its existence). Against the claims that IV Toledo prohibited conversos from holding office, he argues that these councils were not "universal" but "particular," and therefore not binding. Furthermore, "Jews" in that legislation means those not converted, and "of Jewish origin" (*ex Judaeis*) means, according to him, "Judaizers," but not sincere converts.[33]

He concludes by condemning the activities of the followers of Sarmiento (whom he never names, however), and says they are guilty of heresy like the ancient heretics or those of more modern times; and as did Fernan Díaz and Barrientos, he includes here the Hussites of Bohemia, followers of John Hus, who was corrupted by the "perverse doctrine of John Wyclif of England" (as a member of the Council of Basel, Alonso had participated in the condemnation of Hus).[34]

The converso poet Juan de Lucena wrote a fictitious dialogue (at least its general outlines are copied from another work) between the conversos Juan de Mena and Alonso de Cartagena, and the marqués de Santillana (Iñigo López de Mendoza). The author also introduces himself into this discussion at one point, and it is difficult to know whether there is any reality to the reported conversation. In any case, he has Juan de Mena make an unfortunate reference to the "simple and pure life" of the ancestors of the converso bishop, to which he replies with some indignation. Do not think, he says, to alarm me with reference to my ancestors as "Hebrews." For, "if antiquity is nobility, who is so remote? If virtue, who so close? Or if the mode in Spain is that riches are aristocracy, who was so rich in their time? God was their friend, their Lord, legislator, consul, captain, father and son, and in the end, their redeemer." Following a lengthy comparison with the pagans, the bishop then passionately defends the despised conversos. In light of the great virtue of the "Davidites, the Levites, the Maccabees, and the twelve tribes of Israel," he says, "see, see what is a Marrano; a little lower than dirt." In reality, those who are deceitful (he employs a pun here: *marrados,* "deceitful, erring") are rather those faithless Christians who attack them.[35]

Juan de Torquemada was a Dominican and a cardinal, who was in Rome when he heard about the anti-converso riots, He, too, requested and received a "memorial" as background for his own treatise (who the author was is not presently known), which may explain the close parallel between his work and those already discussed here. His little treatise is neither very original nor very profound, being primarily a point-by-point refutation of the charges against conversos, based almost entirely on scriptural arguments, etc. The only original point he makes, perhaps, citing Augustine, is that error is not heresy. Heresy, he adds, is not merely in thought but in will. (Apparently, though this is not clearly indicated, he intends to say that some conversos may be guilty of error in their intellectual understanding of belief, but this is not heresy unless, when the error is pointed out, they continue willfully to maintain it.)[36]

Removed as he was from Spain at the time, he does not go into specific details, as had others, as to important conversos and descendants of such, but does remark that "not only mediocre persons but great ones," of great virtue and religiosity, and both ecclesiastical and government officials, living in "different parts of the world" (does he mean to include himself?) are conversos or descendants of conversos.[37]

There is also a very important text by Alonso Díaz de Montalvo (b. 1405), who held prominent judicial posts under Juan II and Enrique IV and was a prolific author. (Among other things, he compiled the *Ordenanzas reales de Castilla,* which saw five editions in 1485 alone; edited and glossed the *Fuero real,* and also the first edition of the *Siete partidas* [1491].) In 1453 he assisted the commission which condemned Álvaro de Luna to death. Montalvo's biographer has pointed out that the important political treatise contained in his gloss to *Fuero real* 1.4, containing the history of the rebellion of the supposed "count of Dacia," is actually a satirical attack on Luna.[38] (We shall refer to another important work of Montalvo's later.)

This text deals with the situation of conversos holding ecclesiastical and public office. Those who are false he calls "perpetually damned," and recalls once again the old Visigothic laws prohibiting Jews or their descendants from holding office. However, he notes that for the sake of "peace" in the faith, no distinction must be made between "Israelites" (conversos) and

Gentiles if the former are *true* converts. Nor is there any distinction with regard to guilt for the crucifixion of Christ, for which "all are culpable," Jew and Gentile alike (a view shared by many theologians, although he was hardly qualified to pronounce on this). All, Jews and Gentiles alike, are "like lost sheep, but now are converted to (turned to) the shepherd."

If, in fact, there are heretics among the conversos, God will be able to distinguish them and "separate" them from the faithful. But converts are not automatically suspect, for through baptism all—Jew and Gentile— become one body (1 Cor. 12.12) and form one Church, without distinction.

He also notes that Rodrigo Jiménez de Rada had spoken highly of "Julianus Pomerius" and his virtue, and he was of the Jewish people and proclaimed the doctrine of God (converted; indeed, Jiménez does say all of this about Julian of Toledo, but adds that his being of Jewish origin was like a rose flourishing among thorns).[39] Not only should true converts be considered equal to other Christians, they must not be denied any office or Christian honor, and to act contrary to this is against "express law and right."

The same argument used by others (Barrientos, Díaz, Torquemada) is also here: there are many Christian heretics in places like Viscaya (or Bohemia), but not all the inhabitants are therefore condemned as heretics.

Something totally new and of great significance, however, is his argument to those who cite the Visigothic code against conversos' holding public office. He replies, "that law [not the actual Visigothic code, but the supposed medieval Spanish version, *Fuero juzgo*] is not authentic, nor is that book authentic, nor is it observed in Spain, and as happens with the antiquated that law is already replaced by a contrary law: 7 *Partidas tit.* 24, *ley* 6, which is later."[40] The law of *Partidas* to which he refers specifies that those who convert must not be compelled, but should do so of their own free will, and that after conversion all "Jews" (!) shall be honored by everyone in the kingdom and neither they nor their descendants be reproached for having been Jews.

Again, he carefully distinguishes the true converts from those who may be heretics and relapse to Judaism. However, those who are faithful must not be denied any office, and especially those who for five or seven years have been good Christians, and can hardly be called "neophytes" (converts).

Rather curiously, he concludes by condemning the policy of Enrique III (the father of Juan II, for whom Alonso wrote these glosses), at the advice of Pedro Tenorio, the archbishop of Toledo, to restrict converts from holding ecclesiastical and public office, and he combines this with an eloquent denunciation of Toledo for maintaining such pernicious statutes. (Note that this is the exact opposite of what Fernon Díaz and Barrientos both said, claiming to have seen privileges of Enrique III *permitting* converts to hold such offices.)

Finally, he protests that this persecution of conversos is not true zeal for the faith, but a type of malice, and that hatred should be directed at sin and not men. Those who pursue these false notions and laws are the true heretics.[41]

As is well known, the battle against conversos did not end with the Sarmiento affair, but continued well into the sixteenth century and beyond. When the archbishop of Toledo Juan Martínez Siliceo (1546–57) published his *Estatuto de limpieza de sangre* against conversos' holding ecclesiastical office, the famous leading follower of Erasmus in Spain, Juan de Vergara, who himself had been secretary to two previous archbishops of Toledo, wrote a denunciation of the book. In that work, still in manuscript, he raises all the points that had already been made in the fifteenth-century dispute, noting that such discrimination is contrary to the laws of the kingdom and to scripture and natural law, and injurious to "many noble people and *principals de los Rey[nos]*." He adds, as had Fernan Díaz and Barrientos, that it is specifically against the laws of Alfonso X and Enrique III, and finally he notes that not only papal bulls but also Saint Paul in Romans protected the Jews, who are the "adopted sons" (of God).[42]

Ciudad Real

In June of 1449, the rebellion against the conversos spread also to Ciudad Real. The Order of Calatrava, already notorious for its murder and robbery in the city on a previous occasion, was involved also in instigating these riots. (Ironically, the master of the order, Alfonso de Aragón, bastard son of King Juan II of Aragón-Catalonia, was married to a conversa.) more than three hundred men, "armed with many and diverse arms," attacked the conversos, and especially the tax collectors and other officials, and burned a great part of the city. The robbery of houses of conversos, which the officials of the city were powerless to stop, lasted for two days. Some converso officials were killed and their bodies dragged in the public square, exactly as had happened in Toledo.

From the perspective of centuries, one reads almost with more distress than for those killed of the burning of "many books" and "many writings." One can only wonder what treasures may have thus been lost.

The king this time intervened vigorously to punish those responsible, and it was this which elicited the lengthy report of the events in Ciudad Real, ending with a plea for mercy and promises to make "restitution" to those robbed and to restore conversos to their offices (of course, no "restitution" could be made to those who had been murdered). As a result, the king readily granted his complete and unconditional pardon to all the inhabitants of the city, and exemption from punishment for any crimes related to the incident. He did, however, accept the offer of restitution.[43]

Response: The Inquisition, More Riots

All of this gave added power to those who already favored the establishment of an Inquisition. Nevertheless, it is notable that Juan de Torquemada and other religious leaders convinced the pope to issue a bull of excommunication against Sarmiento, but Juan II almost immediately asked for and received a suspension of that bull (October of 1450). Apparently the king sought to regain the support of Toledo. In August of 1451 he actually *confirmed* the prohibition of conversos' holding office in Toledo. The pope then pardoned all the followers of Sarmiento whom he had excommunicated, and restored them to their former offices. Finally, Sarmiento himself was pardoned and restored (already in 1450) to favor.[44]

Beltrán de Heredia would have us believe, for reasons which probably had to do with his own strong anti-Jewish animus, that the establishment of the Inquisition in Castile was due entirely to the "animosity" between Álvaro de Luna and the conversos, and that Álvaro wished to rid himself of his enemies by accusing them of heresy. There is no evidence to sustain such a theory (especially given the fact that Álvaro was himself of converso origin), and in any case the actual battle against the conversos was precisely because they were accused of *supporting* and even instigating the tax policy of Álvaro.[45] The statement of the Franciscan polemicist Alonso del Espina (not the Inquisitor), who incidentally was certainly *not* a "*neófito*" (convert), in 1459 that if there were to be an Inquisition in Castile, many real "Judaizers" would enter the flames and thus be saved from eternal fire does not prove that this judgment was true, and still less that there was any "Semitic" conspiracy between conversos and Jews, as Beltrán claimed.[46]

In 1462, however, almost two decades after the Toledo riots, Enrique IV did petition Pius II to establish an Inquisition in Castile. Apparently there was no response to this request (the pope died soon after). Fernando de Plaza, a Franciscan, in a sermon at court (possibly in 1457, when the king was in Segovia), claimed he had the circumcised foreskins of sons of conversos whom their fathers had secretly circumcised. The king, somewhat skeptical, ordered him to produce the foreskins and the names of the circumcised conversos. It has been claimed that this absurd sermon was one of the main causes of the Toledo riots of 1467, but this seems doubtful.[47]

The converso historian Alonso de Palencia, chronicler of Enrique IV, relates that in 1462 "great disturbances" were caused by Beltrán de Pareja, commander of the castle built by Pedro I at Carmona and brother of the notorious Beltrán de la Cueva, favorite of Enrique (and probable father of "his" daughter Juana). Without referring to the "infinite crimes" committed by this commander, Alonso says, he will mention only his inciting an uprising against the conversos, resulting in robbery, murder, "and the violent perpetration of every manner of infamy," similar to what had happened in Toledo.

Alonso complains that the king should have punished Beltrán, but refrained because of his relationship with his brother and instead sent troops from Córdoba, Écija, and Seville to put down the uprising (Carmona, today a small village, seems an unlikely place for such a major uprising). The converso poet Antón de Montoro, then living in Córdoba, wrote a poem to the king entreating him to act and telling him of the plight of the conversos "accused with less guilt than gusto," who are treated worse than the Muslims. The great jurist Alonso Díaz de Montalvo may also have referred to these riots (or the earlier one) in his legal lexicon.[48]

Alonso de Palencia also says that false rumors circulated in Toledo and other cities that the boy "king" Alfonso, proclaimed at Ávila in 1465 when his half brother Enrique was dethroned by the nobles, intended to persecute the conversos. This caused them to join the supporters of Enrique (1466). The "old Christians" then proceeded "scandalously" against the conversos in Toledo, but he gives no real details of what happened.

The following year, when "king" Alfonso entered Toledo, the hostilities again erupted because the conversos supported Enrique, whose agents were inciting them and promising support if they attacked the followers of Alfonso. The conversos chose as their leader Fernando de la Torre and purchased weapons which they concealed in his house. Among these were muskets and a kind of blowgun (cerbatana), "arms newly invented for the destruction of the human race," according to our chronicler, who adds that the plotting of the "old Christians" against the conversos resulted in their murder and forced exile, none of which was due to any crime on their part but only to envy of the wealth they accumulated "by their work and industry." Alvar Gómez, a converso secretary of the king, entered the church during mass and a quarrel broke out in which a priest was killed. The fight then spread through the city, and houses near the church were burned. Four large streets totally inhabited by conversos were burned. "All" the conversos had their property confiscated and were expelled from the city (a great exaggeration, of course), and Fernando de la Torre and his brother Álvaro were killed.[49]

Other sources reveal a somewhat different picture. A document of interdict against the city, and against Alvar Gómez, the alcalde mayor and former secretary of Enrique IV, was read in Toledo in 1467. This involved the payment of certain ecclesiastical taxes, and charges made against "certain Jews" (conversos?) who had been granted rights as tax farmers on the assessments. Before a compromise could be reached in the ensuing debate, Fernando de la Torre intervened. After further lengthy debate, a group of armed conversos broke into the cathedral with the intent of killing their enemies. Inevitably, open combat resulted yet again. As usual, Pedro López de Ayala headed the "old Christian" cause. During the battle, stores and houses of conversos were burned and the fire spread through a large part of the surrounding neighborhood.

Fernando de la Torre, captain of the converso band, while attempting to escape from the city was captured and imprisoned in the tower of the Church of San Leocadia and hanged the next morning. His body and that of his brother Alvaro were later dragged to the plaza de Zocodover.[50]

Which account is to be believed? No doubt both of them together provide details which are correct, with certain exaggerations.

Conversos were accused of having documents in Hebrew which exempted them from certain "contributions," and other books in Hebrew prohibited by the Church, which books the local Jews were called to examine and describe (not aware of the modern theories of "crypto-Judaism" of the conversos, the Jews were only too willing to cooperate in causing trouble for their hated enemies).[51]

The result was again imposition of restrictive measures and persecution against the conversos. A manuscript source lays the blame entirely on the clergy and government of the city, "who favored the destruction and robbing of the conversos."[52]

Like his father before him, Enrique in 1468 granted a pardon to those who had engaged in the riots, and ordered that no converso be allowed to hold public office (in 1471 he nullified this order). He also personally attempted to pacify the cofradías (religious guilds) of Toledo, divided between "old" and "new" Christians, by uniting two of these and himself becoming a member (a more unlikely "religious devotee" than Enrique is hard to imagine). In 1480, the synod of Alcalá, under the influence of Archbishop Carrillo (who we have seen may himself have been of converso origin), was to prohibit cofradías based on distinctions between "old" and "new" Christians.[53]

Indeed, among the converso officials of Enrique had been Diego González de Toledo ("doctor Franco"), possibly his contador mayor and "oidor" of the Audience, whose son Alonso Franco had been one of the leaders in the battle in 1467, and who owned houses in the judería. He died in 1460.[54]

More Riots

Uprisings against the conversos continued to spread. The riots in Córdoba in 1473 are reported by the converso historians Alonso de Palencia and

Diego de Valera. The converso poet Antón de Montoro of Córdoba, an eyewitness, addressed a sarcastic poem to don Alonso de Aguilar, overlord of various cities in the province, who was then in control of Córdoba and did little or nothing to protect the conversos.

Why should he help them, the poet implies, when they are considered more "Jews than Christians" (stanza 9)? He concludes that the conversos are "willing" to pay Aguilar taxes "and be captives and to serve, / the poor ones, cuckolds and queers," acting deceitfully and accepting every humiliation in order to live (stanza 19; as we shall see, sexual charges of this kind against the conversos were common).[55]

In Jaén, the *condestable mayor* of Castile, Miguel Lucas de Iranzao, who unlike Aguilar did protect the conversos, was murdered in the church for his trouble, and his family terrorized and forced to hide in the castle. Alonso de Palencia laid the blame on Juan Pacheco, the king's favorite, but this is only another instance of that chronicler's antagonism to the officials of Enrique IV. Diego Enríquez del Castillo briefly mentions the uprisings in Córdoba, blaming the conversos and claiming they could no longer live in the city afterward (which is untrue).

Of great importance is the letter of the *condestable* himself, written only a day or so before his assassination. In it, he tells of the scandalous news concerning the riots. The condition and quality of the conversos are such, he says, that there is no reason for such actions. He reminds the officials of their duty and loyalty to the king and the honor of the city. "It would be more just and honest and better if one or some of the said [conversos] who live badly and counter to conscience and the law should be accused and punished by justice, and not do generally against all of them what has been done."[56]

He paid for this good sense with his life.

Alonso de Palencia says that the conversos were "extraordinarily enriched by rare arts" (knowledge and skills) but arrogant in their pursuit of public offices. The bishop (Pedro de Córdoba y Solier), he says, was one of those opposed to the conversos, "supposing them more inclined to avarice than to religion." He criticizes the bishop's "notorious vanity" and lack of judgment.

Some of the anti-converso elements were nevertheless expelled from the city, which only increased the audacity of the conversos. The "old Christians," who Alonso says were "motivated by a certain apparent religious zeal," founded a *cofradía* for charity, the real motive of which was persecution of conversos. When a young conversa maid threw water from a window, and it happened to hit the statue of the Virgin which the *cofradía* was carrying in a procession, a certain ironmonger stirred up the mob by accusing the conversos of impiety.

Predictably, riots resulted. Houses of conversos were burned, and many conversos were attacked. Certain nobles intervened, one of whom killed the ironmonger. The conversos armed themselves "in their most populous *barrios*" (such expressions are an indication of the relatively large size of converso populations in these cities). Many were killed, including girls and women who were cruelly raped, and even the bodies of dead girls were sexually violated by the "old Christians." Many conversos fled the city, mostly to the town of Palma del Rio. However, the riots spread to the towns of Montoro, Adamuz, Bujalance, La Rambla, and Santaella, and would have occurred also in the important city of Baeza if the count had not intervened. (The presence of conversos in these towns is an important clue to the previous existence of Jewish communities, otherwise unsuspected.)

Fear of attack was renewed also in Seville, and in Jerez and Écija the conversos were saved by the lords of these cities. In Seville, beside the usual complaints against conversos, those who had fled from Córdoba were suspected of harboring new "heretics" who came to the city, who also "consumed no small part of the most dear cereals." Indeed, grain shortage was a serious problem, but in much of this complaint we can no doubt see the common distrust of strangers.

Some of the Córdoban conversos who had fled to Palma were sent by the duke to Seville, and upon coming to the city they were attacked and murdered.

Juan Pacheco, master of the Order of Santiago, then in Segovia, also spoke sharply against the conversos, whom he accused of all sorts of crimes and of secretly plotting against the Christian religion (strange accusations coming from this vile lecher; as Alonso rightly says, he was a friend of religion only insofar as it helped him extend his tyranny). Nevertheless, he was unable to persuade the "old Christians" of Segovia, "to whom were notorious the differences of manner which existed in Spain among conversos, even though they were all equal in name" (i.e., some behaved well, others shamelessly). Determined to gain control of the Alcázar of Segovia, and with it the city, Pacheco thus was the cause of hostilities which broke forth between the conversos and their supporters and his followers. Pacheco lost, however, and fled the city.[57]

The Gibraltar Plan

Apparently late in 1473 the conversos from Córdoba who had fled to Seville resolved to go to Gibraltar, but the duque de Medina Sidonia refused their plan, claiming that the conversos could not defend themselves or the city (Gibraltar), a strategic position in the war against the Muslims. He added besides that they were corrupted by "Jewish rites," and thus justly infamous. Others of the conversos who had first gone to Palma, and then also to Seville, determined to go to either Gibraltar or Niebla, while others left for

Flanders or Italy, "in order to save at least the lives of their wives and children and escape the infamy which awaited them in Spain if they were to form separate 'tribes' in the towns where they lived, with the name of *barrios* or colonies of conversos." Still others remained quietly in their homes, but hid their valuables in caves and lived guarded in the recently walled *barrio* constructed by the Jews "before their great disaster" (1391). They secretly established a militia of three hundred light cavalry (*jinetes*) and five thousand armed infantry (of which three thousand were *escuderos* [squires, or simply warriors] and the rest archers or musketeers).[58]

Alonso later relates more details about the Gibraltar enterprise, according to which the duke secretly agreed to the plan and negotiated with a certain Pedro de Córdoba (not, of course, the bishop; apparently a converso) an arrangement whereby the conversos would buy all the "old Christian" houses of Gibraltar and build in addition new ones, at their expense, and maintain an army, also at their expense, to defend the port. The duke agreed to contribute an insignificant sum. When the "friends" of the duke discovered this, they argued against allowing conversos to go there because of their adherence to "perverse rites and Jewish superstitions," and because they suspected that their real intent was to use Gibraltar as a port of embarkation for Egypt and Jerusalem. Even those who did not go to these places would be free to live in Gibraltar as they wished: to circumcise their sons, "pervert" Church discipline with "ceremonies of the synagogue," corrupt children with "ancient fables" of Judaism, etc.

Religious fanatics in Sevilla also accused the conversos of observing not Sunday but Saturday as their Sabbath, of not dealing in business with "old Christians," reciting their "Jewish Psalms" (!) at night in the synagogues— or "at least" of bringing oil for the perpetual burning of the lamps there. Alonso remarks that some conversos may have been guilty of such customs, but the intent of the fanatics was clear: the robbery and murder of conversos, as had happened in Córdoba. Many of the "old Christians" not "contaminated" by these vices, however, went from house to house in an effort to contain the hatred of these "assassins" (*sicarios*). Alonso twice uses this term, which was that applied to the fanatics of Jerusalem in the war of 68–69 C.E., who used "knives" to assassinate Romans. He certainly got the term from Josephus, whose *Jewish Wars* he translated for Isabel.)

Alonso here states well what applies in general to *all* the charges ever made against conversos: "No moderate person doubted that those robbers declared as heretics those they thought to be rich"; in other words, the malicious "old Christians" knew very well that the conversos were not heretics, but cupidity led them to their schemes against them.

One summer day, during a period of siesta when no one went out, a young converso wounded an "old Christian" with a knife in a quarrel. On pretext of avenging this injury, bands of Christians attacked the *barrio* of druggists, where the majority of the perfume shops (owned by conversos) were. The riot quickly spread to the other *barrios*. Some of the leaders of the conversos, along with some of the nobles, hastened to the scene and caught the main perpetrators, hanging two of them.

All of this strengthened the desire of the conversos of Seville to join those of Córdoba in going to Gibraltar. Pedro de Córdoba was convinced that all the conversos of Spain wished to go there, "where by their honorable behavior and Catholic practices they would palpably demonstrate that the Catholic faith is best observed among the conversos," and that in case of danger (from Muslim attack) they would eagerly defend the faith. Many sold their houses, bought ships, and sent their families to Gibraltar, but several were robbed by pirates, who took some women captive. Some 350 cavalry and 2,000 infantry went by land to Gibraltar. Nevertheless, the sharp increase in prices there and the difficulty of buying houses, or finding material to build new ones, as well as quarrels between conversos of Seville and those of Córdoba, caused many to return. Mostly conversos from Córdoba remained.[59] The duke finally expelled conversos from Gibraltar.

So ended one of the most fascinating events in the history of the conversos, and a plan which might well have changed the whole tragic future of the Inquisition.

Not surprisingly, only a few years later, in 1477, when Fernando established the *Hermandad* in Seville, Alonso claims that the conversos protested that it was intended to harm them. Enrique de Guzmán, the duque de Medina Sidonia, in a fit of rage tried to prevent entirely the formation of the *Hermandad,* but Alonso himself (representing the king) negotiated with him. Aiding these "negotiations" was the fact that Alonso's supporters had secretly armed themselves. The duke gave in, and changing his position completely imprisoned four hundred conversos in the Alcazar.[60]

In 1477 the conversos in Ciudad Real complained to Pope Sixtus IV that the sanctions aimed at the "old Christians" who discriminated against them were insufficient. The pope wrote to Pedro González Mendoza, archbishop of Seville, and to Alfonso de Burgos, nephew of Alonso de Cartagena and now bishop of Córdoba, and to a deacon of Segovia, instructing them on the punishment of excommunication for those who discriminated against conversos.[61]

The following year "certain clergy and others" in Seville informed the Catholic Monarchs (who had remained in the city since the birth of their son Juan) that there were many conversos guilty of "Judaizing" in the city. Cardinal Mendoza issued certain laws which every Christian was to obey. Particular attention was given to details of what the clergy must teach their parishioners, and what every Christian must teach his children. Of course, conversos were to be given special attention with sermons designed to convince them of the error of the Jewish rites and the danger of "perpetual damnation" in observing them.

One of the common myths prevalent about conversos (Menéndez y Pelayo, López Martínez, and other writers) is that they received little or poor
instruction in their new faith. On the contrary, if they were so poorly instructed, how are we to explain the abundance of bishops, monks, theologians, and clergy who came from their ranks? The writings of these conversos reveal how very well-informed they, in fact, were. As for the masses of
conversos who did not enter the professional religious offices, such sermons
and other instruction were designed to ensure their Christian training. In
1493 the Catholic Monarchs ordered that, to ensure the continued faith of
the new converts who have "abandoned the ceremonies and rites of the old
law," each local prelate should see that "good men of learning and conscience" be appointed to instruct the conversos.[62] No doubt such measures
were taken earlier.

Alonso de Palencia, in the newly discovered completion of his history,
refers to anti-converso activity also in Toledo in the summer of 1478. The
archbishop, Alonso Carrillo (himself possibly of converso origin), long a
troublemaker, was responsible for stirring up some citizens of the city "under the pretext of religion." "This same pest," Alonso adds, "infected the
minds of the *sicarii* [assassins; see above on this term] against the conversos,
which always caused a just fear among men thus injured, who, exiled during
a long time did not refuse to confront evident new danger, so sweet was the
love of country—especially for those who sought to repent and thus obtain
great fortune. . . ." These somewhat enigmatic remarks apparently refer to
the conversos who were allowed to depart from Toledo (those who wished
to do so) after the attack on the quarter of Magdalena in 1467, with the
express provision that none of them could take their goods out of the city.
Those who remained, apparently, went through the motions of "repentance" to advance their position.[63]

Of great importance, considering that he himself lived and wrote in Seville, is his reference to the activities of Alonso de Aguilar, overlord of the
region and an important noble (Palencia thought him a tyrant). Among the
misdeeds of which he accuses him was his failure to protect the "10,000
conversos" of Córdoba (not at all an exaggerated number, as we see from
his other references to them, the size of their militia, etc.) who were then
being robbed there, and most of whom were *farmers*.[64]

Fernando de Pulgar's Reactions

One of the most important sources we have for the events of the reign of the
Catholic Monarchs is the chronicle of Fernando de Pulgar, a son of a converso, Diego Rodríguez de Pulgar of Toledo, scribe of Juan II. Fernando was
secretary to both Enrique IV and Isabel, as well as official chronicler.

He wrote a sharp letter of protest on the treatment of conversos to Cardinal Mendoza:

> Your lordship surely knows of the new statute passed in Guipúzcoa [!] in which it was decreed that *we* should not go there to marry or to dwell, etc., as if *we* had no other desire than to go and inhabit that fertile domain and that blooming countryside. It seems a little like the ordinance the stonecutters of Toledo made, not to teach their trade to any [converso].[65]

Guipúzcoa is the central Basque province (capital, San Sebastian), and is in fact a beautiful and fertile region. There were Jews there, although not many, but the region may not have been known to Pulgar. Pulgar's satirical point is that it was unlikely that conversos would want to go and live in so far away a place, just as it was highly unlikely that any of them would wish to learn the trade of stonecutting. We see from his twice-repeated "we" that he considered himself to be a converso, although in point of fact, as mentioned, he was the son of one. This is itself important evidence that descendants of conversos felt the hostility and persecution.

He continues to ask, sarcastically, is it not laughable that old Christians "send their sons to serve us as footmen," yet do not wish to marry the conversos whom they serve? Among the conversos he names as having Christian apprentices in their houses are Fernán Díaz de Toledo (the *relator*) and Fernando Álvarez and Alfonso de Ávila, converso secretaries of the Catholic Monarchs, like Pulgar himself. He adds that four "old Christians" were currently receiving instruction in his house, and "more than forty" already had done so.

Most important is another letter from him to the cardinal.[66] Pulgar there refers to the "stupidity so blind" and "blindness so stupid" of the conversos which brought about the recent consequences. Cantera cogently compared this to Pulgar's similar phrase in the first redaction of his *Crónica*, in which he refers to those who insist on "Judaizing" as being possessed of a "blindness so stupid and an ignorance so blind."[67]

Noting that some, indeed, deserve punishment, he reserves the necessity of this for the "*few* who have relapsed, but not for the *many* who have not"; otherwise, "there would not be sufficient wood" for the burning of all the conversos. As Cantera noted, this contrasts poignantly with the chilling opposite expression of the anti-Semitic Bernáldez, also a chronicler of the period, who wrote: "For the fire is lighted . . . it will burn until it reaches the extremes of the driest wood."[68]

The few bad conversos are so, Pulgar says, because of the example of bad "old Christians," and to burn the thousands of good conversos would be "most cruel and even difficult to do" without causing widespread animosity to the ministers of the Inquisition. He estimates that there were in Andalucía alone some ten thousand conversa girls between the ages of ten and twenty who never went out of their houses and knew of no other doctrine than that of their parents (Christianity). He concludes that the Inquisitors of Seville, Diego de Merlo and the "doctor of Medina" (fray Juan de Medina, a Jeronimite), are good men, "but I know well that they will not make such good Christians with their fire as the bishop don Paul [Pablo de Santa María], a converso" and don Alonso [de Cartagena] will with water; and not without cause, for these were chosen by our Redeemer Christ [for their task] but those others [Inquisitors] were chosen by the licentiate our chancellor for theirs."

An anonymous rebuttal to Pulgar, discussed at length by Carriazo and again by Cantera, contains among other things the interesting statement that a certain "member of your nation whom you know," as well as the Franciscan Alonso del Espina, had come among the conversos to instruct them.[69]

Pulgar was criticized for having said that the Inquisitors of Seville acted incorrectly in what they did, as did the queen. He defended himself against these charges, saying that he never wrote such things; although possibly the queen did err in what she ordered or instructed, and the Inquisitors in their proceedings (in other words, he now made the very statements he denied having previously made). He notes that Juan II, although "certainly good," had done wrong in entrusting the city of Toledo to Sarmiento.[70]

In one of his letters to a friend, written from Toledo, Pulgar mentions that Fernán Pérez de Guzmán, author of important biographical sketches of notable people, was told that the converso bishop of Burgos, Pablo de Santa María, had written to an "old condestable [judge] who was sick in Toledo" (Ruy Lope Dávalos), and Pulgar notes the irony of this in a city so full of "notable physicians" (surely a reference either to conversos or Jews). "I don't know whether it can be said now, for we see that the famous odreros [makers of leather bottles] have expelled from here the notable physicians, and thus I believe that now they are provided with many better rebellious bottle makers than native good physicians." Cantera was certainly correct, contrary to the suggestion of Pulgar's editor, in seeing this as a clear reference to the Toledo riots of 1449, and particularly with regard to the bottle maker who was one of the instigators of that riot.[71]

Similarly, Letter XIV refers to the battle over the "purity" statutes in Toledo, and the decrees against conversos' holding public office. The "old Christians," he says, cannot bear seeing wealth, especially new wealth, in the hands of those they consider undeserving of it. (This appears to agree perfectly with what Alonso de Palencia repeatedly wrote.) He complains that many conversos have been forced to leave the city, including one with great knowledge of astrology and astronomy. Demanding that all such people of "low birth" (former Jews) should abandon their honors would result in such absurdities as taking away all offices, tax collecting, etc., which Enrique IV had conferred on them some thirty years earlier. He concludes, "we ought to believe that God created men, not lineages in which they are chosen."[72]

Overlooked by scholars (Cantera, Benito, Ruano, Netanyahu) was one of the most important of all of Pulgar's statements in his letters, that of 1473 to Francisco de Toledo, converso bishop of Coria. The letter contains valuable insights into the events going on throughout Spain at the time, and especially in Toledo. The people driven out of the city make war on it, and those in the city make war with those expelled from it. "And since those citizens are great 'inquisitors' of the faith, it is supposed that heresy has fallen upon the goods of [the count of] Fuensalida," so that they steal those goods and burn and loot everywhere. Those expelled, with the same religious zeal, burn and loot wherever they can. "There is no more Castile," he concludes sadly. The count of Fuensalida, of course, was none other than Pedro López de Ayala, perhaps the most important man of the age. In that very year Enrique sent him to take charge of Toledo, and two years later the Catholic Monarchs were asking the people of Toledo to send representatives to testify to his crimes.[73] It would appear from Pulgar's letter that he had seized property of conversos (as noted above, he led the "old Christians" against them).

According to the bitterly satirical collection of poems written, certainly, by a converso (although scholars cannot yet agree as to which one), *Coplas de Mingo Revulgo,* the religious situation was so deteriorated that one could not distinguish the "flock of Christ" from "that of the other stammerer [Moses] nor of the keen Moor of Mecca." In his gloss to the poem (itself attributed by many to Pulgar), Pulgar explains that because of the lack of effective leadership one can no longer recognize in the Catholic faith who are Christians, Jews, or Muslims, "for according to the laws of the realm, Jews and Muslims should wear [distinguishing] clothing and signs by which to be recognized," but this—like all "good laws"—is now "infirm" and all alike wear the same clothing.[74] However valuable as further evidence that Jews did not, in fact, wear "badges," this is undoubtedly not the meaning of the poem; rather, as we have seen, many Christians were converting to Islam, and the suspicion that Jewish converts to Christianity were not sincere was rampant.

Of great interest also in Pulgar's discussion of the difference between the "law of Christ" and that of Moses, which may shed some light on the reasons for conversion among the Jews. Apparently totally unaware of the ethical teachings of either the Bible or rabbinical sources, Pulgar states that Moses conquered Canaan by force of arms and that "his" law was given to the accompaniment of much noise, trumpets, etc., whereas that of Christ was not given thus but was only a law of humility, charity, etc.

Finally, the *Coplas* refer to the necessity of confessing to the priest all sins and allowing him to "strip the skin" from a penitent in order to save him.

Pulgar refers this task to the Inquisition, so that if by shame, forgetfulness, or ignorance the penitent should neglect to mention a sin, the Inquisitor will force him to remember in order to bring him salvation.[75]

Pulgar definitely changed at least his public position toward the Inquisition. In his earlier writings and private letters, as we have seen, he was adamantly opposed to it. However, as he himself came under suspicion and attack, and as the Inquisition gained power, he became a complete supporter, both in his *glosas* and in the revision of his *Crónica*. Indeed, his earlier open opposition to it may be one more important source in the growing evidence which casts doubt on the accepted theory that the Catholic Monarchs themselves were entirely responsible for initiating the Inquisition (otherwise it surely would have been dangerous for one so close to them to oppose it).

Turning finally to another major work by Pulgar, the *Claros varones,* a series of illuminating but highly romanticized biographical sketches of important contemporary figures, we discover an unusual expression used in his account of Juan de Silva, conde de Cifuentes (d. 1474). Pulgar says he was a "nobleman of pure blood" (*limpia sangre*). There is nothing at all "exaggerated" in Carriazo's statement that this was a strange observation for a converso to make, as Brian Tate objected. Indeed, it is very strange, and certainly in contrast with his sharp criticism of the doctrine of *limpieza* which we have seen in his letters. It may possibly reflect a suspicion of the time that the de Silvas were "tainted" with converso blood, which Pulgar may have wished to deny.[76] Yet another reason for Pulgar's praise of de Silva is that he gave his support and protection to the conversos in Toledo in the 1467 uprising. In 1471 Pulgar's wife, Mercía Fernández, sold to one of de Silva's followers a substantial amount of property, including houses, stores, orchards, etc., which Pulgar had acquired in Toledo from the "master of León, a Jew" (probably a physician), and others. We know that Pulgar lived in Madrid in 1473, possibly until 1487, and this circumstance may explain the sale of his Toledo property.[77]

Another important document concerning Pulgar has come to light. In 1467, the *infante* Alfonso, child brother of Enrique IV, was proclaimed "king" at Ávila by the rebels. Immediately thereafter, Alfonso granted his secretary Fernando de Arce 20,000 *mrs.* of tax money confiscated from Pulgar because he remained loyal to Enrique (among this sum was 6,000 *mrs.* of taxes on the Jewish butchers of Toledo). This document again places Pulgar in Toledo, as we also know from his letters, and precisely at the time of the converso riots there.[78]

To return to Cantera's seminal study of Pulgar, he has shown that the converso author carefully revised chapters 96 and 120 of his *Crónica* to reflect his view that the converso problem was no longer confined to Seville alone (where the Inquisition began), but rather was now a problem of the entire kingdom. (As noted before, perhaps a more correct interpretation is his own change of heart with regard to the Inquisition, not the converso problem, which he surely knew from being an eyewitness of the riots in Toledo was not "confined to Seville.")

Pulgar minimizes or ignores the violence to the conversos in this revision, praises Isabel for routing out the heresy among some who were "Judaizing," and perhaps most important revises his earlier statement that the pope had "*conceded* the authority" to establish an Inquisition in Castile to "the pope *ordered*" its establishment. Cantera correctly concluded that this was to avoid placing the responsibility for the Inquisition on the Catholic Monarchs, an observation which historians of the Inquisition have completely ignored.[79]

Contrary to Carriazo's views, Cantera has also correctly demonstrated that Pulgar was vehemently opposed to the "Judaizers" and other false conversos, both in his letters and in the *Crónica*. More can be said, however. He also stressed repeatedly that these false conversos were few in number. Also, of course, it must be emphasized that he was above all an apologist for the monarchs, a devout Christian, and a supporter of the Inquisition in spite of what he at first had considered its excesses.

Pulgar has given us a very interesting document, the supposed speech of Gómez Manrique, *corregidor* of Toledo and a famous poet, which some believe is almost entirely Pulgar's own creation. Benito Ruano has called this "speech" one of the earliest political discourses in Spanish literature (there were, of course, others much earlier, such as those in the works of Juan Manuel). While it is undoubtedly correct that the literary style is mostly Pulgar's, it seems unlikely that he would have dared to invent entirely the sentiments expressed in it or the fact of the speech, which Manrique and others could easily have challenged. In any event, the speech contains a glowing defense of the conversos:

> We see from experience some men of those whom we judge [to be] born of low blood, whose natural inclination forces them to abandon the lowly offices of their fathers and study science and become great intellectuals [*grandes letrados*]. We see others who have a natural inclination for arms; others for agriculture; others for good and orderly speech; others for administration; and for other various arts in which they have a particular ability according to their natural inclination.

He asks, rhetorically, should all these abandon their natural inclinations which result in these abilities because through them they obtain honors? On the other hand, many descendants of kings and nobles are now of base condition because of their lack of ability. This, too, is natural. "Should we now make valiant [*esforzados*] all those descendants of King Pyrrhus, because their ancestor was valiant? Or should we make wise the descendants of King Solomon because he was the most wise? Or give riches and great estates to those of the lineage of King Pedro of Castile or Dinis of Portugal, because they do not have them, and you seem to think they should have them according to their descent!"[80]

This was a particularly loaded political and social attack. The statement about the descendants of Pedro obviously must have touched a raw nerve at the time, and that about Dinis of Portugal as well, in light of the recent war between that country and Castile. King Pyrrhus, of course, was the famous Greek hero who fought recurrent wars against Rome and Sicily. Plutarch, in his *Lives,* says of him that he might even have been greater but that he was never satisfied with that already achieved and constantly had his eye on new conquests. Did our author have this in mind, perhaps, and was this therefore a clever veiled criticism of the Catholic Monarchs' planned war against Granada? Important, too, is the implicit denial of the *limpieza de sangre* argument: honors or riches belong to those whose abilities show they deserve them, not to those who claim "old" or noble birth.

Baer, who saw Manrique's speech cited only secondhand in Altamira's history of Spain, at first wrote that it was entirely fictitious because Manrique's "anti-Semitism" is well known. Later, having read Cantera's article, but still not having actually consulted Pulgar's *Crónica,* he claimed that the speech was entirely Pulgar's own invention, and appeared to give Cantera himself as the source for this. In fact, Cantera said only that Pulgar's letter of 1478 (no. XIV) was "included almost entirely" in Manrique's speech in the *Crónica.* Even that is an exaggeration, however, for there are only superficial similarities. Nothing permits us to conclude from these that Pulgar entirely "invented" Manrique's speech.[81]

Baer goes on to state, with no indication of a source, that Gómez Manrique, whom he has already labeled "anti-converso" as well as "anti-Semitic," ordered the arrest and execution of several conversos, including Alfonso de la Torre, in 1485. That famous moralist (author of the *Visión delectable,* to be mentioned later) died in 1460, however.[82] Neither Pulgar, nor Fita's study of the Toledo Inquisition of 1486, which Baer cites, gives any support to his interpretation.

In any event, whether Manrique's speech was entirely Pulgar's creation (unlikely) or not, the sentiments expressed were widely shared among at least the intellectuals of the time.

Conclusions

The strong animosity against conversos erupted only in the fifteenth century, and then only in Castile, at least at first. As we shall see, this hostility began to emerge also in Aragón-Catalonia, but only toward the end of the century. This hostility resulted in widespread rioting against the hated converso class. Unlike the famous so-called pogroms of 1391 against the Jews, which in reality were minor in scope and were caused by a small minority of lower-class gangsters who saw an opportunity to rob and vent their general frustrations on the relatively defenseless Jews, the anti-converso riots were organized and were massive, actual battles using sophisticated weapons and machinery of war. Even so, they were confined to Toledo and some Andalusian cities, mostly in the province of Córdoba (Pacheco's efforts to stir up trouble in Segovia briefly ignited violence there, but as we have seen it ultimately failed). We hear of nothing similar in Madrid, or in the "old kingdom" of northern Castile and León.

The instigators in this case were certainly not, as Baer has claimed, "lower class," but on the contrary, bureaucrats and officials, bishops (Toledo and Córdoba) and nobility. The motives were chiefly, if not entirely, jealousy of the wealth and power of the conversos. Both Alonso de Palencia and Fernando de Pulgar, conversos whose devout Christianity was above suspicion, concur in the hypocrisy of the changes of "heresy" trumped up against conversos in general.

This is supported by the numerous defenses written in response to the pernicious "statutes" of Toledo, some by pious "old Christians" such as the extremely powerful Lope de Barrientos or Alonso Díaz de Montalvo. One could scarcely ask for more impressive and authoritative sources than these.

Thus the Christian sources confirm what we already have seen from the Jewish sources, that the overwhelming majority of the conversos were quite sincere Christians, at least as good as the "old Christians" among whom they lived. Had this not been so, people of the rank and reputation of Barrientos, Montalvo, Cartagena—indeed, even Palencia and Pulgar themselves—would not have joined so vigorously in their defense.

The effort to isolate the conversos as a class and to eliminate their influence and power in Christian society failed completely by the time the Catholic Monarchs came to the throne, as the following chapter demonstrates. The attempt to portray conversos as "heretics" whose devotion to the Christian faith was not sincere had also failed miserably, recognized for the sham it was when the previously mentioned defenses began to circulate.

There was but one ploy left to the enemies of the conversos, which was to result in the first and only real manifestation of anti-Semitism in the medieval world, centuries before that doctrine was to make its ugly presence felt in modern Germany and France. This was the pernicious doctrine of "purity of blood" (*limpieza de sangre*), to be discussed in detail in connection with the Inquisition. This was to provide the rationale for the isolation, and eventually the destruction, of the conversos.

The seeds of this hatred, which was to give birth to the Inquisition, were already planted well before the Catholic Monarchs came to the throne. It is doubtful if they ever fully grasped this, and in any case certainly they made little effort to contain the problem. The weak and ineffective reign of Juan II, followed by the even more disastrous one of his son Enrique IV, corrupted the kingdom, weakened it morally and economically, and enabled the anti-Semites to unleash their campaign—not against Jews, but against conversos, a campaign which was to culminate in the fires of the Inquisition.

5

Conversos in Service
of Church and State

Jews already held positions of increasing power in the government of Spain under the Muslims, becoming even prime ministers of the independent city-kingdoms. Some of those, also, were converts to Islam, while others retained their Jewish loyalty. Almost immediately with the beginnings of the Christian kingdoms both in Aragón and in Castile, from the eleventh century on, Jews are found in prominent positions. By the thirteenth century, Jews were no longer mere tax officials but had risen to the highest ranks of royal counsellors and administrators, heads of the king's chancelleries, chief treasurer, and other positions.

It is important to stress this, although not properly belonging to our topic, precisely to point out that it certainly was not necessary for Jews to convert in order to attain high office and political power. That many conversos did so is, therefore, a mere coincidence. Except for the reign of the Catholic Monarchs, and even they were also served by Jewish officials, the number of conversos in the service of the kings never came close to the number of Jews.

We already find isolated instances, perhaps, of such converts in the thirteenth century. Of the nine or ten most important Jewish officials of Sancho IV of Castile, son of the renowned Alfonso X against whom he rebelled to seize the crown, one, Fernán Pérez Maimon, who was holder of the privy seal, may have been a converso.[1] However, I am somewhat skeptical of this claim, and suspect that he was a Mozarab or descendant of Mozarabic Christians (Maimon, correctly Maimūn, is an Arabic name, common to Muslims, Jews, and Mozarabic Christians). Note that he was also the admiral of Castile, a position unlikely to have been held by a converso at that time.

Whether or not Juan Gato, an official of Fernando IV, certainly a member of the prominent Jewish Gato family of Toledo, was a Jew or a converso is uncertain (for Jews to have so-called Christian first names was unusual, but not impossible).

As previously mentioned, Francisco Fernández de Marmolejo of Seville, *tesorero mayor* (chief treasurer) of Pedro I of Castile in 1369 and after, was a converso. Later in the years 1387 to 1390, he was *contador mayor* (approximately the same position, but more important) for Juan I, and also *mayordomo*, or head, of the council of Seville and representative of that city at the *Cortes* of Guadalajara in 1390.

A relative (son?), Alfonso Fernández de Marmolejo, was also a member of the council of Seville and judge of the Genoese quarter of the city (1376–90), and also *tesorero mayor* of Juan I.[2] In 1396, his widow, Juana Dorta, sold an annuity of 5,000 *mrs.* annually from the taxes of the Jews of Seville to the Christian *mayordomo mayor* of Queen Catalina.[3]

Samuel Abravanel was one of the members of that famous family who was in the service of the kings. In 1379, as a "citizen of Seville," he was named *almoxarife*, or chief tax officer, for the entire kingdom (nevertheless, he was ultimately outbid in this office by another Jew of Seville, and then a second time by that man's son). This Samuel was the grandfather of Isaac Abravanel, the famous author. Samuel eventually obtained the position of *contador mayor* of Enrique III.

Very problematic is a poem in the *Cancionero de Baena* attributed to Alfonso Alvarez de Villasandino, a hanger-on at court, who is the most frequently represented poet in that collection. The poem was written around 1391 when the king, Enrique III, was still under the tutelage of his council, and is a criticism of the chaos caused by various avaricious officials, etc. The poet reminds the young king that his late father had always sought out worthy officials, not those who would sell their offices "like a renegade Jew" (converso). Further, the poet refers to an office granted to a "prelate of Osma," who because of his learning became *contador* (a tax official, but hardly *contador mayor*), with the accusation that he apparently purchased his office for 6,000 Aragonese *florins*. He is said to have been "governor of Aragón and Sicily" and to have "conquered" Seville, and thus was worthy to extend his powers as far as Fez. The suggestion was early made, and accepted without question both by the editor of the *Cancionero* and Cantera Burgos, that all this refers to Samuel Abravanel, who around 1391 converted.[4]

In fact, it seems to me there is absolutely no basis for any such conclusion. Abravanel was certainly never a "prelate," nor was he ever in Osma, either before or after his conversion. After his conversion, Abravanel took the name Juan Sánchez de Sevilla (not to be confused with another converso called Juan de Sevilla, who was tried by the Inquisition, as we shall see). He then fled to Portugal, where he returned to Judaism. The assumption of

Baer, repeated also by Netanyahu, that Samuel converted not in 1391 (as stated by the usually reliable and well-informed Abraham Zacut), but "years earlier" is still without proof. In any event, as we shall see, his name appears in the tax record of Juan I in 1379 as still a Jew. The identification of him with Juan Sánchez who was *tesorero mayor* of Andalucía in 1388, while possible, is not conclusive. If so, then he also had a hitherto unknown brother, also in Seville, who converted and took the name Alonso Sánchez.[5]

Menahem b. Zerah, who lived in Toledo at the time, wrote of the kindness of Samuel Abravanel, who assisted him in moving to Toledo, adding:

I saw that those who walk in the court of our lord the king [Enrique II], may his glory be exalted, are a shield and protection to the rest of the people, each person according to his need and position.

However, he noted, many of these Jewish courtiers are lax in their religious observance, prayers, and the like (perhaps a foreboding of Abravanel's conversion).[6]

In 1380 a certain "conde don Alfonso" (probably Albuquerque) gave Abravanel as surety (?) 30,000 *mrs.*, as did the admiral of Castile (these were probably payments against taxes). Abravanel himself paid the king, for debts he owed and "what he had to pay for his *fiadores*" (those who stood surety for the faithful execution of his duties, who could, in fact, be these officials mentioned), 153,191 *mrs.* He was also the treasurer of the queen.[7]

In 1391, when Enrique was still a minor, the duque de Benavente demanded of the royal council that Juan Sánchez de Sevilla (Abravanel) be appointed *contador mayor*, for "he knew much about accounts and dealt with taxes of the kingdom in the time of the kings don Enrique [II] and don Juan [I]." But the archbishop of Santiago argued that this Juan Sánchez was capable of giving the king large sums of money from taxes he farmed, and would be more useful in that capacity than as *contador mayor*, who merely judged the assessment of taxes (actually, that official did much more than that). The argument developed into open armed conflict between the duke and the archbishop, and involved the considerable forces of both.[8]

Records of the reign of Juan I reveal possibly some other conversos. Among the additional sums of taxes to be paid in 1379 by various officials of Toledo (presumably sums collected by them) we find Gómez García, *tesorero;* Ruy Pérez, *desquirel* (I have been unable to find a definition of this office); Sancho Ferrandes, *contador;* Francisco Ferrandes del Marmolejo; and two important Jewish officials, don Yuçaf Pichon and Yuçaf Abenaex of Córdoba. We recognize, of course, the previously mentioned converso Fernández de Marmolejo, *tesorero mayor* of Pedro I and of Juan I. It is possible that Gómez García and Ruy Pérez were also conversos.[9]

It was precisely in the reign of Enrique III that important new noble families began to emerge, many of whom came from Navarre (Mendozas, Ayalas, Stúñigas, and others). We recall that some of these families, the Mendozas and Stúñigas, were among those who were said to have been of converso origin, or at least who had converso members in their families. (Yerushalmi, unfamiliar with the sources and relying entirely on the statement of a seventeenth-century "antisemite," as he himself labels him, falsely concluded that the conversos "forged" for themselves the names of the nobility, such as Mendoza, Guzmán, etc. Aside from the fact that I know of no evidence that the Guzmans were conversos, or that anyone has suggested this, the statement in itself is incorrect, for many noble families in reality did have converso members or were themselves of converso origin.) [10]

From the very earliest emergence of these new aristocratic families in Castile (primarily in Andalucía) they established strong relations with Jews, as officials and administrators of their estates, etc. These rather suspicious relationships may possibly be explained on the basis of converso ties with these families. They also may have led to intermarriage with Jews or with conversos, as early as the end of the fourteenth century (such marriages with conversos were common in the fifteenth century). What is beyond question, in any event, is the unusually strong Jewish connection with these dynasties and the fact that they were "tainted" with converso blood.

Under Juan II there was at least one important converso official, Lope Fernández Cota, royal scribe, who was a member of the prominent Jewish and converso Cota family of Toledo.[11] Others, such as the poet Juan Alfonso de Baena, held minor posts. As noted in Chapter 4, Álvaro de Luna, *condestable* of Castile, was himself of a converso family, as was probably his treasurer and chronicler Gonzalo Chacón.

However, it was during the reign of Enrique IV that conversos rose to prominent posts in the largest numbers. One of these was the previously mentioned Diego González de Toledo, called "doctor Franco," meaning that he was a doctor of laws. He was, as noted, possibly the *contador mayor,* and "*oidor,*" or official in charge of the audience of the king, where petitions, grievances, etc., were presented, as well as claims for payments of expenses (this institution was not, as sometimes claimed, the invention of Isabel). He owned houses in the *judería* of Toledo. We recall that it was his son, Alonso Franco, who was one of the leaders in the battle between the conversos and the "old Christians" in Toledo in 1467.[12]

Far more important, however, was Diego Arias Dávila (d. 1466), who was the *contador mayor* and one of the most powerful, and despised, men in the kingdom. His name originally was Ysaque (Isaac) Abenaçar of Ávila, and he was converted apparently in the preaching campaign of Vicente Ferrer in Segovia in 1411. At first, he was known by the name of Diego Bolante, or Volador, and became at once a protégé of Enrique. He married Juana

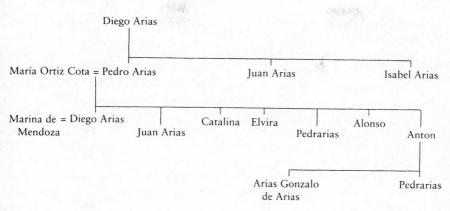

Figure 1. THE ARIAS DÁVILA FAMILY.

Adapted from the complete genealogical table in Francisco Cantera Burgos, *Pedrarias Dávila y Cota, capitán general y gobernador de Castilla del Oro y Nicaragua: sus antecedentes judíos* (Madrid, 1971), facing p. 14.

Rodríguez, who apparently died soon afterward, and then Elvira González of Ávila, also of Jewish background. He became very wealthy, with considerable property which he passed on to his children, including his son Pedro Arias, who held the position of *contador mayor* after him. Pedro died during the siege of Madrid in 1476. Diego Arias, his oldest son, then inherited the position. Enemies of Pedro convinced the king, falsely, of Diego's "treason," for which Enrique had him imprisoned, and he was severely wounded while in prison.

As a result of the efforts of Cantera Burgos, we know a considerable amount about this important family. Figure 1 shows only the first generations of that family (prior to the Expulsion, the limits of our present study). Juan Arias, son of Diego Arias Dávila, became, as we shall see, bishop of Segovia. Pedro Arias, his brother, married María Ortiz Cota, again probably a member of the famous Toledo family. Their son Diego Arias was made lord of Puñorostro, lands created by his grandfather Diego Arias, and married Marina de Mendoza, the illegitimate daughter of the marqués de Santillana (Diego Hurtado de Mendoza). Juan Arias, another son of Pedro Arias, became the first conde de Puñorostro.

Most important of all this family, however, was Pedrarias (Pedro Arias) Dávila, another of the sons of Pedro Arias, who was born probably in the 1460s. He was an accomplished soldier, heading the forces of Segovia and Toledo in the conquest of Oran (in North Africa) in 1509, and he apparently also participated in the conquest of Granada for the Catholic Monarchs. In 1513 he was sent by them to "discover" and govern the "Tierra Firme" in the New World, recently discovered by Balboa. He was known as the *Gran*

Justador, and became the governor of Nicaragua and the founder of Panama.[13]

He married Isabel de Bobadilla, granddaughter of the famous marquesa de Moya, intimate of Isabel. One of their daughters, María de Peñalosa, was promised in marriage to Balboa, but in fact married Rodrigo de Contreras, also governor of Nicaragua. Another daughter, Isabel Arias, married the famous explorer Hernando de Soto.

It is interesting to note that Elvira González (Clara before her conversion) had a sister, Urosol (d. before 1487), who remained Jewish, as did all of her children, including two rabbis and a physician. Another sister, Leticia, also remained Jewish, marrying a Jewish tailor of Segovia. They had only three children, one of whom, Rabbi Mossé, later converted, taking the name Gerónimo de Paz.

The previously cited anonymous anti-converso treatise *Alborayco* states that "old Christians" are oppressed by debt and all manner of subjugation to conversos, who "squeeze them like grapes" (extract money from them), and the same is said "of the unfortunate Diego Arias" in the *Coplas de Mingo Revulgo* (a poetic composition by a converso, although the authorship is debated).[14] The contemporary *Coplas del Provincial* was even more abusive:

> To you friar [!] Diego Arias, queer,
> who were and are a Jew,
> I won't argue with you
> that you hold a great "lordship";
> eagle, castle, and cross [referring no doubt to a coat of arms];
> Jew, where did you get these?
> Because you, [queer], a hood/foreskin
> never had nor have.
> The eagle is of St. John
> and the castle of Emmaus [where Mary is supposed to have died]
> and the cross is of Jesus
> where [at the crucifixion] you were captain![15]

The accusation of homosexuality was one frequently made against conversos, as we shall see, and was merely a general insult. The word *capuç* means "foreskin," but also the hood of a cloak, such as worn by a friar. The satirist's point is that Diego is not such a good Christian as he presents himself to be.

It has been claimed that Andrés de Cabrera, who had been *alcaide* (military commander) of the Alcázar of Segovia in the reignn of Enrique IV, was a converso or of converso origin. On what basis such a claim is made I do not know, possibly his close friendship with Abraham Seneor, court rabbi and Jewish official of Castile, who was later to convert, but this in itself proves nothing. Palencia describes the *alcaide* as a vacillating and ambitious man, whose intimate friend was "Abraham *el Viejo*, a Jew of Segovia of great experience and faithful observer of the laws of friendship," he says with irony (not, as might be expected, "of the laws of Judaism"). Abraham *"el Viejo"* is, of course, Seneor, simply a variant of the Spanish name, both meaning "Elder." [16] (It is also possible that the rumor of Cabrera's converso background started because of his opposition to the efforts of Juan Pacheco to arouse "old Christians" of Segovia against conversos. According to Palencia, the animosity of Pacheco, master of the Order of Santiago—and rumored lover of Enrique IV—toward the conversos of Seville, Córdoba, and Segovia was well known.)

The wife of the *alcaide*, with the interesting (Arabized) name Beatrice de Bobadilla, may more probably be suspected of being of converso background. Fernan Díaz, the converso official who penned the famous memorial of instruction to Lope de Barrientos in the Sarmiento affair, named among the important families of converso origin "those of the Bobadilla," an enigmatic reference that could refer to this woman. Finally, there was coincidentally a converso of Toledo named Alonso de Cabrera who in 1498 donated money for the purchase of a house, apparently for a church or charitable institution of the conversos. Whether or not this Alonso was related in any way to Andrés is unknown.

In any event, Andrés de Cabrera had been persuaded by his friend Abraham Seneor to abandon the cause of Enrique, just before Fernando and Isabel invaded Segovia. His loyalty to the new monarchs was rewarded, and he was eventually given the position of *mayordomo,* or head of the royal household, while his wife became a trusted companion of the queen. In 1480 Fernando and Isabel wrote to Diego de Valera, their converso "master of the chamber," that they wished to confer the title of *marqués* on Andrés. They asked him to inform them in writing of the proper ceremony, which he did in a pedantic reply complete with the history of the office. Whether or not either Andrés or his wife was, in fact, a converso, there certainly were many undoubted conversos who were elevated to such high positions. [17]

When Pedro Arias (Pedrarias) Dávila sought to marry the granddaughter of Beatrice, as previously mentioned, both Abraham Seneor and Pedrarias' uncle, Juan Arias, the converso bishop of Segovia, had to intercede to get Beatrice's consent, for the *marquesa* feared marriage with the grandson of a "heretic" (Diego Arías, whom as we shall see was condemned by the Inquisition). [18]

According to a frequently quoted writer of the seventeenth century, at the court of Enrique in Segovia in 1468 a case of "blood libel" was presented (the accusation that Jews killed Christian boys to use their blood, until then almost unheard of in Spain) against the Jews of Sepúlveda, supposedly acting at the instigation of their rabbi, "Solomon Pichón." If this person existed at all, which I have not been able to verify, he may have been related to the unfortunate Yuçaf Pichon, or Picho, *contador mayor* early in Enrique's reign. During Holy Week, so the complaint claimed, these Jews had seized a Christian boy and performed various "affronts and cruelties" (torture, apparently, since murder is not actually mentioned). The bishop of Segovia, the converso Juan Arias Dávila, whose diocese included the town of Sepúlveda, ordered the arrest of sixteen Jews, no less, supposedly "guilty" of this crime. Some were condemned to death by burning, others imprisoned, and one youth saved himself by accepting baptism.

Fita, who corrected the published version according to an autograph manuscript of the author, discovered a source which indicates that the bishop himself came under criticism and was compelled to go to Rome to defend himself. No doubt the motivation for this attack on the otherwise respected and generous bishop (he gave both an important library and a hospital to the city) was due to the revenge he took for the unjust imprisonment by the king of his brother Pedro Arias Dávila, whom Enrique tortured. The bishop plotted to seize Segovia and turn it over to the rebel forces of Alfonso, Enrique's half brother. In any case, Juan Arias in Rome had to renounce his authority over the diocese, and he remained in Rome, where he died.

Not only the bishop, but his deceased father, Diego Arias, his mother, Elvira González, and other members of the Dávila family were later accused of heresy by the Inquisition.[19]

Whether the charges were brought against Juan Arias because he supposedly favored Jews, as Fita assumed, is questionable. Obviously the Sepúlveda incident never happened; the question is whether any such charges against Jews were ever made, or whether they were a mere invention by the seventeenth-century writer. It is inconceivable that a case like this, the first in Spain, preceding the notorious "Niño de la Guardia" case by some thirty years, would not be mentioned in any contemporary chronicle or other source. Also, the arrest of sixteen Jews in the tiny population of Sepúlveda would have amounted to a substantial percentage of that population, and certainly would have left a record.

The same skepticism, and even more, must attach to the account of Alonso del Espina concerning a similar incident in Valladolid in 1454. Again, it is inconceivable that no notice of it appears in any contemporary source, especially if, as he claimed, the case dragged on for years and involved converso judges of the king's court who were "reluctant" to try it. Instead, this account must be seen as part of his anti-converso propaganda, which was part of his initiative to establish the Inquisition.[20]

Still another converso official of Enrique IV was Alfonso González de la

Hoz, *contador mayor* in 1466.[21] This was an important family in Segovia, members of which became loyal supporters of Isabel.

Undoubtedly, a descendant of the previously mentioned Francisco Fernández de Marmolejo, possibly his grandson, was Pedro Fernández Marmolejo, whose daughter Beatrice had been engaged to no less a person than the son of Rodrigo Ponce de León, *marqués* of Cadiz and famous for his victorious campaign against Granada in the reign of Fernando and Isabel. Alonso de Palencia claimed that Pedro was of a "very elevated" line. Ponce de León, possibly knowing the converso origin of the family, did not consent to the marriage, and finally Beatrice married Pedro Nuñez de Guzmán, brother of the duque de Medina Sidonia.[22]

Converso Officials in Aragón-Catalonia

Not only in Castile but also in the kingdom of Aragón-Catalonia there were numerous converso officials in the fifteenth century, before the reign of Fernando.

The de la Cavalleria (later Caballería) family was one of the most prominent and ancient Jewish families in the kingdom, dating back at least to the reign of Jaime I in the thirteenth century. From that time on members of this family, particularly in Zaragoza, served as government officials, tax administrators, translators, and physicians.

In the discussion of the Tortosa disputation we have already encountered the first converso members of this family, who retained their proud family name after converting. One of those was Juan de la Cavalleria, who was royal purchasing agent of Fernando I, ca. 1414. At about the same time, another member of the family, Fernando (previously Bonafos), was counsellor and treasurer of the king, a position he held at least until 1422.[23]

Luis de la Cavalleria (Caballería) was the treasurer of Juan II in 1416 and after, and continued to lend money to Jews.[24] He was also named treasurer of Navarre by Juan when he ruled that country, becoming treasurer of Aragón-Catalonia when Juan became king there. Pedro de la Cavalleria was named *comisario real* in charge of the treasury (1436) and *maestre racional* (1437). His son Alfonso became vice-chancellor of Aragón (1485).

Other converso officials included Francisco de Santa Fe, son of the notorious Jerónimo (about whom more later), who was *procurador* of Aragón. Fray Vicente Clemente was counselor of the king, and his brother Felipe was secretary of the royal chamber. Both were sons of Moses Chamorro.[25] There were many others, including Jaime Taravau, regent of the royal chancellory.[26]

Luis Sánchez was *receptor* of taxes for Juan II, and treasurer of his son, the *infant* Fernando (later King Fernando, husband of Isabel), beginning in 1465. He was related to Alazar Uluf (actually Golluf, a well-known Jewish family of Zaragoza) and married Jamila, daughter of Azach Avendino and Maria Ezquerra, Jews of Belchite (obviously Maria must have been a convert, probably after marrying). Alazar converted and took the name Luis Sánchez, but he is not to be confused with the treasurer of that name. As noted elsewhere, the converso Tomás García de Santa María, of the Zaragoza branch of that family, married the daughter (Brianda) of this Luis Sánchez.

Alazar's wife also converted and took the name Aldonza Sánchez. According to the *Libro verde de Aragón,* an important early-sixteenth-century source on conversos, when she died her husband, Luis, married again, a sister of the treasurer of Juan II, Luis de la Cavalleria (I), grandfather of Luis de la Cavalleria (II) and father-in-law of the famous Luis Santángel, to be discussed later. By this second wife, Luis Sánchez had a son, Alonso, who became prior of Arguedas and then of Exea.[27]

This Alonso (and not Luis himself) amazingly enough instituted an Inquisition investigation to prove that his family was not of Jewish origin. The result was the emergence of the accusation that his father, Luis, had read Hebrew books and was even a "learned Talmudist" who supposedly taught others, that he read "in Latin" the Bible of the Jews and then translated it aloud in Spanish, etc. (If he were such a "learned Talmudist," one wonders why he did not read the Bible in Hebrew. Like all Inquisition charges, these are obviously false, of course.)[28]

Four of Alazar's brothers also converted (all are called "the Ulufs [Gollufs] of Zaragoza"), taking the names Pedro, Antón, Jaime, and Juan Sánchez. Pedro married a conversa of Tortosa and had several sons: Luis, Gabriel, Miguel, Juan, Alonso, and two others. About two of these, Gabriel and Luis, we shall have more to say in the reign of Fernando and Isabel. Luis Sánchez, as we shall see, was implicated in the assassination of the Inquisitor Pedro Arbués, and on 17 October 1485 he was burned as a heretic.

Converso Officials of the Catholic Monarchs

A special importance attaches to the converso officials in the reign of Fernando and Isabel, obviously, because of the related issues of the Inquisition and the Expulsion.

As already noted, Isabel may have had the support of conversos even before she became queen. The converso chroniclers were not the only ones who were thoroughly disgusted with the corruption of the final years of the reign of Enrique, and many favored his sister to replace the indecisive, if not degenerate, king. Among those present when Isabel was almost secretly proclaimed queen at Segovia were several conversos, including the de la Hoz family and others, chiefly minor officials of the city.

We know, too, from Alonso de Palencia's own account, that he and another converso of Aragón were given the responsibility of bringing the jewels which constituted Isabel's dowry from Juan II of Aragón when she secretly married his son Fernando (there are further rumors of the involvement of Abraham Seneor in arranging this marriage).

However, great caution is necessary in identifying conversos in this period, particularly in Aragón-Catalonia where many Jews were now using "Christian" (Spanish) first names. Thus, in 1485 when the Jewish officials of Zaragoza were gathered in the *Becorolim* (visitation of the sick) Synagogue to arrange the tax assessments, several bore such names (Juan del Portal, a physician; Leon Manyent; Leon Gallur—perhaps Golluf?). In the small town of Almunia de Doña Godina in 1480, Nicolás de la Caballería was named as *procurador* of the Jews, a thing inconceivable if he were a converso (in this regard, some caution must be used concerning several of his family, unless there is absolute proof they were conversos).

In fact, however, the Catholic Monarchs were soon surrounded by converso officials at court and in their personal service, in such roles as confessors, secretaries, physicians, and close companions. A Polish visitor to Spain in 1484 wrote: "I have heard it said that the queen is the protector of the Jews and daughter of a Jewess [he apparently confused Isabel with Fernando!]. I also have observed with my own eyes that she has more confidence in baptized Jews than in Christians and entrusts them with all her rents and taxes. They [conversos] are her counsellors and secretaries, as they are also of the king; nevertheless, instead of respecting them [the Monarchs], they hate them more than anything."[29]

Both Monarchs had conversos, or descendants of such, as their confessors, responsible entirely for their "religious well-being" (we shall discuss these further in the chapter). Three converso secretaries served them: Fernando Álvarez (perhaps the same who received property in 1496 from the Monastery of Santa Clara of Toledo, always on friendly terms with Jews, and who was "pardoned of the crime of heresy"), Alfonso de Ávila, and the much more famous Fernando de Pulgar. The latter, particularly, was the personal secretary of the queen and a member of the royal council. In addition, another converso, Luis de Santángel, was Isabel's financial secretary. He was the cousin of Luis de Santángel of Zaragoza, about whom more later, who was beheaded for his alleged part in the assassination of the Inquisitor Arbués. Our Luis was also implicated, but was "penanced" on 17 July 1491.[30] As previously noted, Gonzalo Chacón, who had been treasurer and chronicler of the ill-fated Álvaro de Luna, was probably a converso. He became *contador mayor* under the Catholic Monarchs.

Special cases were conversos such as Diego de Valera, not only official chronicler but "master of the chamber," an important if ceremonial position, and for a time head of the Armada (as we shall see), and the other chroniclers, Alonso de Palencia and Pulgar.

There were even more converso officials in the service of Fernando in his capacity as king of Aragón-Catalonia. It is strange that the converso chroniclers rarely, if ever, make reference to these (indeed, their bias was heavily Castilian). Alonso de Palencia, for instance, barely mentions Alfonso de la Caballería, referring to him only in 1474, when he met him while with the king in Zaragoza. He describes him as "learned, ingenious, and perspicacious in the discussions" which took place. He also mentions another converso there, Luis González, already secretary to the then prince, Fernando.[31]

Did Alonso know that both these men were conversos? Did they know that he was? We have no indication. Luis González accompanied Alonso to Castellón, and perhaps the facts emerged on this journey. At Castellón Alonso discussed with the Aragonese king all the events and matters of Castile during two nights and a day.

When Enrique, Isabel's brother, died and Isabel was proclaimed queen in Segovia, a noble carried a naked sword before her (as was the custom at a king's coronation). Fernando, still in Zaragoza and hardly having received any word at all from his wife, was perplexed by this ceremony. Luis González, who read him the account, assured him that it was a novelty. Fernando asked Alfonso de la Caballería, described as jurist (legal scholar or judge), and Alonso de Palencia to tell him if ever such a thing had been done for a queen. The surprise was due to the fact that a sword thus displayed was a symbol of punishment against rebels or criminals, and was therefore always carried for a king but not for a queen. Fernando was amazed at his wife's "insolence" and also suspected, wrongly as it turned out, that he was to have little role in the affairs of Castile, much less be its king. In reality, Isabel adored her husband, and never made a decision without consulting him.[32]

Once in Castile with Fernando, Alfonso de la Caballería proved to be rather lukewarm in his support of the rights of the king. It appears yet again that the conversos tended to support Isabel more than Fernando, at least in Castile.

For that matter, converso chroniclers also made almost no mention of other converso officials in Castile itself. Diego de Valera mentions his colleague Alonso de Palencia only once, calling him "a very prudent and believable man" (prudent, maybe, but his "believability" has been called into question more than once, at least with regard to what he wrote of the homosexual activity of Enrique and several of his nobles).[33] Fernando de Pulgar could have told us so much more about many converso officials, bishops, etc. We wonder if this reticence was not, in fact, due to a fear of seeming to glorify conversos.

The question of whether these converso officials had anything to do with Fernando and Isabel's favorable attitude toward Jews can be answered in the negative, of course. Like the majority of conversos, they were ardent Catholics and most were vehemently anti-Jewish (especially was this true with converso clergy, but also with the officials, including even Pulgar).

On the other hand, Isabel may have felt a certain affection for those conversos who were present at her coronation at Segovia, as noted previously. Ironically, however, all of these later came under suspicion by the Inquisition (perhaps it was feared they might have *too* much influence), and one, Gonzalo de Cuéllar, was burned as a "heretic." Nevertheless, as late as 1483 we still find the names of members of these families, along with other conversos (Mexia, Mesa), as officials in Segovia.[34]

Among the conversos of Castile, a special place must be reserved (in hell, some would say) for the previously mentioned Abraham Seneor. This is not the place for the detailed account of his career, except to mention that in 1491 when, in an effort to bring some order to the chaos of separate treasury officials collecting various taxes, a central agency was created, two officials were placed in charge: "Raby Mayr" and Luis de Alcalá. The latter may, in fact, have been a converso, though there is no proof of this. "Raby Mayr" was Meir *Melamed,* a Jew and relative of Abraham, who later converted with him and other members of the family.[35] Later, Abraham and another Jew, Abraham Bienveniste, joined this group of officials, and they remained, after their conversion, in charge of that agency until at least 1494.

Baer's information about Seneor and *Melamed* is confused. He claimed that Abraham was the "chief tax-farmer," in which post he was succeeded by his "son-in-law" Meir *Melamed.* None of this is correct. The English translator of Baer has further added to the confusion by incorrectly inserting the name "Fernando Núñez [*sic*] Coronel" after Abraham and "Fernando Pérez Coronel" after Meir.[36] (The correct forms of these names will be explained below.)

Seneor was both an enormously powerful and an enormously wealthy man. In 1492 he owned property valued at over 1,300,000 *mrs.,* without taking into account numerous other vineyards and properties he owned all over Spain.[37] This, of course, makes him one of the wealthiest men in the kingdom (this was, for example, nearly the same as the amount needed to finance Columbus' expedition). It is thus perhaps not surprising that he decided to convert rather than go into exile. On 15 June 1492, Abraham and his son (name missing in the text, but from another source we know it was Solomon) were baptized, with the king and queen and Cardinal Pedro González de Mendoza serving as patrons. Abraham took the name Fernand *Pé-*

rez Coronel (not "Núñez") and his son Juan Pérez Coronel. At the same time, Meir *Melamed* was baptized with his two sons, and he took the name Fernand *Núñez* Coronel. The Coronels were to become a long and distinguished dynasty, some of whom later left Spain and settled in England, where they converted to Judaism. Seneor (Fernand Pérez Coronel) later served as *contador mayor* for the *infante* Juan, son of Fernando and Isabel.

Capsali wrote that Abraham and his "brother-in-law" (not "son-in-law") Meir *Melamed* converted, "whether by compulsion or willfully, for I have heard 'from behind the curtain' [i.e., secretly] that the queen swore that if don Abraham Seneor would not convert, all the Jewish communities would be converted, and in order to save many from sin he did what he did, and not from his heart."[39] We can undoubtedly discount what this sixteenth-century chronicler may have heard secretly rumored, for Seneor was not, in spite of his official title of "rabbi," such a loyal Jew as all that.

Meir *Melamed* was also an important tax official while still a Jew. In 1491 he and Luis de San Pedro (probably also a converso, perhaps related to the famous author Diego de San Pedro) were appointed chief tax collectors for certain taxes for the entire kingdom for the years 1492–94. The Monarchs did not yet know, of course, that the Jews were to be expelled in 1492 (as we shall see, this was not their plan), and this appointment may have been the motivation for *Melamed's* conversion in 1492, rather than giving up such a lucrative post. His relative, Jaco *Melamed,* was father of the converso monk Antonio de Ávila, author of an infamous anti-Jewish manual for the Inquisition.

Luis de Santángel was actually the name borne by several distinct conversos, one of whom was "reconciled" (pardoned) by the Inquisition in Huesca in 1489 and then moved to Zaragoza, where he married Juana de la Caballería, daughter of the previously mentioned Luis. Another Luis de Santángel was accused by the Inquisition in 1484. He was a merchant of Teruel of no particular importance. The Luis de Santángel who is, of course, famous as one of the supporters of Columbus was the *escribano de ración* (comptroller of the treasury) from 1481 on. His brother Jaime, also a converso, was already in the service of Juan II of Aragón and continued to serve his son Fernando. According to Serrano, Luis was probably the son of Alfonso (converted ca. 1414), one of the brothers of Azarias (the first Luis de Santángel), and was born in Calatayud, but in his youth went to Valencia, where two sons were born to him, also named Luis and Jaime. Eventually he moved to Barcelona.[41]

We know that in 1489, together with a converso judge of Seville, Francisco Pinelo, he engaged in a type of tax farming in speculation on the proceeds of taxes of the *Mesta* (sheep grazing and rearing organization).

As noted above, there was yet another Luis de Santángel, cousin of this one, who was financial secretary to Isabel. He was apparently already in the service of Enrique IV from the beginning of his reign, and perhaps even of Juan II of Casile before him.[42]

The Santángel family in general descended from the fourteenth-century Jew Noé (Noah) Chinillo (d. 1415 or earlier), whose son Azarias converted in 1415 and became the first Luis de Santángel. He was a cloth merchant in Daroca, but was also highly educated in law. One of his daughters married his brother, and the bishop of Mallorca, Pedro de Santángel, was their son. This Luis managed eventually to achieve a fairly high position of influence, becoming a counsellor of the king. He died in 1467. It was his son, also Luis, who was executed in the Arbués affair.

All of the brothers of Azarias (Luis) converted with him, and one of these, Martín de Santángel, was no less than the Inquisitor General of Aragón.[43]

The role of Luis de Santángel, the *escribano de ración*, in connection with Columbus has been much discussed, if often incorrectly. He first met Columbus in Córdoba in 1486 when the latter was received by the Catholic Monarchs. He strongly supported Columbus' cause, and in 1491 finally convinced the queen. He did *not*, as popular legend maintains, "finance" the voyage, any more than Isabel sold her jewels to do so (another myth long ago disproved). However, he did arrange to borrow the 1,140,000 *mrs.* necessary for the voyage, from a variety of sources. One document concerning him refers enigmatically to another sum of 1,500,000 *mrs.* paid to Isaac Abravanel. What this obviously must have been was repayment for that sum which Abravanel loaned the Catholic Monarchs in 1491 for the expenses of the war against Granada. Abravanel could not possibly have had this amount of money himself, and no doubt borrowed in turn from various Jews or Jewish communities.[44]

The major family of conversos in Aragón, of course, was the previously mentioned de la Cavalleria, or Caballería, family. It is impossible to detail completely, nor is there any point to it, the activities of the entire family. Already in 1414 under Fernando I, one of these, Juan, son of Benvenist and the first known converso of the dynasty, was *comprador mayor* (purchasing agent) of the king. His aforementioned brother Gonzalo, also a converso, reached an even higher position as treasurer of the hearth taxes.[45] Pedro de la Cavalleria, the notorious anti-Jewish polemicist, was *maestre racional,* a jurist and counsellor of Alfonso V, in 1437.

One of the most important members of the family was Jaime de la Cavalleria, judge of the *Santa Hermandad* of Zaragoza (the *Hermandad,* or "Holy Brotherhood," was actually an organization of long standing in Castile whose purpose was to protect the peace, but it was reorganized under the Catholic Monarchs into a powerful quasi-religious, quasi-military institution which often caused problems for Jews and conversos). Directly contradicting the express orders of the king and queen, the Inquisitors and officials of Zaragoza prohibited the Jews from taking any of their goods or property when they were expelled in 1492. Further, they seized all debts due to Jews, and particularly those of one of the richest, Juce Chamorro. Jaime, together with other officials (one of whom, Juan Fernández de Heredia, was regent governor of Aragón, so that obviously the king knew of these actions), was in charge of this seizure of more than 80,000 *sueldos* owed to this Jew.[46]

Luis de la Cavalleria was one of the most important government officials, acting as *tesorero general* at least from 1460 to 1469, after which he is simply referred to as "treasurer of the cathedral" of Zaragoza. The last document in which he is cited is dated 1483.[47]

The most important family member, however, was Alfonso de la Cavalleria, son of the aforementioned Pedro. From 1485 on he was vice-chancellor of Aragón (contrary to what Baer wrote, it is not at all certain that it was this Alfonso who together with Alonso de Palencia brought the dowry of Isabel from Juan II of Aragón).[48] His role in the Arbués affair will be detailed in the discussion of the Inquisition, and his role in connection with the Expulsion will also be analyzed later.

Among other officials in Aragón, Sancho de Paternoy, the *maestro racional* (more or less in charge of the royal household) and Gabriel Sánchez, the treasurer of Aragón, were also conversos or descended from conversos.[49] They, too, were implicated in the murder of Arbués.

Because of the importance of Sánchez, further details are of interest. As mentioned above, his ancestor was Alazar Uluf (Golluf) of Calatayud, who converted and took the name Luis Sánchez. When he converted, so also did four of his brothers, all of whom were poor: Pedro, Antón, Jaime, and Juan. Pedro married a conversa of Tortosa and had several sons: Luis, Gabriel, Guillen, Miguel, Juan, Alonso, and others. It was this Luis, a nephew (and hardly grandson, as Baer thought) of the older Luis, who became treasurer of Aragón in 1474 or earlier, and then *baile general* (chief administrator) under Fernando II in 1479. It is possible that he continued to serve as treasurer for a time early in Fernando's reign, for it has been suggested that the initials "L-S" which appear on certain of the king's coins are those of Luis Sánchez, as the letters "G-S" on *ducats* of Fernando minted in Aragón are those of his brother Gabriel.

In 1475 Juan II made Gabriel "lieutenant" (assistant) treasurer of Aragón with a salary of 1,000 gold *florins* (not enormous, but substantial). The following year the king granted him an additional subsidy from the taxes of Sicily. By 1480 he already had replaced his brother as treasurer under Fernando.[50]

The other sons of Pedro Sánchez, brother of Luis, in the service of Fernando were Guillermo (or Guillen), *maestro racional,* Francisco, *repositero mayor* (chief tax receiver), and Alonso, "lieutenant" general treasurer for Valencia.[51] A grandson of Gabriel Sánchez, Francisco Gurrea, later became governor of Aragón.

Jacme (Jaime) de Casafrancha, notary and scribe of Fernando, later (1505) was condemned by the Inquisition in Barcelona. He was an important figure from 1477 on, and was a friend of the converso Juan de Sant Jordi, secretary of Juan II of Aragón (it is curious, incidentally, that the *Libro verde de Aragón* makes no mention of Juan de Sant Jordi). Juan de Sant Jordi, together with his mother, was burned by the Inquisition in 1491.[52]

In 1489 this Jaime made a contract with a German printer of Barcelona to print a book for him (*Lunaris* [?], a calendar). By the time the Inquisition condemned him, he was already "lieutenant treasurer" of Catalonia. His wife also was later burned, and his daughter "repented" and was reconciled. In the sentence against Jaime, it is stated that his father had been reconciled and his mother and other relatives burned.[53]

He and Sant Jordi were accused of having observed all sorts of Jewish customs, and at the time when they were officials of Juan II they were said always to have stayed in homes of Jews or of other conversos and to have disputed the Bible with them. Even in his house in Barcelona, in the still-extant plaza de la Trinitat, Jews had stayed with him more than the three days allowed by city ordinance. Further accusations included his supposed dealings with Jews in Gerona and Montblanch, including his having given money to support two poor Jewish students from Castile. Supposedly found in his house in Barcelona was a writing with the "*Quiria setma*" (Heb. *qeriyat shema*ᶜ, the so-called Jewish creed).[54]

There were several other converso officials of somewhat lesser importance, such as Luis González, grandson of a Jew, *conservador* of Aragón; Juan de Albión, a nephew of Jerónimo de Santa Fe, *alcaide* (military commander) of Perpignan and in 1461 ambassador to France; and Fernando's secretaries in Aragón, Miguel Almazán and Gaspar Barrachina (son of Abiatar Xamós, who converted).

Thus we see that there certainly was no hostility to conversos on the part of the Catholic Monarchs, whether at what Baer chose to call "the court of the fanatical queen" or in Aragón-Catalonia.

Conversos in Church Office

Curiously, it sometimes seems to be as difficult for some modern Christian as for Jewish historians to accept the simple fact, demonstrated here repeatedly, that the overwhelming majority of the Jews who converted did so because they sincerely believed in Christianity and just as sincerely were convinced of the falseness of the Jewish faith.

The success of Vicente Ferrer, for example, and the religious hysteria which his oratory everywhere inspired, are well known. Entire Jewish communities were converted by his fervor, and synagogues were turned into churches. The Tortosa disputation was another factor, leading to the conversion of thousands.

It is not surprising that many conversos chose a career in some form of religious life, and this is a further indication of the sincerity of their Christianity. Many entered monasteries and convents, and if detailed studies were to be made of these (such as has been done only with regard to one monastery of the Jeronimite Order so far), no doubt the extent of converso influence in this respect would be revealed. The same is undoubtedly true for local priests, archdeacons, etc., about whom we have few sources.

By sheer accident, we know of one archdeacon, Juan de Góngora of Jerez, who was a converso. He acquired a manuscript of Rashi's commentary on the Bible, which in turn he gave to the Cathedral of Seville in 1480. The Hebrew inscription on the title page indicates that it was purchased with his money, which appears to mean that he purchased it with the intent of giving it to the cathedral (on the other hand, he may have owned it as a Jew and then decided it was too dangerous, once the Inquisition began, to have a Hebrew book).

Alvarez de Villasandino, the previously mentioned poet (d. 1427), wrote a poem to Gutierre de Toledo, archdeacon of Guadalajara and archdeacon-elect of Toledo, in which he spoke disparagingly of him and compared him to a "small cat" who fights with a lion (normally, this proverb concerns a dog, and it is apparent that the insulting term *gato*, proverbial for "Jew" or converso, alluded to his converso status).[55]

Converso Bishops

Pablo de Santa María and his son Alonso de Cartagena (see below) were undoubtedly the most famous converso bishops.[56] As previously mentioned (Chapter 4), it is almost certain that Gutierre Gómez, archbishop of Toledo, was of converso origin, and probably also Archbishop Alonso Carrillo. Another who certainly was is Alonso de Palenzuela, bishop of Ciudad Rodrigo. Francisco de Toledo was bishop of Coria (1475–79), and in the previous chapter we have already mentioned Fernando de Pulgar's letter to him. According to Pulgar, the bishop's "ancestors" (or possibly grandparents) were Jews who converted. While studying at Lérida he came to the attention of Queen María of Aragón, sister of Juan II of Castile, who chose him to be her chaplain. The queen then sent him to Paris to study for ten years (at the time, the only university where theology could be taught). Francisco preached eloquently in Latin as well as in Castilian, according to Pulgar (sermons in Latin would have been unintelligible to any but the most learned). Like another, more famous converso bishop, Alonso de Cartagena, Francisco was an ambassador, to the kings of France and later also to the papal court. He was also sent to Prague to help deal with the Hussite heresy (with which Alonso was also concerned), and in 1460 to Vienna to convince Frederick III to join the Turkish crusade.[57]

Pedro de Aranda, converso bishop of Calahorra, was president of the council of Castile in 1482. He was the son of Gonzalo Alonso, baptized at the time of Vicente Ferrer, whose other son was Alonso de Burgos, discussed below. We have also previously noted that both Lope de Barrientos and the converso Fernan Díaz de Toledo referred to a bishop of Barcelona, born in Valencia, who lived ca. 1413 and was a converso. This can only be Andrés Bertrán, who fits this description, and was bishop of Gerona (which see then included Barcelona) from 1415 to 1419 (not precisely thirty-six years before Fernan Días de Toledo wrote, but perhaps he knew him before he became bishop). Fernan Díaz' own son Pedro became the first bishop of Málaga.

Alonso de Burgos, the above-mentioned son of the converso Gonzalo Alonso (about whom a later fictitious genealogy was developed to prove his "*limpia*" status), became confessor and chief chaplain of Isabel. In 1476, as part of the instructions of the Catholic Monarchs to their ambassador to the pope, he was specifically ordered to tell the pope concerning the "deeds" of Alonso, master of theology and their chaplain; "this" (what, specifically, and what "deeds," we are not told) was to be their final word on the matter. They also asked that he be given license to give sacraments to all at court. Three years later they made a similar request for Juan de Torquemada, then their confessor, who spent most of the year at court. Alonso de Burgos later became successively bishop of Córdoba, Cuenca, and then Palencia. According to Amador, he wrote an anti-Jewish polemic, *Contra los judíos*, but I have found no confirmation of this and suspect a confusion with Abner of Burgos (Alfonso de Valladolid).[58]

A "special case," the very important Hernando de Talavera, possibly the son of a Jewish (or conversa) mother, will be discussed at the end of the chapter.

As mentioned below, two of the sons of Alfonso de Aragón, bastard son of Juan II of Navarre and half brother of Fernando, and his conversa wife, María, became important Church officials. One was don Alfonso de Aragón, bishop of Tortosa and then archbishop of Tarragona in the reign of Fernando. The second was don Fernando de Aragón, *comendador* of San Juan and prior of Catalonia.

The previously mentioned Luis de Santángel, before his conversion Azarias Chinillo, had a brother who also converted and then married Luis' daughter. Their son, Pedro de Santángel, became bishop of Majorca (however, he was appointed 18 June 1465 and died in November of that year).[59]

The Santa María Family

The most important conversos who were bishops, Church officials, and theological writers for many years to come were members of the Santa María-Cartagena family. These included Pablo, bishop first of Cartagena and then Burgos, his son Alonso de Cartagena who succeeded his father in both positions, and many others.

Juan Díaz de Coca, son of Alonso Díaz, one of Pablo's sons, was bishop of Calahorra. Another important member of this family who was a bishop was Juan Ortega de Maluenda.

Unfortunately, the only monograph on Pablo de Santa María, by the otherwise important scholar Luciano Serrano, is full of misinformation and romantic fantasy. Thus, the claim that as Solomon ha-Levy, rabbi of Burgos, Pablo had established a huge "school of Hebrew studies" which attracted students from all Spain is sheer imagination for which there is not the slightest evidence. Nor is there any evidence that the king (Juan I) elevated him to the position of "chief rabbi" of Burgos. No such position existed, in the first place. Nor is it possible that he could have judged criminal cases among Jews, since that king, in contrast to previous rulers, strictly prohibited rabbis from so doing.[60]

Fernán Pérez de Guzmán, a fifteenth-century author and friend of Pulgar, gives some interesting and no doubt authentic details about Pablo:

> He was a Hebrew [!] of great lineage of that nation; he converted by the grace of God and the recognition he had of the truth, for he was greatly learned in both laws [faiths] before his conversion. He was a great philosopher and theologian, and after his conversion he continued these studies in the court of the pope [Benedict XIII] at Avignon.[61]

No less inaccurate than Serrano is Baer's account, correctly criticized by Cantera Burgos, who wrote the only balanced and factual treatment of this important converso family.[62]

Before his conversion, as Solomon ha-Levy, he was a rabbi in Burgos; hardly "chief rabbi," however, as noted already, and there was certainly more than one rabbi in so important a community. Baer, following Graetz, did correctly state that it was during this time that Solomon addressed several questions in writing to the renowned Isaac b. Sheshet, then rabbi of Zaragoza, and we have Isaac's reply to these. It is clear that they had previously been acquainted, for Isaac speaks of "renewing" their friendship. These responsa all deal with matters relating to the Talmudic tractate *Hulin*, and were written not only with great respect toward Solomon, but in a manner which clearly reveals his high degree of learning. Particularly important is the address on one of the questions, which gives the name of Solomon's father, Çag (Zag) ha-Levy.[63]

It is impossible to date this exchange precisely, except that it was before 1385, when Isaac left Zaragoza for Valencia (nothing indicates that the responsa came from Zaragoza, but we know from other sources of Solomon's connections with that city both before and after his conversion).[64]

The father of Solomon is very possibly the person mentioned in a document already published by Baer. If so, he was the son of Abraham, and in 1359 he and Solomon Bienveniste, *arrendadores* of the king for certain taxes, sold part of that privilege to the Jews of Palencia. According to Serrano, the uncle of Solomon was Meir Bienveniste; certainly not, however, to be identified (as he erroneously did) with the famous physician and rabbi Meir Alguadix.[65]

On another occasion, Isaac b. Sheshet wrote to Judah b. Asher, then also a rabbi in Burgos, expressing his disappointment that the latter had not been able to attend a wedding, but stating that "the exalted don Solomon ha-Levy" had explained to him the reason. Baer (followed here by Cantera) jumped to the conclusion that this Solomon was one other than Solomon ha-Levy of Burgos, perhaps a reasonable enough assumption in light of the fact that Judah b. Asher was also then in Burgos. However, it appears clear that this identification is wrong, for at the end of the responsum Isaac writes that "the exalted don Samuel Bienveniste" has informed him that Judah is now in Soria and soon plans to visit "us" (i.e., Samuel and Isaac), but that nevertheless he decided to send his letter to Judah.

In light of this, in the first place all of what Hershman wrote about the date of the responsum (1386) and the place being Valencia and not Zaragoza, and the wedding referred to being that of Isaac's nephew, is entirely wrong.[66] In fact, the wedding in question took place in Zaragoza in April of 1380, as we know from two letters of the king, Pedro IV, concerning it. These letters grant permission to Juçaf Benvenist of Castile and his family to come to live temporarily in Zaragoza, where Joseph is to marry the daughter of Vidal de la Cavalleria (this family was closely related to the Benvenist family). The second letter refers also to members of the "Abnalazar" (Alazar) family, another well-known Jewish clan of Zaragoza, and gives the important information that Samuel Benvenist (or Benvenist) is the uncle of Joseph, the groom. It is, of course, this Samuel who is mentioned at the end of Isaac's responsum.[67]

All of this casts doubt also on the identification of "the exalted don Solomon ha-Levy" mentioned there, for the Benvenist family was also known by the name Ibn Labī, and Arabized form of "Levy" (there were several Solomons in this family, and it is not now possible to further identify which one is meant in Isaac's letter, but it certainly was not Solomon ha-Levy of Burgos, the rabbi).

There is still further confusion with regard to the Judah b. Asher referred to in the responsum. Baer incorrectly identified him as the *grandson* of Asher b. Yeḥiel, the famous fourteenth-century rabbi of Toledo. However, that Judah died in 1349, long before Isaac b. Sheshet was born. Our Judah was, in fact, the *great*-grandson of Asher, and the son of Asher b. Solomon and his wife, the daughter of Jacob b. Asher (the equally famous author of the *Ṭur*).[68]

Further adding to the confusion is Hershman's error in claiming that this Judah was "interested also in philosophy," and that our responsum states that "Isaac Ahdib" (read Alḥadib), a well-known scholar, had left with Isaac "three pamphlets on the writings of Avicenna," asking that they be forwarded to Judah. In fact, "Ben Sini" in the Hebrew of the responsum is simply a scribal corruption for Ben Sneh, or Ibn Zarza ("bush" in Hebrew and Spanish, respectively), and not Ibn Sīnā (Avicenna). The writings thus referred to are known, and they are by a Jewish scholar, but this is not the place for the lengthy detail necessary to discuss all of this (Baer, probably following Hershman, fell into the same error).

It has been suggested that the don Solomon ha-Levy who is mentioned, together with don Samuel Abravalla, as representatives in an alleged disputation before the pope, in Ibn Verga's chronicle, is our Rabbi Solomon ha-Levy. In fact, it was not a disputation, but a delegation which in 1419 went to Florence to convince Pope Martin V (approved by the Council of Constance) to nullify the anti-Jewish legislation of Benedict XIII. Thus, this Solomon ha-Levy could not possibly have been the rabbi of Burgos, since he was by then already bishop of Burgos and a staunch supporter of Benedict. These facts have hitherto been ignored. Another apocryphal story in Ibn Verga's chronicle concerns yet another ritual murder charge in which a Christian boy was supposedly found dead; in order to prevent Jews from being accused, Solomon placed a mystical (divine) name in the mouth of the corpse and the boy came to life.[69]

The story of Solomon's trip to England (or Aquitaine, more probably) in 1389 and his famous Hebrew Purim satire addressed to Meir Alguadix, hardly the "chief rabbi" of Castile, have often been discussed. Baer's account is completely erroneous, as Cantera realized, and Baer's criticism of Cantera in turn is unjust, for there is not necessarily any "irony" in Solomon's statement that he was imprisoned; he may very well have been held as a hostage. Indeed, his unfortunate experience may have been a contributing factor to his decision to convert.[70]

Another incident of importance was the king's order that Jews of Burgos not be required to provide clothing for the castle, or any other supplies or goods, and that men from the castle not be domiciled in the *judería* against the will of the Jews. In 1388 the Jews of the city, led by Solomon, demanded that this royal order be enforced, to which the king agreed.[71]

There is no point in adding further to the harsh words of Baer in his debate with Cantera over the year of Solomon's conversion. In fact, the evidence seems to sustain Cantera's position that it took place before the so-called "pogroms" of 1391. In any event, Solomon and his family, sons and daughters and brothers, converted. It has been conjectured that he went to study theology then either in Provence or in Paris.

What has not been hitherto noticed is that among those listed as receiving payments from Benedict XIII in March of 1396 was "Pablo de Santa María of Burgos," not yet bishop, of course.[72]

Pablo was elected bishop first of Cartagena (an important see which included all of Murcia) in 1403 (not 1402), and served until 1415. Once again Benedict XIII, whom the previous bishop had renounced, was recognized by Pablo as the rightful pope in the kingdom of Murcia, as he was elsewhere in Spain. As bishop of Cartagena, Pablo exercised strong leadership, instituting the preaching of sermons in every church and advocating resistance to the "schism" of the papacy (there was a claimant in Rome and one in Avignon, Benedict).[73]

Besides serving as bishop of this important see, he was also a major political figure with considerable influence over the young king (Enrique III of Castile), and was *canciller mayor* (chancellor) of the kingdom. He also was personally the teacher of the prince, Juan II, until his fourteenth year. Thus, he was clearly the most influential converso in the kingdom. One of his memorable, we may even say notorious, deeds in his episcopacy in Murcia was bringing Vicente Ferrer there to preach, stirring up anti-Jewish sentiment and leading to the conversion of many Jews there.

In 1406, when Enrique died, his testament was locked in a chest with four keys, one of which was given to Pablo and another to Pablo's brother, Pedro Suárez, *procurador* of Burgos. After at least 1388 this Pedro Suárez de Santa María was a member of the council of Burgos.[74]

Joshua al-Lorqi and Pablo

The most important information we have about Pablo de Santa María's conversion and the Jewish reaction to it comes from Joshua al-Lorqi, who probably came originally from Murcia but lived in Alcañiz (between Tortosa and Zaragoza), according to the *Libro verde de Aragón*. He is not to be confused with the Joshua al-Lorqi who was physician of Benedict XIII, and who translated a medical or astronomical treatise from Arabic for Benvenist b. Solomon Ibn Labī of Zaragoza, and died in 1411. Baer apparently made this mistake.[75] Nor is there any proof that Joshua was literally a "student" of Solomon ha-Levy, as has been suggested.[76]

The importance of Joshua's letter, not so much with regard to Pablo as for its insights into the motives of conversion in general in that period, is such that it should be cited here in some detail.

He begins by suggesting that there were four possible motives for Pablo's conversion:

1. "Perhaps your appetitive soul desired to ascend to heights of wealth and honor," which is a thing all desire, and to enjoy eating any food, and to enjoy the pleasures of Gentile women.
2. Perhaps his investigation of philosophy led him to consider adherents of religion as engaged in vanities (folly).
3. Perhaps he saw the "destruction of our homeland" (Palestine) and the oppression which recently has come upon the Jews as a sign of God's "hiding his face," and he feared that "the name of Israel will no longer be remembered."
4. Finally, "perhaps there were revealed to you the secrets of prophecy and roots of faith and the understanding of these which was not revealed to the 'pillars of the world' [sages] of our people in all the ages of the Diaspora, and you saw that our heritage is a lie."

As to the first reason, he reminds him that when he visited him at Burgos at the time of the wedding of Meir Bienvenist, Solomon had already begun to involve himself in the affairs of the kingdom, "and you made for yourself a chariot and horses and men running to do your will" (not literally; he began to achieve a certain power). Thus, desire for honor and power could not have prompted him to convert. Also, with regard to philosophy, he has "eaten the core and thrown away the peel" (*Hagigah* 15b); i.e., he knows how to distinguish good from bad in philosophical speculation, so philosophy could not have corrupted him.

With regard to the third reason, he reminds him of what is known from the writings of travelers (e.g., Benjamin of Tudela), or the Epistle to Yemen of Maimonides, and reports of merchants, that "the essence of our people today is in the lands of Babylon [Iraq] and Yemen," and in general under the Muslims where the "yoke of another nation" (Christians) is not upon them, and even among the Ethiopians or the (legendary) lands of Prester John.[77] "And in accord with this true supposition, even if the decree of God would be to destroy all the Jews among the Christians, the people would still remain extant and whole, and this would not cause a loss of trust" in God.

Therefore, only the last reason remains, and he says that he knows Pablo has seen Christian books and commentaries "since you are expert in their language" (Latin) which "none of our scholars has seen." (This is an exaggeration, since in fact many Jewish scholars in Spain quoted, often quite respectfully, Christian theological works; however, it does confirm Pérez de Guzmán's previously cited statement that Pablo had studied Christian theology before his conversion.)

He concludes: "In addition to this, there came to me by way of Zaragoza, some two months ago, the excerpt of a letter which you sent to Navarre to Rabbi Joseph Orabuena, and I saw that you believe" that Jesus was the expected messiah. This, incidentally, again proves that Joshua did not himself live in Zaragoza, since the letter came to him "by way of," that is, was transmitted, from Zaragoza.[78]

Joshua says he wishes he could "fly" to Pablo to have his own doubts resolved—doubts which ultimately led also to his conversion. These doubts were:

1. The messiah must be descended from David, but if Jesus was the "son" of God, how could he be the son of Joseph (even if Joseph were of the house of David)?
2. The messiah is to be a king, which Jesus never was; even if, as the Christians say, he was called "king of Israel," the Jews never called him that and there can be no king without a people.
3. The messiah is to redeem the Jews. How has Jesus done this, when the Jews do not believe in him, except only a few, as nothing in number (compared, that is, with the entire Jewish population)?
4. He is supposed to gather the exiled Jews, and yet in the time of Jesus the opposite happened: the Jews went into exile.
5. Jerusalem will be restored by the messiah, yet after Jesus it was destroyed.
5. The whole world is supposed to know God in the days of the messiah, but after Jesus came only a few followed him, and even now the majority of the world is not Christian.

He also raised theological objections to Christian dogma. If Adam was already punished by expulsion from Eden, for example, why should his descendants be punished, by the doctrine of "original sin," contrary to the prophets? (He means thereby Ezek. 18.2–4, etc.)

Indeed, if the death of Jesus was necessary for atonement for the world, why did he pray to avoid it? (See Matt. 26.42.) Moreover, why do Christians hate Jews and accuse them of "killing" Jesus, when his death only fulfilled the will of God and brought such benefit to the world?

However, he admits that virgin birth and resurrection are logically possible, since God can do anything (he cites an Arabic translation of Aristotle's *De coele* in possible support of the Trinity doctrine). Yet God cannot be God and possess a physical, limited body (against the doctrine of Incarnation).

Finally, he concludes with important philosophical questions, revealing at once his own intellectual depth and also the perplexity which drove him to conversion: Is a person allowed to investigate religions in order to discover the "true" one? If so, there is no end to such investigation; but if one follows the religion in which he is born, and it turns out to be "false," how can God punish him for that? Can God punish those who live in places where they cannot know of the "true" religion? ("Angletierra" here is not to be understood as England, but literally "the ends of the earth.") He says that he discussed these things "both with sages of our Torah *and with Christian sages.*"

Pablo replied to Joshua (apparently the beginning of this letter is lost). He explained that since the "Torah of Moses" is the essential religion, it is necessary to investigate by that whether the messiah has come, but it is not "worthy" to investigate Islam, since it is not of "the roots of the Torah of Moses." Those born in "false" religions are obligated to investigate the true one, however. For "after the coming of the messiah the whole world is obligated to conduct itself by *his* Torah" (thereby ignoring entirely Joshua's objection that most of the world is not, in fact, Christian).

However, those who have said that the source of faith is "investigative knowledge" have erred, which seems to hint at his view (expressed in his Christian writings) that simple faith based on trust is not only sufficient but superior to reason. Nevertheless, it is incumbent upon him (Joshua, and by implication all Jews) to investigate, with reason, the truth of "that which suffices for the salvation of the soul" (a concept totally alien to Jewish thought). "And even if he does not enter the holy water [of baptism], through lack of understanding, he will be purified in the immersion of the holy spirit," which if he refuses he should die in his wickedness!

Pablo signed his letter with the enigmatic expression: "Priest after Levite because of the defect of the first, and who seeks a second Levite-hood, and the last is the most precious." The meaning of this is that he became a "priest" (Catholic priest) after having been a Levite (a reference to his Jewish name) and having discovered the defect of Judaism, and seeks now a new "Levitical class," the Christian priesthood. He concludes: "Before in Israel Solomon of the house of Levy did not know God, and now that his eyes behold God he is called Pablo de Burgos," like the apostle Paul.[79]

Other Reactions to Pablo's Conversion

In his sharply satirical letter to his friend Davi Bonet Bonjorn, who also converted and decided to remain loyal to his new faith because of the influence of Pablo, Profiat Duran mentions that Davi had written him about Pablo: "and you said that he was created in the image and form of God, and you made him the pope in your words; I do not know whether he will go to

Rome or remain in Avignon!" This refers to the schism, and Duran sarcastically implies that Pablo could choose to be either the pope in Rome or the pope in Avignon, making fun, of course, of the Christians who could not even decide on the true pope.

Duran adds that, indeed, he knew of Pablo's greatness in astronomy and physics (the epicycle), which is new information as to his learning. Then, however, he proceeds sarcastically: "Give thanks to the messiah [Christ] that he has such [men] in his world. Not in vain did our lord the king [Juan I of Aragón-Catalonia] give to him [Pablo] gifts from his treasury." Nor in vain did "the great and special rabbi among the Jews," Ḥasdai Crescas, "flee" from engaging in debate with Pablo; on the contrary, Duran sarcastically suggests, Crescas gave Pablo "great honor" by visiting him in his palace and being with him constantly out of "love" for him (in other words, Crescas refused to dispute with Pablo and did not visit him).[80]

Netanyahu claimed that Pablo "conceived elaborate plans for the *total destruction* of Judaism in Spain," but there is no evidence for this. The letter to which he referred merely states that Pablo obtained a decree from the king (of Aragón?) that women, or children under the age of fifteen, should not be allowed to wander about in the streets. However, the letter does conclude with the statement that Duran heard a rumor that in Aragón Pablo intended to speak "deceit" about the Jews, but was ordered by the cardinal of Pamplona and two of his assistants, in secret, not to bring evil upon the Jews. The Jewish community there gave Pablo a certain sum of money (a bribe). Duran concludes: "the opinion of the lord pope and all the Church is to give him one of the important bishoprics or to make him a cardinal." Baer claimed that the cardinal of Pamplona was Pedro de Luna, who became Pope Benedict XIII, but Netanyahu correctly disproved this (as we have also seen, Benedict was already pope when Pablo converted) and showed that it was Martín de Zalva, made cardinal in 1390.[81]

In an Inquisition process (1490) against a converso of Cuéllar, a Franciscan friar of Santo Domingo de Silos testified that whenever there was a case between a Jew and a Christian, the Jew was not found guilty but was always favored over the Christian. He mentioned having read a passage by Pablo, bishop of Burgos, in the fifth chapter of his first "additions" to the *Postillam* of Nicholas de Lyra, that, according to the Talmud, whenever there should be a case between a Jew and a Christian, or of "another nation" (the Talmud says nothing about Christians, of course), every effort should be made to convince the judge to decide in accord with Jewish law, or otherwise to find in favor of the Jew.[82]

We see from this evidence the importance of the influence of Pablo's conversion, and the fact that his anti-Jewish polemic, published soon after his death, had a very wide audience. There is no question that on both accounts—the impact of his conversion and the damaging effects of his

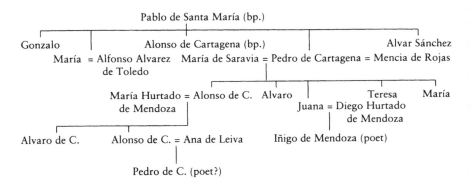

Figure 2. PARTIAL GENEALOGY OF SANTA MARÍA-CARTAGENA FAMILY

anti-Jewish polemic—he was the most "important" of the conversos of Spain.

Ironically, the beautiful cathedral of Burgos where he served as bishop, and where he is buried, which was built by the great Bishop Maurice, an intimate friend of Jews, is decorated conspicuously with two enormous stained glass Stars of David on its front. It is doubtful that they ever caused any pangs of conscience in this fanatic zealot, however.

The descendants of Pablo in the sixteenth and seventeenth centuries, members of by then a long line of illustrious families, published an "Informaciones de nobleza" in which they asserted the immunity of the noble descendants of Pablo to the statutes of *limpieza*, "purity of blood," which barred conversos and their descendants from offices.[83]

According to an anonymous manuscript, of late date, "Memorial de su linaje," Pablo was supposedly a descendant of a "powerful Christian king" on his mother's side, a claim which Cantera has already dismissed. It is said further that Pablo converted in 1390, was made bishop of Cartagena in 1402 (actually 1403), and of Burgos in 1415. Supposedly he converted many ("more than forty thousand"!) Jews and Muslims to Christianity, and died in 1435.[84]

Other Members of the Santa María Family

Pablo's son, who converted with him, Alonso de Cartagena (ca. 1385– 1456), was next in importance to his father.

Although Pulgar calls him "Alfonso de Santa María," and that form is still often found, the only form he himself used was Alonso de Cartagena, and so he is called here. One must use care also to distinguish him from other Alonsos, and Alfonsos, de Cartagena, later members of the same family.[85]

It is surely no coincidence that six times in a single paragraph Pulgar uses the term *limpia* to refer to Alonso; he was "very pure" (*limpio*) in his person and clothes, and everything he did was with *grand limpieza*, and he concludes by observing that the *linpieza esterior* of a man is a sign of his inner nature. No doubt Pulgar was pushing the point that even a converso could be "pure," as noted already in another case.[86]

Indeed, "purity" was something of an obsession in fifteenth-century society, especially, perhaps, among the conversos themselves. Thus, for instance, the converso chronicler Diego de Valera refers to the Franciscan converso Alonso de Palenzuela, later bishop of Ciudad Rodrigo, as having lived so "purely" (*tan limpiamento*) that he overcame objections of some of the order to his being made a bishop.[87]

Alonso de Cartagena's well-known role in the Council of Basel is briefly noted by Pulgar, and also his appointment by Juan II of Castile as ambassador to Portugal to conclude the important peace treaty. Pulgar says he also built the Monastery of San Pablo in Burgos, and "rebuilt other churches and monasteries" in his diocese. This is incorrect, however, for the Monastery of San Pablo was founded in the thirteenth century. Rather, it was the Monastery of San Ildefonso (1456), interestingly dedicated to the memory of a notorious anti-Semite, which was founded by Alonso. Also, together with Alonso de Madrigal ("*el Tostado*"), he encouraged Juan II in building the Monasterio de la Anunciación. Álvaro de Luna, of converso background, opposed the construction, though on what grounds is not clear.[88]

Pulgar remarks also on his great erudition, his translation of Latin works into Castilian, and mentions his famous debate with the Italian Leonardo de Arecio (Leonard Bruno) over Alonso's translation of Aristotle's *Ethics*.[89]

Alonso was certainly no friend of Jews, however strongly he urged, as we have seen, toleration of conversos. In his powerful role as one of the chief advisors of the minor king, Juan II (as mentioned, Pablo was his tutor), he was in a position to insist that the infamous demand of Saint Vicente Ferrer that Jews be forced to live apart from Christians in separate quarters, implemented at once in Aragón, be put into practice throughout Castile. The letter to that effect sent in the name of the young king in 1413 bore three signatures, foremost of which was "Afan. Cartaginensis."[90]

Interestingly, the converso chronicler and author Alonso de Palencia was in the service of Alonso de Cartagena in his youth.[91]

Alonso de Cartagena was educated at Salamanca, where he spent some ten years (to 1406), and emerged a doctor of laws and joined his father, then bishop of Cartagena, as master of the cathedral school there. In 1414, however, he was in the court of Benedict XIII at San Mateo. Did he then participate in the notorious San Mateo and Tortosa disputations? The following year the pope made him dean of Santiago de Compostela, a prestigious appointment.

His most important role, however, was as a government official and ambassador. He headed the Spanish delegation to the famous ecumenical Council of Basel, from 1434 to 1439. Another converso, Juan de Medina, was a representative of the king, together with Juan de Torquemada and others. A relative of Alonso, Gonzalo García de Santa María (probably the bishop, see next page), was another delegate, as was Juan Díaz de Coca, also a member of the family. The famous address which he gave on behalf of the "Spanish nation," to prove that the Christian faith enjoyed greater supremacy in Spain than in England, but actually a clarion call of Spanish nationalism, is well known.[92] Not only did he successfully defend the supremacy of Spain against English pretension (nor should we forget that England was itself plagued at this time by the Wycliff "heresy"), he played a leading role in the council's efforts to suppress the Hus heresy sweeping central Europe.

After the council, he also served as ambassador to the court of the Hapsburg emperor, Albert II, and succeeded in ridding him of his animosity to the council and to the proclaimed pope.[93] We have noted above how in this respect his career paralleled, but was even more spectacular than, that of the converso bishop of Coria, Francisco de Toledo.

In 1435 he succeeded his father as bishop of Burgos, which post he held until his death.

Pope Eugenius IV in 1442 issued a harsh bull condemning the Jews, quite out of line with the attitude of his predecessors of Rome and directly contradictory to his own earlier bull (which has been ignored by scholars) of 1433. No doubt the hand of Alonso can be seen in this, for he had his representatives at the papal court at this time, including the writer of the papal bulls, and also the converso Juan Días de Coca.

This bull claimed that previous bulls favorable to the Jews were being abused by them, and rescinded all papal privileges to Jews and Muslims of Castile, allowing only those conferred by secular law. Specifically included were a prohibition on associating with Christians, bathing with them, and holding office over them (which, of course, was a "secular" matter and could not be affected by any bull); nor could Christians use Jewish physicians. This last, although consistent with a canon (law) of the Basel council, was most hypocritical, for like most popes Eugenius himself had a Jewish physician, Elijah Beer b. Sabetai, the first Jewish doctor to be knighted in Rome.[94]

Alonso's anti-Jewish polemic, and his various writings, will be discussed below.

Amador de los Ríos incorrectly concluded that the converso Santa María family led the "vehement opposition" to the Jews in the fifteenth century. In fact, they were not by any means the most prominent in that regard, and nothing in their polemics compares with that found in such "old Christian" writers as Alonso de Oropesa or Alonso del Espina. For instance, Cantera has shown that Alvar García de Santa María, brother of Pablo, showed no anti-Jewish sentiment at all in his Crónica.[95]

In 1413, Alvar García sold to the Benvenist (or Bienvenist) family of Soria some houses in Burgos which had belonged to his family and then to Juan Hurtado de Mendoza, the *contador mayor* of Juan II. In his testament (1457) he recorded an obligation to Juda Abneredí, a Jew of Navarre, from whom he borrowed 160 *florins* in 1442 when he was in that kingdom by order of its king; therefore, even though he was "not obligated" to repay the debt (for reasons that are unclear), because of the kindness of the said Jew to him he determined to repay it. Nevertheless, not only did it take these fifteen years for him to remember this "kindness," he still did not repay the loan, for a codicil to the will (1458) again makes reference to it. He also was owed a debt of 1,000 *mrs.* by Joseph Bienveniste of Briviesca, by then deceased, as well as a "Bible in rich Hebrew" (possibly this refers to careful writing, or an illuminated manuscript) which he had never returned to Alvar. This Bible was said to be worth "at least 10,000 *mrs.*," an enormous sum. It is of interest to note that the famous "old Christian" writer and nobleman Fernán Pérez de Guzmán dedicated his poetic treatise on virtues and vices to Alvar García, twice referring to him as his good friend. He also wrote a eulogy on the death of Alonso de Cartagena.[96]

Finally, Gonzalo García de Santa Maria, a converso of Zaragoza, was mentioned by Cantera, who was not able to identify him. He was, in fact, the father of the historian of the same name. Cantera's confusion is all the more puzzling, as later in his book he provides accurate details on both father and son.[97]

Neither of these is to be confused, as has often been done, with Gonzalo García de Santa María, another son of Pablo (ca. 1379–1448). He was also eventually appointed to the court of Benedict XIII, and in 1415 was that pope's deputy to Spain, sent to "castigate" the Jews for not observing the papal bull imposing restrictions on them (wearing of the badge, etc.). He became bishop of Astorga (but *not* of Gerona, as Serrano wrote) and then of Plasencia. Renowned as an expert in canon law, he represented Spain in 1416 at Constance, and was elected one of the "six Fathers of the Council" to decide the resolution of conflicts. In 1446 he became bishop of Sigüenza, and died in 1448. His brother Alvar Sánchez was one of those accused of "treason" in 1430.[98]

Tomás García de Santa María was not, as Cantera realized, a brother of Pablo (as wrongly indicated in the *Libro verde de Aragón*). Tate also wrote briefly about Tomás in an article in which he argues, from the fifteenth-century Zaragoza historian Gonzalo García de Santa María's *Dialogum pro ecclesia contra synagogam,* that Pablo was "descended from a sister of Tomás, i.e., he was first cousin to Gonzalo's father."[99] The problem with this statement is obvious, for if Tomás lived in Zaragoza in 1416, according to a source cited by Tate himself, Pablo de Santa María could hardly be "descended" from his sister. (Possibly Tate misunderstood the Spanish word, which means not "*descended from*" but "*related to*.")

Miçer Gonzalo de Santa María (not to be confused with any of the Gonzalo Garcías; *miçer* means educated in law) was the son of Tomás and was baptized as a child with his parents, Tomás and Brianda, the daughter of Luis Sánchez, as previously mentioned (who was *not* an official of Aragón, as Tate thought, but Alazar Golluf, as we have mentioned). According to Tate, Tomás had previously married a member of the de la Cavalleria family, and a son of that marriage then married the daughter from the second marriage, Violante de Santa María. Tate gives no source for this information, and one wonders if he has not confused this marriage with Gonzalo García's marriage to Violante Velvivre, a conversa from Valencia (Cantera has almost nothing on Tomás).

Writings of the Santa María Family

The Santa María-Cartagena family was unquestionably the single most important converso dynasty in Spanish history, and certainly the most prolific (in all respects).

In 1604 Felipe III granted the descendants of Pablo de Santa María (only; not the other branches of the family) the privilege of *limpieza de sangre,* "purity of blood," or equality with "old Christians." Among the romantic nonsense that was written about Pablo was that he was a descendant of the Virgin, and a son of a daughter of Alfonso XI.

While the entire family, in all its branches, contributed much to Spanish history and literature for generations, two other members, in addition to Pablo, are perhaps the best known in the area of literature. These are Teresa de Cartagena, apparently a daughter of Pedro, brother of Pablo, and fray Iñigo de Mendoza, author of the *Vita Christi* (discussed later).[100]

The other famous writers and their works are:

1. Álvar García de Santa María (ca. 1380–1460), a brother of Pablo, who may have converted while still quite young. He also held political posts under Juan II, and in 1405 was declared a noble. He was secretary to the royal council and official chronicler of Juan II. He must have been fairly wealthy, for twice he received from his brother, Pedro Suárez, "some houses" in Burgos, and we hear also of other houses he owned, and still others he purchased from the Bienvenistes (Jews) of Soria, all of these in Burgos.[101]

2. Alonso de Cartagena (previously discussed). As we have noted, he was also politically active. He was already frequently employed by Juan II as an ambassador while he was still dean of Santiago, and also after he succeeded his father as bishop.[102]

3. Alonso de Burgos, a nephew of Alonso de Cartagena, the previously mentioned bishop. (In spite of his erudition, not a single written work is known to have survived.)

4. Juan Díaz de Coca (1388–1477), son of Alfonso Días, another of Pablo's brothers, was bishop of Oviedo and then of Calahorra. In 1440 he farmed out taxes on his property, loans, etc., to a Jew, don Çag el Levi of the castle (held by Jews) of Soria. In 1450 he was chaplain of Pope Nicholas V, and in 1456 he persuaded Calixtus III to confirm Luis de Acuña as successor to Alonso de Cartagena in the see of Burgos. Juan died in Rome.[103]

Major writings of this family in the period which concerns us, i.e., prior to the Expulsion, are:

1. Pablo de Santa María
   a. *Dialogus, qui vocatur Scrutinium scripturarum* (numerous editions, from 1469 to 1591)
   b. *Additiones ad Postillam Nicolai de Lyra* (also numerous editions, from 1481 to 1498)
   c. "Las siete edades del mundo," or "Edades trovadas," historical poem dedicated to Queen Catalina, mother of Juan I
   d. *Suma de crónicas de España* (unpublished), and a brief summary of the years 1343–1454 attributed to him or to his son Alonso de Cartagena
2. Álvar García de Santa María
   a. *Crónica* of Juan II (with additions by Fernán Pérez de Guzmán)
   b. Other minor historical writings
3. Alonso de Cartagena[104]
   a. *Defensorium unitatis christianae* (1943)
   b. *Doctrinal de los cavalleros* (1487, 1492, 1497)
   c. *Alegaçoes fietos contra os portugueses a favor de rei de Castilla e Leão . . . sobre conquista das Canarias* (Lisbon, 1912)
   d. *Regum hispanorum, romanorum imperatorum, summorum pontificum necnon regum francorum anacephaleosis* (1545 etc.)
   e. *Super altercatione . . .* , ed. in *Ciudad de Dios* 35 (1894): 124–29, 211–17, 237–53, 523–42 (and cf. Biblioteca de autores españoles 116:205–32, not mentioned at all by Cantera.)
   f. *Oracional* (critical ed. Silvia González Quevedo Alonso, Valencia, 1983, but lacking the *Apologia sobre el salmo "Iudica me, Deus"* and *Declaracion de un tractado que fizo sant Iohan Crisostomo*, which appeared in the 1487 ed.)
   g. *Un tratado . . . sobre la educación y los estados literarios* (Barcelona, 1979), addressed to the conde de Haro (important)
   h. Translated: Cicero, *De officiis, De senectute,* and *Rhetorica;* Seneca, *Cinco libros* (etc.); Boccaccio, *Cayda de principes*[105]
4. Gonzalo García de Santa María (d. 1521, Zaragoza; *not* to be confused with son of Pablo of same name)[106]

a. *Joannis Secundi Aragonum regis vita* (ed. Paz y Mélia in Colección de documentos inéditos para la historia de España 88 : 174–274)
b. *Arbol de la sucesión de los reyes de Aragón*
c. *Fueros del reino de Aragón*
d. *Evangelios e epistolas de todo el anyo con sus exposiciones en romance* (Zaragoza, 1485; Salamanca, ca. 1488; Portuguese trans., Porto, 1497; critical ed. of Latin and Romance text, I. Collijn and E. Staff, Uppsala, 1908)
e. *Dialogum quendam ecclesiae et synagogage* (Zaragoza, 1497)

Conversos in Royal Families

As we have seen, Lope de Barrientos, an extremely reliable source, stated that the royal house of Navarre had "Jewish blood," for Carlos de Viana was descended through his mother, Blanche, from "pure Israelites."

More important, perhaps, is the intriguing information that the admiral of Castile, don Alonso Enríquez, was descended on one side from Alfonso XI and Enrique II and on the other from "Jews." We shall consider the implications of this shortly.

In addition to these families, it is known that Alfonso de Aragón, bastard son of Juan II of Navarre (himself thus perhaps "tainted" with converso "blood"), married a conversa, as we have previously mentioned. While he was not technically of the "royalty," inasmuch as he was illegitimate, he was the half brother of Fernando, and such a marriage must have been remarked upon.

Alfonso was named master of the Order of Calatrava in Aragón (his banner may be seen in the dining hall of the splendid *parador* at Alcañiz, the castle where the famous "compromise of Caspe" took place), and he played a key role in the intrigues of Juan Pacheco, the notorious marqués de Villena under Enrique IV, who offered the kingdom of Murcia to Alfonso IV of Aragón in 1448. According to the *Libro verde de Aragón,* he fell in love with and eventually married Estenga, daughter of a Jew of Zaragoza with the unlikely name of Amiatar Conejo. After her conversion she took the name María. Their eldest son, Juan de Aragón, became count of Ribagorça. As previously mentioned, their other two sons both became important Church officials.[107]

Jewish Ancestry of Fernando

One of the Jewish exiles from Portugal, who had lived in Seville before the Expulsion, Isaac b. Abraham Ibn Faraj (in the twelfth century Moses Ibn 'Ezra composed poems in honor of members of the Ibn Faraj family), wrote that Fernando was of Jewish descent, adding: "a voice without end [a strong rumor] among the nobility is that he is a grandson of doña Palomba."[108]

The story of Fernando's descent from this Palomba is also told, with elaboration, by the early-sixteenth-century chronicler Elijah Capsali of Candia. According to him, it was the admiral of Castile, Fadrique Enríquez, who had intercourse with Palomba, a married Jewish woman, and she gave birth to a son whom he took and raised as his own, and who succeeded him as admiral. This son then had four daughters whom he married off to "kings and nobles" of Portugal and Spain (one to Portugal and two to Spanish nobles). For the fourth daughter he was unable to arrange a marriage. When he heard that Blanca of Navarre ("donña Franza," France, according to the Hebrew!) had died, he suggested to her widowed husband, Juan II of Aragón, that he marry this daughter, Juana Enríquez, to which the king agreed. It was this same Juan II, formerly king of Navarre, who is said to have been himself descended from Jews and who was the father of Alfonso de Aragón. Fernando was born of this marriage of Juan to Juana Enríquez, and thus was really descended on both sides (however remotely on his father's) from Jews.

Capsali concludes his account by calling down all manner of curses on Fernando, born of that union, because he "destroyed" the Jews. He adds also that Juana Enríquez was jealous of Carlos, prince of Viana (Blanca and Juan's son and rightful heir), fearing that he would inherit the kingdom instead of her son Fernando. Once while playing chess with Carlos, she supposedly insulted him and his French origins, and he replied by insulting the Jews. When Carlos became ill, purportedly the queen had poisoned him, and he died.[109]

While this much is certainly legend (nor is it likely that Carlos would have insulted Jews if his own parents were, in fact, also of Jewish descent), it is not as fantastic as it appears in general. We have seen that Lope de Barrientos had already said that the admiral Alonso Enríquez was of Jewish descent on his mother's side. As mentioned also, there is some evidence that Fernando knew of his Jewish descent.[110]

Juana de Aragón, granddaughter of Juan II, incidentally married Francisco de la Caballería, the grandson of the converso chancellor Alonso de la Caballería.

Did any of this have any practical effect in the reality of daily politics; for instance, influencing the king to favor conversos in his administration in Aragón? It is possible, but it seems unlikely. Apparently the converso officials who came to prominence in such numbers had already begun to achieve power before Fernando became king. They attained, and more important held onto, their positions because of their ability rather than any special favor.

On the other hand, like many conversos and those of converso origin,

Fernando may have had a particular dislike of Jews. This could explain his harsh policy toward the Jews of Zaragoza, for example, in his "own" kingdom, whereas the so-called fanatical queen may have kept such an attitude in check in Castile, where she could serve as a restraining influence on her husband.

A Special Case: Hernando de Talavera

Possibly of Jewish, or converso, background is the famous Jeronimite who was bishop of Ávila, and from 1478 on the confessor of Isabel. In 1479, while prior of the Monastery of Santa María de Prado he was one of two ambassadors sent to Portugal to negotiate the delicate peace, and to investigate the decision of the Portuguese princess, Juana, to enter a convent rather than marry the infant son of Fernando and Isabel (the marriage was to take place when he was of age, of course). The significance of his continuous influence on Isabel was no doubt enormous.

He was perhaps the bastard son of Garcí Alvarez de Toledo, lord of Oropesa, and either a Jewish or a conversa mother, as suggested by Márquez Villanueva; but if so, his relationship to Alonso de Oropesa, legitimate son of that same father, was only a technical one and hardly as close as Márquez would suggest.[111] Hernando was later to become the first archbishop of Granada, when that kingdom was conquered from the Muslims (1492).

His main work that is of interest to us is the *Católica impugnación,* completed in 1480, written, as he says, to combat the book of an "evil heretic" that had appeared (probably in manuscript) in Seville in 1478. Obviously, this "heretic," who concealed his name in his prologue (according to Hernando), was a converso.

Hernando, like his "relative" Alonso de Oropesa, was a severe critic of Judaism as well as of "Judaizing" conversos. As previously noted, he objected to the application of the abusive terms *marranos y marrandíes* to conversos, however, and claimed that the reason such epithets were used was the Inquisition; i.e., the Inquisition itself was a *cause* of hatred and discrimination against all conversos. Indeed, in his dedication to the Monarchs he stated his opposition to having the Inquisition under secular control.[112]

It is possible to reconstruct the arguments of the anonymous treatise of the converso against whom Hernando wrote. The arguments are quite naive: Jesus was a Jew who kept all of the Jewish law, instituted no new laws, etc. While denying that Jesus was a Jew (he was the "son of God"), Hernando devoted his lengthiest chapter (12 *bis*) to an effort to prove that Jesus did innovate laws. The "heretic" apparently denied the division of Jewish laws into "moral, ceremonial, and judicial," which was the distinction made by Alonso de Cartagena (chap. 16).

Very important evidence on the attitude of Spanish Christians at this period toward Jews (not conversos) is found in Hernando's statement that while some *few* Christians hate Jews and even Christians descended from Jews, those who do so are bad Christians and act in sin, whereas the *majority* of good Christians "maintain peace and good love" with the Jews (149). This is precisely the distinction, made by a medieval authority, between anti-Semitism and anti-"Judaism" (the latter of which he himself exhibited) that we have previously sought to make.

We may also see from the complaints of the "heretic" certain things which must have disturbed quite a few conversos of the time: the order of the cardinal (Mendoza) that all Christians must have images of Christ or the Virgin in their homes, the "idolatry" of worshiping saints, entombment in the churches, etc.

In 1480, Alonso de Palencia was one of those who were granted pensions by the intervention of Hernando with the then ruler, Enrique IV. Other conversos who benefited similarly were the secretaries of the king (also later of Fernando and Isabel) Fernando Álvarez and Fernando de Pulgar, and the *contador mayor*, Gonzalo Chacón, who as previously observed was probably a converso.[113]

With regard to the aforementioned distinction between anti-Semitism and anti-Judaism, it is of interest that in 1485 Hernando ordered that the papal bulls prohibiting usury did not apply to Jews (this was generally understood), nor were Jews to be subject to the Inquisition for practicing usury. The Inquisitors of Zaragoza questioned that order, but wrote that they were willing to accept his decision (what authority, other than moral, he had with the Inquisition in Aragón is not clear, however).[114]

According to his chronicler, Hernando succeeded in converting "many" Jews who had fled to Granada to live among the Muslims. One of the tactics he used to convert Jews and Muslims was to guarantee them exemption from any new taxes or tribute. "He showed the Jews that their Law was only a shadow of the clarity of our Faith, and of the happiness of this time of the Gospel, full of the grace and charity of God" (many conversos might have had some reservations about this), writes this historian. "He had a singular grace in opening to them the mysteries of these figures [prefiguration in the Bible], and removing from them the veil of Moses which they had over their hearts. . . ." Nevertheless, his success in converting Jews did not come easily, and the chronicler admits that they knew the Bible by heart and often argued with him, utilizing the interpretation of the rabbis, while he was preaching.[115]

Ironically, and tragically, Hernando himself was accused by his enemies of "Judaizing," and his family was arrested in 1506. He was acquitted of all charges against him in Rome the next year, but died soon after.[116]

Recent documents which have come to light reveal the probable cause of the absurd charges against Hernando. He played a prominent role in the denunciation of the excesses and fraud of the Inquisitor of Córdoba, Diego Rodríguez Lucero (see Chapter 7). Hernando and his sister and nieces (erroneously "brother" and "nephews" in the text) and other members of his household all testified before the Catholic Monarchs against the Inquisition.

Lucero lost no time in retaliating. As an example, he arrested an obviously innocent woman and accused her of having a house known to be a "synagogue," and tortured her to force her to "confess" that "many persons" in the house of the archbishop (Hernando) gathered to hear a "Jewish sermon." Among those supposedly present were the bishops of Almería, Jaén, and "other bishops." [117]

Finally, it has been suggested that Hernando was author of an interesting treatise in defense of the conversos, the argument of which is entirely historical. It notes that Spaniards are descendants of either Mozarabs (which he erroneously described as Christians "mixed with," and the implication is deliberately ambiguous, Muslims) or Jews converted at the time of the Visigoths, or a very few "nobles of the mountains," descended from the legendary Christians who fled to the Asturias when the Muslims conquered Spain. In other words, none of them have anything to boast of in their "old Christian" lineage. In fact, however, it is evident from the text of this rare work that it was written considerably later than Hernando's period, at least in the following generation. [118]

Conclusions

As conversion increased throughout the latter half of the fourteenth and the entire fifteenth centuries, Jewish power continually declined and was replaced by that of the conversos. The conversos were able to attain not only positions in government which had previously been held by Jews—as tax officials, treasurers, etc.—but even higher posts, up to and including those of chancellors of the realm. There was, moreover, an entirely new area of power open to conversos which obviously had never been available to Jews, and that was the Church. The merely "average" pious conversos became in increasing numbers monks and nuns, while others held minor posts as archdeacons and the like. However, those with particular ambition and learning rose to the highest ranks, becoming bishops and even archbishops.

The political (socioeconomic) hostility to the conversos which had already emerged early in the fifteenth century no doubt encouraged an increasing separation of conversos from their Jewish origins and produced a certain hostility on their part toward Jews. The most learned and pious of the conversos, again, exhibited the well-known phenomenon of the zeal of the convert for his new faith and the hatred of his former one. This hatred manifested itself in several polemical works written by them, but these polemics were "anti-*Judaism*" rather than "anti-*Jewish*." The emergence of true anti-Semitism in the campaign against conversos in the late fifteenth century was eventually to have repercussions which would prove disastrous for the Jews as well, resulting in their expulsion.

The converso response to the political crises and riots of the earlier part of the century and to the increased anti-Semitism of the latter part (as we shall see in Chapter 7) was to increase their power base both in the Church and in government. Throughout the latter half of the century, and continuing into the sixteenth century, we find this trend. Although technically beyond the scope of the present study, it is interesting to scan briefly some of the documentation of the Monarchs for the early sixteenth century to see the degree to which converso officials continued to play an important role. The Coronels were, of course, particularly important. Fernand Núñez Coronel, the former Meir *Melamed,* continued his role as tax official, for example for the taxes of Jerez at least until 1503 (he may have died prior to 1506). In 1505 a certain Juan Daza (possibly also a converso, judging by the name and from other sources concerning him), a merchant at court, sought satisfaction for damages suffered as a result of Núñez Coronel's failure to pay for merchandise purchased for the queen in the years 1492–94. Pedro Núñez Coronel, possibly a son or at least a relative, was *arrendador* of taxes for Medina del Campo in 1508. There are references to Fernand's heirs in the years 1522–24, and to his son Luis, preacher (thus, a cleric or friar) of the emperor Carlos V.[119]

Also, there are several records of payments ordered by the Monarchs to recent converts (1492 or after). Some refer to funds taken from conversos, however, as in the 1512 order for payment to a person to be indicated by Cardinal Cisneros to repair some church, from the funds of "newly converted Christians" as authorized by an otherwise unknown papal bull conceding to the Catholic Monarchs two-thirds of the *diezmos* (tithes) of conversos.[120]

Indeed, the Monarchs may have justified such a claim on converso Church revenue on the basis of not only their open support of the missionary campaigns of the Dominicans and Franciscans (although they did not, it appears, have a planned policy of proselytization anything like that of Fernando I of Aragón-Catalonia, for example), but also their constant efforts on behalf of the conversos. An example of these efforts, as early as 1484, was Fernando's personal intervention in the case of a converso in tiny Borja in Aragón who owned some houses in the *judería* in which he could no longer live, not being a Jew, and which he could not sell, because only Jews could own houses in the Jewish quarter and the king was "certain" that no Jew would buy from a converso.[121]

That statement in itself, even if we lacked the evidence of hundreds of other examples which prove the fact, demonstrates another aspect of the "converso crisis" of the fifteenth century which we have discussed repeatedly: the hostile attitude of Jews to the hated converts. This social and economic isolation must have served to further force the conversos into the creation of a minority subculture, accepted by neither Christians nor Jews, which led to the myth of the "Marrano," and resulted finally in patently false charges before the Inquisition, charges which Jews as well as "old Christians" were only too willing to make.

That, however, belongs to a later chapter. We are still at this point in the "age of enlightenment" which, in this case, was to precede the "dark ages" of that anti-Semitism which culminated in the Inquisition and the Expulsion.

As part of that age, the literary and cultural contributions of the conversos merit special consideration, and this is an area which so far has not received the attention it deserves. Along with the work of poets, musicians, novelists, and playwrights, we shall also examine the historical writing of conversos and the important topic of converso contributions to the emerging "humanism" of the fifteenth century, and then survey (the first time this has ever been done) the special case of converso polemics against Judaism.

6

Converso Authors, Chroniclers, and Polemicists

One of the most interesting aspects of the converso phenomenon is the extent of the conversos' contribution to Spanish culture in the fifteenth century and later. The majority of the chronicles were written by conversos, as we already know. Literature was also dominated by them: poetry, drama, novels. Another area of great significance in the developing "humanism" of Renaissance Spain was the translation of classical works, again dominated by conversos. It is, in fact, no exaggeration to say simply that the history of Spanish literature in its "Golden Age" (fifteenth through seventeenth centuries) is virtually the history of converso writers and descendants of conversos. Even Saint Teresa of Ávila, patron saint of Spain and a major author, was a granddaughter of a converso, Juan Sánchez of Toledo (perhaps the one recorded in León Tello's documents of the Jews of Toledo). While considerable imagination is necessary to detect traces of any Jewish "influence" in her writings, this did not deter the Inquisition from suspecting her.[1]

Indeed, the only areas of cultural activity not totally dominated by conversos were religious writing, music, and art. While conversos or their descendants did make major contributions in theology and other religious writing (the Santa María family, San Juan de la Cruz, Juan de Ávila, Benito Arias Montano, and others), this was still an area primarily of "old Christian" activity. In art, the fifteenth and early sixteenth centuries were the period of Spanish genius, almost equaling that of the Italian masters. In music, composers like Morales (also condemned by the Inquisition, but not for "Judaizing"), Vitoria, and others were unequaled, or certainly unexcelled, anywhere in Europe. Yet we know of only two conversos in the entire history of Spanish music, Juan del Encina and possibly Francisco de la Torre (ca. 1470–ca. 1520).[2] This absence of conversos was certainly not because Jews themselves had been uninterested in music, for in addition to the purely liturgical music composed by Jews we know of several secular Jewish musicians in medieval Spain. Why this interest did not carry over among conversos is unclear.

With regard to artists, obviously no converso ever approached the glories of Velázquez, unless those who have argued that "el Greco" was of Jewish background can prove their case (in any event, he was not Spanish). Nevertheless, we know of some converso artists: Juan de Leví (1403) and his brother Guillén, Juan de Altabás, condemned by the Inquisition, and Pedro Salom (or Johan Çalom), already mentioned in connection with converso bookbinders.[3]

However, when we turn to literature the situation is quite otherwise. As noted, virtually *all* of the important writers, poets, and dramatists were either themselves conversos or of immediate converso descent. Many Hispanists, indeed, have claimed to detect a "converso mentality" in the literature. Lacking any precise definition, this term seems to smack at least of romanticism, if not worse, and is largely nonsense. It would seem that whatever is found reflected in Spanish literature of the period is simply labeled "converso mentality." What would be required is a detailed analysis, so far not attempted, of the writers and their work as a whole group, with a view to determining what, if any, Jewish or "converso" influences may have been at work. Amador de los Ríos made the suggestive remark that a certain Hebrew style may be detected in the Spanish writing of some converso authors (see his chapters on some of them in his *Estudios*), which suggestion has never been followed up by philologists thoroughly trained both in Hebrew and in late medieval Spanish literary style. As to "converso mentality," if there are any peculiar specific traits, this would have to be established by careful comparison with the few non-converso literary works written in the same period.[4] Until such work has been attempted, it is best to abandon such meaningless generalizations.

The phenomenon of converso dominance in the writing of chronicles is no less surprising than in belles lettres. Jews in the medieval period in general, and in Spain in particular, were singularly uninterested in historical writing, and the reading of chronicles was generally considered a waste of time or worse. The very few that were produced were self-serving polemics or of the "lachrymose" kind, detailing massacres, etc. Yet suddenly we find converso historians demonstrating great insight and commendable literary style in their chronicles; certainly there can be no question of "Jewish influence" here.[5]

Converso Historians

We have already discussed the conversion of the famous Santa María-Cartagena family. This dynasty, lasting for centuries, produced numerous writers as well as learned religious figures, men and women.

The most famous of the brothers of Solomon ha-Levy (Pablo de Santa María), who converted with him, was Alvar García de Santa María (ca. 1380–1460). Like his brother, he also held important political posts under Juan II of Castile, and in 1408 was already declared a noble, *regidor*, secretary of the royal council, and official chronicler of the king.

His *Crónica* of Juan has already been cited above in connection with the Sarmiento affair, in which his involvement was detailed. In addition, some authorities have attributed part of the *Crónica* of Pedro López de Ayala to Alvar García (the years 1406–20), and part to another converso, the poet Juan de Mena (the years 1420–35). Some have also attributed the *Crónica* of Juan II to this poet rather than to Alvar García. It is interesting that the *Vida beata*, by Juan de Lucena, a contemporary, also a converso poet, calls Mena "the chief chronicler" of the king (presumably Enrique IV, to whom Lucena dedicated this work). A probably unreliable source calls Lucena himself "chronicler of the Catholic Monarchs."[6]

As mentioned previously, even Pablo de Santa María composed a *Suma de crónicas de España* (unpublished), and there is also a brief summary of the years 1343–1454 attributed to him and/or to his son Alonso de Cartagena.[7] (Pablo died in 1435.)

Certain it is that Alonso wrote *Alegaçoes feitos contra os portugueses a favor de rei de Castilla e Leão . . . sobre conquista das Canarias*, defending the king's conquest of the Canary Islands. But his most important history was a general chronicle, *Regum hispanorum, romanorum imperatorum, summorum pontificum necnon regum francorum anacephaleosis* (Granada, 1545).[8]

The previously mentioned Gonzalo García de Santa María (d. after 1510) of Zaragoza, also a member of the family, composed at the request of Fernando II a chronicle of his father Juan II of Aragón-Catalonia (*Joannis Secundi Aragonum regis vita*). In addition, he "revised" Gauberto Fabricio de Vagad's chronicle of the kings of Aragón-Catalonia, published in 1499, which actually was only a translation of that work from Latin into Castilian.[9]

The important Castilian converso historians include the previously discussed Fernando de Pulgar, Diego de Valera, and Alonso de Palencia (1423–92), who at the age of sixteen was already a disciple of Alonso de Cartagena. Until 1453 he was in Rome, then in Seville in the service of Archbishop Alfonso de Fonseca. He became the Latin secretary and chronicler of Enrique IV, completing his *Decadas* (so called because each section covers roughly a decade) in Latin shortly after 1477. Although he was chronicler of Enrique, he despised him and most of the nobility around him, and his work is, as Sánchez Alonso remarked, "a constant condemnation" of the monarch. Indeed, it is responsible for much of the mystique of that king, including the charges of homosexuality and assorted excesses.

Very interesting, in light of his converso status, is Alonso's denunciation of the immortality and decadence of the Holy See, and of ecclesiastical corruption in general.[10]

His second work was the chronicle of the Catholic Monarchs, whom he served with much more enthusiasm. We have already observed that he had little to say about individual conversos, although he is the major source for accounts of the anti-converso riots in Andalucía at the end of the reign of Enrique.

In addition to his official chronicles, he wrote at least ten "books" (i.e., one history in ten parts) on ancient Spain and another ten on the Carthaginian-Roman period, and a total of fourteen separate extant works. His style of writing, moreover, is exceptional; almost modern in characterization of people and description of events, with very sound insights.

Diego de Valera (ca. 1412–88) wrote *Crónica de España* (1482, 1467); *Memorial de diversas hazañas* (chronicle of Enrique IV); *Crónica de los reyes católicas* (his most important work); *Doctrinal de principes,* a political treatise; *Epistolas;* and other previously cited treatises. As a historian he is of far less importance than either Alonso de Palencia or Fernando de Pulgar. As with the former, however, his *forte* was his writing style, and this is most evident in his treatises.

He was the son of Alonso Chirino, a converso physician. He quickly rose to positions of ever-increasing responsibility, and was in charge of the Armada for Isabel and Fernando. In a letter (*Epistolas* 70–74) he reminds them that during the war with Portugal he "armed two ships" and sent them to the command of his son, Charles de Valera (note the French name), who headed the expedition against Guinea. The four hundred slaves Charles captured were seized by the duque de Medina Sidonia, and Diego complains about this. He also complains that although he and Charles were in charge of the Armada for three years he has not received any salary (aside from the not-inconsiderable sum of 10,000 *mrs.*), but lives on the 25,000 *mrs.* which the same duke against whom he complained provides him annually. Diego also wrote a *Crónica* on Enrique IV, but the manuscript, at Seville as late as 1833 and thereafter at the Academia de la Historia in Madrid, is apparently no longer extant.[11]

Brian Tate has attempted to argue that "nationalism" in Spain was introduced by the fifteenth-century *Latin* chronicles; he explained this on the grounds of the "higher level of culture" and "greater sensitivity" to foreign opinion on the part of Latin (as opposed to Romance) authors, but denied that it had any connection with the emergence of humanism.[12] Leaving aside the historical errors in this analysis, e.g., the fact that "nationalism" generally emerged in Spain much earlier than the fifteenth century, the argument is erroneous in the first place. It is not in the fifteenth-century chronicles but in those of the fourteenth century that we discover clear examples of nationalist sentiment. That expression first appears not in Latin but precisely in

Romance *crónicas* and other writings.[13] Finally, the emergence of humanism, which also was a phenomenon of the fourteenth and not the fifteenth
century, most certainly is connected with this new nationalism. There can
be little doubt that these writers, conversos and others, were influenced, for
example, by the "pro-Spanish" sentiments of the great Roman writers of
classical Spain. On the other hand, the sense of unity of Spain and of the
Spanish people was an almost universal theme throughout medieval Spain.

The interesting aspect of this phenomenon in the fifteenth century which
needs to be considered, and so far has not been, is the prevalence of nationalist sentiment in the writings of conversos (to which must be added, of
course, Alonso de Cartagena's previously mentioned praise of Spain and its
precedence over England at the Council of Basel).[14]

Space does not permit a detailed examination of this question here, but
it is clear that the *crónicas,* no less than other writings, of the conversos
definitely exhibit such nationalist sentiments. Certainly it is not to be argued
that the conversos demonstrated more nationalist sentiment than non-
conversos, but since the preponderance of historical and other writing of the
period is, in fact, by conversos, the conclusion is inescapable that they
played a major role in that expression. Conversos very definitely considered
themselves not only Christians but Spaniards, and to some extent at least
the two were seen not only as inseparable but as the ultimate definition of
what a Christian was; i.e., to be a Spaniard was to be the paragon of Christianity. Was there more to it? Were converso authors perhaps attempting to
convince an antagonistic "old Christian" society of their loyalty, both to
their faith and to their nation? Undoubtedly such was the case.

"Jewish Sympathies" of Converso Writers

We have already seen that, with a few exceptions, relations between Jews
and conversos were strained and that they tended to avoid each other, and
all the more so once the "old Christian" enemies of conversos began making
charges that such contacts were taking place and endangering the "purity"
of the faith.

Given this situation, as well as the conversos' desire to advance themselves both socially and economically in Christian society, it is understandable that we find little evidence of any sympathetic attitude to Jews in
converso writing. In fact, what characterizes the chronicles of converso historians, particularly, is that in contrast to previous chronicles written by
"old Christians" there is scarcely any mention of Jews at all. For the modern
historian, this unfortunate fact deprives us of what is usually one of the most
valuable and informative sources concerning the Jews; namely, the refer-

ences in the chronicles. Inasmuch as most of the chronicles of the fifteenth
century were written by conversos, there is little or no information in them
about Jews in this period, unlike earlier periods.

Diego de Valera, for example, hardly mentions Jews at all, while defending the conversos, as we shall see.

Fernando de Pulgar, by contrast, showed some sympathy for the suffering
of Jews in Málaga, at the hands of the Muslims, during the Christian siege
of that city in 1487.[15] We have already discussed his attitude to conversos
and the "Judaizing heresy." It is of interest that the converso chroniclers
avoid references to Jews even with regard to important incidents or prominent men. Jewish officials, of whom there were many, especially in the reign
of Enrique IV and even in that of Fernando and Isabel, are never mentioned.
The result is that we must rely entirely on "old Christian" writers, and on
other sources, for any information about the Jews.

Alonso de Palencia never mentions Jews at all in his long chronicles covering the reigns of Enrique and the Catholic Monarchs (to 1478), even in
the case of events to which he must have been an eyewitness, such as the
Jewish festivities at the reception of Fernando and Isabel when they came to
Seville.

On the other hand, prominent converso writers, as we have seen, rushed
to the defense of conversos when they were attacked, whether physically as
in the riots or simply in polemics written by "old Christian" anti-Semites.
Non-conversos also wrote defenses, as we recall from the Sarmiento affair.
Such defenses were written by Alonso de Oropesa (to be discussed in connection with the Inquisition), Lope de Barrientos, and Alonso Díaz de Montalvo, in his previously cited glosses.

Conversos who penned such defenses included Fernán Díaz de Toledo,
Alonso de Cartagena, Diego de Valera, Alonso de Palencia (in his chronicles), Hernando de Talavara, and Juan de Torquemada (a possible descendant of conversos).[16] An important example of a non-converso writer who
spoke out on behalf of conversos is Fernán Pérez de Guzmán, who used
his description of Pablo de Santa María as an opportunity to defend them
against the attacks of those who claimed that they "are not Christians, nor
was their conversion good [faithful] or useful." He admits that some, especially those few converted by force, are not likely to be as good Christians as
persons born and raised in the faith, just as the disciples of Jesus were not at
first very good believers. However, he does not *generally* believe this to be
true, and adds that he personally knows many who converted of their own
free will and are faithful Christians. Several have entered monasteries and religious orders and instituted needed religious reforms. Others, like Pablo and
his son Alonso de Cartagena, have written books "of great utility" for the
Christian faith (he might have said they also contain vicious attacks on the
Jewish "faith"). If some people suspect conversos of having done such things as

they are accused of, either out of fear or in order to find favor with kings or priests, he replies that zeal for the faith is not so strong now as to produce any such fear among conversos (this was, of course, before the Inquisition).

Nevertheless, he recommends that children of conversos be separated from their parents to ensure that they be raised with the proper zeal. That was a step which the Inquisition, in fact, was to take. Descendants of Christians who convert to Islam in Muslim Spain are so loyal to their new faith, he notes, that they do not return to Christianity even when conquered; why should descendants of Jewish converts to Christianity not similarly remain loyal to the faith? [17]

It should be mentioned that his lengthy poetic composition *Tratado de vicios y virtudes (Las setecientas)* was dedicated to Alvar García de Santa María.

The influence of converso writers on such impeccable "old Christians" as Pérez de Guzmán may be seen in his library. Of the twenty-nine books he owned, five are definitely by conversos (Alonso de Cartagena, Alvar García de Santa María, Diego de Valera), and possibly others as well. [18]

In his important treatise on nobility, the converso Diego de Valera discussed whether converts to Christianity who were nobles (or of high estate) before their conversion retain their status afterward, and answered that not only do they retain it, they increase it to the level of "theological nobility," the highest level. Even though a Jew or Muslim may live virtuously according to his "law or sect," the virtues of the unbaptized are not to be compared with this "theological nobility." Were converts to lose their former status, they would suffer damage rather than enhancement as a result of their conversion. Furthermore, conversion and baptism remove all traces of whatever bad or evil the convert may have done formerly, "not only the guilt but even more the punishment" for which is remitted. However, whatever good they previously may have done is retained.

"And that among the Jews and Muslims there are nobles as among the Christians is obvious to the wise, even though the ignorant think the contrary," he adds. As proof of the nobility of the Jews he cites the fourth chapter of Deuteronomy, "which is another nation so noble?" (Deut. 4.8; *inclytus* according to the Vulgate). In which nation, indeed, were such nobles, for all the prophets, patriarchs, and apostles were Jews, "and finally our fortunate lady St. Mary and her blessed son, God and true man, our redeemer, who chose this lineage [Jewish] as the most noble."

After continuing his poetic praise of various biblical heroes, he recalls that the Jews, it is true, not only lost all their honor because of the "great sin" of not recognizing Christ, they also remain "in the yoke of servitude of all the peoples." However, once converted to the "true knowledge" they regain all their former status, like "those who go out of captivity and recover the liberty they lost."

If those who have converted do not seem to have "recovered" their honor and dignity, strength of body and heart, it is not surprising, "for who now is so powerful that, having been a thousand years in captivity, and going out of it, is able briefly [quickly] to recover?"

However, many royal families are descended from Jews who converted, such as the kings of England, descended from Joseph of Arimathea (!), or the first duke of Austria who was a Jew who became a Christian and "from whom many emperors have come, and today are descended from him the dukes of Austria," or the "noble Gothic kings of the lineage of Abraham, and I do not doubt that many similar examples could be found if we were to diligently search the ancient histories."[19] The legend that the kings of England were descendants of Joseph of Arimathea had already been dismissed by Alonso de Cartagena, it should be noted.[20]

Converso Poets and Satire

Satire was used in the medieval period, as in other eras, as a very effective weapon of criticism. The previously mentioned anti-converso treatise known as the *Alborayco,* comparing conversos to Muḥammad's legendary animal which was neither the one thing nor the other, is an example of a heavy-handed type of satire.

As early as 1408 a satirical work appeared in Portugal; the pretended "renewal" of a law of Alfonso X prohibiting Jews and conversos from holding office (whether this had any influence on the mention of such a law in connection with the Sarmiento affair is doubtful).[21]

Sometime around 1449–50 there was a satirical document purporting to be a letter of Juan II of Castile to a nobleman which uses the term "Marranos" (in fact, prohibited by that very king), granting a "license" to this nobleman to be a Marrano and to use all their "subtleties, arts, traits, and deceits." It also refers to the supposed advice of a previous king to his son (there is no reason to assume, as did the editor of the text, that Alfonso X is meant) that "they" (Jews? conversos?) should not be made treasurers, "nor should any of the 'Pharisees' be taken as *mayordomo* of his houses or councillor of his councils, because the said Marranos, 'Pharisees,' Hebrews, and Sadducees" do many dangerous and harmful things and take the property of their masters for their own uses.

As a Marrano, the "king" promises, the nobleman will "adorn the house of the Torah and adore its image," marry only his relatives, and "not believe, as they do not believe, that which the holy mother Church believes, holds, and preaches . . . [but believe] that there is no other world, except birth and death, as the aforesaid Marranos hold and affirm against the truth." Similarly, he should keep the Sabbath and work on Sunday, lighting candles the night before the Sabbath and washing the plates and utensils and eating special food, or *adafina*.

The "king" further orders that the nobleman's descendants should endeavor to become priests, so that hearing the confessions of "old Christians" they will know their secret sins, and also become doctors and surgeons so they may kill the "old Christians," as Marranos are accustomed to do! It is also good to participate in festivals of the Jews and drink *vino de la baraha* (Heb. *berakhah,* wine of the blessing, which probably refers to wedding feasts). As mentioned previously, from the reference to Pedro Sarmiento in this account, it is clear that this satirical attack originated among his supporters.[22]

The late fifteenth century saw an increasing number of satirical attacks in poetry on conversos. We have already mentioned such verses against the disliked converso official of Enrique IV, Diego Arias Dávila (1436–97), in the *Coplas del Provincial* (possibly the work of Antón de Montoro and Alonso de Palencia, both conversos) and in the *Cancionero* of Gómez Manrique. Other conversos who were satirized in the former work include Juan de Rojas, Alvaron Pérez de Orozco, Juan de Estúñiga, Pedro Girón (who nevertheless was probably not of converso origin), Juan de Valenzuela (the powerful prior of San Juan), Alvar Gómez de Zamora, a fiscal agent of the royal council.[23] Even Fernañ Alvárez de Toledo, the very powerful conde de Alba, is said to have "believed in the true God and was a rabbi in His law."

One of those so accused was said to be "one-fourth Marrano and three-fourths sodomite." The accusation of homosexuality, whether true or false, was common against many at the court of Enrique IV. A recent study has shown that there were forty-nine accusations of this kind generally in the *Coplas del Provincial,* but of the conversos mentioned there a mere 12.5 percent were said to be "homosexuals," whereas 36 percent of the "old Christians" mentioned were so accused.[24] The infamous Juan de Pacheco, certainly not a converso (as often claimed), and Álvaro de Luna, who was, were both accused publicly of this "crime."

Sometimes converso poets were able perhaps to "defuse" such accusations by identifying with them, as in the case of the famous poet Antón de Montoro, to be discussed below. As we shall see, in any case, converso poets were not reluctant to use such accusations against each other. An important element of the satire of the converso poets of the fifteenth century, indeed, was the accusation that their rivals were secret "Jews." Alleging sexual misconduct against enemies, particularly Jews, is an old *topos*.

Juan Alfonso de Baena

The earliest known converso poet is one about whom virtually no information is available aside from what can be gleaned from his work. He was a scribe, or administrative official of some sort, in the court of Juan II of Castile (hardly a "historian," as he has been called). His editor stated that "without any doubt" he was born in Andalucía. We know, in fact, that he was born near Seville, probably in Marchena.[25]

He had at least one brother, Francisco, also an official (of Diego Gómez de Rivera, *adelantado* of Andalucía). Francisco is represented by one poem in the *Cancionero*, of no historical significance (no. 105).

Juan Alfonso collected what he considered to be the best representative examples of poems by his contemporaries, to which he added several of his own, into a *Cancionero* for the amusement of the king and his son Enrique. The work was begun around 1406, but most of the compilations were from the years 1430–40, with parts added between 1442 and 1449.

A lengthy introduction was composed, a dedication to the king, completed apparently around 1433. As all previous editions of this very important and interesting work are faulty, a separate edition based on manuscripts has been published, with a complete English translation (i.e., of this introduction only).[26]

The editor justly compares Baena with the more skilled and far more significant converso poet Juan de Mena, who dedicated his major work, *Laberinto de fortuna*, to the same king in 1443. While Mena's style is obviously superior, Baena's is certainly not lacking in grace, and the *Dezir*, as the introduction is called, is of great interest for the historical details concerning the great Alfonso VIII of Castile, the early years of the life and conditions of the kingdom during the reign of Juan II, and incidentally for information on pharmacy and medicine.

It is interesting to observe that, in the long list of classical literature, scientific, philosophical, and legal works which the author claims to have studied, he mentions the "Old Testament," which he says he read but which is so "deep a cave" that he doubts any can understand it. This is, perhaps, revealing insight into the typical lack of knowledge of Jewish tradition by fifteenth-century conversos.

The editor-translator of the *Dezir* has also correctly called attention to the interesting fact that one of the main purposes of both Baena's and Mena's work was to glorify and defend the *condestable* Álvaro de Luna (of a converso family). Needless to say, such support ultimately did nothing to save Álvaro from his fate, nor did the young king appear to heed at all (if he ever read) the sound advice of his poets.

Baena exchanged several sarcastic poems with a certain Gonzalo de Quadros, in one of which he said he knew the man was in love, but whether with a Christian, Jew, or Muslim was unclear. In another he noted that Gonzalo liked to travel and live in various countries, but the poet expressed his desire to know his true belief, "for it is notorious that you live in Zamora / and others tell me you believe in the Torah" (no. 451, verses 13–14; cf. no. 449).

This backfired on Baena himself when a poet who was his enemy accused him of desiring to marry either the Muslim Usmena or the "Jewess Aben Xuxena or Cohena." The names rhyme, of course, and are probably generic, as the family name Aben Xuxen or Xuxan (Ibn Susan) was very common, as was Cohen. This poet suggested that Baena enjoyed eating and having pleasure with these women, and also with the Muslims of Gibraltar, with whom he ate *çahena* (according to Cantera's note, a food popular among Moroccan Jews on Sundays; it is probably therefore derived from Ar. *ṣaḥn;* thus a kind of ground dish?).[27]

The poet Alfonso Alvarez de Villasandino, not a converso as sometimes stated, who is the most represented in the *Cancionero,* attacked the converso Alfonso Ferrandez (Fernández) Semuel in three poems. The heading of the first calls him "the most witty madman [*loco*] in the world," and the poet says of him that never has there been such a *mesumad* (Heb. *meshumad;* the word became common in medieval Spanish) as he, nor is there likely to be. He says that Semuel has been a Jew forty or more years, "Samuel fyde Salta atras" (an allusion to his former name?). He makes fun of him as he was in his youth and is now in old age.

The final poem is a satirical "testament," written by the poet for this converso, in which after piously leaving gifts to the Church and for the "Crusade" (against the Muslims), he leaves money for the Jews so they will not have to work on the Sabbath (note the anti-Jewish, as well as anti-converso, slander here). He is to be buried with a cross, a Qur'ān, and a Torah, and he instructs that "some *ssamas*" (Heb. *shamash,* custodian of a synagogue and sometimes reader in the services) read in a *Homas* (Heb. *ḥumash,* Pentateuch) and sing a *huynna* (hymn? possibly Heb. *qinah,* lamentation) and a *pysmon* (Heb. *pizmon,* religious poem). He then appoints as executor of his estate a "Jew of good deeds" named Jacob Çidaryo, whom he orders to arrange all of this as a sign of *çedaquá* (Heb. *ṣedaqah,* mercy, justice) and to recite a *tefylá* (Heb. *tefilah,* prayer) until he is buried in the cemetery (no. 142).

There is, incidentally, nothing remarkable about an "old Christian" knowing this much Hebrew, as many Hebrew words were known already in medieval Spanish.

Another Jew, or converso, who aroused this poet's wrath and also that of Baena himself was "Daviuelo," or Davihuelo, against whom there are several poetic complaints, including two addressed by Villasandino to Álvaro de Luna (nos. 183, 184; cf. also nos. 207, 393, 452, and 461; the last three are by Baena). I have been unable to identify this "don Davi," as Baena calls him. He was not a known official of the king, either Jew or converso, and yet must have been an important person.

Important conversos do appear in the *Cancionero,* however. One of these was Ferrán (Ferrant) Manuel de Lando. He addressed a very interesting poem to fray Alfonso de la Monja, master of the Dominican Convent of San Pablo in Seville (later to be the center of the Inquisition), asking whether God existed as a "Trinity" before the incarnation of Christ. The reply, naturally, was that he did (no. 281). Charles Fraker considered this poem a reflection of "Jewish anti-Incarnation polemic," but in fact it was merely a statement of honest confusion on the part of the poet (cf. similar questions by Ferrán Sánchez de Calavera, certainly not a converso, to fray Diego de Valencia, who was, no. 526, and Diego's reply, no. 527). Ferrán Manuel was certainly no heretic, as can be seen from his hymn to the Virgin (no. 568), nor is it likely that he would have known of any Jewish polemic.[28]

Baena attacked this poet in several poems, to which de Lando replied in kind. In one of these, Baena called him "of those of Çadique or of Açuayca" of Seville (no. 361, verses 1–2). "Çadique" is definitely recognizable as a Jewish name, and while no such family is known from the sources concerning Jews in Seville, the name (also Abençadiq, Abençadaque) was common in Toledo, for example. "Açuayca" is more problematic, but could conceivably be a Jewish name.

Ferrán Manuel did not permit his opponent to forget his own converso status, however, calling him "bathed in the water of holy baptism" and, ironically, "pure" (*lindo*) gentleman (nos. 370, 371).

Fray Diego de Valencia (i.e., Valencia de don Juan, in León, where in 1391 the synagogue was totally destroyed by Ferrant Martínez and his gang) was a converso Franciscan theologian and considered to be a very good poet (Ferrán Manuel calls him "crown of the troubadors," no. 376). He was chosen "judge" in the poetic debate between Baena and Ferrán Manuel (no. 377).

One of his own poems was directed against another converso of León called Juan de España, who had apparently been denounced by the Jewish *aljama* (also of Valencia de don Juan?) "for the guilt of Barzilai." This enigmatic statement may refer to Ezra 2.61–62, where priests of that line were declared unclean because they could not find their family records (another possibility, also related to family impurity, would be 2 Sam. 21.8).[29]

"We," the poet continues, were all frightened, "masters, rabbis, and *cohenim*" (priests). The words "*sofar ahenim*" (verse 8) are beyond explanation, but Cantera is certainly correct that "*beçin*" is the Hebrew plural *beṣim*, "eggs," euphemistically "testicles," and therefore Juan de España's "guilt" was that he had none (either literally, perhaps, or figuratively). Furthermore, and this is the biblical allusion mentioned above, he was judged to be a *manzel* (Heb. *mamzer*, bastard), and the "wise men of the Talmud, who are called *çedaquin*" (*ṣadiqim*, righteous), ruled that one without testicles is "not healthy" and that, just as one who is not circumcised (which is the meaning of *mila*, and not as the editor explained it) may not marry.

This ruling, he says, is found in *Pellim* (which appears to be Heb. *pelilim,* in the sense of "judgments, laws"; in fact, the ruling is found in *Yevamot* 70a and in Moses b. Maimon, *M.T., Qedushah,* "Isurey bi'ah" 16.1–3; it is possible that the *Mishneh Torah* was popularly known as "*pelilim*"), by *peçuquen* (*pesuqim,* verses) and by gloss. If Juan does not understand all of this (apparently; Cantera suggested that *caham* is Heb. *ḥakam,* wise), the poet tells him to go to hell (*guehnom;* Heb. *gehenom*) with the wrath of the Almighty (*Saday;* Heb. *Shaday*).[30]

Fernán Sánchez de Calavera (not Talavera), who was *comendador* of the Order of Calatrava for Villarubia (1407–43), and probably not a converso, addressed a theological poem to several important people, among whom was Pedro López de Ayala, and each of them responded to it. The aforementioned Diego de Valencia, described as master of theology and of science, also replied (fray Alfonso de Medina, a Jeronimite, may or may not have been a converso; note also a converted Muslim, former physician of Diego Hurtado de Mendoza, the admiral of Castile, no. 522).[31]

Gonzalo Martínez de Medina, a *veinticuatro* (member of the council) of Seville in 1402, was a converso, brother of the poet Diego Martínez de Medina. The *Cancionero* contains also some poems by Gonzalo, including an interesting statement of faith which incorporates also the *ubi sunt* ("Where are they who lived before?") motif with references to the passing of famous men. His knowledge of history, classical writers, theology, and canon law is also evident in these poems (nos. 337–40 *bis*).

This collection is therefore the first in which satirical poetry against conversos, as well as poems written by conversos, is represented. It is important that we not make too much out of the satire found here, as very little is known about the social condition of conversos in Castile prior to the reign of Enrique IV. Certainly it is not permissible to generalize concerning the "insincere" nature of Baena's own conversion, for which there is absolutely no evidence, nor to draw analogies from the situation of the late fifteenth century, as some have done.[32]

These poems do, however, prepare us for the much sharper invective of converso satire in the period of Fernando and Isabel.

An interesting poem of Baena's which does not appear in his *Cancionero* was addressed to the king as a "satisfaction," or rebuttal, in defense of the converso Juan Marmolejo (related, certainly, to the previously mentioned Fernández Marmolejo family) against the poet Juan Agraz. Of interest particularly are the following lines:

> I swear to you in truth
> that in the midst of the whole universe
> there is not found a converso

> so pervese
> that he does not believe in the Trinity
> nor in what the abbot [priest] says.

The lengthy poem tells allegorically of a *malsín* (Heb. *malshin*, informer) whom the poet met on the road in company with some others, and that they killed him because of his evil ways and "crazy" behavior. The poem concludes with a satiric attack, or analogy, on the evil ways of this "Marrano," clearly his opponent Juan Agraz, including sexual satire best not translated, a forerunner of the kind of sexual satire which we shall encounter in the poetry later in the century.[33]

Suero de Ribera

Another poet of approximately the same period (ca. 1435–40), probably not a converso, was Suero de Ribera. From his pen we have a sharp satire against a "gallant" (courtier, young gentleman) who was a converso, described as a "circumcised young man" (*mançebo;* literally an adolescent, but the word implies a young dandy), who never eats food with olive oil or butter (supposedly despised by Jews and conversos; butter, but not olive oil, would have been forbidden with meat dishes according to Jewish law), and who has a long and reddish nose. The poet accuses him of frequenting the synagogue and being "in the service" of the Torah and familiar with Hebrew.[34]

Antón de Montoro

By profession a tailor (hence his nickname "*El Ropero*"), this important poet of Córdoba was a converso, apparently baptized in his childhood. It has been argued whether his father, who also converted, was or was not Alonso de Baena Ventura and whether he was or was not related to the converso poet Juan Alfonso de Baena. The date of Montoro's birth is unknown; he died ca. 1477, rather a wealthy man. His mother, Teresa Rodríguez (whom he calls by her Jewish name, before her conversion, Jamila), was condemned posthumously by the Inquisition in 1487.[35]

In one of his poems, he clearly alludes to his Jewish ancestors, who used to "enter the holy Temple to adore their Creator," as he, Montoro, now confesses his sins in a church. In another, addressed satirically to his horse (one of his most amusing poems), he refers to his sons and nephews, his "poor father," and his mother doña Jamila, as well as a sister and daughter.[36]

A short satirical poem addressed to Gómez Dávila, an official of Córdoba (probably a relative of the renowned converso Arias Dávila family), complains that as a result of the royal order that only pork is to be sold in the market he must "starve," because of the oath of his ancestors (the Jewish prohibition against eating certain animals, including pigs).[37]

On another occasion a certain cavalier decided to insult him by sending him pork, to which he replied with the lines: "Don't you know I received a certificate of purity [cristiano lindo]?" and yet, he complains, the man sent him "one of those things which the rabbis cursed" (pork). In another poem he replied abusively (with implications of sexual immorality) to a woman who called him a "Jew."[38]

Most interesting, perhaps, is his previously mentioned willingness not only to make a joke of his Jewish ancestry, but also satirically to "accept" the vile insult of being called homosexual used frequently against conversos. In his poem, discussed previously in connection with the anti-converso riots, he used the term "queers" (putos; literally, male prostitutes) with regard to himself and other conversos. Even more astonishingly, in a poem to the intensely pious Queen Isabel he complains that no matter how he endeavors to prove his sincerity as a Christian, "I cannot lose the name of old queer, Jew," i.e., the taint of being a converso.[39]

Like many conversos, he had a particular veneration for Isabel, and addressed very laudatory poems to her, in one including almost as an afterthought mention also of Fernando.[40]

Several other conversos are mentioned in his poetry, some favorably and others not. Among the latter is especially Juan de Valladolid (Juan "el Poeta"), apparently a hated rival. He calls him every conceivable name: fat, a "Jew," robber, a merchant, "impure," "flower of infidels," etc.[41]

A certain military official (comendador) of the duque de Alba was the intermediary in this dispute, and he also despised Montoro, in one exchange of verses accusing him of "sleeping" (being a dreamer), perhaps in exotic isles, perhaps "in the land of Judea, with his stories of rabbis." He calls him an ignorant fool, who "very well knows what is cinqurpul" (cinquipul in another MS; i.e., Yom Kippur).[42] He concludes: "although you now are Antón, first you were Saul" (an allusion, perhaps, to his former Jewish name).

He also says that Montoro well knows what "Sabad" (Shabat, the Sabbath), is and always adores the Torah, and he calls him a "relative of Benjamin [and] brother of don Sentó" (the references are probably to Benjamin of Tudela, the famous traveler, and Shem Tov de Carrión, Jewish writer and poet). He also applies to him the prohibited term "Marrano," and calls him "in any case a Jew, circumcised by the hand of a rabbi."[43]

In still another satire against Montoro, the comendador accused him of many things, such as "observing the Sabbath with your uncles," eating only food ordained by (Jewish) law, "washing the hands from the mouth of a water jug" (Jewish custom required such washing before eating), and not eating pork. "You say over wine your holy Barahá [Heb. berakha, blessing] like one who knows it," and never eat what is prohibited by the rabbi, but only food "watched all night" (refers to *adafina*). The poet confused his customs, however, in accusing Montoro of eating unleavened bread on "the feast of booths" (Sukkot) instead of, correctly, Passover. "You are found enclosed on the good Major Fast [Yom Kippur] with tears and sadness," he says; and he accuses him of "going to *meldar* [this word, entirely Judeo-Spanish, can mean either "study" or "pray"], knowing the law."[44]

Juan de Valladolid

Juan de Valladolid, known as Juan *el Poeta,* "the poet," was another important converso, of interest primarily for the controversy he aroused. His dates are uncertain, but middle to late fifteenth century. He spent his early career in the service of Juan II of Navarre, and later was in Italy (Mantua and Milan, 1458–73, and then in Sicily). He returned to Spain and in 1481 was in Toledo with the archbishop, Alonso Carrillo. Later, he lived in Córdoba, where he came into conflict with Montoro.

Montoro addressed some satirical "advice" to him, in which he says that both he and Juan are Jews, of the same "tribe." In his stinging reply, Juan also dared to use the illicit term "Marrano," but called Montoro also a Jew, "more evil than Lucifer." This apparently caused Montoro to complain to the archbishop of Seville about Juan, and in addition to warn Queen Isabel against him.[45]

(Montoro was not an enemy of all converso poets, however, for he was a great admirer of Juan de Mena, to whom he addressed many laudatory poems.)[46]

A certain "gentleman" once sent a tunic to Juan de Valladolid, by a Jewish messenger, and with it some verses in which he said he sent it with a Jew, whom Juan would well understand, "for you are of one plumage, the Jew and you, Marrano; you will understand his language."[47]

Juan was the subject of several bitter attacks by other poets, no doubt using him as a symbol of conversos generally. Thus, the conde de Paredes (Pedro Manrique, son of Rodrigo, the Master of Santiago, and brother of Gómez) wrote some verses against him in which he said that the papal bull of protection Juan kept with him was easily converted by him into "Talmudic writing," as the holy church was converted, when he entered it, into a house of the "old law" (i.e., a synagogue), and the altar itself, at his touch, was turned into an *atayfor* (Muslim [Ar. *th-f-r?*] term for table) for *adafina*. The alb (white vestment of the priest) is turned into a scarlet gown by his touch, "like those of maestre Samaya / which you, Juan, over the tunic / wore in Toledo." This certainly refers to Shemaya (or Samaya) Lubel, the Jewish physician and official of Enrique IV, who from at least 1465 was chief justice of all the Jewish communities, and thus apparently entitled to wear the scarlet gown of a magistrate. It appears from these lines also that Juan was a priest, perhaps.[48]

When Juan was captured at sea by Muslim pirates from Fez, Pedro Manrique wrote him a very long and abusive poem, accusing him of desiring to go to Palestine, but of being willing to settle for "the house of Mecca, as long as it was not the court of Rome" (the Church). The usual sexual insults are present as well (89). He accused him of being "married" to three wives: Marina (María?), Jamila, and "Axa" (Aisha), common Christian, Jewish, and Muslim names, respectively, which are symbolically the cross, the Torah, and the Qur'ān (93). Thus, he is all three things at once: Muslim for fear of death (among the pirates), Christian for gain, but "Jew—for certain."[49]

Another poet accused him of asking in Naples if his son were Christian or "of the law of Moses," and that poet had already lost a nephew burned by the Inquisition (108–10).

Incidentally, at the end of this collection, in a sexually explicit satire written in the style of Juan de Mena's famous Laberinto, a new word is introduced into Spanish: casijudio, one who is an "almost-Jew," i.e., a converso (154).

Juan somehow apparently managed to arouse the ire of the entire powerful Manrique family. Not only Pedro but his brother Gómez, a renowned poet and nobleman, wrote several sarcastic attacks against Juan. Some of these came also at the time when Juan was a prisoner among the Muslims, and in one of them Gómez calls him a "Hebrew." Earlier, apparently, in Aragón, Juan had sent his own attack to Gómez, to which Gómez replied in the sharpest terms, calling Juan one who is "neither Jew nor Christian but excellent Marrano." To this, Juan replied in a similar vein, calling Gómez an offensive, or importunate, Marrano (marrano hito). Indeed, he closed the poem with the same refrain Gómez had used. Gómez Manrique, of course, was descended from a long line of nobility, but it is possible that Juan knew something about his mother's side of the family, perhaps, which has escaped the notice of modern scholars. In one of these poems to Gómez, incidentally, Juan reveals his contempt for Jews by saying he hunted a boar and put the suckling piglets in a synagogue.

On another occasion, Gómez ridiculed another Juan, a converso ("Jew") jester in the service of his brother Rodrigo Manrique.[50] In both poems he makes vulgar puns on the "hood," or foreskin, lacking in his opponents.

Another "gentleman" addressed some satirical verses against Juan, in which among other things he indicated his pleasure that "the end of a Marrano is a Jewish coffin"; i.e., he dies as a Jew and, presumably, does not receive the Christian reward.[51]

García de Astorga

Apparently this lesser-known poet was also a converso, and he too was accused of "sodomy," an accusation which in turn he applied to others. In a poem to the duque de Medina Sidonia, in reply to such an accusation, he explained that he was guilty of associating with a "bad companion," but not of what he was suspected of. The duke, no friend of conversos, replied that García and his companion had been "clothed" in one day "in a faith like livery in order to pass to Judea"; i.e., they were false conversos whose intent was to live as Jews, or perhaps literally to flee to Palestine.[52]

On another occasion, he sent a pig to a friend, apparently a converso, which the latter sold. García then wrote him some sarcastic verses, in which he said, "Much better it would have been to eat it, and at night vomit it when none could see." He concluded that it was well known that this man "attacks neither old pigs nor Marranos nor suckling pigs, even if he catches them in his hand."[53]

(It is perhaps this "García" who is satirized in the *Coplas del Provincial* as not knowing his real father, for he is the "son of Joel.")

Juan Alvarez Gato

Juan Alvarez Gato (ca. 1430/40–ca. 1509) is another probable converso poet. Although he lived in Madrid, he appears to have been related to the Gato, or Abengato, Jewish family of Toledo (he had a certain connection with Toledo, as in 1480 when he was *mayordomo* of the Convent of San Clemente there and acted on its behalf in a complaint involving the converso official Pedro Arias Dávila). Indeed, it has been asserted that his father was Juan Alvarez, an official of Toledo.[54] He was himself in the service of the powerful Dávila family, first Diego Arias and then his son Pedro, and later also in the service of the Mendozas of Guadalajara.

The editor of his works, who did not suspect his converso origin, wrote that "his religiosity is not as effusive nor as sincere as that of later masters, nor as that of his contemporaries and friends; it is a 'lay mysticism,' so to speak, worldly and philosophical."[55] Nevertheless, most of his poems are religious, with some few of an amorous nature. He was strongly influenced by Hernando de Talavera, the famous monk possibly of converso origin, who was later confessor to Isabel and archbishop of Granada, although there is no proof that Gato was related to him, as has been claimed.[56] Gato married Catalina Alvarez, probably a daughter of the duque de Alba (or, in an unproven hypothesis of Márquez Villanueva, the sister of Fernán Alvarez de Toledo Zapata).[57]

Gato wrote one poem in protest against the unjust imprisonment of Pedro Arias Dávila by Enrique IV. Another concerns, in part, the converso Antón de Montoro.[58]

Rodrigo de Cota

Rodrigo de Cota (ca. 1430/40–d. after 1505), known as "*el Viejo*" or "*el Tío*," was a member of another important Jewish and converso dynasty of

Toledo, about whom there is now considerable information available.[59] It is strange that Cantera Burgos completely overlooked the letter of Enrique IV (1456) to his treasurer in Burgos and Toledo, Alonso Cota, who was, of course, the father of the poet.[60] Of interest also is the merchant Alonso Martínez Cota, his wife Leonor Martínez de San Pedro, and their son, another Rodrigo Cota, scribe of Toledo (ca. 1493). Was this the same Rodrigo who was condemned by the Inquisition prior to 1499?[61]

One of the members of this prominent family, the merchant Francisco Cota, got into trouble in 1470 when all of his property and (unspecified) "offices" were taken from him and given to a certain *contador* because Francisco had given aid to "the enemy Portugal" with whom Castile was then at war. However, by 1474 he appears to have recovered, for in that year he is listed as a tax farmer of ecclesiastical taxes for Uceda. In 1487 he is listed as *tesorero*, and his son Ferrand Suárez (!) was preparing to marry the niece of a clergyman in Toledo. In 1489–90, however, he was investigated by the Inquisition and probably sentenced to death, as this is the last we hear of him.[62]

From the documents of Toledo we learn another bit of interesting information concerning Sancho Cota "*el Viejo*" and his son Rodrigo, later a jurist (not to be confused with our poet). In 1462 the "princess of Castile" (Isabel, who later became queen) ordered the governor of Toledo to release Sancho and Rodrigo from prison, where they had been confined because another son of Sancho, Alfonso de la Cuadra, *alcalde* of Ávila, had "justly" cut off the hand of a certain squire.[63]

There was another Sancho, a later member of the family in the period of Carlos V, whose memoirs have been published.[64]

Cantera relates the details of marriages and alliances between the Cotas and the powerful converso family, the Arias Dávilas. It is apparently the occasion of the marriage of one of these, perhaps Pedro Arias, with one of the noble Mendozas (apparently with one of those of converso background) which was the cause of Cota's bitter if somewhat obscure satire, the *Epitalamio burlesco*. There are veiled references to the presence of many Jews, or conversos, at the wedding feast (some of the family names are identifiable as those of well-known Jews).[65]

Apparently Cota wrote another poem attacking the Arias Dávila family, which caused Antón de Montoro, the previously discussed converso poet, to reply with a stinging attack against Cota. Montoro says that Cota's poems were worthy to have come from the pen of Lope (de Estúñiga, apparently, an "old Christian") or Juan de Mena; or, "not to increase the schism" (between "old" and "new" Christians), "from one who, without sophistry, praising the holy chrism [of baptism] desires to attack the synagogue." In other words, he compares Cota to those conversos, all too common, who from overzealous piety became bitter enemies of Jews.

Furthermore, Cota desired to present himself as "very Christian," in spite of his "black parentage"; i.e., he tried to conceal his own converso origin. Indeed, Montoro openly hints at the Jewish family of Cota, "those of Medina *hu*, of those of the Benatavé; and of those, don Mosé, your grandfather [was] don Barú [Barukh]." This somewhat enigmatic line seems to imply that the family originated in Medina (del Campo?), though the word "*hu*" ("it" in Hebrew or Arabic) is difficult to explain, and that the family was originally called "Benatavé." It so happens that we do encounter the similar name aben Atabe, or Ataben, with three distinct individuals all named Yuda (Seville, 1405; Seville, 1476; and Carrión, 1489); yet whether this is mere coincidence or not is unclear.[66] One of the family, don Hia, was involved in the complaints brought against Ferrant Martínez, who eventually caused the "pogroms" of 1391. Others are mentioned in the fifteenth century: Mayr Abentabe in Cádiz (1490), and, in fact, a don Mosé Abenatabe (1455) in Seville.

The poem is replete with ironic allusions to Cota's "*limpio*" status (supposed purity), and to his grandfather who summons the family to slaughter pork on the Sabbath. In one puzzling stanza (10) Montoro says that while it may have been easy to drop the "aben" from his name, it is not so easy to liquidate the *cota* (a word with many meanings) and thus all enter (to judgment) to the *baile*, "choosing *el al heel*," words which make no sense unless we accept Costa's suggestion that a Hebrew phrase was intended; in that case, perhaps *el ha Elohim* (to God, to judgment; cf. Exod. 22.7, 8).[67]

Finally, the difficult question of whether Cota was the author of the first act of the *Celestina* (see below, Fernando de Rojas) or not is best left to experts to debate.[68]

Juan de Mena

Juan de Mena (b. Córdoba, 1411; d. Torrelaguna, 1456) is certainly the most famous of the converso poets. He was educated at Salamanca and Rome, and was one of the first to show an interest in classical (Roman and Greek) authors. He made the first Spanish translation of the *Iliad*, for example. He was a member of the council of Córdoba, and was a protegé both of Álvaro de Luna and Juan II.

One of his major contributions to poetry was the use of what is called *arte mayor* meter (octets of eleven- or twelve-syllable verses, with *abbaa cca* rhyme), the theory of which was later elaborated by Juan del Encina. For this reason, the renowned grammarian Antonio de Nebrija (1444–1522) compared Mena to Virgil.

Another, less exaggerated, reason is that his most important poetic composition, the *Laberinto de fortuna* (or *Las trescientas*, because it contains [nearly] three hundred stanzas), was inspired by Virgil. It was dedicated to the king, and also praises Álvaro de Luna and other nobles. Another lengthy and famous poem by Mena is *La coronación,* dedicated to the marqués de Santillana.

Juan II asked him to write some verses criticizing the nobles who rebelled against the king, and he also wrote a very pious poem of praise to God which expresses his devout Christian faith. Far more extensive are his "secular" poems, including many love poems.[69]

In one short poem he appears to ridicule the "old" (Jewish) Law, but concludes by praising the Jews:

> At first, with hair and nails cut,
> they were permitted to marry among themselves,
> its [the Law's] afranchised captives
> the Jews; and purified,
> were the Israelites made
> pure, cleansed and blessed,
> consecrated to their law.[70]

Note here the repeated use of the term "pure" applied to Jews.

As was the case with some other conversos (e.g., Alonso de Palencia), he sharply criticized the religious hypocrisy of the times, and long before Luther he attacked the custom of selling indulgences and of making "saints" for payment. The *Coplas de la Panadera,* a poem on the battle of Juan II and the *infantes* of Aragón, has been attributed to him; as also to Rodrigo de Cota or Iñigo de Estúñiga.[71]

Juan del Encina

Juan del Encina (ca. 1468–ca. 1529), already mentioned as one of the greatest composers of the Spanish Renaissance, was even more important as a poet and as something else: the fateful year 1492, in addition to all the other things which marked it, was also the birth of modern theater, since in that year Juan del Encina produced his first *Ecologia (Egloga).*

Encina's secular poems were strongly influenced by biblical style. In his *Arte de poesía castellana,* the first work devoted to analysis of Spanish poetry, he cites Saint Jerome that many biblical books are written in Hebrew meter (which, of course, is not true, and proves that Encina knew no Hebrew), and that according to Christian authorities Hebrew was more ancient than Greek (this non sequitur seems to have been intended to indicate that Hebrew was the earliest poetry).[72]

His *Eglogas* are *autos,* or religious dramas with secular elements, and while they certainly do not compare with the entirely secular *Celestina,* which rightly deserves the title of the first modern play, they are of some interest. It has also been observed that since he composed music as well as dances for his plays, it may be said that he really originated the form which was later to develop as the *zarzuela*.[73]

In his *Egloga cuarta*, dedicated to the Catholic Monarchs and the *infante* Juan, after the Expulsion, he praises the Inquisition for glorifying the Christian faith, and also praises the Expulsion: "already it is not known in your kingdoms what Jews are; and now the hypocrites are recognized and each one given what he deserves." The latter is a reference to the "false" conversos, of course.[74]

Even more anti-Semitic is his *Egloga tercera*, an *auto* of the Crucifixion. Here he refers to the "cursed Jews" (line 101), "that cruel people" who crucified Jesus (line 121), "infernal people" (line 217), and "cursed Jewish people, transgressors of the law" (lines 218–19).[75]

Iñigo de Mendoza

Not to be confused with the far more famous Iñigo *López* de Mendoza, marqués de Santillana and also a poet who lived at roughly the same period (1398–1458), was the religious author fray Iñigo de Mendoza, of converso origin.

It is again to Cantera Burgos and his work on the Santa María–Cartagena dynasty that we owe our knowledge of the life of this important writer (and yet Cantera's work has been generally ignored, once again, by "literary scholars").

He was born probably in Burgos, shortly after 1430, the son of Diego Hurtado de Mendoza (grandson of Pedro de Cartagena).

It appears that he made enemies, and was accused of "hypocrisy" and of somewhat too much knowledge of women and secular pleasures for a friar; as well, perhaps, as being ridiculed for his "Jewish" background.

His poetry was not entirely religious, but certainly nothing "scandalous" is to be found in the secular poems which have survived. No less an authority than Rodríguez Puértolas has attributed to him the satirical *Coplas de Mingo Revulgo*, however, although it appears with insufficient basis.[76]

His most important work (assuming that he was not, in fact, the author of those *Coplas*) was his poetic *Vita Christi*, dedicated to his mother, Juana de Cartagena. The work is not without anti-Jewish polemic, though like most Christian writers he refrains from accusing the Jews of "deicide." Nevertheless, he calls them a "crude people of evil mouth" and "crazy" (because they do not realize that the "ceremonial laws" are only "figures" of Christianity).[77]

In another major religious poem, *Coplas de la veronica*, he does, however, write of Jewish "guilt" in the crucifixion; at least he says that the Jews do not know their father (God) and are cruelly punished because of what was done by an enemy people (the Romans) at their "command" in crucifying Jesus. He continues then with a general tirade against the Jews: they are without understanding, lost, exiled, without contrition, and he calls them "evil Pharisees," "false," "malicious."[78]

Thus, this member of a renowned converso dynasty demonstrates his intense anti-Jewish feeling.

Pedro de Cartagena

Very problematic is the identity of the "Cartagena," according to the *Cancionero general,* or "Pedro de Cartagena" in the *Cancionero castellano.* Some have mistaken this poet for Alonso de Cartagena, son of Pablo de Santa María and his successor as bishop of Burgos, while still others have argued that he was Pedro, the brother of that Alonso. These opinions are obviously erroneous, particularly given the fact that our poet wrote poems both to fray Iñigo de Mendoza and to Queen Isabel.

Another suggestion is that he was the "*caballero* de Cartagena," Pedro (about whom very little is known), or that he was the son—legitimate or not—of the converso Garci Franco, who was a member of the council of Juan II and brother of Antonio Franco, treasury official of the Catholic Monarchs. This suggestion was tentatively accepted by Cantera, not overlooking the difficulty that the relationship with the Franco family is by no means established.[79] It is this Pedro who is buried in the Cathedral of Burgos, and not the brother of Alonso.

His poetry is hardly "erotic," as Cantera described it, but he did write several simple and ordinary love poems. There are poems of other genres, however, including one of advice to his father, and another to his relative fray Iñigo de Mendoza, reproaching him in the name of the king (Fernando, surely), for reasons which are not evident from the poem. Finally, there is a poem praising Isabel.[80]

Diego de San Pedro

Virtually nothing is known of the life of this author, in spite of the fact that he wrote one of the most famous of all Spanish works, the romantic novel *Cárcel de amor* (Prison of Love), first published in 1492, after an earlier novel, *Tratado de amor.* Members of the San Pedro family of conversos are found in Toledo in the fifteenth century, including also a Diego, but probably not the author.[81]

He was a judge in the service of Enrique IV, and aside from this nothing is known of his life or career. His famous novel influenced both the converso Fernando de Rojas and the possible converso Cervantes.

In addition to his novels, he was a poet of some style and repute, and his poems naturally are about love. He did compose a not insignificant religious poem, however.[82]

He was not above writing some very scatological verses, indeed not unlike those found in Arabic poetry of the medieval period.[83] Nothing in any
of his work deals either with conversos or with Jews.

Juan de Lucena

We have already mentioned (Chapter 4) the fictitious dialogue between Juan
de Mena, Alonso de Cartagena, and the marqués de Santillana composed
by the converso Juan de Lucena. Very little is known about his life and
career, however. The situation is complicated by the fact that the name was
quite common, and in fact there are several fifteenth-century conversos
named Juan de Lucena (see also Chapter 7).

The first known printer of Hebrew books in Spain was named Juan de
Lucena. In 1476 he established two presses, one in the tiny village of Montalbán and the other nearby in Toledo, both of which printed only Hebrew
books, and especially those in demand among Jews in (Muslim) Granada.
Juan had a typesetter named Iñigo de Burgos (undoubtedly a converso), and
later he worked with the Christian printer Pedro de Monbil until 1481 when
they both were investigated by the Inquisition, at which time Juan and his
sons fled to Portugal and finally to Rome. Among the books which Juan
printed in Spain were Aaron ha-Kohen, Orḥot ḥayim, and Isaac al-Fāsī's
Halakhot (both important legal works by Spanish Jewish authors), as well
as Maimonides' Mishneh Torah (complete?), the entire Bible, and several
Talmudic tractates, and also (possibly) a prayer book for Yom Kippur. Of
all these, however, only isolated pages and fragments survive because the
Inquisition destroyed the books.[84]

This Juan de Lucena, the printer, was in fact the same as the converso
author, and it was in Portugal that he printed his own Vita beata (the fictitious dialogue previously mentioned).[85]

In Rome, Juan entered the service of the future Pope Pius II, and served
also as protonotario apostolica and consejero (a kind of ambassador) of the
Catholic Monarchs, but his letter against the Inquisition (discussed in the
next chapter) aroused the wrath of Alonso Ortiz who in 1493 in Seville
published his attack on it.[86]

In the 1491–92 records of houses and other property formerly owned by
Jews in Toledo, and then in the possession of the cathedral chapter, the name
of Juan de Lucena appears as currently living in a house in the barrio of
Chapinería. In 1493 he bought other houses, in the barrio of Santo Tomé
(well known as an area of conversos), which had belonged to the heirs of
"Rabbi Samuel the Neopolitan" (the sale was not apparently completed until 1494).[87]

Although he was the author of some other minor works, none of these is
of any particular interest for our purposes. As Gilman has observed, however, his criticism of those Christians who pray in Latin without understand-

ing what they say ("two-footed donkeys") is significant, as is his conclusion
that God also does not understand them, for he understands only "the
speech of the heart," an idea reminiscent both of Maimonides and of the
Talmud itself.[88]

Finally, there remains the intriguing question of whether or not Juan de
Lucena was related to the enigmatic "Martín de Lucena," supposedly a physician of Juan II. Gilman had no doubt that this Martín was, in fact, the
father of Juan; however, in Serrano y Sanz's documents, cited by Gilman,
the name is instead Francisco de San Martín, quite another person.[89]

Ibn Verga relates an interesting account concerning the Expulsion (discussed in Chapter 8, below), and concludes by stating that "on that day
there came there a certain sage of our seed called maestre Martin de Lucena," who advised the Jews not to offer any bribe to the queen because the
evil monk working against them would be hanged the following day. We
know of such a person who was, in fact, tried by the Inquisition, but there
is absolutely no evidence that he was related to Juan de Lucena, much less
his father.[90]

Francisco de Villalobos

Francisco López de Villalobos (1474–1519), to give him his full name, was
an important converso author, and physician to the duque de Alba and (in
1509) to Fernando himself.

He was the author of various works, including some comedies.[91] For our
purposes, it is sufficient to call attention to those excerpts and anecdotes
which have already been noted by Gilman,[92] and translated by him. One of
these, apocryphal or not, has Villalobos in a church being accused by a
woman of causing her husband's death, when a young man enters urging
the doctor to attend to his ill father. Villalobos points out that he is being
castigated by the woman as a "Jew" who killed her husband, and that above
the altar is "another lady" holding her head in her hands because he (i.e.,
the Jews) killed her son. "And now you want me to come and kill your
father!" the unfortunate converso is supposed to have concluded.

More to the point, and authentic since he wrote it himself, is Villalobos'
observation about a French correspondent whose style of writing he ad-
mired, concluding with the remark "and his vengefulness is that of a Marrano." As we have seen, conversos could, indeed, exhibit a good deal of
passion and vengeance in their poetry.

Fernando de Rojas

As we have noted, certainly the famous "tragicomedy" known simply as *La
Celestina* is the greatest masterpiece of fifteenth-century Spanish literature,
and the first true modern play in European literature generally. Unlike most

of the pre-Shakespearian dramas, for instance, it is also one which well stands the test of time and is as rewarding for the modern reader, or audience, as it was when written.

Whether or not it is possible to claim that Fernando de Rojas was himself a converso, or more correctly descended from converso origin, it must be admitted that Stephen Gilman, in spite of certain irritating stylistic mannerisms and posturings in his writing, has done a tremendous service in restoring this hitherto virtually unknown author.[93] More than this, he has set the author and his work in the proper social and historical context, and unlike most literary scholars has demonstrated insight into the converso situation (although, like many, he seems too inclined to accept Inquisition records at face value and believe the myth of "crypto-Judaism").

It is a relief, nevertheless, that Gilman has correctly refrained from attempting to find manifestations of that situation in the play itself, which must be accepted on its own terms without seeking any "hidden allegories." In only one instance, in the final "concluding word" of the author, does Rojas mention Jews at all. There, in a manner which now shall come to us as no surprise (for we have already encountered zealous anti-Semitism in converso writing), he writes of "the false Jews [who] spat" in Christ's face.[94] Gilman nevertheless seems to have missed the point of this passage, which is only somewhat milder than those we have previously encountered by conversos. As in those, Rojas is here totally identifying himself, in an overly zealous manner, inasmuch as "old Christians" rarely if ever made such statements, with his Christian faith.

He has nothing to hide, and there is no "ultimate irony." Like a good Christian, with the fires of the Inquisition raging around him (indeed, it had already apparently claimed members of his family), he sought to clearly separate himself from any possible suspicion of "Jewish sympathies."

"Converso" Authors Who Were Not

The rush to find conversos hiding behind almost every written work in the late medieval period in Spain did not begin with Castro. In fact, erroneous identification of supposed converso authors goes back to another Castro (no relation), the well-known eighteenth-century bibliographer Rodríguez de Castro, who in turn was followed by Amador de los Ríos and others who should have known better (indeed, Rodríguez de Castro's misinformation on Jewish authors of medieval Spain continues to mislead many).

For example, many important legal works were compiled in the reign of Alfonso X of Castile. One of these, *Flores de derecho,* was said by de Castro to have been written by Mosé Çarfaty (Moses Ṣarfatiy), who he claimed was a converso.[95] In fact, it appears that this Jew, not a converso, only made a copy of the work, probably for a ruler, at a later date.

The real author of the *Flores* was one maestre Jacobo "*de las Leyes*," probably Giàcomo Giunti, an Italian.[96] Amador did not hesitate to claim that not only was "Mossén Zarfati" (*sic*) a converso, but that maestre Jacobo himself was a Jew.[97]

It also appears that de Castro was the first one responsible for the persistent, but false, claim that the notorious anti-Semite Alonso del Espina was a converso.[98] Alonso de Oropesa has been wrongly claimed as a converso, as well.

The famous Catalan poet, actually born in Valencia (1397), Ausias March, has recently been claimed to be of a family "of Jewish origin," a fact supposedly revealed by a cryptic line in one of his poems. The same writer suggests that the name "Ausias," very unusual, derives from King Uzziah (Isa. 1.1), no less.[99] In fact, there is absolutely no evidence for any of these conjectures.

Similarly remote are Gilman's claims that Alonso Núñez de Reinoso ("Spain's first reviver of the Byzantine novel") was a converso, and absolutely false is his addition of Jorge de Montemayor, of a distinguished line of old nobility, to the list (suspect, if not absolutely impossible, is also Alonso Martínez de Toledo).[100]

Nothing is gained from such unfounded speculations, and the danger which results is that serious scholars may refrain from the necessary research to establish the identity of actual converso authors.

Fifteenth-Century Humanism and the Conversos

The introduction of "humanism" into fifteenth-century Spain is generally attributed to an unlikely source, Alfonso V of Aragón-Catalonia, who conquered Naples in 1443, thereby opening Spain to the influence of Italian humanism and the Renaissance. Indeed, his court became a great center for literature and scholars, Italian, Aragonese, Catalan, and others. Italian and French influences in art and music also began to manifest themselves.[101]

Some of these influences, at least increasing references to classical authors and themes, began to appear in Castile also in the reign of Juan II and even more in that of Enrique IV. Nevertheless, it was probably not until the already learned (fluent in Latin and Greek, for example) Isabel took the crown that humanism and classical influence really came into full flower. However able a ruler her husband Fernando may have been, it is doubtful that anyone could accuse him of being too much of a scholar, and in any case Castile certainly took the lead in this area in the united monarchy.

Penna has commented that veneration for antiquity was less pronounced in Spain than elsewhere in Renaissance Europe because of the "Arabic and Hebrew influences" that resulted in more of an emphasis on "newness."[102] This seems to be a misunderstanding of a particular element in Arabic literary, especially poetic, theory which did, in fact, stress innovation as opposed to slavish imitation of "classical" Arabic poetry. In Hebrew poetry as well, contrary to the interpretation of some scholars that it was nothing but imitation of the Bible, the emphasis was on innovation in both vocabulary and themes. Nevertheless, both Muslim and Jewish culture, particularly in Spain, emphasized veneration for antiquity, particularly classical Greek learning, in a manner unequaled anywhere in the Christian world. It was, after all, Arabic and Hebrew translation which first gave to Europe its knowledge of Greek philosophy, science, and medicine. Arabic and Hebrew writings are replete with references to these, and with expressions of great veneration for the "ancients" and their wisdom.

Indeed, it is perhaps something of this Jewish attitude, for example, which found its expression in the enthusiasm of conversos for classical authors.

There may be more to this peculiar converso love of classical authors, particularly Cicero, than mere enthusiasm for the "new" humanism. In his masterful study of the Renaissance, Denys Hay has suggested that the discovery of Cicero's true character, which Hans Baron attributed to Petrarch, opened the way for an escape from the narrow-minded renunciation of nature, love, and all things of "this world" which characterized Christianity.[103] It may be that converso writers, while certainly devout Christians, nevertheless rejected, or at least felt uncomfortable with, this particular aspect of Christianity, which was totally incompatible with their former Jewish way of thinking; a mode which it would have been very difficult to change, in contrast to a mere change of belief.

Another factor which certainly influenced the conversos was education. The overwhelming majority of conversos simply continued the trades and way of life they had before their conversion. Some more ambitious ones sought both economic and social advancement in commerce or minor government posts. Many entered the service of the Church, either as clergy or in one of the monastic orders. Neither choice required any particular education (indeed, as much of the clergy, even in the fifteenth century, was illiterate, the influx of conversos, most or all of whom were literate, may have significantly increased the level of clerical sophistication).

As anti-converso hostility increased, and of course especially once the Inquisition was established, the shrewder and more intelligent conversos sought ways in which to protect themselves. Basically there were three options, none of which guaranteed safety but all of which at least provided some possibility of it: the Church, government service, or the intellectual life (as a writer, poet, historian, etc.). Advancement to high level in any of these areas required education, and the usual path in fifteenth-century Spain was the famous university at Salamanca. It was there, sometimes beginning as young as twelve (or even younger), that students went to isolate themselves from the world for a period of years. Students of that age, of course, do not make such choices for themselves; the choice was that of a wise parent, who thereby gave at least temporary shelter and protection to young converso children, with the hope of their attaining a distinguished career which might permanently protect them from the fires of the Inquisition.[104]

Another factor which certainly must not be underestimated was the influence of the great scholar-pope, Nicholas V (1447–55), who established the most important private library of the Christian medieval world, some five thousand volumes, and who paid for the translation of numerous Greek classics.[105]

Still, as Schevill correctly noted, it was inevitable that men who immersed themselves in the study of the classics would have their faith in the infallible dogmas of Christianity shaken to a greater or lesser degree.[106] This certainly was to be the case at least in the sixteenth century with some of the famous scholars who were of converso descent, and perhaps as early as the fifteenth century.

Even the "humanism" of fifteenth-century Spain could sometimes work against the Jews, incidentally. For example, the translations of Josephus (such as that of the converso Alonso de Palencia, and others) made accessible to Christians yet another source for polemical propaganda. Fernán Pérez de Guzmán, for example, wrote very critically of King Solomon. He also mentioned that Josephus claimed that Solomon wrote "more than three thousand books," and that when the Jews were asked where all these volumes are now (either Pérez de Guzmán asked them, or he is reporting what he has heard from other sources), they responded that when Nebuchadnezzar conquered Jerusalem he burned all these and other books.[107]

In a sense, we may say that "humanism," or at least the use of classical material, is found first in the work of an early medieval converso, Petrus Alfonsus, the former Moses ha-Sefardy. Most of the sources utilized in his *Disciplina clericalis,* which became one of the most famous books in Europe for centuries afterward, were Arabic, but several were classical. Nevertheless, our present concern is with the fifteenth century, and in this period it appears that Alonso de Cartagena, son of Pablo de Santa María, was the first to make extensive use of classical authors. In addition to some references of importance in his own writing, he translated Cicero, as well as a portion of a work of Boccaccio.[108] It is undoubtedly no accident that he chose Cicero's *De officiis* as one of the works to translate, inasmuch as that work discusses the nature of virtue and focuses on "practical" virtue as the highest good, and it also stresses the duty of the philosopher to involve himself in affairs of state. Boccaccio's work, too, it should be noted, was a very practical one.

In addition to his translations of classical work, attention should be called to his original treatise on education and literary studies, which has been recently edited.[109]

The most important of the converso "humanists," however, was the chronicler Alonso de Palencia.[110] This importance, exemplified by his translations of classical works, Latin and Greek influences in his own writing, etc., has been hinted at by many authors but not thoroughly investigated by any.[111]

In addition to these influences in his chronicles, his translations of Petrarch, Domenico Cavalca, and Josephus and his own treatise *De synonimis elegantibus* (Seville, 1491) are works so rare as to be virtually inaccessible. It is doubtful whether the world would benefit from reprints of these, but surely they demand careful study in the context of a broader analysis of conversos and humanism which remains to be done. Of his other works, mention should be made of *Guerra e batalla campal de los perros y lobos,* a satirical attack on the nobility of both sides in the struggle of Enrique IV's reign.[112]

Juan de Mena's translation of Homer's *Iliad* has already been noted, and also Juan del Encina's of Virgil.[113]

Juan de Lucena wrote a very interesting letter addressed to a secretary (which one is not stated, but in any case a converso) of the Catholic Monarchs. The letter contains generally fascinating information on grammar, Latin, etc., of great interest for the subject under discussion. Lucena there states that he himself while in Rome "exchanged my Castilian grammar with the children for their Italian." He complains bitterly of the decline of Latin in Spain: "Who knows what Latin literature Castile has lost?"[114]

In connection with our observations on Cicero, it should be mentioned that Gonzalo de la Caballería, converso son of Bienvenist and brother of Juan, who was *comprador mayor* of Fernando I of Aragón (1414), and who himself became a treasurer of the kingdom, translated *De los oficios* and *De la amistad,* though both are now lost.[115]

The Moral and Political Aims of Converso Writers

Soria has aptly remarked that in Renaissance humanism, which of course, characterized all of Spain and not simply the Aragonese court in Sicily, "we encounter two fundamental ambitions: the quest for an equilibrium of culture and the enthusiasm of a return to the [classical] sources. The humanist is not a philosopher," but instead a moralist.[116] This is quite correct, and may be readily seen in the writing of the period, including that of the conversos, whether in personal letters, poetry, chronicles, or the kind of treatises composed by a Diego de Valera or Alonso de Palencia, for example.

There is little point in searching for any "Jewish" (much less Arabic) influences in the writings of conversos, aside from the satirical and always derogatory use of certain common Hebrew words which already were part of Spanish vocabulary that we have encountered in the poetry. Conversos, once again, were not Jews, not even "crypto-Jews," but Christians. The intellectuals among them, few enough given the enormous number of fifteenth-century conversos, expressed themselves either in the most pious of theological and devotional literature or in the humanistic style of the age; in either case, in a manner no different from, and indeed learned from, that of "old Christian" models.

Nor was the humanism of the fifteenth century, at least in Spain, a "secular humanism" of the sort which might arouse the wrath of an Inquisitor (of either the fifteenth- or the twentieth-century type). For all their sincere admiration of Cicero, Virgil, and numerous other classical authors, the converso writers of the fifteenth century, at least, retained a strong religious feeling and absolutely orthodox Christian views.

Soria was correct; the humanist was not a philosopher, but a moralist. The one probable converso who may be thought to have been a philosopher, Alfonso de la Torre (1417–60), falls really into that category of moralist as well. His *Visión delectable de la filosofía y artes liberales* is an adaptation and revision of Maimonides' famous and truly philosophical work, *Guide of the Perplexed*.[117] De la Torre may have been influenced by Maimonides, but in the end his work is in no way comparable to the *Guide*. It is rather an allegorization of and an attack on those customs and manners, as much as ideas, which are perceived as irrational. The liberal arts, freed from what he interprets as the corruption inflicted upon them in the medieval period, are the focus of his book, rather than Aristotelian truths.

It was to be nearly a century before Spain produced intellectuals who could truly be called philosophers, and few if any of those were of converso origin.

As we have seen, the goal of converso authors of the fifteenth century was something entirely different. Their concerns were morality, as reflected in their interpretation, at least, of the classical sources and the Bible, but with only passing reference to Christian theological tradition; and politically, the glorification of the new Christian empire which Spain would be, an empire again based on the twin models of the Bible and classical political wisdom, and headed by a glorious Christian queen (and her husband, what's-his-name) whose virtues were only slightly less than those of the Virgin Mary, to whom they often compared her.

Diego de Valera frequently refers to the "prophecy" of Spain, that the country would be united under the scepter of the Catholic Monarchs, and not only Spain but other countries (of the Muslims) as well. Juan de Lucena, discussing grammar, Latin, etc., concludes with a discussion of culture in general and launches into praise of Isabel as "splendid Diana," "wife, mother, queen," who fights our battles, oversees our kingdom, judges our quarrels, devises new clothing, listens to music, watches bullfights (it was precisely this which aroused the wrath of her confessor Hernando de Talavera); "she goes, and goes, and never stops." She is a creature of heaven on earth, the heart of a man in feminine form, etc.[118]

Not one of these converso writers, it should be noted, is known to have taken any active part in the defense of the conversos against the physical attacks, or even the polemics, against them. Only Pulgar, mildly, and Lucena, more forcefully, criticized the Inquisition. Not only is there no "converso mentality" in the literature of the century, there appears not to have been any uniform converso group identity among the intellectuals.[119] With the exception of the satirical poems, usually satire directed against other conversos, there is virtually no reflection of an individual writer's own converso status (Pulgar, as we have seen, is an exception). The fifteenth-century converso is writing not as a converso, but as a Spanish Christian humanist.

Converso Anti-Jewish Polemic

Conversos themselves, at least those whose conversion was motivated exclusively by religious zeal and conviction, were the worst enemies of Jews.

It is a fact that medieval Spain was virtually entirely free of the kind of anti-Jewish religious polemic that is to be found in the works of medieval Christian writers in Europe generally. Prior to the thirteenth century, of the more than twenty major anti-Jewish polemical works that have survived in published form (there are others in manuscript, or which have not survived), only three originated in Spain: Petrus Alfonsus (also a convert), an anonymous twelfth-century work, and Martin of León. To these may be added, with some qualifications, Lucas of Túy. It is only from the thirteenth century on that we find any significant amount of such polemic in Spain, almost entirely from the pen of Dominicans (Ramón de Peñafort, Ramón Martí, and others), themselves inspired in large measure by the activity of Jewish converts in France and Provence.

In the fourteenth and fifteenth centuries, however, there is a veritable flood of such polemics, written by or inspired by conversos: Abner of Burgos (Alfonso de Valladolid), Pablo de Santa María, Jerónimo de Santa Fe, Pedro de la Caballería, Pablo de Heredia, and others. The most notorious "old Christian" polemicists, Alonso de Oropesa and Alonso del Espina, certainly were personally acquainted with and influenced by conversos.

Not only textual exegesis or theological topics could serve as material for such polemic, but even Jewish customs and rituals. The "new" polemic moved slowly but surely from the former arena of attack on "Judaism," specifically the Bible and Talmud, to the area of true anti-Semitism, attacks on Jews.

An important element of the anti-Jewish activity and attitude of the conversos was the production of manuals or guides for the Inquisition, intended to enable the Inquisitors to "detect" (or, more correctly, to fabricate) supposed "Jewish practices" of those whom they wished to condemn as heretics.

Outside of Spain we already have an example of this in the famous "guide" of the French Inquisitor Bernard Gui. An interesting example produced for the Spanish Inquisition of the fifteenth century, is the work of Antonio de Ávila, a converso Dominican friar possibly from Segovia, who wrote for Torquemada himself a lengthy explanation of the Talmud and of Jewish "rites" and practices.

We do not, however, have any real information as to the effect of the polemic of such conversos upon Jews themselves, in terms of either leading to further conversions or (possibly) demoralizing further an already weakened community. Only in the case of Joshua al-Lorqi (Jerónimo de Santa Fe, see Chapter 5) do we know that Pablo de Santa María convinced him to convert. Both Pablo and, earlier, Alfonso de Valladolid elicited significant Jewish responses to their polemical writings, but the impact of these on the general Jewish population is unknown.

Netanyahu writes that Ḥayim Ibn Musa, an important anti-Christian polemicist, stated in his book (1456) in a "matter-of-fact style" that the ignorant people "are persuaded by the Christians and especially by the converts." Yet in fact, this is *not* what he wrote; rather, "the foolish, who do not know the way of disputation, are persuaded by the *words* of the Christians and especially by the *books* of those who change their faith," specifically mentioning Petrus Alfonsus and Abner (Alfonso de Valladolid). As Netanyahu further on correctly says, this shows that these *books* were known to Jews; but it does not demonstrate, as he suggested earlier, that conversos themselves had any particular success in persuading Jews to convert.[120]

The earliest known Jew who converted to Christianity in Spain was Isaac Iudaeus ("the Jew"), who was sent by Rome to Spain in 378. In the fragments of his preserved writings, nothing of "anti-Jewish" (or "anti-Judaism") polemic is found, however.[121]

Petrus Alfonsus (or, more correctly, Pedro Alfonso), formerly Moses ("ha-Sefardy" according to later tradition), was baptized in the cathedral of Huesca in 1106. His birthplace and details of his early life are unknown, and there is no reason to refer to him as "rabbi," as later tradition did. Four years after his conversion he wrote his important polemic against Jews and Muslims.[122] The novelty of this work lies in its being the first in Spain to accuse Jews of "deicide" in the crucifixion, i.e., they knew Jesus to be God when "they" crucified him. Furthermore, his attacks on Talmudic and other rabbinic traditions depart also from earlier polemic by being based on the alleged contradiction between these sources and reason and science.

This polemical "dialogue" became one of the most important sources for later medieval polemic, not only in Spain but throughout Europe.[123] Ramón Martí and the conversos Alfonso de Valladolid, Pablo de Santa María, and Jerónimo de Santa Fe all used it. Thus, it would be no exaggeration to say that this single work largely changed the direction of anti-Jewish polemic.

In spite of the important influence of Pedro's work, however, there appears to have been little or no Jewish response to it. This is undoubtedly primarily due to the fact that it was written in Latin, a language unknown among the Jews of Spain at the time.

By far the most important polemicist, from the Jewish point of view, was another convert, Abner of Burgos, a rabbi, who took the name Alfonso de Valladolid (ca. 1270–1347).[124]

It has been claimed that he was also a physician, although on insufficient evidence. As previously mentioned, I have discovered that before his conversion he was a scribe and bookbinder for the *infanta* Blanca, granddaughter of Alfonso X and *señora* of the Monasterio de las Huelgas of Burgos. A "Rabbi Abner," certainly he, is recorded also as being in Valladolid, at the same time that "Mosseh Narbon," none other than Moses Narboni, the famous commentator and philosopher, was also (temporarily) in that city.[125] After his conversion, about 1320, Alfonso continued to live in Valladolid. According to Amador, he served as sacristan of the cathedral there. It appears that he continued to enjoy the patronage of the *infanta* Blanca, for she is said to have been responsible for urging the translation into Spanish of his main anti-Jewish polemic, "Wars of the Lord."[126]

Baer has given generally a correct account of Alfonso's polemics, to which only some additional bibliography and new information need be added.[127]

In addition to his main polemic, *Moreh ṣedeq* in Hebrew (lost), of which only the Spanish translation survives, Alfonso is known to have written numerous other works. One of these, *Maldiciones de los judíos* (Paris B.N. MS. Esp. 43, fols. 1–11), deals with the "curses" of the Jews against Christians and supposedly anti-Christian statements in rabbinical writings, etc. Another work, *Libro de las tres creencias* (Madrid B.N. MS. 9302, fols. 1–50), is currently the subject of research by an outstanding Spanish scholar, Carlos del Valle Rodríguez. Another attributed work is not, apparently, by him: *Libro declarante* (dealing with the Trinity; Escorial MS).[128]

According to one perhaps not entirely reliable author of the last century, Alfonso also wrote a *Libro de las tres gracias,* to explain the creed, a *Concordia de las leyes,* and a gloss on Abraham Ibn ʿEzra's important commentary on the Ten Commandments. In addition, that writer and other authorities have claimed that a Spanish translation of Alfonso's "Wars of the Lord" (*Batallas de Dios*) was found at one time in the library of a monastery in, or near, Valladolid.[129] Finally, various Hebrew letters of Alfonso have been edited by Rosenthal.[130]

An important Jewish source concerning Alfonso is the contemporary poet Samuel b. Joseph Ibn Sason of Carrión (near Valladolid). In the introductory poem to his *maqamah* (rhymed prose work), he mentions that it was written "at the time of the dispute between Rabbi Joshua and Abner, for at that time the troubles increased and labor was much in the land and the enemy almost consumed us except that the Lord was with us."[131] Undoubtedly this "Rabbi Joshua" was the famous Joshua Ibn Shuʿayb (so his name is correctly spelled) who later achieved renown as a preacher. He was a student of Judah b. Asher in Toledo, and the teacher of Menaḥem b. Zeraḥ. (The controversy over Jewish prayers and their reference to Christians, which led to a ban on such prayers by Alfonso XI, was also due in no small measure to Alfonso's writing, and Ibn Sason also mentioned this; but this is not the place to detail that issue.)

The Jewish reaction to Alfonso, as mentioned, was immediate and vast. He was considered a most dangerous enemy; indeed, apparently, *the* most dangerous enemy of Judaism at the time. (The work of the Dominican friar Ramón Martí, *Pugio fidei,* was also in Latin, and thus unknown to Jews, aside from its use in the Barcelona disputation with Naḥmanides in a secondary manner; Chazan has demonstrated that, contrary to the speculations of Baer, this work did *not* influence Alfonso.) Some of his Jewish opponents began referring to him as "*Av ḥosheq,*" or "father of darkness," an antonym of his original Hebrew name, Abner, "father of light."[132] Among those who attempted to refute his ideas were Joseph Shalom, Isaac Nathan, Moses Narboni, Shem Ṭov Ibn Shapruṭ, Moses ha-Kohen of Tordesillas, Isaac Polgar and Isaac Israeli of Toledo, and, of course, Ḥasdai Crescas. No other single polemicist, "old Christian" or convert, has ever produced so formidable an array of respondents. There can be little doubt that it was not so much *what* Alfonso said as in *what language* he said it, since he chose to do most of his writing in Spanish rather than Hebrew (or Latin, of course), and this meant that his work could be widely read by all sorts of people.

Of particular interest, because so much attention has been paid to it, is a small treatise later expanded into a book against Alfonso, written by Isaac (Ibn) Polgar.[133] He notes that it is not enough that the Jews are caught be-

tween "enemies and oppressors," Christians and Muslims, but "now men
from among our people have gone forth and added themselves to our enemies." He apparently disputed in person with some of these conversos, possibly including Alfonso himself, and his friends asked him to record these
disputes in writing. Although he does not specifically refer to Alfonso, we
may judge from the book some of the themes of their debate (such as the
length of the exile, the coming of the messiah—which Isaac correctly says is
not a cornerstone of the Jewish faith, although his coming is to be expected,
nor should anyone be amazed at its delay). Only once does he mention
Alfonso directly:

> One time I was united with a certain man, by my soul, fluent in knowledge of
> the ways of religion and also philosophy which he comprehended fully, and
> his heart inclined to turn from our Torah. His name previously [before he
> converted] was Rabbi Abner.

He then reports an actual debate they had concerning allegorical statements
in the Talmud or Midrash. Isaac concluded by saying to him that such statements are not in the category of commentary on the Torah and commandments, which constitute the true Talmud, but rather allegories or hidden
wisdom about which we are not to concern ourselves at all.[134] The remainder of the book is concerned with attacks on philosophy, astrology, etc., of
little value.

It may be seen what a weak and altogether ineffective attack this was by
one praised as a "great scholar" against so shrewd an opponent as Alfonso.
The other responses, with the possible exception of that of Moses ha-Kohen,
are little better.

Of particular importance is the lengthy treatise on astrological determinism, predestination, etc., written in Spanish and summarized at length
(in Hebrew) by Baer, as a response to Polgar. This debate, and the influence of Abner's Christian views of determinism and predestination upon
the renowned rabbi and philosopher Ḥasdai Crescas, need still further
investigation.[135]

Another interesting convert was the previously mentioned (Chapter 3)
Profiat Duran, whose name prior to his conversion in 1391 was Israel b.
Moses ha-Levy. He was baptized in Perpignan, but had a change of heart
and returned to Judaism after leaving that city. He began calling himself
"Efod," and so titled two of his books (the still unpublished *Hoshev efod*
and the published *Maʿaseh efod*). While this name is usually explained as
an acrostic (*aniy Profiat Duran,* or *amar Profiat Duran*), this is unlikely,
and it probably is to be explained by the Talmudic statement "the *efod*
[priestly breastplate] atones for the error of idolatry" ('*Araqin* 16b, cf. *Ze-
vaḥim* 88b, *Lev. R.* 10.6, *Song of Songs R.* 4.4, and Baḥya b. Asher on

Exod. 28.4); i.e., he sought atonement for his own conversion and for others in his generation.

He was also an important mathematician and astronomer (numerous works still in manuscript), as well as a Hebrew grammarian of importance, who dedicated his *Ma'aseh efod* to Moses (Ibn) Zarzal, or Zarzar, physician of Enrique III.

There is no need here to enter into a detailed discussion of his major work, *Kelimat ha-goyim* (Shame of the Gentiles), a lengthy anti-Christian polemic which focuses entirely on traditional Christian theological notions, arguments based on biblical texts (including the New Testament), etc. While not lacking in originality, this work properly belongs to the area of Jewish polemic against Christianity and not to our topic. It is of interest, however, that a former convert was bold enough to write such a work, even in Hebrew and under a disguised name. The fact that his citations of the New Testament are entirely in Spanish, and without specific reference to chapters or verses, is also proof that he expected his Jewish audience to be totally familiar with the New Testament, and in Spanish.

The work of his which is most important for our purposes is the satirical letter *Al tehiy ke-avotekha* (Be not like your fathers). The exact date of the letter is impossible to determine (usually said to be 1396, but Netanyahu has shown that this is based on a misunderstanding; nevertheless, it clearly was later rather than earlier, after 1391 and almost certainly after his letter to En Joseph Abraham).[136]

It has also been accepted as fact (so also Netanyahu) that the letter was intended generally as propaganda against the conversos. It is also said that the "Christian authorities" condemned to death anyone who distributed the letter to conversos; however, supposedly, this was only after those authorities learned of the true (satirical) nature of the letter from the commentary written on it by Joseph Ibn Shem Ṭov. Netanyahu at least correctly rejected this last part as fictitious, noting that with accomplished Hebraists among the conversos (he might have said among Christians generally), they hardly needed "sixty years and the help of a Jewish commentator to make this decision."

However, the entire account of the letter is based on the claim of its sixteenth-century Italian Jewish editor, Isaac 'Aqrish, and is very suspect. At best, we may accept Netanyahu's conclusion that this account reflects only an older tradition that Christians in Spain knew the letter, which they called (in Spanish transliteration) *Alteca boteca*.[137] We know of no documentary evidence that any attempt was made to prevent the "distribution" of the letter.

Strangely, however, Netanyahu ignored altogether the actual occasion for this letter, which was the conversion of Duran's longtime friend Davi (David) Bonet Bonjorn, who lived in Gerona. He was the son of Bonet Davi

Bonjorn, a physician in Perpignan and famous astronomer. (Baer claimed that it was "Magister Bonet Bonjorn" who converted, confusing the son for the father.)

Apparently Davi Bonet Bonjorn converted at the same time that Duran did, probably also in Perpignan. Later they both repented of their conversion and determined to go to Palestine to return to Judaism (Baer wrote that it was "inconceivable" that Duran could have "paid obeisance to alien gods," i.e., converted, but Emery has conclusively proven that he did). Duran waited (in Perpignan?) for his friend to come from Avignon, but in the meantime Pablo de Santa María (who, *contra* Baer, was not responsible for Davi's conversion) in Avignon convinced Davi to remain a Christian, and Davi wrote Duran about this decision. It was then that Duran wrote his satirical letter, "Be not like your fathers," and sent a copy also to the famous Castilian rabbi and physician Meir Alguadix.[138]

The previously discussed Pablo de Santa María, bishop of Cartagena and of Burgos, was certainly the most famous of the conversos from a theological point of view, and author of what has been characterized as the most profound work, *Scrutinium scripturarum.* The popularity of that book is shown by the repeated printed editions in the fifteenth century alone.[139] Besides this work, his *Additiones ad Postillam Nicolas de Lyra,* commentaries on the work of perhaps the most famous medieval Christian biblical commentator, also saw several additions after 1473. Influenced primarily by Thomas Aquinas, he was also clearly dependent on Ramón de Peñafort and, especially, Ramón Martí. Thus, he claimed that "proof" of Christ can come not only from the New Testament, and "Old" Testament citations correctly understood, but from Talmudic and other Jewish authorities as well.

There is really nothing very new in his arguments which cannot already be found in those of Aquinas, Peñafort, Martí, and other polemical works. The "redemption" of Israel is to be understood spiritually, and not in a physical sense (and so, of course, will come when Jews recognize Christ). The Law, or Torah, contains ceremonial commandments and moral commandments, and only the latter are eternally binding.

Of interest is his statement in the concluding section of the work, as an example of Jews' "blindness" in their false calculations about the coming of the messiah, that the date mentioned by Maimonides (in *Igeret Teiman*) for the coming of the messiah (1210 c.e.) in fact was "about" the time of the appearance of Saints Francis and Dominic, and "who can calculate how many souls have been redeemed" by the preaching of those orders! Another example is the calculation of Naḥmanides (Moses b. Naḥman), which was followed exactly by "R. Levi Begner" (i.e., de Bagnols; Levy b. Gershon), of 1358. At that time, he admits, the Jews were in fact held in great honor in Spain. He then cites the well-known story of the "miracle" of the crosses of Ávila and Abner of Burgos, in 1295, which apparently happened deliberately to confound such false messianic calculations and prove the truth of the Christian faith.[140]

Pablo's writings may have had a significant impact on later Christian authors, but as previously noted they aroused no particular reaction among Jews at all, and that primarily if not entirely because they were in Latin.

Alonso de Cartagena, Pablo's son and successor as bishop, dealt with some typical Christian polemical themes in his previously mentioned defense of conversos. With traditional Christian love of dividing things into threes, he distinguishes first three classes of nobility: theological, moral, and natural or civil. The biblical Jews, he says, were distinguished by all three classes, in the priesthood, kings, and judges and other heroes.[141] However, those who refuse to recognize the true eternal King (Christ) lose their claim to royal title and dominion (an allusion, however veiled, to the famous debate over Gen. 49.10), and those who deny the "celestial Jerusalem" (the Church, which is "our mother") become captives and servants of the earthly cities (thus have the Jews, he implies, lost their dominion and become "servants" of Christians; of course, the fact that the very allegory of "heavenly" and "earthly" Jerusalem was invented by Jews he seems to have forgotten).

Next he distinguishes three kinds of servitude, as earlier he had done with nobility: natural, civil, and theological. Reverting to the old typology of Sarah and Hagar, he states that the perfidious Jews who maintain the literal law are descendants of Hagar, whereas the Gentile Christians are the true sons of Sarah and of the typology of Isaac. "Natural" slaves are those, inferior by nature, destined for slavery according to Aristotle (or, more correctly, according to his not altogether accurate understanding of Aristotle, based, of course, on the inferior medieval Latin translations). "Civil" slaves are those provided for by the law. The third type, "theological," are slaves by reason of sin. This "sin" consists in stubbornly maintaining the laws of Moses, and even more, being guilty of "infidelity." Alonso did not, however, as his editor claimed, accuse the Jews of "deicide," a charge, as noted, very rare in Christian writing, but made by Pedro Alfonso.[142]

Jerónimo de Santa Fe turned from being an intelligent and devoted, if somewhat skeptical, Jew to a zealous enemy of Jews. His chief anti-Jewish polemic, the Latin text of which has been published, was based on his presentation at the Tortosa disputation "in August of 1413." He was, incidentally, baptized by Saint Vicente Ferrer, whose later canonization was based in part on the special merit of having converted this Jew in the small and lovely medieval town of Alcañiz.[143]

This treatise, *Hebraeomastyx*, consists of "proofs" that Jesus was the messiah, etc., and in the second part, attacks on the Talmud. The Hebrew version of the work, with the title *Sefer ha-piqurim* (Book of Heresies), was not apparently written by him, but during his lifetime. Virtually all of Jerónimo's ideas were taken directly from Ramón Martí's *Pugio fidei*.

Unlike the previous books written in Latin, this book, in its Hebrew version, prompted an immediate and significant Jewish response. Those who reacted to it included Vidal Benvenist of Zaragoza, whose work fortunately (since the Vienna MS of *Sefer ha-piqurim* no longer exists) contains the entire Hebrew text of Jerónimo, with a chapter-by-chapter rebuttal;[144] Isaac b. Qalonymos Bongodas (Bonjudas) Nathan (who was the author of the first Hebrew biblical concordance); Solomon b. Ṣemaḥ Duran;[145] Moses Botarel (possibly); Ḥayim Ibn Musa; and Isaac Abravanel (in a work written after the Expulsion).

The second part of Jerónimo's work, the attack on the Talmud, has been analyzed recently by Moises Orfali, with excerpts from the work itself and comparisons with Talmudic and other rabbinical sources.[146] As is to be expected, Jerónimo was not above falsifying and distorting his sources. For example, he accuses the Jews of having a law which permits them to "steal and sell men," and cites *Sanhedrin* that a father who sells his son, or a master his student, is not to be punished. In fact, the case deals with the biblical law of an Israelite slave, and states that one who steals an Israelite for such a purpose is not punishable until he takes possession of him and "uses" him (as a slave); but a father who sold his son (only in the biblical period when such laws applied) was, in fact, exempt. In another case he cites the same tractate to the effect that "one who adores an idol through love or fear is exempt," without adding that the text further states that if he accepts the idol as his god he is certainly punishable.[147]

Finally, the previously discussed de la Cavalleria family of conversos produced one of the most anti-Jewish spokesmen of the period, Pedro (d. 1461). His father Bonafos (Fernando after his conversion) converted at the Tortosa disputation and at once became the treasurer of the king. In 1415, the year the disputation finally concluded, Fernando I interceded with the pope (Benedict XIII) to obtain a benefice for Pedro.[148]

As noted already (Chapter 5), Pedro was *maestre racional* in 1437, a jurist and councillor of Alfonso V. According to the *Libro verde de Aragón*, his son Alonso had been born a Jew, named Bonafos (after Pedro's father), and thus both Pedro and his son must have converted, perhaps together with Pedro's father. This son, Alonso (Alfonso), as noted already, became vice-chancellor of Aragón under Fernando II. Another son, Jaime, was condemned by the Inquisition in 1504. There were also at least two daughters.[149]

In 1447, Pedro attempted to prove that he was *not* of Jewish descent, but in spite of the testimony of nobles that he was supposedly an "old Christian," the conversion of his father is proven fact (thus, the *Libro verde* was in error in stating that he was a brother of Bienvenist and husband of the divorced wife of Luis de Santángel). Pedro was assassinated during the rebellion against Juan II of Aragón in 1461.[150]

His infamous anti-Jewish polemic, *Tractatus zelus Christi contra iudaeos, sarracenos et infideles* (1450), was published in Venice in 1592.[151]

Pablo de Heredia, born a Jew in Aragón, converted probably in Rome. He died before 1490. His most important work is a curious book, published in Rome ca. 1480, which purports to be a "translation" of *Epistolae de secretis Neumiae fili Haccanae* (copy at Madrid, B.N.).[152] Pablo claims in his introduction (fols. 1v–2r) that the work is a translation from Hebrew of two letters, or treatises, by "Neumie" (Neḥemiah? Neḥunya?) the son of "Haccane" and by Haccane the son of Neumie. In fact, the work is entirely a forgery, the creation of Pablo himself (it should be noted, however, that an early medieval Hebrew mystical treatise, *Sefer ha-bahir,* has the alternate title *Midrash R. Neḥunya b. ha-qanah,* and it is entirely possible that this provided Pablo with the names of his heroes).

The treatise itself cites the "*libro gale razaya*" and "*Niggherth hazadoth*" about the conversations reported in the Talmud between Antoninus of Rome and Rabbi Judah "*ha-qodesh,*" redactor of the *Mishnah.* These titles are also forgeries by Pablo (the first is not to be confused with the *Galey razaya* which is an authentic important sixteenth-century qabalistic work probably composed in Turkey). The second title is apparently an attempt at "*Igeret ha-sodot*" (letter of secrets), a standard term for any number of works. The errors in spelling of simple Hebrew words are an indication of the real ignorance of Hebrew of the author.

Pablo himself interjects "proof" of the Incarnation from the Zohar (Deut. 11; fol. 5r), and also makes the usual claim that "holy, holy, holy" represents the Trinity.

He raises the usual polemic (fol. 7v) about the "virgin" of Isaiah 7.14. He discusses three Hebrew words, *nahara, bethula,* and *alma;* the first is an adolescent girl, whereas *bethula* is virgin (this much he at least got correct), but *alma* (simply "young woman"; used in Isaiah) is adolescent and virgin both. Here he mentions an earlier book of his, *Ensis Pauli,* in which he discussed this.[153]

His references to such midrashic works as "Mechelta" (*Mekhilta;* fol. 22r) or "beresith rabba" (fol. xxxv r; unpaginated, but written in by hand, in the second part of the book) is no proof that he himself read these works, for he probably took the references from earlier polemical literature. The second part (fol. 53ff., his own commentary on the work he supposedly "translated") also cites the "magistri Cabbale" that the Hebrew term *Adonay* refers to "God the Father," and *Elohim* to "God the Son." Needless to say, no known qabalistic treatises ever make such a statement; but this, and the reference to the Zohar, is an interesting example of an early polemical use of qabalistic sources in an attempt to "prove" Christianity.

There remains only to be mentioned Juan "*el Viejo*" (the aged one, apparently because he wrote his work at an advanced age in Toledo), supposedly another convert at the hands of Vicente Ferrer. If so, he was already "elderly" when he converted, for in 1416 he wrote his *Memorial de los misterios de Cristo,* as it is known. It appears that he was fairly well versed in Jewish sources, including the early mystical *Sefer yeṣirah.* The main argument of the work is to prove that Jesus is the messiah, and the virginity of Mary. Of interest, too, is his assertion that the year 1391, which had been calculated by the father-in-law of the important Alazar Golluf of Zarargoza to be the year when the messiah would appear, but which was actually the year of the "pogroms," was the year when the true messiah (Christ) brought Jews into the fold of the Church "by force." Juan also wrote a Christological explanation of Psalm 72.[154]

Alfonso de Zamora was a converso who was baptized in 1492 and went on to become one of the most prolific Christian writers of the early sixteenth century. As such, he is outside the boundaries set for our discussion, but it is important to mention him in connection with the famous Complutensian (so-named because published at Alcalá, Compluto in Latin, 1514–17) Polyglot Bible, which includes also the Hebrew text and Targum Onkelos (vols. 1–4) and a Hebrew lexicon and grammar, composed by Alfonso (vol. 6). He was aided in his translation and editing by two other conversos, Pablo Coronel (born Segovia, ca. 1480, died 1534) and Alfonso de Alcalá, of whom little or nothing is known. Pablo could hardly have been a "well-known Talmudist" before his conversion, as nineteenth-century writers have claimed, since he was a mere child in 1492. Alfonso de Zamora, although an accomplished Hebraist, was an anti-Jewish polemicist.[155]

The conversos were, as previously noted, the worst enemies of the Jews. While there is no doubt that the works of Ramón de Peñafort and Ramón Martí, both "old Christians," were the most damaging anti-Jewish polemics written, they were in Latin, a language known only to the learned. The converso writings were often in Spanish, and thus had far-reaching consequences. Alonso del Espina, for instance, could not possibly have written his book without these works (although he also wrote in Latin). Also, the converso polemicists brought even more dangerous use of distortions and half-truths derived from Jewish sources into the arena of polemics. Even as late as 1651 the Christian Hebraist Johannes Buxtorf II included among his *desiderata* for disputing with Jews not only Ramón Martí and Espina but also Jerónimo de Santa Fe, the *Zelus Christi,* and "Paulus de Sancta Maria" (Pablo).[156]

Converso "Religiosity"

We have seen that many of the converso polemicists had degrees of knowledge of Jewish sources ranging from excellent to mediocre or worse. The converso poets, on the other hand, appear to have had far less knowledge of Jewish religious practices, other than the most common laws and customs which even "old Christians" knew about.

We have already mentioned Amador de los Ríos' interesting suggestion about possible Hebrew stylistic influences on some converso poetry, a suggestion which nevertheless needs to be treated with some caution. Even more skepticism, and indeed complete denial, is necessary with regard to the suggestions of some (Lida de Malkiel concerning Juan de Mena; Márquez Villanueva for Juan Alvarez de Gato) about "Talmudic influences" on the work of these poets. (Gato, it should be remembered, was the grandson of a convert, and certainly raised with no knowledge of Jewish sources whatever.) This is, once again the "converso mentality" idea, seeking to find "Jewish influences," and where none exist, to invent them.

The ignorance of some conversos as to Jewish matters was remarkable. The previously mentioned Pedro de la Caballería, for instance, a major anti-Jewish polemicist, referred to Maimonides, as did all Christian sources, as "Moses the Egyptian." He did not know that Maimonides was born and educated in Córdoba, Spain, and assumed instead that there was a "Córdoba" in Egypt where Maimonides lived. (Perhaps even more surprising is his confusion concerning the supposed advice of Saint Vicente Ferrer, who died in 1419, to the Catholic Monarchs in 1492 that they expel the Jews.) [157] We have also already noted (Chapter 4) Pulgar's apparent lack of familiarity with elemental Jewish ethics.

Even those conversos who had considerable Jewish learning, such as Pablo de Santa María (presumably also his son Alonso, although he nowhere demonstrates it), completely rejected that knowledge, including in Pablo's case even the use of the text of the Hebrew Bible, favoring entirely Christian interpretation based on erroneous understanding. In his poem on the history of the world, for example, he has a serpent, who is "Lucifer" (!), tempt Eve in the Garden of Eden and, following Origen (not named, however), has Eve tempt Adam to eat the "apple" (the Bible does not specify what fruit it was). The man is "good" but Eve is evil. While "sin," a non-Jewish concept, is mentioned, however, the Christian doctrine of "original sin" is not. Furthermore, he says that from Shem is descended "Israel with all the Hebraist" (civilization, religion), "even though now after holy baptism all are intermingled with other lineages," which seems to allude to the Christian doctrine of "True Israel." The laws given at Sinai were "ceremonial," some with promises of reward and others as prohibitions.[158] Thus a former Talmudic scholar writes as though he never opened a Hebrew book in his life.

Important testimony to the "religiosity" of conversos, particularly of the overwhelming majority who were neither writers nor polemicists, comes from Alonso de Palencia, who claimed that "the majority" of conversos in

Andalucía still expected the coming of the messiah, and when notice reached them that off the coast of Portugal, near Setúbal, an unusual whale was seen chasing a ship, they concluded it was the biblical Leviathan sent as a sign of the imminent appearance of the messiah. It is difficult to know what to make of such testimony; obviously the facts themselves are correct (Alonso seems to have been an eyewitness, for he describes in detail this interesting encounter with the whale), but the interpretation may be slanted. It would always be possible for a converso to say that such statements about the "coming" of the messiah referred to the anticipated second coming of Christ. Indeed, it is quite probable that a number of ordinary conversos, not very well informed in any case about Jewish tradition, confused the two things. Elsewhere the same author says that conversos of Burgos were considered very observant Christians, and he mentions the Santa María family, all "virtuous men, whose example the *majority* of the conversos of Spain [not just Burgos] follow in the road of good." Certain instances of "infamy," nevertheless, have been found in Calahorra, Osma, Salamanca, Palencia, León, Zamora, Ávila, Segovia, Cuenca, and Sigüenza. More serious are the "crimes" of some in Toledo, Córdoba, Seville, and Jaén, whereas many are "accused" of crimes in the diocese of Badajoz.[159] It is interesting that in these latter cases he is not discussing any lack of religious sincerity, much less "Judaizing," but actual crimes, of which we know that these conversos were accused. However, "infamy" clearly refers to religious matters, and this reference simply appears to be to hearsay evidence about the accusations of the Inquisition.

An interesting Christian doctrine which seems to have been particularly influential among learned conversos was the "mystic body" concept, according to which all believers are one body, and which, indeed, may have its origin in Jewish tradition of communal responsibility (*keneset Yisrael; kelal Yisrael;* "kol Yisrael ʿarevim zeh le-zeh," [all Israel is responsible one for the other]). This doctrine of the mystic body, in any case, was already used by Pedro Díaz de Toledo, first bishop of Málaga, son of the converso Fernan, the *relator* of Toledo, and was to continue in the seventeenth century.[160]

There is also a considerable amount of evidence that has already been mustered in previous chapters which demonstrates the sincerity and devotion of conversos to their new religion. For instance, we have seen that conversos often were active in support of various religious and charitable institutions, and either formed their own *cofradías,* as such groups were called, or contributed to the support of those already in operation, like that of Santa María la Blanca in Toledo, founded by Doctor Nuño Alvarez de Cepeda (a canon of the cathedral of Seville) in 1478, in connection with the church which had previously been a synagogue. Among the founding members of this *cofradía* were several conversos, in fact, including various physicians, the *mayordomo* of the archbishop, some members of the Cota family, and various merchants and craftsmen. In 1488 another group of Toledo conversos established a chapel in the Monastery of San Agustín.[161]

"Dio" vs. "Dios" as Supposed "Jewish" Usage

It has frequently been claimed that conversos scrupulously avoided using the expression *Dios* for God, which they thought to be a plural form, using instead *Dio*, a nonexistent "singular" form. One author has even incorrectly stated that Jews were guilty of the same error.[162] In any case, it has become commonplace to assert that this was done to avoid "Trinitarian" implications.

In fact, the form *Dio* is entirely unknown in Jewish sources from medieval Spain (Shem Ṭov de Carrión, for example, uses *Dios* in his *Proverbios morales,* and other cases could be cited). Linguistically, of course, the Spanish *Dios* is merely an adaptation of the Latin nominative form *Deus,* and no "plural" is implied at all. Indeed, Christian texts always refer to *Dios* in the singular, as God, and clearly distinguish between this usage and the Trinity. One scholar has suggested that because the plural form is the same as the singular (*Dios*), the "Jews" (!) accused the Christians of polytheism for not using the singular *Dio* (from the Latin accusative *Deum*).[163] There is no evidence to sustain this theory, and it would be absurd to insist on the grammatically incorrect use of an accusative singular in place of the nominative merely to avoid the appearance of "polytheism." In addition, as previously stated, Jews did not know Latin and certainly were not such experts in Latin grammar; conversos, or at least the converso authors, on the other hand, did know Latin and certainly would not have made such errors. Also, this theory is wrong because a plural form of *Dios* in fact exists—*dioses* (in the sense of "gods")—and was used in medieval Spanish.

In only two works which *may* have been composed by Jews in fifteenth-century Spain, the *Poema de Yosef* and a Spanish translation of Judah ha-Levy's *Kuzari,* does the form *Dio* appear. The problematic nature of these texts, and of their dating, does not allow us to conclude positively that they reflect actual Jewish usage, however.[164]

Unquestionably, however, we have evidence that conversos used, or at least were accused of having used, the form *Dio.* This all appears in Inquisition processes, and as usual these are highly suspect of being falsified Christian testimony. The earliest recorded instance I have been able to discover is the process of Alfonso de Toledo, a monk of the Jeronimite Order, in 1487 (discussed in Chapter 7, below), who was reported to have said that man must serve God, using the term "el Dio." Yet in the testimony immediately following, he is reported to have said "Dios" on another occasion.[165]

Another accused converso in the same period is said to have referred to serving "Dio." [166]

In the notorious case of the conversion of Juan de Ciudad, discussed also later, a Jew, Isaac Arrondi, is reported to have used the form *Dio* (1489). In the same year, another converso supposedly stated that he believed only in "el santo dio." In 1498 another converso is supposed to have referred to the laws given "por mano del dio" to Abraham. [167]

It is interesting to note that the Catalan form is *Deu* (also French), which might be supposed to have influenced some of this usage, especially in those Inquisition cases (such as that of Juan de Ciudad) which were in Aragón-Catalonia. Also, the form *Dio* in early Christian Spanish texts is attested. [168]

We may conclude either that this was another example of false testimony against conversos accused by the Inquisition, or, perhaps (and this appears remote), that some conversos actually used this form to distinguish a "singular" from a "plural" deity; in which case we would have to assume a complete ignorance of Spanish grammar, as well as theology, on their part.

It should be mentioned that the form *Dio* is found, usually but not exclusively, in Spanish works written by Sefardim in the seventeenth and eighteenth centuries. These were, however, almost exclusively Portuguese Marranos—i.e., Christians of Jewish descent—living in Amsterdam.

7

The Inquisition

The general impression that the Inquisition in Spain was a product of the reign of the Catholic Monarchs is erroneous. The reason for this error is not hard to discover; the majority of the books dealing with the Spanish Inquisition begin with the fifteenth century, as though it emerged at that time without any antecedents.

In fact, there were two Inquisitions in Spain, the earlier one centered in Aragón-Catalonia, and the fifteenth-century "Spanish" Inquisition. Yet another misconception shared by many, including not a few scholars, is that the Inquisition was established and run by "the Church." Thus, a recent translator of Eimeric's Manual for Inquisitors asked, but did not attempt to answer, "Why did the *Roman* Inquisition [his emphasis] last longer in Spain than elsewhere?"[1] The question reveals several erroneous assumptions: (1) that there was a "Spanish Inquisition," (2) that it was "Roman," i.e., directed from and controlled by the Church in Rome, an *opus romanum*, as he calls it; and (3) that the Inquisition lasted longer in medieval Spain than elsewhere (ignoring, for example, Italy).

Even the Spanish Inquisition of the fifteenth century, as we shall see, can scarcely be called "Roman," for it soon achieved a complete independence of the Church and even a defiance of the papacy.

Origins of the Inquisition

The original Inquisition was established by a bull of Alexander III at III Lateran, the ecumenical Church council, in 1179, attended by the bishops of Tarragona, Gerona, Barcelona, Vic, Tortosa, Lérida, and Seu d'Urgell, from the kingdom of Aragón-Catalonia.

The purpose of the Inquisition was solely to act against Christian heretics who were deemed to be corrupting the faith from within.

In Spain, the first secular act (initiated not by Church authorities) was a document of Alfonso II (1194) of Aragón-Catalonia against the Waldensian heretics. In 1197 at the council of Gerona, Pedro II confirmed this act and added, for the first time, the penalty of burning at the stake.[2]

Throughout the thirteenth century, also, the Inquisition was concerned with Christian heretics, primarily the Albigensians. Three papal delegates met in Montpellier in 1206 and nearly gave up all efforts to convert the Albigensians, when the (Spanish) bishop of Osma, Diego de Azevedo, arrived on his return from Rome. He urged the legates rather to give up their wealth and preach in a state of poverty to the common people, using his subprior Domingo de Guzmán as the example they should follow. From this memorable meeting emerged the Dominican Order, or the "preaching" friars, which also took control of the Inquisition. However gentle the bishop's urging was, a crusade was proclaimed against the Albigensians.[3]

The Jews, therefore, had no role whatever in the activities of the Inquisition. True, the Church had concerned itself with the possibility of conversion of Christians to Judaism, or the possibility of converted Jews relapsing to their former religion. Gregory I had already set down the rule which was to become canon law that baptism could not be by force. However, Innocent III in 1201 modified that rule considerably. While admitting that baptism by force could not be sanctioned, he noted that baptism is a sacrament, which automatically takes effect, and thus once a Jew has been baptized he must be considered a Christian and must remain so, even where force was used. Nicholas III, in 1278, took the next crucial step in deciding that those who through fear, even if not absolutely coerced, were baptized and then returned to their "Jewish blindness" should be handed over to the secular authorities to be condemned to death (this was confirmed in 1378 by Nicholas IV).[4]

Menéndez Pelayo claimed to find the law that any Christian who became a Jew would be burned already in the *Furs* (law code) of Valencia (1240). It is not there, however, but is instead in the *Fuero real* written for Alfonso X of Castile-León. The immediate source appears to be a forgery, the *Fuero juzgo,* purporting to be a translation of the Visigothic code of law. Similarly, the *Siete partidas,* largely written by Ramón de Peñafort, a canonist, for Alfonso, proclaimed the death penalty for any Christian "so unfortunate as to become a Jew," or who "sometimes becomes insane" and converts to Islam.[5]

Llorente also provided some false information concerning the origin of Inquisition activities in Aragón-Catalonia, citing documents of 1225 and 1228. However, the first is simply Jaime I's well-known "Peace" law, in which paragraph 22 merely excludes heretics from its protection; it has nothing to do with the Inquisition. The document of 1228 is the same. However, the Church council of Tarragona of 1233 (which came after, and clearly as a result of, Gregory IX's bull of 1232 to Esparrago, bishop of Tarragona, cited by Llorente) did establish certain relevant laws; e.g., a prohibition on the possession of translations in "Romance" (the vernacular) of the Bible, either the "old" or "new" testaments; a stipulation that no heretic or suspected heretic should hold public office; and the granting of exclusive jurisdiction to local bishops to try suspected heretics. This last was to prove a source of considerable controversy with the renewal of the Inquisition in this kingdom in the fifteenth century. This document, therefore, is the first so far known which clearly indicates the establishment of the Inquisition on Spanish soil.[6]

In 1257, some Dominicans in fact arrested and tried some Christian heretics in Lérida. Some were condemned to death and their goods confiscated for the Crown. However, Jaime I revoked the confiscation and pardoned at least one of the condemned altogether. The following year a deceased knight was condemned for heresy in Porta and his body was exhumed and burned. In 1263 several Christian heretics were condemned in Perpignan, including the widow of Arnau Eimeric (related to the later famous Inquisitor?). Of particular interest to us is the restitution by the king of "*bona fama*" (good name) and return of confiscated property, in 1265, to a Christian of Gerona because the accusation of his having observed rites and customs of Jews was not proven. Nevertheless, a few months later he was again in trouble and was again absolved by the king of charges he had entered the house of a Jew in Gerona contrary to orders that he was not to have contact with Jews.[7]

Baer attempted to portray the king as a zealot for the faith: "Throughout his reign he cooperated with the papacy, vigorously persecuting the heretics in his kingdom." However, this portrayal is not substantiated by the sources. In fact, far from cooperating with the papacy, he was in constant conflict with the pope. Clement IV severely condemned the king for desiring to divorce his second wife (who Jaime claimed was infected with leprosy) and for keeping a concubine. The pope also demanded that he not allow "Saracens" (Muslims) to remain in his kingdom at all, and that he "repress the Jewish mischief," which he certainly did not do.

On the other hand, Peter Linehan appears to have been unaware of the relevant sources we have mentioned, including the Tarragona council, and incorrectly claimed that the "burden" of the suppression of heresy "had been shouldered by the secular power in 1233 and not entrusted to the bishops and to ecclesiastical assemblies which [i.e., such "entrusting"] hardly ever occurred." This is directly contradicted, as we have seen, by the Tarragona council.[8]

Ramón de Peñafort, a Dominican born in Catalonia but educated in Bologna, was the major anti-Jewish figure of thirteenth-century Spain. After he had completed his malicious work in writing the Castilian legislation (*Siete partidas*) which for the first time in Spanish codes expressed hostility to Jews, although fortunately it remained only a reference work with mere advisory status at best, he returned to his native Catalonia to wreak similar havoc. We have encountered him already in regard to the efforts to censor Hebrew books and as a major figure in the disputations. In 1242, together with "other wise men," he succeeded in persuading the Council of Tarragona to issue a decree that heretics should be turned over to the "secular arm," i.e., the government, to be burned at the stake, while those who recanted were, mercifully, to be imprisoned for life![9]

The most important document in the foundation of the Inquisition, however, is the bull *Turbato corde* (1267) of Clement IV, sent to the friars. For the first time, Jews are specifically mentioned:

> With a troubled heart we relate what we have heard, that [several reprobate Christians] have abandoned the true [Catholic] faith and have wickedly transferred themselves to the rites of the Jews. This is obviously the more reprehensible since it makes it possible for the most holy name of Christ to be more safely blasphemed by enemies out of his own household [Jews]. We have been informed, moreover, that this is not without injurious effect on the said faith [Christianity], and it should therefore be countered by means of quick and appropriate remedies.
>
> We command your organization [*universitati vestrae;* your Order is probably a better translation] [by apostolic writing, to search out heretics within your territories, by the authority of the Apostolic See], to make diligent and thorough inquiry into the above, through Christians as well as through Jews. Against Christians whom you have discovered to have committed such things you are to proceed as against heretics. Against Jews whom you may find guilty of having induced Christians of either sex to join their execrable rite, or whom you may find doing so in the future, you shall impose fitting punishment. By means of appropriate ecclesiastical censure you shall silence all who oppose you. If necessary you may call on the secular arm.[10]

Synan correctly has suggested that this bull was directly influenced by the previously discussed Barcelona disputation(s). However, he neglected to mention Clement's letters against the Talmud and ordering the censorship of Hebrew books.[11]

In fact, none of this proved to be effective, for although a commission of Dominicans, including Ramón de Peñafort, was appointed to investigate Jewish books, the Jews were soon able to convince the king, who was anything but anti-Jewish, of the falseness of the charges against them. The Inquisition failed to take any action against any Jews at all, so far as we know.

Thomas Aquinas, also a Dominican and a major theologian, played a crucial role in the development of efforts to missionize among Jews and Muslims. Full details on this activity as it relates to Spain remain to be discussed elsewhere. Recently, a Spanish writer has agreed that Aquinas was intimately involved in the missionary efforts of the second half of the thirteenth century, and he contends that the "Gentiles" of Aquinas' *Summa contra gentiles* are not merely pre-Christian pagans, as often claimed. He concludes that he intended by this term the "Oriental [Muslim] infidels," or those of Aragón. However, his conclusions are unsatisfactory. He does not mention Jews at all, and while Aquinas' work is hardly a strong anti-Jewish polemic, it is at least in part that. This author claims, without any evidence, that Aquinas distinguished the "action of the Church" from civil power in the Inquisition, and that it was "foreign" to his thinking to permit the Church to utilize the secular arm in all circumstances; nevertheless, he approved the Inquisition, "although without enthusiasm." [12] In fact, we know that Aquinas, no particular friend of Jews in any event, was heavily influenced by the harshly anti-Jewish polemic of Ramón Martí's *Pugio fidei*. In any case, it is unlikely that the Dominicans would have carried out their Inquisition with such enthusiasm lacking the full support of so important a member of the order and the most important theologian of the Middle Ages. [13]

In France around 1280 some Jews accepted baptism during a riot in the town of La Marche, and later they sought to return to Judaism. As noted, this return was now against canon law, following the ruling of Innocent III. Apparently the local Inquisitors imprisoned them for over a year and then asked the pope, Nicholas IV, what should be done with them, to which he replied that they should be treated as Christian heretics since they had not been forcibly baptized but "voluntarily" became Christians. Deplorable as such actions may have been, they were due not to some "peculiar" definition of force on the part of the Church, but rather to the legal distinction that the action of a sacrament takes effect in spite of circumstances, and as Innocent III wrote, the "impress" of Christianity is still upon the baptized person, however unwilling. [14]

In November of 1281 the archbishop of Canterbury, John Pecham, complained to Edward I that some of the Jews converted to Christianity had relapsed to Judaism. He demanded their punishment by the "secular arm," using the traditional claim that although Jews cannot be compelled to convert, once they are Christians they must not be allowed to relapse (the traditional phrase "like dogs to their vomit" is used in at least one letter). Some of the converts fled and took refuge with the Jewish community of London and received the protection of the constable of the Tower of London until a new writ could be issued. This *cause célèbre* led to a general complaint in 1285 against relapsed converts, and may have been a cause of the expulsion of the Jews from England a few years later. [15]

Honorius IV responded to the accusation of 1285 in his bull *Nimis*, complaining of Jews who converted and then returned to practicing Judaism in the very parish where they had converted, while others were aided by Jews to flee the country and go where they could live openly as Jews (return to their "perfidy").[16]

We hear of few such incidents yet in Spain, but in 1284 Pedro III in fact *forbade* the Dominicans to proceed with investigation of Jews in Barcelona accused of harboring Jewish converts who had a change of heart and sought to return to Judaism.[17] An important text, ignored by historians of the Inquisition, reveals that in 1286 Alfonso III gave authority specifically to the secular officials, but not Church officials, at the behest of the Dominicans themselves, to punish any heretics in the kingdom. Nothing is said about Jews or any "Judaizing" heresy.[18]

Most astonishing, perhaps, was the grant of royal protection by Jaime II in 1311 to Juçef Maçana, a Jew of Barcelona, exempting him from persecution by the powerful Inquisitor Juan de Lotgerio (or Llotger, the Catalan spelling), who had been instrumental in suppressing the Templars. Such persecution was directed at Jews who had converted and relapsed to Judaism, or who had encouraged Christians to convert to Judaism.[19]

Earlier, Philip the Fair of France had written to Jaime II informing him of his action in seizing the goods of the Templars (accused of heresy and a whole host of crimes), and urging that king to do the same. Philip's action had the blessing of the pope (Clement V), but Jaime nevertheless replied that he "marveled" at Philip's actions and that he would take no such action without orders of the pope. He wrote the pope for instructions, but before the pope received the letter he had already sent "permission" to move against the Templars in Aragón. Jaime then promptly forgot his scruples, and Juan de Lotgerio and fray Guillermo, both Franciscans, urged action against the Templars. The king ordered such actions throughout his kingdom.[20]

Nevertheless, the following year (1304) the king wrote to the Inquisitor Bernardo de Podio expressing his displeasure over the latter's proceedings against *Jews* in Tarragona.[21]

The activities of the Inquisition decreased considerably with the eradication of the Cathar heresy, and although heresy among Christians was by no means over, the Inquisition now turned its efforts, through the preaching campaigns of the Dominicans and the Franciscans, to "propagation of the faith" among Muslims and Jews. In fact, this activity had only very limited success in the fourteenth century among Jews, and virtually none among the Muslims of Spain (even less in North Africa).[22]

The most significant figure in the Inquisition of the fourteenth century was, of course, Nicolás Eimeric (sometimes spelled Eymerich), born in Gerona in 1320. A fanatic of indomitable energy and religious zeal, according to his biographer, he entered the Dominican Order at the age of fourteen. Although he quickly rose to a position of importance and eventually became Inquisitor General, there was opposition to him almost from the beginning of his career. Thus, although he was confirmed in his post by the bishop of Porto and the papal legate of Innocent VI in 1358, the chapter of the Dominican Order deposed him in Perpignan in 1360 and named his enemy Bernat Ermengol as Inquisitor General. By intrigue and manipulation he was named at the chapter meeting in Ferrara as vicar-general of the order for Aragón in 1362, and shortly thereafter resumed his post as Inquisitor General. His excesses in that position resulted in severe condemnation by the king.

The major concern of the Inquisition at the time were the supposed "heresies" of the doctrines of Ramón Lull. Juan I of Aragón-Catalonia, who became king in 1387, continued the opposition to Eimeric and the royal support of Lull's doctrines. In 1389 Eimeric had a papal audience at Avignon to discuss the case, and this seems to have lasted a considerable time, since in 1390 the council of Barcelona wrote to the pope against Eimeric, virtually calling for his removal. Shortly thereafter, they in fact demanded of the king that Eimeric be expelled from the kingdom of Aragón-Catalonia. Perhaps he was, for soon he was found in Valencia (a part of the kingdom, but maybe the exile did not include Valencia), and the council again complained to the pope of his excesses there. In 1391 the city council of Valencia complained of his persecution of the "Lullists" there. The following year the king deposed him from his office also in Valencia, and as Inquisitor of Aragón. As perhaps the final insult, the king established a school for Lullist doctrine in his palace in 1393.[23]

Most of the works of Eimeric are still in manuscript. One of these mentioned a scholar of Valencia among the heretics, one Antonio Riera, with some items of interest relating to Jews. Supposedly he had calculated, according to "prophecies," the time at which all Jews must be exterminated without leaving a single one in the world! Second, he had said that the time would come when the Laws of Jews, Christians, and Muslims would be reduced to only one Law (religion). Finally, in spite of his desire that Jews be exterminated, he had supposedly said that the Jew who believes (i.e., in his own "Law") with good faith would be saved.[24]

It is easy to understand why these points would be considered heretical, even the unique statement that all the Jews would be exterminated, for the Church never advocated or envisioned any such thing (the sole exception hitherto was the fanatical Saint John Chrysostom).

Eimeric's chief importance and lasting influence, however, was his famous manual for the Inquisition, *Directorium inquisitorum*. There he refers to the possibility of Jewish heresy in regard to their own faith:

> If any Jews be found who, by word of mouth or deeds, should deny what is common to us Christians and to them, as when they verbally assert that God is not one or indicate it by deeds through sacrificing to demons . . . they ought

to be prosecuted and punished by bishops and Inquisitors of the faith as heretics against their own law and as promoters [*factores*] of heretics against the
law of Christ.[25]

That Jewish "orthodoxy" was theoretically subject to the jurisdiction of the
pope was a long-recognized doctrine, but this is the first time that we find
the Inquisition seeking to exercise such control.

In relation to this statement of Eimeric, it is instructive that in 1352 in
Valencia a Jew who was a renowned physician, Moses the son of Jacob
Porpoler, was accused by the Inquisition of having taken part with other
Jews in their houses in casting lots (fortune-telling, "per sorticatores re-
periri"), which was contrary to the Christian faith, since it "smacked of
heresy," and was also, the king reminded him, prohibited by Jewish law. In
return for the payment of a fine, Pedro IV exempted him from any further
punishment, in recognition of the services of his father, "stivalerii nostri"
(apparently a shoemaker; cf. Aragonese *estivalles*).

That same year the king provided the Dominicans in Barcelona with
5,000 *sous* from the fine imposed on Jews of Valencia condemned for heresy by Hugo (de Fenollet, bishop of Valencia and chancellor of Aragón-
Catalonia from 1348 to 1356), possibly the same case.[26]

There were other manuals of the Inquisition even before Eimeric's famous
one, however. Elsewhere I have already discussed briefly Bernard Gui's earlier manual as it relates to Jewish practices, in connection with the Albigensian heresy. Pedro de Albalat, archbishop of Tarragona (1238–51) and also
a friend of Ramón de Peñafort, strongly supported the Dominicans. Probably at the synod of Pamplona in 1241 (in any case, around that time),
Pedro issued what has been described as "the first document worthy of the
name of a manual of inquisitorial procedure." It contains nothing concerning Jews or Jewish practices, however.[27]

Ramón de Peñafort, Pedro's friend and protégé, took an active part in
the Inquisition immediately upon his return to Spain and prior to his election as master general of the Dominican Order, being involved, for example,
in the investigation of charges of heresy against the bishop of Urgel, Ponce
de Vilamur (ca. 1250–52), and of the Waldensians shortly thereafter. As
yet, however, he confined his anti-Jewish sentiments to his prolific and dangerous legal codes.[28]

In 1354 there took place an extraordinary meeting of the representatives
of the Jewish communities of Catalonia and Valencia (later, also Aragón) in
Barcelona. This was not, as Baer assumed, a reaction to the "Black Plague"
of 1348, although one of the problems discussed related to the general possibility of consequences to the Jews from pestilences, but rather was due to
the necessity of dealing with various perceived threats to the Jews. The most
important of these was, in fact, the danger of the increasing conversion of

Jews, who "have gone over the pass" (converted) and "exchanged their glory [Judaism] for shame." This is the document which we have already discussed, and partially translated, at the end of Chapter 2.

Various measures were enacted at that time by the representatives of the Jewish communities, and as usual all of these (that is, the practical ordinances) had the approval of the king.

Most important in the context of our present discussion, considering the fact that Jews for the first time were beginning to have some significant contact with the Inquisition and were understandably fearful of what its consequences might prove to be, was the concern that "investigation of heresy" should not include the Jews, except in such matters as should be equal for all faiths, such as the denial of God or of revelation. It was also urged that if a Jew assisted a Christian heretic, the charge of heresy should not automatically be applied to the Jew. This, they explained, is because "it is impossible to place in the boundaries of heresy a Jew who is justified [in what he says] in accord with his faith."[29] In other words, if a Jew were to deny the Trinity, etc., in discussions with a Christian heretic, this ought not to be considered "heretical" in terms of Jewish belief. However, they acknowledged that a Jew may merit punishment by the *civil* authorities for aiding a Christian heretic. Obviously, their chief concern was that Jews fall under the jurisdiction not of the Inquisition, but rather of the civil courts, where the law already offered them some protection (witnesses, etc.).

Very interesting at about this time is the case of Ramón de Tárrega. He was baptized at approximately the age of eleven, and his parents also converted (perhaps after his birth; Fort i Cogul conjectured that his parents returned to Judaism, since he was not baptized until that age; however, this is unlikely, as there was a good deal of controversy about the validity of baptism of converts before the age of eleven and it is probable that his parents were baptized and then had him baptized when he reached the appropriate age). He entered the convent of Cervera and then pursued advanced studies, as a Dominican, at the convent of Barcelona, where Nicolás Eimeric was his student. He was assigned to Palma (Majorca) in 1355, and then was named lector of logic (perhaps also medicine) at the convent in Lérida in 1357, and finally returned to Cervera to teach theology (1365–66). It was, apparently, at that time that he got into trouble for "errors" in his teachings and writings. Nicolás Eimeric, his former pupil and now Inquisitor, attempted to get him to retract his errors, to no avail. In 1368 papal intervention, while condemning his errors, absolved him from having to recant.

However, the case was soon reopened, but in the midst of the investigation (1371) he was found dead in his room in the monastery at Barcelona, in suspicious circumstances which suggested either murder or suicide. His works, including some alchemical works attributed to him but probably by Ramón Lull, were burned.[30]

Certain Jews in Traust in 1357 were condemned to perpetual imprisonment by the Inquisition, at the instigation of a priest, and these obtained conditions of pardon from the archbishop of Zaragoza and the king. Those conditions required a payment of a fine for their release. Some, however, refused to pay after they were released, and Pedro IV had to order them to make payment.

In 1367 in Barcelona two Jews were burned and a Christian was imprisoned on charges of having sold consecrated hosts to the Jews (throughout the Middle Ages, though rarely in Spain, Jews were suspected of doing awful things to consecrated hosts).[31]

Pedro IV in 1359 sent orders to the Inquisitor Bernard de Podio of Provence that any Jew who abandoned the "Jewish blindness" for the "light of Christ" and then relapsed "like a dog to its vomit" was subject to the Inquisition, and noted that many such were fleeing from Provence and elsewhere to other cities in the kingdom (Aragón-Catalonia) and there continued to live "according to the Jewish perfidy." Therefore, at the request of this Inquisitor, the king granted him authority to investigate such cases *throughout the kingdom* and to incarcerate and punish offenders in accord with canon law.[32]

Nevertheless, the chief concern of the Inquisition in the latter part of the fourteenth century was the previously mentioned "Lullist heresy," with the result that little attention was given to conversos.

In the second half of the fifteenth century, the city council of Barcelona attempted to gain some control over the activities of the Inquisition by requesting from Eugenius IV in 1446 the appointment of a special Inquisitor, a native of Catalonia, but the request was not dealt with before that pope died in 1447. Finally in 1459 the papal office in Avignon granted it and appointed a special Inquisitor for Barcelona.[33]

It was this precedent which the council and citizens of that city were to cite in their futile opposition to the unified "Spanish" Inquisition in the reign of Fernando and Isabel.

Jews and the Inquisition

Contrary to general myth, the Inquisition never had any specific jurisdiction over Jews, nor did it ever harm Jews in any way, with the exception of the specific matter of Jews influencing Christians to convert. Over a century ago Lea already put this quite correctly:

> The Inquisition had no jurisdiction over the Jew, unless he rendered himself amenable to it by some offence against the faith. He was not baptized; he was

not a member of the Church and therefore was incapable of heresy, which was the object of inquisitorial functions. He might, however, render himself subject to it by proselytism, by seducing Christians to embrace his errors and this was constantly alleged against Jews, although their history shows that, unlike the other great religions, Judaism has ever been a national faith with no desire to spread beyond the boundaries of the race.[34]

If somewhat overstated in several respects, this formulation nevertheless is essentially correct. As specific proof may be cited a letter of Jaime II (1292) to the Inquisitors, noting that they were, in fact, "proceeding against Jews of Gerona and Besalú and other places," and reminding them that "it is not our intention for you to introduce an inquisition against the Jews for heresy, since they are not of the Catholic faith or law, and since if some of them should act against the law they are punished by us, we order you to desist" from investigating Jews.[35]

One of the extremely rare cases where a Jew was arrested by the Inquisition happened in Zaragoza in 1365 when three Jews (including two members of the prominent and influential Caballería family) protested that fray Gómez de Luna, a Dominican, had imprisoned a Jew on orders of the Inquisition.[36]

However, as we have seen, the Inquisition could intervene in cases where Jews aided conversos to return to Judaism, or assisted Christians to convert. Such a case occurred in Tarragona in 1312 when ten Jews were condemned by the archbishop for their part in aiding two German Christians to convert to Judaism and flee to Toledo. Jaime II sentenced the ten to banishment and confiscation of their property. One of the condemned Jews was Senton (Shem Ṭov) Falco, later the rabbi of Majorca and a renowned scholar. In April of 1313, however, the king revoked the sentence against eight of the Jews, among whom was Falco, and they were permitted to remain in the kingdom but not in Tarragona.[37]

The same archbishop was responsible for a process against the Jews of Montblanch in 1313 for assisting a converso to return to Judaism. This time the king intervened and ordered the archbishop not to punish all the Jews of Montblanch, but only those actually guilty. Once again, he finally remitted a portion of the fine imposed, already a very lenient sentence.[38]

Finally, in 1323 the king, for payment of 15,000 *sous*, pardoned some twenty-one Jews of Tarragona and Valls who had been condemned. Baer conjectured that this was a retrial of the earlier Tarragona affair; however, there is nothing in the text to support this conclusion, and the ten years which had elapsed make that unlikely, nor did Baer pay attention to the fact that Jews of Valls as well as Tarragona are named or that the names of the Jews are not the same as in the earlier case.[39]

In 1326 the king gave permission to a Franciscan friar to keep some books confiscated from certain Jews of Calatayud accused of heresy. The books were a Hebrew Bible, "a book called *sarasin*" (surely *Shorashim*, probably the well-known Hebrew grammar by Qimḥi), and various Talmudic tractates. The king noted that the friar knew Hebrew.[40]

We hear, however infrequently, about other actions against Jewish heretics, as when Jaime II assigned all the revenues obtained by the Inquisition in a case against "certain heretics of the Jewish *aljama* of Calatayud" to his daughter Maria (then a nun at Sijena).[41]

As had his predecessors, Pedro IV continued to insist that the Inquisition generally had no jurisdiction over Jews. Thus, in 1379 he wrote a strong letter to the bishop of Gerona protesting a case in which the Inquisition had arrested a Jew and was extorting money from him. The king reminded the bishop that "the Jews are our treasure and under our general protection," and must not be unjustly oppressed or harmed by anyone, "for except in certain cases the investigation [?] and punishment of Jews pertains to us and to no other."

Alfonso IV continued the policy of his predecessors, and in 1416 ordered the Inquisitors of Perpignan not to have any jurisdiction over Jews. The queen reiterated this in 1421. Pope Martin V also issued a strong statement in 1422 particularly relating to the Jews of Spain. The papal legate wrote from Lérida prohibiting the Inquisition of Aragón from molesting Jews. Nevertheless, one Jew (possibly a converso?), Bonafos Roget of Perpignan, was condemned.[42]

As noted in a previous chapter, Jews often voluntarily gave information to the Inquisition against conversos, particularly in the fifteenth century. So in 1484 the king wrote to the Inquisitors of Aragón-Catalonia concerning such information given by certain Jews there, ordering that the rabbi and "sacristan" of the synagogues and other Jews should be further interrogated as to the truth of these matters.[43]

Elijah Capsali of Candia, relying on firsthand accounts of exiles from Spain he met while in Venice, states that the Inquisition imposed a *ḥerem* (ban) on all Jews in their synagogues compelling them to inform of anything, "great or small," which they knew about the conversos. This, of course, could not have been imposed without the agreement and cooperation of the Jews themselves.[44]

Not all Jews cooperated, however. Solomon Ibn Verga also relates that Judah Ibn Verga, perhaps an ancestor, was arrested in Seville by the Inquisition so that he would inform them who the conversos were who were guilty of "Judaizing." However, he fled to Lisbon, where he was again arrested and tortured and finally died.[45]

The anonymous account of the Expulsion, written perhaps by an Italian Jew and probably dependent on the above accounts (contrary to Marx, the editor), states that the Inquisition required the Jews "in every city" to announce in the synagogues the *herem* concerning anyone who knew of a converso who gave money for lamps in the synagogue, or any other religious purpose. The Dominicans (*dorshim*) preached in the synagogues before the scribes of the king and imposed an oath upon the Jews to inform on any of these matters.[46]

Many documents of the Inquisition processes of Toledo in the last decade of the fifteenth century indicate that Jews did testify against conversos, often as hostile witnesses. Some may have had personal animosities to settle, but there is no doubt, as we have earlier seen, that the majority of Jews had no love for the conversos.[47]

While Jews in some places were compelled to give testimony on pain of excommunication (*herem*), we see clear evidence that many were only too eager to do so. Fernando de Pulgar refers to the false witness given by many Jews in Toledo:

> And because in this case of heresy they received Jewish and Muslim witnesses and servants and infamous and vile men, and by the word of these many were seized and condemned to the fire. There were in this city some poor and vile Jewish men who because of enmity or malice gave false testimony against one of the conversos, saying that he had seen him "Judaizing." And, knowing the truth, the queen ordered them judged as false [witnesses], and eight [such] Jews were stoned [or] torn to pieces.[48]

In this remarkable account, it will be seen that Isabel herself knew that Jews were giving false testimony against conversos. This is again one of the sources ignored by modern "experts" on the Inquisition.

In some cases, the animosity of Jews against conversos was at least partly due to economic matters, as for example in Trujillo in 1489 when the accused had owed money for taxes to a Jewish official who had seized his houses and property for nonpayment. In others, it was a matter of professional competition and jealousy, as when some Jewish physicians testified in the case of a converso surgeon of Ocaña.[49]

Jews Pay the Tuition of a Friendly Inquisitor

Not all of the contacts between Jews and the Inquisitors, even in the period of the early Inquisition of Aragón-Catalonia, were hostile, however. A very important document, unfortunately lacking any date and with the crucial name of the Inquisitor removed (it was apparently Petrus de Fonte Luporum, Inquisitor General from 1405 to 1412), is a letter written by the poet Solomon de Piera on behalf of the Jewish *aljama* of Zaragoza to all the other Jewish communities of the kingdom.[50]

The letter reminds them of the dangers in which the Jews found themselves because of the Inquisition, due to the accusations of heresy against conversos, "almost as though he who turns his face to the wall to pray is considered a heretic and unbeliever" (that, indeed, was precisely one of the charges found in the Inquisition manuals, as this was considered a Jewish form of praying). Though it is not said specifically in the letter, the implication is obvious that Jews themselves were under suspicion of influencing the conversos.

"Therefore all the inhabitants of the land are dismayed [cf. Exod. 15.15] because of the oppression of the distress [caused by] the Inquisitors." However, he says, God has seen fit to cause mercy to be shown to the Jews by "the kings and counselors of the land . . . and especially the *honorable sage the Inquisitor General has dealt wondrously with us*," and all the Inquisitors in the land have been influenced by him. "He also spoke good things of us from the day when God desired to confound us," influencing others "to give us rest from the anger of the speech and slander of the people and calm us from the days of evil." (This no doubt refers to the animosity against Jews which, to some extent, continued from the events of 1391.)

Now this Inquisitor has decided "to go to Avignon to become elevated in the degrees of a *maestre* of theology and to enclose himself in its ascent, and since the nature of the affair requires the daily expenditure of considerable sums [to realize his plan], the man has entreated us to provide for him a blessing from that which comes to our hands" and also to write the other Jewish communities to request money for this purpose. "And we, seeing that his mercy was wondrous to us in times of sorrow, and always all the day he stood ready to strengthen us in his wisdom and understanding—and these are things which have no measure for their reward," have agreed.

This incredible document, totally ignored by Baer and other scholars, reveals that the Jews were quite willing to reward those who supported them and intervened for them. It hardly needs to be said that this generous protection of the Jews by an Inquisitor General in the fifteenth century, and the no less generous response of the Jewish communities in paying at least part of the expenses for his advanced schooling, are hardly consistent with the general myth concerning either the Jews or the Inquisition.

Veracity of Inquisition Records

Many writers, Jewish and non-Jewish, accept at face value every record and testimony in every Inquisition process. Accordingly, the myth of "crypto-Judaism" is the more extensively perpetuated the more these cases are written about, especially by scholars unfamiliar with the whole picture of Jewish-Christian relations in medieval Spain, and the converso problem in general.

At first glance, the evidence of these records seems damning, indeed. Conversos are accused of a whole litany of practices which are termed "Judaizing" (e.g., lighting lamps or candles on Friday night, wearing "clean clothes" on the Jewish Sabbath, observing the "great fast" [Yom Kippur], eating unleavened bread on Passover, and even observing the holiday of Sukkot, which requires building—outdoors and in full public view—a booth [*sukkah*] adorned with branches, in which all meals are eaten for a week).

However, common sense and careful consideration of these charges reveal how absurdly false most, if not all, of them actually are. Almost all the charges were made by "old Christians," who seem peculiarly familiar with Jewish religious customs, which coincidentally just happened to be only those outlined in the manuals of the Inquisition. Never do we find, in fact, charges of observing less hazardous and less public religious practices which are not mentioned in the manuals but were no less important in Jewish life.

Second, the charges were usually made about incidents which supposedly took place years before the Inquisition opened the case, sometimes twenty or more years. Why did these zealous "old Christians" wait so long to inform the Inquisition?

Finally, seldom if ever is there any corroborating testimony of more than one witness to these "crimes," which appears peculiar in light of the open and public practices of which the conversos were accused. In the case of building a *sukkah*, for example, the entire town would have known and observed such activity.

Logically, too, these charges rarely make any sense. In the first place, none of these conversos was forced to become a Christian. They all willingly decided to convert, and as we have seen, it was precisely this which caused the rabbis to decide that they were in a totally different category from the forced converts of the earlier medieval period in Germany or France. Therefore, how are we to explain this sudden "zeal" for observing Jewish religious practices, a zeal which they certainly failed to exhibit when they chose to convert to Christianity? This is a particularly compelling argument in the case of these first-generation conversos, within a few years of their conversion, at a time when there was still no reason for them to despair at their situation, nor any nostalgia for the remembered customs of their youth.

Also, these conversos surely knew the danger of any such practices. If there had been any doubt in the minds of those who converted long before the Expulsion (i.e., in the 1460s to the 1480s), there certainly was no longer room for such doubt after the Inquisition was established in Castile. By the late 1480s, condemned "heretics" were being burned in large numbers all over Castile. Surely only an insane person could have imagined that it would be possible to practice openly and in public such notorious Jewish religious customs.

What about those cases where the accused conversos, according to the records, confessed to the "crimes" with which they were charged? The answer to that is easy; whether or not torture was used, which we shall discuss, the fear of death was enough to cause many to confess to anything. A confessed heretic usually got off fairly easily, with no longer the punishment of perpetual imprisonment but simply that of being condemned to a life of constant public ridicule and penance. That was certainly better, nevertheless, than being burned alive.

Of course there may have been some few who were actually guilty of the charges. Some such cases will be discussed here. Generally, where the reliability of the testimony seems more valid than usual, and where the accusations are not a mere laundry list of charges drawn from the standard manuals, then we might *consider* the possibility that the charges are valid.

Some conversos were intent on leaving Spain and returning to Judaism in another land, as many already had done earlier. Their numbers were few, however, and they must have been further discouraged by the *uniform insistence* of the Sefardic rabbis in those countries that such conversos were to be considered "complete Gentiles" who required full conversion before they could return to the Jewish fold.

Furthermore, even assuming that such conversos were determined to maintain their adherence to the Jewish "religion" while still in Spain, the Jewish law very clearly specifies that in time of persecution, and particularly of danger to one's life, only when one can act in private and in complete secrecy is it necessary to refrain from violating Torah prohibitions (such as kindling a fire on the Sabbath, which nevertheless could be done by a Gentile servant). There would thus have been no reason for such flagrant displays of public Jewish piety, guaranteed as they were to bring *certain death.*

An example of the kind of thing which could lead to condemnation was the case of a converso in 1527 who was accused of blasphemy because when he tried to collect a debt which he had recorded in a book, the debtor, denying the debt, said, "Is your book the Gospel?" to which the converso replied that it was more true than the Gospel. For this "crime" he was condemned to attend mass on a holiday, standing with a candle in his hand and a gag on his mouth. He was then to give the candle to the church.[51]

After reading countless Inquisition "processes" (trial records), one's eyes begin to glaze over. The accusations have a monotonous sameness to them.

That the litany of identical charges, no matter the city, is invented and totally false would be obvious, one might assume, to all who read them. Nevertheless, those who wish to cling to the romantic "crypto-Judaism" theory do not see this, or pretend not to.

Where did the knowledge of such Jewish practices come to the Inquisitors? They were provided with detailed manuals, of the kind already referred to written by Eimeric and others. Even more detailed information was available to the fifteenth-century Inquisition, such as the manual prepared by the converso friar Antonio de Ávila for Torquemada himself. Antonio's father was Jacob *Melamed,* brother of the infamous Rabbi Meir who later converted with Abraham Seneor. In that manual we find details of *precisely* these practices which in fact appear repeatedly in the Inquisition processes.[52]

An important and informed Catalan scholar has called attention to the nineteenth-century discovery of certain Catalan manuscripts belonging to Jews of the fifteenth century, found in a house in Barcelona in the former Jewish quarter (*Call*). He insists, however, that at least one of these, which he carefully edited, was a prayerbook of conversos. The only possible evidence to support such a conclusion is the exclusion of certain benedictions from the "silent devotion" (eighteen benedictions) of the daily prayer, and the undeniably problematic order of the rest. This may be explained, however, as simply an alternative ritual of some kind (perhaps qabalistic) or as being due to ignorance on the part of the writer of the manuscript. Riera assumes, probably correctly, qabalistic influence on the inclusion of seventy-two verses from the Psalms "which are Yours" (i.e., the divine name of seventy-two letters). If this is so, and were it to turn out to be correct that the manuscript is a prayerbook of conversos, this would further confirm my suggestion that *qabalah* influenced the conversos.[53]

More important is the testimony deduced by the same author of "confessions" by conversos, all from Valencia, to having recited "Jewish prayers." Only three of those cases belong to the fifteenth century, however (1481, 1491, 1492). All of these consist of the conversos having recited, in Catalan, a psalm, either 91 (two cases) or 46.8, and the *Shema*ᶜ—or more correctly, the first sentence of that so-called "creed"—in a garbled mixture of Hebrew and Catalan. It is again possible, however, that these accusations originated with the Inquisitors, and the accused were compelled to "confess."

The most curious testimony comes from a 1512 trial, where a conversa confessed to having recited the "Ten Commandments in Hebrew," and then recited a lengthy Catalan poem which has only the Hebrew refrain *barahu barahu simo* (bless, bless His name) in Catalan transliteration. This poem, however, is in fact the famous "Eḥad miy yodeᶜa," sung at the conclusion of the Passover meal. It is highly unlikely that even the most ignorant converso could have confused this with the Ten Commandments, so that we have again an example where the Inquisitors took a text, which they did not understand, and put it in the "mouth" of an accused converso, identifying it as something it obviously is not.[54]

Several of the supposed "Judaizing" customs, the mere accusation of which could lead to being condemned as a heretic, were nothing other than popular superstitions with no basis in Jewish law or custom whatever. Examples of these may be found in the manual of such customs in Toledo;

see particularly the reported practices concerning marriages, death customs, etc. (such as providing a jar of water and a candle for the "departed soul" of the dead; or, on the contrary, pouring out all the water in the house).[55]

As we have already seen, Jews and conversos were sometimes popularly imagined to avoid certain foods or to prefer certain others. The preparation of some of these was, in itself, sufficient to lead to condemnation for heresy. An Inquisition process relates in detail the preparation of special food for the Sabbath, which was made by a Christian servant for her conversa mistress (who must have been very foolish to have done such a thing). After providing the complete recipe, the servant testifies that this Sabbath dish was called *adafina*. We have already encountered that term in some of the converso and anti-converso poetry of the fifteenth century, to which we may add the verses of the conde de Paredes, attacking a converso, in which he says that even the holy altar, by his touch, becomes a table for *adafina*. The term is also found in a rebuttal to the converso poet Juan Alfonso de Baena. The fourteenth-century Christian poet Juan Ruíz had already used the word, but not in a Jewish context at all. When Baena himself refers to one of his poets as "mi adefyna," it seems to be in the sense (sarcastically) of "delightful companion," or the like.[56]

The word, which I have elsewhere explained as being probably derived from Arabic *dafina,* "covered," refers to a kind of stew, of vegetables or meat, covered and cooked all night so that it can be eaten warm at the Sabbath noon meal (since cooking on the Sabbath was prohibited). It is mentioned often in connection with the Inquisition; not surprisingly, in the aforementioned manual of Antonio de Ávila, and in the famous "Niño de la Guardia" case (to be discussed), and also in the 1486 trial of Juan Arias Dávila, the bishop of Segovia, where his father, the famous government official Diego Arias, was accused of eating "*adefina*" (so?) on the Sabbath.[57]

Grave dangers increased for the conversos and Jews when, both as a result of continuously increasing conversion to Christianity and the establishment of schools for the study of Hebrew among the Dominicans and Franciscans, a more sophisticated knowledge of Jewish sources became possible. An example may be seen in the judgment of the Inquisitorial court in Huesca in 1489 (a case discussed later in detail) where the court cited as an example of Jewish deceit of Christians "that which is said and recited in *bava camma* in cap. *hagazel*" that Jews, in order to protect themselves, may falsify an oath. Such an opinion is, indeed, given in *B.Q.* 113a, but the court neglected to note that it was there *rejected* by Rabbi ʿAqiva, who said Jews must not do this because of "sanctification of the Name" (i.e., the requirement to behave so as to bring glory to God in the sight of Gentiles).

The same Inquisitional decision cited a similar statement in *Nedarim* (chap. "arba nedarim"; possibly 28a?), as well as "rabi Moyse" (Maimo-

nides) "en madda en las licions de ydolatria cap. VII et X" (i.e., *M.T., Mada*ᶜ:
ʿA.Z.). Interesting, too, is the reference to "Rasba cap. CCCXXXVI,"
which of course is Ibn Adret; however, the statement cited does not relate
to any of his extant responsa (possibly it refers to his commentary on *B.Q.*,
but this is not clear, and the "chapter" number corresponds to no present
text). Even more problematic is the reference to a commentary of "rabi
Yaco" on the laws of Talmud Torah, ch. XXXVIII (presumably thus referring to Maimonides' Code, but there is no such chapter; "Yaco" could be
any of several Jacobs).[58]

The representatives of the Jewish community of Huesca very ably answered all these charges, made against Jews, not conversos, although they
pretended not to know who "Rasba" was (!) and denied that he could have
made a ruling contrary to the Talmudic law requiring obedience to the laws
of the kingdom.

Punishment by the Inquisition

Since, according to canon law, the Church could not actually shed blood,
the condemned "heretic" was turned over to the "secular arm," i.e., the
government, for a death sentence to be carried out. Nevertheless, the actual
form of execution, death by burning, was not known in secular law and was
one totally contrived by Church authorities (as noted above, the *Fuero real*
based itself on a forged text, surely of ecclesiastical origin). Furthermore,
the Inquisitors themselves were present and joyfully participating at the *autos de fe* (acts of faith), as these public celebrations were known. They were,
indeed, celebrations and public spectacles. The condemned, both those sentenced to death and the others, were led in procession, usually barefoot,
through the streets before a jeering mob, their "crimes" and sentences were
publicly read and long sermons preached, and then the fires were lit. These
events became ever more popular as a kind of holiday event (in sixteenth-
century Madrid, the king and queen sat on a balcony over a bakery in the
Plaza Mayor, eating pastries while enjoying the spectacle).

The theological excuse for the horrible death by burning was that the
corrupted soul of the unrepentant "heretic" would be better served, and
possibly saved, by punishment in this world than by eternal damnation in
the next.

There was always the possibility that the condemned would "repent" at
the very last minute. In this event, he or she would be spared death by the
flames and given the special "grace" (so it was called) of garroting: death
by strangulation. They were just as dead, but their souls went straight to
paradise.

The smart ones—those who after prolonged torture and imprisonment "confessed" their sins—were called *reconciliados,* or "reconciled" to Holy Mother Church. They, too, were marched in the processions, forced to wear tall caps (sometimes pointed, sometimes not) and long sacklike robes which were called *sambenitos*—actually a loose tunic on which was painted a large red cross, often in the form of an X (the so-called cross of St. Andrew). After the *reconciliados* had heard their crimes read aloud to the assembled public, their *sambenitos,* with their names inscribed, were hung in the church of each penitent sinner, and even after they had died, the *sambenitos* remained there for *centuries* afterward to mock the descendants of the heretic.[59]

Another punishment which could be imposed was perpetual imprisonment for those whom the Inquisitors did not wish to condemn to death. Whether this was literally "perpetual," i.e., until death, or whether it was possible to bribe one's way out of prison eventually, is unclear from the sources.

In any case, property of those condemned was always confiscated, and ultimately the abuses led to confiscation of converso property on general principles, as we shall see.

Others, who either had died or had fled in order to escape persecution, were condemned "in statue" (or, later, "in statute"; both terms are found), which means that they were burned in effigy and a standing death sentence was issued should they ever be apprehended. Those "heretics" already dead, or the ancestors or deceased relatives of "heretics," would have their bones dug up and publicly burned.

Lesser penalties were sometimes imposed, especially in the early years of the general Spanish Inquisition, for what were judged to be less grave "crimes." These included such things as obligatory attendance, often in penitent garb, at masses, donations to the local church, etc. Suspect or condemned "heretics" were also deprived of all public or ecclesiastical office; such positions were increasingly becoming restricted to "old Christians" in any case.

When the Inquisition was established in a particular town, sermons would be preached announcing this joyous event, and a "grace period" would be given during which all heretic conversos (sometimes even "old Christians") were supposed to voluntarily come and confess their sins. When this failed to produce the desired results there began the series of secret informing, imprisonment and confiscation of property in the hopes of eliciting "confessions," torture, and outright fabrication of charges.

It will become patently clear, if it is not now already, that the root cause of all this was by no means a sincere belief that all, or even a majority, of the conversos were "heretics" or "crypto-Jews," but rather the desire both to totally eradicate the converso class from an "old Christian" society, many of whose members considered competition from them too powerful to endure, and also to enrich the growing bureaucracy of the Inquisition by the confiscation of as much property as possible.

All of this was concealed by the hypocritical veil of zeal for "God's work."

Establishment of the Inquisition in Castile

As we have seen, the original Inquisition operated exclusively in the kingdom of Aragón-Catalonia. It is still unclear why no effort was made to expand its activities into Castile-León in the thirteenth century, for at least in León the Albigensians were very much present, and there is evidence of some activity also in Castile. In the fourteenth and early fifteenth centuries as well, heresy was every bit as prevalent there as in Aragón-Catalonia. Of course, the absence of an official Inquisition does not mean that no attempt was made to control heresies, always a problem in medieval Spain. Nevertheless, even the tremendous influence of Vicente Ferrer in Castile brought no attempt at the introduction of the Inquisition.

In some respects, the origin of its establishment may be traced to the converso Alonso de Cartagena, son of Pablo de Santa María, who obtained a decree at the Council of Basel in 1434 branding as heretics those conversos who kept Jewish practices, and allowing the Inquisition to investigate and punish them. This, of course, was nothing other than a reaffirmation of long-standing policy, but it is significant that it was the head of the Castilian delegation, and a converso, who was responsible for it.

More important, inasmuch as that decree was actually ignored in Castile, was the political struggle between powerful converso clans (the Santa Marías, the Dávilas, and others) and Álvaro de Luna which apparently gave him the idea of suggesting to the king that the Inquisition be established. In 1451 Juan II appealed to Pope Nicholas V to this effect, and the pope readily agreed. Only the downfall of Luna and his execution in 1453 prevented the actual establishment of an Inquisition.[60]

In 1478 Pope Sixtus IV sent a letter to the Catholic Monarchs noting that throughout Spain certain persons who had been baptized were relapsing to the "superstitions and perfidious dogma" of Judaism, and not only were continuing in heresy themselves but were influencing others, infecting them with their "perfidy." Noting that the king and queen had *requested* the power to act against these heretics, the pope complemented their zeal for the faith. Therefore, three *bishops* or supervisors and *other priests,* friars or not, but either doctors of canon law or bachelors or masters of theology, were to be appointed as Inquisitors in "certain cities." It must have taken well over a year for this letter to reach Spain (not unusual), or else there may have been prolonged negotiations after it was received, as Baer suggested, since the Catholic Monarchs did not act on it until 1480. Nevertheless, in 1479 they had already instructed their ambassadors to the pope to ask that Jacobo Reda, a Sicilian Franciscan, be appointed for life to head the Inquisition in Sicily (under their rule).[61]

Flórez attributed the establishment of the Inquisition in Castile to the influence of Tomás de Torquemada on the queen, since he had been her confessor in her early youth and during the reign of her brother Enrique IV, and had made her vow that if she became queen she would make it a principle concern of state to investigate heresy.[62]

Thus it was in 1480 (not 1481, as often stated) that the Inquisition was established in Castile. Fernando and Isabel immediately sent a letter (27 December) to Seville, observing that there "have been and are some bad Christians, apostates, heretics, and *confesos*" (another term for conversos) in the kingdom who "have turned and converted, and do turn and convert, to the sect and superstition and perfidy of the Jews," etc. The pope has listened to their supplication to remedy this by authorizing the appointment of "two or three" individuals as Inquisitors. (It should be noted that Sixtus IV was himself a former Franciscan friar, whose family obtained his election as pope because of their outstanding loans to various cardinals.) In fact, as we have seen, the papal letter authorized the appointment of three *bishops* and other priests, scholars of either canon law or theology. From this it is apparent that the pope was sensitive to the complaints already made earlier in Aragón-Catalonia that the Inquisition was acting independently of Church control and appointing unqualified officials.

To begin with, the Catholic Monarchs more or less followed at least part of the papal instructions, appointing the Dominicans Miguel de Morillo, master of theology, and Juan de San Martín, prior of the Monastery of San Pablo in Seville. There were thus only two Inquisitors, and not a bishop in sight.[63]

Already in the previous months the queen alone had written another letter warning that no one should interfere with the activities of the Inquisitors. A second letter, in November, is more significant, for it refers to "bad and unfaithful Christians" who in order to live "more freely in their infidelity" desire to leave the kingdom for Muslim Granada "and other parts" and become Jews or Muslims. She ordered that no such persons be given aid, but that they be seized and their goods confiscated.[64]

The first actual tribunals of the Inquisition were at Seville, Córdoba, Jaén, and Ciudad Real. Lea was undoubtedly correct that there was yet no tribunal in Segovia, because it was resisted by the converso bishop Juan Arias Dávila. In 1484 Rodrigo de Orense was appointed Inquisitor in Toledo. No doubt the resistance of the bishop of Segovia to the establishment of the Inquisition there was a major cause of his denunciation and trial, previously mentioned. After the Expulsion, Torquemada also presented charges against another converso bishop, the aforementioned Pedro de Aranda, bishop of Calahorra and head of the *Concejo* of Castile. He and his bastard son, the Protonotary Apostolic of Alexander IV (Borja; a Spanish pope), were tried by that pope and sentenced to life in prison in Rome.[65]

Juan de Torquemada (d. 1468), bishop of Cádiz, Orense, and León and cardinal of San Sixto, uncle of Tomás, was one of the key figures of the Inquisition, in spite of his earlier defense of conversos. It is often claimed that he himself was a converso, apparently on the basis of Pulgar's statement that Juan was born in Burgos and "his ancestors [*avuelos*] were of the line of Jews converted to our holy catholic faith." However, Domínguez Bordona has objected that he was born not in Burgos but in Valladolid, nor was he of Jewish lineage; rather, a son of Alvar Fernández de Torquemada, *regidor* of Valladolid, and grandson of Pero Fernández de Torquemada, the son of Lope Alfonso de Torquemada "whom Alfonso XI knighted on the day of his coronation in Burgos." However, Domínguez (among other writers who have dealt with the subject, e.g., Cantera Burgos, Baron, and others) forgot that *abuelos* does not only mean "grandfathers" but also means ancestors in general. True, Alfonso XI of all rulers is not likely to have knowingly knighted a converso, but it is entirely possible that Pulgar was correct in stating that some of Torquemada's *ancestors* were of Jewish origin (Netanyahu, *Origins,* p. 433 gives additional sources). In any case, the converso background of Juan de Torquemada would have been very remote at best, and that of Tomás so far removed as to make repeated modern claims that he was a converso absurd. Tomás, whatever the truth of his influence on the queen in establishing the Inquisition, was not named Inquisitor General (for all Spain) until 8 April 1491 (although appointed for Castile in 1483).[66]

These observations are important because of the repeated attempts, highly suspect in their motivation, to claim that the excesses of the Inquisition were due to conversos themselves. I know of absolutely no evidence of the involvement of proven conversos in the Inquisition in any manner except as victims.

Inquisition Viewed by Converso Authors

Alonso de Palencia, chronicler of Enrique IV and of the Catholic Monarchs, a converso, reports that in 1481 in Seville there began the punishment of conversos of that city, those who, "like the rest of the Andalucían" conversos, were "known to be rebellious against the catholic faith." He adds: "The [old] Christians nevertheless vacillated in naming those suspected of heresy and accused the lower class [*plebe*] of conversos of being more infected than their leaders." The Inquisitors apparently knew better and punished the wealthy leaders along with the rest, imprisoning them in "murky cells." He continues:

> These cases were much more terrible than in any other part of Seville [i.e., the province] because here was the beginning of the Inquisition and because from day to day the crimes increased and there were discovered the evils and traditions [customs] of the conversos which directed their wicked designs, to the great harm of the name of Christian.

Many found a pretext to leave the city, but "close to sixteen thousand" were victims of the Inquisition, so that the city was "almost uninhabited," between those who fled and those who were killed or otherwise punished.

He later returns to the subject in general, commenting that the establishment of the Inquisition, necessary to combat heresy, nevertheless resulted in impoverishment of the kingdom (at a time when money was desperately needed for the war against Granada). Here, the figure is no longer the enormous one previously mentioned, but five hundred who were burned in the city of Seville in the space of three years. The majority of the women among the conversos adhered to Jewish customs, he claims.[67]

The converso Diego de Valera blamed Enrique IV for the heresy rampant in the kingdom: "The laziness and fluctuation and little care which the king don Enrique had, whether for the service of God or the good of his kingdom, gave open license to the evil ones to live according to their free will; from which resulted not only that many of those recently converted to our holy faith but also some of the old Christians departed from the true path." Some openly "Judaized," and others adopted heretical opinions. Even though some of these were burned in the reign of Juan II, the errors and heresy continued in the reign of Enrique, "and even until now it is believed that among some the heresy of Durango persists; among them is the *comendador* fray Alonso de Malla [Mella] of Zaragoza, brother of Cardinal Juan de Malla." (The Durango heresy was a kind of "communistic" movement which believed in a "more perfect order" to come.)

Fernando and Isabel summoned there in 1480 a council of religious officials, among whom were Hernando de Talavera and Tomás de Torquemada. "With the counsel of these, there were appointed in all the cities and towns, not only of these kingdoms of Castile and León but in all others subject to them, most notable and prudent men to head the Inquisition."[68]

One of the most important sources is that of the converso historian and author, secretary of Isabel, Fernando de Pulgar. As Cantera Burgos amply and correctly demonstrated, contrary to the opinion of Carriazo, the text of chapter 120 in the latter's edition of the *Crónica* is the original version which Pulgar later revised, incorporating material from chapter 96, as chapter 77 of the version found in B.A.E.[69]

In the earlier version, Pulgar discussed the Inquisition only as it was first established in Seville, noting that it was headed by a "Dominican friar," whom he doesn't name (according to the chronicler Bernáldez, this was fray Alonso de Ojeda), assisted by "religious doctors" of Valencia and Burgos and by Juan de Medina. This Inquisition was established because "many Christians of Jewish lineage began to 'Judaize' and to keep Jewish rites." In the revised version, the Inquisitor General is named, Tomás de Torquemada, confessor now of Fernando. (As noted before, the fact that Tomás was not named to this post until 1491, which Cantera apparently did not know, gives us a date for this revision.) Torquemada then appointed Inquisitors "in all the other cities of the kingdoms of Castile, Aragón, Valencia, and Catalonia." He adds that provision was made to allow all "heretics" to come and confess and be "reconciled" to the Church, which many did; more than fifteen thousand men and women. (It is possible that the number sixteen thousand given by Alonso de Palencia was a confusion also with the number reconciled, not burned.) His statement in the first version that some three hundred men and women were burned in Seville alone is now revised to two thousand in "some cities and towns," with others condemned to perpetual imprisonment. Others were sentenced to various penances, including the requirement that they always wear colored crosses on their clothing, on breasts and shoulders. They and their children were deprived of all public offices.

Also, the Inquisition proceeded against those already dead, "because it happened that some of these in their lives had incurred this sin of heresy and apostasy"; their bones were dug up and publicly burned and their property and the inheritances of their descendants were seized by the Crown.

Many fled to Portugal, "the country of the Muslims" (Granada), and "other places" in the kingdom, according to the first version. Italy, France, and other kingdoms are added in the revision. These were condemned *in absentia*, and their property seized "for defense of the faith" according to the first version, or solely for the war against Granada in the revision.

Significantly, the first version states that some of the relatives of those imprisoned or condemned complained to the Catholic Monarchs that "such Inquisition and execution was not done, which it must be, according to justice," i.e., it was carried out unjustly, and in particular they complained that the bull which the sovereigns had requested from the pope applied only to conversos, but not to "others." By this, they apparently meant that the Inquisition did not apply to "old Christians" who might also be suspect of heresy. They also protested the manner of testimony, the torture, and the general cruelty of the authorities. They insisted that gentle reason be used instead, and particularly objected to burning as heretics those converted to Christianity who insisted that they were true Christians.

The cardinal (Mendoza, archbishop of Seville) and other bishops assembled, at the order of the Monarchs, and drew up rules to deal with these matters.

All of this is missing in the revised version, and reduced to a mere sentence, to the effect that some objected to the "manner of the processes and execution of the sentences"!

Finally, the first version states that in the diocese of Seville more than three thousand houses of such accused heretics (or those who feared being accused) were abandoned, and this depopulation and the diminution of taxes were pointed out to the Monarchs, who responded that "purifying the kingdom of that sin of heresy" was a "service to God and themselves" (the Monarchs). In the second version, the number of abandoned houses is four thousand for Seville, Córdoba, and other cities of Andalucía, and the statement is added that because communication between conversos and Jews in those cities was seen to be "somewhat" of a cause of the heresy, no Jew—on pain of death—was to be allowed to live in that land any longer.

This refers to the edict of expulsion for the Jews from Andalucía in January of 1483.

The anonymous continuator of Pulgar's *Crónica* wrote:

> In this time was born in Spain another evil, because many of the Jewish people lived intermingled in the kingdom among Christians, and some of those Jews whom fray Vicente [Ferrer] had converted with his preaching, in public maintaining the way of Christians and thus appearing, kept Jewish ceremonies, because of which these most Christian rulers were saddened. In order that our lord Jesus Christ should not be continuously crucified, and desiring to purge their kingdom of this pestilence,

they appointed Tomás de Torquemada as Inquisitor General.[70]

For comparison, we have the work of Andrés Bernáldez, one of the most notorious enemies of Jews in fifteenth-century Spain, also a chronicler of the Catholic Monarchs and chaplain of the archbishop of Seville, Cardinal Mendoza. He devoted a chapter of his chronicle to the establishment of the Inquisition in Castile. He claims that the "Mosaic heresy" rampant in the kingdom began in 1390 (*sic;* 1391) with the robbery of "the *judería*" (as if only one was robbed) due to the preaching of Vicente Ferrer (who did not enter Castile until the 1400s).

This totally confused "historical" information is followed by a diatribe against the Talmud, which had such a hold on the Jews that Vicente was able to convert only a "few" of them (actually he converted thousands), but the people of Castile killed many (he has, of course, confused the pogroms of 1391 again with the later missionary campaign of Ferrer). Many were then baptized, but many of those later went to Portugal and other kingdoms and returned to Judaism, while others went to places in Spain where they were not known and became Jews, according to him. The "majority" of the conversos, he claims, were "secret Jews, and were neither Jews nor Christians, although baptized; rather heretics and without law [religion]."

He adds that when the Monarchs came to Seville, a certain Dominican, fray Alonso (de Ojeda, head Inquisitor), was responsible for initiating the Inquisition, convincing the cardinal to establish "certain ordinances" against heresy. But "two years" passed and nothing happened. "Those who sought to excuse themselves from baptizing their children did not baptize them, and those who did baptize them washed them in their houses" after they returned (to "remove" the baptism).

There follows a long list of "Judaizing" charges of the usual kind, concerning the "Jewish food" eaten by conversos, etc. The usual anti-Jewish charges are also found: Jews and conversos "smell bad" both because of the food they eat and because they are not baptized; many nuns were "violated" by conversos: they practice "arts and deceits"; etc.

The only important information to emerge from all of this is that fray Alonso and other Dominicans (no doubt Bernáldez himself played a major role) did everything possible to "convince" the king and queen of the "Jewish ceremonies" observed by conversos.[71]

"Purity of Blood": Anti-Semitism and the Inquisition

It has become fashionable not only among Jewish writers but even among some non-Jews (increasingly in Spain) to label as "anti-Semitism" any real or imagined manifestation of anti-Jewish sentiment in any period of history. This is anachronistic, of course; in a literal sense because the term and the concept did not come into existence until the nineteenth century, and in a descriptive sense because "anti-Semitism" refers to the hatred of the Jews as a people because of imagined "racial" characteristics which are judged to be inferior or subversive. Non-Jewish expressions of disagreement with, or even hostility to, what is (incorrectly) perceived to be the "Jewish religion" is not anti-Semitism. Second, there was not, before the modern period, a theory of biological race, or the understanding that the Jews constituted such a race. Even the Spanish term raza, infrequently employed in some medieval texts, does not carry this connotation (thus, some people of Hispanic, i.e., Latin American, origin in this country quite properly refer to themselves as members of "La Raza," in the sense of "people" or ethnic community).

With the increasing anti-converso (and not anti-Jewish; the distinction is important) sentiment of the fifteenth century, however, an uncanny precursor of true anti-Semitism in the modern sense emerged. This was the development of the doctrine of *limpieza de sangre*, "purity of blood," which we have already briefly mentioned. It is crucial to understand this doctrine and how it relates to the attitudes toward conversos, the Inquisition, and the Expulsion.

As we shall see, the increasing hostile attitudes and actions toward conversos elicited protests from some "old Christians" of the kind we have seen already in connection with the riots of the fifteenth century. The objection was that once converted, a person is a Christian, without distinction from any other Christian. This was, indeed, canon law, as well as the theological teaching of the Church. There was no legitimate way to rationalize the hatred for, and discrimination against, conversos. Therefore, slowly there emerged the insidiously clever doctrine that it was not the *religion* of the convert which really was objectionable; rather it was the tainted "Jewish blood" which somehow created a *racial* inferiority. This justified the discrimination against conversos, their exclusion, or attempted exclusion, from secular and ecclesiastical offices, prohibition against marrying with "old Christians," etc.

Thus, the anti-Semitism which was directed in the latter part of the fifteenth century against the conversos was launched on two fronts, or with two ends: first, the extermination of as many as possible under the false pretense that they were "bad Christians"; and second, the social isolation and persecution of those who could not be burned, by the doctrine of their racial inferiority and corrupting influence on the "pure" Christians. The parallels with modern anti-Semitic manifestations are too obvious to need comment.

The target of this campaign, once again, was not at all the Jews, who continued to live the normal life of cordial relations with their Christian neighbors they had always enjoyed (although tensions began to manifest themselves at the end of the century in some places). The "final solution" in this case was to be not the annihilation of Jews, but their expulsion, and that solely because it was claimed—again falsely—that they were a corrupting influence upon the conversos.

Apparently the Colegio de San Bartolomé of Salamanca, founded by the archbishop of Seville, was the first to introduce laws of *limpieza* in Spain, in the bulls of foundation of the school requested from Benedict XIII in 1414 and Martin V in 1418. These included the provision that no one of Jewish origin, however remote, could be admitted to the college.[72]

Interesting in light of the furor aroused by the *limpieza de sangre* controversy is the fact, as noted in Chapter 5, that several royal persons were descended from conversos, including Fernando himself. While not common knowledge, this was certainly known to informed clergy, as we have seen.

One of the earliest general references to the law appears in the statutes enacted by the chaplains and sacristans of the church of Belmez, in the dioceses of Córdoba, around 1463. The laws of the Order of Santiago, enacted by Alfonso de Cárdenas in 1480, ordered that no person, Jew or Muslim, recently converted, nor descendants of conversos for a hundred years previously, should marry or permit their children to marry another converso until the fourth generation, but marry only "with pure old Christians and each one according to his estate and manner," for in this way they will be "intermingled clearly and with true love" (!) into the catholic faith, "for just as they were purified by the water of baptism from original sin," so they will thus be saved from "infamy" and error from their previous descent. (The order, like other religious-military orders, owned vast amounts of territory to which these laws applied.)[73]

The most analyzed situation so far, however, applies to the Order of San Jerónimo, the "Jeronimites." According to the sixteenth-century chronicler of the order, in 1483 (an error, of course) the Inquisition was established, which caused "much difficulty in the one part [Aragón] and in the other [Castile]," in Castile "because of the many Jews who were there, a rich and powerful people, which had with it many subjugated old Christians, [which caused] no little affront and even damage to Christianity." Almost certainly he did not mean "Jews," but rather conversos, a distinction which some modern writers still fail to make. It is interesting to note that the anti-Jewish attitude of this author did not save him from being investigated himself by the Inquisition, a fact to which his being a student and friend of the converso Benito Arias Montano no doubt contributed.[74]

In 1484, Rodrigo de Orense (not "Orenes"), general of the order, was called to be the Inquisitor of Toledo. The council of the order voted to allow him to accept the position, and also to forbid anyone from holding such an office unless permitted by the order, except if the king and queen should expressly order it. In this, we can already see a certain uneasiness in the order about the Inquisition (Orense nevertheless refused the post).

Another meeting was held in 1486, at which a major concern was to "purify" (limpiar) those suspect of heresy, "like the Israelite nation, seen by all the world to be exiled, debased in perpetual dishonor and infamous punishment for the atrocity of their murder of the son of God," a punishment which will endure until the fulfillment of the "prophecy" that will result in the conversion of the Jews. Meanwhile, the "Jews" (conversos) make every effort to intermingle among Christians, by entering either the clergy or the nobility, in order to escape their abasement. Many have entered the order and have even achieved a certain reputation for themselves. The document accuses them of hypocrisy and malicious intent in doing this, to which the Inquisition helped "open the eyes" of members of the order. The converso "heresy" was found throughout the order, it claimed, and especially in Guadalupe, where the chief monastery was located. As a result, the Inquisition was to be given free rein to search out and punish all such heresy within the order. The king ordered them to guard against the "wolves in sheep's clothing," i.e., the conversos guilty of heresy, who sought refuge in the monasteries. Therefore, they decreed that the "new Christians" no longer be permitted to enter the order at all. The Dominican fray Tomás de Torquemada, later to become Inquisitor General, was now already put in charge of several Inquisitors to investigate heresy in the order, and it was reported that the queen "heard with pleasure" these rules of the order.[75]

Immediately, Innocent VIII issued a letter in which, while taking note of the seriousness of the problem, he pointed out that the decree of the order was contrary to the previous bull of Nicholas V, and ordered that no such distinctions may be made between conversos and "old Christians" (he did not, of course, use these terms, unique to Spain). However, the former might be excluded from holding offices in the Church or in the order.[76]

In 1457 Alonso de Oropesa had been elected general of the order, and again in 1462. He was extremely powerful in the kingdom, particularly in the affairs of Enrique IV.[77] His most important work was his defense of conversos, coupled with a polemical attack against Jews and Judaism, begun shortly after 1450 and completed in 1465, *Lumen ad revelationem gentium et gloria plebis Dei Israel*.[78]

He refers to the Visigothic forced conversion of the Jews and argues that even at that time many of the converts were guilty of "Judaizing" (possibly, but there is no evidence of this), and that certain clergy defended them and argued that such forced conversion was against canon law and they should be allowed to return to Judaism (chapter 51). Throughout, he refers to the controversy over the recognition of conversos and the discriminatory attitude of those who sought to deny them ecclesiastical offices, which attitude he disavowed. He blamed "old Christians" for this, and especially their jealousy of the conversos for attaining important administrative posts in the Church.[79]

Very important is the observation of Díaz y Díaz that Alonso "was sure that there were some [conversos] who apostasized, but all of his book gives the idea that these were *few*" (my emphasis).[80]

Alonso deduced from Saint Augustine that, since the term "people" can apply only to those with a law and a concept of justice (which according to Augustine the Romans did *not* have), "one may conclude that in those times only the Jewish people was in truth the people of God, whereas the others were idolaters . . . they served and obeyed only God truthfully and were in consequence an authentic republic" (135). Furthermore, individual Gentiles who observed justice through natural law could be said to have been included in "Israel," and thus the Jews "prepared the way for salvation for all the Gentiles" (151).

In spite of the numerous positive references to Jews and Judaism, Alonso of course could not separate himself from the "official" view of Jews in his age. He thus denounces in no uncertain terms the "perfidious Jews" who speak "against our faithful," but warns his readers that this refers only to those who "remain in Judaism." However, the "faithful of that people who are found with us in the Church must be treated equally and in peace with other Christians, including those who are *supposedly* bad [i.e., supposedly bad conversos; my emphasis], just as are treated those of us found to be equally bad" (246).

Perhaps as a result of Alonso's work, the above decree of the council of the order was not accepted by all members of the order, many of whom objected to barring admission to conversos and even their descendants. Fray García de Madrid, a personal friend of the general, worked especially against this decree and again brought forth the bull of Nicholas V which declared that any such distinction was contrary to the unity of the Church, and that anyone seeking to make such distinctions would be excommunicated.[81] Rodrigo de Orense was moved by this papal bull, and also consulted with the "many" learned conversos in Castile, and ordered the previous decree of the order set aside. A major feud erupted, which even involved the Catholic Monarchs. In August of 1486 Gonzalo de Toro was elected as the new general, a former Inquisitor who had "seen the value" of purifying the order of conversos. In the argument in favor of observing the papal bull, a book by Alonso de Oropesa was cited (undoubtedly the above book) which argued for just such unity. However, it was argued, the decree of the council sought to discriminate on this ground not against conversos but only, in accord with the Inquisition, against those guilty of heresy. When reminded that the decree excluded all converts, heretics or not, the response was that no doubt there are some "holy, pious, learned, excellent" men among the conversos, but the decree is not obliged to consider these "rare accidents," but rather the general nature of the converts. The council allowed itself to be convinced by these arguments, and in spite of the fact that the Catholic Monarchs had sent requests asking that the decree be revoked, the order decided not to revoke it.[82]

Diego de Zamora, who had been in the service of Cardinal Mendoza and had acted as controller and secretary of the order, carried out the segregation of Jews from conversos in the Jewish quarters of Gaudalajara and Álcalá (1480–82), for which the Jews supposedly composed a prayer against him (doubtful). Nothing indicates that he himself was a converso, other than the suspect testimony of converso members of the order who were themselves under suspicion and later burned, and yet Beinart concluded that their testimony was "undoubtedly true." He also stated as fact that Diego de Zamora was a "Jew," whereas this was the evidence of only *one* monk, himself suspected of "Judaizing." In fact, Diego was vindicated by the Inquisitorial court.[83]

Another monk, Diego de Marchena, was also accused of "Jewishness," which he had supposedly sought to confess to Diego de Zamora, but the latter refused to hear the confession. He was burned at the stake in 1485 (not "1488"), but not before he had "testified" against Diego de Zamora. The "evidence" was apparently transparent enough so that even the council was not convinced of Zamora's guilt, yet on the basis of such flimsy testimony Beinart concluded that both monks were relapsed conversos, and that their trial was only symptomatic of a "return to Judaism" within the order the extent of which "it is difficult to assess." On the other hand, the more judicious remarks of Sicroff on this same case should be noted, especially his skepticism of the "evidence" against even Diego de Marchena on a matter which was supposed to have happened some *eighteen years* previously. At least one "old Christian" monk of the Guadalupe monastery vigorously defended the conversos, stating that most of them were good Christians.[84]

Another monk, Alfonso de Toledo, was the son, or grandson, of a converso. He was accused of maintaining "contact" with Jews, learning the so-called Jewish creed, reciting "Jewish oaths," and apparently suggesting to his Jewish relative, Samuel Valenci, that they flee to Turkey.

This Samuel Valenci was not, as Beinart assumed, the same as the famous Rabbi Samuel Valanci who was involved in the case of the brother of the renowned Rabbi Abraham Saba in 1485. First, note the difference in spelling—"Symuel *Valenci*" and "*raby* Simuel *Valanci*"—which is significant in these documents, which are very precise. Second, Rabbi Samuel Valanci is described as having lived in Zamora. He was given a house in Valladolid after the trial of Saba's brother, and died in 1487. Samuel *Valenci,* on the other hand, not a rabbi, is described as a resident of Toledo in the records of this process against Alfonso de Toledo in 1487.[85]

In 1496 the council of the order again met to consider a letter of Pope Alexander VI again directing that no conversos or their descendants to the fourth generation be accepted into the order (the popes could not seem to make up their minds). A lengthy and detailed objection to this letter was written, again calling attention to the bull of Nicholas and denying the legality and even the authority of Alexander's letter.[86]

We have noted that at the outset of his article Sicroff, who made a thorough study of the records for the Guadalupe monastery, was not nearly so gullible as Beinart in accepting *prima facie* evidence of "Judaizing," although we may reject as dubious his own conjectures as to why conversos may have entered the order, or whether or not they liked pork (there is no physiological reason why a converted Jew would have an aversion to pork);[87] but the conclusions he reached about the nature of the Inquisitorial processes should be underscored and remembered by all who deal with the Inquisition:

The *vaguest sort* of denunciations were often set down in these depositions.

. . . it should be noted that it was quite common for accusers to become in turn the accused, the very same or similar sins they had alleged of others now being attributed to them. *At no time should it be taken for granted that a vehement denouncer of others would necessarily be a most trustworthy Christian himself.* (94; my emphasis)

Nevertheless, the records do reveal some apparent evidence of Jewish practices. If a first-generation converso monk was accused of being circumcised, he could easily excuse himself by the obvious explanation that he had been born a Jew and all Jews were circumcised; but monks born of converso parents, unless born before they had converted, who nevertheless were circumcised had to come up with ingenious if fantastic explanations. The most amusing was the claim by one that it was a result of a childhood prank when friends tied him up and cut his member, so that he was "a little bit circumcised" (rather like being a little bit pregnant) (96–97).

One friar had preached that Mary did not know she had conceived the son of God, and that other virgins had also conceived. Although he was tried not once but twice for heresy for this, he was completely acquitted. Still another speculated on the "channel" by which Mary conceived, and concluded it was the normal one by which women conceive. More "orthodox" monks argued against this that Christ was "incorporeal God" and as such needed no place to enter the womb of Mary. When another suggested a traditional interpretation that the conception was through the ear of Mary, the (supposed) converso monk repeated incredulously, "¿por la *oreja?*"— "through the *ear?*" (105–6).

One monk was accused of having entered a synagogue, which he readily admitted, expressing his pleasure in having gone to see the Torah displayed (99). It apparently never occurred to the Inquisitors that a devout Christian might have felt pleasure in just such a thing, or that, indeed, Christians had often frequented synagogues.

On the other hand, accusations of inattentiveness at prayer, or forgetting certain ritual formulas, may easily be discounted as proof of "heresy." Sicroff himself appears to have forgotten his own caution and to have believed some of the more obviously ridiculous charges. The conclusion that masses of "cohesive Judeo-Christians" (i.e., conversos) were everywhere infesting the order and generally corrupting Christianity with their "secret Judaism" is completely unfounded and unsupported by all the evidence.

Such discriminatory legislation as was enacted by the powerful Jeronimite Order was not, of course, limited to that order. As a result of the controversy over *limpieza* statutes in Toledo, for example, the archbishop, Alonso Carrillo, is reported to have called a special council to deal with the problem. All records have disappeared, except for one citation of the deci-

sion of that council, noting that many *cofradías* and religious institutions
had barred conversos. Inquiry is made as to the "progeny" of applicants
(which would seem to indicate that descendants of conversos were also
barred). The council declared such rules invalid, however, and prohibited
them under the threat of excommunication.[88]

Alexander VI's contrary position has already been noted, confirmed in
his letter (12 November 1496) to Torquemada, in which he authorized him
to exclude *all* descendants of Jews, not just first-generation conversos, from
the Monastery of St. Thomas Aquinas in Ávila. Ironically, the monastery
was built exclusively from the proceeds of goods confiscated from "suspect"
conversos.[89]

The persecution of conversos in the religious orders did not cease as a
result of the efforts of those like Alonso de Oropesa and others opposed
to it. On the contrary, it continued well into the sixteenth century, as attested by the letter of Francisco López de Villalobos, a famous converso and
court physician to Fernando from 1509 on, to the general of the Franciscan
Order (probably Vicente Lunel, elected in 1535), in which he complained
to him of the treatment of certain converso monks of the order who came
from France to visit some of the Spanish monasteries (the fact that they
were living in France was in itself probably due to their desire to escape
the persecution of the Inquisition). The duque de Alba particularly persecuted them, and Villalobos objected that such treatment was not permitted by previous generals of the order, and especially because "these
[conversos] we know certainly are a pillar of those who sustain the Church
of God." The descendants of previous "heretics" have been "purified by
fire," and among them now "are excellent men of great example and doctrine." Furthermore, many of them willingly go to preach the faith in Muslim lands and die a martyr's death. He complained also that the duke
maintained a *cofradía* which refused to admit conversos.[90] When the Jesuit
Order was established, initially there was no prohibition on admitting conversos, but then in Toledo toward the end of the century such a decree was
promulgated.[91]

Further research is needed on other monasteries and religious orders, and
certainly concerning the various *cofradías,* and the converso policy.

Having thus put in motion a policy of social and economic discrimination
based on the fiction of racial impurity, the enemies of the converso class
were now ready to move to the final step, the Inquisition. We understand,
of course, that although the papal bull and other documents refer to the
king and queen's having "asked" for the establishment of the Inquisition,
they did not initiate this on their own. No doubt, as we have seen, it is
correct that Tomás de Torquemada was one of the instrumental forces behind its establishment, but just as certainly he did not act alone. In fact, the

motivation for the renewal of the Inquisition came from all those groups
who feared and despised the conversos, including some, like Cardinal Mendoza, whose own families were "tainted" by converso "blood."

The Inquisition at Work: Castile

What follows here cannot pretend to be more than a representation of the
activity of the Inquisition in the fifteenth century. Even working within the
limits of the period up to the Expulsion, with references to processes in
the following years only where those are particularly important or shed light
on the pre-Expulsion converso situation, the documentation is vast. To give
a thoroughly detailed account would require at least a volume as large as
this one.

Nevertheless, the historian is frustrated at every turn both by the lack of
research on the hundreds of thousands of extant documents which yet remain to be studied, and by the loss and destruction, often (as in the previously cited case of Llorente's stealing and burning records) willful, of documents which should exist. The material here presented should still provide
a more complete picture than that which so far has been attempted.

Córdoba

The Inquisition was established in Córdoba in 1482, with three canons appointed to serve as Inquisitors. The Jewish, and converso, communities of
fifteenth-century Córdoba were very significant, much larger than has been
imagined. We have already seen that entire streets and districts of the city
were populated solely by conversos, and that in the riots they were able to
muster a militia of thousands of men. There were, of course, conversos living in the smaller towns and villages in the diocese, as we may learn from
the accounts of those riots and from other sources. The animosity toward
the conversos had been fueled by the riots, and by the ill-fated Gibraltar
plan, so that the acceptance of the Inquisition there must have been in-
stantaneous and enthusiastic on the part of much of the "old Christian"
population.

Apparently few records prior to the Expulsion have survived, but in the
years 1484 to 1486 two justices and two public scribes were deprived of
their offices for "Judaizing," and in the same period some ten *reconciliados*
were granted postponements on their taxes because their goods and property had been confiscated by the Inquisition.

That others were condemned in Córdoba prior to 1492 there can be no
doubt. In the records of the trial of Juan de Pineda of Toledo, *comendador*

of the Order of Santiago, a witness mentioned that about that time, ca. 1486, in Córdoba a certain Juan de Madrid was condemned for observing Jewish practices, and when he was led to a platform outside the church in order to abjure his heresy, he said: "I must now die one death, but it is better to die now than to die another time [in the 'hereafter']. I say that the law of Moses is the best, and in it men shall be saved." The people standing there then stoned him. (Baer, who discussed this incident, invented the fiction that "the whole city was split into two camps, and open warfare broke out between the Christians [!] and the conversos"; apparently he confused this incident with the earlier riots.)[92]

On 5 January 1492 twenty-five men were burned and seven women, together with the remains of two already deceased "heretics."[93]

In 1499 the Inquisitor (Pedro Guiral, dean of Guadix) was replaced and charged with fraud and extortion. The new Inquisitor, Diego Rodríguez Lucero, was hardly better. He began attacking also members of prominent "old Christian" families, the clergy, etc. On one day in 1504 he burned 107 people, preaching in the cathedral that all had died "as Jews," and on another day in 1505 another 27 were burned.[94]

In the protest to the queen which resulted from Lucero's excesses, it was stated that it is "very difficult" to believe all the charges of "Judaizing" against the old Christian nobles, clergy, and others; yet apparently few had any "difficulty" believing such charges against conversos.

Among those accused by Lucero, as we shall see, was Hernando de Talavera, the aged archbishop of Granada and former confessor of the Catholic Monarchs, who may or may not have been descended from conversos, as already noted. He was arrested, as were his sister, two nieces and their daughters, and all his servants. Naturally, as a result of torture, these testified against Hernando. The absurd charges included that of keeping a "synagogue" in his palace. Only when the pope himself intervened in 1507 was the archbishop finally released, but he died almost immediately.[95] In 1508 Lucero was finally removed from his post. He died peacefully in Seville.

Lucero's evil influence extended also to the Inquisition of Jaén, where, as its historian aptly noted, the Inquisitors "imagined the existence" of a large converso population secretly practicing Judaism. (Perhaps a misprint occurred in the text further on, for that author says that the documentation confirms the existence of a converso population but "it does not further signify that this Converso population was sincere in its Christianity," where perhaps the author intended "insincere"; English is neither his native language nor that of his editors.)[96]

Virtually the only complete process relative to our period which has come to light from Córdoba is from the years 1502–4, against Juan de Córdoba

Membreque, a judge of the city. The charges originally were the result of information from his female Muslim slave, Mina. The details are such that one might imagine that the charges were at least partially true. Juan and several others were accused of having observed "the fast of the Jews" (Yom Kippur), not eating all day until a star appeared at night, and holding prayer services that day at which sermons were preached (supposedly by a former rabbi). The details of the prayers and ritual appear to be correct. What is of greatest interest is the report, confirmed by many witnesses, of the content of the sermons.[97]

According to the testimony, this included the reading from a *book* the statement that Elijah would come and take all the *"confesos"* (converted Jews preserving certain Jewish beliefs) who observe the Jewish fasts to the "promised land," where they would first cross two rivers, one of milk and one of water, and they would be bathed in one of these (the one of water, one assumes). All of the men and boys would become the same age: twenty-five (what was to become of the women and girls is not stated). The heavens would open, the sun and moon "die," the sea turn to blood, and all the trees dry up. In the "promised land," first cousins and other relatives would be permitted to marry each other (it should be mentioned that the Jewish laws permitting such marriages, prohibited by canon law, were a constant source of scandal to the medieval Church).

Some of this is found also in the testimony against another accused, Ynes, daughter of Juan Esteban of Villa de Herrera, in 1500.[98]

These details, and the fact that the witnesses testified that they did not understand all the prayers, which were in Hebrew, and that they described the prostration which is part of the Yom Kippur service, the wearing of white robes, washing of hands, etc., *might* appear to prove the "accuracy" of the charges. In fact, of course, all of these charges are patently false and simply derive, again, from Inquisition manuals and general knowledge of the most important of Jewish holidays. The only possibly believable charges concern the strange book mentioned.

Most amazingly, the accused did very little to defend himself against the charges. He and eight others were condemned to death.

The most questionable aspect of the entire case is the enormous number of witnesses—ninety-three, no less. It seems incredible that these conversos would have been so careless as to allow ninety-three "old Christians" to witness a Jewish service. (In fact, in the later protests which resulted in Lucero's being removed from office, it was established that *all* the condemnations in Córdoba under his direction were fraudulent. This again should serve as a caution to those who are so gullible as to believe Inquisition processes.)

At one time, twenty-five *sambenitos* hung in the "patio of oranges" (near the Postigo de la Leche) of the cathedral, beginning with that of a man burned in 1486.[99]

Jaén

Again, the actual records of the Inquisition for Jaén are lost (1483–1526), but other documentation has permitted Coronas Tejada to provide us with some information.

Among this is the notice of several members of a religious *cofradía* who were accused (ca. 1503–8) of "Judaizing." They were variously condemned by the Inquisition to burning and other punishments.

As previously mentioned, the notorious Inquisitor of Córdoba, Lucero, was responsible also for the Inquisition in Jaén in the years 1499 to 1507. However, the Inquisition was at work earlier, and already in 1486 the sources indicate that it acted against many people there. One Diego Rodríguez Abenbarca was condemned *in absentia* and burned in effigy in 1486, and his son and grandson were persecuted by the Inquisition into the sixteenth century.

Coronas speaks of 256 "Jews" and 208 conversos condemned. It is difficult to know what to make of such a statement, since, as mentioned, the Inquisition had no jurisdiction over Jews. One wonders if he means "old Christians" accused of "Judaizing," and thus called "Jews," but this seems unlikely. The other possibility is that, like many Spanish writers, he confuses "Jews" with "conversos," and for some reason uses the term *conversos* to refer only to descendants of first-generation converts. In his book on the Inquisition of Jaén, which by no means supersedes the earlier article, he appears to have retracted some of his more questionable statements, including this reference to "Jews" tried by the Inquisition, and the unsupportable claim of "secret synagogues" operating in the city. The book provides some scant details of an uprising in 1473 against the conversos, about which we should like to know more. Further details of the few extant records of the early sixteenth century are also provided. Generally, however, it is of use primarily for the later Inquisition.[100]

Toledo

Fernando de Pulgar provides the following information about the Inquisition of Toledo:

> In this year [1485] the Inquisition continued which had begun against the Christians of Jewish lineage who began to "Judaize." In the city of Toledo some men and women were found who secretly observed Jewish rites, who in great ignorance and danger to their souls kept neither the one nor the other law [religion] correctly, because they were not circumcised like Jews . . . and

although they observed the Sabbath and some Jewish fasts, they did not observe all the Sabbaths nor all the fasts, and if they observed one rite they did not observe another, so that they were false to both laws. It happened in some cases that the husband kept certain Jewish ceremonies and the wife was a good Christian, and that one son and daughter would be good Christians, and another hold the Jewish opinion. Thus, in one house there was a diversity of belief, and one would hide from the others.[101]

This important testimony, again hitherto ignored, would seem to be believable. Pulgar was a highly placed government official and certainly in a position to know the situation. We recall that he himself owned property in Toledo. It is certainly not inconceivable, particularly in Toledo, which had a large Jewish population and where Jews and Christians continued to live on the most cordial terms until the very eve of the Expulsion, that some conversos felt safe in occasionally observing Jewish customs, such as some Sabbath observances or the like, if we remember that we are speaking for the most part of first-generation converts (on the other hand, those who "were not circumcised like Jews" were obviously born to already converted parents).

Believable, too, is his statement that in some houses one or more members of a converso family would secretly observe some Jewish practice and hide it from others of the family. Such things happen also in the modern period. However, we must be careful not to extrapolate from this testimony about a unique situation in Toledo to other localities in Spain.

Even more important is Pulgar's statement that "because in this case of heresy, testimony is received from Muslims, Jews, servants, infamous and vile men, and because of this some were imprisoned and condemned to the penalty of burning, there were found in this city some Jews and poor and vile men who, from enmity or malice, gave false testimony against some conversos saying they 'Judaize.' Knowing the truth, the queen ordered them [the false witnesses] judged, and eight Jews were apprehended and tortured."[102] We have already mentioned that Jews were only too willing to testify against conversos, a willingness which increased as time produced more and more converts and it became increasingly clear that the overwhelming majority of them had no desire to return to their people or practice their law. It is interesting to learn that Isabel, always concerned about justice, ordered the punishment of those Jews who were caught giving false testimony. Nevertheless, as we know from the documents summarized by León Tello, this did not discourage others from similarly testifying, in their desire to wreak vengeance on those whom they viewed as traitors to their people.

The Inquisition was established in Toledo, as Pulgar says, in 1485, under the direction of Vasco Ramírez de Ribera, archdeacon of Talavera, and Pedro Díaz de la Costana, a canon of Burgos. Supposedly in June, at the feast

of Corpus Christi, some conversos planned to attack the Inquisitors and
their officials and kill them, but the plot was discovered. Under torture, they
"confessed," but were let off with fines—highly unlikely if they had, in fact,
been guilty.

As usual, the rabbis were ordered to pronounce bans of excommunication in the synagogues against anyone with knowledge of "heresy" among
the conversos who did not testify against them.

Alonso de Palencia says that the people of the city, "fearing the poverty
to which the city would be reduced" if the Inquisition were established,
and recalling that "three or four times" previously the infamous conduct of
"Judaizers" had resulted in great damage, worked hard to impede the establishment of the Inquisition. The queen herself had to interfere to convince
the city.[103]

The first "heretics" burned were Sancho de Ciudad and his wife, María
Díaz, and their son and his wife, and Pedro González de Teba and his wife
(both from Villa Real, later Ciudad Real).

At an *auto* in February of 1486, 750 *reconciliados* were in the procession, bareheaded and barefoot (but because of the great cold they had a
kind of sole to wear under their feet) and with candles, and a large crowd
of onlookers ridiculing them. There were two other such processions in February, four in March, five in April, two in May, two in June, two in August,
one in October (at which all the property of deceased heretics was declared
forfeit to the Crown), and two in December. In January of 1487, another
seven hundred marched in procession, and in March, twelve hundred from
Talavera, Madrid, and Guadalajara. In May, fourteen men and nine women
were burned.

In July of 1488 another twenty men and sixteen women were burned,
and also deceased "heretics," whose property was confiscated from their
heirs. Another *auto* in July saw the burning of a cleric and two Jeronimite
friars. In May of 1490 eighteen men and three women were burned, and
five men and six women condemned to perpetual imprisonment. The following day "more than four hundred" deceased were condemned, and
"many books of the heretics were condemned, and false Bibles" (as Fidel
Fita, that amazing scholar who uncovered these records, commented, "how
many Hebrew codices of great value were destroyed in this manner!").

"On this day was burned in the plaza a woman who was a very famous
heretic," reads a document, "who said publicly that she desired to die in the
Mosaic law and that there is no other truth but that. Thus she died saying
'*Adonay*' [Heb., Lord]."

Finally, in July of 1492 some five people were burned, and others condemned to perpetual imprisonment.

Also, during these years (up to 1492) many more were burned in the city
by the Inquisition of Toledo, but they were inhabitants of other cities.[104]

In fact, the records edited by Fita, ignored as they have been, reveal only the tip of the iceberg. In León Tello's collection of Toledo documents are many others, drawn primarily from the national archive in Madrid. It is interesting to observe once again that numerous Jews testified against the accused conversos (one such witness was the same Rabbi Pérez, a doctor, who was himself later accused in the infamous "Niño de la Guardia" case). In other cases, condemned conversos testified against others.[105]

The primate of Spain, then archbishop of Toledo, Pedro González de Mendoza, was shown an order from the Catholic Monarchs in 1486 that all property of suspected "heretics" who fled the city, even if they had paid taxes to the cathedral or monastery, was to be seized until the owners were condemned (no mention of the possibility that they might be found innocent). Some such property was nevertheless sold, after it had been seized, to private parties.[106]

In 1488 a conversa of Ocaña was tried and, apparently, tortured by the Inquisition. A lengthy prayer (in Spanish) was supposedly "discovered" among her possessions which definitely was of Jewish content and very similar to fast-day or penitential prayers. We must reserve judgment on the veracity of this information, however.[107]

Concerning Spanish prayers, there is also the testimony of a (conversa?) of San Martín de Valdeiglesias (outside of Madrid, a town which had an important Jewish community) who testified that when she was a girl, a Jew from Segovia had come to her parents' home and while there asked her if she wished to buy from him a book of prayers, written in Spanish. She did so, but her uncle later told her the book was "against our holy faith." She also testified that she had once gone to the synagogue with the daughter of the duchess (de Infantado) and other girls.[108]

The previously mentioned Juan de Pineda, a converso of Córdoba, *comendador* of the Order of Santiago, later living in Toledo, was tried by the Inquisition on charges that he had said that the Turkish sultan was the messiah promised to the Jews and that he would conquer Castile (we shall consider this topic in Chapter 8). He also was accused of having said that the conversos of Villareal (Ciudad Real) were good Christians who "erred and did not now what they did" in converting.[109]

Opposition to the Inquisition

The Catholic Monarchs wrote (1485) letters to the justices and officials of their cities, including the cathedral of Toledo and religious authorities, noting that certain people were falsely interpreting the bulls of Sixtus IV and Innocent VIII with regard to the Inquisition, and arresting and trying people incorrectly in accord with this false interpretation. They ordered that all such letters and documents of arrest and trial be examined in their chamber.[110] This, of course, reflects criticism of the Inquisition, no doubt by some of the more powerful conversos, and attempts to check its excesses.

The previously discussed converso author Juan de Lucena, counselor of the Catholic Monarchs and ambassador to England, etc., wrote a letter criticizing the methods of the Inquisition. The letter, written sometime between 1482 and 1492, but almost certainly after 1485 when the Inquisition began in Toledo, produced a condemnation of its "errors" by a canon of Toledo, Alfonso Ortiz (published in 1493, but probably written earlier).[111] At present, we can only guess as to how much other opposition of this kind came from prominent conversos.

In Burgos in 1493 several "Judaizers" were condemned, and as a result the merchants of the city demanded that no such burnings take place in the city itself, to which the Monarchs agreed, though in July they had to be again reminded of this. *Sambenitos* were nevertheless hung in the cathedral.[112]

It has already been noted that opposition to the excesses of two powerful Inquisitors in Córdoba led to the removal of both of them.

Inquisition in Seville

We have already seen how important the converso community of Seville was in the fifteenth century, and the troubles that resulted there. The city was itself of great importance to the Catholic Monarchs, who visited it almost immediately at the beginning of their reign, and according to the chronicler Bernáldez, the Dominican friar Alonso (de Ojeda) of San Pablo at that time preached a sermon against the conversos, and he and Cardinal Mendoza and others informed the rulers of the "great evil and heresy" which existed in the city because of the conversos. According to that writer many of the conversos did not have their children baptized (whether this was something he actually knew is questionable).

Instrumental in establishing the Inquisition in Seville, he says, were the bishop of Cádiz, the ecclesiastical judge of Seville (Pedro Fernández de Solis), "and another official" (Diego de Merlo). Among the first condemned were Diego de Susán, who had been a "great rabbi," Manuel Sauli, and Bartolomé (or Benito) de Torralva. Many conversos fled to Granada, Portugal, Rome, and elsewhere. Bernáldez states that in 1488 alone, over six hundred conversos were burned and five thousand (!) reconciled in Seville. (As we have seen, Pulgar in the first version of his chronicle had said that three hundred were burned in Seville, but gave no specific year; one would assume he meant over a period of several years.)[113] The "Susán" case will be examined here in some detail, as it is the most famous and is typical of the mythology surrounding the Inquisition.

When the Inquisition began in Seville, many of the prominent citizens, conversos and "old Christians," united to resist it. According to an anonymous source, of dubious authenticity and date, they decided to rebel against the Inquisitors with armed bands and "take vengeance on all their enemies." Of the names of the conspirators mentioned, only three are of obvious Jewish origin: "Susán, father of the legendary Susan" who was called the *fermosa fembra* (beautiful female), a certain "Abolofia, the perfumer," and Foronda, called simply "an old [former] Jew." The name Susán is undoubtedly derived from the well-known Ibn Sūsan family, an important Jewish dynasty. It is unlikely that the first name "Susan" is real for the supposed daughter, since the name is neither Hebrew nor Spanish. "Abolofia" is an obvious corruption of Abulafia, also a well-known Jewish name but never in that form. "Foronda" cannot be explained at all, and is undoubtedly fictitious. In fact, all of these characters were entirely fictitious, as we shall see.

Our "source" abruptly skips any details of the rebellion and goes immediately to the burning of Susán, stating that he had a Christian daughter, *enamorada y reqrebada* (probably *requebrada;* both words mean the same: "enamored"), who accused her father, "[she] being the friend [lover] of d . . . [name missing in the MS]." The (titular) bishop of Tiberias, Reginaldo Romero, made her a nun, but she left the convent and had illegitimate sons by her lover and then "came to such misery" that she was the lover of a druggist (*especiero;* perhaps less a discriminatory aspersion on druggists than a hint that he was a converso, common in Andalucía especially).

From such flimsy evidence and vague sources (even Bernáldez, although chaplain of Mendoza, who was named cardinal of Seville in 1486, is not to be trusted) there developed over the centuries a legend which is still firmly believed by many in Seville and recorded in some tourist guidebooks. According to the legend, the daughter of Diego de Susán, "Susana" now instead of simply "Susan," was in love with a Christian knight and because of him betrayed her father and the others involved in the plot. After her father was burned, she entered a convent but soon left and followed a life of shame until, before dying, she repented and ordered that after her death her skull be placed over the door of her house as a warning. There it supposedly remained, for hundreds of years (!), in the calle del Artaud (now, in fact, called calle Susona [sic], at the beginning of the callejón del Agua).[114]

Needless to say, none of the documents so far brought to light concerning either the Jews or the conversos of Seville substantiates any of this in any way.

As previously mentioned, the Jews were ordered expelled from Seville, and all Andalucía, in 1483. However, not all of them left (nevertheless, 1487 is the last we hear of even a single Jew in the city). From the extant documents, the name of a converso, Alfonso Fernández Abenxuxén, in 1407 proves the existence there (probably) of a branch of the Toledo Jewish Ibn Sūsan family (Arabic *Shūshan*, pronounced Sūsan in the Mozarabic dialect and written as Xuxen or Xuxan in Spanish).[115] There is, however, no mention of an Abulafia in Seville from the thirteenth century through the fifteenth (although the name is found in other cities, of course), to say nothing of any "Foronda." There was a Saul (first name) in 1252, but not "Saulí" as a family name.[116]

The *existence* of Diego de Susán is nevertheless without doubt, for in 1478 Queen Isabel appointed him *regidor y veinticuatro* (one of the councilors) of Seville in recognition of his services. Yet in 1479 his name is not mentioned among the *regidores* of the city in another royal document. The earliest reference to him is as a merchant in 1465. He may, indeed, have been a converso, but the rest of the legend is wholly without foundation. Since he is not heard of after 1478, it seems probable that he died in that year, or before the Inquisition was established in Seville.[117]

In 1482 Isabel wrote to the Inquisitors and to Juan de Medina (an important monk of the Jeronimite Order, one of the first Inquisitors and later a bishop) complaining that in certain yards near the monasteries of San Bernard, the Trinity, and San Augustin, conversos were being buried according to Jewish rites, in Jewish garments (probably the white gown), and without a cross in their hands. This was witnessed by many and was "public and notorious" knowledge. If this were true, she ordered, then these monasteries and their grounds were to be confiscated for the royal treasury. As usual, one may conjective whether or not ulterior motives were behind these charges.[118]

One Jewish chronicler, Joseph Ibn Ṣadiq, reported on the beginning of the Inquisition in Seville:

> In that year [1482] the judges of the king in the province of Seville and in all the kingdom of Aragon and Castile began investigations against all the *anusim* on the subject of religion, and they searched after them and found that some of them believed in the religion of the God of Israel, and all of them [!] were judged [to death] by burning and their possessions to the king. This is what is written: "A third I will bring into the fire" [Zech. 13.9].[119]

He adds the words "see the commentary of Rashi at the end of this book"; apparently in the text of the complete book, which has not survived, that commentary was added. On that passage "Rashi" (Solomon b. Isaac) says: "some of the proselytes [to Judaism] of the idolaters will suffer the tribulations of the days of the messiah and the wars of Gog and Magog with Israel [the Jews] and thus will be tested and proved that they are true proselytes, for first many of them will return to their evil way [former religion] and join with Gog, as it is written in the *agadah*." Apparently Ibn Ṣadiq, by citing this commentary, intended to allude to the tribulations of the Inquisition, which forced many of even the would-be "returners" (penitent apostates) among the conversos to revert to being good Christians.

The most important Inquisition process concerning Seville was that of the converso Juan de Sevilla (not to be confused with the aforementioned Samuel Abravanel, who converted and took the name Juan Sánchez de Sevilla),[120] who "confessed" in 1485 that at the age of twenty-five when he was apprenticed to the Jewish silversmith Mayr Abenbilla (well-known from other sources) he kept certain Jewish ceremonies, as he did when he afterward returned to the house of his father and mother. At the age of twenty-two he was with (apprenticed to?) a Christian headdress maker, and saw that he observed Jewish ceremonies and kept a Jewish youth in his house.[121] Afterward, he was also in the house of "Alfonso Lopes, *toquero*" (headdress maker; Christian? converso?) and observed that he and his wife kept Jewish customs. Later, some six or seven months following the massacre of conversos in Toledo (1467), he moved to that city where for twelve years he lived with (but was not, apparently, married to) a conversa, Mari Alvares, by whom he had a daughter. He considered returning to Judaism and attended synagogue on Yom Kippur. Mari Alvares also had a son from a previous union (with Ysaque Varquete), and that boy had been baptized but was sent to live with his father in Guadalajara, where he observed Passover and even sought to obtain unleavened bread (*maṣah*) from Jews of Toledo, which they refused for fear of punishment for providing this to a converso. The case ended with Juan being condemned to death.

Inquisition in Other Castilian Cities

Obviously it is impossible in the limited space here to detail all of the activities of the Inquisition in Castile. Entire books have been written on some of these, and although most of the documentation relates to the sixteenth century or later, some information of interest for our period is to be found also.[122] Essentially, the general picture which emerges is not affected by the accumulation of details.

A typical case is that of the trial of a converso in Talavera in 1486, curate of the Church of San Martín, against whom there was testimony that a Jew had given him a Hebrew book, and also that the accused had provided money for oil for lamps in the synagogue. Precisely these accusations turn up over and over again in the Inquisition records. What stretches credulity is not that one or two conversos might have been so indiscreet, especially in the first years before the Inquisition was established, but that literally thousands should have continued to do such stupid acts, knowing that this could result in their own death.

A contemporary source states that the first *auto* of the Inquisition in Valladolid was on 19 June 1489: "eighteen persons were burned alive, and four dead" (i.e., deceased who were exhumed and burned). The names are listed, and it is noted that some had been arrested the previous year.[123]

In the important diocese of Soria-Osma, which included towns with a major Jewish population in northern Castile, the Inquisition was established in 1486. Thanks to the efforts of Carrete, the full texts of the Inquisitorial processes for this diocese have been published. There are some interesting documents here, including those showing the famous Jewish government official Abraham Bienveniste testifying against conversos, including the "protonotario de Lucena," son of Juan Ramírez de Lucena who may have been related to the famous poet Juan de Lucena. The father himself (deceased) was accused of having given wine to Jewish relatives in the castle (as in several communities, the Jews in the city lived in the castle), and of having "repented" his conversion.[124]

Interesting accusations include several relating to the use of Hebrew, either speaking Hebrew, praying in Hebrew, or owning and reading books in Hebrew; expressing a desire or plan to go to Palestine (three cases); converting only for the sake of the children or because of debts; one case involved a man who converted but still had relations with his Jewish wife (though not, of course, living with her).[125]

Interesting testimony concerning the (supposed) claim of believing that the Turkish sultan is the messiah will be discussed later in connection with the Expulsion.

However, in general these records also indicate the same kinds of standard accusations: attending synagogue or not attending mass, giving oil for synagogue lamps, or wine to Jews, saying Jewish prayers or blessings, etc. There is little that is believable about any of the charges contained in the documents. Even the charge about the Turks is clearly a standardized Inquisition accusation (see above on the Toledo Inquisition).

Segovia and the "Niño de la Guardia" Case

As previously noted, an attempt to establish the Inquisition in Segovia in 1485 was apparently resisted, but it was in operation at least by October of 1490. Already in that month there was a case involving Gonzalo de Cuéllar, a converso and *regidor* of the city who had already been burned. His relatives—don Mosé de Cuéllar and his brother don Abraham and Rabbi Abraham, son of Moses, all residents of Buitrago—owed 393,000 *mrs.* (a considerable sum) to the deceased. The officials of the Inquisition sought to interrogate them and found them among some Jews in an inn they owned in Medina del Campo, but they refused to admit that they were present until one of the other Jews finally pointed them out. It being the Sabbath (what these Jews were doing in an inn on the Sabbath is unclear), they explained they could not bring their accounts or even discuss financial matters. The judges and officials therefore waited until night, when the Sabbath was over, at which time a Jewish broker of Segovia, Isaac Galfón (of a well-known family), produced his account books in order to prove that these Jews had already paid part of the debt. Nevertheless, the officials insisted on verifying this, and meanwhile ordered the seizure of all money and property of the above-named Jews for the remainder of the amount due. Rabbi Abraham further had to swear an elaborate oath that they were not lying.

This condemned Gonzalo (López) de Cuéllar was one of the officials who, in December 1474, received the young Isabel in the Alcazar of Segovia and accompanied her to the Plaza Mayor where she was proclaimed queen.[126]

Extant records do not permit an accurate idea of the activity of the Inquisition in Salamanca, but in 1488 at least one woman, Aldonza González, widow of Juan García de Nieva, was burned, and in 1490 several conversos were condemned.[127]

The most famous case, of course, was the ritual murder charge known as the "Niño de la Guardia" (boy of La Guardia) case. Ritual murder charges against Jews were not new, going back to the twelfth century in England, France, and Germany. Briefly, when a Christian boy disappeared, or was rumored to have disappeared, Jews were often accused of having murdered him, sometimes in a "ritualistic" manner by stabbing or even crucifixion. There had not been such charges in medieval Spain, however.

Baer provides an almost correct summary of the study published by Fita concerning this case. However, the boy was killed not "about eleven years" but only *two* years before the trial, as Fita explained (another possibility, which seems to be supported by the Spanish testimony Fita later published, is that the *age* of the boy was eleven years); also, nowhere is it said that the residents of La Guardia who were imprisoned were conversos; indeed, at least some of them were "old Christians." As to Baer's question of why the prisoners were brought to Segovia when jurisdiction belonged to Toledo, that very question had been raised by the defending lawyers and the explanation given that the archbishop of Toledo had relinquished authority to the chief Inquisitorial court (at Segovia). Again, Baer asked why the trial was transferred to Ávila, to which the simple answer is that Ávila, not far from Segovia, was the seat of the Inquisitorial court and this was a most important case (all of this was discussed in other articles by Fita).[128]

Nevertheless, some details must be added, and other corrections made, to Baer's account. In August of 1490, Torquemada wrote the Inquisitors of Ávila about the arrest of the Francos of La Guardia and of Moses Abenamías of Zamora. The Francos, incidentally, appear to have been Jews, not conversos.[129] As part of the initial proceedings, a witness testified that he heard a monk speaking, half in Hebrew and half in Spanish, to Yucé Franco, the accused, who told the monk he was imprisoned for having killed a *nahar* (Heb. *na'ar*, youth) "*por otohays*" (Heb. *oto ha-ish*, that man = Jesus), and that this should be told to Abraham Seneor, head of the Jewish community.[130]

On 17 December the Inquisitorial court of Ávila met, and was composed of an abbot of León, fray Fernando de Santo Domingo (a Dominican), and special judges, including Torquemada himself. Yucé Franco, described as a Jew, along with other Francos, Mosé Abenamías (Ibn Nahmias, a Jew) of Zamora, and Juan de Ocaña and Benito García of La Guardia, apparently "old Christians," were the defendants. Yucé was accused of speaking openly with Christians and telling them the law of Moses was the true law by which "salvation" can be attained, and other such "false and deceitful" things. He was not, as Baer thought, accused of trying to "convert conversos to Judaism." Worse, he was accused of joining with others, Christians and Jews, in crucifying a Christian boy on Good Friday, and also of stealing a consecrated host (for good measure, one supposes).

All these charges were made by *one* Christian man, with no supporting testimony. Franco denied the charges as being the greatest falsehood in the world. Two attorneys were appointed to advise and represent the accused. It would seem that they represented him well, claiming that he was entitled to exemption from the jurisdiction of the court at Ávila on the grounds that he was a resident of Toledo; that the charges were vague and should be dismissed (vague in that dates and places were unspecified); and most important that the defendant, being a Jew, was guilty of neither heresy nor apostasy and according to canon law should not therefore be tried by the Inquisition. To this the court replied that, in spite of his oath to the contrary, they had his "confession." Among the names mentioned in the "confessions" obtained are Yuçá Tazarte, a doctor, and "Rabbi Peres" of Toledo, also a doctor, to whom the consecrated host was supposedly given. If this were true, it is amazing that this doctor was not arrested and charged; indeed, his name appears as a witness in another Inquisitional process in Toledo in 1485, just two years before these events were supposed to have occurred.[131]

In 1491 the Jews of Ávila petitioned the Catholic Monarchs and the royal council concerning this trial against certain heretics and two Jews, Ça and Yucé Franco, which they considered a scandal against their community. Fearing attacks from the Christians, they demanded protection, to which the king and queen responded by taking the Jews under their immediate protection and ordering that no one molest the Jews. (This, incidentally, almost certainly reveals that the Monarchs knew these charges to be false; otherwise, their wrath would have been unleashed against all the Jews.)[132]

The complaint that the tribunal had no jurisdiction was taken care of neatly by obtaining a letter from Cardinal González de Mendoza, archbishop of Toledo. The trial then continued all summer. On 21 October, new charges were brought against Franco that, when crucifying the child, he made blasphemous remarks against the Christian faith. Following brutal torture, on 16 November (not 14, as Baer says), Yucé Franco and his father Ça (the one mentioned in the above protest from the Jews of Ávila), Benito García, Juan de Ocaña, and Juan Franco were all burned at the stake.[133]

Less gullible than Fita, who in spite of his immense erudition and general admiration for the Jews was inclined actually to believe this case, Lea correctly noted that the whole series of "confessions" was the creation of the torture chamber. No child was, in fact, reported missing and no body was ever found.[134]

A Catalan translation of the summary of the "evidence" (against only one of the accused, Benito García, with no mention of the others; was he Catalan, perhaps?) was printed almost immediately in Barcelona in 1491, and a copy of it was included by Carbonell, the royal archivist and archivist of the Inquisition of Aragón-Catalonia, in his records.[135]

The details concerning torture in this case permit us to briefly consider the question generally. Llorente already devoted some space to a discussion of methods of torture employed by the Inquisition, and yet some modern apologists have tried to deny or minimalize its role.

Yucé Franco was tortured on the rack, and the Inquisitors were themselves present at the brutal torture which took place. They told the prisoner that any pain, loss of blood, mutilation, that resulted or even death, was his responsibility, not theirs.[136]

Generally, prisoners were kept in dark and filthy cells, hot in summer and freezing in winter, infested with rats, snakes, and worms. Water and fire were routinely used as methods of torture, as well as the rack and the pulley. Some prisoners were so weakened, or their feet so burned, that they could not walk to their own death at the stake and had to be carried.[137]

Pico della Mirandola and the Spanish Inquisition

A major figure of the "humanist" Renaissance, Giovanni Pico della Mirandola, in 1486 at the age of twenty-four delivered his now famous *Oration on the Dignity of Man*. Often incorrectly hailed as a manifesto of "tolerance," the speech nevertheless appealed to Jewish, Christian, and even Muslim authorities to support his central thesis that man himself is the most worthy subject of man's study, and that man should be free to choose his own way of life. Among other things, he comments on the tradition that Moses gave "a more secret and true explanation of the laws" (i.e., the so-called oral Torah, which Pico mistakenly thought to be the esoteric teachings of the *qabalah*, which greatly influenced Pico). Not surprisingly, the pope condemned Pico's ideas and he fled to Spain.

On 16 December 1487 Innocent VIII wrote an incredible letter to the Catholic Monarchs condemning Pico, "alienated from holy Christian doctrine," and saying that "he is a false prophet." The pope praised Fernando and Isabel for their fight against the Muslims and "heretics" (i.e., conversos and "old Christians") among whom he mentioned also Pico. Indeed, a papal bull of 14 August had condemned Pico's teachings as *perfidiam judaeorum*. Therefore, the pope ordered that he be incarcerated and all his goods seized; too late, however, for by then Pico was already in France writing his "*apologia*."[138]

Pico was, in fact, more than slightly acquainted with Jews and Jewish teachings. In Italy his tutors in Hebrew, and in Jewish texts, had been the famous Elijah del Medigo of Candia, who was a lecturer at the University of Padua, and Yoḥanan Alemano, a German Jew of great learning. Alemano wrote a commentary on Song of Songs, parts of which he read (in Hebrew) to his pupil, who was "much impressed" by it.[139]

The irony of the papal condemnation is that, while greatly admiring some individual Jews, such as his teachers, Pico himself condemned what he called also the "Jewish perfidy." He was scarcely a champion of toleration, yet his dangerous espousal of even esoteric religious doctrines of the Jews led him perilously close to the fires which burned ever more intensely.

The Inquisition at Work: Aragón-Catalonia

Tomás de Torquemada was made Inquisitor General for Aragón-Catalonia in 1483, the appointment being confirmed by Pope Sixtus IV, a mere formality, of course. A year later he had already established the Inquisition in Zaragoza and Barcelona, and took charge of that in Valencia.[140] Alonso del Espina, prior of the Monastery of San Domingo de Huete, was appointed by Torquemada to act as Inquisitor of Barcelona in July in 1487 (he was not the same Alonso del Espina as the anti-Jewish author of the notorious *Fortalitium fidei*). The city council of Barcelona refused to swear the required oath of absolute obedience to the Inquisition, however, objecting strongly on the basis of papal permission formerly given for the establishment of a special Inquisition for Barcelona which would be independent, but to no avail. A compromise was finally reached after repeated recriminations between the council and the king. Resistance continued even after the formula of the oath was agreed upon. Furthermore, some of the conversos obtained documents from the pope exempting them from investigation, all of which hindered Espina's efforts.[141]

Alonso del Espina used his office for his own program against Jews, as well as conversos, and immediately set about isolating Jews from contact with *all* Christians, not just conversos (thus, for example, in Tortosa and Tarragona, under his jurisdiction along with Barcelona, Jews were required to live separated from Christians). In Tarragona twenty-seven conversos were immediately condemned.[142]

In 1486 the Inquisitor Juan Franco informed the Barcelona council of the king's intent to expel the Muslims from Granada and also to punish "Judaizing." The letter stated that the king was engaged "in the conquest of the infidel Moors and in expelling them from that part of his kingdom" (i.e., Granada, not yet conquered). As befits a "most Christian king," he also intended to punish all heresy "and especially some conversos who spontaneously were converted from the Jewish to the Christian law" but were still corrupted by "Jewish error." (The use of the qualifying adjective "some," *algunos* conversos, is significant.) Almost at once the council responded in a letter to Franco denying that he had the right to act in the city or in the diocese, and furthermore stating that they did not believe that "all the conversos are heretics." They ignored the specific statement about "some" conversos, possibly because they feared action would be taken against more than "some," or because generally they resisted the Inquisition's being imposed upon them.[143]

It was this resistance which led to the appointment of Torquemada, and strengthened the king's resolve to extend the Castilian Inquisition to all of his kingdoms. The Barcelona council, even after being forced to accept, still protested the usurpation of their authority and asked the king at least to order the Inquisitors not to exceed their authority.[144]

One "heretic" had already been condemned in February of 1486, and in December of 1487 the first procession under the new Inquisition consisted of only twenty-one men and twenty-nine women, all "reconciled." The first *auto* in January saw only four burned alive and twelve in effigy. A platform was erected in the plaza del Rey (behind the cathedral) where sermons were preached and the condemned were burned.[145]

The totally ignored eyewitness account of the official archivist provides us, of course, with the only absolutely reliable record we have of the operation of the Inquisition.

23 May 1488:   Three women were burned, one of whom was the wife of Lorenç Bedos, a physician of the royal household. Twenty others were condemned "in statue."

8 August: Another ten (one of whom, from Sardinia, was not of "Jewish origin" but merely a Christian heretic; he was not burned but imprisoned).

16 August: Espina led a procession and preached a sermon, as did an Augustinian monk, and thirty-four men and eighty-six women "confessed" and were "reconciled."

9 February 1489:   Two men and a woman were condemned, one of whom repented at the last moment and was strangled. Some thirty-seven others were also condemned, one of whom was royal secretary to the governor of Catalonia.

13 March: Nine burned (one a non-converso).

April (no date):   Nine "reconciled."

21 October: Nine burned.

23 March 1490:   Two burned, and then well over a hundred others (one was none other than Gabriel Miro, who had been chief physician of Juan II, along with his wife).

10 June 1491:   Some 126 burned.

13 October: One burned (a Jew who had been baptized and then became a Muslim) and thirty-nine "reconciled"; another thirty-nine condemned to perpetual imprisonment.[146]

Carreras nevertheless provides some other figures: the first public *auto* was 14 December 1487, involving twenty-one to twenty-three men and twenty-nine or thirty women. Not all were conversos, however. He gives the name "Badós" for the widow of the physician to Juan II, burned 23 May 1488. There were numerous letters from Fernando in 1490 complaining of continued opposition of the clergy to the Inquisition. On 10 June 1491, the powerful ex-royal secretary, Juan de Sant Jordi, was condemned, along with his wife, Angelina, and her sister Aldonça Boscá and others. According to Carreras, Juan fled and was burned "in statute" (in effigy); but I do not know where he got that information, since Carbonell, who was there, says he was burned in person.[147]

In Tarragona on 18 July 1489 there was a procession of twenty-seven "reconciled" (mostly women). These were required to swear "formulas of abjuration," confessing to having observed the "laws of Moses" or "rites and ceremonies of Jews" and swearing faithfulness to the Church and the pope. In 1490, a total of fifteen were burned and four condemned to perpetual imprisonment (including a doctor and his sons; his wife was burned). There was a plague in Barcelona, which interrupted the activities of the Inquisition there. Apparently not wanting to waste his time while in Gerona Espina set to work there. On 14 February 1490, under the direct supervision of Espina, some thirty-three were burned.[148]

In 1488 the Catholic Monarchs went to Zaragoza to hold the *Cortes* (parliament), primarily with a view to revising the traditional Aragonese system of criminal justice to enable them to have more direct control. They consulted a native of the city who was learned in law, the aforementioned converso vice-chancellor Alfonso de la Caballería. He is described as "very learned, a man of good prudence and well instructed in the laws and customs of that kingdom."[149] His family, however, was to become embroiled in the Inquisition.

An important example of the patent falseness of so much of the Inquisition testimony concerns the charges which were made against Alfonso and his father Pedro de la Caballería in 1485 (by which time Pedro was deceased). The Inquisition had been established in Zaragoza in 1482, but was suspended and reintroduced in 1484. The case involving the powerful de la Caballería family was one of the first.

A certain Jeuda Zunana, a Jew, called also "Noderço" (one of the rabbis of Zaragoza in 1492 was Solomon Zunana), testified that he was of the household of Pedro and Alfonso and that he had rented for them places in the "great synagogue," and in other synagogues, in the city, and that "Bienbenis" (Benveniste) de la Caballería of Zamora, Pedro's uncle, had obtained from Alfonso "certain books of the Talmud and a Bible in Hebrew."

Even more damning was the testimony of a Jew that he had seen Alfonso in Ocaña (near Toledo) in the house of Moses Azaradel (Abenzaradiel, probably) speaking with the famous Rabbi Isaac de León, the teacher of the witness. This much is obviously false, for that great scholar would not have dared risk such a thing, and certainly not in the remote and tiny village of Ocaña where it surely would have been noticed. Later, in May of 1492, a Jewish tailor of Zaragoza testified that Isaac de León, supposedly in Zaragoza, had maintained cordial relations with Alfonso and went to his home to speak with him. Isaac, who had died in 1490, as previously mentioned was head of a yeshivah in Salamanca. He lived in Toledo (Pulgar) in the 1480s, where he died, and was never in Zaragoza as far as we know. (Baer, misunderstanding the source, made him a rabbi of Ocaña.)

In April of 1492 (this investigation lasted that long), Rabbi Levi aben Sento of Zaragoza testified that the Inquisitors had ordered him to preach three sermons telling the Jews to inform the Inquisition of anything they knew concerning "Judaizing" on the part of conversos. A certain Jewish official then told the rabbi of the "help" which Alfonso supposedly had given the Jews in matters concerning taxes, etc., and how in a private conversation he had "confessed" his secret Jewishness. What makes this doubly suspicious is that the rabbi did not come forward until the edict of Expulsion had been issued; obviously, his motive was revenge against converso officials for not aiding in rescinding the edict.

More believable is the testimony of another Jewish official that he had spoken to Alfonso to complain about the taxes imposed on the community, and Alfonso had agreed (in return for payment to him of the enormous sum of 1,000 gold *florins*) to do what he could. When the Jew asked for better surety for this promise, Alfonso took a Bible and opened it to the "Ten Commandments" and asked the Jew if he believed in them. When he replied affirmatively, Alfonso swore by the commandments to do what he had promised. This is hardly proof of any "Judaizing heresy" on his part, of course, nor is it stated that the Bible was Hebrew. Other testimony, also by Jews, concerned Alfonso's brother Jaime who had supposedly visited a synagogue, after having disguised himself to visit a Jewish widow whom he knew.

In 1486 a Christian priest had accused various powerful conversos, including Gonzalo García de Santa María and even the officials Juan and Luis de Santángel and others of ridiculing a crucifix in a ceremony. Obviously all such accusations, including those against the de la Caballería family, arose out of personal jealousy and animosity. Pedro de la Caballería particularly, author of a notorious anti-Jewish polemic, and, as we have seen, a man who went to great lengths to try to "prove" that he was not even of Jewish origin, was hardly guilty of "Judaizing."[150]

The Inquisition was meanwhile at work elsewhere in Aragón-Catalonia as well. Thus, in Calatayud, a Jew accused a converso of having said that he became a Christian only because someone struck him in the synagogue, and that he regretted it, and also that he gave money for a Hebrew prayer to be recited at his mother's grave.[151]

Papal Opposition to the Inquisition

Not only was there continued opposition in Barcelona to the Inquisition, but the bull of Sixtus IV (18 April 1482) complained that the Inquisition in Aragón-Catalonia was engaged less in investigating heresy and the salvation of souls than in greed for profit. He noted that "true and faithful Christians" had been imprisoned, tortured, and condemned as heretics on the false testimony of enemies, envious people, servants, and other "vile" and unworthy persons.

Because of the many complaints he had received, and indeed because of his own certain knowledge of this, the pope ordered that in the future the Inquisitors must act together with episcopal vicars and other diocesan officials, as had been ordered in previous papal letters. Specifically, the accused were to be given the names of their accusers and the testimony of witnesses against them; they were to have the right of legal counsel and defense; imprisonment was to be only in the episcopal prisons; and, most important, the right of appeal of any abuses to the pope himself was to be guaranteed. Finally, those guilty of heresy should be given the right privately to confess and be absolved and be given *secret* penance, free of any public humiliation. This important document, which has often been ignored by scholars, indicates that the pope was well aware of the abuses of the Inquisition. On the other hand, it seems to have been as much ignored by the Inquisition as it has been subsequently by scholars.[152]

Conversos played a key role in obtaining this bull, and in December Fernando wrote his governor in Valencia that one Gonsalvo de Gonsalvo Roys was particularly instrumental, and ordered his *arrest* pending oral instructions to be given by (the converso official) Luis de Santángel. Not content with this, the king protested directly to the pope and flatly refused to allow the bull to take effect, insisting on maintaining control of the Inquisition.[153] Thus did his "most Catholic majesty" show his respect for the pope.

In 1485 the Catholic Monarchs noted that "some persons" had influenced both Sixtus IV and Innocent VIII to issue various bulls against the activities of the Inquisition, which were injurious to the "holy faith" and (especially, perhaps) to the royal treasury. Therefore, they ordered that anyone presenting any papal bull or letter whatsoever having to do with the Inquisition be arrested and the document sent to them to be examined.[154]

Nevertheless, there was continued strong opposition in Aragón and Valencia, as well as Catalonia, to the Inquisition. It was hoped that an end could be brought to the confiscation of property, which would result in ending the Inquisition (this fact alone reveals that it was common knowledge that "zeal for the faith" was hardly the motive for the Inquisition). It was necessary for the Monarchs in 1484 to issue an order forbidding suspect "heretics" from leaving Spain, and even this met with resistance as being contrary to the laws, but Fernando was firm and ordered that the Inquisition was above the law and that now *no one*, suspect or not, could leave the land without permission of the Inquisition.[155]

Teruel

The tyranny of Fernando is perhaps nowhere more evident than in his abusive measures against the ancient and important city of Teruel when it refused to admit the Inquisitors. He ordered the nobles of Aragón to supply troops to besiege the city and arrest all its inhabitants. Failing to obtain sufficient forces, he brought in Castilian troops from Cuenca and elsewhere before the city finally submitted.[156]

Already in 1486 the Inquisition was hard at work there. The usual litany of false charges against conversos emerged, perhaps more extensively documented here than elsewhere, which reveal animosity against a converso because of overcharging on the price of a mule or some such thing, "suspicion" of old Christian servants, economic jealousy, etc. One prominent merchant was accused because, having spent a week doing business in a small village, he left at once to return home on Sunday without waiting to hear mass. Therefore, obviously, he was a "Judaizer." One woman, Violante de Catorce, from a well-known Aragonese Jewish family, fled out of fear of the Inquisition. A conversa, she was condemned "*in absentia*" for having observed the Sabbath, Yom Kippur, etc. Nor, as usual, did deceased "heretics" escape. Their graves were destroyed and their bones publicly burned.[157]

Assassination of an Inquisitor

Gaspar Juglar and Pedro Arbués were appointed Inquisitors in 1484. Juglar soon died, however, amid rumors that he had been poisoned by conversos. This left Arbués.

Pulgar reports that there were "many" false conversos, very wealthy, and that some held public offices. They claimed that they were such good Christians that an Inquisition was not necessary. "Others, who knew that it was more serious, sought to escape by killing one judge whom they believed had solicited this Inquisition, more from animosity which he had for them than zeal for the faith. Motivated by this diabolical intention, they took advantage of a time when this Inquisitor was saying Matins before the altar of the chief church of the city of Zaragoza [Catedral de La Seo] and two men with covered faces entered and killed him." They were apprehended and burned, as were "some others who kept Jewish rites" in cities throughout the kingdom.[158]

This was the notorious assassination of Pedro de Arbués. Among those implicated in the murder (1485) was a grandson of the famous convert Jerónimo de Santa Fe, and he committed suicide in prison. His body was burned and the ashes were thrown into the river.[159]

Many important conversos and even some "old Christians" were implicated, including the officials, discussed elsewhere, Gabriel Sánchez and Luis de Santángel (who is not to be confused with the Luis de Santángel condemned by the Inquisition in Teruel in 1486), and others. Some fled to Tudela, in Navarre, and thus escaped, but others were caught. The punishment was severe: their hands were cut off and nailed to the door of the cathedral of Zaragoza and they were then beheaded and quartered. In 1489 the property confiscated by the Inquisition, including certain houses of Luis de Santángel in various cities, was given to the sister of Arbués for the expenses of her marriage. Francisco de Santa Fe, as mentioned above, the grandson of Jerónimo, the assessor of the governor of Aragón, was arrested and threw himself from his prison wall. Luis de Santángel was beheaded and his head publicly displayed on a pole, while his body was burned. In 1488 Juan de la Caballería was also put on trial, but he died in prison in 1490.[160]

What is truth and what fiction in all these charges? Certain it is that the Inquisitor, later made a saint, was murdered. To this day it is "common knowledge" in Spain that the conversos conspired to assassinate him, and it is unquestioned, even by scholars, that all of those accused were guilty. No doubt some conversos were involved in the plot, but we cannot ignore the authoritative testimony of Pulgar that "old Christians" were also involved. Few, if any, were tried, however, and not one was murdered or otherwise punished. Once again, the trials were used as a convenient way of getting rid of powerful converso officials.

The Juan de Ciudad Case

In about 1465 a certain Juan de Ciudad, an "old Christian" (not, as Baer thought, a converso; the word *confeso* in the text refers to a witness, not to the accused), came to Huesca and met with Abraham Bivagch (which is the correct spelling of his name, not "Bibago," etc.; he was author of a famous philosophical treatise) and Abraham Almosnino and stated his desire to convert to Judaism.[161]

He was hidden in Huesca for a few days, while Abraham Bivagch assembled ten of the leading Jews of the city and they spoke with Juan about his desire to be circumcised. Among the Jews involved in Juan's circumcision (and possibly also that of his son) were Jewish students from Castile and Portugal who were in the city, probably to study with Bivagch.

Meanwhile, the Jews of Huesca were involved in yet other difficulties which came to the attention of the Inquisition. One case concerned some, two of whom were rabbis, who had made a vow to convert to Christianity and then had fled to Zamora, or elsewhere in Castile, and Portugal. The second case involved a Jew who had converted in Portugal, and now lived openly as a Jew in Huesca, being housed in the hospital of the Jews. The entire Jewish council of eighteen met to discuss these cases. When the Inquisitors imposed the usual threat of excommunication on all Jews who knew about such matters, the Jews refused to accept the threat and left the synagogue.

Juan de Ciudad meanwhile convinced Bivagch and the others of his sincerity, having earlier sought to convert in Valencia, Zaragoza, and Calatayud, without success, and was circumcised. The Jews gave him money and he left "for the Levant" (or Jerusalem, according to other testimony) to live as a Jew.

Most damaging, perhaps, was the testimony of a learned Jew, Açach Rondi, that Bivagch had told Juan that in order to be circumcised he must "remove and purify" himself of all "Christianity" by washing his head thoroughly. In the decision of the Inquisitorial court it is mentioned that when Jews receive *garines* (i.e., *gerim*, proselytes) they "debaptize" them in water and by cutting the nails, "as is proven in *Yoreh de'a* chap. 270"—actually chap. 268, which states the real requirement, namely that proselytes, like all who are immersed, must cut their hair and nails. The representatives of the Jewish community very ably answered these charges.

In 1489 several of the Jews who had been involved were condemned to death. Açach (Isaac) Bivagch, brother of the then deceased Abraham, converted to Christianity at the last minute so that he could die the quicker death of strangulation (garroting) rather than by the fire.

Other testimony by Jews revealed that still other Christians had come to Huesca from various parts of Spain to live as Jews, including a young man of about twenty-five years of age who was a great Talmudic scholar and preached as a rabbi in the synagogues. (Huesca, today a remote, if beautiful, small town, was the capital of Aragón.)[162]

The Inquisition in Valencia and Majorca

In 1464 several conversos of Valencia, some of whom had lived as Jews previously in Córdoba, were accused by the Inquisitors of conversing with Jews, particularly about the messiah "whose coming they await," and of planning to go to Israel where they would be "saved," meanwhile planning to go to Constantinople, Venice, or elsewhere, and eventually to "the land of the Turks" where Jews live. Some of those accused did, in fact, confess to having already made journeys to Venice, but these were primarily legitimate business trips. One stated that he had been a Christian for twenty-five years. Other accusations emerged, including that one had gone either to Venice or Cairo (!) and there had been seen wearing "Jewish clothing." A daughter of one converso claimed in testimony that she had seen letters from Constantinople which stated that the messiah was already born and living near that city.[163]

In general there is little to add to what Lea has already, remarkably, uncovered concerning the Inquisition in Valencia. Jaime Borell had been appointed Inquisitor by 1474, but little was actually done until 1481 when Cardinal Rodrigo Borja (later Pope Alexander VI) convinced the pope to remove the independence granted the Valencia Inquisition and put it under the control of the vicar general, archdeacon of Valencia. In 1482 Fernando provided "ample" salaries for the officials and growing bureaucracy of the Valencia Inquisition.[164]

Nevertheless, the activity temporarily came to a halt in 1482 (Lea conjectured that conversos managed to convince the pope to intervene, but he also suggested that Sixtus IV himself sought to maintain control of the Inquisition and the lucrative possibilities provided by appeals to the pope; however that may be, we have already seen that he did, indeed, attempt to intervene). As already noted, however, Fernando strongly objected to this papal interference, and according to Lea the king threatened retribution against the entire Dominican Order, having already banished the Inquisitor of Catalonia, Francisco Vital, for taking bribes.

Even the royal council for the Inquisition in Valencia complained about the sequestering of property of those arrested but not yet tried, much less condemned. The king insisted, however, that he should not lose anything which was "his." The conversos themselves came up with a solution whereby a kind of general bond was posted against the confiscation of property of those who might later be condemned.

As previously mentioned, the Inquisition did have jurisdiction over Jews in those cases where they were accused of "corrupting" Christians. Such a case was that of Solomon Çaporta of Murviedro (1488), accused of inducing a Christian to convert.[165]

Resistance to the Inquisition continued as the *Corts* protested that the procedures used violated the laws and ancient privileges of the kingdom. The king was outraged, just as he had been by similar claims in Catalonia, and adamant that the Inquisition continue to operate in Valencia, but it took a year and more unseemly battles before anything could be done. In the face of the king's wrath, further opposition finally proved futile. By 1488, some 983 "heretics" had been reconciled, including 100 women who were wives or daughters of those already burned.[166]

As we have previously mentioned, a large portion of the Jews of Majorca already converted in 1391. Many of those who did not fled the island to go to North Africa. Nevertheless, Majorca's Jewish population was certainly not entirely gone by 1488 when the Inquisition was established there, as has been erroneously claimed.[167] In addition to Jews and the large number of conversos already in the capital city (essentially the only place they were allowed to live), there was an influx of others from Aragón-Catalonia, Valencia, and even Córdoba and elsewhere in Castile. A *cofradía* of conversos, already founded in 1401, was reestablished in 1410 as the *cofradía nueva de San Miguel arcángel*.[168]

It has been estimated that at the beginning of the reign of Fernando there were between twelve hundred and fifteen hundred conversos in Majorca, chiefly engaged in commercial activities. The Inquisition was established there in 1484, but only a relatively small number, a total of eighty-five in the first twenty-eight years, were burned.[169] During the "grace period" many conversos, "persuaded by a great rabbi," according to one source, publicly confessed their "sins" and were absolved on condition of paying huge fines to redeem their sequestered property.[170]

Giving "Order" to the Inquisition

As we have seen, there was mounting opposition to the excesses of the Inquisition from many quarters, from the various popes, from ecclesiastical authorities, from some "old Christian" sources (particularly the officials and the *Corts* of the kingdom of Aragón-Catalonia, but also from the "lower aristocracy" of Andalusian cities), and certainly from the conversos themselves.

In order to deal with this, the Catholic Monarchs in 1488 assembled in Valladolid all the Inquisitors from each town and city of the entire kingdom in order to "put order in the Inquisition," i.e., to impose their absolute control. Pulgar wrote of this:

> There were found many Jews, vile men, who gave false testimony against certain conversos, in order to have them executed [as he already previously said, in Toledo several such Jews were arrested]. Also, they [the Monarchs] named Inquisitors to be sent to certain dioceses to carry out the Inquisition in a judicial form, to punish those guilty and purify [*apurazen*] them of all the Jewish rites which they observe, and purify [*alimpiasen*] the land of that evil and iniquitous inclination which some hold.[171]

That same year, at the *Cortes* of Zaragoza, the Catholic Monarchs noted that they had been informed that "many persons of Jewish lineage, whose fathers and grandfathers had become Christians" in the kingdom of Aragón-Catalonia, were not good Christians and maintained Jewish customs. Therefore, they had sent Inquisitors to all these kingdoms (actually, already in 1484). In November of 1484, the *Diputación* (Council) of Aragón had petitioned the Monarchs that the Inquisition be stopped, or at least made to function in accord with Aragonese laws. This request was completely ignored.[172]

Confiscation of Property

It has been often suggested that a chief motive, if not indeed the main one, of the Inquisition was the confiscation of wealth and property. The avarice in seizing property is attested by such statements of contemporaries as "he who owns an estate should take into account that he has fire with it" (que el que tenía fazienda feziese cuenta quen tenía el fuego consigo); i.e., he is in danger from the Inquisition.[173]

In a letter of instruction in 1519 from Charles V to his papal envoy, to prevent Pope Leo X from "liberalizing" Inquisition procedures, the envoy was instructed to argue that reform would give credence to the claims of conversos about avarice.[174]

Ladero Quesada unearthed some actual figures for sums of money (not including, apparently, property) seized by the Castilian Inquisition alone in the years 1482–91.

Toledo:	930,000 *mrs.*
Córdoba:	1,641,500 *mrs.*
Valladolid:	1,121,524 *mrs.*
Seville:	300,000 *mrs.*
Sanlúcar de Barrameda (1488):	2,091,850 *mrs.*
Chillón (1489):	1,306,599 *mrs.*
Baena (1489):	1,724,840 *mrs.*
Condado de Niebla (1491):	531,210 *mrs.*[175]

While most of this money was used for the war against Granada, by no means all of it was. The salaries and vast expenses of the Inquisition itself came from the money and property seized from conversos, and in 1484 the Catholic Monarchs ordered that not only the property of those condemned, and those who had fled, was forfeit but also all outstanding debts due to them. From 1490 to 1493, confiscations of the Inquisition of Jaén amounted to 3,288,479 *mrs.*[176]

Another use for such seizures was to give the property or money to various people upon whom the Monarchs wished to bestow favors. For example, in 1487 the Monarchs promised to Alonso de Quintanilla some money and land from this source, and we encounter such donations fairly frequently in the records.[177]

In Córdoba in that same year a group of suspected conversos fled and their property was confiscated, but they petitioned the king and queen for its return and the petition was granted. They had to pay a total of 1,200,000 *mrs.* to "redeem" that property, however. A similar decision was made in 1493 with regard to property of some conversos in Ciudad Real, and we have already cited examples of this elsewhere.[178]

The excesses and abuses in such confiscations, frequently protested by conversos and even "old Christians," are evident in such things as the grant of seized property to the sister of the Inquisitor Pedro Arbués for her marriage. Another example is the case of Rodrigo de Toledo, who in 1490 obtained a special exemption of imprisonment for debt because all his goods had been confiscated when he was reconciled, but he was to pay his debts when he could.[179]

Finally, in 1491 the Monarchs ordered that no property be seized from *reconciliados* who had paid "compensation" (ransom) and that all money from property seized from those condemned to perpetual imprisonment, or reconciled after the "grace period," be used to construct the new city of Santa Fe (in Granada).[180]

Part of the complaints against Lucero, the Inquisitor of Córdoba in 1506, was that although the Catholic Monarchs had decreed that goods and property seized from "heretics" by the Inquisition should be used for the costs of the war against Granada, that war had long since ended and the seized property was now going to the Inquisitors, their officials, and relatives. The Inquisitor General, Diego de Deza, archbishop of Seville, was also implicated in the same charges.[181]

Condemned to Death

Far worse than forfeiture of money and property, of course, was the fate of those condemned to death by burning, or mercifully by strangulation. We recall that Pulgar, certainly a well-informed source, stated that more than fifteen thousand were "reconciled" and some two thousand burned "in some cities and towns" (he does not say whether this was just in Andalucía, however), and also that in the diocese of Seville alone some three thousand houses were abandoned by conversos who fled (a figure he later revised to four thousand for Seville, Córdoba, and other Andalusian cities).

Diego de Valera, at least as knowledgeable and reliable a witness, wrote that by the time he completed his chronicle (1487?) "more than" fifteen hundred had been burned and more than four thousand "reconciled." Like Pulgar, he adds that many had fled, "some in the land of the Muslims [thus worded, this can only mean Granada], others in Portugal, others in various parts." A later interpolation adds that "until the year 1520" in the diocese of Seville more than four thousand had been burned, and more than thirty thousand "reconciled." Zurita added a handwritten note: "This chronicler does not know what he says, because between the living and the dead and those absent condemned as 'Judaizing' heretics there were more than one hundred thousand only in this archdiocese of Seville, along with those reconciled."[182]

On the other hand, Alonso de Palencia, who at the time was actually living in Seville, wrote of sixteen thousand who either had fled or were condemned in 1481 alone, as previously mentioned. In the years 1481–85, according to him, five hundred were burned. Pedro Barrantes Maldonado, a writer of the early sixteenth century, relates that "in a brief period" more than fifteen thousand were "reconciled" and almost two thousand men and women burned.[183] A nineteenth-century author, on the basis of certain records, gave the following estimates of the numbers burned in Seville:

1482: 88
1483: 88
1484: 88
1485: 88
1486: 88
1487: 484 (together with other Andalusian cities)
1488: 88
1490: 32[184]

Of course, these figures are suspicious, especially since virtually the same number is given for each year.

Kamen, on the other hand, certainly exaggerated wildly in his claim that "tens of thousands" of conversos were burned. He himself cited figures gathered from various sources which, while incomplete, show how absurd this claim is (see table).[185]

	Burned	In effigy	Other
Toledo (1485–1501)	250	500	5,400
Zaragoza (1485–1502)	124	32	458
Valencia (1484–1530)	754	155	1,071
Barcelona (1488–98)	23	445	421
Mallorca (1488–1729)	120	496	664

Since no sources are, in fact, named, it is difficult to know where he got these figures, but several of them are ridiculous. Thus, from Fita's documents alone, we know that 95 were burned in Toledo between 1485 and 1492, and thus surely more than 250 for the years indicated. Like other scholars, Kamen never read the most important source for the Catalan Inquisition, the memoirs of its archivist Pedro Miguel Carbonell, which indicates that actually 293 were burned in Barcelona alone; as for the other categories, we have little or no information.

To this table, however inaccurate, we must add:

	Burned	In effigy	Other
Jaén (1483–95)	560	380	5,444
Cuenca (1489–91)	45	2	46

and, as previously noted, 25 burned in Córdoba in 1492, and 27 in Tarragona in 1484.[186]

Nevertheless, while the total burned by the Inquisition in the years up to and including 1492 was probably closer to thousands than tens of thousands, the impact of this catastrophe upon the converso community, and also upon the economy of Spain, must have been enormous.

Inquisition Legends and Modern Mythology

The Inquisition is the stuff of which legends are made, of course. It was by no means only the conversos who were its victims, for the "Holy Office" continued its gruesome work until it was abolished by Napoleon in 1808, although the Inquisition did not actually end completely for several more years. After the seventeenth century the Inquisition focused mostly on other kinds of heretics, particularly Protestants, rather than on "Judaizers." Legends about conversos and the Inquisition persisted, nevertheless.

In the former Jewish *barrio* of Santa Cruz in Seville in the seventeenth century, for instance, the legend existed that the Jewish messiah had taken the form of a fish in the Guadalquivir river in order to escape the persecution of the Inquisition.

This was also apparently the period of the birth of the legends concerning the "*Chuetas*" of Majorca, the sometimes real and sometimes imaginary descendants of conversos who have so captured modern romantic attention.[187]

Still as late as the end of the seventeenth century, however, some "Jews" (i.e., "Judaizers," either descendants of conversos or heretics accused of Jewish practices) were being burned in Córdoba; and, in fact, twenty-six such people were burned in 1721. Inquisition activity of this kind continued in Gibraltar until 1820.[188]

Conclusions: Lessons of the Inquisition

While this chapter, lengthy as it is, cannot of course pretend to be a thorough history of the Inquisition, it at least brings to light material elsewhere ignored. Indeed, almost all the scholarship on the Inquisition since Lea has been completely inadequate with regard to medieval Spain. We have seen, for example, the absolute necessity of considering what Baer and others have falsely called the "papal Inquisition," i.e., the Inquisition in the kingdom of Aragón-Catalonia in the thirteenth and fourteenth centuries, as a forerunner of the Castilian and "Spanish" (united kingdoms) Inquisition of the fifteenth. Only such a focus, taking into account the *entire* history of the Inquisition in medieval Spain, can permit us to make sense of such things as the fierce opposition not only to the methods but to the very establishment of the Inquisition in the fifteenth century.

It cannot be overemphasized, either, how important it is to understand that the Inquisition never had jurisdiction over Jews, except in the special cases noted. This fact the Jews themselves knew very well: that they had nothing to fear from the Inquisition. Indeed, the Jews in fifteenth-century Spain were only too happy and willing to use the Inquisition for their own purpose, which was to avenge themselves on the hated conversos whom they rightly considered to be their enemies, who had totally abandoned not only their religion but their people.

An example of this attitude may be seen in the almost gloating tone of the words of Isaac ʿArama, commenting on Deuteronomy 28.64 as a prediction of the Inquisition and the persecution of the conversos,

> for even though they became intermingled [assimilated] with those Gentiles completely, they do not find peace or rest among them, for they [Gentiles] will always revile and shame them and devise against them thoughts and complaints [charges] in matters of faith; and always they are suspect in their [Gentiles'] eyes as "Judaizers" [mityahadim], and they subject them to tremendous dangers, as was in all the period of time of these innovations, and all the more in this present time in which their smokes [of the Inquisition] have ascended to the heavens in all the kingdoms of Spain and the islands of the sea [Sicily, Majorca].

He concludes, in words reminiscent of those already cited of Joseph Ibn Sadiq (see above on the Inquisition of Seville) that a "third of them has been consumed by fire," a third tries to hide, and the rest live in fear and terror.[189]

This is, to be sure, virtually the only reference to the Inquisition that we have by a Jewish scholar living in Spain at the time. Nevertheless, it reveals what must have been a general attitude that the conversos deserved what happened to them. It also demonstrates clearly that ʿArama knew that the charges of "Judaizing" were false.

That is more than most modern scholars are willing to admit, of course. Compelled by the romantic myth of "crypto-Judaism," a myth for which there is not the slightest factual evidence, these scholars insist on accepting at face value the "records" of the Inquisitional processes as if they were true.

As one reads the hundreds of documents which so far have been edited, however, it becomes increasingly obvious that the charges against the accused conversos or their descendants were so patently fabricated that it is difficult to understand how anyone could believe them.

In the Inquisition of Cuenca in 1490, for example, of a total of thirty-five processes, eleven were against women, and of these women, seven were already deceased when the charges were brought. We have seen that it was not all uncommon for charges of "heresy" to be brought against people, men and women, long dead. It is strange that they were not accused while they were still living and could, theoretically, have defended themselves.

In Cuenca, as elsewhere, the charges consisted of the usual litany: observing Yom Kippur, lighting Sabbath candles, separating a portion of dough before bread is baked (a Jewish law actually of minor significance, but one likely to be observed by a pious woman), not eating pork or rabbit or seafood without scales, blessing the children, etc. The only interesting accusation in all of these documents is that one of the women was supposed to have said at mass: "Pan y vino veo y en la Ley de Moysén creo" ("Bread and wine I perceive, and in the law of Moses I believe"), quite a witticism to imagine that a conversa would have been so daring as to utter publicly at mass.

There were no Jews at all living in Cuenca after 1391, so there can hardly be any question of supposed Jewish influence on these conversos (if, indeed, they were that; for there is no proof given). Many of them, judging from their names, came from other cities: Castillo, Ávila, Murcia, Madrid. It is very likely that this "outsider" status, with the suspicion that all small towns have for such people, may have been a major factor in the charges brought against them, and this very well may be the case in a number of Inquisition accusations elsewhere.[190]

What is of importance is that in *all* of the countless records of accusations which are available thus far, the situation is the same. The accusations are almost always of an identical nature, relating to well-known Jewish laws and practices of the kind specifically outlined in the manuals of the Inquisition. In vain do we look for some novelty in these charges, of some individual accusation which might be believable as the act of a "secret Jew," or at least of a converso somehow reluctant to abandon certain customs of his childhood. There are many possibilities, and yet none of these are ever brought forth as original and unique charges which might make us believe that here, at last, is a real case.

We have already mentioned the extreme danger, and therefore the folly, of actually engaging in such easily seen and public practices as those of which these conversos were accused, such as public congregational services on Yom Kippur, lighting Sabbath candles, and the rest. A converso would have had to be insane to imagine that he could do such things without detection, knowing full well that detection would bring certain death.

There is no doubt whatever, therefore, that the *overwhelming majority*, nearly all, of these accusations are totally false. Only the extreme bigot, or the most zealous apologist for the conversos, can possibly continue to maintain otherwise.

Are we to conclude, then, that there were absolutely no "Judaizers," no "crypto-Jews," at all among the conversos? Such appears to be the position of Netanyahu, for example, and this goes too far to the opposite extreme.

Logic would suggest to us, and some of the Inquisition testimony seems to confirm, that at least in the early years of the fifteenth century when thousands had converted because of the preaching, or their fear, of Vicente de Ferrer, many were not sincere converts. We have seen that some gave as a reason for converting their being in debt (apparently this means they hoped to gain better economic status), and others said they converted for the sake of their children, i.e., to give them better prospects as Christians. Nevertheless, such a lack of sincerity in conversion and the adherence to certain Jewish customs, whether from reverence or superstition, can be postulated only for the period before the Inquisition became fully established and operational. Once the "fires were lit," and it became common knowledge that *any* practice or statement which could lead to the slightest suspicion of "Judaizing" meant the penalty of death, then that such conversos would dare to engage in these things defies belief.

The possibilities for any truly "insincere," or repentant, converso were many: he could flee to Muslim Granada or even North Africa, or some other Christian land; he could move to another Jewish community where he was not known and simply live as a Jew; or, finally, he could continue to live openly as a Christian, waiting either for conditions to improve or else for the opportunity at some future time to leave Spain. From our sources we have seen, indeed, that some conversos did exactly these things. Their numbers were few, however, for the vast majority of conversos were, indeed, sincere converts who lived as very good Christians.

All this, as we have seen in previous chapters, was well known to Jewish scholars and rabbis not only in the fifteenth century, but even in the fourteenth, in relation to the conversos of that time. Those authorities criticized the apostate Jews for not taking the opportunity to flee to Granada or to North Africa as some did. Those authorities decided, as early as the fourteenth century, with the decision being reviewed and reaffirmed constantly in the fifteenth, that such apostates were no longer part of the Jewish people and that they certainly were not "forced" but *willful* converts.

These were radical decisions, brought about by radical conditions, which had never before existed among the Jews. The ordinary Jewish people, now made doubly zealous by their determination not to convert in the face of mounting pressure and hostility, accepted the scholarly interpretation of the conversos' status. It was this which impelled them to willingly testify to the Inquisition against these converts, testimony which they *knew* to be false, in order to eradicate the hated enemy. After all, their law instructed them that it is an obligation to kill such a one with your bare hands on Yom Kippur which falls on a Sabbath (thereby making the day doubly "holy").

Nor did these apostates, the conversos, behave in a manner which was calculated to arouse any sympathy for them among the Jews. On the contrary, they exalted themselves in their new power as Christians. They used every opportunity to attack and defame their former "coreligionists," and were authors of the most damaging anti-Jewish polemics, bringing with them into their new faith a dangerous knowledge of Jewish religious and legal texts which they could turn against them. Neither Ramón Martí's *Pugio fidei* nor Alonso del Espina's *Fortalitium fidei,* the two most potent anti-Jewish polemical works ever written, could have been composed were it not for the numerous converso polemics and the information provided the authors by conversos.

The tragedy of the Inquisition, for the Jews of Spain, was that while they used it for their program of eradicating their hated converso enemies, the "old Christian" forces who were the minority of fanatic zealots responsible for its initiation developed their own program of racial anti-Semitism. Originally directed against conversos only, as a theoretical base for their planned annihilation, this hatred was soon unleashed on the Jews themselves.

As we shall now see, the same element which produced the revival of the Inquisition in Spain brought about the Expulsion of the Jews from Spain.

8

Expulsions of the Jews

The title of this chapter is not an error, for there was not just one expulsion of the Jews in Spain but three.

Up to this point, we have seen that a considerable amount of mythology surrounds the topics with which we have been concerned: the conversos, their relationship to Jews, the Inquisition, etc. It should not therefore be surprising that myth has also distorted the understanding of the Expulsion (for now, we shall confine the discussion to the general order expelling all Jews from the Spanish kingdoms in 1492).

Challenging that myth, particularly as it relates to the "anti-Jewish" character of Fernando and Isabel, may be the most difficult task faced in this book.

A proper understanding of the issue requires a knowledge of the history of the reign of Isabel's brother, Enrique IV, and even back to the beginning of the Trastámara dynasty. Some of that has already been presented here, though only in the context of the struggle against the conversos. My complete description of the details of the relationships between Jews and Christians during those reigns will have to await my future work.

Nor is there room for a detailed analysis of the situation of the Jews even in the reign of the Monarchs. Important discoveries no doubt remain to be made, and therefore much of what is stated here will have to be fleshed out and even to some extent, perhaps, revised in the future.

"They are the first years of the incipient Spanish nationalism . . . the unity of faith was an integral part of the new political unity. . . . How would it have been possible to tolerate that the unity would not be complete for the fault of a small group of inhabitants of Spain?"[1] So writes an authority on the *Visigothic* period and its persecution of the Jews, and the "final solution" (conversion or exile) at the hands of a tyrannical ruler, Recared. Yet the words could equally apply to the situation in Spain at the end of the fifteenth century and the national spirit of unification following the conquest of Muslim Granada.

Otherwise, however, the situation of the Jews in Visigothic Spain was hardly analogous to that in the later medieval period. Centuries of harmonious relations, the much-discussed *convivencia,* had intervened. Even the fanatic preaching of Vicente Ferrer, resulting in the voluntary conversion of thousands of Jews, did not lead to any strain in relations between Christians and Jews on the "normal" level of ordinary citizens.

Who, then, deserves the "blame" for the change in that situation which took place at the end of the century, and for the drastic decision to expel the Jews? Many think they obviously know the answer to that question, but the real answer may come as something of a surprise.

The Character of Fernando and Isabel

One of the most damaging results of careless scholarship, particularly by Jewish authors, has been the blackening of the reputation of the Monarchs, in total disregard of the sources. Baer, particularly, unleashed pages of invective and rhetoric against them, usually denouncing both rulers equally. Only occasionally did he single out Isabel as "the fanatical queen." Later, he refers to fifteenth-century "slanderers and rumor-mongerers" who unfairly sought to distinguish between the "proud and bigoted" queen and the "kindly Ferdinand, who was said to have Jewish blood in his veins."[2] The remark about "blood" aside, it is a fact that Fernando was of Jewish descent, as we have seen. Unknown to Baer was the fact that a Jewish chronicler, Elijah Capsali, had written this, and that he also had placed the blame on Isabel alone, who supposedly "forced" Fernando against his will to persecute the conversos (for which there is not the slightest evidence).[3]

Most recently, in a book unfortunately marred on nearly every page by errors, José Faur stated that the very title "Catholic Monarchs" was claimed by the rulers as a symbol of their animosity to Islam and Judaism; this in spite of the fact (unknown to Faur) that the title was conferred *upon* them by Pope Alexander VI only in 1496, long after the Expulsion.

Netanyahu, too, blamed the entire anti-Jewish policy on one of the rulers only, but this time it was the king. Fernando saw the "Jewish situation" as not only a problem, but an "opportunity" for his own "self-aggrandizement;" he was a "master at political criminality, while . . . playing the role of a man of piety."[4] Netanyahu claimed that the expulsion of the Jews from Andalucía (1483) was calculated to gain support for the war against the Muslims (48), yet this overlooks the very real fear which existed of Jewish collaboration with Granada, a fact which is attested by the sources.

But Netanyahu also did not spare Isabel, and like his teacher Baer he refers to the "haughty, fanatic and often ferocious queen," but this interesting description is mitigated somewhat, perhaps, by the assurance that she had "a mystic vein in her soul" (if one is not too concerned about mixed metaphors; 55, 56). That Abravanel's view of the queen was harsh (long after he himself had left Spain, of course; see 280, n. 61) is important historical information concerning *him,* and it would have sufficed to state that.

Concerning the statement of the converso chronicler Fernando de Pulgar, in reference to the establishment of the Inquisition in Seville in 1480, that Isabel had done what a Christian ought to do, but ought not to do more than what God commands (implying thereby a criticism of that action), Cantera correctly noted that this attribution of responsibility to the queen alone is counter to what Pulgar said in his *Crónica,* where he had learned the lesson that all royal acts must be credited equally to both Monarchs.[5] This is a lesson not learned, for instance, by Lea, whose history of the Spanish Inquisition constantly blamed Fernando alone for its various acts.

Pulgar was the personal secretary of the queen, and therefore probably knew her better than many others did. Although his characterization of her may be somewhat romanticized, nothing suggests that she was "fanatical" or "haughty," much less "ferocious." What he says is of significance:

> She was much inclined to do justice, although it was imputed to her that she followed more the way of rigor than of piety, [but] this she did to remedy the great corruption of crimes which she found in the kingdom when she succeeded to it. . . . This queen was the one who eradicated and removed the heresy which was in the kingdoms of Castile and Aragón of certain Christians of Jewish lineage who began to "Judaize," and she caused them to live like good Christians.

Of course, here he neglects what he noted elsewhere, that this was done through the torture and burnings of the Inquisition; but the point that Isabel was firm but just, and concerned with redressing the anarchy of the reign of her brother Enrique IV, is undoubtedly a correct portrayal.[6]

How different Isabel really was from the false image of a religious zealot and "fanatical" queen may be seen from the letter of outrage which her confessor, Hernando de Talavera, wrote her about her participation in the festivities in Barcelona early in 1493 when the Monarchs had successfully negotiated the return of Rosellón and Cerdaña by the French to Spain. The irate confessor went into a tirade about the "illicit licentiousness" of the dancing and the conduct of the French and Spanish women, the cruelty of the bullfights celebrated, etc. Nor did he spare the queen for her behavior, comparing her to Vashti (the queen of Ahasuerus in Esther) or the queen of Sheba. This love of music and dancing apparently had always been a part of the court. In the middle of the first disastrous campaign against Granada in 1483, for instance, the king and queen went to Córdoba with their entire court, and Diego de Valera describes in detail the dancing and playing of instruments on several occasions there. Isabel danced with one of her women and Fernando danced with his (male) cousin.[7]

More to the point, perhaps, is how the Jews themselves perceived the Monarchs. At the beginning of their reign when they entered Seville they were greeted by "grand amusements" on the part of the Muslims, and "the Jews with their Torahs received well these monarchs." This was in contrast to the terrible insults which the Christians poured upon Fernando, especially, for several years despised as a "foreign" (Aragonese) ruler. Isabel alone had been similarly well received by the Jews of Ávila with their Torah scrolls and with trumpets and drums when she was proclaimed queen there in 1474.[8]

The most important thing is not these ceremonial displays, or even the magnificent gifts which the Jews of Barcelona bestowed upon the Monarchs, but how, in fact, the rulers dealt with Jews throughout their reign. Here the record speaks for itself, and it is a record which Baer, for example, ought to have known. Hundreds of archival documents dealing with the Jews were painstakingly edited by the great Spanish historian Suárez Fernández, long before Baer's final revision of his work was completed, and yet Baer continued to ignore this important source.[9]

To those published documents may be added many more which have since come to light, or which previously were available from other sources. All of these will be detailed in my future book; however, suffice it to say that they uniformly demonstrate a consistent attitude of scrupulous justice on the part of the Catholic Monarchs in all their dealings with Jews. Two exceptions stand out: The *Cortes* of Madrigal (1476) imposed certain anti-Jewish restrictions, most notably with regard to usury, but its laws also contained an interesting stipulation that no Jew was to permit a "Tartar" (Tatar) or Muslim or any "other person" to convert to Judaism. The Tatars were to be found mostly in the Ottoman Empire, but apparently there were also some in Spain, possibly in the Muslim kingdom of Granada.[10] The second exceptional legislation was the proclamation of the *Cortes* of Toledo (1480) that all Jews and Muslims throughout the kingdom must live separated from Christians in special quarters (*juderías*). According to the eyewitness Alonso de Palencia, the Monarchs took this drastic step chiefly under the influence of Hernando de Talavara, aided by Tómas de Torquemada.[11]

Nevertheless, throughout this period the Monarchs continued to extend their personal protection to Jews and their property whenever there were any signs of disturbances or local acts against them.

Very important for revealing the actual attitude of the Monarchs toward Jews, as late as 1490, is a letter to the officials of Bilbao in Vizcaya concerning a complaint from the Jews of Medina de Pumar. The Jews "by canon law and the laws of our kingdom are tolerated and suffered [to live] and do live in our kingdom as our natural subjects, buy and sell and contract quietly and peacefully, and as our natural subjects and vassals" are under royal protection. The issue at hand was that the officials of Bilbao had enacted a law that no Jew could stay overnight in the city, on penalty of a 2,000 mr. fine. This decree created a great hardship for Jewish merchants coming to the city, and the Monarchs, saying that it was totally contrary to their law and interests, ordered that it be revoked and Jews be permitted to stay (though not to live) in the city.[12]

Nevertheless, in the same year an order was issued to officials of Medina del Campo reminding them of the law of the *Cortes* of Toledo whereby Jews could not own or work in shops, etc., outside of the *judería*. That law was not being observed, and the Monarchs ordered that it should be. However, when the Jews pointed out that the *judería* there was far from the center of town, the Monarchs rescinded the order and allowed Jews to have stores in the plaza.[13]

In 1491, poor Jews of Guadalajara chose representatives to protest that, although some of them were so poor they scarcely had food to eat, they were taxed at the same rate as rich Jews. The Monarchs saw the justice of their complaint and ordered the officials of the Jewish *aljama* to apportion taxes accordingly.[14]

From these and numerous other similar examples that could be cited, it appears in reality that the "Jewish policy" of the Catholic Monarchs, while essentially based on their concern for justice, sometimes fluctuated according to the demands and desires of local authorities. It also depended to a large degree on the Jews themselves; i.e., whenever the Jews protested a particular practice, if the Monarchs recognized the injustice involved they always responded favorably. On the other hand, if local authorities urged the enforcement of anti-Jewish ordinances and the Jews did nothing to protest, the royal policy favored the authorities.

Local Conditions and Danger Signs

While an abundance of documentary evidence proves that throughout most of Spain the normal state of positive relations between Christians and Jews did not change substantially up to the very moment, literally, of the Expulsion, there were some notable exceptions, in Ávila, with its very large Jewish population, where there were repeated acts of discrimination and even minor acts of violence.

In the diocese of Toledo, on the other hand, things continued normally. Jews continued to serve as tax officials of various towns and in the city itself. In the late 1480s and early 1490s there were even Jews in charge of collecting taxes on religious objects (priestly vestments, "pontifical bread" and wine, etc.). The *mayordomo* (official in charge of the estate) of the important Monastery of Santa Clara, which always had maintained good relations with Jews, was a Jew.

Nothing seems to have changed, either, with regard to the rights of Jews to demand and obtain justice. In 1490, for example, a Jew of the town of Santa Ollala obtained from the court the right to collect money owed him on the sale of some property. Another was granted "justice" for having been imprisoned for no fault during a dispute between the countess of Plasencia and a noble.

Right up to the eve of the Expulsion in 1492 Jews continued to own stores, buy and sell property, hold stores in partnership with Christians, on which they paid taxes to the chapter of the chapel of Pedro Tenorio in Toledo, etc.[15] That there was no thought of expelling the Jews as late as December of 1491 is shown, incidentally, by the fact that the Monarchs confirmed the appointment of "Rabbi Mayr" (possibly Meir *Melamed*) and a converso, Luis de San Pedro, as officials in charge of the taxes (*alcabalas* and *tercias*) of Toledo for the years 1492–94.[16]

Certain danger signs were nevertheless beginning to appear. In 1491 the Jews of Plasencia, which had perhaps the largest population of Jews of the kingdom, complained that "some *caballeros* and [other] persons" of the city and other towns in the province, because of hatred and animosity, were wounding and killing Jews and seizing their persons and property. The Monarchs agreed to take the Jews and their property under their protection, notice of which was to be posted in public places. Similarly, the Jews of Zamora were given royal protection because of a friar, Juan de Santo Domingo, who preached against Jewish usury and put a ban of excommunication on Christians who talked with Jews or had any dealings with them. The Jews feared attacks upon themselves (the small *judería* of Zamora was located outside the walls of the city and was thus vulnerable to attack). The Monarchs further ordered an investigation of this friar because his ban was contrary to papal bulls.[17]

A strange incident in Trujillo reveals the peculiar situation of the Jews at the time. A quarrel broke out in the synagogue, and the *alcalde* came and arrested the Jews involved. While they were in his house for judgment, other Jews (apparently outside in the streets as well as those inside) began fighting with each other with stones and swords. Christian knights of the city took sides, "some favoring some of the Jews, and others the others." These knights in turn brought their armed followers into the fight. The Monarchs ordered an investigation, with seizure of the persons and property of those involved.

The next month certain Jews constructed a new platform (*escalera;* literally, staircase) in the synagogue for the purpose of reading the Torah. Other Jews protested to Abraham Seneor, who ordered it taken down and the former reading platform to be used as it had been (we recall that he was chief judge of the Jewish communities). He imposed a fine of 7,000 *mrs.,* a third of which was to be used for the war against Granada and another third for the *Hermandad* (the "Holy Brotherhood," about which see below). This was ignored, so he issued a new order and increased the fine, which was also ignored until he appealed to the Monarchs.[18] (This is an indication, incidentally, of the great "leadership" of this Jewish official.)

The *Hermandad* was a society which already had a long history. Originally organized on local levels to provide some protection against the robbery and murder which took place as a result of the general anarchy prevailing throughout much of the fifteenth century, there was now a unified *Hermandad* operating both in Castile and, separately, in Aragón. That of Aragón was officially organized by Fernando in 1487, composed of those communities which chose to join, with the purpose of the administration and execution of justice and keeping the peace. In the revision of its laws in 1488, the king determined also to extend its jurisdiction over certain crimes committed by Muslims and Jews (there was also a substantial Muslim population in Aragón). The most serious of these was, as always, any act of sexual relations with a Christian woman. No specific penalties were imposed; every crime was punished in accord with local law and custom.[19]

Among the ordinances enacted by the *Hermandad* of Castile, meeting at Madrigal in 1479, was one requiring that no Jews be allowed to wear silk trim or scarlet cloth or gold or pearls or other such adornments on their clothing. The king and queen specifically exempted "don Abraham Seneor of Segovia" from these restrictions, for the "many good and loyal services" he had performed. However, Solomon, Seneor's son, petitioned the Monarchs that previous privileges had been granted by them exempting not only Abraham but all his family and those in his service from any decrees against Jews, and therefore he requested that the exemption from this ordinance of the *Hermandad* be extended also to the wife of Abraham and his sons and their wives. The Monarchs agreed and so ordered.[20]

While these are the only instances so far known to me of intervention of the *Hermandades* in affairs of Jews in the reign of the Catholic Monarchs (there were some in previous reigns), they are sufficient to indicate that this was certainly one source of the increasing anti-Jewish hostility.

In Catalonia, too, there were various incidents similar to those which occurred in some of the Castilian communities. Thus, in 1489 the officials of Tortosa, "zealous for the Christian religion," imposed certain restrictions on Jews and Muslims, including the requirement that they live in separate quarters which were to be enclosed and have only one gate. No Christian could enter Jewish houses on their "feasts" (Sabbaths and holidays) to light their fires, prepare food, or perform any work for them. When the "body of Christ" (the host) or a statue passed in procession in the street, Jews and Muslims must prostrate themselves or at least remove their caps. Jews and Muslims could not leave their quarters on Sundays or Christian holidays until midday, after services were concluded. An exception was made, somewhat hypocritically, for tailors or other craftsmen, who were to be accompanied by a "boy" (servant) of the Christian for whom they were to do the work. Jews and Muslims could not sell to Christians meat forbidden by their own law (this was not enforced, however). They were also required to wear "badges."[21]

Obviously, the truth of the matter is that the situation of the Jews in the late fifteenth century was extremely complex. In many cities, and indeed whole provinces, nothing changed in the essentially cordial and normal relations which existed between individual Jews and Christians or between the two communities in general, or in the role of Jews as governmental and tax officials. Indeed, the Monarchs also continued to be served by Jewish officials, although there were nowhere near as many nor in as important positions as had been the case with previous rulers. Also, this role was increasingly taken by conversos.

On the other hand, we have seen that there were signs of growing tension, and that in several localities (Ávila, Plasencia, and elsewhere) the increasingly independent and often violently inclined *caballeros* were the instigators. Their role in the *Hermandades* is also obvious. Some friars were also stirring up trouble against the Jews, as in Zamora and also in Segovia. Church officials, at whatever level, on the other hand, did *not* seem to share in any significant way in anti-Jewish feeling or acts. The worst enemies of the Jews in this respect were the conversos who became archbishops, bishops, and theologians, or were authors of notorious anti-Jewish polemics, as we have seen.

The Jews themselves were not without a certain degree of blame. Not only were they in many cases reflecting the general lawlessness and violence of the time, with many instances of Jewish crime against other Jews and even against Christians, but they generally continued to behave in a very "high-handed" manner, apparently oblivious to the changes taking place around them. Again, the total lack of effective Jewish leadership throughout the second part of the century is obvious.

What is certainly clear, although it can only be generally outlined in the few examples given here, is that the Monarchs were scrupulous in their treatment of Jews, individually and collectively. The exceptions discussed were the result of actions taken by the democratic parliament, the *Cortes,* to which they merely gave their consent.

The War against Granada

Space here does not permit a detailed account, which again has to be reserved for the future, of the campaign for the conquest of the last independent Muslim stronghold in Spain, the kingdom of Granada. Lukewarm and abortive efforts in the reign of Enrique IV had failed to make any real progress in this campaign. Indeed, all the monarchs of the fifteenth century had found it prudent to continue the policy of benign neglect toward the Muslim kingdom, and remained basically content with collecting what tribute they could.

Nevertheless, there was some evidence already of the religious fervor which was ultimately to unleash itself in the final "crusade." The *converso* historian of Juan II, Alvar García de Santa María, tells us of a campaign in 1410 when a priest carried the crucifix to remind the soldiers "that as he died for us, we must die for him and for our faith, destroying the heresy and sect of the infidel Moors." [22]

In the early years of their reign, beset with rebellion amongst their own nobles and the war with Portugal, the Monarchs were in no position to do much about Granada. In fact, they *paid* tribute to the Muslim kingdom. However, in 1482 Alhama was conquered by Rodrigo Ponce de León, marqués de Cádiz, and the next year the war against Granada began in earnest. The disastrous campaigns of that year cost the lives of many nobles, including the master of the Order of Calatrava, and many others were taken captive by the Muslims. It was not a complete failure, however, for the important city of Ronda surrendered in 1485, and lesser towns were also taken. [23]

Early in the fifteenth-century campaigns we find at least one instance where a *converso* was involved. The aforementioned chronicler Alvar García de Santa María relates that in 1408 the *alcalde* of Christians and Muslims (i.e., judge in cases between them) of Córdoba informed Juan II of the death of the king of Granada, Muḥammad VII, and sent a Muslim representative of Granada to the court, together with "Maestre Alonso, alaqueque [alfaqueque], un converso del dicho don Alonso Fernández," the *alcalde.* [24] Contrary to what might be assumed, *converso* here refers not to a Muslim convert to Christianity, always referred to as "*tornó cristiano*" or sometimes "*tornadizo,*" but rather to a converted Jew. This makes good sense, for some Jews still knew Arabic in the fifteenth century, but a converted Jew would be preferred if possible for translating delicate matters between Christians and Muslims.

The possibility needs to be considered that Jews were themselves involved in a very significant manner, as *caballeros,* in the actual battles. According to Suárez Fernández, Jews, like Christians, who had more than 30,000 *mrs.* were required to own a horse and arms.[25] While Jews in Spain always had weapons, and in the early medieval period fought in the armies, it still seems doubtful that they participated in the Granada campaign. If they did, there would again have arisen the possibility of Jews fighting against Jews, for undoubtedly there were Jews in Muslim Granada who fought.

Whether or not they actually fought, they certainly contributed money. In 1484, certain Jews gathered at the home of the dean of the "church" (cathedral?) of Toledo and, in compliance with the bulls of the crusade against Granada, voluntarily gave money, "because of certain allegations and pious charges" against them of usury on loans. Among these was at least one probable converso, don Mosé Manrique, and also the widow (Jewish) of don Çag Abençaçon, who had been an official of Juan I.[26]

Fernando and Isabel did not wait for such voluntary contributions, however. Already in that year they imposed compulsory taxes on the Jews, and the *procuradores* (delegates) of the Jewish communities of Castile and León assembled under the direction of Abraham Seneor and allotted a total of 16,000 *castellanos del oro* for that year (at the rate of 486 *mrs.* per *castellano;* a significant sum). In return, they were promised exemption from all other taxes.

Nevertheless, not all the communities sent *procuradores,* and apparently some of these did not agree to this sum, which was virtually imposed by Seneor. He therefore was authorized, through his agents, to seize property and goods for public sale to meet the apportionment if these communities refused to pay.[27]

In cities directly threatened by Muslim attack, such as Jerez, Jews contributed to the salaries of the guards of the city (1482) along with other inhabitants.[28]

The Monarchs lost no time in demanding the payment of the taxes. In a letter (1485) to the Jews of Burgo de Osma informing the Jews of that diocese, which included Soria and other towns, of the amount due for each community, the sum of 18,000 *castellanos* is mentioned. Similar letters were sent to the Jewish *aljamas* of the provinces of Córdoba, Palencia, Burgos, etc.[29] In 1490, the rulers ordered an additional payment of 10,000 *castellanos,* bringing the total for that year to 20,000.

Besides these taxes, Isabel had earlier borrowed money from some Jewish sources. In 1483 she borrowed a total of 238,000 *mrs.* from various individual Jews of Soria for the expenses of the war. Nine are named, most of whom gave 30,000 *mrs.* or more apiece.[30] Certainly there were similar loans in other communities. We have already mentioned that the Monarchs borrowed the enormous sum of 1,500,000 *mrs.* from Isaac Abravanel in 1491, and that this was repaid him by the converso Luis de Santángel (on their behalf). Santángel also arranged loans from the *Mesta,* or sheep-herding association.

Some of the Jews' loans were actually repaid in the years 1489–92, including 1,100,000 *mrs.* to the Jews of Soria, 700,000 to Trujillo, 40,000 to those of Badajoz, 33,000 to those of Arana, and 10,000 to Palencia.[31] There are records of other such repayments as well.

In 1482 a special tax of one gold piece (*castellano*) per person was imposed on all Jews and Muslims in Castile and León in support of the war, according to Pulgar, who does not say whether this was in addition to the community tax.[32]

Jews in the Muslim kingdom suffered along with the Muslim population during the campaign. During the siege of Málaga in 1487, famine swept the city. The inhabitants were forced to eat the carcasses of horses and asses, and bread was not to be found at all. Pulgar says: "The *gomeres* [a derogatory name for the Muslims] entered into the houses of the Jews in the city and robbed them of their provisions, and it reached such a state that some of the Jews died of hunger."[33]

The fifteenth-century Jewish chronicler Ibn Ṣadiq referred to the conquests in the kingdom. "In this year" (1482; actually 1480), he says, "the king ordered in all his kingdoms to distinguish between Israel and the Gentiles in their dwelling places and in all their settlements." This statement, which refers to the *Cortes* of Toledo, must be separated—as the printed text fails to do—from the following:

> Ronda, Marbella, Cartajima, *Q-s-a-r-h* [Cascares?]—all these cities in all of the region of *ha-Sharqiah* [i.e., Ar. *al-sharqī,* "Eastern" Spain] in the kingdom of Mulai Abu'l-Ḥasan, king of Granada, our lord the king don Fernando took in the year 1485. In [5]246 [A.M.] which is [1]485, on 18 Ḥeshvan [October 18], there was a rain in the land for sixty days and sixty nights; truly, from the [biblical] flood until now there is no memory among those of this generation of hearing or seeing a great wonder like this.
>
> In 1487 there was no rain for nine months. By divine providence the price of wheat was [reduced to] 90 gold *mrs.* and barley 45. In 1487 our lord the king took *T-r-a-g-h* [Torrox?] and Vélez Málaga and besieged the city of Málaga, the praised city on the coast of the western sea, on Sabbath, 29 Av, 18 August 1488, and he besieged it four months and captured all the people of the city, almost twelve thousand Muslims and among them almost four hundred Jews; and the [Jewish] communities ransomed them at great expense. . . .[34]

As may be seen, this contemporary Hebrew source contains important information not known from any other source. The famine in Málaga, previously mentioned by Pulgar, who was present at the siege, is also mentioned by Jewish chroniclers. Thus, Abraham Ibn Ardutiel notes that there had been a terrible drought all year (as Ibn Ṣadiq mentions also), and the siege began in the summer and lasted four months. Abraham Zacut claims it lasted a hundred days, and that the famine was so bad that even "fourteen thousand" of the Christian soldiers died; a wild exaggeration unsupported by other sources. The Christian army, on the contrary, was well supplied. The sixteenth-century chronicler Elijah Capsali of Candia, perhaps with access to Pulgar's account, wrote that the famine was so bad that the inhabitants of the city "ate their horses and donkeys and camels."[35]

There are many more interesting details concerning the Jews in Málaga and elsewhere in the kingdom of Granada, the ransom of Jewish captives, etc., which cannot detain us here. Something which is of importance for our present discussion is the document of surrender of Almería and the surrounding territory, which stipulated that any Christians who had converted to Judaism and were living in the Muslim territory had one year either to return to Christianity or to leave Spain. As we have already previously noted, many Christians in fact had fled to Muslim Granada to become Jews or Muslims.

The Jews of Granada were included in the general terms of surrender, and those who had formerly been Christians (i.e., conversos who had fled there) were given a month's time to leave. Since in this case no statement was made about returning to Christianity, as was permitted for former "old Christians," this would have meant leaving Spain entirely, since a converso who reverted to Judaism and was caught in a Christian country would be subject to the death penalty.[36]

We have seen that at least one contemporary Jewish chronicler, Ibn Ṣadiq, spoke in admiration of the conquest and with terms of veneration for Fernando, particularly. Some of the Jews in Castile, at least, such as those of Huete, joined in the general rejoicing over news of the conquest of a city (which one is not stated) in Granada, taking their Torah scrolls out in procession.[37] For very good reason, Spain's Jews still very much considered themselves loyal subjects.

Expulsions from Andalucía and Aragón

The edict of expulsion of 1492 referred to the expectation of Fernando and Isabel that they would be "content" with the order that the Jews should leave the towns, cities, and other places of Andalucía.[38] This would appear to indicate that the Jews had already been expelled earlier from that region. It has also been suggested that when Columbus made the enigmatic reference to the Monarchs' having expelled the Jews in the month of January, he somehow confused it with the earlier expulsion from Andalucía.[39]

That this earlier expulsion actually took place, at least in parts of Andalucía, seems apparent from a document concerning the farming of certain taxes on wood, etc., in Seville in which it is stated that the Inquisitors had proclaimed the expulsion of all Jews from the city and diocese on 1 January 1483, giving them thirty days in which to leave. Later, it is stated that there was no farming of taxes on Jewish wine or meat for that year because there were no Jews.[40]

The exclusive responsibility of the Inquisitors for this expulsion is explicitly confirmed by a document of the Monarchs of 1485, expelling a Jew and his wife from Córdoba for having "Judaized" among conversos and encouraging them to flee to Granada to live as Jews.[41]

In January of 1483, Mayr Aben Sancho and Moses Aben Semerro, two Jews of Jerez de la Frontera, reported to the city council rumors that at the instigation of the Inquisitors the Jews of Seville and its diocese were being forced to leave. It was reported by one of the members of the council that some Jews from there already had rented property in Jerez. That same month the council asked the master of the Order of Santiago about this, and he confirmed the reports, but said that for the time being nothing should be done. In August the council received a letter of the king ordering the expulsion of the Jews from Jerez also. However, in February of 1484 the Monarchs (jointly) issued a suspension of that order for six months, until 7 July. It is not known, however, whether this expulsion was ever enforced, or whether it was totally revoked.[42]

In July of 1484, the Monarchs instructed the *bachiller* (legal official; probably a converso) Luis Sánchez to investigate the complaints of Jews who had been forced to abandon their property when they left Seville, as well as complaints concerning unpaid debts. Again in September, Jacob Cachopo, *procurador* of the former Jewish *aljamas* of Seville and the diocese, petitioned the Monarchs concerning the property Jews had abandoned when they left. Many Christians had seized this property unjustly, and the king and queen ordered the restitution of all such property and the payment of all outstanding debts to the Jews. The Jews were under royal protection.[43]

Although the Jews were expelled from Seville, and perhaps also from Jerez, in April of 1485 there still existed Jewish *aljamas* in Córdoba and Maguer, "which disappeared the following year," according to Suárez. In March of 1491 the former Jews of Seville were permitted to sell any property which remained there.[44]

Nevertheless, doubt is cast on the *total* expulsion of Jews from Córdoba by the fact that we find don Yuçe Abenaex, *recaudador mayor,* living there in 1488, 1491, and 1492. While his position may have been important enough to warrant an exemption, it is doubtful that he would have continued to live in a city totally free of Jews. In 1490, Ysaque Aben Semerro, the former *arrendador* of Seville mentioned above, and his relative Moses and Mayr Abenatabe and his son were all living in Cádiz, and a Jew of Portugal was granted the right to live in Córdoba.[45]

According to a late source (mid-sixteenth century), some four thousand Jewish houses were abandoned in Seville and Córdoba alone.[46]

In 1484, Fernando wrote the *merino* of Zaragoza about the complaints of the Jews which their *procuradores* had presented to the king concerning the violations of certain privileges they had. The king ordered Alfonso de la Cavallería, vice-chancellor of Aragón (a converso), and García Sánchez, *tesorero general*, and also a converso, to investigate. In the end, having convened the *Cortes* to meet in Tarazona, the king decided to deal with the complaints personally when he came to that city. Meanwhile, the *merino* was ordered to do nothing against the Jews of Zaragoza.[47] In the same year the king wrote that the "devoted Inquisitors" had informed him that Jews in the village of Cella, near Teruel, did not live separate from Christians as they were supposed to, and therefore great "dangers in offense to divine majesty and damnation of the souls of Christians" result from the "participation and conversation" between Christians and Jews. The king thereupon ordered that all Jews leave the village within eight days, and that in whatever place they went (in Spain) they wear a colored badge.[48]

This was all perhaps only a prelude to the disastrous blow which fell on 12 May 1486, equal to that of the expulsion of the Jews from Andalucía, when Fernando ordered the expulsion of all Jews from the archbishopric of Zaragoza and the bishopric of Albarracín ("Santa María de Albarracín"), noting that since

> all the danger which has resulted to Christians from heresy has come from the conversation and practice with which Jews have received those of their lineage, there is no other suitable remedy to separate them than the manner in which this has been done in the archbishopric of Seville and the bishoprics of Córdoba and Jaen.

This order was probably directly related to the assassination of the Inquisitor Arbués in 1485, which unleashed a furor of anti-converso hostility, *autos de fe,* etc., in 1486 and after. It was also probably the result of the previously mentioned complaints the king had received.[49]

Nevertheless, we may not conclude from these isolated examples, important as they were (Zaragoza was the major Jewish center of Aragón, and Seville and Córdoba were important areas of Jewish population in southern Spain), that there was as yet any plan to expel all the Jews from Spain. As previously noted, in December of 1491 Fernando and Isabel still appointed

Jewish tax officials to act for the years 1492–1494, thus indicating that even at that date they had no intention of expelling the Jews.

The Expulsion of 1492

Not only is there no evidence the Monarchs had any preparations in mind for the expulsion of the Jews, the Jews themselves apparently had no foreboding of the impending disaster. In April of 1492, actually the month after the decree was announced but probably before it was received, Jews were still buying property, stores, etc., from Christians in and around Toledo, and selling to Christians. No doubt the same was true everywhere.[50]

Contemporary accounts relate that on 30 April, with the blowing of trumpets and in the presence of various officials at the palace of Sante Fe in Granada, it was proclaimed that the Jews must leave all the kingdoms of Spain by the end of July (in fact, the decreee was issued 31 March, not in April).[51] On that date, 31 March, the Monarchs wrote to the count of Ribadeo informing him of the edict. This letter is important because it adds some specific information: that they were informed *by the Inquisitors* and "from other parts" that the earlier remedies (separate *juderías*, expulsions from Andalucía and Zaragoza) had been of no avail, and only expelling the Jews completely would stop the "evils and harm which come to the Christians from participating with and conversation with the said Jews," who continue to "pervert" them (words almost identical to those in the decree).[52] Thus, if we did not already suspect it, we here have proof that it was the Inquisitors who were responsible for the Expulsion.

Bernáldez, the fanatical anti-Jewish chronicler, claims that the Monarchs were convinced of the "perpetual blindness" of the Jews and of their being the cause of the "Mosaic heresy" (of the conversos), and so ordered that the Catholic faith be preached to all the Jews. Those who would convert would be allowed to remain in the realm, while the others would have to leave within six months (he erred in saying the Jews were given a six-month reprieve, probably confusing this with the expulsion from Andalucía, for it was only three). There follows another of his long tirades against the Talmud, after which he says that all this preaching was of no avail, for the rabbis preached the opposite to the Jews.[53]

In Barcelona, the royal archivist and archivist of the Inquisition wrote that the Jews were expelled from all of Spain "like a deadly plague."[54]

Fernando himself, in a letter of 1494 to Jaca granting two former synagogues there to the university (school of arts), refers to the expulsion of "perfidious Jews" from the kingdom, since the Jews were "servants" of the king and the goods of the servant belong to the master, which justified the king's seizure of all the property that had belonged to the Jews there.[55]

Nevertheless, this generally was not the policy where the Monarchs acted jointly with respect to the Jews. On 26 April and again on 20 May they ordered the repayment of loans to various Jewish *aljamas* and individuals, loans which had been made as far back as before 1475, when they were still princes. Among these were debt to Luis de Alcalá (probable converso) and Rabbi Meir *Melamed,* the *recaudadores mayores.*[56]

The anonymous continuator of Fernando de Pulgar's chronicle of the Catholic Monarchs (cited already in conjunction with the Inquisition) made some interesting observations also about the Expulsion:

> There remained moreover in these kingdoms another pestilence [besides the Muslims]: a great number of Jews who were spread out and scattered in all the kingdoms, and these Jews collected the taxes of the kingdom by which they took advantage of and destroyed many Christians, becoming rich and loaning on usury the most that they were able.

Because of all this, according to the author, the Monarchs decided to expel all Jews except those who converted. "More than one hundred thousand, besides the children they took," left the realm, according to his estimate. He asserts that they took for truth and certainty what their rabbis told them: that the sea would open for them as at the exodus from Egypt. When they saw that this did not happen, many returned and were baptized. Others later were robbed on the ships, and after such misfortunes many returned to Spain and became Christians.[57]

Jewish Accounts of the Expulsion

An anonymous lamentation by an eyewitness (the editor called it a "chronicle," but in fact it is more a prose eulogy) is typical of the lachrymose tendency of Jewish portrayals of tragic events. It applies every imaginable biblical cliché to express grief at the "destruction" of the Jewish people. Also notable is the application of biblical expressions referring originally to the exile from the land of Israel to the current exile from Spain; e.g., "for He lowered us from our dwelling-place and uprooted us from our land" (cf. Deut. 29.27 [28]). The author compares Fernando to Sennacherib and Nebuchadnezzar, no less.[58]

The scribe of a manuscript of an important Hebrew literary work from Spain wrote the verse "the Lord will bless you" (Jer. 31.22 [23]) and marked the word for "will bless you," which has the numerical value of 252 in Hebrew; thus, the year 1492 (240 added to the Hebrew year). The scribe said he found this written in his father's hand, and that in that year "all the congregations of Spain were expelled in the month of Av, for on Friday the tenth of Av sixteen ships left the coast of Cartagena carrying Jews, in addition to many others who left earlier."[59] We shall return to the question of the Hebrew date of the Expulsion.

Elijah Capsali, a sixteenth-century chronicler, blamed the Expulsion solely on Fernando, who pursued the Jews with a "drawn sword" and "did not recall the covenant of brothers—behold, Esau [the Gentiles] is a brother of Jacob—and deceived us twice, taking our money and now our birthright" (cf. Gen. 27.36). Even in his "factual" account of the Expulsion, he mentions only the king: *he* decided to expel the Jews; in February *he* ordered the scribes to write the decree; etc. Only after giving, in Hebrew translation, the entire text of the decree did he mention as an afterthought that the messengers of the king *and queen* carried the decree throughout Spain.[60]

Capsali's version of the decree is more a paraphrase than a real translation, however. Among the serious errors it contains is the statement that three months were given, from 1 May to the end of June, *during* which all Jews had to leave, and that the decree was issued "in the fifth month [!] called February in their language." In fact, the decree was issued on 31 March (although Capsali was at least consistent, giving the Hebrew date of 5 Adar, which was 4 February in 1492), and stated that by the end of July, not June, the Jews must leave. In the Hebrew dates he gives, the time limit for leaving Spain was from 9 Iyar (which was 5 May) to 9 Av (2 August). Capsali further adds the gratuitous information that a *señal real* (royal sign) was placed on every Jewish house; for which we have no evidence. Another false statement is that any Jew remaining would either be killed by "hanging on a tree" or forced to convert, and that anyone who wished to convert within three months could remain in Spain. He furthermore totally distorts the reality of how Jews were treated after the decree was issued, claiming that Christians to whom the Jews owed money pursued and whipped them, and that no judge enforced payments of loans due to Jews. As we have seen, this is entirely false.[61]

This chronicle has apparently been the source of a widely believed legend that the Jews were expelled from Spain on 9 Av (Tishah b'Av), a notorious date on which traditionally both Temples were said to have been destroyed, and which therefore is commemorated as a fast day. Among those who believed this legend and perpetuated it was the Jewish historian Graetz, who noted that the time of departure was actually 31 July, which was 7 Av (this is correct), but that the Jews asked for an additional two days' delay to make up the full three months promised and thus, prophetically and coincidentally, the actual departure fell on 9 Av. A more modern scholar, Rosanes, assumed that the decree itself was somehow delayed (for a month), believing Capsali's date of the end of June, instead of July, to be correct.[62]

Another Jewish chronicler, who himself lived in Spain, Abraham Ibn Ar-dutiel, wrote that the Jews were "expelled from the land of Castile [!] by the king don Hernando and the counsel of his *cursed wife,* Isabel the *wicked,* and the word of her counsellors." According to him, the edict was issued on the first of the Hebrew month of Nisan, which thus was turned from a time of rejoicing to sorrow. (It is the month in which Passover is celebrated; Capsali also talks about the sorrowful Passover that year. 1 Nisan was 30 April in 1492, an entire month *after* the edict was actually issued.) He agrees that three months were given for the Jews to leave Spain, but says nothing at all about the ninth of Av.[63]

Abraham Zacut, generally a more reliable writer and less given to emotional hysteria, wrote: "we have seen with our eyes like this [like the expulsion of the Jews from France] in the expulsion from Spain, Sicily, and Sardinia." Further on, he says that in 1492, on the first of January, Granada was captured and "then the decree of the expulsion" of the Jews was issued, and "after four months the edict was announced at the end of April" that the Jews must leave within three months, which was 7 Av. This is somewhat more accurate, but again introduces the false date of 7 Av, as well as January for the decree, instead of the end of March. However, we recall Columbus' statement that the Jews were expelled in January. It is perhaps remotely possible that the decision was made in January and the actual decree not issued until 31 March, perhaps because of the task of cleaning up and rebuilding the captured city of Granada.[64]

Zacut adds the further statements that his ancestors, who had come from France, all withstood the "persecutions" in Castile and remained faithful Jews. "I also, God enabled me and my son Samuel to sanctify His name" (i.e., to remain Jews), and they went to North Africa, but were twice captured (on the voyage?). Some of the exiles, he says, went to Turkey and some to North Africa (especially Fez and Oran), "and famine and plague went after them so that almost were all of them lost [note carefully the wording: not that "almost all" were lost]. But the majority from Castile went to Portugal because they were not able to go by sea and hasten themselves [in leaving]." This apparently means that they did not have time to arrange sea passage. He continues that they gave a tithe of all their money as a tax to enter Portugal. "Further, [they paid] a *ducat* for each person, in addition to three *ducats* for permission to pass through the provinces [of Spain]; they also gave a fourth of all money they brought in [to Portugal], and some of them close to a third, and even those who had [almost] no money at all gave a ransom of eight *ducats,* and if not they would be imprisoned."[65]

An anonymous account of the Expulsion, written perhaps by an Italian Jew, has been edited by Alexander Marx. According to this, the decree was issued in January (which would appear to indicate his dependence on Zacut, and indeed he also says it was after the conquest of Granada, as did Zacut). The Jews were given three months in which to leave, with the decree being announced on the "first of May," and the date on which the Jews were to leave was "the day before" the ninth of Av (which would have been 1 August).

More important than these erroneous details are the names of various rabbinical scholars living at the time in Spain; nevertheless, these are known to us already, of course. Also indicating his dependence on Zacut is the peculiar spelling of "Bizcaya" (if that is what it is), and thus the account had to have been composed after Zacut had written his, and certainly could not have been in 1495 as Marx assumed.[66]

Abravanel, although he wrote his account many years after the Expulsion, was also an eyewitness. In the introduction to his commentary on Kings, cited frequently later in this chapter, he stated that the edict caused great sorrow among the Jews. Some went to Portugal and Navarre, which were close, but they encountered many tribulations: "bribery, hunger, and plague." Others went by ship, and many were captured and sold as slaves. Still others drowned when ships sank, or were killed when ships were "burned" (by pirates?), a fact mentioned in no other source.

Ibn Verga relates that he heard from "elders" among the exiles that plague spread on one ship and the captain deposited the passengers on a deserted place where most died of starvation, but others set out on foot to find food. In one such case the wife died and her husband carried his two sons until they, too, died. He proclaimed to God that in spite of all efforts to force him to abandon his faith "I am a Jew and will remain a Jew, and nothing that you bring against me shall avail" to cause him to give up his faith.[67]

If Capsali is to be believed, many Jews left Spain in ships of "Bizcayans" (Basques; it is this statement which enables us to decipher the peculiarly spelled term in Zacut and the aforementioned anonymous Italian writer), Catalans, Castilians, and even Genoese and Venetians; for when news of the Expulsion went forth "ships came from the four corners of the earth to carry the Jews." They did so not out of the goodness of their hearts, of course, but in the expectation of enormous profits.[68] The anonymous Italian account also states that ships from Genoa came to carry the Jews, but the crews of several of these robbed the Jews and sold them to the "famous pirate of that time, who was called the Corsair of Genoa" (possibly the *real* "Columbus," who was a famous pirate). Those who arrived safely in Genoa were robbed by the people.[69] As we shall see, Jews from Granada did, indeed, leave on a Genoese ship.

Capsali further claimed that the decree of the Expulsion was "bad in the eyes of the ministers and dukes and other nobles of the kingdom, for *all of them* [!] loved the Jews like the apple of their eyes," but they were unable to save the Jews.[70] This is, of course, a great exaggeration, but there is some truth to it. Several of the nobles, at least, still maintained the traditional cordial relations with Jews, and many had Jewish officials in their service. Did they, in fact, make any effort to prevent the Expulsion? At the present time, we have no knowledge of any such efforts. However, the following discussion may confirm it.

Contemporary Jewish Attitudes to the Expulsion

In another context, Yerushalmi has written a perceptive analysis of Ibn Verga's attitude to kings and their relations with Jews in general, which attitude was entirely positive (as was characteristic of Spanish Jews, in fact). With regard to the Expulsion, however. Yerushalmi is puzzled that Ibn Verga "never budges from this basic position." He continues that "not once do we hear" in the *Shevet Yehudah* that the Expulsion was due to a "fundamental change in attitude" on the part of the Monarchs. (Possibly we do not hear this because there *was* no fundamental change. Ibn Verga places the blame on a growing religious fanaticism and popular hostility toward Jews, and while this is not the sole cause, the sources certainly confirm that it was a major one.)[71]

Yet Ibn Verga, as Yerushalmi notes, at one point seems to place the blame on Isabel. In chapter 44 he wrote that the queen's confessor (Torquemada) convinced the queen to "forcibly convert" all the Jews or expel them, and she entreated the king that this be done. Possibly this account is entirely fictitious, as Yerushalmi observes (Ibn Verga's modern editor believed that everything in that chronicle was fiction, which it is not), yet that the Inquisitors played the major role in the Expulsion there can be no doubt. More important is the statement which follows in Ibn Verga:

> And the Jews when they heard [this] went to one of the ministers of the king, who was a great admirer of them [the Jews], as was the case with Jews in Spain who were loved by the kings and the ministers and all the [Christian] sages and their scholars and were greatly honored [by them]. And the Expulsion did not come about except by reason of some of the people of the land who said that because of the Jews and their coming to power the prices of food had increased. So also the Expulsion came about because of the priests . . . who preached every day bad things against the Jews. *But by the other sects of the Christians the Jews were honored,* as though they dwelt on their [own] land, and greatly loved by them, as is known to the elders [of the Jews] of Spain.[72]

The reference to "preaching" or "preachers" in Hebrew nearly always pertains, in Christian context, to the Dominicans (sometimes, though usually not, Franciscans are also included). Thus, Ibn Verga confirms what is already known to be true from other sources, that the Dominicans particularly, and to a lesser extent the Franciscans and some Augustinians, were stirring up the hatred against the Jews, whereas other "sects" (other monastic orders, and the clergy in general) remained on quite friendly terms with the Jews.

Ibn Verga concludes his account with the story of a "learned man of our seed" (i.e., a converso), Martín de Lucena, who told the Jews not to offer any bribe to the queen because the next day the evil priest (Torquemada?) would be hung, and so it was. This, of course, is totally false, unless another priest, of whom we do not otherwise know, was intended. Martín de Lucena, however, was real enough and he was tried by the Inquisition in 1481. This fact does not, *contra* Yerushalmi, lend any particular credence to the whole account, but it does raise the question whether this much of the account refers, not to the Expulsion of 1492, but rather to that of 1483 from Andalucía.

Nor does Ibn Verga say anything which would permit us to conclude that he, like some modern historians, considered Isabel a "bigoted queen" (the words are Yerushalmi's). The blame, according to Ibn Verga, is neither the king's nor the queen's but Torquemada's. If, as suggested, the historical reality behind the account was the expulsion from Andalucía, then the blame was, indeed, entirely the Inquisitors'. On the other hand, if he mixed together both expulsions, his statement lends further support to our conclusion that the Inquisition was largely responsible also for the later one.

Overlooked entirely by Yerushalmi was Ibn Verga's other important statement as to the cause of the decree, which he says was due to seven things: "the sins of our fathers" (the usual homiletic explanation for any evil); length of the exile, compounded with the desire of the rulers to spread their faith; the crucifixion of Christ (blame for it?); the "three great jealousies," manifested among Jews, of the Christian religion, of Gentile women, and of money; swearing of false oaths (which Ibn 'Ezra had warned would lengthen the exile); the arrogance of some Jewish officials; and fights among Jews themselves (literally, physical violence, which indeed was a constant problem).[73]

This is very perceptive, and in fact it must be seriously considered that such things did lead to increasing anti-Jewish sentiment among the "middle classes," which sentiment the friars used to spread their propaganda. Thus, these things may very well have been a major "cause" of the Expulsion.

Abravanel, of course, was a propagandist interested in religious homily and in saving his own reputation (his role in the Expulsion will be considered below). Writing many years after the fact, he appears to have blamed both Fernando and Isabel, but especially the king (not the "bigoted queen").

Thus, in the original *uncensored* introduction to his commentary on Deuteronomy, hitherto ignored by scholars, he wrote:

> The Lord aroused [read *he'ir*] the spirit of Ashmedai head of the destroyers
> [*maḥbelim*], the terrible king who rules the kingdoms of Spain due to the
> abundance of sins. And he [was] mighty as oak trees to expel all the Jews from
> all the boundaries of his land, great and small.[74]

Ashmedai is the mythical name of the "head of the demons," though he is never mentioned as a ruler, and in the famous story of his encounter with Solomon is depicted in a rather benevolent manner (*Giṭin* 68a). The use of the (corrected) term *maḥbelim* here certainly refers not to Song of Songs 2.15, but rather to Isaiah 54.16 and even more certainly to the *midrash* ("from this we learn that permission was given to the destroyers [demons] to destroy" [*Num. R.* 14.31]).

Similarly, in his introduction to his commentary on Kings (in all printed editions) he writes that the "king," only, having conquered Granada, determined to repay God for the victory by expelling the Jews from all his kingdoms. Only in the following paragraph does he mention that the queen "stood beside him to encourage him" in his resolve.[75]

Important testimony comes from another eyewitness, who says that in his old age he came to Castile (possibly from Portugal) to find "rest," and then the king, "may his bones be ground to dust" (cf. *Lev. R.* 25.8), together with his "accursed wife" Isabel, expelled the Jews. From the year 1478/79 "when they investigated the thing, they began to burn the *anusim,* both the living and the dead, and took counsel to strengthen their faith, the king and queen with their priests."[76] The reference to the year (the Hebrew chronogram *Raḥ"l* probably signifies *Rahmana lișlan,* "May the Merciful One save") is puzzling. In 1479 Fernando's father, Juan, died, and he became king of Aragón. However, more than likely there is confusion here with 1480, the year when the Inquisition, in fact, began.

Naturally, there was also a strong eschatological or "messianic" aspect to the Jewish understanding of the Expulsion. It was, in fact, the greatest disaster which had befallen the Jewish people since the exile from their original homeland, Palestine. As such, it is indeed surprising that it did not arouse more comment than so far has come to light. Nevertheless, several scholars have already called attention to this eschatological aspect of the Jewish effort to deal with the catastrophe, particularly in qabalistic writing.

Bonet de Lattes (Jacob b. Immanuel Provensaliy) of Italy, for example, predicted that the messiah would come in 1505. He also told Pope Leo X that the expulsion of Jews from Spain and Portugal (1496) was the plan of God so that the Jews would go to Israel, or "near there" (e.g., North Africa, the Ottoman Empire).[77]

Abravanel, in spite of the fact (as will be made clear) that he did nothing while in power in Spain to prevent the Expulsion, afterward showed great concern. Apparently repenting of his earlier zeal for power and fortune, he now turned to messianic calculation and polemic, and was not above plagiarizing from a variety of sources. From Abraham b. Ḥaya, an important twelfth-century writer, he took the idea of the "conjunction" of certain planets which was to occur in 1464, from which time, in reality, the persecution of the conversos began! These persecutions were worse than those endured by any other people, and they fell upon those who once were of the "seed of Israel," but abandoned the Torah and "mingled with the Gentiles" but found no rest, for "the hand of God was [against] them as a consuming fire," referring to the Inquisition. "Thus, many in the land of Spain, who were more than the number of those who went out to Egypt [more than six hundred thousand], they investigate them and say, 'You deny the Christian faith and believe in the Jewish faith.' This evil decree [persecution] began at the time of the conjunction [1464] and still its hand is outstretched" (it still continued in 1496 when Abravanel wrote these words). Even the Jews who remained always faithful were punished for no reason and expelled.[78]

Possible Motivation for the Expulsion

We have already discussed the main reasons which led to the decision to expel the Jews. In addition to the "official" reasons given in the edict itself, chiefly the supposed influence of Jews upon conversos and Christians in general, there was the growing hostility toward Jews manifested in the events we have earlier described. The Inquisition (specifically, Torquemada) was the chief instigation, as well as the religious military orders and certain of the nobility. In addition, certain influences from outside of Spain cannot be discounted.

A factor which may have had an influence on Spanish attitudes in the late fifteenth century was the anti-Jewish sentiment of various Dominican and Franciscan friars in Italy, which led to the expulsion of Jews not from major cities but at least from several smaller communities there. As noted below, Jews were, however, expelled from Trent, a major northern Italian community.

It is possibly these expulsions to which Abravanel refers in his previously cited commentary on Daniel:

During the last thirty-two years there were renewed against the Jews in every place great and evil tribulations, such as had not been seen before, not to them and not to any people from the time Adam set foot on the earth until this day. No eye has seen, nor could the imagination picture, the torrents of evil which

come to all called by the name of Israel. . . . The rulers of the earth, without reason or cause,

expelled the Jews from their lands. Among those he enumerates are Germany, Russia, "Lombardia" (the general region of Lombardy in Italy, probably, specifically, Trent), Tuscany, Provence, Sicily, Sardinia, and all of Spain.[79]

Ibn Verga also relates in "1490" there was an expulsion from Savoy and Piedmont, as well as "Lombardy," Sicily, Russia, and Florence. Both authors refer to an expulsion from "Russia." In fact, it would appear that this is the expulsion of the Jews from Kiev in 1482–83, and finally from all of Lithuania in 1495, just two years before Abravanel completed his above-cited book.[80]

In 1475 there was yet another blood libel (the charge that Jews were using Christian blood, usually of children, for ritualistic purposes) at Trent, only a few years after the Jews had once again been expelled from Mainz. The bishop had the entire Jewish community at Trent burned alive, an event commemorated in later printed engravings. Jews elsewhere were massacred and many expelled.

Isaac Ṣarfaty, a Jew of France though born in Germany, wrote from his security in Turkey urging his fellow Jews to flee to that land rather than to continue to bring suffering, "guilt, and sin" upon themselves by "living under [the rule] of Gentiles [Christians] instead of Muslims." He went on to praise Turkey and the quality of life and luxury possible there for Jews.[81]

Turkey was, indeed, a growing problem for Christian Europe, and particularly for Spain. In 1481 the Catholic Monarchs ordered the Mediterranean fleet to prepare for the conquest of Otranto. Further orders went out to raise money for the planned invasion. They also obtained from Sixtus IV a bull granting indulgences to all who aided the fleet in the war. Fernando de Pulgar relates, in the context of the intervention of the Monarchs in 1482 in the wars with Italy, that the Venetians concluded peace treaties with the Turks, which caused Fernando of Sicily to do the same. Sicily, especially, was in "grave danger" of destruction as a result.[82]

Certainly the conquest of Constantinople by the Turks, which shook the whole Christian world, had repercussions in Spain. Aside from calling attention to the references in Alonso del Espina, who claimed that messianic fervor was aroused among the Jews because of this, no one has so far discussed this, however. The only tangible proof I have found is the interesting poem of Fernán Pérez de Guzmán, dedicated to the marqués de Santillana, also ignored by historians. Later on, Abravanel spoke of the possible conversion of the Turks to Judaism, an idea he stole without acknowledgment from Shem Ṭov Ibn Shem Ṭov.[83]

We have already seen in some of the Inquisition testimony that some conversos had claimed that the sultan of the Turks was the messiah. Alonso del Espina, in the above-mentioned passage to which Baer has already called attention, also wrote that the Jews claimed to have found an "Aramaic commentary" which stated that biblical Yavan (usually understood to be Greece) is 'Uṣ, and that Constantinople therefore is the "daughter of Edom" (Lam. 4.21). Abravanel, indeed, cites this very translation.[84]

In one of the aforementioned Inquisition cases involving conversos of Valencia, one of the witnesses testified that letters had arrived from Constantinople which proved that the messiah was born, and she further said that he was now a young man (fadri) and lived on a mountain near Constantinople, but no one who was not a circumcised Jew might see him. Another claimed that those conversos who leave the "part of the Jews" (i.e., Spain) and go to Constantinople have "much good," but that they believe that those (conversos) who remain "in these parts" (Spain) do not obtain even a measure of garbanzos (ciurons), "because in these parts there is much spilling of blood" (scampament de sanch). Therefore, those who were circumcised, even if they were "Christians by nature" (i.e., sons or descendants of Christians), if they "turn to the good part" (become Jews) will receive both good and salvation of their souls. The "others" (who do not become Jews) will receive neither. Another testified that when they go to "those lands" (of the Turks), they will ride on horseback over the Christians, and it is said that the Antichrist will come, who is the Turk, who will destroy the churches of the Christians and turn them into stables, but he will show much honor and reverence to the Jews and their synagogues.[85]

In the interesting testimony concerning Fernando de Madrid (1491–92, already deceased), various "messianic" accusations were made, including the statement he supposedly made that the "Antichrist" would appear in the city of Palos. Other testimony stated that a Jew, one Rabbi Huça Facel, a Portuguese, had letters indicating the messiah would come in 1489, when there would be "all one law."[86]

The officials of the Inquisition, who as we have seen were not above forging "testimony" against conversos, also forged letters supposedly written by the Jews of Spain to Constantinople and the reply. Whether or not they were the work of Archbishop Siliçeo of Toledo (1546–57), they are said to have been the cause of his obtaining from Pope Paul III the order that no converso could hold any benefice in the church of Toledo. The forged "reply" of the supposed "prince of the Jews of Constantinople" advised the conversos to seek revenge on the Christians for the Expulsion and their conversion by becoming doctors (the implication being that they would kill their patients), priests, and Church officials to "pervert" the Christian religion, etc.[87]

Another aspect of the Turkish problem was that news which reached Spain of "miraculous" discoveries of "holy relics" may possibly have further inflamed religious zeal and anti-Jewish feelings. The sultan at Constantinople sent an annual tribute to the pope (as is well known, the chalice used today by the pope when saying mass at the Vatican on special holidays is made of gold from a melted-down saddle of one of the sultans). One year the sultan sent along with his tribute various holy relics, such as the supposed head of the spear which pierced Christ during the crucifixion, and other "relics" such as the sponge of water and vinegar used, etc. Already in 1484 there had been "discovered" in Rome the notice, in three languages, which hung on the cross, proclaiming Jesus "king of the Jews," which notice was personally venerated by the pope.[88]

Legendary "Causes" of the Expulsion

Fita stated that the infamous "Niño de la Guardia" case, previously discussed, was a chief cause for the expulsion of the Jews (it is amazing that that great scholar, generally very favorably inclined toward the Jews, actually believed those charges). It is certainly correct, as Fita stated, that the edict itself confirms that fear of Jewish "tainting" of Christian beliefs was a major factor in the decision; yet it is also true that only a few months prior to the edict, in December of 1491, the Monarchs were willing to grant royal protection to the Jewish community of Ávila. Thus, desire for religious and political unity in Spain was demonstrably *not* the chief cause of the Expulsion, contrary to the old position which was advocated also, as we have seen, by Lea and others. Indeed, the fear which Jews themselves had of Christian attacks against them may have induced the Monarchs to consent to the idea of expelling them in order to prevent a more serious catastrophe: extermination.

In any case, the decision to expel the Jews, although no doubt secretly planned by the Inquisition and others at least for months, was clearly something which came late and very much as a surprise to the Monarchs themselves.

One of the more fantastic stories which have been advanced as a "cause" is that of a converso physician of the king, maestre Ribas Altas, who in fact we know had already been burned by the Inquisition much earlier, since at the *auto* of his mother in Zaragoza in 1488 there is reference to his previous burning. Nevertheless, the record of this mother's *auto* also relates the same obviously fictitious story about him, that he had a gold ball in which was a painting of the crucifix and of the physician himself apparently kissing the posterior of the image, and that the *infante* Juan (son of Fernando and Isabel) saw this and reported it to his father, who supposedly then decided to expel the Jews.[89] The obviously false nature of this story scarcely needs comment; it is unbelievable that, even if such a picture existed, a converso would be foolish enough to show it to the *infante,* nor would there be any reason to blame the Jews for this impiety of one converso.

According to Klein (who must be read with caution), the *Mesta* (sheep-herding organization) in the reign of the Catholic Monarchs began a campaign to force its authority over local cities and over individual tax farmers of the local sheep tolls, "Jewish concessionaries," according to him. "For centuries" (no less!), enmity existed between the sheep owners and these Jews. "There is every reason to believe that Jorge Mexía, the energetic attorney-general of the Mesta . . . had not a little to do with the edict for the expulsion of the Jews." However, whereas we may accept Klein's apparent evidence that Mexía was "constantly" at the royal court, he offers no evidence whatsoever to support his other statements.

This supposed dominance of tax collecting for the *Mesta* on the part of Jews "for centuries," if true, ought to have been substantiated. As it is, I know of only *two* Jews who were ever involved in the taxes of the *Mesta,* both in the thirteenth century: Zag de la Maleha and Abraham al-Barjilūnī. There may well have been some "enmity" against them, but they were both so powerful that it would not have mattered. The single example of a case in the fifteenth century which is relevant was in 1485, and involved charges by the *Mesta* against the town of Arnedo and Bienveniste Abayud, the Jewish collector there of *Mesta* tolls. He was certainly a very small fish, and we can hardly conclude from this that there is any basis for Klein's theory.[90]

Jewish Leaders and the Expulsion

What role did the leaders of the already weakened Jewish community play in trying to avert the disaster of the Expulsion? Very instructive is the statement of Abraham Ibn Ardutiel, himself one of the exiles (though only a child at the time):

> The *majority* of the Jews and their great men and judges sat in their houses and exchanged their religion [converted] for the religion of a foreign god, abandoning the well of living water and the King of the world, and served other gods whom they knew not. . . .

He continues that only a few of the leaders chose to leave Spain with their people, those who "set their faces to die for the sanctification of the Name and made themselves 'abandoned,' whether to death or [other] punishment." It is difficult to know what is meant by this, however, for no one was killed or even threatened with death; other exiles, such as Zacut, spoke of "sanctifying the Name," by which they meant that they chose to leave Spain and remain Jews.

The most important of these, Ibn Ardutiel says, was Isaac Abravanel, "who sanctified the Name in public before the eyes of the king and minis-- ters, he and the sage and philosopher don Solomon Seneor the elder," who was the brother of Abraham Seneor. It is possible that Solomon was not the brother but the *son* of Seneor, who indeed was named Solomon; on the other hand, the identification of him as "the elder," implying also a younger man of the same name, may indicate that he really was Abraham's brother. In any case, we know nothing else of him. Ibn Ardutiel concludes that the sages of Spain, all of them and their students (in fact, there were not many), were greatly beneficial and an example to the Jews.[91]

Capsali invented an even more romantic story, which also has become part of popular mythology, that "the sage like Daniel," Abravanel, went to the king and queen together with Abraham Seneor and other "sages of Israel" and pleaded with them to annul the decree. When they saw that Fernando would not hear them, they wrote to Isabel, and Abravanel "wrote harshly to her and did not display honor for the monarchy since his soul was prepared for death." Abraham Seneor supposedly also wrote the queen. Isabel experienced a great "dread," no less, when she read Abravanel's words.[92]

This tale is also reported by the previously mentioned anonymous Italian writer, who may have derived his account from Capsali, and who adds the interesting detail that Seneor was "attended by a retinue on thirty mules." Nevertheless, he adds that the renowned scholar Isaac de León used to call Abraham Seneor *Soneh or* (Heb., hater of light) because he converted. No doubt that rabbi did call Seneor by this term, but it had nothing to do with his conversion, since Isaac de León died two years before the Expulsion and the conversion of Seneor. This indicates that Isaac well understood the nature of Seneor and his devotion to the Jewish people!

The anonymous account adds information not found in Capsali or any other source, namely, that an agreement to nullify the decree was almost completed (in return for a payment of a large sum of money) "when it was frustrated by an official of Santa Cruz" (probably Torquemada, Inquisitor General and prior of the Monastery of Santa Cruz). The queen replied to the Jews that this decree was "in the hands of God," and supposedly stated that *she* was not responsible, only the king. The total falseness of this state-ment is, of course, obvious to anyone with knowledge of the relationship between Isabel and Fernando.[93]

The only value in that account, therefore, is the mention once again of Torquemada, adding to our previous knowledge of his implication in the Expulsion. Nevertheless, we may ask what truth there is to these late legends that figures such as Seneor and Abravanel attempted to obtain the nullifi-cation of the decree. Netanyahu writes eloquently that "the moment when Abravanel and his colleagues pleaded with the king for the life of their people was one of the most critical in Jewish history," and yet he admits that we have no details, only that "many years later" there are "tales and legends" about it (he cites only Capsali).[94]

However, Abravanel himself claimed, many years later in the introduction to his commentary on Kings, that "I called my friends, those who see the face of the king, to petition for my people, and the nobles assembled together to speak to the king with all might to annul the books of anger and wrath and his thoughts which he thought to destroy the Jews." The king resisted all these efforts, however, in spite of three meetings which Abravanel says he had with the king and the offer of a huge sum of money. Netanyahu adds that the king told Abravanel that it was not his decision alone, but also that of "the queen of Castile"; however, it is unclear where Netanyahu got this impression, which is not in the text and is, interestingly, the exact opposite of the anonymous account mentioned above. Furthermore, Isabel was never called "queen of Castile" by anyone in Spain, least of all her husband. She was queen of all Spain, and Fernando was king of Spain, and they acted on all things jointly. It is also hard to explain why Abravanel, and Netanyahu after him, were under the mistaken impression that the lives of the Jews were in danger; with respect to Abravanel it would appear that this is pure religious propaganda intended to arouse sympathy for the Jews and admiration for his own "bravery."[95]

Nevertheless, all of this romantic story falls apart under the harsh light of historical scrutiny. In the first place, is it conceivable that such a momentous undertaking would have been carried out without consulting Jewish leaders and communities throughout Spain? Yet no record, no hint, of any such activity exists, nor has any mention of all this ever surfaced in the writings of any Jew who actually lived in Spain at that time, or who was an adult exile.

Furthermore, Netanyahu incredibly ignored a crucial passage on the very page of a source which he elsewhere cites. There, in Abravanel's reply to the scholar Saul ha-Kohen, written in Venice in 1507 just before Abravanel's death, he writes:

> All these commentaries and compositions I wrote after I left my homeland, because before that all the days that I was in the courts and palaces of kings [i.e., first in Portugal and then in Spain] occupied in their service I had no opportunity for study and I did not know a book and spent in vanity my days and my years in confusion to acquire wealth and honor. And indeed that wealth was lost in an evil manner, and honor is removed from Israel.[96]

This self-portrait is confirmed by the almost identical words, again ignored by Netanyahu, which Abravanel wrote in the previously cited introduction to his commentary on Kings: "also the wealth and honor which a man acquires and live by I acquired in their [the Catholic Monarchs'] courts and palaces; therefore was the Torah slackened [ignored; cf. Hab. 1.4] and the work withheld [of writing the commentary], and because of the service of the kings of the Gentiles who are not of the children of Israel I forsook my inheritance, the kingdom of Judea and Israel and the explanation of their stories."

All this proves, from Abravanel's own words, that he had no other interest than fame and fortune while in Spain. It also, incidentally, indicates that he wrote none of his books and commentaries (except Joshua, Judges, Samuel, and the beginning of Kings) in Spain.

Second, in the documents published long ago by Suárez Fernández (which neither Netanyahu nor his mentor Baer read closely, though both casually cite the book) there are, in fact, several relating to Abravanel at this period. There is also an important document published by *both* Baer and Suárez which Netanyahu ignored.

On 22 May 1492, the king and queen (acting, as always, together) wrote to a certain official informing him that Abravanel had called to their attention a number of outstanding debts to the Crown and instructing that these be collected. Abravanel was then still acting as an official of, and at the request of, the duque del Infantado, Íñigo López de Mendoza.[97]

On 31 May, the Monarchs granted permission to Abravanel and his wife and sons to take 1,000 gold *ducats* out of the kingdom with them, along with "other jewels of silver and gold" and other goods. Fernand Nuñez Coronel (formerly Meir *Melamed*) paid on behalf of the Monarchs 1,000,000 *mrs.* (an enormous sum) to Yuçe (Joseph) Abravanel, Isaac's nephew and son-in-law. In June the king and queen intervened, at the request of this don Yuçe Abravanel, to order the justices of Plasencia to release certain goods of his brother Jacob and his wife.[98]

Yuçe had complained that the duque de Plasencia had put a lien on certain property of his wife and his brother for taxes he had collected and not given the duke. However, Yuçe had as his *fiadores*, to prove that he had paid, the converso (?) Luis de Alcalá and Fernando Nuñez Coronel, no less. Jacob Abravanel further complained that 140 cows were taken from him and sent to Portugal, where he could not go to reclaim them (since by order of the Expulsion decree he had to leave Spain by way of Valencia). The Monarchs also ordered that his cows be restored; presumably he sold them before he left Spain.

At the end of July, the Monarchs issued orders to the converso treasurer Luis de Sepúlveda concerning certain claims of fraud against either Isaac or, more probably, Yuçe. Most significant is a document of 6 October (long after the Expulsion) noting that a hold had been placed on all debts due to Jews who *still remained in the kingdom,* including various debts to Isaac

Abravanel, and instructing that these now be released (paid). This, incidentally, proves that Abravanel did *not* leave Spain with the rest of the Jews.[99]

It is also hardly likely that Abravanel and his family would have continued to receive such favor and protection if he had intervened in any way to nullify the edict, much less if he had written such "harsh words" to the queen.

A similar picture results with regard to the documents relating to Abraham Seneor. In May the Monarchs responded to his petition concerning certain problems with the farming of taxes. After his conversion, in June of 1492, they named him *contador mayor* of their son, the *infante* Juan.[100]

None of this is conceivable if we are to believe that these men, Abravanel and Seneor particularly, intervened in some sort of secret plot, least of all with the nobles of the realm, to convince the king and/or queen to annul the edict. Certainly, it is inconceivable that Abravanel could have spoken, or written, harshly (like a great prophet of old, in the hyperbole of Netanyahu) to the queen.

There were also rumors that Alfonso de la Caballería, son of the infamous Pedro (author of a harsh anti-Jewish polemic) and vice-chancellor of Aragón, had worked to assist the Jews concerning the edict. As we have seen before, his father had attempted to obtain documentation that he was of "pure Christian" origin, and it is hardly likely that the son of this Jew-hating converso would suddenly evidence such concern for the plight of the Jews. There were other charges against him besides that one, possibly that he was implicated in the plot to murder the Inquisitor Arbués, although this is not certain. All this we learn from a letter of the king in June (no date) of 1492 addressed to the officials of the Inquisition in Aragón, noting that bulls and letters had been received from the pope on behalf of Alfonso and his family and parents. Accordingly, the king ordered their protection against Alfonso's "enemies in this city [Zaragoza] and kingdom." One of the charges which these "enemies" had raised was that he attempted to act in some unspecified way concerning the decree of Expulsion ("also because of acts done by him concerning our service and the benefit of this kingdom; as [also] for the expulsion of the Jews, concerning which it is said he gave them to understand that he delayed it").

Beinart, who edited this text, insisted that Alfonso was a great hero of the "Jewish" people, risking his own life in an attempt to get the decree annulled (nothing in the text supports any such interpretation; the charge was only that there were rumors that he had *pretended* to have intervened) in his "great love for his people." Yet Beinart himself cited earlier Inquisition testimony against his hero, that Alfonso was asked to intervene by some Jews with regard to a simple tax and that he promised to do so in return for a payment of 1,000 gold *florins*. Where was his "great love" for "his" people then? Had he really intervened concerning the decree of Expulsion, he surely would have demanded millions.[101]

A family chronicle by a relative of Alfonso, who himself remained a Jew and was one of the exiles, provides very important information. According to this, Alfonso was hardly a "hero" of the Jewish people; on the contrary, he is described as one of the "enemies of Israel" (the Hebrew term is a technical one, meaning those who seek actively to harm the Jews) who *influenced* Fernando in the decision to expel the Jews. He refers to him as "messer Alfonso, son of messer Pedro the idolatrous apostate [*meshumad;* see Chapter 1 on the term] who converted, he [Pedro] and his father don Fernando [Bonafos de la Caballería] and all his house in the days of the priest frau [Catalan for friar] Vicente [Ferrer], the uprooter of Israel." Of the whole family only two brothers, don Vidal de la Caballería, father of the author of this chronicle, and don Solomon did not convert.

As Hacker observed, it is not entirely correct to say that Pedro (author of the *Zelus Christi,* previously discussed) converted, since his mother was a Christian who married Pedro's father after the latter converted. Thus, Alfonso was the *grandson* of a converted Jew on his father's side. By Jewish law (even modern Reform rabbis would agree), there is no way such a person could be considered "Jewish," and thus Beinart's romanticism about Alfonso's love for "his" people is without any foundation.

The author of the chronicle continues to state that Alfonso "thought evil against the people of God" and counseled the king to "destroy the name of Israel from the land" (expel the Jews). He further adds that Abraham Seneor and his relative Meir *Melamed* converted, "and who [could see] these heads [of the people] go out to evil culture [convert] and not go out [likewise convert]?" (The wording is an allusion to the well-known statement about Moses going to meet his father-in-law Jethro; who could see this leader leave the camp and not follow him?)[102]

Alfonso, as well as the converso Gabriel Sánchez, another royal official, was, as already noted, indeed implicated in the assassination of the Inquisitor Pedro Arbués. Certainly those charges were totally false, but they led to his trial in 1485. Remarkably, undoubtedly because of his powerful position, he was acquitted, and soon after that he was himself involved in establishing the Inquisition in Barcelona. As noted elsewhere, the Catholic Monarchs consulted him also in Zaragoza in 1488 concerning the Inquisition.[103] All of this was undoubtedly known to Beinart.

To sum up, there is no solid evidence whatever that any of the "Jewish leaders," much less grandsons of converts, did anything whatever to bring about the annulment of the edict of Expulsion. On the contrary, such "leaders" as Abravanel, Seneor, and *Melamed* were solely concerned with their own power and fortunes. The latter two converted rather than face the loss of these, and while Abravanel eventually left Spain, he did so only after remaining behind for months in order to secure his personal fortune. We have already seen that the rabbinical leadership was weak and ineffective, and indeed the majority of what important rabbinic scholars there were in the latter part of the fifteenth century had already died before the Expulsion.

Sale of Property prior to Leaving

If the policy of the Catholic Monarchs toward the Jews was one of persecution and hostility, as popular myth imagines, then we would naturally expect to find that the Jews would be expelled without being permitted to take anything with them; indeed, that their property, if not their goods, would be seized by the Crown. In fact, not a few uninformed writers have stated just that. As we shall see, the facts are quite the opposite.

In the documents we begin already to find records of numerous sales of property by Jews to Christians almost as soon as the edict was issued, These include the sale of stores, etc., as well as private houses.

Contrary to the claims of Baer and others, these documents demonstrate that such sales were treated as legitimate ones, under normal conditions, with the payment of normal prices and in some cases quite substantial sums.[104]

On 14 May Fernando issued an order (this one was for Aragón-Catalonia, but obviously similar orders were issued jointly by the Monarchs for all of Spain) that when the Jews left during "all the month of July" (the edict specified that by the end of July all Jews were to be gone) they and their *goods*—i.e., movable property—were under his royal protection, and that no one should molest or rob the Jews or threaten their lives or cause any danger to them or their goods. In Aragón, don Martín de Gurrea, lord of Argavieso, was given the job of guarding the Jews and punishing any who violated the order with a fine of 10,000 gold *florins* (an enormous sum). These orders were faithfully carried out, although in some cases the Jews had to pay for this protection, and de Gurrea himself received a substantial sum.[105]

The Jews, of course, still had to pay their tax assessments for 1492. Of particular interest is the case of Ezmel Abnarrabi of Zaragoza (a distinguished Jewish family), whose wife, Alazar (normally a man's name!), acted as agent to sell all his debts to the king, and on behalf of the king to sell them to his *comisario* for Jewish affairs. The debts were mostly in bushels of wheat, which he had lent almost entirely to Muslims in various towns of Aragón.[106]

As previously noted, the Inquisitors of Zaragoza, together with officials of the city, contradicted the king's express orders and prohibited Jews from taking any goods or property with them. Apparently this prohibition was ultimately rescinded.

Throughout Castile there were numerous instances of the sale of property by Jews. In the town of Béjar, near Salamanca, Jews sold vineyards, houses, etc., to Christians for "certain, just," and agreed-upon prices (which, in fact, appear to have been very fair). The vineyards of some of the Jews were adjoining those of various clergy. In Ávila some 107 heads of households (approximately 535 individuals) are recorded as having left; the majority of the Jews apparently had converted, since the total Jewish population in 1492 in the city was "close to 3,000." The cemetery was given to the newly founded Convent of Santo Tomás, largely converso. One of the synagogues was bought at public auction by a clergyman.[107]

In May, the Monarchs, noting that the Jews complained that they were not able to pay and collect debts before the end of July (the Jews in Spain not only lent money to Christians and Muslims, they also frequently *borrowed*), ordered that all local judges in each community investigate such debts and have them promptly and justly paid.[108]

In many cases, the expulsion of the Jews created some financial hardship for local communities and individuals who thereby lost income. In Ocaña in 1514, for example, the *comendador* Juan Sarmiento received compensation from the royal treasury for the income he had lost from the butcher shops of the Jews.[109] No doubt there were other such cases.

Although Jews were specifically permitted to sell their property, and to take movable property with them, no one in Spain (Jews included) was supposed to be able to take gold or silver out of the country. This prohibition extended also to "*cosas vedadas*" (prohibited items, judged to be of special value, weapons, etc.; often exceptions were made, and Jews were frequently the collectors of taxes on these). The obvious question arises, if Jews were permitted to sell their property, what good did this do if they could not take the money out of the country? One solution would be to convert the money to goods, but in fact, as we shall see, the prohibition was generally ignored.

In September of 1492 the Monarchs complained to the *regidor* of Medina del Campo that he had allowed Jews to take gold out of the country, and that similar violations were occurring elsewhere in the diocese of Toledo. In fact, Jews everywhere had done this.[110]

The facts concerning money taken out of Spain by the Jews emerge chiefly in documents dating after the Expulsion. Thus, as an example, in 1508–9 the Monarchs purchased some houses in Carrión which a local man had obtained from Solomon Harache (of a distinguished Jewish family). In those same years, they ordered repayment to the heirs of Rabbi

Abraham Amarax of Segovia for "the part which belonged to them" of a loan he had made to the Monarchs in 1489. Half of that sum belonged to the rabbi's mother, which she could not receive now because she had been guilty of taking money out of the country at the time of the Expulsion. Obviously, of course, the heirs of the rabbi were conversos, and even his mother had returned to live in Spain as a Christian.

In 1518 there was a payment to heirs of Pero Juárez de la Conche, called Jaco Jalión, who had been a Jew of Segovia, for loans he had made to the queen in 1489 and 1490, which had not been repaid at the time of the Expulsion because of the prohibition on taking out money (as in the above case, he had also returned to Spain and converted). A pardon for having taken out money was also extended to his sons Cristobal and Fernando, merchants, and his daughters Isabel (former wife of the surgeon Juan de Ávila) and Catalina, wife of Alvaro de Piña, a merchant, all living in Segovia. In the previously mentioned case of Rabbi Abraham of Segovia, whose son claimed repayment of his father's tax payment for the war against Granada because his father died before 1492 and his mother had then gone to Portugal, it was stated that she had been guilty of taking *cosas vedades* out of the country. In 1525–35 payment was ordered for the heirs of Rabbi Davi de Arévalo of Ávila for loans to the king and queen, given in his name by Davi Abraham Cerrula to Fernando de Ayala, tax official of Ávila, in 1489. Such records are perhaps only the "tip of the iceberg" in reflecting such things as loans by Jews to the Monarchs, money taken out during the Expulsion, and Jews who returned to live in Spain as Christians.[111]

Another example of a famous Jew who was able to take considerable wealth and books with him (unlike other Jews, who complained of having to leave books behind) was Judah Bienveniste, probably of Toledo. When he arrived in Salonica, he established the first library in Ottoman Turkey, which unfortunately was destroyed by the fire of 1545.[112]

Synagogues and other communal property (this would have included cemeteries, schools and what yeshivot existed, hospitals, and any other community buildings) could not be liquidated as a general rule, however. The Jewish cemetery of Toledo, which was outside the city, was given by Isabel to the cathedral chapter of the city in December of 1492. The cemetery of Ávila, as previously noted, was given to the Convent of Santo Tomás, and one of the synagogues was sold to a clergyman. Other property abandoned by Jews in Ávila, Coria, Salamanca, and Ciudad Rodrigo was given by the Monarchs to the duque de Alba (it is thus interesting that a good portion of the enormous wealth of this noble family derived from Jews). The *synoga vieja* (old synagogue) of Toledo was given by the Monarchs to two men to be sold at auction, and the famous *sinagoga mayor* was given to the

Order of Calatrava. The cemetery of Tauste was given to an official by the king, "in recognition of services." Even the Torah ornaments and other synagogue decoration were seized in Zaragoza and later sold, some as late as 1507.[113]

Protection of Jews during the Expulsion

On 14 May 1492, the Catholic Monarchs wrote to all the nobility and Church officials of the entire kingdom that the Jews, having been ordered to leave by the end of July, and fearing possible attacks and robbery of their goods, etc., had appealed for protection (we have already noted the order of Fernando to Aragón-Catalonia, on the same date, concerning this), which was now granted. Jews and their property were taken under royal protection and security, and no harm was to come to them or their possessions. The notice was to be posted publicly in all towns and cities, and punishment for violation was to be a fine of 10,000 *mrs.* for each violator. Later documents of the king which have recently come to light show that he extended protection to the Jews for forty days after they left Spain, as well.[114]

On 30 May orders were issued as to how debts by Jews to Christians or Muslims, or debts of these to Jews, were to be paid. All officials were ordered to summon all such debtors and arrange payment, in cash or property of equivalent value. Jews who owed debts not yet due were to leave security for future payment of such debts, and all debts *to* Jews were to be paid before July, on pain of severe fines. In Béjar, all property of Jews and debts owed to Jews were taken under the protection of Alvaro de Zúñiga, duque de Plasencia and Béjar and *justicia mayor,* who ordered a strict accounting.[115]

In June the Monarchs instructed the officials of the town of San Vicente de la Barquera in Cantabria, hardly a major city or center of Jewish population, concerning the petition of Yuçe Farache (Harache) of Dueñas, who was owed 20,000 *mrs.* for certain work he had done in San Vicente. It was explained that unless he received payment he would be unable to leave the kingdom by the date decreed (unable to afford passage, apparently), and the judges were therefore ordered to hear the case and administer justice in a speedy and truthful manner to Yuçe. No suggestion was made that he could just as well walk across the border to Portugal, not that far from Dueñas.

This Yuçe, it should be noted, was certainly a relative of another Cantabrian Jew, Abraham Farache (Harache), who had but recently been condemned for blaspheming the Virgin, and he was probably also related to the aforementioned Solomon Harache of Carrión.[116]

The Catholic Monarchs also gave instructions concerning the Jews of

Maqueda and Torrijos, including those who wished to become Christians, that all should be helped and well treated. They also ordered that the "second synagogue" of Torrijos be used as a mosque after the Expulsion, that Muslims could live in formerly Jewish houses, and that the synagogue of Maqueda should be guarded until a decision as to its use or disposal could be made. An inventory was made of all Jewish property, and all debts to Jews or of Jews were to be paid. Jews were to be allowed to sell their property, and Isaac Abravanel was to be in charge of collection of debts.[117]

Even after the Jews had left Spain, the Monarchs continued to investigate whether their orders concerning the protection of the Jews and their property had been scrupulously observed. Thus, for example, on 27 July 1492, Lorenzo Gascó, a judge, and Jaime Agramut were sent to Valencia to look into matters relating to the Expulsion. Their detailed report is worth quoting in part:

> Most magnificent Lords: we left Castellón [de la Plana; a coastal town north of Sagunto] and arrived at [Sagunto] where we were told at length of everything which at that time had been done concerning the matters of the Jews, both in this city of Valencia and in the aforementioned town of [Sagunto], and particularly that in those matters of the Jews the only judges were the *baile* and the justice of that town, and no other official had anything to do with it; and thus was ordered by the lieutenant governor to those judges, that in these matters they should administer complete justice, and should any doubt arise they should appoint a jurist as assessor, if the lord king had not designated such; but the truth is that the judges appointed whomever they wished. . . .

The text continues to state that micer Pere Valsanell arrived at Murviedro (Sagunto) and informed these investigators that the Jews had been required to pay all taxes and debts due. Afterward, they met with Abraham Legem, *adelantado,* and "Devosal" (probably Moses Devosal), Jews of Castellón, who agreed to discuss these matters, but only before Valsanell or "micer Ros" (?), but not Pere Miquel, assessor of the regent and governor, whom they "considered very suspect." This request, however, was refused and the regent-governor was asked to instruct Pere Miquel who should be appointed assessor to deal with the matter of taxes.[118]

The Jews Leave Spain

The sources presently available enable us to obtain a fairly good picture of the actual departure of Jews from Spain, although they are by no means complete and therefore the picture must necessarily remain somewhat unclear.

Jerez de la Frontera, in Andalucía, once a proud Jewish community, was probably quite small in the fifteenth century. In 1492 some twenty Jews chose baptism rather than exile (the previous year only one Jew had been baptized), and even after the Expulsion some Jews who remained were baptized: one in 1493 and two in 1494 (in spite of the order, not all Jews actually left in 1492, as we have already seen).[119]

In the former Muslim kingdom of Granada, Jews of the cities of Granada and La Alpujarra were allowed to take 4 *doblas* each for their maintenance, and were sometimes granted special permission to take addition sums of money. Jews left Granada from Málaga and Almería, on a ship belonging to Genoese owners, as early as June. They converted their capital and property into bills of exchange or they purchased silk, taking enormous quantities of silk with them for eventual resale. In Almería alone, Jews purchased 3,176 pounds of the finest silk, at a value of 26 *reales* per pound (1 *real* being worth 31 *mrs.*). Of course, the export of this silk was taxed, but even so the profits realized would be substantial. One-tenth of all goods taken out of the country was also paid as a tax by the Jews of Granada. Specially appointed "committees" responsible to the Crown oversaw the restrictions on what Jews could take out. Large sums of money were realized in illegal goods seized from Jews.[120]

Ysaque Perdoniel (or Perdonel) was a Jew of Granada who served as an official to the last Muslim king, "Boabdil." The latter requested of the Catholic Monarchs a special privilege allowing this Jew to take with him all his property, money, jewels, etc., when the decree of Expulsion was issued. The king and queen readily agreed, and included also his wife, children, and (Jewish) servants in the privilege.

In all, some thirty-eight Jewish males are listed as having embarked from Málaga, and seventy-six from Almería (together with the value of their property and the taxes each paid). Even assuming that each of these males was the head of a family (not likely, of course), this would mean that not more than 560–570 Jews chose exile rather than conversion. It is true that some had already gone to live in other parts of Spain after the conquest.[121]

Specific details about the departure of Jews from Castilian communities, including the all-important one of Toledo, if they exist, are not yet known. For Plasencia, however, which was the major center of Jewish population, we have the following interesting account:

> Some Jews, when the time for selling their goods ended, went about day and night in desperation. Many [of the exiled] returned from the road and wherever they were and received the faith of Christ. Many others, in order not to be deprived of the homeland where they had been born, and not to sell their property for a low price, were baptized; some with sincerity and others to accommodate themselves to the time and protect themselves with the mask of

the Christian religion. Others returned from the roads, seeking baptism if their houses and property would be restored to them, returning the purchase money, and to many this was granted.[122]

Similarly, a historian of Segovia described the moving scene of "those miserable ones" who filled the fields of the *Hosario* (site of the Jewish cemetery), visiting and praying at the graves of their ancestors before leaving. Even at such a time "certain zealous religious and secular" Christians could not resist the temptation of going there to preach to the Jews in a last effort to convert them. Some few, indeed, were baptized on the spot, which henceforth was called *Prado santo*, but the rest chose exile.[123]

In Catalonia, most of the Jews also left by ship. Between 26 July and 8 August (in spite of the firm order that all Jews were to be out of Spain by the end of July), Jews of Tortosa went either to Alfacs (Port Alfaques) on the coast, or to Salou (just south of Tarragona, from which port Jaime I in 1229 had launched the conquest of Majorca). Others went to Ampolla, a port directly east of Tortosa, from which many of the Aragonese Jews also embarked. Other ports of embarkation used by Catalan Jews were Barcelona and Valencia.[124]

We recall that the overlord of Argavieso, Martín de Gurrea (of a family with a long history of relations with Jews), was directly responsible for the protection of the Jews of Aragón. He appointed numerous officials to assist in conducting them safely from Zaragoza, as well as from Daroca, Huesca, and other towns. The Jews of Jaca, for example, went to the port of Tarragona. The majority of the Aragonese Jews, apparently, went overland to Navarre.[125]

In Santa Coloma de Queralt, in Catalonia, as late as May of 1492 Jews and Christians were still entering into business partnerships. These, of course, now had to be liquidated. Jews also had to pay off and collect all debts and sell their property. Most of this was done in an orderly fashion between 12 and 23 July, and houses and land were sold to Christians for fair prices, as elsewhere.

Particularly touching, and significant in revealing the true state of Jewish-Christian relations on the local level, is a document dated 17 July in which a Jew, Vital Symeon, provided money for the establishment of a charitable institution (*almoina*) for the Christian poor, noting that his "Christian brothers" had always treated him with respect and honor. Vital was one of the commissioners named by the Jews to sell property of those who had already left before 17 July, in order to pay the taxes for 1492 that had already been apportioned the previous year by the duke. However, the duke remitted the considerable sum of 700 *livres* in taxes to the Jews. As we have seen, this did not necessarily happen elsewhere.[126]

We have some scattered information also about Jews departing from Valencia. On 15 June Galcerán Adret and Pablo and Juan Salvador, merchants, undoubtedly conversos, contracted with a ship called the *San Pedro* to transport 250 Jews from Murviedro (Sagunto). Again on 20 June these same merchants arranged for another ship, the *Santa María*, to transport an additional 400 Jews (obviously this was not the same as Columbus' famous ship). Their destination was Naples or North Africa, and the price charged for each person for the voyage was 36 *sous* (*reals de Valencia*). Half of the total sum was paid by Alhonor Anshom Zoir, a Jew of Teruel, and the remainder was to be paid by Samuel Esdra of Sesma, erroneously described as "of the kingdom of Aragón" in the source (Sesma is in Navarre, and in 1463 that part of Navarre had been given to Castile), acting as *procurador* of the Jews of "Vila de Gerica" in Valencia (i.e., Jérica, northwest of Sagunto), within eight days after the ships' landing in Oran (Algeria), with the male passengers remaining on the ship until the sum was paid. Three hundred Jews had contracted to continue on to Naples. In addition, the passengers had to pay for bread, water, and salt provided by the ships, and for any extra baggage or merchandise they took.[127]

The Jews were expelled, of course, not only from Spain proper but from all its kingdoms and possessions. Essentially, this meant Sicily and Sardinia. At the present, there is nothing to report on Sardinia, but in Sicily the Jews were also given a three-month extension, from the original date of 18 September 1492 to 18 December. (It took a surprising amount of time for documents and other information to travel short distances, and the original edict of expulsion did not reach Sicily until 29 August, so that obviously a different date had to be set for the expulsion there than for the rest of Spain.)

Jews apparently had paid a substantial sum for the privilege of this extension, however. Further delays postponed the final departure to 12 January. For reasons not at all clear, the policy which the Monarchs applied for the Jews in Spain was changed with regard to those of Sicily, and they were forbidden to liquidate their holdings and convert them into gold, silver, or jewels; however, they were able to convert them into utensils and other movable property or into "less valuable" clothing.[128]

Jews from Sicily went primarily to the kingdom of Naples, then independent of Spain. Others chose more remote areas, such as Gallipoli (many of the exiles were slaughtered by sailors on the ships on the way there). In 1494 the French conquered Naples, with severe persecution of the Jews following, including massacres. The majority of the Sicilian exiles, however, went to the Ottoman Empire.[129]

We have already previously mentioned something of the Jews who went to Portugal, and among whom were the vast majority of the exiles from Castile. The tragic story of their brief sojourn in that country and their expulsion from it must await future treatment. Similarly, the interesting and important story of the "Sefardim," the Jews who left Spain, and their descendants, and their dispersion virtually throughout the world is a subject to which I hope to return in the future. That story, too, has never been fully told.

Jews Who Returned

In August of 1498 the Monarchs issued a proclamation in which they noted that the Inquisitors claimed that many Jews who had converted were secretly observing Jewish rites and adhering to the "law of Moses," for which they were condemned as heretics. Many of these had fled to "other parts" to escape punishment, and therefore it was ordered that none of these be allowed to return to the Spanish kingdoms on pain of death.[130]

It should be noted that this text refers specifically and exclusively to conversos, and not to Jews. It has frequently been claimed that Jews were forbidden to return to Spain on penalty of death. There is no document presently known to me, nor any source whatever, which confirms this. Of course, once expelled, Jews were not permitted to return unless they agreed to accept baptism and become Christians. As we have already seen, many did just that, some even while on their way out of the country. Many others returned from the lands of their exile, immediately and over the next several years.

Bernáldez, chaplain of Cardinal Mendoza and anti-Jewish chronicler of the Catholic Monarchs, cites a letter from "Rabi Mair" (Meir *Melamed*) to Abraham Seneor which supposedly stated that thirty-five thousand Jews were expelled (see Appendix B on the number of Jews expelled). He then adds some significant information:

> And of the rabbis whom I baptized on their return from there [those who returned to Spain], which were ten or twelve, one was very keen of nature. He was called Zentollo, and was from Vitoria, and I gave him the name Tristan Bogado.

It is also interesting to observe that even this anti-Semite, remarking that during the Expulsion the rich Jews bore the cost of the journey for the poor, had to admit that the Jews acted toward each other "with much charity."[131]

One of the Jews who converted before the Expulsion, Yuda Abensabad of Maqueda (near Toledo), taking the name Juan Calderón, went to Fez in 1492, where another Jew saw him dressed as a Jew and wearing the "sign of a Jew" (badge) like the other Jews there (this is important testimony, incidentally, that the Jews in Muslim Morocco had to wear a badge). The Jew who gave this damaging testimony himself returned to Spain and converted. Calderón also returned, but only to sell his property and move to

Portugal. He was tried *in absentia* by the Inquisition in 1509–10, and the former Jew from Fez testified against him. A Jew from Jerez who had gone to Portugal in 1492 also returned to his former home, we learn, and was baptized. No doubt there were others who did the same.[132]

The *fuero* of Vizcaya (1452, revised in 1526) contains a reference to the privilege granted by the Catholic Monarchs whereby, since "all" the inhabitants of Vizcaya were *hidalgos* and of *limpia sangre,* no converted Jews or Muslims or their descendants were permitted to live in the territory (we recall Pulgar's sarcastic remarks about the prohibition against conversos' living there). Since, however, many people were coming from other lands, especially Portugal and "other parts remote from these kingdoms of Castile," a law was enacted requiring such settlers to inform officials of their genealogy. According to the accompanying letter of Queen Juana, dated 1511, the prohibition was specifically to prevent conversos who were fleeing the Inquisition elsewhere in Spain from taking refuge in Vizcaya. It would, of course, also have the effect of discouraging former Jews from returning.[133]

There may even have been cases of Jews returning surreptitiously to live in Spain without benefit of conversion, though obviously we know of no such.

Fanciful Theories of Consequences of the Expulsion

Although we are done with the story, we still are not done with mythology, however. One of the most commonly accepted myths is that the Expulsion "crippled" the Spanish economy, in a way from which it never really recovered. It is pointless to cite the numerous historians who have shared this notion, including a surprising number of Spaniards (e.g., Sánchez-Albornoz). One example, significant for the undoubted influence it exerted, was the statement of Klein that "the Jews formed the largest group of merchants in Spain familiar with money economy, and handled most of the operations of foreign exchange." Their expulsion supposedly led to a long period of "confusion" in the wool trade until the coming of the Flemish.[134]

This is misleading. The Jews never at any period in medieval Spain had any monopoly on a money economy, and while they shared in that economy they played a very insignificant role indeed in "foreign exchange," and an even lesser one in the wool trade. In fact, there is very scant evidence of any involvement of Jews in that trade at all, other than as retail merchants of cloth.

Klein greatly exaggerated the importance of the wool industry in medieval Spain in general; but, largely because his book was one of the very few in English dealing with Spain, one suspects, it had an enormous and lasting influence even on Spanish historians.

Details of the actual role of Jews in the economic life of medieval Spain will also have to await my future book, which of course will be greatly indebted to the many careful studies of a growing number of competent Spanish economic historians. Their work has uncovered a wealth of material on this aspect of Jewish life, and still other information remains to be tapped from a host of Jewish sources.

Meanwhile, suffice it to say that while Jews were involved, often in a very significant manner, in virtually every trade, occupation, and profession in Spain, they by no means dominated or had a controlling share in any, including even medicine. Contrary to popular imagination, the Jews even played a decidedly *small* role in moneylending. In every case, there were far more Christians loaning far greater sums of money than there were Jews.

Spain's economy, while it undoubtedly suffered in some areas, and particularly on the local level, certainly was in no sense devastated by the expulsion of the Jews. Recently, Stephen Haliczer has also argued against the devastation thesis, and noted that, indeed, the Christian economy of Spain was flourishing in the fifteenth century before the Expulsion. While this may need some correctives in certain areas, more to the point is his observation that the *constant conversion* of large numbers (the majority, in fact) of the Jews prevented the Jews from playing a crucial role.[135]

On the other hand, the impact of the converso problem on the economy of fifteenth-century Spain has not been dealt with at all. No one so far has paid the slightest attention, for example, to Pulgar's previously cited testimony that the Inquisition forced many conversos to flee the country, and left some four thousand abandoned homes in Andalucía alone, causing severe economic deprivation throughout the kingdom.

The fanatical zeal of the anti-converso campaigns particularly in Córdoba and Seville unquestionably devastated not only those cities but the entire surrounding region. Seville eventually recovered, but it would appear that Córdoba, particularly, never did. The city remains even today a pale shadow of what it must have been in the fifteenth century, to say nothing of the tenth.

The Expulsion: Conclusions

It is necessary to stress, in the remote possibility that the point has been missed, that almost everything previously written concerning the Expulsion of the Jews from Spain is incorrect (the single exception is the extremely valuable study by Motis of the expulsion from Aragón). Baer, in particular (and also his disciples), can be accused of disregarding sources—even published ones—which contradict his thesis. Perhaps no other topic in Jewish history has been so much the subject of distortion and propaganda, and it is difficult to find any similar case of sober historians employing the kind of hysterical invective which has been used to characterize one or both of the Monarchs. Not surprisingly, additional sources which have since come to light only further prove that the Monarchs were hardly the "fanatical" tyrants they were imagined to be.

We have seen that, on the contrary, they continued the centuries-old policy of protecting the Jews and, above all, administering justice. The Jews themselves knew this, of course, and turned to the Monarchs in the expectation of such justice.

This does not mean that there were not very real tensions and very real hostility toward the Jews in the latter half of the century. Indeed, to some extent the situation of the Jews in Spain had already deteriorated in the late fourteenth century, a deterioration which reached a peak in the religious zeal of Vicente Ferrer and coincided with the anti-Jewish policy of Benedict XIII, the pope recognized in Spain. As we have seen previously, the preaching of Ferrer and the Tortosa disputation called by the pope led to the massive conversion of Jews.

There can be no doubt that this unprecedented conversion of the *majority* of Spanish Jews during that century created an equally unprecedented situation of hostility, directed first toward the conversos and ultimately toward the Jews themselves.

The emergence of true anti-Semitism, i.e., hatred of Jewish "racial" and personal characteristics and of the *people* and not the religion, centuries before it was once again to break forth in Europe, is the key to understanding the topics with which this book deals. The motivating factors were, as usual, many, including economic and social jealousy of the new "converso class," religious bigotry, etc. This was clearly a new manifestation, however, in that the efforts of the bigots were frustrated by the official teaching of the Church, and by the many Church leaders who insisted on its strict application, according to which no distinction could be made between "old" and "new" Christians. In order to carry their mission to its ultimate disastrous conclusion, therefore, the enemies of the conversos had to develop a counter theory, the pernicious idea of "racial purity," *limpieza de sangre*. Accordingly, it was not that the conversos were not "good Christians," for in fact everyone knew they were, but that inherent characteristics corrupted them ("Jewish blood"), and through them would corrupt all of Christian society. The only solution to this imagined threat was, first, the total isolation of conversos in society, and, finally, their complete elimination through the fires of the Inquisition.

It will be noted that for this scheme to work it was necessary to propagate several myths: that the conversos were insincere, indeed, false Christians; that conversos as a class sought to control the country through control of ecclesiastical and secular offices; and that conversos were corrupted by their Jewish racial origin, a corruption which would contaminate "old Christians" unless isolated and finally exterminated.

The initial support old Christians provided the conversos seems to have declined sharply as a result of the long period of uprisings and actual warfare between them and their enemies which devastated and exhausted Castile and Andalucía, at least, and had repercussions also elsewhere in Spain. No doubt the arrogance of many, if not most, of the conversos themselves did not help their situation, and the open hostility of the Jews toward their former "coreligionists" certainly must have confused many a Christian.

The Inquisition, as we have seen, soon became (if, indeed, it was not already so intended from its establishment) the tool of the anti-Semitic elements determined to eradicate the converso "threat." Its excessess finally aroused the indignation and opposition of many throughout Spain, and not only because it also began to attack solid "old Christians" who were important members of society. Indeed, at least in Catalonia, there was strong opposition to the establishment of the Inquisition at all.

This opposition was bound to fail, however, and particularly because Torquemada and his supporters already had the ear of the Monarchs and had succeeded in convincing them of the dangerous heresy represented by the conversos.

The truth is that the Catholic Monarchs, occupied first with putting down the strong resistance on the part of their own nobility to Fernando's rule, then with the war with Portugal, problems in Aragón-Catalonia, and finally the war against Granada, almost certainly had no "master plan" for the unification of the faith in their kingdom, as some writers have imagined. They no doubt gave as little attention as possible to the matter of the conversos and the Inquisition, except when Fernando in particular saw the Catalan resistance as a challenge to his own authority. Their own converso advisors and numerous converso officials were very good Christians indeed, and as for the rest, the Monarchs appear to have been content to allow the Inquisition to deal with the problem as it saw fit. The Jews certainly made no objections, and in fact cooperated willingly with the institution which they saw as just punishment for the apostasy of the hated conversos.

Anti-Semitism, once unleashed, eventually had disastrous repercussions for the Jews themselves, however.

While that which I had long suspected, namely, that it was the Inquisition generally and Torquemada specifically who were responsible for the idea of the expulsion of the Jews, has now been conclusively proven by letters of the king himself, we cannot overlook the importance of the other elements detailed at the beginning of this chapter. These included the increasing hostility of the lesser nobility, described as *caballeros* (knights), toward the Jews, including the constant troubles in such an important town as Ávila with its major Jewish population. Second, there is the evidence of the anti-Jewish sentiment stirred up by the preaching, once again, of some Dominican friars throughout the kingdom. All of this, while it was certainly *not* typical of Christian-Jewish relations at the time (a point which must be stressed), helped create an atmosphere in which Torquemada and his supporters could carry out the final part of their scheme: the total elimination of Jews from Spanish society. That they succeeded completely is demonstrated from the various letters, especially of Fernando, previously cited, as well as from the text of the edict of Expulsion itself. The version sent to Aragón, differing in significant ways from that of Castile, refers to the influence of Jews upon Christians, leading many of the latter to "abominable circumcision, blaspheming the sacred name" of Jesus, and abandonment of the "evangelical doctrine" and holy faith. Jews are further accused of teaching Christians their law, "its precepts and ceremonies and causing them to keep the Sabbath and holidays." [136]

Of course, in all these texts "Christians" actually means the conversos, as there is little or no evidence of Jewish proselytizing among "old Christians" at this time. The charges were, of course, almost entirely false; as we have seen, there were very few incidences of cordial contacts between conversos and Jews, and the overwhelming majority of conversos were good Christians; if for nothing else, because of the fear of the Inquisition.

Nevertheless, this propaganda served Torquemada and his followers, and it is evident that they were able to convince the Monarchs of the truth of these claims. If the Jews were the source of all these troubles, then the logic of removing this "heresy" and cause of social unrest from the kingdom was apparent. The inevitability of that fateful act had little to do with the Monarchs themselves and everything to do with the events set into motion long before they came to the throne.

Afterword

Once again, the thesis (or theses, for there are more than one) of this book must be clearly stated. Massive conversion of Jews to Christianity began in Spain not in the fifteenth century but in the fourteenth; there were, of course, individual cases even earlier. The preaching campaigns of the Dominicans and Franciscans resulted in Jews willfully abandoning their ancestral faith and becoming Christians. There is no doubt that some also converted out of fear of the kinds of violence that often accompanied these compulsory sermons in the synagogues, and certainly the attacks in the summer of 1391 resulted in more such conversions. Such converts, and *only* such, could be viewed as *anusim* ("forced converts," but in this case not literally compelled but converted from fear). It was with regard to these first-generation converts, and a minority of the total that had converted, that Jewish authorities held out some hope that they would return to the Jewish people. They had every opportunity to do so, but most chose not to. When that fact became clear, along with the fact that the overwhelming majority of converts both before and after 1391 (and nearly all during the fifteenth century) had unquestionably abandoned their faith and their people, for whatever motives, the rabbis determined that they were *meshumadim* (apostate Jews). More than that, they created an entirely new category of those *who abandoned not just their "religion" but their people,* and had become complete Gentiles. This was a drastic step, nearly without precedent in Jewish history, to exclude large numbers of people from the Jewish camp. Contemporary rabbis took such a step because they knew without doubt that these conversos, nearly all of them, no longer considered themselves as part of the Jewish people and had no intention of ever returning. Understanding the various categories and terms applied to the converts, both in Jewish and Christian sources, is extremely important, and that is why so much attention was given to this (see below, the section on reviews, for more about this).

I had hoped that my discussion of terms used for conversos would end the false notion that *Marrano* means "pig" (1–2), but of course that did not happen and even scholarly articles continue to make this mistake.

Salo Baron inexplicably cited a supposed text of Profiat Duran (a converso who returned to Judaism; he is mentioned elsewhere here, see especially 36–37), who in his anti-Christian polemic *Kelimat ha-goyim* allegedly wrote that Jews called followers of Jesus by the term *Marrano*, which he relates to the idea of altering or twisting the meaning of biblical texts, and thus the

"Gentiles" also call Jews who believe in Jesus by this term.[1] But this statement does *not* appear in Duran's cited work, nor anywhere else as far as I know.

Among the responsa I cited (26), I overlooked another by Nissim Gerundi concerning the reliability of the testimony of a Jewish transgressor. Nissim replied that he is believed only on matters in which he is not suspect of transgression, *unless* he is an "apostate [*meshumad*] to idolatry" (that is, a convert) or publicly desecrates the Sabbath, in which case he is like an "apostate [with respect to] the entire Torah."[2]

Another thesis of the book is that several factors led to the massive conversions of the fifteenth century: despair over the length of the exile with no sign of the coming of the messiah, the extremely successful missionary campaign of Vicente Ferrer that resulted in the conversions of entire Jewish population of several cities, the change in social structure (particularly the formation of a new nobility that lacked the traditional cordial relations with Jews), and the decline of Jewish leadership—rabbis who converted, closing of yeshivot, et cetera. With the enormous increase in the number of conversos (the majority of the Jewish population converted before the end of the century) there came an increasing distrust and finally hatred of the conversos among *some* (a minority, but a powerful one) of the "old Christians." This led to riots and, in Toledo, outright civil war. The attempt to remove conversos from public and religious offices, and to prevent them from ever holding such offices, failed and this led to the determination to reinstitute the Inquisition.

The *alleged* purpose, the justification, for this was the existence of widespread "heresy" among the conversos, for which there was no evidence whatever. The *real* purpose was the eradication of the hated conversos from Spanish society. Obviously false charges were invented to achieve this purpose, and from their side Jews, who hated the conversos as their worst enemies, willingly testified falsely against them. This is not a theoretical hypothesis of my own, but proven fact. In the thousands of Inquisition processes, could there have been a few that were true? Possibly, but that does not mitigate the fact that the vast majority (nearly all) of the charges were false. What is also most obvious seems to have been most overlooked: my statements that even if some converts had intended to be "bad Christians" and had merely converted for convenience, the terror of the Inquisition did not permit them that luxury and they had to become very good Christians indeed just to stay alive. Second, if any had such peculiar "devotion" to Jewish customs (and not very important ones at that), nothing would have prevented them from going somewhere else, across the border to Muslim Granada or to Portugal or to Navarre, and there returning to Judaism (as some few did). Why would they remain as Christians and risk their lives merely to observe such trivial things as lighting lamps on Friday night?

Logic, however, cannot be expected to stand in the face of the continued romantic myth of "crypto-Jews."

Further on the decline of rabbinical leadership in the fifteenth century (see 53–54, and Leadership in the index), note the strong words by Joseph b. Shem Ṭov Ibn Shem Ṭov in the introduction (1451) to his translation of the polemical work of Crescas: "believers have been removed and men of science [learning] have been lost, [and] only those who do not know the law of the God of the land have been left."[3] Two of the most notorious "Jewish leaders" of the late fifteenth century were, of course, the much despised Abraham Seneor and his relative Meir *Melamed* (see index for references). A far less favorable view of Seneor than that expressed by Capsali (see 130) was given by David Messer Leone, also early sixteenth century, who complained about "court rabbis" who had been appointed by the rulers in Spain even though they were not expert in learning or judging the law, nor careful and "fearing sin," such as the "notorious" case of the rabbi in Castile "whose end testified on his beginning" (that is, his conversion showed that he was not a pious Jew).[4]

Rabbi Samuel Valanci of Zamora, who as I have noted is not to be confused with the notorious converso Samuel *Valenci* (54), was accused of having befriended and given money to Rabbi Mayr Araye, son of Rodrigo Contador (or Juan Contado), a Christian of Córdoba who had fled to Granada and converted to Judaism. This is another instance of "old Christians," and some conversos, who went to the Muslim kingdom in order to become Jews.[5]

Among the families of nobility who were of converso descent or that included converso members (93), the *mayordomo* Juan Hurtado de Mendoza was also married to María de Luna, a cousin of Álvaro de Luna and thus a member of a converso family (none of the information on the families listed there is in Netanyahu, incidentally).

Juan de Torquemada wrote, as I observed (98), a not very original work defending the conversos; yet Netanyahu devoted no less than sixty-four pages to it.[6] The remote possibility, at most, of his Jewish ancestry is turned by Netanyahu into making him a "Marrano" and his book a depiction of "Marranos' own view of themselves"; of course, Netanyahu ignored important information concerning Torquemada's actual family (225 here), and his statements at the bottom of 421 are erroneous. (I was gratified to note an Internet message board that discusses the allegations of certain French anti-Semites that the Jews were themselves responsible for the torments of the Inquisition, noting that Torquemada was a converso, in response to which my statement about his actual genealogy was cited as rebuttal. I only regret that Netanyahu was not more careful about this.) According to Netanyahu, Torquemada "became known as Spain's leading Dominican," although he admits he lacks direct evidence for this assertion (422). Nevertheless, of importance is Netanyahu's statement that by calling the opponents of the conversos "Ishmaelites," Torquemada wished to show that "he viewed them not only as foes of the conversos, but also as enemies of *all* Christians" (434, my emphasis). Relying heavily on Netanyahu, yet another summary of Torquemada has recently appeared, including some quotations, in translation, from the work itself.[7]

Somewhat confusing, perhaps, is the statement I made concerning Luis Sánchez (148); what I meant was that this Luis Sánchez was the former Alazar Golluf, and not to be confused, as Tate did, with the other Luis Sánchez who was a government official in Aragón (see 132).

Fernando's Jewish Grandmother

Fernando's Jewish ancestry has been frequently hinted at, or asserted, by various popular writers, and largely ignored by scholars. In the same year in which my book appeared, David Romano, a highly respected Spanish scholar of Jewish history, wrote an article on the subject in which he cited some admittedly unreliable evidence concerning this, except for the statement of Lope de Barrientos and an important new source, to be discussed.[8] Romano, who admits that he trusts no source that is not a document indicating place and date (165 n. 5), therefore rejects even the possibility of this testimony as historical and insists that references in various Jewish encyclopedias must be "corrected." But is this really the case? Lope de Barrientos was an important bishop and generally a reliable source who certainly knew the king and queen well. As I mention in my book, he also asserted that the royal family of Navarre had "Jewish blood" (Romano took no notice of that claim; is it more "reliable" than the claim about Fernando?). This curiously coincides with the statement of a later Jewish chronicler, Elijah Capsali (151 of my book), although it should be noted that with regard to Fernando, that chronicler confused Fadrique Enríquez with his father Alonso as the admiral of Castile. Barrientos would not have dared to make such statements, in writing in an official document, if he were not certain of their veracity.

Romano could not have seen my book, of course, so he is not to be blamed for failing to take into account the important testimony of a Jew from Seville that I cited (150–51). Note that this is not mere hearsay evidence, but a report that he says was circulating "among the nobility." Finally, Romano introduced important new testimony (169), the *Memorial de cosas antiguas* attributed to Diego de Castilla, the contemporary dean of Toledo. This statement unequivocally states that the admiral Alonso Enríquez was the son of "a Jewess of Guadalcanal who was called doña Paloma." Romano is also incorrect in saying that this is "the first (and only?)" mention of the name Paloma (170), since the Jewish writer from Seville also gave her name. In short, far from being conclusively proven false, the claim of Fernando's Jewish descent is clearly proven to be correct, and no encyclopedias need to be changed.

Conversion and Conversos

Evil Philosophy—"Averrosim" Revisited

I discussed the claim of Baer and his followers that philosophy, particularly so-called "Averroism," was responsible for the decline of Jewish religiosity generally and the massive conversions in particular, and showed how false such an idea is (61–65 here). Much remains to be written on this subject, to which I hope to return soon. With regard to what I wrote about Ibn Laḥmis (or Alami, as he was also known), that Baer ignored the fact that he "blamed not the philosophers but the rabbis" for the depressed Jewish condition (61), I find that at least one scholar concurs.[9] I also cited Netanyahu's views on philosophy (63). It is distressing to see that in *Origins of the Inquisition* he has taken a more extreme, and completely wrong, position that, first of all, "Averroism" was a "denial of religion," and that although adherence to it did not "incline" Jewish philosophers to convert, as soon as there was a threat of "mortal danger" they saw such conversion as "an acceptable solution" (211). Again, I must emphasize what I wrote, and which remains unchallenged: *not one single philosopher is known to have converted,* whereas a great many rabbis did.

Abraham Bivagh (ca. 1465), a rabbi and philosopher who lived in Huesca and Zaragoza, and whose own brother Isaac converted in 1489 (as noted here, 160), wrote in defense of philosophy: "and if someone should say that there are scholars who have investigated this art [philosophy] who have converted and are evil men and sinners and of bad character, we reply to this that we also see others who do not investigate and who have no knowledge at all of demonstrative sciences [knowledge], and are called scholars because they immersed themselves in the holy knowledge of the Talmud," even though they did not truly understand the metaphysical statements therein, and they also are evil men who have converted.[10]

A recent article asserts that Isaac Abravanel (who, of course, wrote his commentaries long after he had left Spain) distinguished two groups of conversos, those loyal to the Christian faith and those who were not, but also a third group, the "Averroistic conversos," to whom he refers as "the heretics."[11] The author cites the following passage from Abravanel as proof: "As a consequence of the persecutions, many of our People rejected their religion and this means heresy. Because of the malfeasance of the gentiles and their use of force, many Jews left God and because they left their law and did not adopt another religion [the talmudic scholar Rabbi Yishak] used the word heresy."[12] (The "Rabbi Yishak" alluded to in the author's obscure interjection is Isaac Napaa in *San.* 97a.) Abravanel also wrote in the name of that sage that until all the nations of the world, "and in particular, the wicked kingdom," are afflicted with heresy (the messiah will not come). Abravanel explained: "He is possibly speaking of Rome [all of Christianity] as where the number of heretics will increase, as we see happening today in the kingdom of Spain where the heretics and apostates in their various countries have increased, and where they are burned in the many thousands because of their heresy, and when all the priests and bishops [not archbishops, as translated in the article] of Rome seek to enrich themselves and take bribes, and are not concerned with the fate of their religion for they too are branded with heresy."

In fact, nothing in this statement refers to "Averroists"; rather, the unusual verb *nitfaru* derives from the common Greek loanword *Apiqoros* ("Epicurean, heretic"), and was used by Abravanel to explain "heresy," Jews who abandoned God "since they were Epicureanized and not integrated in any religion," as Netanyahu translated. Netanyahu was also entirely correct that it refers, not to "Averroism," but to the "medley of views and attitudes which had typified Jewish apostates at all times."[13]

Abravanel and Other Jewish Attitudes toward Conversos

What was Abravanel's real position with regard to the conversos and the Expulsion? He suggested that the passages in Obadiah about "redemption" may refer to the generation of Spanish exiles or their descendants "and perhaps were also written about those Jews who no longer practiced their religion as a result of persecutions and destructions, and who stayed in France and Spain in the thousands and constituted large communities there. They will return to worship their God, as some are doing today, and by so doing the prophecy will be fulfilled" (Abravanel, comm. on Obadiah 1.20). By "France" he must refer to Provence, of course. His reference to the "some" who are already returning means those conversos or their descendants who already, after 1492, were beginning to flee Spain and Portugal.

As Netanyahu correctly noted, Abravanel clearly stated that when the conversos (whom he called "Jewish criminals," *poshqei Yisrael;* see Netanyahu, *Marranos,* 79 n. 1 on this term) had been Jews they observed the commandments, "but now in their Gentilehood they do not a thing of this," that is, they do not observe any of the commandments (Abravanel, comm. on Isa. 44.5; cited Netanyahu, *Marranos,* 180). Abravanel claims that they wished to show themselves "imbued with the new faith as real Gentiles of Christian origin" (see 181), a statement reiterated in his commentaries. But ironically, these conversos who "sought, they and their descendants after them, to be like complete Gentiles, it is not so, for always the families of the lands [Christians where they live] will call them Jews, and by the name of Israel will they be known against their will and they will be considered Jews and will be accused of 'Judaizing' (*mityahadim*) in secret, and by fire will they be burned because of this" (Abravanel, comm. on Ezek. 20.32; Netanyahu, *Marranos,* 184). Abravanel also denounced conversos for intermarrying. Yet, as part of his apocalyptic-messianic "vision" of history, he believed that a time would come when the conversos, both *anusim* and *meshumadim,* or their descendants, would begin to perform some commandments secretly and would be condemned for this by the Gentiles. This would cause some of them to flee the lands of their persecution. As Netanyahu quite rightly stated, all of this was to happen "at the end of days," and was not a description of something that Abravanel currently observed.

It is important to recognize that Abravanel used two terms in describing conversos and their descendants: *anusim* and *meshumadim.* The latter term applied primarily, if not exclusively, to those converts who deliberately separated themselves from the Jewish people by willful conversion and total rejection of the commandments and of the Jewish people. *Anusim,* on the other hand, was a term that traditionally referred to compulsory converts, those converted against their will (Netanyahu discussed this term, *Marranos,* 78, and correctly noted that it was almost never used by Jewish writers in Spain to refer to conversos, but nowhere does he remark on the unusual and repeated use of the term by Abravanel). Can we conclude that Abravanel considered the conversos, or even some of them, to be truly *anusim*—forced converts? The answer is undeniably, No. Repeatedly, he makes it clear that the overwhelming majority, if not indeed all, of the conversos are "sinners" and "criminals" who are completely cut off from God and the Jewish people. Only those descendants of conversos who at the "end of days" will finally flee their persecution and go to other lands to live again as Jews can be considered in the category of *anusim.* We must conclude that his use of the term to apply generally to conversos is simply lack of precision, influenced probably by the common usage in Italy, where he lived, and elsewhere in the lands of refuge where the Spanish exiles had gone (compare the statement cited by Netanyahu, *Marranos,* 197). The other possibility, suggested by Netanyahu (195), is that he considered *anusim* to be those conversos who continued to live as Christians out of fear of punishment, although they may not have sincerely believed in Christianity, whereas the *meshumadim* were those who were willful and devout Christians. Nevertheless, of course, both "groups" were complete and observant Christians, if for no other reason than that the Inquisition forced them to be.

There is, indeed, some inconsistency in Abravanel's views expressed in different writings, and at times even within the same commentary. Netanyahu called attention to such inconsistencies (192 ff.), and other examples could be added. Inconsistency, in fact, is found in several of Abravanel's statements on important matters, such as his views on the coming of the messiah and the final "redemption."[14]

Although lacking in the historical knowledge necessary to understand the situation of conversos in Spain, Shaul Regev, who has elsewhere distinguished himself in interpreting philosophical texts, recently wrote an article that requires consideration.[15] However, the usual religious biases appear to have influenced his views. Thus, conversos were all "coerced," but the author offers his own peculiar definition that "only if there is a direct cause-and-effect relationship" between the coercion and conversion, and only if a "connection" with Judaism is maintained, "can the convert be considered a converso" (119). This is, of course, ridiculous, for the term converso *means* "convert," and no distinction can be made in this term as to the motive of the convert, much less alleged "connection" with the Jewish religion. What is most distressing is the *deliberate distortion* of the views of fifteenth-century authors whom he cites. Thus, he mentions a commentary of "R. Joseph ibn Yehieh" that everyone who is circumcised "will ascend to heaven" (119). The author to whom he refers was, in fact, Joseph (b. Solomon) Ibn Yaḥya, not "Yehieh" (Israeli writers notoriously err in transliteration of names, but surely he ought to know that "Yehieh" as a Hebrew name is impossible; he gave no identification for this "Yehieh"). He was born in Portugal (1425), but fled to Spain (!) in 1495 to escape compulsory conversion in Portugal, and then finally to Italy, where he died in 1498. There is absolutely no evidence that the statement about circumcision that Regev cites has anything to do with conversos; surely the mere fact of being circumcised (which all first generation Jewish converts were, of course) does not guarantee a place in heaven.

While correctly noting (he seems to have learned something, at least, from Netanyahu; see above on Abravanel) that Spanish Jewish "scholars, preachers, and Biblical commentators" did not (usually) use the Hebrew term *anū s* for "converso," but rather extremely derogatory terms such as rebels, criminals, et cetera, he insists that "it is quite possible" that first-generation conversos still were secret Jews (119, 120). Anything is, of course, "possible," but the indisputable fact is that very few if any such converts maintained any "Jewish customs," clandestinely or otherwise. Convoluted syntax aside, it is difficult to know what to make out of the statement that "generally speaking, the conversos are referred to in a derogatory manner, while the conversos are seen in a positive light because they were forced to convert," and again, "Jews who are forced to convert and who, nonetheless, benefit from this conversion in various ways are seen in a positive light" by contemporaries, and to be told that "this is the view of Netanyahu as well" (122)! No, it certainly is not, nor does it make any sense. Aside from some instances in 1391 (and even those were rare), there were no "forced converts" in Spain, and every convert of course "benefited" from conversion, socially and sometimes materially.

Worse than this, however, is the distortion of the position of Abravanel, who we are told considered even second and third-generation conversos as "an integral part of the Jewish people" (120), citing out of context his aforementioned commentary on Ezekiel 20:37, that God will bring the uncircumcised sons and grandsons of conversos into the tradition of the covenant; yes, but according to Abravanel this would only happen at "the end of days" and only after they had repented, as we have seen. Regev claims to have found "many examples" of what he calls "positive, apologetic comments" about conversos in the writings of Spanish Jewish scholars (122), and yet he can only cite one, Abravanel, whose ideas he distorts to fit his theory. Not every statement found in a biblical commentary refers necessarily to the conditions in Spain or to the Jews or conversos at that time. Thus, Regev cites a comment by Abravanel about those who "in the course of our period of exile" have, because of persecutions, distanced themselves from their Jewish roots (123). The "course of our exile" does not mean just Spain, but the whole history of Jews in the lands in which they were dispersed, and Abravanel undoubtedly had in mind such things as the persecution of the First Crusade period. Certainly Abravanel, like all Jewish scholars, believed that truly *forced* converts were exempt from performance of commandments (except those that they could perform secretly or without danger to life, an important distinction Regev failed to note), but this does not permit us to conclude that his "attitude towards the *conversos* is not at all negative" (125). We have seen how negative it was; in fact, he considered them to be "sinners" and "criminals" and totally cut off from God and the Jewish people. Of course he believed that at the time of "redemption" those descendants of conversos who truly repented would be "redeemed."

Not content with this misrepresentation of Abravanel's views (again, without once citing Netanyahu, other than the false claim that he shares Regev's peculiar interpretation), he then cites "R. Yitzhak Karo" (that is, Caro, the correct transcription of the name) as one who "similarly emphasizes the loyalty of the *conversos* to Judaism" (128). Regev quotes the first part of a passage from Caro's *Toldot Yiṣḥaq* about those who convert because they can no longer endure suffering and practice idol worship publicly but secretly worship God "because they continue to believe in the principles of the Jewish religion" (actually: "because in their hearts are the principles of the law of Moses").[16] But he conveniently ignored the rest of the statement, which *condemns* these alleged secret Jews, because in their hearts they think that they will live in peace clinging to two religions (but not really believing in either). These converts follow two laws, "the divine law which is in his heart and the law of idolatry in his hand [deeds]," and Caro concludes by saying that God will *absolutely refuse to forgive* such converts. Such selective quotation in support of a theory is unacceptable scholarship. Netanyahu was correct, and Regev wrong (see also my statements, 69 and 72–73, on the true nature of Caro's attitude).

By now, we are not surprised that the same kind of distortion is applied to yet another writer, Abraham Saba, who we are told also "expresses admiration" for those conversos who still observed some Jewish practices (129). Inasmuch as Saba lived not in Spain but Portugal, and wrote after the expulsion of Jews from that country, I did not consider him relevant to a discussion of conversos and the Jews of medieval Spain. But for the real position of Saba, see Netanyahu.[17] Once again Regev is impressed with Saba's argument about circumcision, that if Jews in the exile should be persecuted so that "they are not able or permitted to perform the commandments of Jewish law," they can fulfill the law merely by observing the commandment of circumcision. Yet this situation never applied to the Jews in Spain, who at *no time* were prevented from completely observing their laws or customs. Clearly, Saba did not have in mind the conversos of Spain, whatever else he may have meant. (The remainder of Regev's article deals with writers who lived in the Ottoman Empire, and thus is of no relevance to the topic.)

Converso Polemic and Literature

Jewish responses to converso polemic were rare, and thus it would be important to edit the manuscript of Vidal Benvenist to which I referred (196). There is still no adequate analysis of these various works.

As noted in the preface, scholars continue to ignore the important details in the book about converso writers, chroniclers, and poets, and in general the discussions of such things as converso "religiosity," humanism, et cetera.[18] Netanyahu also said nothing about any of this. Ignored also is the theme of homosexuality as a form of ridicule used by converso poets against each other, and sometimes even satirically by a poet referring to himself (see Homosexuality in my index for this, and in general). Another theme that I touched upon briefly was the praise of Isabel in converso poetry and writing (for example, see here, 171, 179, 187–88). There is now an important article by Gregory B. Kaplan that deals with this theme in more detail.[19] It begins with a historical introduction on the situation of the conversos in the reign of Enrique IV, including reference to Montoro's poem concerning the anti-converso uprising in Carmona in 1474 (see also my book, 102, and on Juan Álvarez Gato, see 174; I am gratified that Kaplan appears to have accepted my suggestion that Gato was probably a converso). The attempted "deification" of Isabel in late-fifteenth-century prose and poetry generally has been remarked upon, but it is perhaps particularly noticeable in converso writing. Kaplan quotes also two poems by Iñigo de Mendoza glorifying the queen "as if she were the Virgin," and also the laudatory poem by Montoro (see my reference to that, 171). Important is Kaplan's conclusion: "The existence of a corpus of converso poetry dating from 1474–1480 in which Isabel is consistently deified, and the lack of contemporary Old Christian examples which portray Isabel in this manner, suggests that the converso poems share a common motivation" (296). This laudatory poetry was only possible, perhaps, before the establishment of the Inquisition in Castile destroyed whatever hopes the conversos may have had for improved status under the "glorious queen."

The Córdoba Uprising

On the 1473 uprising against conversos in Córdoba (103–5), see also Manuel Nieto Cumplido, and on conversos in Córdoba generally Miguel Ladero Quesada.[20] The eminent historian points out that the majority of conversos in the city were middle-class artisans, which incidentally appears to be true of conversos generally. Quesada's brief remarks on the Gibraltar plan are somewhat inaccurate (196–97), and it is regrettable that he did not see what I wrote (compare also Netanyahu, *Origins*, 1122–26, a correct account).

Conversos: New Literature

Remarkably little new work dealing with conversos in medieval Spain has appeared. *Judíos, Sefarditas, Conversos: La expulsión de 1492 y sus consecuencias,* edited by Ángel Alcalá (Valladolid, 1995) is a collection of articles on various topics, of uneven quality, few having to do with the title of the book. Of interest is Julio Valdeón Baruque, "Motivaciones socio-económicas de las fricciones entre viejocristianos, judíos y conversos" (69–88), who revisits the theory that Jews and conversos were viewed as financial "oppressors" (through collection and administration of taxes) in the fourteenth and fifteenth centuries, which allegedly contributed to anti-Jewish feeling and to animosity toward the conversos in the fifteenth century. The theory of Jews and conversos as "oppressors" has also been advocated by Angus Mackay, *La España de la Edad Media: Desde la frontera hasta el imperio 1000–1500,* translated by Salustiano Moreta (Madrid, 1991), who comments on inflation from 1460–1470, with a concurrent rise in taxes for which "presumably" Jews and conversos were blamed (202). Netanyahu also sees this as a (the?) major cause of "Jew hatred" in medieval Spain. On what basis such suppositions rest is never stated by the advocates. Ladero Quesada, among others, has long ago disproved such theories. In the same book in which Valdeón's article appears, Henry Kamen argues *against* the myth of Jewish financial power and the alleged economic deterioration of Spain after the Expulsion (*Judíos, Sefarditas, Conversos,* 420–33), although few historians any longer accept that old claim (see what I wrote about this here, 312–13).

Other articles repeat once again well-worn claims of "crypto-Jewishness" of conversos, or deal with themes that go beyond the Expulsion. There is again a Spanish translation of an article by Netanyahu attacking the late

Claudio Sánchez Albornoz for views that he no longer held in his later years (Netanyahu has thus weighed in against both Américo Castro and Sánchez Albornoz, consistent perhaps with his view that Spain was perpetually "anti-Semitic"). Probably the most useful contribution to this collection is the publication, once again, of the texts of the edicts of Expulsion from Castile and Aragón (*Judíos, Sefarditas, Conversos,* 125–33), both already widely available (for Aragón, the indispensable work of Motis Dolader is essential, see Works Frequently Cited).

On the (probable converso) philosopher Alfonso de la Torre (see here, 187), there is now an important new study, Luis M. Girón-Negrón, *Alfonso de la Torre's Visión Deleytable: Philosophical Rationalism and the Religious Imagination in Fifteenth Century Spain* (Leiden, 2001), of which I have written a review (to appear in *AJS Review* sometime in 2003, apparently).

A new edition of Pablo de Santa María's historical poem (see here, 149) has appeared: *La creación de un discurso historiográfico en el cuatrocientos castellano: Las siete edades del mundo de Pablo de Santa María,* edited by Juan Carlos Conde (Salamanca, 1999); note also *History and Literature in Fifteenth-century Spain: An Edition and Study of Pablo de Santa Maria's Siete edades del mundo,* edited by M. Jean Sconza (Madison, 1991). There is now an edition of *Los sonetos de Francisco de la Torre,* by Soledad Pérez-Abadín Barro (Manchester, 1997). Peculiarly, she has separated the "sonnets" from the rest of his poetry, which is not included. There is also a new edition of the poetic works of Juan de Mena: *Obras completas,* edited by Miguel Ángel Pérez Priego (Barcelona, 1989). Another edition of the poetry of Anton de Montoro has appeared: *Cancionero,* edited by Marcella Ciceri, with introduction and notes by Julio Rodríguez Puértolas (Salamanca, 1990); see here 373 notes 35 and 36 for the editions I used (I regret that I did not then have access to this edition).

The most authoritative edition of all fifteenth-century Spanish poetry, however, is that of Brian Dutton, which was still in preparation for publication when I consulted with him. I have now added to the notes the references to various poems in his published edition.

For some reason, there have been several new studies, of uneven quality, dealing with the Arias Dávila clan: *Arias Dávila: Obispo y mecenas Segovia en el siglo XV,* edited by Ángel Galindo García (Salamanca, 1998); David M. Gitlitz, *Los Arias Dávila de Segovia: Entre la sinagoga y la iglesia* (San Francisco, 1996); and Giorgio Testuzza, "Fuga di un 'Marrano'? Dalla Spagna a Roma: Juan Arias Davila vescovo di Segovia (1461, 1497)," *Rassegna mensile di Israel* 64 (1998): 41–52.

On the *Celestina,* of course, there is constant new research. Important on the "converso origin" is Donald McGrady, "Calisto's Lost Falcon and Its Implications for Dating Act I of the Comedia," in *Letters and Society in Fifteenth-century Spain: Studies Presented to P. E. Russell on his Eightieth Birthday,* edited by Alan Deyermond and Jeremy Lawrance (Llangrannog

[Wales?],1993). And from a different perspective see the important study by Ciriaco Morón Arroyo, *Celestina and Castilian Humanism at the End of the Fifteenth Century* (Binghamton, N.Y., 1994).

The Inquisition Revisited

When the book was written, few authors (aside from the pioneering work of Lea) had considered the origins of the Inquisition in Catalonia, instead focusing on the Inquisition in the fifteenth century and beyond. Sadly, this is still the situation. Only two new books consider Catalonia at all: Miguel Juan Blázquez, *La Inquisición en Cataluña: El tribunal del Santo Oficio de Barcelona, 1487–1820* (Toledo, 1990), and Joan Bada i Elias, *La Inquisició a Catalunya: Segles XIII–XIX* (Barcelona, 1992); but single volumes obviously cannot hope to do justice to such a span of centuries, a problem with almost every book written on the Inquisition. Promising is Miguel Angel Pallarés, *Apocas de la receptoría de la Inquisición en la zona nororiental de Aragón, 1487–1492* (Monzón, 1996), which I regret that I have been unable to see. The same is true of José Enrique Pasamar Lázaro, *Los familiares del Santo Oficio en el distrito inquisitorial de Aragón* (Zaragoza, 1999). For Valencia, in addition to Jordi Ventura, *Inquisició espanyola i cultura renaixentista al País Valencià* (Valencia, 1978), there is Ricardo García Carcel, *Origenes de la inquisición española: El tribunal de Valencia 1478–1530* (Barcelona, 1976), although as noted in my book (398 n. 163) the first tribunal there was in fact in 1461. For Andalucia, worth noting is Juan Gil, *Los conversos y la inquisición sevillana* (Seville, 2000), two volumes, and Juan Antonio Alejandre García, *Palabra de hereje: La inquisición de Sevilla ante el delito de proposiciones* (Seville, 1998). An important general work is José Ramón Rodríguez Besné, *El consejo de la suprema inquisición* (Madrid, 2000). Benzion Netanyahu, *The Origins of the Inquisition in Fifteenth Century Spain* (New York, 1995) will be discussed below in detail; his *Toward the Inquisition: Essays on Jewish and Converso History in Late Medieval Spain* (Ithaca, N.Y., 1997) contains mostly reprints of articles already published elsewhere (some of which have also been translated into Spanish in various conference paper collections, et cetera). Edward Peters, *Inquisition* (New York, 1988), basically an homage to Lea, again attempts to deal with the entire history of the Inquisition through the nineteenth century, in a mere 362 pages. It does, however, have some useful bibliographical references. Most of the work recently published deals, in fact, with the Inquisition after the fifteenth century, including such collections as *Cultural Encounters: The Impact of the Inquisition in Spain and the New World*, edited by Mary Elizabeth Perry and Anne J. Cruz (Berkeley, 1991), while some other books are worthless or nearly so.

Carlos Carrete Parrondo, *El Judaísmo español y la inquisición* (Madrid, 1992), is worth reading. There are some minor errors, such as the incorrect statement that "don Ya'aqov Saddiq" (that is, Jacob Çadique of Uclés) was a converso (56); he was not, but rather a Jew, and he was not the "author" of *Libro de los dichos de sabios,* but the translator (from Catalan) of that work by Jahuda Bonsenyor. But the book contains some interesting new information relating to the "Niño de la Guardia" case (77 ff.). Carrete correctly states that the absolutely false nature of the accusations is obvious; see my discussion of this case (here, 248–51). He might have avoided such inaccuracies as that Abraham Seneor was the "chief rabbi" of Castile (79), following Baer's incorrect characterization. The book includes, incidentally, an appendix of documents that relate almost entirely to Jews, not conversos or the Inquisition, and which are, of course, valuable.

A peculiar and popularized book, *Inquisición. historia crítica* by Ricardo García Carcel and Doris Morengo Martínez (Madrid, 2000), barely touches on the medieval Inquisition at all. It is hard to see what is either "historical" or "critical" in this work, aside from some mild implied criticism of Netanyahu. It also comes dangerously close to something like another "apology" for the Inquisition (192–93). Such books, to say nothing of *Historia de la inquisición Española (1478–1834)* by Jaime Contreras (Madrid, 1997) in eighty pages (!), are of no scholarly value. John Edwards, *The Spanish Inquisition* (Stroud, England, 1999) is another brief general history. His work, including numerous articles, is always interesting, although chiefly on the post-medieval Inquisition (see also my discussion of his "review" of my book below).

For Cuenca, in addition to the article I cited (399 n. 190), see also Carrete, "Dos ejemplos del primitivo criptojudaismo en Cuenca," *El Olivo* 13 (1989): 64–69. On Teruel (see 397 n. 157), I should also mention Manuel Sanchez Moya, "La inquisición de Teruel y sus judaizantes en el siglo XV," *Teruel* 18 (1957): 145–200, an important article; and see below on Inquisition testimony in Teruel.

Pedro de Aranda, a converso and bishop of Calahorra was, as noted (135, 225), charged by Torquemada with heresy and sentenced in Rome in 1498; there is now a new article on this, including also the trial of 230 other conversos there at the same time.[21]

Of the new work on the Inquisition, the best by far is Henry Kamen, *The Spanish Inquisition* (New Haven, 1998), which is a revision of his earlier work on the subject. The origin of the Inquisition, as I observed (203), was in a bull of Pope Alexander III in 1179. Kamen states that the Inquisition was established in Aragón in 1232 (43), and in a footnote asserts that I "mistakenly" dated the foundation to 1179, but that "no such body existed then"; but the papal bull did exactly what I said, and was confirmed at III Lateran.[22] However, that was the origin of the Inquisition against the Albigensian, Cathar, and other Christian heresies; the actual establishment of the Inquisition in Catalonia (not "Aragón") was in 1232, as noted already in my book (205).[23]

Kamen then jumps immediately to the fifteenth-century Castilian Inquisition, providing correct details about its beginnings (on Medina del Campo in 1480, Kamen, 45; see my book, 224). Almost uniquely among recent writers, he rightly emphasizes the falseness of claims of "Judaizing" among the conversos: "on what evidence did the tribunal [the Inquisition] justify its existence? Historians have tended to accept without question the reason given by the Inquisition, namely, that the conversos were judaizing. The fact is that apart from a handful of scattered cases there was no systematic evidence of judaizing" (45). As Kamen rightly notes, even the fiercest enemies of the conversos, such as Alfonso del Espina, "could point only to unsubstantiated rumours and allegations."

Why, then, was there an Inquisition? If it was generally known that the conversos were, in fact, sincere and good Christians, why were they falsely accused, tortured, and burned? Kamen suggests that "there is much to be said" for the argument that Fernando wished to consolidate his power; however, contrary to Netanyahu's thesis, he asserts (rightly) that there is nothing to substantiate the idea that the king sought this by "directing opposition against the converso elite." Indeed, it would be very puzzling were that the case, since that very elite provided the officials who ran his government, particularly in his native kingdom of Aragón-Catalonia (Kamen, 56, also notes that from the beginning of Fernando's reign conversos had supported him).

Kamen never answers his own question, nor does he explain exactly how the king "consolidated his power" through the establishment of the Inquisition. After a digression on the Inquisition in Seville and the legendary account of Diego de Susán (it is surprising that Kamen, who footnotes my work on virtually every page of his early chapters, overlooked what I wrote, 245–46, about that case), he concludes that Fernando took steps in 1481–82 to assert control over the appointment of inquisitors in Aragón, and that his aim was to bring the Inquisition there under his own control "so as to come into line with practice in Castile" (48–49). But how, exactly, did this serve his alleged purpose of consolidating his control in general? Fernando was already independently the ruler of that kingdom, and the reintroduction of the Inquisition there, far from helping consolidate his power, actually resulted in widespread rebellions. The most serious instance of rebellion was in Teruel (Kamen, 51; my book, 257–58), but hardly less serious was the resistance of Barcelona. In 1484 the Council of Deputies of Aragón invited the aid of the duke of Híjar and other nobles in an attempt to stop the imposition of the Inquisition.[24] In 1484 Fernando instructed the cardinal of Gerona to obtain a papal bull authorizing the Inquisition there (Sesma, 81 ff.). On resistance to the Inquisition in Valencia (Kamen, 53) see further details here (261).

In fact, as I have more than once commented, nearly every action concerning the Inquisition, as with most other matters, was taken jointly by Fernando and Isabel. The failure of many scholars to understand this simple fact is astonishing. (One need not be a revisionist feminist historian to wonder if at least part of this is the unwillingness to imagine that Isabel did anything but sit home and knit; those who have carefully studied her career know that, if anything, she was more active and powerful in ruling than Fernando.) It is also important to emphasize, as few writers have, that the fifteenth-century Inquisition was not a "papal" initiative, but was specifically requested by the Spanish rulers (see here, 223; this is not correctly stated, for example, by Carcel and Morengo Martínez, 31). Thus, it is really incorrect to refer to this as a "papal Inquisition," which seeks to transfer blame for its actions to the Roman church (I do not mean to imply that Kamen made such an error).

The basic explanation for the hatred of conversos, by a *minority* of the "old Christian" class, and for the establishment of the Inquisition in the fifteenth century, lies in a combination of religious fanaticism and socioeconomic envy (see above, 106, 222–23, and 262–63). Kamen refers to my "plausible" argument in this regard (61), but adds that it is difficult to accept greed as the only motive; yet I did not, of course, say that it was. Absolutely correct, on the other hand, is his observation there that the oft-repeated claim that (the rulers) sought to impose religious uniformity in the kingdom, and thus established the Inquisition, is false. As Kamen repeatedly says, and Netanyahu failed to appreciate, the rulers never ceased to protect the Jews (paradoxically, this was true even with the issuance of the edict of Expulsion, as we have seen). These are important points, and Kamen's book should be required reading for all who write in the future on the conversos or the Inquisition (his book, like mine, was the object of some unfortunate "reviews" by writers ill-qualified to discuss the subject).

Once unleashed, the Inquisition became a bureaucracy that was no longer under the control of anyone, including the rulers, and whose officials saw an opportunity to attain almost unlimited power while filling their purses with the wealth of "suspect" conversos. At the height of its corruption, the Inquisition began to seize the property of wealthy conversos on general principles, even before they had been accused. The excesses of the Inquisition were not a late development, but began at once with its establishment in Andalucia. Converso officials themselves protested; for example, Fernando de Pulgar (my book, 110, and see 358 n. 66 for the published source, which Kamen, 69, cites from the manuscript, apparently not having seen that I already quoted this and that it has been published, and also omitting the conclusion of the statement; see also here 240–41 for further criticism by Pulgar). Kamen there also borrowed my reference to Juan de Lucena (who was not "apparently" but definitely a converso, see here 180 ff.) and his letter opposing the Inquisition (see 244). Incidentally, on Juan Ramírez Lucena (see 248), there is an article by Máximo Diogo that discusses his family in detail, but adds relatively little of importance to the information already known.[25] Nor did he comment on Paz y Mélia's erroneous identification of him with Juan de Lucena (see here 377 n. 86).

Victims of the Inquisition—Again

Unfortunately, Kamen also did not use the testimony of the official archivist of the Barcelona Inquisition, and so erroneously claimed that "throughout 1488 it burnt only seven victims, and in 1489 only three" (53), having overlooked the specific details I gave from that source as to the actual figures (254), which were considerably more. Kamen objects (329 n. 117) to my criticism (265) of exaggerated figures, in his earlier book, of conversos burned by the Inquisition generally, saying that I "omitted the supporting references" and then concluded that he had not read the references. This is unfair, since what I actually wrote is that he exaggerated in claiming that "tens of thousands" were burned, and yet gave figures that clearly contradict this; the only source that I said (correctly) that he had not used was the memoirs of the official archivist of the Barcelona Inquisition. In any case, my criticism can now be retracted, because he has substantially revised his estimate (Kamen, 58–60). The only other criticism of me (328 n. 66) by this distinguished scholar is that I identified Alonso de Ojeda as head inquisitor of Seville (229), for which Kamen says he finds no evidence; yet if he had consulted my notes (or, indeed, the text itself) he would have seen that the source is the chronicler Bernáldez.

"Victims" also of the Inquisition were the numerous manuscripts, including Bibles, which were burned (see here, 242), a subject almost totally ignored in work on the Inquisition; however, on the burning of books by the Inquisition at Salamanca in 1490, see Lea, *History of the Inquisition in Spain* III, 480 (cited also by Moshé Lazar, introduction to his fine edition of *Biblia Ladina Escorial I. J.3* [Madison, 1995], xi; an edition of Escorial ms. I.i.3, the letter "j" being merely the archaic form of writing "i." Lazar consistently confuses medieval Spanish, which this is, with "Ladino," which is Spanish written in Hebrew letters). Lazar mistakenly wrote that this action, in 1492, "followed" the decree of 1497 which he cited (x–xi). Incidentally, many of the things that Kamen discusses in regard to the Inquisition of the sixteenth or seventeenth centuries have their corresponding elements in the earlier medieval Inquisition (see, for example, books and the subentries and "booksellers and Inquisition" in his index, and compare books and censorship in my index; there is, however, no reference in Kamen to these earlier examples). I have only mentioned aspects of Kamen's book dealing with the medieval Inquisition or conversos; the majority of his book is in fact on the

post-medieval Inquisition. It is a splendid example of careful research and
even more carefully considered conclusions.

Veracity of Inquisition Testimony—Again (see here, 216–21)

Perhaps the most important contribution of Kamen's new book is his agreement that the testimony against accused conversos was false. "The majority
seem to have been dragged before the court on the basis of neighbours' gos-
sip, personal malice, communal prejudice and simple hearsay" (62), and as
he observed, much of the testimony was about things that were alleged to
have happened years before the trial took place. No better statement about
the "believability" of Inquisition testimony can be made than this: "Very
little convincing proof of Jewish belief or practice among the conversos can
be found in the trials" (63). As Kamen notes, the Inquisition officials had
little clear idea of what Jewish practice was, and this is because (as I have
shown) they relied almost entirely on manuals drawn up by ill-informed
people, so that there is a monotonous sameness in the accusations. Kamen
comments also on the numerous abuses of the process, including, of course,
torture; in one case in Jaén a girl of fifteen was locked in a room, stripped
and beaten until she agreed to testify against her own mother (74). Examples
such as this, incidentally, should silence those who claim that the inquisitors
were controlled by regulations that limited torture; while such rules may
have existed, they were routinely violated. Cases of financial gain, such as
the confiscation of converso money and property for the personal enrich-
ment of Inquisition officials, could be listed in tedious detail (Carrete, *Judaísmo español*, 71, provides other examples, although he does not accept
the legitimacy of such accusations).

In an important article on the Inquisition in Teruel (which appeared too
late for inclusion in my book), John Edwards discussed Jewish testimony
against conversos of that community.[26] I have already referred to the frequent instances in which Jews testified, willingly and sometimes under orders, against conversos. It is important to emphasize Edwards's statements
that these charges in the Teruel cases were those found in "the standard list
of offences used by the Inquisition prosecutor" (336), and again, charges
"taken directly from the prosecutor's sheet"; for example, that because Jews
keep certain customs, the accused converso is charged with having kept
those customs on general principles, with no proof (337). While only one of
the accused was actually burned at the stake, the others being tried *in absentia,* the Jewish testimony in these cases did not result in the death of the
other conversos, as often happened. Edwards's article, informative as it is,
contains some errors, such as the lengthy excursus (339–41) on the anonymous Christian polemic *Censura et confutatio libri Talmud,* written probably at the same time as the *Alborayco* discussed in my book; he confused Fita

as the discoverer of this instead of Loeb—it was Loeb who asserted the 1488 date and Fita who followed him. Also, relying on inadequate sources, he wrongly concluded that the Jewish community of Teruel, "like those elsewhere in the Crown of Aragon" (344), suffered severe losses in 1391, wrong on both counts, and contradicted by his statement that according to a letter from the queen to local officials there were threats to the community "but no major outbreaks of violence" (345). Nevertheless, the article adds important additional evidence of Jewish willingness to condemn conversos by repeating the standard false accusations found in the Inquisitors' manuals. Perhaps he has moved away to some degree from the antagonistic approach of his review of my book.

Thus, we have two major scholars of the Inquisition who now agree that the charges in these cases were generally, or always, *false* and that testimony against conversos was tainted.

Carrete, who nevertheless is one of those who continues to maintain the "crypto-Jew" myth of the conversos, also noted instances in Uclés where Jews testified against conversos (*Judaísmo español*, 60), yet he did not comment on the patently deliberate false nature of these accusations. However, he did so comment on the equally false testimony given by Jews in Huete (98). Added to the important examples, as noted in my book, which he earlier provided from the sources he published relating to Soria, we see a growing record of such false testimony.

"Purity of Blood" Revisited

One of the most important developments in the war of certain "old Christians" against the conversos, and which as I have stated was in fact the first manifestation of true anti-Semitism in medieval Spain (in medieval history, for that matter), was the doctrine of "purity of blood" (see especially 229–36 and *limpieza de sangre* in the index). I stated that the first instance of such laws was at Salamanca in 1414 and 1418 (230), but in the Spanish translation of Albert Sicroff, *Los estatutos de limpieza de sangre* (Madrid, 1985), it is claimed that these laws were a later insertion into the texts of the papal bulls (117–19 n. 101), information not in the original French edition of that book. This seems plausible, in fact, since both of these dates appear far too early for such demands.

Incidentally, it should be mentioned that an important source, *Discurso sobre los estatutos de limpieza de sangre* by Agustín Salucio (1523–1601) has been republished in a limited facsimile edition (Cieza, 1975). In spite of many efforts, I was unable to obtain a copy.

Kamen has written an insightful article objecting to the often sensationalist characterization of Spain as "racist" and "obsessed" with the notion of *limpieza*.[27] Yet, again as I have demonstrated, fifteenth-century Spain was in fact very much obsessed with the idea of "purity," which was a kind of catchword for "old Christian" orthodoxy as opposed to (alleged) converso heresy (see "purity" in the index). While certainly agreeing with Kamen that these statutes represented essentially a power struggle, it is hard to concur with his statement that "race or religion was secondary" (20). The whole point of these laws was to exclude any Christian of even remote Jewish descent from public offices, study at certain schools, religious posts, or marriage with "old Christians," purely because of the taint of "Jewish blood." If Kamen is correct, as in general he is, that these restrictions (usually) had no judicial or legislative force, he nevertheless ignored, also in his book, what I wrote about the laws of the Order of Santiago of 1480 (231). These were not theoretical nor merely restricted to members of the order, but had the effect of law for the very considerable territories that it controlled, and prohibited marriage between conversos and "old Christians" down to the fourth generation, even for those who had Jewish ancestors as far back as one hundred years. Incidentally, not only Kamen (see also *Spanish Inquisition*, 235) but also Netanyahu ignored this source, and while casually mentioning the meeting of the Jeronimite Order in 1486 which I there discuss, Netanyahu says nothing about the content of what was discussed at the meeting (*Origins*, 1060).

A new source has come to light, a previously unnoticed order by Nicholas V in 1479 directing that Diego de la Caballería of Toledo, a converso and member of a prominent family, be allowed to join the military Order of Calatrava, which had laws against allowing "descendants of Jews" in the order.[28]

Carrete Parrondo, as cited in Kamen's article (20), is also wrong that in 1486 the king and queen *opposed* the adoption of a statute of *limpieza* by the Jeronimite Order; see the actual statement by Fernando as I cited it (232), which is quite the opposite. While Kamen is perhaps correct with regard to the sixteenth century and beyond, caution is necessary in applying these conclusions to the fifteenth century. In fact, even with regard to the sixteenth century, it seems that Kamen somehow overlooked the evidence I presented about Francisco López de Villalobos (236), and about the statutes of the Jesuits. Poignantly, this converso physician wrote that the descendants of "heretics" (conversos) had already been "purified by fire," in itself a critical comment on the "purity" statutes.

A recent article by John Edwards also contains much erroneous information.[29] For example, (citing Hillgarth, who is responsible for the error) that in Vizcaya province all immigrants of Jewish origin were banned after 1482 (183; for the facts, see my book, 224–25); the incredible statement that "Hebrew scriptures" contain "the idea of a person's sins being visited on his or her descendants, including those still unborn at the time of the original commission" (184, ignoring such famous references as Ezek. 18:2–4, 20; compare Jer. 31:29–30); the erroneous statement that "religious corporations, such as the military orders" did not concern themselves with purity laws until "about 1500" (194; see my book, 231, and above on the Order of Calatrava); that the Toledo cathedral continued to employ Jews as tax-farmers in spite of the laws (195), when in fact those laws never applied to Jews. In spite of these errors, there is interesting material on the post-medieval period.

I must emphasize the importance of what I wrote, that "having put in motion a policy of social and economic discrimination based on the fiction of racial impurity, the enemies of the converso class were now ready to move to the final step, the Inquisition" (236). It was only a small and inevitable step that led this same group of "old Christians," minority though they may have been, to hatred of the Jews whose "impure blood" was after all the alleged cause of the contamination of the "pure" Christian race. That step brought about the expulsion of the Jews. Thus, if Spain of the sixteenth century was not "obsessed" with a "frenzy" about purity, it is only because there were no Jews left to hate, and the descendants of conversos already met the conditions of fourth (or more) generation of "purification."

Expulsions—Some Notes

I had hoped, in vain as it turned out, that attention would be paid to the completely new information provided about the war against Granada and Jewish involvement (279–82). Given the scarcity of sources we have about that in general, at least the important information from contemporary Jewish chroniclers should be significant (281–82). It must be emphasized, in light of suggestions (or dogmatic assertions) by some trying to connect the final expulsion of Jews with the conquest of Granada that there is absolutely no evidence for such a theory. On the contrary, Jews completely supported the campaign, rejoiced publicly at its success, and praised the king and queen.

On the first expulsion of the Jews, in 1483 from Seville, the sources show that this was a proclamation of the Inquisition (283), but Netanyahu distorted this into a decision by "the Kings" (monarchs), and included Córdoba and Jaén in this alleged decision (1088). Some, but by no means all, of the Jews were in fact expelled from Córdoba sometime after 1485. All of the remaining details about the expulsion of Andalucian Jews that I included there are entirely overlooked by Netanyahu, who nevertheless correctly realized the role of the Inquisition in the expulsions from Andalucia and also from the dioceses of Zaragoza and Albarracín (not "Albarrazin"), but it is curious that he characterized Baer's statement about this as "extreme," there is nothing extreme about it, it is correct. Concerning the expulsion from Jerez, I wrote that it was unclear whether it was ever enforced or perhaps revoked

(283). I had not yet seen Lunenfeld's article in which he shows that it was, in fact, permanently revoked due to the intervention of the *corregidor* (administrator of the town), who interceded on behalf of the Jews.[30]

Relevant to the letter of the monarchs to the count of Ribadeo proving that the Inquisitors were responsible for the expulsion order (here, 285), Pilar León Tello quotes a similar letter to the count of Aranda.[31] Note also the contemporary Jewish chronicler Ibn Verga who blamed not the rulers but the Inquisition for the decree (here, 291).[32]

I should also like to call attention to two sections in my book, "Jewish Accounts of the Expulsion" (286–90) and "Contemporary Jewish Attitudes to the Expulsion" (290–93), both of which contain information from Jewish sources that, for the most part, have not been discussed elsewhere (even for Capsali, who has been briefly mentioned by some Spanish writers, no mention has been made of his "version" of the edict of Expulsion). Particularly important is the incisive analysis by Ibn Verga as to the reasons for the Expulsion (291), which, along with the rest of what I wrote there, remains unnoticed by subsequent writers. On the "messianic" aspects of Jewish response (292, 295), see also the index and the notes cited there. The sources cited from Abravanel (292, 293) are also not mentioned by other writers, including even Netanyahu. While calling attention to things, it is important to emphasize what I wrote: "Thus, desire for religious and political unity in Spain was demonstrably *not* the chief cause of the Expulsion" (296). The only *stated* reason for the Expulsion, repeated in letters and in the edict itself, was the alleged "influence" of Jews upon conversos.

Among the various myths concerning the Expulsion, it should now be clear that not all the Jews left in 1492 (some, including the Abravanels, remaining for months or longer), that in spite of the supposed prohibition on taking money with them many did so, and that in general it is incorrect that Jews were forced to leave in abject poverty after losing all their property and possessions.

With respect to expulsions from other countries, it is possible that "Russia" in fact is Rossano, near Calabria in Sicily (294).[33] Expulsions from North Italy took place between 1463 and 1473, and it is possible that "Florence" in Ibn Verga should be "Provence."[34] There were also expulsions from Parma and Milan in 1488 and 1490.

I wrote that there is no document that confirms the old myth that Jews were forbidden to return to Spain on penalty of death. In fact, there is a document that specifically *encouraged* Jews to return (and accept baptism, of course), a letter from the monarchs in November of 1492.[35] I did not go into great detail on the Jews who returned to Spain in the decades following the Expulsion because this was not, of course, the theme of the book.

There is nothing new of importance to add to the literature concerning the Expulsion. Motis Dolader, an outstanding Spanish historian, in addition to his brilliant two-volume study of the expulsion from Aragón (see Works Frequently Cited), has also published *La expulsión de los judíos de Zaragoza*, which I should have mentioned, and an important article that provides new sources for conversions at the time of the Expulsion and after.[36] Finally, mention should be made (solely because of its publication in a prestigious journal) of a peculiar article apparently promising to explain "anomalies" in the text of the Expulsion decree; however, there is nothing here that has not already been known, including some information culled from already published work.[37]

Netanyahu's Book and Mine

As I noted in the Preface to this new edition, when Netanyahu's *Origins of the Inquisition* appeared just after my own book was published I assumed that it would entirely replace my much smaller volume. After all, he had worked on this for many years, even before he published the first edition of his *Marranos* (1966), in the Foreword of which he had promised "a scrutiny of all related testimony [relating to conversos] contained in the non-Hebrew documents." Even if by "documents" he had meant only manuscript or archival sources, this still has not been realized in the new book. Space does not permit reference to all of the sources overlooked, some of which are referred to below; for example, in discussing chronicles of the reign of Juan II (628 ff.), he neglected the *Repertorio* of Escavios (my book, 353 n. 10; to be sure, he sometimes cites excerpts from it contained in secondary works, unaware that the text itself has been edited) and Chacón's *Crónica de Álvaro de Luna*. Similarly, with regard to the chronicles of Enrique IV (904 ff.), he was unaware of the *Cuarta decada* by the converso chronicler Alonso de Palencia, and overlooked information I cited about Alonso (159 and elsewhere). Even editions of Hebrew sources are often overlooked (this was true of his *Marranos* as well).

I am deeply indebted to Netanyahu, and agree far more than not with most of his conclusions in his earlier book, *Marranos of Spain* (the few points of disagreement I have already indicated). This new book, however, praised by some as a "magisterial study" or other laudatory phrases, is a complete disappointment, as other critics also have noted.[38] In another context, the author himself wrote what could, ironically, be used to describe his own book: "it was often hard to tell facts from falsehoods, and it was especially hard for those who preferred to have the falsehoods regarded as facts" (56). Even the title of the book, *Origins of the Inquisition in Fifteenth Century Spain,* is misleading, for the book deals only with Castile, ignoring Aragón-Catalonia almost entirely (this includes also Valencia and Murcia as well). I will pass over what reviewers have noted, and is obvious, the constant use of outdated editions of sources when new and even critical ones exist, and the citation of secondary literature (rare enough in any case) that is also years out of date.

An example of how serious this lack of knowledge of recent scholarship can be concerns the laws of Valladolid (which he calls "Catalina") of 1412 (191 ff.). Netanyahu overlooked, among other things, an important article by Eleazar (or Eliezer as he elsewhere spells it) Gutwirth, in which he discusses "the chronicle" of Juan II (there was more than one, however, he considered only that of Alvar Garcia de Santa María).[39] There he cites the passage concerning the ordinances, although with an error in translation: "The noble queen, following the commands of her conscience, had to proclaim her ordinances throughout all her provinces (*en todo su provincia*)," which should rather be translated "in all of her *province*," singular, referring to the territory under her personal control (380). The entire subject of the ordinances is complex and requires much fuller treatment than either I or Netanyahu have given it. Baer was convinced that the laws were a "monkish plot" to enslave the Jews, although what "monks" were involved he did not say. Netanyahu has merely substituted his own arch-villain Pablo de Santa María for Baer's monks (this is not to say that some of what Netanyahu wrote about the origins of the ordinances, for example, 197–99, is without merit). Neither author has bothered to note that, in fact, the ordinances (some of which were only for the city of Valladolid, while others were, it is true, intended for the whole kingdom) were never enforced. Thus, there was an absolute prohibition on Jews holding any office, including tax collecting, or serving as physicians to Christians. Yet Jews continued everywhere in both capacities, and as usual the royal physicians were also Jews.

Netanyahu's book is marred throughout by the "lachrymose conception of Jewish history" carried to absurd extremes. The first chapter is a summary of what he perceives to be "anti-Semitism" from the Bible to the Middle Ages. The first part of the second chapter deals with Visigothic Spain (an incomplete and often erroneous survey; see my *Jews, Visigoths & Muslims in Medieval Spain,* not cited by Netanyahu, of course, who probably had completed his book before this was published). The second part of the chapter contains the most incredible misstatements of fact: no Jews lived in northern Spain after the Muslim conquest, nor did they live in any of the territories reconquered from Muslims in the eighth and ninth centuries (54, both claims, of course, are false). Indeed, the only Jews Netanyahu knows about are allegedly "small groups as migrants" from northern Europe (of course, since according to him there were no Jews already living in Spain).

False also is the claim that Jews "negotiated" their settlement in Spain, which was a land of the kings, princes, and grandees, "who, the Jews believed, owned the land and all its assets to dispose of in any way they wished" (66). The Jews, of course, believed no such thing, for it is completely untrue. The country "belonged" to the kings only in a theoretical manner, for most of the land was owned by towns, monasteries, various overlords and individuals. Jews themselves were free and independent landowners, already in this early period. Also false is the assertion that "Christian Spaniards" restricted, if not "totally cut off," their economic ties with Jews (67). Not even Baer made such an absurd claim. Finally, it is false that "most Jews" who engaged in moneylending (at least to the end of the fourteenth century) were of the "lower classes," although in the last paragraph he contradicts himself and says "lower middle class," which also ignores numerous published studies (69). There were no "professional" Jewish moneylenders, but Jews of all classes loaned money, either on a regular or at least occasional basis (they also borrowed money from Christians and Muslims).

There are many other flaws in the opening chapters. Here we meet for the first time an error that, astonishingly, not one single reviewer or critic of Netanyahu has remarked upon: the idea of "kingship by divine right" in medieval Spain, found throughout the book; for example, "since Alfonso X, Castile's kings had endeavored to transform their rule into a government by divine right" (1023). There simply was no such a thing in the medieval period, and especially not in Spain, where kings were carefully held in check by the parliament.[40] As de Jouvenel observed, the misconception of a medieval arbitrary and divine authority is "grossly inaccurate" but "deeply imbedded" in the minds of those who seek to use it for their own purposes in *rewriting history*. Later, Netanyahu discusses the statement of Álvaro de Luna in 1445 at the *Cortes* of Olmedo, and quotes Carlyle that this was an "emphatic" statement of the doctrine of divine right (594–95); however, Carlyle was overly enthusiastic about a "doctrine" that still did not exist in law or practice. That John of Salisbury or other theorists may have argued that kings rule by divine grace does not make this an accepted doctrine, nor one that had any legal force. Netanyahu's repeated reference to an alleged "absolutism" of the Spanish rulers is part of his even more erroneous notion that all of them were "anti-Semitic" and oppressed the Jews.

Since Netanyahu's book purports to deal only with the "origins" of the Inquisition in the fifteenth century, it would be unfair to complain that he totally ignores information, presented in my book, about the earlier Inquisition in Aragón-Catalonia, or conversions in the thirteenth and fourteenth centuries (nevertheless, he does discuss some of the latter, again with errors). However, even with regard to the fifteenth century, my statement about the change in attitude toward Jews and conversos being due in large measure to the "new nobility" of the cities finds no counterpart in his book (not surprising, given his lack of utilization of recent studies), nor does the information about Juan Pacheco and the other nobles who demanded restrictions and the imposition of an Inquisition in Castile in 1465 (here, 51).[41]

In spite of the importance of the defense of the conversos by Lope de Barrientos, and the considerable space devoted to this by Netanyahu (610–18), he failed to include *any* of the things that I mentioned (93), and incorrectly states that what Barrientos discussed "was not a Jewish issue, or one that concerned the conversos only," and that the words "Jews" or converts "are not even mentioned in this connection" (614). That this is false is quite evident from what I wrote (92–93). He also overlooked information about the converso archbishop of Toledo, that there were many other prelates of converso origin, and the other information from Fernan Díaz mentioned there (my book, 94, 95). To my statement that the manuscript by Alfonso González de Toledo, addressed to Barrientos (96), has been overlooked by all, we may now add also Netanyahu.

Netanyahu's account of the anti-converso rebellion in Ciudad Real in June (not July) of 1449 is also wrong (330–31; see 100–101 of my book), primarily due to the fact that he apparently relied upon the editor's description of the documentary source rather than the source itself (see 356 n. 43 where I give citations of both).

Even more surprisingly, *all* of the information contained in my section "Response: The Inquisition, More Riots" (101–4) is missing in Netanyahu's book; thus, his statement that the sources available "are extremely curt and deficient" is pointless (798), since he overlooked the most important ones. Concerning the assassination of Miguel Lucas de Iranzo, the *condestable mayor* of Castile, I cited a letter written by him which, as noted, is "of great importance" about the conversos and the riots (104). Netanyahu nowhere mentions this. Ignored also is the establishment of the *Hermandad* ("brotherhood") in Seville, and the fear of the conversos that it was intended to harm them, and so all the rest of the information on that page (107). The completion of the history of Alfonso de Palencia, with its important material on the anti-converso activity in Toledo in 1478 (108), is unknown to Netanyahu. Fernando de Pulgar, the converso secretary of Isabel, is apparently not considered important enough to merit full discussion of his reaction to the treatment of conversos (903; compare 109 in my book). Since he did not know that Pulgar's letters were long ago published, he completely overlooked the first letter to Mendoza, and he also ignored the rebuttal to Pulgar (my book, 110), although it was discussed by Cantera, whom Netanyahu sometimes read, and indeed he overlooked all of the material which I cited (110–11), and most of what follows. Netanyahu claims that Pulgar wrote the speech of Gómez Manrique (900 and 1300 n. 17), but this is of course incorrect (see 113–14 in my book), and as usual Netanyahu has ignored important studies.

Since his book is not really about conversos (although, in fact, he devotes pages to that topic), it is perhaps understandable that he has little if anything about the Arias Dávila family (my book, 120–24), barely mentioning Diego

Arias Dávila (716 and a totally false statement on 1024). He does not mention Pedrarias Dávila at all (my book, 121), and confuses the name Pedrarias with Pedro Arias, the son of Diego (787). Of course, most of the other information about important conversos, the Santa María family, and so on, is missing in Netanyahu's book, although he does write extensively about Pablo (Paul of Burgos, as he calls him), again with some erroneous details. To begin with, he was not "chief rabbi of Burgos" before his conversion, as Netanyahu claims (168), an error traceable to his earliest biographer (see what I wrote about Pablo, 136–44). Equally erroneous is the assertion that in the second half of the fourteenth century "theological disputations between Jews and Christians *abounded* in Spain, especially in Castile" (there was *one*, in Ávila, and another in Pamplona, in Navarre).

Netanyahu continues with his "reconstruction" of the conversion of Pablo, according to which he was somehow magically aware of the impending 1391 attacks and "called a general meeting" of the Jews of Burgos at which he suggested that conversion was the only way to escape their hopeless situation (170). Having gone thus far with his "conjecture," or fantasy, it is an easy step to add that "most notables" of the Jewish community agreed with Pablo and decided to convert (171). There is, of course, no basis whatever for such "conjecture," and nothing of the kind happened. In fact, as I noted, the Jewish community of Burgos enjoyed special privileges from the king precisely in the years just before Pablo's conversion, and its members were hardly in despair over their status (138–39); second, Pablo's conversion certainly took place before the attacks in 1391 and was solely the result of his own conviction of the truth of the Christian religion.

It is surprising, however, that Netanyahu barely mentions Hernando de Talavera (see here, 152–54 and index), whose importance is obvious (on 1024 he mentions Talavera's treatise, without apparently having bothered to read it; Kamen also mentions him only briefly, 70–71). Thus, it is perhaps not surprising that Netanyahu overlooked the statement by Alonso de Palencia that the rulers took the drastic step of segregating Jews and Muslims from Christians chiefly on the advice of Talavera (see here, 274). There are now some important new studies on Talavera.[42] Nor does Netanyahu mention Pablo de Heredia, a definite converso and polemicist (here, 197). Netanyahu does, however, devote pages to Alonso de Palencia, yet he overlooked the sources I discussed (159). But Netanyahu's book is nothing if not verbose; thus, he devotes six pages to Diego de Valera's treatise on nobility (578–83), the same information that I managed to convey in less than two pages (163–64), but he failed to mention the important biographical background I discussed (160) or the important letter to Fernando and Isabel. Similarly, in a later discussion of Diego, Netanyahu overlooked his criticism of Enrique IV for the heresy then rampant in the kingdom (897–99; 226 of my book). However, I also overlooked, as he did, another letter of Diego to the king in which he gave several reasons for the discontent in the reign, one of which (no. 5) is the lack of justice felt by "all the peoples." Gregory Kaplan is undoubtedly correct in seeing this as an allusion to the uprisings against conversos in Carmona in 1462 and Enrique's failure to punish those responsible.[43]

Coming at last to the "origins" of the Inquisition in the fifteenth century (book 4, 923 ff.), which is the alleged theme of the book, we find that he managed to ignore the interesting account of the Jews of Aragón-Catalonia having paid the tuition for the Inquisitor General to advance his studies (my book, 215–16). In his very inadequate discussion of the important revision by Pulgar of his *Crónica*, Netanyahu altogether missed the crucial statement in the first version that relatives of condemned conversos complained to the king and queen that the Inquisition acted unjustly (902–3; bottom of 227 in my book). His discussion of the Jeronimite Order and the Inquisition is also inadequate, overlooking everything mentioned here (231–32). The segregation of Jews and conversos in Guadalajara and Alcalá is not mentioned (233). Most amazingly, perhaps, given its importance and the fact that Baer and Beinart both referred to him (however incorrectly), there is no mention of the events involving Samuel Valenci (234), or the meeting of the council of the Jeronimites in 1496 to consider the pope's letter with regard to "purity of blood."

Netanyahu blames the establishment of the Inquisition on Fernando, "aided," perhaps by his "spirited wife" (at least she is no longer the "bigoted queen"), although it was really "the racists" who permeated Spanish society who are to blame (1005). But Fernando not only knew this, he supported it, for "he realized that . . . they were giving vent not only to their own feelings, but also to those of *large masses of Spaniards*" (1017, my emphasis). There is no evidence to support such a false generalization, of course. This is true of the statements on the following pages; throughout the book, in fact, the reader is required to accept the most audacious statements simply on Netanyahu's authority. In fact, the reader can well skip most of chapter 1 in this section, "The Major Causes of the Inquisition," which contains grossly inadequate information or completely distorted ideas. Chapter 2 further outlines the author's theories of "racism," to be discussed below, again without substantiating support, and may safely be ignored.

Much of the other information concerning the Inquisition in Castile is missing, and it goes without saying that so is all, or nearly all, of the information relating to the Inquisition in Aragón-Catalonia (252–60 here). Only with regard to the assassination of the Inquisitor Arbués does Netanyahu offer some insights (much better than those of his disciple Alcalá), but his assumption that *all* of the accusations against the conversos were made up, apparently at the instigation of the king, no less, is absurd (1164 ff.; 258–59 here). As I observed, "no doubt some conversos were involved in the plot, but we cannot ignore the authoritative testimony of Pulgar that 'old Christians' were also involved" (259). However, that the king would have conspired to have his own most important officials, conversos all, killed on invented charges is not worth considering.

In my section "Conclusions: Lessons of the Inquisition" (266–70), I quoted the identical text by Isaac 'Arama that Netanyahu also cited (929), with nearly an identical translation. He overlooked the statement by Joseph Ibn ṣadiq that I quoted, however, that a third (of the conversos) has been consumed by fire, a third tries to hide, and the rest live in fear and terror, the *only reference* to the Inquisition by a contemporary Jewish scholar in Spain ('Arama, of course, was nearly a century earlier).

In his "Sidelights and Afterthoughts," he discusses one version of the apocryphal letters from Constantinople to the Jews of Spain (1065–66), ignoring the other sources (295 here). Again, the lack of awareness of source material concerning these letters, let alone secondary studies, is astonishing (compare 1311 n. 2 of his book with 404–5, notes 85, 87 of my book).

"Racism," Medieval Anti-Semitism, and Nazi Germany

Salo Baron coined the memorable phrase "lachrymose conception of Jewish history" to describe the all too prevalent attitude of many Jewish writers, according to which the entire history of Jewish-Christian relations has been marred by "anti-Semitism" and persecution. This was to a great extent the attitude already of the first modern Jewish historian, Heinrich Graetz in the nineteenth century. Just as it appeared that a more rational approach, coupled with objective and solid historical research, was beginning to emerge in the twentieth century, a new wave of lachrymose sentiment has become popular, beginning in this country with Gavin Langmuir and taken up by others. Most recently, Robert Chazan, *Medieval Stereotypes and Modern Antisemitism* (Berkeley, 1997) argues that the entire medieval Christian attitude, from at least the twelfth century or earlier, was "anti-Semitic," and that if this did not cause modern racial anti-Semitism, it laid the groundwork for it. The careful distinction that other scholars (myself included), Jewish as well as Christian, have sought to make between anti-Jewish sentiment and racial anti-Semitism is dismissed outright by Chazan.[44]

The predominant contemporary Jewish misconception of perpetual Christian "anti-Semitism" has been fostered also by Zionist ideology, according to which a normal existence of Jews under Christian domination is impossible. It is little realized, especially among Spanish historians, the extent to which Baer's attitudes, for example, were shaped by this ideology. Baer did not undertake to write on the history of the Jews in Spain from any great admiration for Spain, nor even yet to relate dispassionately the intricacies of that history over a period of centuries, but rather to dispel the commonly perceived notion that Jewish history in Spain was "different" from that of, say, medieval Germany or France. He was determined to show that, on the contrary, Jews in Spain suffered "anti-Semitism" and persecution no less than in other Christian countries. If he needed to distort and even deliberately misinterpret historical fact in order to accomplish this goal, the end certainly justified the means. Normalization of Jewish life, much less living in harmonious cooperation, under Christians in the *galut*, the "Exile," was absolutely unthinkable for this Orthodox and Zionist ideologue.

Baer's followers, Beinart and Netanyahu, and more recent successors, have continued this mythology. Some other Israeli writers are equally convinced of the "anti-Semitic" nature of Christian-Jewish relations throughout history, and especially in Spain. Thus, in a recent article Alisa Meyuhas Ginio, could write that in medieval Spain "Old Christian society rejected the New Christians" and "extended their traditional distrust and enmity towards the Jews to their descendants—the *judeoconversos*."[45] It is demonstrably false that all (or even the majority) of "old Christian society" were opposed to conversos, much less to Jews. Continuing, this author asserts that a "norm" of fifteenth-century Spain was "the condemnation of Judaism and its adherents as enemies of the Christian faith" (131). Far from being a "norm," such an idea was, as I have demonstrated, extremely rare. With increasing assuredness as the article progresses, she then states categorically that from the mid-fifteenth century "social rejection of the New Christians became *unanimous*" (134, my emphasis). Words do have meaning, and writers need to think about what they are saying (the remainder of the article rehashes well-known concepts that do not need to be "rediscovered").

Netanyahu is the most representative, and yet the most extreme, example of this attitude. His massive tome begins with a lengthy discourse on the "anti-Semitism" of medieval Spain. We are told (incorrectly) that Jews in the eighth and ninth centuries did not live in the reconquered parts of Christian Spain, but were either "killed" by Christians or fled south to Muslim territories (*Origins*, 54). Even more radically, he states that "no Jew could live in Christian Spain after the Moslem conquest" (56). Both of these statements are simply false. We then hear that Jews were "terrified" even in eleventh-century Christian Spain, when there were "massacres" and "pogroms." One may be forgiven for wondering why Jews lived in Spain at all, if this were so. In fact, of course, there were neither "massacres" nor "pogroms" in Christian Spain at the time, and the Jews benefited equally with the Christians from the liberal policies of local laws that recognized their rights, laws that were merely confirmed by local lords and by the kings. They, like Christians, owned land and participated fully in the economy of medieval Spain. Later in the medieval period, according to Netanyahu, the Jewish revenue agents were treated as "objects of massive exploitation" by the king (71). Far from being so exploited, of course, the Jewish tax farmers and treasury officials enjoyed a wealthy lifestyle and privileged status in society.

But it is the fourteenth century that particularly saw the ultimate persecution of Jews, according to Netanyahu. Not only did Pedro I and Enrique II unleash horrible "excesses" against the Jews (the latter "showing the Spaniards for the first time how Jews may be butchered by the hundreds in the cities," 125), but the "pogroms" of 1391 caused the greatest losses to Jews in the entire European Middle Ages (127). Those familiar with the devastating massacres of Jews in Germany and Austria in the fourteenth century, for instance, will be surprised at this statement. We are told, however, the policy of "Jew hatred" needed an ideology in order to be carried out, and that ideology was "the (sic) deicide": "it was thus against the Jews as killers of Christ that the war against Spanish Jewry was launched" (128). Later, he asserts (again, with no evidence) that the entire Jewish people was blamed for "the crime of the Crucifixion," but that the converso bishop Alonso de Cartagena absolved them of this and blamed only "a few" (548–49); even this is incorrect (see what I wrote about this, 195). The fact is, contrary to the hysterical claims of some Jewish authors, that in the whole history of medieval Christian polemic or exegesis, less than a dozen references are to be found that accuse the Jews of killing Christ. Thus, whatever "war" was supposedly launched against Jews, this was not the ideology on which it would have been based.

The half-mad Ferrant Martínez, an archdeacon (not priest, as Netanyahu describes him), supposedly saw Enrique as "embarked on a policy of extermination which alone, he thought, could rid Spain of its Jews," but he was soon disappointed by the inexplicable "reversal" of Enrique's policy, and this "bitter disappointment was shared by the *majority* of the common people" (129, my emphasis). We then are told that the "Jew hatred" of Martínez and of the masses who followed him was the product of "a long social evolution" and that this is "of course unquestionable" (147). Not only is this very much questionable, it is an unproven and totally unsupported allegation. Indeed, we have no knowledge of what the "majority" of the common people, in medieval Spain or any other country, thought about anything. Other outrageously false statements are passed off as fact, such as the claim that the "notables" of the Jewish community of Burgos joined in a mass conversion in July of 1391 (171), for which there is not a scrap of evidence (some Jews in Burgos did, it is true, convert, but there was hardly a mass conversion of Jewish "notables").

According to Netanyahu, by 1410 the Christians of the cities, as well as the peasants and people of the countryside, were "seething with hatred for the Jews" (180), which enabled Benedict XIII to unleash his campaign for conversion "and draw the *Christian world* to his side" (182, my emphasis).

The antipope's policy, we learn, "would endear him to the *great majority* of the people" (183, again, my emphasis). The reader will look in vain for footnotes to offer any substantiation for these astounding statements, since, of course, there is no evidence for any of this. Thus, we are not surprised upon reaching Netanyahu's sweeping conclusion that "parallel to the Spanish tradition of Jew hatred there ran a tradition of hatred for Jewish converts" (266). This is no casual remark, but one which the author has obviously considered carefully, as indicated also by the fact that he put the entire statement in italics for emphasis. However, few careful historians would agree with this view. Nothing in the history of Christian-Jewish relations in medieval Spain provides any support for talking of a "tradition," no less, of "Jew hatred." On the contrary, there is overwhelming documentation that proves the opposite. Nor is it even correct to mention such a "tradition" of hatred of conversos. As I have indicated, and most Spanish historians concur, the animosity toward conversos, which in any event was only in the fifteenth century, was limited to a small minority of the population. Even the sources discussed by Netanyahu demonstrate this (the incident to which he refers in Burgos in 1392, where *some people* persecuted new converts hardly justifies talk of a "tradition" of animosity).

But this is not all; Spanish society of the fifteenth century (perhaps, indeed, of the whole medieval period) was "sick with an all-pervading hatred for the Jews and prepared to believe any calumny about them" (827). In his lengthy concluding "Sidelights and Afterthoughts," Netanyahu repeatedly returns to this theme, for example, the "boundless hatred that filled the thinking of the Spanish racists" (1052).

It would be superfluous and require more space than is possible here to disprove the absurd idea that Spain, in the fifteenth or any other century, was "sick with an all-pervading hatred for the Jews." I have already presented much evidence to prove the contrary (nowhere, of course, does Netanyahu substantiate his statement with any source, since there is none). He chose to ignore, for example, Ibn Verga (whom, in fact, he never cites), whose clear statement that only the Dominicans and Franciscans were preaching against Jews "but by the other sects of the Christians the Jews were honored . . . and *greatly loved by them,* as is known to the elders [of the Jews] of Spain" (my book, 290; and note there Yerushalmi's great astonishment that in general there is no mention by Ibn Verga of any "fundamental change" in the attitude of the monarchs toward the Jews; there is no mention of it because there was no such "change"). Unlike Netanyahu and Yerushalmi, Ibn Verga— who actually lived in fifteenth-century Spain—did not consider Isabel a "bigoted queen." How little "hatred for Jews" pervaded Spain may be seen in the cases of Jewish-Christian cooperation which I mentioned at the very time of the Expulsion (for example, 309).

There is overwhelming evidence against the idea that "anti-Semitism" was prevalent in Spain even at the end of the fifteenth century. Ignored by Netanyahu is the example I cited of Fernando and Isabel's letter to Bilbao in 1490, noting that the Jews are "our natural subjects, buy and sell and contract quietly and peacefully" and are under royal protection (275). These are the very words, incidentally ("quietly and peacefully") which Abravanel later used to describe the *general situation* of Jews in Spain (introduction to his commentary on Daniel). As I noted, while the situation of cordial relations between Jews and Christians remained generally unchanged, there were signs of growing tensions in some communities (278). I also observed that church officials, with the exception of converso bishops and polemicists, for the most part did not share in the anti-Jewish feeling or acts that began to manifest themselves. Another important example that indicates how little "racism" or "anti-Semitism" existed in fifteenth-century Spain is the fact that Jews who were worth more than 30,000 *mrs.* were required to own horses and arms, just as Christians of the same status. While Netanyahu could not, of course, have seen what I wrote about that (280), he did see the source I cited there, yet made no comment on this.

There are many additional examples that could be mentioned; for instance, the repeated intervention of the *corregidores* (town administrators) on behalf of Jews in the late fifteenth century.[46]

I am not alone in my distress at Netanyahu's extreme position. Kamen, a cogent and careful scholar of the entire history of religious intolerance, correctly observed, discussing the medieval converso situation as background to the later period, that "it is also clear that in the greater part of [fifteenth-century] Spain there was practically no conscious separation between" the groups of "old" and "new" Christians, and the conflicts between them "were motivated more by political than religious questions," specifically, "in order to benefit an elite which desired to protect its monopoly of power and influence."[47]

Yet even Kamen, in an earlier article, apparently accepted the common Jewish misunderstanding about "anti-Semitism" in Spain: "As the western region with the longest experience of Jewish culture, *Iberia breathed anti-semitism through every pore.* It was a common, vulgar response to almost any communal or personal friction."[48] This is simply incorrect. On the contrary, it is remarkable that in most incidents of "communal or personal friction" between Jews and Christians there is little or no indication of any *generalized* anti-Jewish sentiment or rhetoric. The conflicts were, in fact, "communal" or "personal," and had little to do with the Jewishness of the opponent (exceptions, of course, were the attacks of 1391 and some isolated incidents in the fifteenth century). It is possible, however, in the context of the article, that Kamen referred to the sixteenth century, and by "anti-Semitism" he meant the continued hatred of and attacks against descendants of Jewish converts. More correct is his statement that "the existence and growth of discrimination should not be misconstrued as a triumph of racialism in Spain" (*Spanish Inquisition*, 235).

That the *Inquisition* was truly anti-Semitic, in the full technical modern meaning of that term, is, of course, undeniable (see what I wrote about this throughout, but especially 314–15). Even in this regard, however, it is equally undeniable that—as I wrote (315), and no less an authority than Kamen concurred with my statement (*Spanish Inquisition*, 26)—the king and queen had no "master plan" for the unification of the faith in Spain; therefore, to use that as an "explanation" for the Expulsion is as false as using a theory of alleged "anti-Semitism" throughout medieval Spain. As Kamen rightly observed there, "The king and queen were neither personally nor in their politics anti-Jewish." Once unleashed, the forces of the Inquisition brought about the expulsion of the Jews, but the expressly stated reason for this was not "anti-Semitism" but the claim (however false) that Jews were influencing conversos in daily contact.

Spanish "Anti-Semitism" and Nazi Germany

As with several other writers, Netanyahu equates what happened in medieval Spain with Nazi Germany; however, he fails to make the distinction that the racial "purity of blood" statutes, few in number as they were, were directed only at conversos and not Jews. Indeed, he says: "thus, in Germany as in Spain four centuries earlier, racial theory largely replaced religious doctrine in justifying discrimination against *the Jews*" (1053, my emphasis). There was no instance of the *limpieza* doctrine being used in any attempt at discrimination against Jews in medieval Spain, only conversos. But that does not deter Netanyahu from writing that both "Spanish antisemitism" and German Jew-hatred "produced *race* theories about the Jewish *persons* aimed at their annihilation" (1085, emphasis in the text). Thus, it is no longer the conversos alone against whom racial theories were directed, but also (or even primarily) Jews, and the aims of the Spanish "antiSemites" and the Nazis was the same: annihilation of the Jews. The perplexed historian will wonder what evidence there is of any effort, or plan, ever to "annihilate" the Jews of Spain, but as we have seen, for Netanyahu this was the constant aim of medieval rulers, especially Pedro I and Enrique II, and of Benedict XIII, and even of some conversos, such as Pablo de Santa María. This smearing of an entire nation, Spain, by false association with Nazi Germany is unconscionable.

Others have fallen into the same error, without the excesses of Netanyahu's rhetoric. Thus, the American scholar Yosef Hayim Yerushalmi wrote that the same general conditions applied to the "two colonies" (!) of Jews, medieval Spanish and modern German: exclusion of students from colleges or student organizations, books listing names of aristocratic families of Jewish origin, similar laws of racial "impurity," and so on. Having correctly remarked that German racial anti-Semitism developed independently of that in medieval Spain, he nevertheless concluded that Jews in both "societies" suffered the same history: an early period of relative acceptance marked by "great assimilation" and access to important civic and economic positions, which aroused increasing resentment and "racial hatred," leading ultimately to racial discrimination that eventually became institutionalized in law. Yerushalmi qualified his comparison only with the observation that "the Inquisition . . . was not the Gestapo; the Spanish and Portuguese anti-Semites were not the Nazis. There is a question of genocide here. The most virulent theoreticians of *limpieza* never preached the physical extermination of the new Christians."[49] That, of course, is also false; the adherents of the theory of the racial impurity of conversos certainly did envision their "physical extermination," which became the goal of the Inquisition.

The essential point which both Yerushalmi and Netanyahu failed to realize, however, is that the *limpieza* doctrine in fifteenth-century Spain (continuing, of course, for centuries after the Expulsion) was directed *only* at conversos and not at Jews. The only connection between Jews and conversos was the repeated, and essentially false, accusation that Jews were "constantly" conversing with and thus perhaps influencing the new converts. This was the charge that Torquemada used to convince the monarchs that expulsion of the Jews was the only solution. This solution, it needs to be stressed, was not "anti-Semitism" but pragmatism. No other accusations were made against Jews, no "undesirable" characteristics mentioned, other than the alleged influence on conversos. As we have seen, normal daily life for the Jews went unchanged and normal cordial relations with their Christian neighbors continued as it always had right up to the very eve of the Expulsion. The effort to characterize medieval Spain, the most tolerant society in which Jews found themselves, as "anti-Semitic" is not only patently false but grotesque and malicious.

Eliezer Schweid, an Israeli Zionist essayist, has also written an oft-printed article on the subject.[50] The opening part of this long essay has some interesting historical information on the comparison of the experience of the Jews of Germany with the Spanish expulsion, although ignoring the literary aspects discussed below. Leo Baeck, rabbi of Berlin and imprisoned in the Theresienstadt concentration camp by the Nazis, was one of those who made the comparison, and also the famous statement that "the Jewish people have ancient eyes" (a long memory). Promising is Schweid's attempt to see beyond the rhetoric, for instance, his observation that the Expulsion did not fundamentally alter the status of the Jewish people under Christian or Muslim rule, and in this respect differed from the Holocaust (*Wrestling Until Daybreak*, 301).

Correctly, he also noted that the Expulsion "constituted a shattering crisis of leadership" and that Jewish leaders had not adequately foreseen what was happening (302).

He abandons these sound observations, however, and proceeds to demonstrate the similarities with the Holocaust, or at least with the Nazi treatment of Jews. Notable are his remarks that "hatred of the Jews assumed a new dimension in Spain, bearing some similarity to racial anti-Semitism," explaining that the "stubbornness" of the conversos "to remain Jews in secret" was responsible for the "racial metamorphosis" of Spanish anti-Semitism (from religious "hatred" to racial; 304–5). Netanyahu would no doubt approve. Another alleged similarity is that "because of the number of Jews in Spain, the extent of their integration, and their failure to assimilate" they, like the German Jews, became an "overly burdensome" problem to the people and rulers. How curious: Yerushalmi blamed "anti-Semitism" in Spain on the fact, at least in part, that Jews *did* assimilate, and Schweid on the fact that they did *not*. Fortunately, the author is on surer ground when he differentiates the two experiences, the Expulsion and the Holocaust, on the basis of subsequent Jewish response, noting that while there was some Jewish response to the Expulsion, it was muted, religious, and tradition-oriented, whereas the response to the Holocaust has been more "organizational" than individual, lacking in the emotional or religious sentiment of the earlier response (310). If, indeed, the "voice of the people itself" is not heard in response to the Holocaust (311), I might add that this is because Jewish cultural and sociopolitical life in general is almost entirely "organizational" today, worked out in large impersonal bodies claiming to "represent" the Jewish people, and to this should be added an appalling lack of education, even with respect to recent Jewish history, much less traditional culture and values.

The false comparison of the treatment of Jews by the Nazis and medieval Spain has a long history in Jewish popular writing: plays, fiction, and journalism.[51] Although having its origins in popular misconceptions dating back centuries, the myth served to enforce Zionist propaganda even prior to the Holocaust.[52]

The real differences between Spain and Nazi Germany are obvious to anyone who knows anything about medieval Spain: Jews were not only protected but granted full equal rights with Christians throughout most of medieval Spanish history; the overwhelming majority never "assimilated," contrary to Yerushalmi. While there were instances of discriminatory laws and restrictions (particularly in the late medieval period), these were nothing to compare to the anti-Jewish laws of Germany prior to the "final solution." Contrary to Netanyahu, there is no evidence of virulent "anti-Semitism" on the part of Spanish rulers; and, most important, there was never any policy of extermination of Jews in Spain.

Reviewers—Reading and Not Reading

Normally, it is perhaps not a good idea to respond to reviewers. There is an increasing tendency on the part of those asked to review a book first to agree to do so, even if they have little or no qualifications for dealing with the subject, and second to read hastily and look for things to criticize in order to demonstrate their own "brilliance." Rarely has the reviewer actually read the entire book, and more rarely has he understood what he has read. While there have been many positive and favorable reviews of my book, some have made dangerously false statements or so distorted what I said that the record must be set straight. This also provides an opportunity to clarify still further certain important statements in the book.

Mark Meyerson accused me of things that I did not say or that he misinterpreted.[53] Although disagreeing with what he thought I had written, he cited not a single source or fact to support his contentions. The statement is then made that, supposedly according to my interpretation, the Inquisition was "merely a tool of the conversos' Old Christian political enemies"—a statement that cannot possibly be justified from reading the lengthy and careful analysis of the reasons that I gave for the Inquisitions (plural) in Spain. Meyerson is amazed that I am "incredulous" that old Christians should have recognized Jewish practices (that is, the inquisitors' manuals). Yet, of course, I never said such a thing. Obviously, and especially in Spain, many old Christians were well aware of Jewish customs. The issue is quite different. It is that in all of the thousands of Inquisition "processes" (trials of alleged Judaizing converts), the same—and only the same—Jewish practices are charged against the accused. Is it not curious that there is never a different custom or observance for which a converso was charged, especially given the wide variety from which something could be selected?

Finally, he says that he does not know what to make of my suggestion that the Expulsion might have been undertaken in order to protect the Jews from extermination (296). I agree that perhaps this was not as carefully worded as it might have been. What was intended, and what I thought to be clear, was that there was some reason for the Jews to be apprehensive about this, since extermination of the *conversos* was already very much under way, and inasmuch as it was the Inquisition itself that demanded the expulsion of the Jews, *perhaps* Fernando and Isabel agreed to this at least in part to prevent what the Jews themselves feared and what the monarchs also did not desire. I clearly stated, however, that this was not the explicit reason given for the Expulsion, rather, the alleged contact between Jews and conversos.

In another review, J. N. Hillgarth, though more a general medievalist than a specialist on Spain, and certainly not at all on Jewish history, unleashed his considerable fury, accusing me of things that I never wrote and never

intended, for example, claiming that I accepted part of a statement about
conversos as "good Christians" while "rejecting the reference in the same
source to contemporary conversions, impelled by fear."[54] What I actually
wrote on the page cited was that the chronicler "distinguished between the
recent conversos who had converted from fear . . . and those who had been
converted by the preaching of Vicente Ferrer, who became 'good Christians,
better than those who were converted by force and fear" (68, last paragraph)—quite different from Hillgarth's distorted reading. I neither "accepted" nor "rejected," I simply quoted the source. Jumping to the fifteenth
century, skipping over three-fourths of the book, he asserts that the kings of
Castile and Aragón "allowed all forced converts to return to Judaism either
in Spain or in North Africa," a statement that perhaps can be excused as the
misunderstanding by one with little familiarity with medieval Spanish Jewish history (see 37–38 of my book for the facts). It is, of course, absurd, particularly with regard to North Africa, where Spain at the time had no control whatever. Perhaps Hillgarth was confused by what I wrote elsewhere,
that Christian authorities were willing to allow forced converts *in 1391* to
return to Judaism (343 n. 61), but this was not the case in the fifteenth century, as I there indicated quite clearly. What in fact was the case, and what I
stated, is that when Fernando and Isabel became aware of cases of forced
baptism, such converts were allowed to return to the Jewish fold. That is, in
those rare instances where conversion was compulsory, and could be proven
to be such, the conversions were nullified, since this was a violation both of
Church and civil law. Any converso, compelled or not, could of course have
fled to Muslim Granada or North Africa and returned to Judaism without
"permission" of the rulers. That few did so is an important indication of the
real status of the conversos.

The "processes" of the Inquisition trials, as stated above, are routine and
monotonous, and only the most gullible reader can remain convinced of the
authenticity of their charges. This, too, is a point made repeatedly by Netanyahu and other scholars, and one with which I am fully in accord. Yet
Hillgarth opines that these records were merely for use "within the organization" (of the Inquisition) and not "public propaganda," a notion he borrowed from my citation of the book of Blázques Miguel (324). While this is
arguable, his statement that "falsified records would, therefore, have been
counterproductive" is incorrect. One who has never examined even a single
record of an Inquisition trial, and certainly has not spent years doing research on them, may be forgiven for not understanding their nature. However, the statement that falsification—not of the "records" but of the charges
made—would have been "counterproductive" is incredible. They were
hardly "counterproductive": they led to the burning of countless thousands
of falsely accused conversos, and that, of course, was the purpose. It was no
secret to anyone then, in the fifteenth century in Spain, that the overwhelm-

ing majority of the conversos were very sincere Christians (at least, and I repeatedly make this point in the book, after the Inquisition was established
when they had no choice). If the Inquisition was to accomplish its "secret"
goal of eradicating the conversos from Spanish society—a goal which, again,
Netanyahu long ago correctly emphasized in his book *The Marranos*—then
they of necessity were compelled to falsify testimony and charges against
them. This is not a matter of conjecture on my part, but a record of fact.

What to make of Hillgarth's claim that the responsibility of the Inquisition
for the expulsion of the Jews from Andalusia in 1483 is not "clearly stated"
in the document cited escapes me (283). Again, I quote what I wrote: "[in
this document] it is stated that the Inquisitors had proclaimed the expulsion
of all Jews" from Seville (in fact, as is made clear, most but not all of Andalusia). Perhaps he was misled by Netanyahu's incorrect interpretation of
the same incidents in which he turned it into an order of the "kings," not the
Inquisition (*Origins*, 1088), but the document speaks for itself. In the following paragraph, however, I introduced evidence totally ignored by Netanyahu. This includes the statement that "the exclusive responsibility of the
Inquisitors for this expulsion [from Andalusia] is explicitly confirmed by a
document of the Monarchs of 1485," which I then cite. The next paragraph
again offers the testimony of two Jews, in a Spanish source that Hillgarth
should be able to read, that the "Inquisitors" had ordered the expulsion.
Thus, had he read to the end of the page, or even the middle of the page, perhaps he would have found the sources for which he was looking.

Hillgarth apparently accepts the old interpretation of the Expulsion as being the scheme of Fernando and Isabel, for reasons unknown. He is satisfied
merely to ridicule me for portraying the Monarchs "as 'rois fainéants,' ma-
nipulated by Torquemada," which "is not the least problem" in the book.
Not only is the statement about my "portrayal" of the rulers false (as is evi-
denced on virtually every page where they are mentioned), but had he read
carefully he might have discovered that not only the evidence which I presented proves conclusively that Torquemada was responsible for the idea of
expelling the Jews from Spain, but that in fact one of the most eminent medieval historians of Spain, Motis Dolader, discovered and published a document that proves this beyond the possibility of any further discussion (this is
now generally accepted by all careful Spanish historians).

Finally, Hillgarth dislikes the fact that I said in connection with an incident
involving one convert in Córdoba around 1486 that Baer "invented the fiction" that the entire city split into two camps and open warfare broke out as
a result. I am sorry this distresses Professor Hillgarth, but it is a fact, Baer did
say that, and no such "warfare" took place nor is there a single source to
confirm this. Hillgarth thinks, indeed, that the source mentions a grave
threat of civil war, which it does not, and a mere "*slip of the pen*" by Baer
turned the threat into a reality. The very emotionally worded description of

a city divided into "two camps" and "open warfare" between them seems to me more than a "slip of the pen." Nevertheless, I clearly stated there that "apparently [Baer] confused this incident with the earlier riots" that had taken place in Córdoba. Hillgarth appears somehow not to have seen that sentence, or perhaps it was just a "slip of the pen" that caused him to ridicule me by selective quoting.

At least John Edwards has the credentials to discuss the Inquisition and the situation of the conversos in Spain, and so I assumed that his review, which included also a discussion of Netanyahu's book (also attacked), would be balanced and would show an understanding of what the book is about.[55] This was an expectation in vain, however. He begins by taking me to task for using "without acknowledgment" the term "religiosity," which he attributes to Gavin Langmuir, in a book that I had not even read at the time. This is curious, as I am not aware that Langmuir invented the word, which appears in any standard dictionary. Edwards exaggerates my alleged criticism of Baron and Yerushalmi, without demonstrating in any way why I was wrong in what I said (he is "sure" that Baron used some sources that are nevertheless not cited in his work). I take second place to no one in my admiration of Baron (if I am anyone's "disciple," in Edwards's patronizing language, it is surely Baron, who for many years was a close personal friend and mentor), but when he was wrong about something I do not refrain from saying so.[56]

But how well has Edwards, in fact, read my book? He claims, incorrectly, that it "plunges at once in the later medieval period," covering ground "similar" to Netanyahu's. I certainly hope that the average reader of this book does not share these distorted ideas, and realizes that most of the first three chapters, and a great deal of the remaining ones, deal with the thirteenth and fourteenth centuries and that the book (as demonstrated above) contains a great deal of information altogether lacking in Netanyahu's. Edwards, to be sure, "compliments" me on my "linguistic expertise" and "known linguistic and literary skills," although he claims that this leads only to disappointment when it comes to defining terms, for example those relating to conversos. Yet every one of the terms which he thinks has not been discussed has, in fact, and perhaps too hasty a reading caused him to overlook this (see, for example, 23, the entire first chapter, and the terms *anus,* converso, *meshumad, mumar,* and especially *tornadizo*—the term he particularly accuses me of not having defined—in the index; see particularly 354 n. 21 on that).

More astonishing is his claim that, like Netanyahu, I somehow failed to mention not only "the continued presence" of the Muslim kingdom of Granada, but of other Muslim communities in Christian Spain. In fact, not only are both of these things mentioned several times in the book (although it is not about Muslim Spain or Muslims in Christian Spain), new information is given relating to Christians ("old" and "new") who fled to Granada, to the war against Granada, and to Jews and later conversos there. One wonders why an index is provided if careless reviewers are not going to bother to consult it, even if they are unwilling to completely read the book. Edwards still believes that Juan de Torquemada was "of converso parentage," because Netanyahu said so, in spite of what I wrote to prove the contrary (another section of my book that he overlooked). It is perhaps just as well, since in a section that he did read, or at least glance over, he came to the conclusion that the poets and writers I discussed "are presumed not to have been conversos," when in fact all of them were. I would not object if this were his opinion, but in the context it reads as if this were *my* statement, that they were not conversos. No wonder he finds the detailed analyses of these writers and their works "more a series of jottings than a coherent discussion," since he appears to have skimmed it so hastily. Had he consulted the notes, he would have seen that the poems, for example, were carefully analyzed in consultation with the late Brian Dutton, the greatest authority on the subject. His condescending characterization of me as "a literary specialist" is remarkable (360). Of some sixty-nine published articles I have written, a mere eighteen deal with poetry and literature. True, few historians in general, and even fewer in Jewish history, concern themselves with literary sources at all, but as I have often written, I believe this to be a grave mistake. In any case, my writing on these topics scarcely makes me a "literary specialist," any more than my book on Maimonides and some articles on philosophy make me a "philosophical specialist."

At this point, I am no longer surprised to read such things as that I gave a "somewhat garbled" account of the Inquisition manuals of Bernard Gui and Eymerich (lest I again be accused of missing something, I will here call attention to Shaye Cohen's important new article).[57] The former I mentioned only once (210) and the latter quoted once (209–10), but gave no "account," garbled or otherwise, of these because they are basically irrelevant to the Spanish Inquisition. (Incidentally, I call attention to another article dealing with Gui and some well-known cases of conversion in Provence, which contains a serious misrepresentation of a responsum of Ibn Adret that the author sought to use to justify the killing of an apostate in Lérida and of apostates in general by Jewish law; obviously the responsum says no such thing.)[58]

Edwards, with characteristic arrogance, accuses me also, like Netanyahu, of having ignored "the work of innumerable scholars" who have done what "apparently" we have not, that is to consult manuscripts in archives. It is curious that it is precisely my utilization of numerous manuscripts and archival sources that one of Spain's greatest historians, Motis Dolader, singled out for praise in his review. No matter, Edwards has already shown how little concerned he was to read footnotes or even consult the index. Netanyahu and I are also both faulted (denounced with vitriolic scorn, in fact) for not having "peeped" into neighboring Portugal or France in our discussion of the Inquisition, never mind that neither of these countries was in any way the subject of our studies (the Portuguese Inquisition, of course, as Edwards well knows, was established long after the Expulsion from Spain). On the other hand, I did devote pages to the earlier Inquisition in Provence, but Edwards seems somehow to have overlooked that also. Even further afield, we should have considered the entire subject of suppression of heresy "throughout Western Europe, both before and after the Reformation." That is a daunting task, ably undertaken by other scholars, and I gladly relinquish the topic to Edwards, who appears competent to discuss the entire history of the Inquisition throughout the world in a few pages.

All of the long list of things concerning the Inquisition and its operation that Edwards claims were not "properly discussed" are, in fact, detailed in my book (365). That the processes of the Inquisition can be valuable sources for such things as "personal and social beliefs . . . conflicts and economic difficulties" is, of course, obvious and has been mentioned by many historians. That is not the point. At issue is whether these records are *believable* and *reliable* sources for the "religiosity" (*pace* Langmuir) of fifteenth-century conversos. They are not, of course. Edwards concludes his "review-essay," or diatribe, with the startling conclusion ("Dare one say it") that some Christians may actually have believed in their religion and wanted to share it, while some Jews may actually have wanted to change. Yes, of course, and his point is? Inadvertently, he seems to have come at last to accepting one of my major premises, that most Jews *did* convert of their own free will, out of conviction and not under duress.

Lest the reader by now assume that all reviews have been negative and vituperative, not to say based on hasty and careless reading, I certainly wish to acknowledge the numerous very positive reviews that have appeared. The most important of these are by the two scholars most qualified to discuss the book, Henry Kamen and Miguel Ángel Motis Dolader.

In his review, Kamen says: "This book is of capital importance for a history of the conversos," written with "scrupulous scholarship based on a profound knowledge of the Hebrew, Latin and Spanish sources."[59] Following this, he sets forth succinctly and accurately the main contributions of the book. He states: "Roth for the first time introduces concrete data stripped of ideology." He acknowledges that there are some weaknesses in the manner of writing at some points, which I readily admit and can only plead that the pressure to complete the manuscript and have it published before I had really intended had much to do with these problems. "Despite this," he concludes, "the book presents a careful, solidly researched and (to me) thoroughly convincing exposition. . . . It is one of the most important contributions made in very many years to a study of the controversial last decades of the Jews in Spain."

In an interesting article dealing with literary topics, Dayel Seidenspinner-Núñez discusses my book in connection with other recent related studies.[60] He alone, of all the reviewers, comments on the two chapters devoted to conversos as authors, political statesmen, and Church leaders; chapters that necessitated considerable research and present much new material not to be found elsewhere. (Unfortunately, he like many historians errs in referring to the converso chronicler Fernando de Pulgar as "Hernando del Pulgar," thus confusing him with a famous military figure; an error I repeatedly warn against in the book.) This author, moreover, understands what some other reviewers did not, the nature of the polemical works and the Inquisition records. "The inflammatory rhetoric of the anti-converso tracts undermines the credibility of their exaggerated claims. . . . Roth underscores the necessity of reading Inquisition documents with a wary and critical eye. . . . *Clearly their efficacy as stock accusations outweighed any relation these allegations might bear to concrete circumstance*" (8, my emphasis). I can only wish this had been as "clear" to other reviewers (except, of course, Kamen, who understands this very well).

Turning finally to the lengthy review-essay (in the true sense) by Motis Dolader, one of the foremost medieval historians in Spain who has also written extensively on Spanish Jewish history, carefully and thoroughly surveyed the entire book, accurately presenting the major points (a minor typographical error, 1106, is that the Jews did not recover from the decline of leadership until the nineteenth century, *siglo XIX,* which of course should be XV).[61] It is gratifying to note that Professor Motis read carefully also the section dealing with converso historians, authors and poets. Unlike Edwards, he understands that the poets named were, of course, conversos. Unlike Hillgarth, he also understood correctly my position with respect to the Monarchs, and writes that he concurs with my view that the attribution of fanaticism to the rulers is erroneous (1109). He rightly warns against naïve acceptance of propagandistic statements intended for public consumption in some documents that do not reflect the actual attitude, or behavior, of the rulers. Also correct is his statement, emphasized in many of his other publications, that the Expulsion must be seen at least partially in light of global changes that were taking place at the end of the medieval period (I also emphasized this, including the expulsion of Jews from other countries in the same period). Motis also commented on the "nuclear idea" that I stressed of the decline of subsequent cultural activity among the exiled Jews, resulting primarily in qabbalistic speculation, responsa and legal works, and translations of Hebrew classics. Finally, he comments on the extensive notes, corroborating and validating "every one" of my statements, including references not only to published sources and literature, and research that I undertook in numerous Spanish libraries and archives (all of which he names). It is gratifying to read such a thorough and careful analysis of my work from a scholar who in everything he writes demonstrates reasoned judgment based on solid and always innovative research.

Appendices

Abbreviations

Notes

Works Frequently Cited

Glossary

Bibliography of Norman Roth's
  Writings

Index

Appendix A
Critical Survey of the Literature

It will already be obvious to the reader that many of the theories, as well as the handling of factual information, of previous writers who have dealt with the issues of conversos, the Inquisition, and the Expulsion are to be treated with extreme caution, if not rejected outright. While it has been necessary throughout the book to criticize specific points, it seemed best to confine to a separate appendix the critical treatment of the literature as a whole, where those who wish to consider such details may do so.

Yitzhak (Fritz) Baer is the best-known writer on the Jews of medieval Christian Spain. His editing of documents (*Die Juden*), in fact not chiefly his own work but that of a number of Spanish scholars whose collaboration he never fully acknowledged, provided a valuable collection of sources. On the other hand, his later synthetic treatment of the general history of the Jews in Christian Spain, written in Hebrew and translated by others in a very abridged English version (*History of the Jews*), is not only marred by severe biases and distortions but replete with errors and omissions. This is not the place to enter into a lengthy discussion of these, except to remark that Baer was, among other things, afflicted with a "metaphysical" conception of Jewish history, colored by both his own personal religious convictions and his Zionist ideology. According to this view, no Jewish life outside the land of Israel could be normal, no Jewish contact with a dominant Gentile population could be even relatively free of discrimination and persecution.

Such metaphysical conceptions also affected his understanding of the situation of conversos. An example is his statement that "conversos and Jews were one people, united by bonds of religion, destiny and messianic hope," and that, indeed, this is the chief value of the Inquisitional records (incorrectly suggesting that they support this erroneous conception). We have seen how completely false this view is. Equally false is his claim that the conversos became hated by "the Christians" (*sic*) when it became apparent that they were "intellectuals, Averroists, and nihilists" who believed in no religion at all.[1] This is one of Baer's best-known theories, that Jews of Spain became "Averroists," thus deviating from some presumed norm of traditional Jewish life, and this corrupted them into converting to Christianity. That thesis is, however, both ideologically and historically false.

Methodologically, Baer is even more seriously to be faulted for his distortion of documentary and other historical evidence. Had he carefully read the documents which his Spanish collaborators assembled, as well as the many thousands of other sources which he never consulted (in addition to those which have come to light only recently), he could not but have realized that the position taken on almost every page of his *History* was contradicted by those sources.

Baer's chief student, Haim Beinart, perceives the situation of the conversos in very similar terms. According to him, the conversion of thousands of Spanish Jews was due to a "wave of despair" which swept the Jewish community (how could there have been such despair when, according to Baer, Jews and conversos shared such optimistic belief in "destiny and messianic hope"?). Nevertheless, the converso community used its profession of Christianity "only as a cover," according to Beinart. The Jews in Spain regarded the conversos as "brethren in the truest sense, brethren who, in a moment of weakness, had relinquished [the people] Israel and whose reversion [to "Judaism"] it was a duty to encourage."[2]

Another student of Baer saw things in an entirely different light, and in this and other respects parted with his mentor. Benzion Netanyahu had already written his definitive statement on the true nature of the "Marranos" (conversos) in his first edition before Beinart wrote his above-cited statements. There, Netanyahu correctly sums up the conclusive evidence of a multitude of Hebrew sources: "the overwhelming majority of the Marranos were Christians"; that is, they were complete and willing adherents to the Christian faith.[3] Netanyahu's interpretation of the whole question of the nature of the converso problem, of their relation to Christianity and of Jewish attitudes to them in the fifteenth century, is entirely correct. My only quarrel has been with some particular details, or possibly incorrect interpretations in a few instances of a particular source. In addition, as I had already demonstrated in an earlier article, and repeated and expanded upon here, *exactly the same situation and attitudes* prevailed already in the fourteenth century.[4] It must be understood once and for all: conversos were not "crypto-Jews"; they were Christians, who chose completely to separate themselves from the Jewish people, and not just from the Jewish "faith."

Contemporary Jewish historians who are less than familiar with the sources, Spanish or Hebrew, have not hesitated nevertheless in making judgments. Even Salo Baron, rightly acknowledged as the "dean" of Jewish historians in the modern period, who nevertheless had only a secondary knowledge of this topic, criticized Netanyahu's book unfairly. Baron's student, Yosef Yerushalmi, stated that he "firmly disagrees" with Netanyahu's position, without ever explaining why.[5] He did raise what logically would appear to be one valid consideration, namely, the reliability of the rabbinic responsa.

To deal with that consideration here briefly, and I have already further clarified this in detail in the text of the book, the responsa (Hebrew *she'elot u-teshuvot*) were legal decisions rendered by outstanding scholars who actually lived in Spain and were part of the Jewish community. Such decisions are obviously to be given more credence than the romantic notions of later rabbis in other lands (Yom Ṭov Ṣahalon, etc.) who had no such firsthand experience with conversos. With one or two possible exceptions, all the sources analyzed by Netanyahu, and all those which I have here discussed, fall within this category of total reliability and firsthand experience. It is not an acceptable method of historical research to rely upon such sources only when they support one's personal theories and to reject them as "unreliable" when they do not.

It is interesting to observe that Spinoza, who was an astute observer of the Jewish situation and whose own family had lived in Spain and Portugal before "returning" to the Jewish fold in Amsterdam, stated that when the Jews of Spain were forced to convert or go into exile, a large number became Catholics. "Now, as these renegades were admitted to all the native privileges of Spaniards and deemed worthy of filling all honourable offices, it came to pass that they straightway became so intermingled with the Spaniards as to leave of themselves no relic or remembrance" as Jews. "But exactly the opposite happened to those whom the king of Portugal compelled to become Christians, for they always, though converted, lived apart, inasmuch as they were considered unworthy of any civic honours."[6]

It would appear that Spinoza had a far better understanding of the real situation of the Spanish conversos than many modern historians.

Since Spanish scholars have made such considerable contributions to the entire history and culture of the Jews of medieval Spain, it is surprising that they have not done more to advance our understanding of the converso problem. For the most part, their work in this area is either popular in nature and of little value, polemical, or generally superficial. Antonio Domínguez Ortiz is one of the leading authorities, and yet he has concentrated almost entirely on the situation of descendants of conversos after the Expulsion. Nevertheless, he is one of a growing number who have come to accept Netanyahu's position. For example, in his critique of Caro Baroja, *Los judíos en la España moderna* (and his similar views in *La sociedad cripto judía en la corte de Felipe IV*), he objects to the emphasis on "crypto-Jews" which relegates to the background the real conversos "who were by number and quality much more important" than any minority of "crypto-Jews."[7] This is absolutely correct, of course.

Américo Castro has played an important role in identifying (often with no apparent evidence, almost mystically) converso poets and authors, and in almost every case later research has proved him to be either correct or probably so. Nevertheless, some of his other theories were at best speculative.[8]

Nicolas López Martínez's study is of limited value and to be used with caution.[9] Only Francisco Cantera Burgos, a noted scholar of Jewish history and culture of medieval Spain (though somewhat deficient as a Hebraist), has made a significant contribution. His various studies are cited throughout the present book.

Literature on the Inquisition

If some controversy, and considerable misunderstanding, exist with respect to the converso situation, this is even more the case with regard to the Inquisition. Far more heat than light has been generated in the numerous articles and books on the subject. Almost without exception, writers have advocated personal ideological bias instead of the results of sound research. Examples include anti-Catholic bias (Lea, especially); anti-Protestant (Llorca); apologetic (Pinta Llorente and others); Marxist (Saraiva, Kamen).

Overly simplistic "explanations" have been given, such as that of Castro, according to which supposed Jewish legal procedures gave rise to the Inquisition, or the claims of Sánchez Albornoz that it was totally a Jewish invention.[10] Similar views were repeated by López Martínez, and in the anti-Semitic article of "Gabriel, duque de Maura." An example of a more important work is that of Sebastian Cirac Estopañan, cited in Chapter 7 for its sources alone (his work shows an even worse anti-Semitic bias). Even as respected a scholar as Ramon d'Abadal blames anti-Jewish legislation of the (Visigothic) XII Toledo Council directly on the "converted Jew" Julian, bishop of Toledo (a convert or descendant of converts), and remarks that here began the "trajectory of intolerance" which conversos centuries later injected into Renaissance Spain (the Inquisition).[11]

As to the few Jewish scholars who have written on the Inquisition, Baer's notions about German versus Roman legal theories, etc., are ill-founded. Baer also relied on the testimony of obviously biased sources, without discussing these biases, and failed to report facts and evidence accurately. Beinart too readily accepts at face value every false accusation in every Inquisition record. Netanyahu is discussed in the Afterword.

Turning from polemicists to earlier historians of the Inquisition, we note the tendency to "blame" the Inquisition on purely political motives. Thus, such nineteenth-century historians as von Ranke and Hefele tried to portray it as part of Fernando's ambition to gain absolute authority over the nobles and clergy (it is no longer conceivable for a serious historian to maintain any such theory). Llorente, too, blamed the Inquisition on Fernando and on Pope Sixtus IV, with the supposed motive this time largely financial—to seize the riches of "heretics"—but also political: to gain control over the state in the case of the king; to expand his power in Spain in the case of the pope.[12]

There is absolutely no proof to support such theories, widely accepted as they have been, and a great deal to counter them. For example, all property seized by the Inquisition did *not,* as we have seen, go to the Crown. Also, the Inquisition was surely not an institution calculated to gain control over the state, even if there were reliable evidence that this was Fernando's intent.

A wealthy American businessman and amateur historian of considerably ability, Charles Henry Lea, accomplished at the turn of the century what would be absolutely impossible today for someone not a member of the academic "union": he wrote what remains nearly a century later the most authoritative and accurately researched history of the Inquisition (both the general European one and the Spanish one). However, there are also some conceptual errors. Lea also understood the motives to be part of an effort by Fernando (whom, alone, he "blamed" for the Inquisition) to organize and centralize control of the institutions of Spain. The Monarchs were, according to him, determined that the Inquisition should owe "obedience to the crown much more than to the Holy See."

While Lea was certainly correct, on the other hand, that the creation of the General Supreme Council of the Inquisition, modeled after the other administrative national councils created by Fernando and Isabel, and the appointment of Tomás de Torquemada as Inquisitor General were both innovations not previously known to the Inquisition, it is still incorrect to conclude that the Monarchs desired to exercise autocratic control over the Inquisition (nor could they had they wanted to).

This is not to deny, certainly, that the papacy fully supported the Inquisition at least initially, and in theory it was the pope and not the Monarchs who appointed the Inquisitor General. Yet the Inquisition soon became such a powerful and self-sufficient bureaucracy that neither papal nor royal power could possiby "control" it.

Llorente's account of how the Inquisition started in Castile is incorrect, incidentally; it was Sixtus IV himself who initiated it, by sending the papal delegate, Nicolo Franco, with a bull to Fernando and Isabel instructing them that Nicolo was to prosecute false conversos. In fact, the Monarchs ignored the papal bull, and it was at Seville in 1478 that Isabel (alone, without Fernando) confirmed the forged privilege of Frederick II of Sicily granting the Inquisition there the right to seize a third of all property of condemned heretics (the Inquisition, not the Crown, seized the property). Alonso de Ajeda, prior of the Dominican Convent of San Pablo in Seville, tried in vain to convince Isabel to establish an Inquisition in Castile. These facts seriously challenge most of the theories so far presented.[13]

In spite of the importance of Lea's work (and his earlier general study of the medieval European Inquisition), and his commendable control of sources, many of which had to be laboriously copied by hand for him and sent from Spain, it should be pointed out that he was a historian neither of medieval Spain nor, of course, of Jewish history. Indeed, he was concerned not primarily with the conversos, but rather with the institution of the Inquisition itself. He had, therefore, little enough to say about conversos at all, and virtually nothing about Jews other than a summary of secondary material on their general history in Spain.

By the early part of this century, therefore, research on the Inquisition had stalled at an apparent consensus (contrary to evidence) that it was part of a political plot by Fernando to gain control over the institutions of Spain.

Critique of Recent Studies

Miguel de la Pinta Llorente (I do not know whether or not he was related in any way to the earlier Llorente) *La Inquisición española y los problemas de la cultura y de la intolerancia* deals only with the Inquisition of the sixteenth to the eighteenth century and demonstrates a strong Catholic bias; his work is apologetical and of little value. Jean Plaidy, *The Growth of the Spanish Inquisition,* a novelist (literally), again deals only with the period after 1492, and her book cannot be recommended. (For an apologetic, but nevertheless scholarly, treatment of the Inquisition after 1492, see Juan Manuel Ortí y Lara's *La Inquisición,* to be compared with the work of Llorente, Lea, etc., for that period.) Paul Hauben's *The Spanish Inquisition* is merely a reprint of selected readings of limited value, with inadequate editorial commentary, so that it cannot even be recommended as an undergraduate textbook. Cecil Roth's *The Spanish Inquisition* is again a popularized account dealing with the whole history of the Inquisition; it is an adequate introduction for the post-1492 era only, although with some errors even for that period.[14]

Henry Kamen's *La Inquisición española* (Barcelona, 1979), is a Spanish translation (by Gabriela Zayas) of his *Inquisition and Society in Spain,* with apparently some revisions by the author. Like most other recent studies, it is derived from a selective reading of secondary material, with little or no attention to sources. It, too, attempts to deal with the whole history of the Spanish Inquisition to the nineteenth century, in one slim volume. Again like all other modern writers, Kamen totally ignores the Inquisition in Aragón-Catalonia, not only for the period prior to the Monarchs but even in the fifteenth century. While some of the Marxist (mis-)interpretations of the English version have been removed from the translation, other errors persist, particularly with regard to the history of the Jews.[15]

The most disappointing of all the more recent studies is a volume of collected papers, the previously cited *Inquisición española y mentalidad inquisitorial.* No fewer than twenty-eight scholars, some of whom are important, contributed to this volume of conference papers, yet the results are extremely disappointing. Every single paper is based, again, entirely on secondary material, with the often amusing result that authors cite each other. There is neither new information nor new insights, and the editor's introduction is the most interesting of all the contributions.

The danger of arriving at conclusions not supported by the sources is to be seen again in Juan Blázquez Miguel's *Inquisición y criptojudísmo*. Essentially an authority on the later Inquisition (postmedieval), he offers judgments on the "crypto-Judaism" of conversos of the fifteenth century, a subject about which he is ill informed. These conclusions are again drawn from secondary material, much of it thoroughly outdated. In spite of a commendable mustering of some secondary literature on Spanish Jews, the author's own knowledge of Jewish life and religious observance in medieval Spain is insufficient to allow him to make such conclusions.

There is certainly merit to his argument that the "processes" of the Inquisition were not written for public propaganda, but like so many other authors he ignores the overwhelming proof of the falsity of the charges in these records. His ignorance of Jewish law and customs, on the other hand, is the source of many serious errors. He puts forth, for example, a theory that pork was "prohibited" in the Bible because the ancient Jews were nomadic shepherds. In fact, there is no specific prohibition of pigs as such; rather, they are included among *types* of animals prohibited as food, and the theory about Jews as "nomadic shepherds" makes no sense. He also cites such things as a supposed prohibition on sexual intercourse for a week after marriage and fasts unknown in Jewish tradition. With regard to factual matters relating only to the Inquisition, there are also serious errors, such as his belief that there was no opposition in Spain to the medieval Inquisition, when, in fact, there was tremendous opposition (as we have seen, Llorente devoted an entire book to the subject). So, too, his statement that the Inquisition could act against Jews who said that "Jesus was only a man and that the virgin was not a virgin" is wholly erroneous. Were that so, *every* Jew would have been condemned by the Inquisition. Exactly the opposite was the case: Jews were not to be subject to the Inquisition precisely because such beliefs were legitimate to their religion. Finally, like other modern authors, he ignores the earlier Inquisition in Aragón-Catalonia.[16]

Coming, finally, to works on the Inquisition in that kingdom, a professor of Spanish literature, Ángel Alcalá Galve, who was the editor of the previously mentioned collection of papers, has written a popularized account of the murder of the Inquisitor Arbués (see my discussion of that case). This is yet another apologetic defense of the Inquisition; its prison cells were supposedly "better" than secular ones (we have already seen how false that is; if it were so, why was every effort made to transfer prisoners to ecclesiastical, i.e., non-Inquisition, prisons where conditions were better?); that "perpetual imprisonment" never lasted longer than six years; that torture was severely restricted; that the *autos de fe* (where unrepentant "heretics" were burned to death) were merely public acts of "national affirmation"; etc. Like all the other modern writers on the Inquisition, he ignored the most important source of all for that kingdom: the memoirs of the official archivist and secretary of Torquemada.[17]

The only book so far which has attempted to deal accurately with the Inquisition in Catalonia (though not Aragón) is Eufemià Fort i Cogul's, *Catalunya i la Inquisi-*

ció. It has some merit and ought to be consulted more than it has been by other writers on the Inquisition in general. Nevertheless, as with all the other books since Llorente and Lea (with the exception of those which actually publish documents relating to specific cities), this author also relied almost entirely on secondary sources. Thus, it shares the fault of being mostly a popularized summary of a selective reading of that literature. It shares also another fault (which is also true of the papers in Alcalá's previously mentioned collection): an almost complete neglect of Jews and conversos (one very brief chapter is devoted to "Jews and Judaizers"). Following a few false generalizations about Jewish life in medieval Catalonia, the author does aptly observe that even those who (may have) converted out of fear during the campaign of Vicente Ferrer ultimately became convinced of the truth of Christianity.[18] Other authors have either ignored or flatly denied the sincerity of the conversos; Blázquez, for example, fails to mention any of the converso bishops or theologians.

We come, finally, to Juan Blázquez Miguel's newest book, *La Inquisición en Cataluña, el tribunal del Santo Oficio de Barcelona (1487–1820)*. It hardly needs stating that a book of 396 pages cannot hope to do justice to the Inquisition even of Barcelona for the entire period covered. On the other hand, the Inquisition prior to 1487 is, once again, ignored completely.[19]

For the Inquisition of Catalonia, there is only Fort's inadequate study, and for Barcelona the brilliant article of Carreras. On Aragón, see the Aferword.

Majorca (part of the kingdom of Aragón-Catalonia, of course) has not been dealt with except in a couple of articles (the books on the Jews of Majorca, all inadequate, treat only of the postmedieval Inquisition).

For Valencia (again, part of the same kingdom), Manuel Ardit's, *La Inquisició al país Valencià* is a popular treatment of an important subject which needs more research. Although it is limited entirely to the period of the Catholic Monarchs, it sheds little light even on that subject. The author does acknowledge the existence of an "antiga Inquisició aragonesa," but does not devote any attention to it.[20]

Stephen Haliczer's, *Inquisition and Society in the Kingdom of Valencia, 1478–1834* would, from its title, appear to be at last that much-needed thoroughly researched history for this area. Unfortunately, it is devoted entirely to the modern Inquisition (chiefly sixteenth and seventeenth centuries), and while it is excellent for that subject it is not relevant to the period with which we are concerned.[21]

In addition to the sources for Valencia which I have used in the chapter on the Inquisition, I am aware of the superb dissertation of Subirats, as well as some articles he has written. Other material may be found in various articles by others.

One of the difficulties, as always when dealing with medieval Spain, is getting access to sources; those that have been published are often harder to obtain than unpublished ones. This was the case with an important source on the Inquisition in Valencia, found in a nineteenth-century book on the history of Castellón, which I was able to obtain only with great difficulty (thanks to the courtesy of the magnificent library of the Madrid Ateneo, a private organization). However exciting it may be to do research in the archives, scholars must not neglect such equally important published materials.

Blázquez, again, has brought forth a recent study entitled *El tribunal de la In-*

quisición en Murcia. A carefully researched investigation into the medieval Inquisition of Murcia would, indeed, be welcome; this book falls short of that. It deals only with the late sixteenth through eighteenth centuries. One needs in addition to read carefully the brilliant studies of Torres Fontes, as well as other very important work of Murcian scholars.[22]

A great shortcoming of most of the recent studies relating to the Spanish Inquisition in general, or to specific territories and cities, is that they attempt to deal, in a few pages, with the entire history of the subject down to the modern period. The result is, of course, doomed to be superficial. Another example is José Martínez Millán's *La hacienda de la Inquisición,* which, while promising to deal "only" with the period 1478–1700, focuses almost entirely on the seventeenth century. It is indeed useful, even important, for that period, but of no value for the medieval Inquisition. Rafael Gracia Boix followed up his previous collection of documents for Córdoba, cited frequently in the present book, with a new collection entitled *Autos de fe y causas de la Inquisición de Córdoba.* It is, again, devoted entirely to the later period, and not only adds nothing new for the fifteenth century but is by no means as useful for that as his previous work was.[23]

The best work on the medieval Spanish Inquisition, therefore, after more than a century of research, remains those studies of Llorente and of Lea. In that regard, it is fortunate that Lea's volumes have at long last been translated into Spanish.

The chapter on the Inquisition in the present book, although not pretending to completeness (indeed, there are several important articles and even some sources which have not been cited due to limitations of space), at least has the merit of dealing with the *entire* subject, the origins of the Inquisition, its operation in Aragón-Catalonia as well as in Castile, etc. It also takes into consideration, for the first time, sources which have been ignored by all other work on the subject.

A complete and thorough history of the medieval Inquisition in Spain cannot, of course, be accomplished in one chapter. It is therefore to be hoped that serious scholars in the future will take up the challenge of this task, at least taking into account the sources here utilized, as well as the myriad studies and sources not mentioned (although most were consulted). After a century or more, it is surely time for a new history of the medieval Inquisition of Spain.

Limpieza de Sangre

Américo Castro again pioneered in bringing to light the importance of the doctrine of "purity of blood" (incidentally, no such expression as "*pureza de sangre*" exists in any of the sources, in spite of the invention of this phrase by some modern writers). *Limpieza,* or "purity," was in fact a far more important concept than even Castro or anyone else has grasped, and as we have seen, it was central to late-fifteenth-century thought in many ways. (The incorrect statement of Tate as to the meaning, and importance, of Pulgar's repetitive use of "purity" has already been commented upon [Chapter 5, n. 85].)

However, Castro, useful as his work was, arrived at many erroneous and in fact dangerous conclusions, seeking to base this concept (as he did also with the abuses of the Inquisition) on a Jewish foundation. These notions were cogently criticized in an article by Netanyahu.[24]

Sicroff's French book on the subject, as previously mentioned (Chapter 7, n. 73), is of no value for our period. His articles on the discovery of actual documents relating to the early "*limpieza*" statutes and the Jeronimites, followed by other documents published by Beinart, on the other hand, are extremely valuable (Beinart's interpretation is however, incorrect).

What remains to be done, then, is, first, a thorough and updated history of the medieval Inquisition in *all* of Spain, and one which presents the facts without bias and without the unquestioning acceptance of every report of Inquisitional processes.

Second, a thorough literary-sociological analysis of the cultural contributions and worldview of the converso writers as a group. Such a study will also need to consider linguistic elements, such as the possible (if unlikely) influence of Hebrew.

Finally, perhaps, a thorough reexamination of the "*limpieza*" issue, utilizing all of the published and unpublished sources, and with a comparison with postmedieval developments.

As noted in the text, one of the things which must be done is to continue the useful (with respect to uncovering and publishing documents but, for only one of the monasteries of one order) work of Sicroff and Beinart in searching out the importance of conversos, questions of "*limpieza,*" etc., in the monastic orders of the fifteenth century.

Appendix B
Jewish and Converso Population
in Fifteenth-Century Spain

Naturally it would be important if we could confidently give an accurate estimate of the number of conversos in Spain, at least in the fifteenth century. Unfortunately, our sources simply do not permit this. For example, mention has already been made of the fact that in all the documents examined by León Tello for Toledo, not just for the city but for the entire diocese (including many small towns where Jews lived in relatively large numbers), the names of very few conversos are found. Are we to conclude that there were hardly any conversos in fifteenth-century Toledo? Such a conclusion would be totally false, for we know from the "Sarmiento affair" that conversos made up a very substantial portion of the population of Christian Toledo. The same is true for Córdoba, where we have more information on conversos than we do on Jews themselves.

Netanyahu has attempted to argue for a large figure of conversos, starting as early as the persecutions of 1391 which resulted in the conversion of many Jews. *How* many? Netanyahu cites Abraham Zacut that more than 4,000 converted in 1391, but he questions the reliability of that estimate; not that it is too large but rather too small. This assumption he bases on the previously mentioned letter of Hasdai Crescas, according to which "the number of converts in Seville alone exceeded 4,000."

However, Crescas' letter said nothing of the sort; only that there were (he estimated) "six or seven thousand households" (i.e., total number of Jewish households) in Seville, of whom many were killed, some were sold to the Muslims as slaves, but "the majority of them converted." Now, if we accept the generally agreed-upon figure of between five and six people to a medieval household, this would result in a figure of at least 30,000 Jews in Seville (a figure which Netanyahu easily accepts as accurate; he also notes that the sixteenth-century historian Zúñiga—hardly "the historian of Seville," however—also claimed that 4,000 Jews were "killed" in 1391 there). These figures are patently ridiculous, however.

Nevertheless, Netanyahu insisted on believing them because of the "authority" of the Catalan rabbi (who, as far as we know, was never in Andalucía in his life). "Can it be assumed," he asks, "that . . . the leader of Aragonese [Catalan] Jewry would not know the approximate number of Jews" in far-off Seville? The answer, of course, is yes, it certainly can be so assumed. Not only was he never personally in Seville, his letter itself is remarkably unreliable. According to the letter, there was an enormous massacre of Jews also in Toledo, something which is unconfirmed by other sources. He also claims that there were some 1,000 Jewish households (at least 5,000 Jews) in the city of Valencia, a figure which is absolutely beyond possibility.[1]

Assuming for the sake of argument that Crescas' estimate that some 4,000 Jews were converted in Seville is correct, the question arises, how would it be possible, not in the few days during which the riots there actually took place, but even in a month or a year, to baptize 4,000 people?

Reliable Spanish historians are of some help to us in the case of Seville, however. Ladero Quesada has estimated the total Jewish population in the city in the four-teenth century at 400 families, or about 2,000 individuals, with only about 70 families remaining after 1391. Collantes estimated the Jewish population within the main *judería* of Seville at the end of the century at 450–500 individuals. Still, it must be remembered that many Jews lived in other neighborhoods outside the main *judería*. However, these estimates nevertheless represent a more rational figure, based on reliable if incomplete evidence.[2]

"Authority" hardly enters into the consideration of the reliability of medieval sources on such matters. Thus, Enrique III, king of Castile (and certainly "authori-tative"), wrote in 1395 to the chapel of the cathedral in Toledo that officials there would no longer receive 48,800 *mrs.* from Jewish taxes because the *judería* had been "robbed and destroyed."[3] Yet we know absolutely that this is untrue, for life in the (not one, but many) Jewish quarters of Toledo continued as usual after 1391, and there is no evidence of any "destruction," other than robbery.

For Valencia, we have an abundance of documents, letters from the king, reports from his officials in the city, etc. These show how unreliable Crescas' letter actu-ally is. For example, he states that 250 Jews were killed in the city, whereas, the official report gives the figure of "about" (fewer than) 100. Indeed, the report says that so many were baptized that they ran out of holy water; yet if Crescas' figure of 5,000 Jews baptized were correct, an entire reservoir of water would have run dry!

To turn from the conversions of 1391, for which we have no reliable figures, to those of 1411–12, the preaching campaign of Vicente Ferrer and the Tortosa disputation, Netanyahu discusses the obviously rounded-off estimate of Zacut of 200,000 and notes that this is exactly the figure given by Joseph Ibn (not "ben") Ṣadiq in his earlier (1487) chronicle, from which Zacut obviously copied, as he copied other information. Then Netanyahu cites the interesting statement of Isaac Abravanel (long after the Expulsion) that the number of conversos persecuted by the Inquisition was "larger" than that of the Israelites who left Egypt; at least 600,000 according to tradition, but according to Netanyahu as many as a million or *more* could possibly be the figure.[4]

This allegorical estimate of Abravanel, it should be noted, is not for the total Jewish population of Spain, but only for conversos tried by the Inquisition; thus, not even the total number of conversos, for only a minority of them were ever so prose-cuted. Nevertheless, considering that the program of the Inquisition was nothing less than to effect the elimination and total eradication of the converso element in society, its perpetrators certainly made every effort to destroy as many conversos as possible. It might then be argued that as much, say, as 25 percent of the conversos were so dealt with by the Inquisition. This then would yield a total number of two million conversos, according to Abravanel's statement. Even Netanyahu rebelled at that fig-ure as being "quite inconsistent" with the available data.

Turning from wild speculation to actual fact, we have a very interesting Hebrew letter written from Spain to the Jews in Lombardy (Italy) in 1487 which provides very important information, presuming that it is authentic and was accurately copied (it has been misprinted, however). The letter refers to the Jews "of our kingdom," which probably means not all of Spain but only Castile. It states that in that year the "king, although he is just and righteous," imposed a tax on the Jews for the war against Granada of 14,000 *castellanos del oro*. This much we know from other sources, previously discussed. However, this letter alone provides the crucial information that the tax was at the rate of 1 *castellano* for each head of a household. If this is correct, it then becomes easy to estimate the Jewish population, since we have a nearly complete war tax list of the Jewish *aljamas* of Castile for 1480, only seven years prior to the letter. That list gives the figures in *maravedís* rather than *castellanos*, but from another source we know that the conversion rate was 489 *mrs.* per *castellano*. The total, therefore, is 9,078 *castellanos* (or heads of households), resulting in an approximate Jewish population of 54,468 for Castile. The above-cited letter gives a figure of 14,000 *castellanos* (heads of households), or at least 70,000 individuals, which is quite possible, since the tax list of 1480 is not complete.[5]

It must, however, be stressed again that all of this depends on the reliability of the assertion in that letter, which so far is unconfirmed by any other source, that the rate was 1 *castellano* per head of household. That our tax lists are woefully incomplete is already obvious from numerous other sources on the Jews in various communities. An anonymous eyewitness lamentation on the Expulsion, for example, states that there were 277 "holy communities" of Jews in Castile, and further on repeats this: "the communities of Castile, whose sign as to their number was 'the holy seed was its stump' [Isa. 6.13]" (the numerical value of "seed," *zera'*, is 277).[6] Even this figure is ambiguous, as we do not know whether the writer considered "Castile" to include León and Andalucía, or only one or the other of them, or Castile alone.

If the above figures for Castile's Jewish population are correct, however, we can see how absurd the estimates are for the number of Jews expelled from Spain. Loeb, for example, estimated about 160,000 from Castile alone. Unlike Netanyahu, however, he already expressed distrust of Abravanel, whose account is extremely vague "for a man who loved precise detail." Loeb exaggerated the Jewish population of Aragón, Catalonia, Majorca, Sicily, and Sardinia, which he included in his estimate of 300,000 Jews expelled from the Spanish kingdoms. On the contrary, however, if Loeb's estimate for those expelled only from Castile were at all accurate, then it would appear that Abravanel *underestimated* the population of Jews in the rest of the kingdom (there were almost certainly more Jews in the total kingdom of Aragón-Catalonia, including Valencia, than there were in Castile). It is not clear, incidentally, that Abravanel did include the Jews of the rest of the kingdom in his figure, since he speaks of those Jews who went to Portugal and Navarre, and these were primarily, if not exclusively, Jews expelled from Castile.[7]

We have already discussed the estimates of fifteenth-century sources such as Bernáldez, and the anonymous continuator of Pulgar's chronicle who estimated that over 100,000 Jews left (Castile? Spain?). Indeed, if we combine the estimated figure of Bernáldez of approximately 160,000 Jews living in Castile and 170,000 in Aragón-Catalonia, then we again arrive almost exactly at Loeb's figure of

300,000. Nevertheless, this appears an impossibly large figure, and certainly the figures given for *exiles* from Spain by these sources are unacceptable.

The previously discussed anonymous account of the Expulsion, possibly by an Italian Jew of the sixteenth (?) century, states that 120,000 went to Portugal alone. Earlier he says that there is little agreement as to the number of exiles, but that the generally accepted estimate is 50,000–53,000 families. This would be about 150,000–165,000 individuals.[8]

Estimates for Aragón-Catalonia are even harder to arrive at than for Castile. For the city of Jaca, Romano had estimated a Jewish population in 1377 of between 425 and 474, but Motis Dolader demonstrated that it was considerably less, between 270 and 305. In 1471 there were 73 Jewish houses, however, which would mean a minimal population of 355. For some other Aragonese Jewish communities, Motis provides the following estimates (1492): Zaragoza—1,400; Huesca—550; Fuentes de Ebro—400; Ariza—300; Calatayud—300. At the time of the Expulsion, the Jewish community of Zaragoza contracted for 2,400 individuals to embark by ship, while those of Calatayud and Fuentes de Ebro contracted for 300 each. However, as Motis correctly indicates, it is not possible to conclude that these figures reflect the actual number of Jewish exiles of those cities. Either they were hypothetical maximum estimates, or they include Jews from other regions who joined those of the cities mentioned. The total Jewish population of Zaragoza he estimated to have ranged from 1,702 to 2,070 (as always, the figures depend on the theoretical number of persons per household; between 3.7 and 4.5 in his estimate, based on a known factor of 460 Jewish houses). In addition to the fact that many Jews of these towns left by foot for Navarre, and not by ship, a factor which Motis did not take into account was the last-minute conversion of a substantial number of those Jews who therefore did not leave at all.

The actual documented number of exiles who set out for various ports is:[9]

Albarracín	214–710
Ariza (and other towns)	300
Ariza itself	170–200
Belchite	9–12
Calatayud (etc.)	300
Daroca	55–140
Epila	163–271
Fuentes de Ebro	300
Huesca (etc.)	600
Jaca	270–330
Teruel	200 (?)
Zaragoza (etc.)	2400

However, Joseph Ya'aveṣ, one of the exiles who later went to Italy, wrote that the number of exiles was "close to 3,000 householders," *including* those of Sicily.[10] This would result in a figure considerably less than 18,000 individuals for the exiles from the Peninsula alone, which seems entirely too small. It may be concluded that the *total* Jewish population of Spain proper could have been between 200,000 and 300,000. Whatever figure is accepted, clearly the *majority* of those persons chose conversion rather than exile.

get some information from figures on individual communities, previously discussed in this book.

Thus, in 1477 in Seville 400 conversos were imprisoned in the Alcázar. As noted, there were four large streets in the city which were entirely inhabited by conversos (this information, as noted, came from Alonso de Palencia, who actually lived in the city at the time). Therefore, it may be that the above Spanish scholars' estimates on the size of the Jewish population of Seville in the fifteenth century are, in fact, too low. Alternatively, it may be that large numbers of conversos moved into the city from other communities. In any case, it would perhaps be no exaggeration to assume that close to a third or more of the city's population was composed of conversos.

In Córdoba in 1473 the conversos were able to raise a militia of 5,000 infantry and 300 light cavalry, and it is known that there were about 10,000 conversos in the city in 1478.

Similarly, in Gibraltar (ca. 1473) there was a converso militia of 2,000 infantry and 350 cavalry. Certainly only young and able-bodied men (and boys, of course) fought in these militias, and an extreme estimate, therefore, would be that these figures comprise no more than one-half of the total *adult male* population of conversos.

For the present, this is as close as we shall be able to come to any kind of estimate. If we ever have exact and reliable figures for the number of conversos burned by the Inquisition, and if we could be sure that the oft-cited statements (Isaac 'Arama and others) that a third were burned were true, we would then be able to estimate more correctly the total converso population.

For the present, our impression from a detailed investigation into the sources and the material presented in this study is that the *overwhelming majority* of the Jews in Spain converted during the years 1400–1490. Thus, if there was a total of, say, 250,000 Jews by the end of the century, there must have been at least three times that number of conversos. This would result, in other words, in a population of close to one million Jews at the end of the fourteenth century, a figure not at all inconceivable.

Appendix C
Major Converso Families

Converso Families Named by Lope de Barrientos and Fernan Díaz de Toledo

Alarcón
Albares
Anaya
Araujo (Arroyo? cf. also Aruque in Toledo; same?)
Ayala
Barrionuevo
Bernáldez (Bernaldes)
Carrillo
Cervantes
Cuéllar
Fernández (family of Diego Fernández de Córdoba, *mariscal* of Juan II of Castile)
Fernández Marmolejo
Hurtado de Mendoza (not the sons of Iñigo López de Mendoza, Diego Hurtado and Hurtado de Mendoze, but probably the family of Juan Hurtado de Mendoza, connected with the de Luna family, who was the *mayordomo mayor* of Juan II)
Luna (the Castile branch)
Luyan
Manrique
Mendoza (the Mendozas and Ayalas all descended from a certain "Rabbi Solomon" and his son don Isaque de Valladolid, according to Lope de Barrientos)
Miranda
Monroy
Motiçon
Ocampo
Osorio (Ossorio)
Peña Loza
Pestin
Pimentel
Porra
Roja
Sandobal
Santi-Esteban
Sarabia

Saucedos (Salcedos)
Soli
Sotomayor
Valdez

Most Frequent Converso Names in Toledo

Alcocer	Montalván
Alonso	Nuñes
Alvares	de Ocaña
de Avila	Ortis
del Castillo	de la Peña
de Córdoba	Prado
Cota	Pulgar
Cuéllar	Rodrigues
de Cuenca	de la Rua
Dias	Sanches
Dueñas	San Pedro
Faro, Haro	de Segovia
Ferrandes	Serrano
de la Fuente	de Sevilla
Funesalida	Sorge (Sorje)
García	de Toledo
Gomes	de la Torre
Gonçales (González)	Torrijos
Husillo	de Ubeda
de Illescas	Vasques (Vázquez)
Jarada	de Villa Real
de León	de la Xara (Jara)
Lopes	

Source: Francisco Cantera Burgos, Introduction, *Judaizantes del arzobispado de Toledo* (Madrid, 1969), xxxiii. Names are for years 1485, 1495, 1497; for these and later periods, see also José Gómez Moreno, *Cristianos nuevos y mercaderes de Toledo* (Toledo, 1970).

Abbreviations

ʿA.Z.	ʿ*Avodah zarah* (tractate of Talmud, in standard eds.)
B.A.E.	Biblioteca de autores españoles (series of volumes)
B.A.H.	*Boletín de la (real) academia de la historia*
B.M.	*Bava Meṣiʿah* (tractate of Talmud)
B.N.	Paris, Bibliothèque Nationale
Madrid, B.N.	Madrid, Biblioteca Nacional
B.Q.	*Bava qamah* (tractate of Talmud)
CODOIN	Coleccíon de documento inéditos para la historia de España
CODOINA	Colección de documentos inéditos del Archivo de la Corona de Aragón
J.Q.R.	*Jewish Quarterly Review*
M.T.	Moses b. Maimon, *Mishneh Torah*
N.B.A.E.	Nuevo biblioteca de autores españoles (series of volumes)
Lev. R.; Num. R.	*Midrash Rabbah* (Leviticus; Numbers)
P.A.A.J.R.	*Proceedings* of the American Academy for Jewish Research
R.A.B.M.	*Revista de archivos, bibliotecas y museos*
R.E.J.	*Revue des études juives*

Notes

Introduction

1. Much has, of course, been written on all these subjects; for the revival of Hebrew, see, e.g., my "Jewish Reactions to the 'Arabiyya and the Renaissance of Hebrew in Spain," *Journal of Semitic Studies* 29 (1983): 63–84. Some aspects of Hebrew poetry and secular literature are dealt with, for example, in my "The Lyric Tradition in Hebrew Secular Poetry of Medieval Spain," *Hispanic Journal* 2 (1981): 7–26, and "The 'Wiles of Women' Motif in Medieval Hebrew Literature of Spain," *Hebrew Annual Review* 2 (1978): 145–65. In Spanish, the important works of Millás Vallicrosa, Gonzalo Maeso, Carlos del Valle Rodríguez, Angel Saénz Badillos and others should be consulted.

2. Norman Roth, "Jewish Collaborators in Alfonso's Scientific Work," in Robert I. Burns, ed., *Emperor of Culture: Alfonso X of Castile and His Thirteenth-Century Renaissance* (Philadelphia, 1990), 59–71, 223–30.

Chapter 1. Marranos and Conversos

1. *Cortes* 2:309; also in *Ordenanzas réales* (ed. *Colección de códigos,* 273; ed. *Códigos españoles* 6:265) (see Works Frequently Cited).

2. *El Fuero de Brihuega,* ed. Juan Catalina García (Madrid, 1888), 151. *Fueros de Aragón,* ed. Gunnar Tilander (Lund, 1937), 160–61, no. 271. *Fuero real de España* (Madrid, 1781), 2:339–41 (see the gloss of Alonso Díaz de Montalvo there, only in this edition) = F.R. IV.iii.2 (*Códigos españoles,*Vol. 1); *Siete Partidas* (Madrid, 1807) VII.xxiv.3, 6.

3. See the extensive discussion in the Anchor Bible translation of 1 Corinthians by William Orr and James Walther (Garden City, N.Y., 1976), 366. See also standard eds. of the Vulgate; the medieval Spanish version, *Nuevo Testamento,* ed. Thomas Montgomery and Spurgeon W. Baldwin (Madrid, 1970). José O'Callaghan, *El nuevo testamento en las versiones españoles* (Rome, 1982), lists no variant readings. For some of the fanciful etymologies of "*Marrano,*" see Joan Corominas, *Diccionario crítica etimológica de la lengua castellana;* I. S. Révah, "Les Marranes," *R.E.J.* 118 (1959): 29–77; Netanyahu, *Marranos,* 59 n. 153 (see Works Frequently Cited).

4. Francisco Cantera Burgos, "Fernando de Pulgar y los conversos," *Sefarad* 4 (1944): 319; English translation as "Fernando del [*sic*] Pulgar and the Conversos," in Roger Highfield, ed., *Spain in the Fifteenth Century* (New York, 1972), 296–353.

5. Text in B.A.E. 13:231b; cited also by Américo Castro, *España en su historia,* 213 (see Works Frequently Cited).

6. *Beit ha-behirah,* '*Avodah zarah* (Jerusalem, 1964), 61.

7. Moses b. Maimon, *M.T., Mada',* "Teshuvah" 3.9; *Neziqin,* "Roseah" 4.10.

8. Ibid., *Mada',* "Akum" 2.5; *Shoftim,* "Mamrim" 3.2.

9. Netanyahu, *Marranos,* e.g., 17 n. 45, where a responsum cited in the name of Isaac al-Fāsī (the correct title of the collection should be *She'elot u-teshuvot ha-geonim*), but which in fact may not be his (cf. Joel Müller, *Mafteah le-teshuvot ha-geonim* [Berlin, 1891], 11 n. 14), refers to *mumar,* "apostate," not "convert" as Netanyahu said, whereas the responsum of the *geonim* which he cites refers to the case of a *meshumad,* "convert." Cf. also 18, end of n. 47, where *mumar le-hakh'is* is also incorrectly translated "convert." In some few late-fifteenth-century responsa, *mumar, meshumad,* and *anūs* are used interchangeably, it is true (see 50, n. 135 and 59 n. 153; there Netanyahu correctly says that the term *meshumad* was more derogatory than *mumar,* and was applied to a "willful and complete" convert). The best discussions so far of these various categories are Netanyahu, *Marranos,* 8ff., 19–22, 59; S. Assaf, "Anusey Sefarad u-Portugal," *Zion* 5 (1932): 19–60 (rpt. in his *Be-ohaley Ya'aqov* [Jerusalem, 1943 and rpt., s.a.], 145ff.); and Jacob Katz, "Yisrael af-'al-piy she-hata Yisrael hu," *Tarbiz* 27 (1958): 203–17.

10. Netanyahu, *Marranos,* 22 n. 55; cf. also Katz, "Yisrael af 'al piy," 214. Later on, Netanyahu correctly refers to the "rarity" of the use of the term *anūs* in Spanish Jewish sources (78 n. 1). Note that "Rabenu Tam" (Jacob b. Meir) of France clearly distinguished his attitude toward an *anūs* from that toward a *meshumad* (source cited by Netanyahu, 9 n. 19); cf. Jacob's *Sefer ha-yashar,* no. 536, dependent probably on the geonic responsum mentioned above, a source overlooked by all who have cited this).

11. Solomon Ibn Farḥūn, *Mahberet ha-'arukh,* ed. S. G. Stern (Pressburg, 1844), fol. 2d, and Zunz's note there, which correctly suggested that the author originally wrote *Rūmī*—which means "Christian" in Arabic, hence "Syriac" in the context— and a later copyist, mistaking it for *Roma,* changed it to *Edom* in Hebrew.

12. Moses Ibn 'Ezra, *Kitāb al-muhādara wal-mudakāra,* ed. (Judeo-Arabic) and trans. (Hebrew) A. S. Halkin (Jerusalem, 1975), 48–49, lines 43–46; cf. *Sotah* 47a (in uncensored eds. of the Talmud) and *Sanhedrin* 107b (also uncensored).

13. Judah ha-Levy, *Kitāb al-radd wa'l-dalīl fi'l-dīn al-dhalīl* (so-called *Kuzary*), ed. (Judeo-Arabic) David H. Baneth and Haggai Ben-Shammai (Jerusalem, 1977), 139; cf. *Sefer ha-Kozary* [*sic*], trans. (Hebrew) Judah Even-Shemuel (Jerusalem, 1973), 144.

14. Abraham Zacut, *Sefer yuhasin,* part 1, fol. 15a (see Works Frequently Cited). The comments of Nahmanides to which he there refers may be found in Moses b. Nahman, *Peirushey ha-Torah* to Exod. 12.42, end (in standard "rabbinical" Bibles with commentaries; critical ed. Charles Chavel, 5th ed. [Jerusalem, 1969], 1:341); however, cf. his commentary on Gen. 42.7, where he disagreed with Rashi, and see Chavel's note there (232).

15. Simon b. Ṣemah Duran, *Sefer magen avot,* "philosophical section" (Livorno, 1785; photo rpt., Jerusalem, [1969]), fol. 31a.

16. *Sha'arey sedeq* 3.6.11 (where it is attributed to 'Amram *Gaon*) (see Works Frequently Cited); *Hemdah genuzah,* no. 54, end (attributed to Naṭronai), and cf. no. 86 (see Works Frequently Cited); also *She'elot u-teshuvot ha-geonim "ha-yashan,"* no. 313 (erroneously *mumar* instead of *meshumad*) (see Works Frequently Cited), and Rashi (Solomon b. Isaac), *Pardes ha-gadol,* fol. 61 col. b.

17. Yom Ṭov Ṣahalon, *She'elot u-teshuvot ha-hadashot* (Jerusalem, 1981), Vol. 2, no. 107.

18. According to one of the greatest Jewish preachers of Spain, in a book of sermons completed in 1489, despair over the delay of the coming of the messiah was a cause for conversion of many: "although we believe that the redeemer, our messiah, will come, nevertheless his coming is delayed, and every ignorant man who would know that the messiah will not come in his time and that the time already delayed shall be further delayed, very few [of them] would remain Jews." Shem Ṭov Ibn Shem Ṭov, *Derashot* (Salonica, 1525; photo rpt. Jerusalem, 1973, Hebrew University, ha-Faqulṭeh la-madaʿey ha-ruaḥ, ha-ḥug le-hisṭoriah shel ʿam Yisrael), 41 [fol. 21a]; cf. the different version in Marc Saperstein, *Jewish Preaching, 1200–1800* (New Haven, 1989), 183.

In later chapters, we shall see that this concern with the delayed messianic redemption, and attempts to calculate the coming of the messiah, were used both by "old Christian" and converso polemicists. I have dealt with some aspects of the messianic speculation in my "'Seis edades durará el mundo': temas de la polémica judía española," *Ciudad de Dios* 199 (1986): 45–65.

19. No fully satisfactory treatment of this important subject has been done; see Jeremy Cohen, *The Friars and the Jews* (Ithaca, N.Y., 1982), who, however, failed to consider some major figures and sources (also all of the sources later discussed in this book). He summarized his belief that the entire "mendicant mission" was only one means of implementing the new "anti-Jewish ideology" and as such was "hardly adequate" (226). Of course, Christian desire to convert Jews is scarcely "anti-Jewish ideology," and the question of the inadequacy of that effort is precisely what needs to be considered but was not (cf. in general my review of that book in *J.Q.R.* 74 [1984]: 321–25).

Much better in most respects is Robert Chazan, *Daggers of Faith* (Berkeley, 1989), for which see my review in the *Catholic Historical Review* (1990): 119–21. Our present concern throughout this book is only with Franciscan and Dominican relations to conversion and conversos.

20. Text of the ordinances frequently published; e.g., Baer, *Die Juden* 2:264–70 (see Works Frequently Cited); León Tello, *Judíos de Toledo* 1:446–49 (see Works Frequently Cited). (Baer did not, of course, assemble the majority of the documents published in his collection, although he took credit for them, and appears not to have read many of them, or at least to have forgotten them, when he wrote his *History*.) See Baer, *History of the Jews* 2:167–69; the offensive statements about "Church Militant," "monkish policy," etc., are a faithful translation of the original Hebrew text of his *History*. For the dangerous situation of the Jews in Murcia at this time, and the young king's efforts on their behalf, see the documents in Torres Fontes, "Los judíos murcianos," especially 111–13, 114–16 (see Works Frequently Cited).

21. María de los Llanos Martínez Carrillo, *Revolución urbana y autoridad monárquica en Murcia durante la baja edad media (1395–1420)* (Murcia, 1980), 54ff. Francis Oakley, *The Western Church in the Later Middle Ages* (Ithaca, N.Y., 1979), 262.

22. Julio González, *El reino de Castilla en la época de Alfonso VIII* (Madrid, 1960), 2:573, lines 13–14; cf. ibid., 520, the *fuero* of Uclés (1179). The interpretation that these refer to Jewish conversos is that of Francisco Cantera Burgos in *Sefarad* 22 (1962): 88.

23. Rubió y Lluch, *Documents* 2:9–11, no. 12 (see Works Frequently Cited).

24. Hernando de Talavera, *Católica impugnación,* ed. Francisco Marquéz Villanueva (Barcelona, 1961), 82–83.

Chapter 2. Early Phase of Conversions: Thirteenth and Fourteenth Centuries

1. See Chap. 1 n. 23 (Régné, no. 2427, cited this from another source, with uncertain dating). Régné, no. 2624 (see Works Frequently Cited).

2. Régné, nos. 731, 732, and the text edited by Ambrosio de Saldes, "La orden franciscana en el antiguo reino de Aragón," *Revista de estudios franciscanos* 2 (1908): 597–99.

3. Baer, *Die Juden,* Vol. 1, no. 117; Régné, nos. 734, 735, 736, 740, 746.

4. Régné, no. 2650.

5. Ibid., no. 2670; no. 2719, no. 2862. This Jaime Pérez is not to be confused, of course, with the anti-Jewish polemicist of the same name (fifteenth century).

6. Rubió y Lluch, *Documents* 1:129–30, no. 119; 2:81, no. 82.

7. Torres Fontes, "Los judíos murcianos" 111–13, Doc. 6; Baer, *Die Juden* 2:320, no. 306.

8. Régné, no. 2670; *Usatges de Barcelona,* ed. Joan Bastardas et al. (Barcelona, 1984), 108–9 (us. 75).

9. Régné, no. 3023.

10. In addition to the previously cited, though both somewhat inadequate, studies of Jeremy Cohen and Robert Chazan, see the relevant chapters in Baron, *Social and Religious History,* especially Vol. 9 (see Works Frequently Cited), and Robert I. Burns, *Muslims, Christians and Jews in the Crusader Kingdom of Valencia* (Cambridge, Mass., 1984).

11. An excellent statement of this doctrine appears in the Preface to the 1899 English translation of the N.T. of the official Catholic version of the Bible, the Douay-Rheims translation (photo rpt., 1976); namely, the "Old Testament" alone is divinely inspired, whereas the "New" has no such claim and depends entirely on the "witness" of the Church as to its authority. (The errors in citing the Hebrew Bible in the "New Testament" have not, of course, been dealt with satisfactorily.)

12. On the First Crusade, the best work is Robert Chazan, *European Jewry and the First Crusade* (Berkeley, 1987). See, however, the important critique by Ivan G. Marcus in *Speculum* 64 (1989): 685–88. (Chazan does not mention William II.)

13. Norman Roth, "Jews and Albigensians in the Middle Ages: Lucas of Túy on Heretics in Leon," *Sefarad* 41 (1981): 71–93. The most recent article on the Albigensians, from a different perspective entirely, is Joseph Shatzmiller, "The Albigensian heresy in the eyes of contemporary Jews" (Hebrew) in *Tarbut ve-ḥevrah be-toldot Yisrael bi-mey ha-beinayim* (H. Ben Sasson memorial volume) (Jerusalem, 1989), 333–52. On the general background of Jews and Christian heretics, see also David Berger, "Christian Heresy and Jewish Polemic in the Twelfth and Thirteenth Centuries," *Harvard Theological Review* 68 (1975): 287–303.

14. On Nicholas Donin and the censorship of the Talmud, see Yitzhak Baer, "Investigations of the disputations of Rabbi Yeḥiel of Paris and the Ramban" (He-

brew), *Tarbiz* 2 (1930): 172–87; Isidore Loeb, "La controverse de 1240 sur le Talmud," *R.E.J.* 1 (1880): 247–61; Noel Valois, *Guillaume d'Auvergne, évêque de Paris* . . . (Paris, 1880), 118–37; Judah Rosenthal, "The Talmud on Trial," *J.Q.R.* 47 (1956): 58–76, 145–69; Ch. Merchavia, *ha-Talmud be-re'iy ha-noṣrut* (Jerusalem, 1970), 229–40 and passim. See also Joseph Shatzmiller, "Did Nicholas Donin initiate the blood libel?" (Hebrew), in *Meḥqarim be-toldot ʿam Yisrael ve-Ereṣ Yisrael mugashim la-ʿAzriel Shoḥet* (Haifa, 1978), 4:175–82, and Robert Chazan, "The Condemnation of the Talmud Reconsidered (1239–1248)," *P.A.A.J.R.* 55 (1988): 11–30. Chazan, virtually alone, cited the important letter of Innocent; cf. Solomon Grayzel, ed. and trans., *The Church and the Jews in the XIIIth Century* (Philadelphia, 1933), 241–42, 275–81.

15. Fernando Valls i Taberner, ed., "El Diplomatari de Sant Ramón de Penyafort," *Analecta sacra tarraconensia* 5 (1929): 286–87, no. 28 (cf. Régné, no. 216), rpt. in Ramón de Peñafort, *Diplomatario*, ed. José Rius Serra (Barcelona, 1954), 149–50.

16. Valls, "El Diplomatari," 287–88, no. 29; already published in CODOINA 6:161–66; cf. Régné, no. 249. The second document of 1264 is in Francisco de A. de Bofarull y Sans, "Jaime I y los judíos," *Congrés d'historia de la corona d'Aragó* 2 (1913): 882, Doc. 50. The prohibition against using violence to force Jews to hear sermons is in Joaquim Miret i Sans, *Itinerari de Jaume I "el conqueridor"* (Barcelona, 1918), 342 (not mentioned by Valls).

17. Solomon Ibn Adret, *She'elot u-teshuvot*, Vol. 1 (Vienna, 1812; photo rpt. Jerusalem, 1976), no. 315.

18. Ibid., no. 763 (for the source he cites, see *Seder ʿolam*, ed. B. Rattner [Vilna, 1897], chap. 3, p. 9). For the categories mentioned, see the text of Maimonides translated in my *Maimonides: Essays and Texts* (Madison, 1985), 50.

19. Ibn Adret, *She'elot u-teshuvot*, Vol. 3 (Livorno, 1778; photo rpt. Jerusalem, 1976), no. 352.

20. Cited in Isidore Loeb, "Polémistes chrétiens et juifs," 238 (see Works Frequently Cited).

21. Ibn Adret, *She'elot u-teshuvot*, Vol. 5 (Vilna, 1884; photo rpt. Jerusalem, 1976), no. 66 (and in the name of a "*gaon*" it is found also ibid., Vol. 7 [Warsaw, 1868], no. 411); for the *geonic* sources, see above, Chap. 1, n. 16. Netanyahu's statement that "the dominant Geonic view [was] that conversion does not change only one's *religion* but also one's *peoplehood*" is entirely too broad (*Marranos*, 17 n. 45). Indeed, quite the opposite was the general opinion; namely, that the convert *remained* a Jew in terms of "peoplehood" (cf. Katz, Yisrael af-ʿal-piy," 73). With the exception of this ruling, apparently by Naṭronai, Katz was quite correct in saying that only in the medieval period did some legal authorities reverse the *geonic* attitude and require ritual immersion of a repentant convert (Katz did not cite any of the sources under consideration here, however).

22. Solomon Ibn Adret, *Teshuvot ha-meyuḥasot le-ha-Ramban* (Warsaw, 1883; photo rpt. Jerusalem, 1976), no. 180.

23. Müller, *Mafteaḥ*, 77; cf. *Shaʿarey ṣedeq* 3.6.28.

24. Moses b. Naḥman, letter in defense of Maimonides, in Moses b. Maimon, *Qoveṣ teshuvot*, ed. A. Lichtenberg (Leipzig, 1859), 3:9d; critical ed. of the text in

Monatsschrift für Geschichte und Wissenschaft des Judentums 9 (1860): 184–95; rpt. in Moses b. Naḥman, *Kitvey ha-Ramban,* ed. Charles Chavel (Jerusalem, 1963), 1:346. Chavel there says the quotation is not from the well-known work of El'azar, *Roqeaḥ.* Incidentally, the opinion of Jonah b. Abraham Gerundi cited in the responsum under discussion, according to which a convert who returns to Judaism does not require testimony before a court of three (like a proselyte) and that his wine is permitted, is almost certainly that referred to also by Aaron ha-Kohen of Lunel in the name of "ha-R"IT" that a convert who repented does not require a court of three and his wine is permitted. Undoubtedly the text originally had "ha-R"IY b. Avraham," and was corrected to "ha-R"IT" (Yom Ṭov b. Abraham Ishbīlī). No such decision is found in the responsa of Ishbīlī, and the parallel opinion here of Jonah b. Abraham Gerundi confirms the identity (Ishbīlī, of course, lived after Naḥmanides and could not have been cited by him); cf. Aaron ha-Kohen of Lunel, *Orḥot ḥayim* (Berlin, 1899), 2:245–46.

25. See the article, "*Murtadd*" in *Shorter Encyclopedia of Islam* (Leiden, 1953), especially section b.

26. *She'elot u-teshuvot ha-geonim "ha-yashan,"* no. 284 (see Works Frequently Cited).

27. This, in fact, was so; see Rashi's position and the reason for it discussed by Jacob Katz, *Exclusiveness and Tolerance* (Oxford, 1961), 71–72. Katz, however, was unaware of this contrary opinion of R. Tam, nor did he see Urbach (see next note), although he listed that book in his bibliography.

28. Text ed. from MS by Ephraim Urbach, *Ba'aley Tosafot* (Jerusalem, 1968), 204–5. Urbach apparently did not know of the abridged citation of this in the responsa of *geonim* (above, n. 27); cf. also Müller, *Mafteaḥ,* 11 n. 14, who already identified the author as Isaac b. Samuel. Netanyahu, *Marranos,* 17 n. 45, mentions both the first responsum, attributed to al-Fāsī, and the opinion of Isaac Dampierre, without realizing that these are in fact the same text (cf. also ibid., 19 n. 50). The language of the text as found in the responsa of the *geonim,* mixed with that found in the text edited by Urbach, is also cited in *Tosafot* on *'A.Z.* 26b, "Aniy shoney." See also "Teshuvot . . . Mishpaṭim" in Moses b. Maimon, *M.T.: Mishpaṭim* (end), no. 36.

29. Nissim b. Reuben, *Ḥidushey ha-Ran . . . B.M.* (Jerusalem, 1973), 126 (on *B.M.* 71b); Moses b. Naḥman, *Ḥidushey ha-Ramban* (Jerusalem, 1928; rpt. 1975), 2:66–67; *She'elot u-teshuvot ha-meyuḥasot,* no. 224 (definitely by Naḥmanides). Ibn Adret does not follow Naḥmanides in considering a convert "still a Jew" with regard to these various laws, but rather ruled that his corpse defiles, etc., because he is still a *person,* although not a Jew (see the previously cited responsum of Ibn Adret, Vol. 1, no. 191).

30. Meir Ibn Abī Sarwī, *Ḥidushey talmidey* [sic] *Rabenu Yonah . . . 'A.Z.* (Brooklyn, 1955, bound with Jonah Gerundi, *Ḥidushey . . . Sanhedrin*), 36–37.

31. Rashi, cited in Aaron ha-Kohen of Lunel, *Orḥot ḥayim* 2:54; from there also by Joseph Caro, "Beit Yosef" to *Ṭur, Even ha-'ezer,* no. 42. Caro apparently did not see the reference also in Judah b. Asher, *Zikhron Yehudah,* responsa (Berlin, 1846), f. 52b, citing apparently a MS of Rashi which may have circulated in Spain. Aaron ha-Kohen, indeed, may have learned of this decision from Judah in Toledo

while he was there. See Rashi (Solomon b. Isaac), *Teshuvot* (New York, 1943), no. 171.

32. Ibn Adret, *She'elot u-teshuvot*, Vol. 1, no. 1162 (repeated verbatim in *She'elot u-teshuvot ha-meyuḥasot*, no. 142).

33. *M.T., Ishut:* "Nashim" 4.15; cf. Netanyahu, *Marranos,* 71 and 151 n. 48.

34. Ibn Adret, *She'elot u-teshuvot*, Vol. 7 (Warsaw, 1868; photo rpt. Jerusalem, 1976), no. 267.

35. Ibid., Vol. 5, no. 240. Isaac b. Sheshet, *She'elot u-teshuvot*, no. 43 (see Works Frequently Cited) (see Hershman, *Rabbi Isaac Ben Sheshet* 220 for the date [see Works Frequently Cited]).

36. Yom Ṭov Ishbīlī, *She'elot u-teshuvot*, ed. Joseph Kafiḥ (Jerusalem, 1959), no. 21.

37. See Norman Roth, "'*Am Yisrael:* Jews or Judaism?" *Judaism* 37 (1988): 199–209.

38. *M.T., Mishpaṭim:* "Naḥalot" 6.12; cf. also Moses b. Maimon, *Teshuvot,* ed. Alfred Freimann (Jerusalem, 1934), no. 202; ed. Joshua Blau (Jerusalem, 1957–61), Vol. 2, no. 375.

39. Ibn Adret, *Teshuvot she'elot* (Rome, ca. 1470; rpt. Jerusalem, 1976), no. 292; repeated verbatim in *She'elot u-teshuvot*, Vol. 7, no. 292. The responsum of Haye (Hai) is to be found in *She'elot u-teshuvot ha-geonim "ha-yashan,"* no. 137; *Ḥemdah genuzah*, no. 52; *Teshuvot ha-geonim*, no. 23 (see Works Frequently Cited). (Both of the latter collections attribute it rather to Naṭronai, which appears to be correct, and the text in *Ḥemdah genuzah* appears to be the most accurate. In *Sha'arey ṣedeq* 4.3.25 it is attributed to Rav Ṣadoq.) The text of Ibn Adret's responsum is also found in Louis Ginzberg, ed., *Ginzey Schechter* (New York, 1929), 2:122, but with erroneous source citations by the editor.

40. *She'elot u-teshuvot ha-geonim "ha-yashan,"* no. 138; *Ḥemdah genuzah*, no. 53; cf. also *Sha'arey ṣedeq* 4.4.5, and Rav Bibiy, "Sefer basar 'al gabey geḥalim," *Jahrbuch der jüdisch-literarischen Gesellschaft* 5 (1907): 63 (Hebrew page), no. 9, and ibid. 7 (1909): 329 (it is unfortunate that this important work has escaped the notice of modern scholars). Yet there seems to be a contradictory opinion that descendants of converts *may* inherit; see Netanyahu, *Marranos,* 17 n. 45.

41. *M.T., Neziqin:* "Roṣeaḥ" 4.10–12, only in the uncensored editions (Rome, 1480; rpt. Jerusalem, 1955; or Constantinople, 1509; rpt. Jerusalem, 1972). There is a different text of 'A.Z. 26 cited in the commentary of Joseph Caro ("Kesef mishneh") in the *M.T.,* which has *apiqorsin* instead of *minin,* and this text apparently is the one which was used in the later printed eds. of the *M.T.* For Maimonides' explanations of the term, see my *Maimonides: Essays and Texts,* 50.

42. *Ṭur, Yoreh de'ah,* no. 158.

43. Ibn Abī Sarwī, *Ḥidushey talmidey Rabenu Yonah,* 37–38. See Ibn Adret, *Ḥidushey . . . Ḥulin* (4b–5a) in detail.

44. Joseph Ibn Ḥabib, citing Ishbīlī, as quoted in Joseph Caro, "Beit Yosef" to *Ṭur, Yoreh de'ah,* no. 268, end.

45. See Netanyahu, *Marranos,* 53ff., 72, 152–54. Ishbīlī's decision, although cited by fifteenth-century authorities, is not mentioned by Netanyahu.

46. Baer, *Die Juden,* Vol. 1, no. 213 (Baer failed to identify Jucef).

47. Nissim b. Reuben, *She'elot u-teshuvot* (Rome, 1545), no. 47.

48. Pedro López de Ayala, *Crónica . . . Enrique III*, B.A.E. 68:177, chap. 20.

49. Baer, *Die Juden*, Vol. 2, nos. 248, 253, 254.

50. Crescas' letter is found in Samuel Ibn Verga, *Shevet Yehudah*, ed. Wiener, 128 (see Works Frequently Cited). Reuben b. Nissim's statement is in Hershman, *Rabbi Isaac Perfet*, 194–96 (in spite of the fact that it was first published in 1936, and then again by Hershman, Baer did not know of its existence).

51. Baer, *Die Juden*, Vol. 1, nos. 408, 431, 432, 412, 413, 414, and pp. 659–60 (the statement of Queen Violante).

52. Lluís Marcó i Dachs, *Los judíos en Cataluña*, Castilian version (Barcelona, 1977), 191.

53. Atansio López, *Obispos en el Africa septentrional desde el siglo XIII* (Tangiers, 1941), xii–xiii (see the review by F. Cantera Burgos in *Sefarad* 4 [1944]: 427, in general).

54. The temporary conversion of Isaac: Jaume Riera, "Le-toldot ha-RIVaSH begezeirot 151 [1391]," tr. Frank Talmage, in *Sefunot* 17 (1983): 11–18. Riera drew several unfounded conclusions there, both as to Martin's actions and the "crimes" of which Isaac was accused (only the singular "crime" appears in the texts). Isaac's responsum to the rabbi of Majorca, *She'elot u-teshuvot*, no. 51.

55. Simon b. Ṣemaḥ Duran, *Tashbeṣ* (Lemberg, 1891), Vol. 1, no. 58, and see also no. 61. Baer's misinterpretation, *History of the Jews* 2:463 n. 12.

56. Isaac b. Sheshet, *She'elot u-teshuvot*, no. 107; Simon b. Ṣemaḥ Duran, *Tashbeṣ*, Vol. 3, no. 227.

57. Profiat Duran, *Ma'aseh efod* (Vienna, 1865), 195.

58. Isaac b. Sheshet, *She'elot u-teshuvot*, no. 11 (see on this also Netanyahu, *Marranos*, 29–30).

59. Ibid., no. 61.

60. Simon b. Ṣemaḥ Duran, *Tashbeṣ*, Vol. 1, nos. 63 and 66. Both responsa are discussed in detail by Netanyahu, *Marranos*, 33–37, and cf. 23ff. on Isaac b. Sheshet. See also Hershman, *Rabbi Isaac Ben Sheshet*, 245. Neither is it correct, as stated by Netanyahu, that Duran wrote the second opinion "many years later" than the first; either they were written in the same year or, as Hershman cogently argued, the first was written in 1392 and the second in 1404–5.

61. Netanyahu completely misunderstood this, and wrote that Duran here rejects the opinion that the Christian authorities considered the *anusim* to be actually Jews. This is not to say that the authorities "did not care any more about the Christianization of the Marranos," as Netanyahu claimed. He appears to have confused the situation of the *anusim* after 1391 with that of the Marranos, the true converts, of the fifteenth century. The authorities were not, of course, ever concerned with the "Christianization" of the former group, whom they recognized to have been literally coerced and forced into baptism—especially was this true in Majorca—and whom they were willing to allow to return to Judaism if they so desired. Duran's complaint is that many did *not* so desire, and these should no longer be viewed as *anusim*. The signs by which to differentiate between the two groups, he suggests, are whether they desecrate the Sabbath publicly even when not forced to do so, and whether they make any effort to leave. As to those who have left and then returned to Spain to

live there as Christians, "and the matter of complete converts [*meshumadim*], for whom I find no remedy," he asks the rabbi of Majorca to inform him if he thinks differently.

62. Simon b. Ṣemaḥ Duran, *Tashbeṣ*, Vol. 3, no. 312; cf. Netanyahu, *Marranos*, 42–43 and sources cited there, n. 120, on the persecution of 1435.

63. Simon b. Ṣemaḥ Duran, *Tashbeṣ*, Vol. 2, no. 60. For the dating, see Isidore Epstein, *The Responsa of Rabbi Simon B. Zemah Duran* (1930; rpt. New York, 1968), 96.

64. Simon b. Ṣemaḥ Duran, Vol. 2, no. 201; the cited opinion of Aaron ha-Levy should be in his commentary to Ibn Adret's *Torat ha-bayit*, but I was unable to find it discussed there at all. See Epstein's somewhat too broad statement of Duran's rejection of Aaron's opinion, *Responsa* 31n.

65. Simon b. Ṣemaḥ Durah, *Tashbeṣ*, Vol. 3, nos. 40 and 43.

66. Ibid., no. 47; cf. Netanyahu's analysis, *Marranos*, 38–41, and see especially n. 101 there. In this instance, his analysis is entirely correct. Yet another case involved a man who had left his family and all his property in Majorca and fled, and the Christians took everything in his house and forced his wife to convert. She then hired passage for herself at great expense on a boat to North Africa, even though the Christians promised to pay her the sum stipulated in her marriage contract if she remained (*Tashbeṣ*, Vol. 2, no. 176; overlooked by Netanyahu).

67. Ibid., Vol. 2, no. 139; the source, not given in the text, is *Ḥidushey ha-Ramban* on B.M. 71b (col. 66b of the edition I have cited previously; see above, n. 29).

68. Ibn Adret, *She'elot u-teshuvot*, Vol. 7, no. 179.

69. Moses b. Naḥman, *Teshuvot*, ed. Charles Chavel (Jerusalem, 1975), no. 2.

70. Ibn Ḥabib, "Nimuqey Yosef" on *Sanhedrin* there (printed in standard eds. of the Talmud with the laws of al-Fāsī).

71. Ishbīlī, *She'elot u-teshuvot*, no. 159.

72. Ibid., no. 67.

73. Nissim b. Reuben, *Derashot ha-RaN*, ed. Leon Feldman (Jerusalem, 1974), 155.

74. Joseph Ibn 'Aknin, *Hitgalut ha-sodot ve-hofa'at ha-meorot*, ed. (Judeo-Arabic) and trans. (Hebrew) Abraham S. Halkin (Jerusalem, 1964), 446, line 15ff.

75. Baer, *Die Juden* 1:350.

76. Joseph Ibn Naḥmias, *Peirushey* ([Jerusalem?], [197–?], 15 (commentary on Jer. 31).

77. León Tello, *Judíos de Toledo* Vol. 2, index, s.v. "conversos."

Chapter 3. Conversos and Crisis: The Fifteenth Century

1. Juan Torres Fontes, "Los judíos murcianos" 107–10 (Doc. 4) and cf. 87. The same text, addressed to Toledo, in León Tello, *Judíos de Toledo* 1:444–46, and elsewhere. Nevertheless, we find Jewish tax collectors and officials in Alba de Tormes in the years 1408–10, and elsewhere in the kingdom.

2. María de los Llanos Martínez Carrillo, *Revolucción urbana y autoridad monárquica durante la baja edad media* (Murcia, 1980), 57.

3. Pérez de Guzmán, *Generaciones y semblanzas*, ed. Tate, 39–41 (see Works

Frequently Cited). See on this period, *inter alia,* Eloy Benito Ruano, *Los infantes de Aragón* (Madrid, 1952).

4. Juan Torres Fontes, "La política exterior en la regencia de d. Fernando de Antequera," *Anales de la universidad de Murcia: Filosofía y letras* 18 (1959–60): 56. C. Baronius—O. Raynaldus, *Annales ecclesiastici* (Lucca, 1738–56), 30:139, no. 16, citing Raphael Maffei Volaterranus; translation in Edward A. Synan, *The Popes and the Jews in the Middle Ages* (New York, 1965), 143. On Volaterranus, see H. Hurter, *Nomenclatur literarius,* Vol. 2 (Innsbruck, 1906), cols. 1324–26.

5. Baer, *Die Juden* 1:793–94, no. 487 (cf. also no. 490, to Benedict XIII); 834, no. 516, on the 1416 mission. Jerónimo himself, with a certain Salvador de Aguas (undoubtedly a converso), was responsible through his preaching for the conversion of the Jews of the village of Alcañiz, at the behest of Benedict. "Not even fifteen houses of Jews" remained (ibid., 810).

6. The text has been frequently published; e.g., Baer, *Die Juden* 2:264–70; León Tello, *Judíos de Toledo* 1:446–49, etc. See the outrageous remarks of Baer, *History of the Jews* 2:167–69.

7. Joseph Ibn Ṣadiq, "Qiṣur zekher la-ṣadiq," in Adolph Neubauer, *Mediaeval Jewish Chronicles* (Oxford, 1887), 1:98; Abraham b. Solomon, ibid., 110.

8. Angus MacKay, "Popular Movements and Pogroms [*sic*] in Fifteenth-Century Castile," *Past and Present* 55 (1972): 36, and cf. 38.

9. See, for example, Collantes de Terán, *Sevilla,* especially 226ff. (see Works Frequently Cited).

10. *Memorias de don Enrique IV de Castilla* (Madrid, 1835–1913), Vol. 2: *Colección diplomática,* 366, 376 (no. 7), 431ff. See the interpretation of William D. Phillips, Jr., *Enrique IV and the Crisis of Castile, 1425–1480* (Cambridge, Mass., 1978), 78 (Phillips correctly noted the converso problem as part of the crisis, but stated the entire situation in altogether too modern a political conceptual framework).

11. See Marc Saperstein, *Jewish Preaching, 1200–1800* (New Haven, 1989), 169–70. The "Great Synagogue" is problematic, since the *sinagoga mayor* was converted into a church, probably in 1410 (this had nothing to do with the totally fictitious legend of a host desecration, as Saperstein thought). The only remaining synagogue was called, in fact, the *sinagoga menor,* or "Minor Synagogue." Perhaps Ibn Shem Ṭov was simply confused as to the name.

12. Jocelyn N. Hillgarth, *The Spanish Kingdoms* (Oxford, 1976), 1:407.

13. Francesch Carreras y Candi, *L'aljama de juhéus de Tortosa* (Barcelona, 1928), 56–57 (text in Catalan).

14. Carreras y Candi, "L'Inquisició barcelonina," 131 n. 3 (see Works Frequently Cited). The papal texts were edited by Beltrán de Heredia, "Las bulas de Nicolás V," 37–38, 41–44 (see Works Frequently Cited).

15. Baer, *History of the Jews* 2:426. Introduction to *Halikhot 'olam* (Sabioneta, 1567) cited by Ḥayim (Joachim) Z. Hirschberg, *Toldot ha-yehudim be-Afriqah ha-ṣefonit* (Jerusalem, 1965), 1:288; cf. David Conforte, *Qore ha-dorot* (Berlin, 1846; photo rpt. Jerusalem, 1969), fol. 27b.

16. For Isaac de León, see the responsum of Jacob Ibn Ḥabib in the collection *Zera' anashim,* ed. David Frankel (not Ḥayim Azulai, as sometimes stated) (Husiatyn, 1902), "Even ha-'ezer," no. 43, fols. 33b–42a. See also Zacut, *Sefer yuḥasin,*

fol. 226a. On Isaac and his uncle, both in Toledo in 1483, see León Tello, *Judíos de Toledo* 2:419; and see generally Marx, *Studies*, 90 (see Works Frequently Cited) (he claimed Isaac headed a yeshivah in Toledo ca. 1447, but he would have been only twenty-seven at the time; hardly likely). Marx did not consult the important responsum of Ibn Ḥabib mentioned above. Baer, *History of the Jews* 2:374, makes Isaac "the famous rabbi of Ocaña," a tiny village near Toledo! The philosophical MSS mentioned here, completed in the yeshivah of Ibn Shem Ṭov, are now in the Freiburg Universitätsbibliothek; see *Verzeichnis der orientalischen Handschriften in Deutschland*, ed. Hans Stridel: *Hebräische Handschriften*, by Ernst Roth (Weisbaden, 1965), 68–69. Yaʿaveṣ on the "many" yeshivot, introduction to his *Or ha-ḥayim* (Lublin, 1912; rpt. Israel, s.a.), 8.

17. Zacut, *Sefer yuḥasin*, fol. 226a (Freimann, in his introduction to the rpt. ed., fol. I, misunderstood the text and claimed that Zacut said that Samuel was a student of Aboab; in fact, he said that he himself was Aboab's student. Freimann generally made several errors in his introduction there). Samuel Valanci is not to be confused with Samuel *Valenci* of Toledo, involved in an Inquisition process in 1487; to add to the confusion, Rabbi Samuel Valanci was also involved with the Inquisition in 1486! Both of these will be discussed in Chapter 7.

18. Abraham Ibn Megash, *Kevod Elohim* (Constantinople, 1585; facs. rpt. Jerusalem, 1977), fol. 47 (48)a. On Aboab, see Zacut, *Sefer yuḥasin*, fol. 226a. He was a pupil of Isaac Canpanton, and hardly his "colleague" as Marx erroneously wrote (*Studies*, 90 n. 15). Ibn Habib, in the previously cited responsum, gives interesting information about him.

19. See S. Poznánski, "Le colloque de Tortose et de San Mateo," *R.E.J.* 74 (1922), especially 18–22, 34–39, 160–64; L. Landau, ed., *Das apologetische Schreiben des Josua Lorki* (Antwerp, 1906). Further details also in Chapter 5, in the discussion of Pablo de Santa María.

20. Baer stated that the pope "invited" participation, when, in fact, it was a command. The text of the letter, in French translation, in Poznánski, "Le colloque de Tortose," 168, and cf. also *R.E.J.* 75 (1923): 74. The most complete study to date, with the text of the Christian "protocols," or account of the disputation, is Antonio Palacios López, ed., *La disputa de Tortorsa* (Madrid-Barcelona, 1957), 2 vols.; yet he made no reference at all to this letter. The Hebrew accounts have been translated, with helpful notes (although some minor errors in the introduction), by Jaume Riera i Sans, *La crònica en hebreu de la disputa de Tortosa* (Catalan) (Barcelona, 1974).

21. Baer, *History of the Jews* 2:170–210. Further discussion will be in my book on relations between Jews, and Muslims, and Christians.

22. Bonafed's poem in Baer, *Die Juden* 1:797–98, and the epigram of de Piera (the correct spelling) ibid., 798. Baer's discussion in *History of the Jews* 2:211ff. is somewhat confused and erroneous.

23. Solomon de Piera, *Divan* (poetry), ed. Simon Bernstein (New York, 1943), iv.

24. See Baer, *Die Juden* 1:410, 503, 506, 507, 598, 603, 754, 777, 986–87. Important new information on the entire family is in Manuel Serrano y Sanz, *Orígenes de la dominación española en América*, N.B.A.E. 26 (Madrid, 1918), especially clxxxv ff. on Benvenist and his sons, and Francisca Vendrell, "Aportaciones

documentales para la estudia de la familia Caballería," *Sefarad* 3 (1943), especially 129ff. (neither author used the documents in Baer, however).

25. In addition to the above, see the articles and studies cited by Vendrell, "Aportaciones," 130–31 (all from Bernstein's introduction to the *Divan*, cited above). Other material remains to be investigated.

26. See de Piera, *Divan*, ix and n. 21, and top of x. Bernstein there criticized Graetz for the error in identification of the two Vidals, which error Baer simply repeated.

27. Vidal b. Labī Benveniste, *Meliṣat ʿofer ve-Dinah*, ed. Gerson Soncino (Constantinople, 1516). The Rimini 1525 ed. contains the same poem by Gerson Soncino (both eds. are in the collection entitled *Divrey ha-yamim shel Mosheh rabenu*). Subsequent eds. omitted the poem, nor is the name of the author (Vidal) mentioned in these early editions. Excerpts may be found in Ḥayim Schirmann, *ha-Shirah ha-ʿivrit bi-Sefarad u-ve-Provans* (Tel Aviv, 1956), 2:603ff. Schirmann's introduction (592–94) correctly distinguished between the two Vidals.

28. See Vendrell, "Aportaciones," 130, and Bernstein's introduction (vii) on Samuel (unnoticed by Vendrell).

29. See Bernstein's article cited in the introduction to *Divan*, x n. 22 (also overlooked by Vendrell). Incidentally, Baer's claim that the aged Bonastruc Dezmaestre of Gerona "welcomed" Vidal Joseph's conversion is totally without basis, and hardly consistent with what we know about that man (*History of the Jews* 2:212).

30. See the partial English translation of these lines in Baer, *History of the Jews* 2:215 (while the incorrect translations noted in the text above in brackets are, of course, the fault of Baer's translator, he himself nevertheless approved that translation). Vidal's reply to de Piera, first published by Kaminka, is reproduced in A. M. Habermann, "Igerot Shelomoh de Piera le-Mosheh ʿAbbas," *Oṣar yehudey Sefarad* 7 (1964): 24–26 (an article with some errors). Habermann apparently did not know that Vidal also converted, and so, like Baer, interpreted the poem as " proof" of de Piera's own conversion. He then adds to the confusion by suggesting that de Piera "returned" to Judaism in Monzón, with no proof whatsoever. Strangely, there is no reference to any of the poems discussed here in Heinrich Brody, *Beiträge zu Salomo da-Piera's Leben und Werken* (Berlin, 1893).

31. Baer, *History of the Jews* 2:483 and n. 29.

32. Millás Vallicrosa's review of Bernstein's edition, *Sefarad* 7 (1947): 187–88.

33. De Piera is known to have lived later in Monzón, where he wrote several poems, one of which is dated 1417; cf. Schirmann, *ha-Shirah* 2:576, no. 1, and Habermann, "Igerot Shelomoh de Piera," 26 n. 8.

34. Text in Baer, *Die Juden* 1:688–89; cf. Brody, *Beiträge zu Salomo da-Piera's Leben und Werken*, 13.

35. Schirmann, *ha-Shirah* 2:620, says he was the last great poet in Spain; however, he perhaps underestimated the number of poets in this period. Bonafed was not, as Patai and others have thought, the rabbi of Calatayud mentioned in the responsa of Isaac b. Sheshet (see Joszef Patai, *Mi-sefuney ha-shirah* [Jerusalem, 1939], 69).

36. Solomon Bonafed, *Divan*, ed. A. Kaminka, in *Mizraḥ ve-maʿarav* 2 (1895): 114; see also Patai, *Mi-sefuney*, 72–73.

37. Kaminka, *Mizraḥ*, 115–16.

38. Solomon Bonafed, "Shirim ve-melisot le-ha-rav [sic] Shelomoh . . . Bonafed," ed. A. Kaminka, in *ha-Tsofeh le-ḥokhmot Yisrael* 12 (1928; photo rpt. 1972): 35. This important letter is not mentioned in Baer's lengthy discussion of Bonafed, *History of the Jews* 2:212ff.

39. Ibid., 38–39 (see especially lines 36–45); translated in Baer, *History* 2: 217–18. (There are, again, several errors in the English translation. Lacave, with a superior knowledge of Hebrew, has correctly translated the poems in Baer, *Historia* 2:481 [see Works Frequently Cited]).

40. The work has been edited: *Peirush A"B,* ed. Dov Rappel (Tel Aviv, 1978).

41. Baer, *History of the Jews* 2:224.

42. Bonafed, "Shirim," 40; excerpt only, in Baer, *History of the Jews* 2:223.

43. Hershman, *Rabbi Isaac Ben Sheshet,* 181–82, who misread Alcala for Alcolea, near Lérida. Already in 1352 Shaltiel was named as one of the twenty-six *ne'emanim* (councilors of the Jewish community) of Gerona (I. Loeb, "Actes de vente hébreux originaires d'Espagne," *B.A.H.* 6 [1885]: 57).

44. Text of Francesch's letter in Israel b. Moses ha-Levy (Profiat Duran), *Igeret ogeret* (Breslau, 1844), following the end of Duran's letter, also with the letter of Bonafos there. Critical ed. of Francesch's letter (only) by Frank Talmage in Isadore Twersky, ed., *Studies in Medieval Jewish History and Literature* (Cambridge, Mass., 1979), 344–46. On Astruc Rimokh in 1391, see Baer, *History of the Jews* 2:131, and cf. Baer, *Die Juden* 1:808.

45. See Carreras y Candi, *L'aljama de juhéus de Tortosa,* 98–102, also on other converts of Tortosa.

46. Baer, *History of the Jews* 2:239–42. Text of Solomon Ibn Laḥmis, *Igeret musar,* ed. A. M. Habermann (Jerusalem, 1946), 32, 38–39.

47. Ibn Laḥmis, *Igeret,* 41, 44.

48. Profiat Duran, *Ma'aseh efod* (Vienna, 1865), 14.

49. Ibid., 14 and 40–41.

50. Netanyahu, *Marranos,* 97ff., 100, 108 (n. 63a), 113. On Abravanel's attack on the positions of Crescas and Albo, see Aviezer Ravitzky, *Derashat ha-Pesaḥ le-R'Ḥasdai Crescas* (Jerusalem, 1989), 15 n. 18 (and also n. 17). Of this criticism there is not a hint in Netanyahu's *Don Isaac Abravanel,* 3d ed. (Philadelphia, 1972).

51. Joseph b. Shem Tov Ibn Shem Tov, *Kevod Elohim* (Ferrara, 1556; photo rpt. Farnborough, England, 1969; and also Israel, s.l.s.a., with handwritten corrections to the text), fol. 26a–b. Cf. Netanyahu, *Marranos,* 97–98 (he incorrectly identified the folio number of his brief citation as "2ab"). Zacut, *Sefer yuḥasin,* fol. 223a.

52. See Baer, *Die Juden,* Vol. 2, no. 305; cf. Miguel Ángel Ladero Quesada, *La hacienda real de Castilla en el siglo XV* (Universidad de Laguna, 1973), 278. Moses Alashqar (born in Spain 1466, died in Turkey 1542) composed a lengthy rebuttal of Shem Tov Ibn Shem Tov's criticism of Maimonidean philosophy, *She'elot u-teshuvot* (Jerusalem, 1959), no. 117. There are numerous manuscripts of the works of Shem Tov and his son Joseph in the Pamplona cathedral which should be edited.

53. León Tello, *Judíos de Toledo,* Vol. 2, nos. 634, 641.

54. Ibid., no. 679.

55. Netanyahu, *Marranos,* 240 and 255ff., gives the unacceptably high estimate; the low figures are those of Miguel Ángel Ladero Quesada, *Historia de Sevilla,* [no.] 2: *La ciudad medieval (1248–1492)* (Seville, 1976), 124, and Collantes de Terán,

Sevilla, 207. Already before 1391 conversions began in Seville, and several conversos received charity payments from the city. In 1412 a salary was paid to a Christian preacher to teach Christian law and faith to both "old" and "new" Christians. By 1426 there were numerous converso artisans and tailors (about twenty-three altogether) living in the *barrio* of Santa Cruz (see Antonio Collantes de Terán Sánchez, "Un pleito sobre bienes de conversos sevillanos en 1396," *Historia, Instituciones. Documentos* 3 [1975]: 169–85).

56. Wagner, *Regesto,* 24, Doc. 46 (see Works Frequently Cited).
57. Collantes de Terán, *Sevilla,* 207 n. 32, and 209.
58. Ibid., 90.
59. See Baer, *Die Juden* 2:302 and 303; Collantes de Terán, *Sevilla,* 90–91, 445–46 (Appendix V), and also 93.
60. Baer, *Die Juden* 2:320, no. 306.
61. Manuel Nieto Cumplido and Carlos Luca de Tena y Alvear, "El Alcazar viejo, una repoblación cordobesa del siglo XIV," *Axerquia* 1 (1980): 246.
62. Coronas Tejada, *Conversos and Inquisition in Jaén,* 17, 19 (see Works Frequently Cited).
63. Documents referred to may conveniently be consulted in Carlos Carrete Parrondo, *Fontes iudaeorum regni Castellae,* [no.] 1: *Provincia de Salamanca* (Salamanca, 1981), 276 (nos. 276 and 277). Carrete did not indicate that Gil González (Dávila), author of the account of the synagogue, wrote in 1618. See there also nos. 289, 322, and 342 on the hospital.
64. Glosses to *Fuero real* (Madrid, 1781 ed. only) 2:325.
65. Loeb, "Polémistes chrétiens et juifs," 232–33 (incidentally, the text quoted on 233, "contra Xpistianos qui ad rritus transierient," which Loeb could not identify, is the decretal of Boniface VIII, *Liber sextus* 5.13.2, that the Inquisition is to proceed against Christians who convert to, or return to, Judaism. The bull of Sixtus IV, which Graetz cited in his article in *R.E.J.* 20 [1890]: 237–43, merely quotes this decretal).
66. Loeb, "Polémistes chrétiens et juifs," 238.
67. Cited by Torres Fontes, "Los judíos murcianos," 73.
68. Loeb, "Polémistes chrétiens et juifs," 239.
69. Ibid., 240–42 (Loeb completely misinterpreted this passage).
70. Isaac ʿArama, *ʿAqedat Yiṣḥaq* V, 30a (cited by Netanyahu, *Marranos,* 147); Isaac Caro, *Toldot Yiṣḥaq* (Warsaw, 1877; photo rpt. Jerusalem, 1978), fol. 76b (cf. Netanyahu [167] on Caro; however, there is no "different view" here, and both authors accurately reflect the Christian polemic).
71. Simon b. Solomon Duran, *She'elot u-teshuvot Yakhim ve-Boʿaz,* Vol. 2 (Livorno, 1782), no. 19.
72. *Tashbeṣ,* Vol. 3, no. 47.
73. Simon b. Solomon Duran, *Yakhin ve-Boʿaz,* Vol. 2, nos. 19, 31; cf. Netanyahu, *Marranos,* 64–65. Nevertheless, in spite of these claims, we know that intermarriage between conversos and "old Christians" took place on a significant scale.
74. Responsum in Zvi Hirsh Edelmann, ed., *Hemdah genuzah* (Königsberg, 1856; photo rpt. Tel Aviv, 1971; not to be confused with the collection of responsa of *geonim* of the same title), fols. 13a–16b.

75. Cf. Netanyahu, *Marranos*, 54–64.

76. Isaac Caro, *Sefer Toldot Yiṣḥaq* (Warsaw, 1877; photo rpt. Jerusalem, 1978), fol. 71b (col. 142a); Netanyahu, *Marranos*, 72.

77. In the collection of responsa entitled *Zeraʿ anashim*, ed. David Frankel (Husiatyn, 1902), "Ḥoshen mishpaṭ," no. 59.

78. *Memorias de don Enrique IV* 3:364–67, nos. ii, iii, iv, vii. For the decretal, see n. 65 above.

79. Régné, nos. 1206, 2616.

80. Ibid., nos. 2987, 3120.

81. Baer, *Die Juden* 1:539–40 and 541–42.

82. Ibid., 202, no. 4; Antonio Benavides, ed., *Memorias de d. Fernando IV de Castilla* (Madrid, 1860), 2:280.

83. Antonio Chabret, *Sagunto, su historia y sus monumentos* (Barcelona, 1888), 2:341–42 (the date should be 1393 instead of 1396); cf. also José M. Madurell Marimón, "La cofradía de la Santa Trinidad de los conversos de Barcelona," *Sefarad* 18 (1958): 72–77, Doc. 5, which contains the text of Juan's decree and the decree of Queen María.

84. Rubió y Lluch, *Documents* 2:59–60, no. 63.

85. Baer, *Die Juden* 1:205–6; Régné, no. 3016.

86. Régné, no. 3259.

87. Régné, no. 3363.

88. Manuel Serrano y Sanz, "Notas acerca de los judíos aragoneses en los siglos XIV y XV," *R.A.B.M.*, 3a ép., 37 (1917): 334–35; Lea, *History of the Inquisition* 1:257 (see Works Frequently Cited), on Juan's involvement in the Arbués affair.

89. Manuel Serrano y Sanz, *Orígenes de la dominación española en América*, N.B.A.E. 25 (Madrid, 1918), xxxi and cccclvii, no. 19.

90. Serrano, "Notas," 335, 338.

91. Baer, *Die Juden* 1:835, no. 518; Serrano, *Orígenes*, xxxi.

92. Shlomo Simonsohn, "La 'limpieza de sangre' y la Iglesia," translated in *Actas del II congreso internacional, Encuentro de las tres culturas* (Toledo, 1985), 305.

93. Serrano, "Notas," 338–39, 340–41, 343.

94. Pedro Sanahuja, *Lérida en su lucha por la fe* (Lérida, 1946), 98 and n. 1 (this is an extremely rare book, apparently not available in the United States, and hardly to be found even in Spain).

95. Ibid., 100–101 and 202, Doc. 6; and 104–9.

96. León Tello, *Judíos de Toledo* 2:184 (e.g., Ferrant Peres, converso; Esteban Arroyal and Alonso Días Abensaboca, *conversos*), 186 (Johan Ferrández Abzaradiel).

97. Ibid., 201, 208, 286 (nos. 881 and 882).

98. Ibid., 339, 357, 212 (no. 714).

99. Juan Alfonso de Baena, *Cancionero de Baena*, ed. José María Azáceta (Madrid, 1966), no. 511.

100. Suárez Fernández, *Documentos*, 246–48 (see Works Frequently Cited); León Tello, *Judíos de Toledo*, Vol. 2, nos. 1386, 1388 (she did not mention Suárez, however).

101. Oropesa, *Luz para conocimiento de los gentiles*, 264 (my emphasis), 276 (see Works Frequently Cited).

102. Torres Fontes, "Los judíos murcianos," 73–74, 75.

103. Baer, *Die Juden* 2:153,

104. Collantes de Terán, *Seville*, 208n. 39.

105. Bernáldez, *Historia de los reyes católicos*, 599 (see Works Frequently Cited).

106. Enrique Cantera Montenegro, "Solemnidades, ritos y costumbres de los judaizantes de Molina de Aragón a fines de la edad media," *Actas del II congreso internacional, Encuentro de las tres culturas*, 68.

107. Carlos Carrete Parrondo, "Fraternization between Jews and Christians in Spain before 1492," *American Sephardi* 9 (1978): 15–21 (many examples need to be added to those adduced there).

108. From documents discussed by Elies Serra i Ràfols, "Oficis i eines al segle XIV," *VII Congrés d'historia de la corona d'Aragó* 2:567, and ignored by all others who have written on this subject.

109. Vicente Castañeda, "Ensayo de un diccionario de encuadernadores españoles," *B.A.H.* 141 (1957): 518 (Guillermo was *not* "included in a list of penitents of the Inquisition"; he misread his source), 532 (cf. Pedro Miguel Carbonell, *Opúsculos inéditos* [CODOINA 28], 10–11). The basic source, to which Castañeda refers, is José M. Madurell-Marimón and Jorgé Rubió y Balaguer, *Documentos para la història de la imprenta y librería en Barcelona* (Barcelona, 1955), where the index should be consulted for all these conversos.

110. Madurell and Rubió, *Documentos*, 70* (and see there 34* and 36*–37* on other possible conversos).

111. Ibid., 38*, 18–19, 21, Doc. 10, and 60–61, Doc. 28; cf. Carbonell, *Opúsculos inéditos*, 29, 32.

112. Carbonell, *Opúsculos inéditos*, 32; cf. Castañeda, "Ensayo," 534–35 and the numerous references in Madurell and Rubió.

113. Madurell and Rubió, *Documentos*, 109, Doc. 49, and cf. 40*. For Majorca, see Alvaro Santamaría Arández, "En torno a la situación de los judíos conversos de Mallorca en el siglo XV," *Boletín de la sociedad arqueológica luliana* 31 (1953–60): 193.

114. León Tello, *Judíos de Toledo* 2:381, no. 1070.

115. Juan Torres Fontes, *De historia médica murciana* (Murcia, 1981), 1: 62–64.

116. Juan Torres Fontes, "Riesgo de Izag Cohen y ventura de Alfonso Yáñez Cohen," *Estudios en memoria del profesor d. Salvador de Moxó, En la España medieval*, Vol. 3 (Madrid, 1982), 653–64.

117. Collantes de Terán, *Sevilla*, 408.

118. His *Menor daño de la medecina* and *Espejo de la medecina* (Seville, 1506, etc.) were given a modern edition by A. Paz y Mélia (Madrid, 1945), and the first work (only) a critical edition by María Teresa Herrera (*Acta salmanticensia* 75, Salamanca, 1983) but with no mention that the author was a converso, much less the father of Diego de Valera. See also A. González Palencia, *Alonso Chirino* (Madrid, 1944–45). See more on Chirino in the Afterword.

119. Antonio de la Torre, "Un médico de los reyes católicos," *Hispania* 4 (1944): 66–72; Baer, *Die Juden* 2:520–21 (the process of Fabricio). The legend of Ribas Altas, another converso, will be mentioned in Chapter 8.

120. "Chronicon de Valladolid," CODOIN 13:194; Suárez Fernández, *Documentos*, 441.

121. Santamaría Aréndez, "En torno a la situación de los judíos," 192.

122. Régné, no. 2881; Tomás García was one of those pressured by Fernando I to convert in 1413; see Francisca Vendrell, "La política proselitista del rey d. Fernando I de Aragón," *Sefarad* 10 (1950): 351–52.

Chapter 4. Conversos and Political Upheaval

1. Angus MacKay, "Popular Movements and Pogroms in Fifteenth Century Castile," *Past and Present* 55 (1972): 34 and 35, Table 1.

2. While appearing to criticize Baer's (correct) statement that only in the late 1440s was the converso problem revealed in its full gravity, and Márquez Villanueva's (equally correct) statement that deteriorating economic conditions were a cause of popular unrest, MacKay unwittingly provided solid evidence which in fact completely substantiates the latter hypothesis, and admitted finally that from 1440 to 1449 "there is little evidence of serious popular agitation" (ibid., 52–53, 54–57, 58). We only need substitute "no" evidence.

3. See Carriazo's introduction to Gonzalo Chacón's *Crónica de don Alvaro de Luna*, ed. Juan de Mata Carriazo (Madrid, 1940), xxvi ff. Carriazo did not suspect Chacón's converso origin, but the name Chacón—later Coronel—was that of a renowned converso dynasty. Gonzalo's father, Juan, was *alguacil* of de Luna in 1429, and may have been the first converso member of the family. Note that Chacón speaks twice with considerable sympathy of the "great persecution" of conversos in Toledo (ibid., 244). On de Luna's Jewish ancestry, see *Sefarad* 14 (1954): 110n. 26.

4. Pedro Carrillo de Huete, *Crónica del halconero de Juan II*, 325–32 (see Works Frequently Cited); cf. Nicholas Round, *The Greatest Man Uncrowned: A Study of the Fall of Don Alvaro de Luna* (London, 1986), 24–25. For the *pragmática*, see Fermín Caballero, *Noticias de la vida, cargos y escritos del doctor Alonso Díaz de Montalvo* (Madrid, 1873), 47. Francisco Cantera Burgos, *Alvar García de Santa María y su familia de conversos* (Madrid, 1952), 77ff., 427–33; and cf. also briefly Round, *Greatest Man Uncrowned*, 63–64 (which adds nothing to what Cantera already said).

5. Chacón, *Crónica*, 334, 381–83. Some additional details involving Alonso, and his brother Pedro de Cartagena, and their dealings with Sarmiento after he left Toledo following the 1449 riots, may be found in Cantera, *Alvar García*, 165–68, 423–27, and 474. These add nothing of real importance, however. Surprisingly, Cantera said virtually nothing about Alonso de Cartagena's famous defense of *conversos* (to be discussed below).

6. *Crónica del rey don Juan II*, B.A.E. 68:661. Cota was apparently the father of a famous jurist, also named Alonso, who was burned by the Inquisition in Toledo in 1486 (see Fita, "La Inquisición toledano," *B.A.H.* II [1887]: 299). A document of Toledo in 1491–92 refers to the house of "Alfon Cota" in the Alcava (*barrio*) and a house in Rúa nueva in which Cota and "Alfon" de San Pedro lived. These were probably members of the same families (Cota and San Pedro) mentioned here (see León Tello, *Judíos de Toledo* 2:556).

7. Cf. Baer's brief summaries of the events, *History of the Jews* 2:279–81, but

his claim that it was the "lower classes" who rebelled against the conversos is not supported by the sources. The letter of Nicholas V to Juan II condemning Sarmiento is cited by Beltrán de Heredia, "Las bulas de Nicolás V," n. 27. Further information on the status of the conversos and their involvement with de Luna can be found in Round, *Greatest Man Uncrowned*, 171–80, with the most important new information being on the Díaz de Toledo family; and cf. also 204–7, and on the part played by Alonso García de Guadalajara, brother of the converso historian Diego de Valera, 186–88. However, Round was apparently unaware that de Luna was himself of converso descent, which makes his "tolerance" of conversos somewhat less surprising.

8. He was not, of course, the same Juan de Ciudad, also a converso, who got into trouble with the Inquisition in Aragón (as we shall see), but he probably is the one mentioned in the documents summarized in León Tello, *Judíos de Toledo* (see index). See also generally Eloy Benito Ruano, *Toledo en el siglo XV* (Madrid, 1961), 35; Carrillo, *Crónica del halconero*, 511ff.; Lope de Barrientos, *Refundición de la crónica del halconero*, ed. Juan de Mata Carriazo (Madrid, 1946), cxcii–viii; and Chacón, *Crónica de don Alvaro de Luna*, 244. The "Chronicon de Valladolid" (CODOIN 13:19) states that houses (plural) of Cota were "robbed and burned," and that Fernando Alonso Salinero, Alvaro de San Pedro, and "another" were also killed.

9. Carrillo, *Crónica del halconero*, 521, 523.

10. Pedro de Escavias, *Repertorio de principes*, ed. Juan Bautista Avalle-Arce, *El cronista Pedro de Escavias*, University of North Carolina Studies in the Romance Languages and Literatures 127 (Chapel Hill, 1972), 206. Baer distorted the entire incident. Thus, there was no arrest of conversos, no trial, no torture under which they supposedly "confessed" to "Judaizing" (*History of the Jews* 2:278).

11. Benito Ruano, "Del problema judío al problema converso," *Simposio Toledo judaico* (Toledo, 1972), 2:5–28; rpt. in his *Los origenes del problema converso* (Barcelona, 1976), 28.

12. The text of the statute has been frequently published: A. Martín Gamero, *Historia de la ciudad de Toledo* (Toledo, 1862), 1036–40; Baer, *Die Juden* 2: 315–17 (partial edition); Alonso de Cartagena, *Defensorium unitatis christianae*, ed. Manuel Alonso (Madrid, 1943), 357–65; Benito Ruano, *Toledo en el siglo XV*, 191–96, and again in his "La 'Sentencia-Estatuta' de Pero Sarmiento," *Revista de la universidad de Madrid* 6 (1957): 277–306, appendix (rpt. in his *Los origenes del problema converso*, 85–92). For the sake of convenience, I cite the text as in Benito Ruano, *Toledo en el siglo XV* (here, p. 142; further references in parentheses in the text).

13. See Benzion Netanyahu, "Did the Toledans in 1449 Rely on a Real Royal Privilege?" *P.A.A.J.R.* 44 (1977): 104–5, and 116–24 for the points below.

14. On the riot in Toledo in 1108, see my "New Light on the Jews of Mozarabic Toledo," *AJS* (Association for Jewish Studies) *Review* 11 (1986): 198–99 (there, on p. 199, I erroneously wrote Alfonso VII instead of Alfonso VIII, who of course was the king who confirmed the *fuero* in 1174). See now Netanyahu, *Origins*, 369.

15. On the legend of the Jewish "betrayal" of Toledo in 711, see my "The Jews and the Muslim Conquest of Spain," *Jewish Social Studies* 37 (1976): 145–58, and "Jews and Albigensians in the Middle Ages: Lucas of Túy on Heretics in León."

16. See the introduction to Francisco Cantera Burgos and Pilar León Tello, *Los judaizantes del arzobispado de Toledo* (Madrid, 1969), xxxiii. See also Appendix C of the present volume.

17. The claim that these were all conversos was made by Beltrán de Heredia, "Las bulas de Nicolás V," 26 n. 6. León Tello also stated that almost all were conversos (*Judíos de Toledo* 1:209). Francisco Marquéz de Villanueva, in his introduction to Hernando de Talavera's *Católica impugnación,* claimed that Barrientos was a converso, which he certainly was not, and even added Alonso de Oropesa (to be discussed in detail later) to the list!

18. See José Amador de los Ríos, *Historia . . . de los judíos* 3:125 (see Works Frequently Cited); Benito Ruano, *Los origenes del problema converso,* 52–53. On Francisco de Toledo, see Chap. 5, but see Netanyahu, *Origins,* 1230 n. 12.

19. Text edited by Luis Getino, "Vida y obras de Fr. Lope de Barrientos," *Anales Salmantinos* 1 (1927): 182 (further references in parentheses in the text; for the correct year of Barrientos' birth, see "Chronicon de Valladolid," 14).

20. *Crónica del rey don Juan II,* 608.

21. Barrientos, *Contra algunos zizañadores,* 195–96; this is all taken verbatim from the memorial of Fernan Díaz, prepared for Barrientos. On efforts after the conquest of Granada to reconvert Christians who earlier had fled there and become Muslims, see Miguel Ángel Ladero Quesada, *Granada después de la conquista* (Granada, 1988), 350; and on the missionary activities of Hernando de Talavera in this regard, José de Sigüenza, *Historia de la Orden de San Jerónimo,* 2d ed. (Madrid, 1909), 2:306–7. Such Christian converts were also called *tornadizos,* but this was confusing, as Jewish and Muslim converts to Christianity were also so called; therefore, these Christian apostates were more specifically referred to as *elches* (from Ar. *ʿilj,* infidel; cf. Felipe Maíllo Salgado, *Los arabismos del castellano en la baja edad media,* 2d ed. [Salamanca, 1991], 146–48). Examples of such apostasy may also be found in Juan de Mata Carriazo, *En la frontera de Granada. Homenaje al profesor Carriazo,* Vol. 1 (Seville, 1971), 244, and see 282, 283 and 246ff. Neither he nor other authors mention the sources here referred to. For the poems mentioned here, see *Cancionero de Baena,* ed. José María Azáceta (Madrid, 1966), nos. 107 and 565. The Catholic Monarchs in 1480 enacted a law against Christians in Andalucía aiding Muslims or supplying arms to them, and also against "bad Christians" who go to Granada to become Muslims *or Jews* (*Ordenanzas reales* 1.12.4, in *Los códigos españoles* [see Works Frequently Cited] 6:284; *Colección de códigos,* 293).

22. The Stúñigas (Estúñigas) were, of course, an extremely powerful family. Pedro de Estúñiga, conde de Plasencia, was chief justice of Juan II. Alvaro was the first duque de Plasencia and the chief justice of the Monarchs.

23. Barrientos, *Contra algunos zizañadores,* 199; the text is cited from the earlier corrupt edition of Fermín Caballero by Castro, *España en su historia,* 539, and note the anecdote there concerning a cousin of Fernando, Sancho de Rojas, which indicates that the king knew of his Jewish descent. According to Barrientos, de Rojas himself was of a converso family. (See Fernando de Pulgar, *Claros varones de Castilla,* and Galindez de Carvajal's genealogical additions to it, on Sancho de Rojas, bishop of Palencia; see also the details on further discussions of this by Castro, and lack of inclusion in histories of this crucial information on Fernando's background,

in Nicasio Salvador Miguel, *La poesía cancioneril. El 'Cancionero de Estúñiga'* [Madrid, 1977], 85–86 nn. 4, 6.)

24. See the numerous references to Fernan Díaz in Carrillo, *Crónica del halconero*, and in Barrientos, *Refundición* (see the index to the latter volume for both works). He was somewhat more important than his title implies. Santiago-Otero has confused him ("Ferrandus Didaci, relator," listed among famous conversos in a Toledo manuscript) with the canon Fernando Díaz de Carrión (Reinhardt-Santiago, *Bibliotéca bíblica,* 140 [see Works Frequently Cited]). Alfonso Álvarez, a cousin of the *relator,* became *contador mayor* of Castile in 1445, and the great jurist Alonso Díaz de Montalvo was at one time a pupil of Fernan Díaz (Round, *Greatest Man Uncrowned,* 172, 182).

25. Another remote possibility might be Gutierre Álvarez, also called Gómez de Toledo, who was archbishop in 1442 and died in 1446. He wrote *De santissime trinitate,* a treatise against Jews (in all eds. of his works). Nevertheless, the strongest suspicion falls on Gutierre Gómez, because of both his mother's name and the relationship of the family to other conversos, on which see Fernando de Pulgar, *Claros varones,* ed. R. Brian Tate (Oxford, 1971), 87 n. 77.

26. Manuel Alonso, in his reprint of this account in Alonso de Cartagena, *Defensorium unitatis Christianae* (Madrid, 1943), added the parenthetical identification of Juan Gómez as Julian (353), but this is impossible since no Visigoth—least of all a Jew—could have had a Spanish name.

27. Text of Fernan Díaz edited by Fermín Caballero, in *Noticias,* 243–54; rpt. in Alonso de Cartagena, *Defensorium,* 343–56. There is a lengthy analysis by Nicholas Round, "Politics, Style, and Group Attitudes in the '*Instrucción del Relator,*'" *Bulletin of Hispanic Studies* 46 (1969): 289–319, which is chiefly a summary of the work and sheds little light on it or on its context. Caballero's edition (see n. 23) is perhaps not to be trusted, and a critical edition would be welcome, taking into account also the manuscript discussed below (see n. 30).

28. Marcos García de Mora ("Marquillos"), "El memorial contra los conversos del bachiller Marcos García de Mora," ed. Eloy Benito Ruano, *Sefarad* 17 (1957): 320–51; rpt. in Ruano, *Los origenes del problema converso,* 103–32.

29. Marquillos, "El memorial," 331; Ruano, *Los origenes del problema converso,* 113.

30. Alonso González de Toledo, "Judíos y cargas publicas," Madrid, B.N. MS. 1181, fols. 129r–154v (further references in parentheses in the text).

31. See, e.g., León Tello, *Judíos de Toledo,* Vol. 2, index. s.v. "Carrillo"; note especially nos. 1090, 1092 (who was the later archbishop; same as "Carrillo, Alfonso" in her listing), and no. 1135 on the condesa de Alba.

32. Alonso de Cartagena, *Defensorium,* 191ff., 196, 206–8.

33. Ibid., 228ff., and cf. especially 231, again on the Basel manuscript of the Toledo canons. See, e.g., 239: "Nam hii ex iudeis sunt, cum ad iudaycam cecitatem per vomitum redeunt"; and see especially 242 and 259. Note that this was also the opinion of Barrientos in his very interesting "response" there (327).

34. Ibid., 286–87. He also refers to the Durango heresy, mentioned above in the discussion of Barrientos (all these things have been ignored by those who have written on these subjects).

35. Juan de Lucena, *Libro* (or *Diálogo*) *de vita beata,* ed. A. Paz y Mélia (so he

spelled his name, not "Melia" as it is usually written), *Opúsculos literarios de los siglos XIV a XV* (Madrid, 1892), 146, 148.

36. Juan de Torquemada, *Tractatus contra Madianitas et Ismaelitas,* ed. (Latin) Nicolás López Martínez and Vicente Proaño Gil (Burgos, 1957), 50. (The introduction to the work is marred by the typical anti-Semitism and other errors which characterize López Martínez.)

37. Ibid., 51.

38. Caballero, *Noticias* 51. In his gloss to *Partidas* I.vii.1 there is an apparent contradiction in Montalvo's defense of Luna, which was satisfactorily explained by Caballero (53–54).

39. Rodrigo Jiménez de Rada, *De rebus hispaniae* 3.13, in his *Opera* (Madrid, 1793; rpt. Valencia, 1968), 60. Nevertheless, the great archbishop was hardly an enemy of Jews; see my "Rodrigo Jiménez de Rada y los judíos: La 'divisa' y los diezmos de los judíos," *Anthologica annua* 35 (1988): 469–81. On Julian and the Visogothic laws see my *Jews, Visigoths & Muslims in Medieval Spain* (Leiden, 1994).

40. There is no question that his statement about the *Fuero juzgo* not being authentic is correct; cf. the authorities cited by Rafael de Floranes, "Vida y obras del dr. d. Lorenzo Galindez Carvajal," CODOIN 20:293–94 n. 1. On the authority of Montalvo, see ibid., 304–5 and notes.

41. *Fuero real* (Madrid, 1781 ed. only), 339–52, glosses to IV.iii.2.

42. Juan de Vergara, "Contradicción del Estatuto de Toledo," manuscript, Universidad de Salamanca MS. 455, fols. 70–87 (on Juan de Vergara, see the important article of J. Goñi in Luis Moreno Nieto, ed., *Diccionario enciclopedico de Toledo y su provincia* [Toledo, 1977], 502–6).

43. Luis Delgado Merchán, *Historia documentada de Ciudad Real* (Ciudad Real, 1907), 399–406 (Doc. 12); cf. Delgado's description of the events (158–63), not always accurate or in agreement with the text of the document.

44. Text of Nicholas' bull in Benito Ruano, *Toledo en el siglo XV*, 215–16; cf. 76 on the pardons, and Juan II's letter, 222–23. Note that all of this disproves Sicroff's claim that the pope *renewed* his condemnation of Sarmiento's "Sentencia" (Albert A. Sicroff, *Les controverses des statuts de "pureté de sang" en Espagne du XVe au XVIIe siècle* [Paris, 1960], 63).

45. Beltrán de Heredia, "Las bulas de Nicolás V," 33–34.

46. *Fortalitium fidei*, fol. 182v (cited ibid., 35). That Alonso was not a converso was already known to careful scholars, but has been conclusively demonstrated by Benzion Netanyahu, "Alonso de [*sic*] Espina: Was He a New Christian?" *P.A.A.J.R.* 43 (1976): 107–65 (he did not, however, cite Beltrán's article there).

47. Diego Enríquez del Castillo, *Crónica*, B.A.E. 70:130; cf. Tarsicio de Azcona, *Isabel de Castilla* (Madrid, 1964), 377–82. Mario Méndez Bejarano, *Histoire de la juiverie de Seville* (Madrid, 1922), 144, made the claim that this was the chief cause of the 1467 riots.

48. Alonso de Palencia, *Crónica de Enrique IV* (= *Cuarta décadas*), Vol. 1, trans. A. Paz y Mélia, B.A.E. 257 (rpt. Madrid, 1973), 136; see generally Miguel Ángel Ladero Quesada, "Judeoconversos andaluces en el siglo XV," *Actas del III coloquio de historia medieval andaluza* (Jaén, 1982), 30–31. Antón de Montoro,

Cancionero, ed. Francisco Cantera Burgos and Carlos Carrete Parrondo (Madrid, 1984), 121ff. (there is no reason for Carrete's belief that this poem was addressed to Fernando; see 25). Alonso Díaz de Montalvo, [*Repertorium*] ([Seville], [1477]), s.v. *"Bellum,"* col. b (extremely rare; I consulted the copy at Madrid, B.N. *Raro* 225). What he says there is somewhat obscure, however, and may not refer to this at all.

49. Alonso de Palencia, *Crónica* 1:195, 215–16.

50. Benito Ruano, *Toledo en el siglo XV,* 93–100.

51. See the letter of Pedro de Mesa, canon of Toledo, in *Memorias de don Enrique IV de Castilla* (Madrid, 1835–1913), 2:545–51.

52. Cited by Benito Ruano, *Toledo en el siglo XV,* 100 (cf. his *Los origenes del problema converso,* 135–51, which, however, adds nothing new).

53. See "Anales de Garci-Sánchez, jurado de Sevilla," *Anales de la universidad hispalense* (Seville) 15 (1953): 50. On the Alcalá synod, see Benito Ruano, *Toledo en el siglo XV,* 136. See generally on all of this *Memorias de Enrique IV* 2:551–53; León Tello, *Judíos de Toledo* 1:236 and 472–79 (Doc. 60).

54. *Memorias de Enrique IV* 2:76 n. 1; Benito Ruano, *Los origenes del problema converso,* 139; León Tello, *Judíos de Toledo* 2:332, no. 935. On "doctor Franco" see Francisco Cantera Burgos, "El poeta Cartagena . . . ," *Sefarad* 28 (1968): 13–15, and on his son Alonso and the riots, 22–23.

55. Diego de Valera, *Memorial de diversas hazañas,* B.A.E. 70:78–79. (The *Crónica* of Alonso will be discussed in detail below.) Diego incorrectly gave the date of April 1474, but according to Pedro de Escavias (*Repertorio de principes,* 230 and cf. 90–94) it was in March of 1473 (which is correct); See also Diego Enríquez del Castillo, *Crónica,* 214. Antón de Montoro, *Cancionero,* 113ff.

56. Pedro de Escavias, *Repertorio de principes,* 174–75.

57. Alonso de Palencia, *Crónica de Enrique IV,* Vol. 2, B.A.E. 258 (rpt. Madrid, 1975), 85–88, 89, 96, 93–94. Alonso also claimed that Pacheco instigated the Córdoba riots (129).

58. Ibid., 96.

59. Ibid., 129–30.

60. Alonso de Palencia, *Crónica de Enrique IV,* Vol. 3, B.A.E. 267 (rpt. Madrid, 1975), 21; cf. 2:303.

61. Shlomo Simonsohn, "La 'limpieza de sangre' y la iglesia," translated in *Actas de II congreso internacional. Encuentro de las tres culturas* (Toledo, 1985), 305–6.

62. Fernando de Pulgar, *Crónica de los reyes católicos,* 334; idem, *Crónica de don Fernando é doña Isabel,* 331 (see Works Frequently Cited) on the laws of 1478; text of the 1493 decree in Augustín Millares Carlo, "Indice y extractos de los libros de cédulas y provisiones de Archivo y Museo de Madrid," (Ayunatmiento de Madrid) *Revista de la biblioteca archivo y museo* 6 (1929): 319, no. 167. See also above, Chap. 3, n. 55.

63. Alonso de Palencia, *Cuarta década,* Latin text ed. José López de Toro (Madrid, 1970), 54; somewhat free Spanish trans. idem (Madrid, 1974), 65. On the exiled *conversos* from Toledo in 1467, see Benito Ruano, *Los origenes del problema conversa,* 145.

64. Alonso de Palencia, *Cuarta década,* Latin text, 71–72; translated vol. 85–86.

65. Fernando de Pulgar, *Letras*, ed. J. Domínguez Bordona (Madrid, 1958), 137, no. 31; F. Cantera Burgos, "Fernando de Pulgar y los conversos," *Sefarad* 4 (1944): 297; English translation used here is that in Roger Highfield, ed., *Spain in the Fifteenth Century* (London, 1972). Incidentally, the letter to Pedro Navarro, reproduced in facsimile and discussed by Carriazo in the introduction to his ed. of Pulgar, *Crónica de los reyes católicos*, lxiv–xx, is not by him but by Fernán *Pérez del* Pulgar, and was written not in 1484 but in 1509. He was an altogether different person, author of *Breve parte de las hazañas del excelente nombrado Gran Capitán*. There is no evidence that he was in any way related to Fernando de Pulgar. (Carriazo, of all people, should have known this, for he had already edited and discussed this very letter, correctly, in 1926, in an article reprinted in his previously cited *En la frontera de Granada*, 75 ff.)

66. Pulgar, *Crónica de los reyes católicos*, xlix–li; Cantera, "Fernando de Pulgar y los conversos," 306–10. Carriazo had great difficulty in deciphering this extremely simple and legible text which was reedited by Cantera.

67. Pulgar *Crónica de los reyes católicos*, 335, lines 8–9.

68. Cantera, "Fernando de Pulgar y los conversos," 307–8.

69. Ibid., 319; cf. Pulgar, *Crónica de los reyes católicos*, liii–lv. Cantera was undoubtedly correct that Letter 21 was Pulgar's reply to that attack (incidentally, the text of Augustine which Cantera could not identify in the first letter is here specifically mentioned: Epistle 149).

70. Pulgar, *Letras*, 85–89; Cantera, "Fernando de Pulgar y los conversos," 321–29.

71. Pulgar, *Letras*, 21, no. 4; Cantera, "Fernando de Pulgar y los conversos," 331; cf. Pérez de Guzmán, *Crónica del rey don Juan II*, B.A.E. 78:662, and Manuel Alonso's introduction to Alonso de Cartagena, *Defensorium*, 25.

72. Pulgar, *Letras*, 63, 66, 67.

73. Ibid., 120–21, no. 24. Cantera briefly mentions it, but not this passage. On López de Ayala and Toledo, see Benito Ruano, *Toledo en el siglo XV*, 277, no. 72, and 281 (unfortunately, he made no use at all of Pulgar's letters).

74. *Coplas* 10, in Pulgar, *Letras*, with his glosses, 172–73. In addition to Pulgar, the *Coplas* have been attributed to the conversos Rodrigo de Cota and even Juan de Mena. J. Rodríguez Puértolas argues that the author was fray Iñigo de Mendoza, who was a descendant of conversos, which is possible if unproven. Rodríguez made the common error, found even in the writings of historians, of referring to Pulgar as "Hernando del Pulgar," i.e., Fernán Pérez del Pulgar, called Hernando; as previously mentioned; see Rodríguez Puértolas, "Sobre el autor de las *Coplas de Mingo Revulgo*," *Homenaje a Rodríguez Moñino* (Madrid, 1966), 2:131ff.

75. *Glosa* to *Coplas*, in *Letras*, 224, 227–28.

76. Pulgar, *Claros varones*, 39; Carriazo in Pulgar, *Crónica de los reyes católicos*, xxv, and Tate's observation on this, *Claros varones*, 92 n. 118.

77. León Tello, *Judíos de Toledo* 2:399, no. 1113. On Pulgar in Madrid, see Carriazo, introduction to *Crónica de los reyes católicos*, xxx.

78. León Tello, *Judíos de Toledo* 2:374, no. 1047 (she did not seem to be aware of the significance of these documents concerning Pulgar and made no comment on them even in the introductory study; indeed, in the index this second document does not even appear under "Pulgar").

79. Cantera Burgos, "Fernando de Pulgar y los conversos," 334ff., with the parallel versions of the chapters from each recension.

80. Pulgar, *Crónica de los reyes católicos,* 348–49. Benito Ruano, *Toledo en el siglo XV,* 127 n. 29.

81. Baer, *History of the Jews* 2:339 and 495 n. 14.

82. His *Visión delectable,* influenced by Maimonides, was first published ca. 1484 (see the works on him cited in my *Maimonides: Essays and Texts,* 138 n. 17).

Chapter 5. Conversos in Service of Church and State

1. So according to Jocelyn N. Hillgarth, *The Spanish Kingdoms, 1250–1516* (Oxford, 1976), 1:301. He is not mentioned, however, either by Baer or by León Tello.

2. Isabel Montes Romero-Camacho, "Notas para el estudio de la judería sevillana en la baja edad media," *La ciudad hispánica durante los siglos XIII al XVI, En la España medieval,* Vol. 10 (Madrid, 1987), 358 and table, 362 and 360 (she did not mention that Alfonso was *tesorero mayor* of Juan I, however). Francisco is not even mentioned in Luis Vicente Díaz Martín, *Los oficiales de Pedro I de Castilla* (Valladolid, 1975).

3. Emilio Mitre Fernández, "Los judíos y la corona de Castilla en el transito al siglo XV," in Salvador Moxó, ed., *Estudios sobre la sociedad castellana en la baja edad media, Cuadernos de historia,* Vol. 3: *anexo* of *Hispania* (1969): 353.

4. Juan Alfonso de Baena, *Cancionero de Baena,* ed. José María Azáceta (Madrid, 1966), 1:126, verse 80, and no. 57, verses 97–120. See Azáceta's notes (127), and F. Cantera Burgos, "El Cancionero de Baena," *Sefarad* 27 (1967): 95.

5. *Colección de documentos para la historia del reino de Murcia,* ed. Juan Torres Fontes (Murcia, 1963–), 7:169–72. See Baer, *Die Juden* 2:246 n. 2, and *History of the Jews* 1:378; Netanyahu, *Don Isaac Abravanel,* 266–67; and Zacut, *Sefer Yuḥasin,* fol. 225. On Alonso, brother of Juan Sánchez, see Miguel Ángel Ladero Quesada, *Andalucía, de la edad media a la moderna* (*Cuadernos de historia*) Vol. 7 (1973), 54.

6. Menaḥem b. Zerah, introduction to his *Ṣedeh la-derekh* (Warsaw, 1880; photo rpt. Tel Aviv, 1962/63), fol. 4a. He did not, however, "dedicate" his work to Abravanel, as Baer thought.

7. Luis Suárez Fernández, *Historia del reinado de Juan I de Castilla* (Madrid, 1977), 2:257–58.

8. Pedro López de Ayala, *Crónica del rey don Pedro,* B.A.E. 66:168.

9. Julio Valdeón Baruque, ed., "Un cuaderno de cuentas de Enrique II [*sic;* Juan I]," *Hispania* 19 (1959): 110–11.

10. Yosef Hayim Yerushalmi, *From Spanish Court to Italian Ghetto* (New York, 1971), 62.

11. León Tello, *Judíos de Toledo* 2:224 (note that Gonzalo Rodríguez de San Pedro, whom she queried " ¿converso?" [227] was his nephew).

12. *Memorias de don Enrique IV de Castilla* (Madrid, 1835–1913), 2:76 n. 1. See also León Tello, *Judíos de Toledo* 2:322, no. 935.

13. See the detailed account of his activities, with many documents, in Manuel Serrano y Sanz, *Orígenes de la dominación española en América,* N.B.A.E. 25 (Ma-

drid, 1918), cclviii ff., and very briefly in Francisco Cantera Burgos, *Pedrarias Dávila y Cota, capitán general y gobernador de Castilla del Oro y Nicaragua: sus antecedentes judíos* (Madrid, 1971).

14. See A. Paz y Mélia in Alonso de Palencia, *Crónica de Enrique IV* 3 : 251, also with the poem alluded to in the *Coplas*. The text of *Coplas de del Provincial* cited there is incorrect; see below. Alonso de Palencia, who certainly did not like him, called Diego Arias a converso of obscure lineage, who began his career as a tax collector for the then prince Enrique, eventually gaining control of his finances (39–40).

15. The text according to a manuscript (*coplas* 41–43) in Cantera Burgos, *Pedrarias Dávila* 30:

> a ti fraid Diego Arias puto,
> que eres i fuiste Judio,
> contigo no me disputo
> que tienes gran señorio;
> águila, castillo i cruç,
> Judio, ¿de dó te viene,
> pues que tu p[uto] capuç
> nunca le tuvo ni tiene?:
> el águila es de san Juan
> i el castillo de Emaús,
> i la cruç es de Jhesús
> donde fuiste el capitán.

Not everyone was so ill-disposed toward Dávila. The renowned poet Gómez Manrique, himself of the nobility, penned a lengthy poem to him, prefaced by a flattering introduction. Nevertheless, even this poem implies that Dávila was taken with wealth and possessions (R. Foulché-Delbosc, ed., *Cancionero castellano del siglo XV*, Vol. 2 [Madrid, 1915], 85–91; Gómez Manrique, *Cancionero*, ed. Antonio Paz y Mélia [Madrid, 1885], 2:65–84, with introduction, not in Foulché's ed.).

16. Alonso de Palencia, *Crónica de Enrique IV* 2:112.

17. Letter of Fernando and Isabel and Diego de Valera's reply in Mario Penna, ed., *Prosistas castellanos del siglo XV*, B.A.E. 116 (Madrid, 1959), 18–20. Cf. also Alonso de Palencia, *Cuarta década*, Latin text, 182–83; translated vol., 213–14.

18. José Gómez-Menor, *Cristianos nuevos y mercaderes de Toledo* (Toledo, 1970), 31, on Alonso. On Francisco de Bobadilla, whose daughter's marriage was arranged by Abraham Seneor and the bishop, see Eleazar Gutwirth, "Elementos étnicos e históricos en las relaciones judeo-conversas en Segovia," in Yosef Kaplan, ed., *Jews and Conversos* (Jerusalem, 1985), 96. Gutwirth calls him a converso, without giving proof. On the intercession of Seneor and Juan Arias in Pedrarias' marriage, see Cantera Burgos, *Pedrarias Dávila*, 20–21.

19. Diego de Colmenares, *Historia de la insigne ciudad de Segovia* (rpt. Segovia, 1921), 3:302; corrected (only slightly) by Fidel Fita, "La Inquisición de Torquemada," *B.A.H.* 23 (1893): 421–22. On the Inquisition and the Dávilas, see Chap. 7, and Gutwirth, "Elementos étnicos," 86, 88, 90, etc., and also Cantera Burgos, *Pedrarias Dávila*, passim.

20. On Espina's charges, see Fita, "La Inquisición de Torquemada," 422 (only

on the host desecration of Segovia, however), and Baer, *History of the Jews* 2: 287–88. Baer saw neither Colmenares nor the important article of Fita.

21. See Gutwirth, "Elementos étnicos," 92 and n. 33.

22. Alonso de Palencia, *Crónica de Enrique IV* 2:25, 27. Paz y Mélia, unaware of the converso origin of the family, noted that in 1387 Pedro Ponce de León sold to Alonso Fernández de Marmolejo the hamlet of Bornos granted his family by Alfonso X (3:281). This simply means that there was a converso member of the family already in 1387 (or earlier), and it is not surprising that Rodrigo forgot, or never knew, of his ancestor's relations with that Marmolejo.

23. M. Serrano y Sanz, "Notas acerca de los judíos aragoneses en los siglos XIV y XV," *R.A.B.M.*, 3a ép;., 37 (1917): 334, 338. Other conversos of the family include Gaspar (1414) (335) and Luis, "canónigo [church official] de la Seo [cathedral]" (1492) (345). Note also the previously mentioned brothers Gonzalo and Juan (ibid., 334–37, 341.) See generally Vendrell's aforementioned "Aportaciones" 115–54 for additional details on some of these.

24. Serrano, "Notas acerca de los júdios aragonesas," 338.

25. Lluis Marco i Dachs, *Los judíos en Cataluña* (Barcelona, 1977), 108.

26. Francesch Carrera y Candi, *L'aljama de juhéus de Tortosa* (Barcelona, 1928), 108. See on other converso officials, etc., Amador de los Ríos, *Historia . . . de los judíos* 3:207–9, and 213–14 on conversos who fought on behalf of the king against the Catalans in 1462 (see Works Frequently Cited).

27. Felipe Mateu y Llopis, "Los recursos económicos de Juan II en Lérida y Tarrega durante las turbaciones del principado en 1465," *Hispania* 2 (1942): 413–15 (the whole article contains much information on Jews). There are several serious errors in Serrano y Sanz, *Orígenes de la dominación española* concerning the early Sánchez family, not least of which was his assertion that Luis' name before his conversion was "Alazar Usuf," and that he was a member of the important (Jewish) Alazar family rather than of the Golluf family. On Azach Avendino, Maria Ezquerra, and Alazar "Uluf" (Golluf), see *Libro verde de Aragón*, 17–20 (see Works Frequently Cited).

28. José Cabezudo Astrain, "Los conversos aragoneses según los procesos de la Inquisición," *Sefarad* 18 (1958): 276.

29. J. García Mercadal, ed., *Viajes de extranjeros por España y Portugal* (Madrid, 1952), 319.

30. León Tello, *Judíos de Toledo* 2:601, no. 1711. Concerning the problematic identity of Fernán Álvarez, see Francisco Márquez Villanueva, *Investigaciones sobre Juan Álvarez Gato* (Madrid, 1960), 63; Lea, *History of the Inquisition* 1:259 (see Works Frequently Cited). On Luis de Santángel's role in arranging loans for the *Mesta* (sheep-herding association) during the conquest of Granada, see Miguel Angel Ladero Quesada, *Castilla y la conquista de Granada* (Granada, 1987), 217.

31. Alonso de Palencia, *Crónica de Enrique IV* 2:146–47.

32. Ibid., 161–62, 168.

33. Diego de Valera, *Crónica de los reyes católicos*, ed. Juan Mata Carriazo (Madrid, 1927), 75.

34. Gutwirth, "Elementos étnicos" 92 n. 33 (and add to that Gonzalo de Cuéllar, to be discussed later in connection with the Inquisition in Segovia); see also Suárez Fernández, *Documentos,* 208 and passim.

35. See Miguel Ángel Ladero Quesada, *La hacienda real de Castilla en el siglo XV* (Universidad de Laguna, 1973), 56; also the documents in Amalia Prieto Cantero, *Casa y descargos de los reyes católicos* (Valladolid, 1969), 391 (fol. 207) and 403ff. (fols. 346–49). Luis de Alcalá, it should be noted, was *regidor* of Madrid, and was named, along with *Melamed* (Fernando Nuñez Coronel), as *fiador* (trustee) by Joseph Abravanel in his difficulties in 1492 (Baer, *Die Juden* 2:416). That Meir was not the son-in-law of Seneor was correctly pointed out already by Marx, *Studies in Jewish History and Booklore*, 92 n. 28 (the original version of which Baer repeatedly cited). Netanyahu, *Don Isaac Abravanel*, 54, 279, made the same error. The conclusive proof comes from the chronicle, or memoir, of a member of the family, which says that Abraham "and his relative don Meir" converted; if Meir were his son-in-law, that source surely would have said so (see Joseph Hacker, "Keroniqot ḥadashot ʿal geirush ha-yehudim mi-Sefarad," in Salo W. Baron et al., eds., *Sefer zikaron le-Yiṣḥaq Baer* [Jerusalem, 1979–81], 222); cf. also Capsali, *Seder Eliyahu* 1:181, 210 (see Works Frequently Cited).

36. Baer, *History of the Jews* 2:316. Suárez Fernández may have been the source for this, since he surprisingly made the same mistake; *Documentos*, 49.

37. M. Ladero Quesada, "Los judíos castellanos del siglo XV en el arrendamiento de impuestos reales," in Salvador de Moxó, ed., *Estudios sobre la sociedad hispánica en la edad media* (*Cuadernos de historia Anejo de Hispania*) 6 (1975): 430 (rpt. in Ladero's *El siglo XV en Castilla* (Barcelona, 1982), chap. 5).

38. The contemporary "Chronicon de Valladolid" in CODOIN 13:195. On some of the Coronels in Spain immediately after the Expulsion (possibly the sons of Melamed?) see Gabriel González, "The Intellectual Influence of the Conversos Luis and Antonio Coronel in 16th Century Spain," in William D. Phillips, Jr., and Carla Rahn Phillips, eds., *Marginated Groups in Spanish and Portuguese History* (Minneapolis, 1989), 71ff. (however, he makes no specific connection of these with either Seneor or Melamed). See now also Carlos Álvarez García, "Los judíos y la hacienda real bajo el reinado de los reyes católicos," *Las tres culturas en la corona de Castilla y los Sefardíes* (Salamanca, 1990), 112–17; genealogy of part of the Coronel family, also with the correct form of names (the documents discussed have already been repeatedly edited and nothing new is added there).

39. Capsali, *Seder Eliyahu* 1:210.

40. León Tello, *Judíos de Toledo* 2:556, no. 1561; cf. also 529, no. 1472, on Diego de San Pedro, and 511, no. 1424, on *Melamed*'s earlier activities. On Jaco *Melamed* and Antonio de Ávila see Gutwirth, "Elementos étnicos," 100, etc.

41. Serrano y Sanz, *Origenes de la dominación española*, xcii–iii; cxiv ff. on Luis of Teruel; xcix on the family background. On the conversion of Alfonso de Santángel, see Francisca Vendrell, "La política proselitista del rey d. Fernando I de Aragón," *Sefarad* 10 (1950): 353.

42. Ladero Quesada, *La hacienda real*, 223. In 1494 the property of both men was declared safe and free from seizure by the Inquisition in Toledo. At that time they are described as "belonging to the Cardinal of Spain" (Pedro González de Mendoza), i.e., probably, under his protection; León Tello, *Judíos de Toledo* 2:592, no. 1670.

43. Serrano y Sanz, *Origenes de la dominación española*, lxxiv–vi, lxxxvi. See

also the text of *Libro verde de Aragón*, cited there from a manuscript, cccxciv ff.
Meyer Kayserling's claim in his book *Christopher Columbus* (New York, 1894) that
Luis and Leonardo were "grandsons" of Azarias and received permission from him
to dig for treasure in his house is wrong, being a confusion with the sons of one of
Azarias' brothers. There is no evidence they found anything, much less that it was
used to finance Columbus' voyage (Serrano [lxxxvii–lxxxviii]). See also the documents relating to the first Luis (Serrano [ccccxcvi ff.]). However, from references in
Francisca Vendrell, "La política proselitista," 353–54, it would appear that the conversion of Azarias and his brothers was in 1414 (cf. also Baer, *Die Juden* 1:807).

44. Serrano, *Orígenes de la dominación española*, cxvii, cxxxiii ff., cxxiv. Events
in the life of Luis after 1492 are reported there (cxli ff.). On Abravanel's loan to the
Catholic Monarchs, see Ladero Quesada, *Castilla y la conquista de Granada*, 299.
The reference to Santángel's repayment is in Serrano.

45. Serrano, *Orígenes de la dominación española*, clxxxv n. 1, and clxxxviii–
clxxxix.

46. Ibid., lvii–iii (he is not even mentioned by Baer).

47. Ibid., clvi–ii.

48. See Baer, *History of the Jews* 2:305 and 321. In 1514 the Monarchs ordered
payment to the heirs of Alfonso de la Caballería of a salary due him from 1502;
Amalia Prieto Cantero, *Casa y descargos de los reyes católicos* (Valladolid, 1969),
495 (fol. 220).

49. Serrano, *Orígenes de la dominación española*, cxxviii. On the Sánchez
family, see *Libro verde de Aragón*, 20–28.

50. Serrano, *Orígenes de la dominación española*, cliii–cliv, clvi (most of the
important information is in the notes), and see the text from *Libro verde* there (dii
ff.). See also Cantera Burgos, *Alvar García*, 379, and especially Felipe Mateu y Llopis, "Los recursos económicos," 413ff.

51. Baer, *Die Juden* 1:610ff.; Mateu, "Los recursos económicos," 415 n. 9.

52. Pedro Miguel Carbonell, *Opúsculos inéditos* (CODOINA 28:54).

53. Ibid., 165, 169. On the printer and his book, see José M. Madurell Marimón,
Documentos para la historia de la imprenta y librería en Barcelona (Barcelona,
1955), 134–36.

54. Carbonell, *Opúsculos inéditos*, 170–87, and see the "process" of his wife
Blanquina there (201–14).

55. Francisco Cantera Burgos, "Nueva serie de manuscritos hebreos de Madrid,"
Sefarad 19 (1959): 36–42. The poem in R. Foulché-Delbosc, ed., *Cancionero castellano del siglo XV*, N.B.A.E. 22 (Madrid, 1915), 2:397, no. 721; also in *Cancionero de Baena* (Madrid, 1966), no. 162. For the proverb about a dog, see Foulché
(78, 303), and on the pejorative meaning of *gato*, Márquez Villanueva, *Investigaciones sobre Juan Álvarez Gato*, 52 (he overlooked this poem).

56. Information on all members of the Santa María family in Cantera Burgos,
Alvar García. The converso bishops known, but only some of them, are listed by
Brian Tate, ed., *Fernando de Pulgar, Claros varones* (Oxford, 1971), 105 n. 195. He
also lists "Alfonso de Valladolid," without any information. I suspect Tate has confused him with Abner of Burgos (Alfonso de Valladolid), who, while a converso,
certainly was not a bishop.

57. Pulgar, *Claros varones*, ed. Tate, 68–71 and his notes (this ed. only).

58. Luis Suárez Fernández, *Política internacional de Isabel la católica* (Valladolid, 1965), 1:318. On Alfonso de Burgos, see José Amador de los Ríos, *Historia de la literatura española* (Madrid, 1861–65), 6:308 (where he is called "Alonso de Vargas," whereas in *Historia . . . de los judíos*, it is, correctly, "Burgos"; Alonso de Cartagena was also sometimes referred to as Alonso de Burgos). See also Cantera Burgos, *Alvar García*, 522, that Alfonso was a Dominican.

59. Serrano, *Orígenes de la dominación española*, especially lxxvi.

60. Luciano Serrano, *Los conversos d. Pablo de Santa María y d. Alfonso de Cartagena* (Madrid, 1942), 11.

61. Fernán Pérez de Guzmán, *Generaciones*, 91–97 of Domínguez Bordona ed.; 28–32 of Tate ed.

62. Baer, *History of the Jews* 2:141ff.; Cantera Burgos, *Alvar García*, 63.

63. Isaac b. Sheshet, *She'elot u-teshuvot*, nos. 187–92; Baer, *History of the Jews* 2:139–40.

64. See Hershman, *Rabbi Isaac Ben Sheshet*, 180–91. Hershman's objections to Graetz's identification of the Solomon ha-Levy of these responsa with the later convert (Pablo) are entirely unfounded, however. Nothing is said about the length of friendship between the two rabbis, and it is certainly not impossible for a man in his late fifties (Isaac) to have a friendship with one in his "early thirties" (Solomon), as Hershman believed.

65. Baer, *Die Juden* 2:189–90, no. 197. Serrano, *Orígenes de la dominación española*, 15 n. 13.

66. Hershman, *Rabbi Isaac Ben Sheshet*, 229, and cf. 26 and 31.

67. Baer, *Die Juden* 1:485–96, no. 329.

68. Baer, *History of the Jews* 2:465 n. 23 (cf. the original Hebrew text, *Toldot ha-yehudim bi-Sefarad ha-noṣrit* [Tel Aviv, 1965], 525 n. 57); see Hershman, *Rabbi Isaac Ben Sheshet*, 165 n. 77.

69. Ibn Verga, *Shevet Yehudah*, ed. Wiener, 79ff., and 94; ed. Shochet, 109ff., 126 (see Works Frequently Cited). Shochet in his notes (201) could not identify either Solomon ha-Levy or Samuel Abravalla; on the latter, see León Tello, *Judíos de Toledo* 2:173, no. 603 (again, a caution to Baer's and Shochet's claims of the fabrication of Ibn Verga's chronicle). On the delegation to Florence, see Umberto Cassuto, *Gli ebrei a Firenze nell'età del rinascimiento* (rpt. Florence, 1965), 23–24 and the source cited there.

70. Baer, *History of the Jews* 2:140, and see 473 n. 38. In addition to the sources cited there, the satirical letter appears also in L. Landau, *Das apologetische Schreiben des Josua Lorki* (Antwerp, 1906), 21–22, Hebrew section.

71. Cantera Burgos, *Alvar García*, 19–20 (text).

72. Manuel Milian Boix, ed., *El fondo "Instrumenta miscellanea" del Archivo Vaticano* (Rome, 1969), 261, no. 568 (overlooked not only by Baer, but surprisingly also by Cantera).

73. Serrano, *Los conversos*, 43–44, 47ff.; María de los Llanos Martínez Carrillo, *Revolución urbana y autoridad monárquica en Murcia durante la baja edad media* (Murcia, 1980), 126–27. Juan Torres Fontes, "Fechas murcianas de Pablo de Santa María," *Murgetana* 51 (1978): 87–94, published some interesting documents on this phase of his career, but nothing relating to Jews or *conversos*.

74. Cantera Burgos, *Alvar García*, 353–54.

75. See Moritz Steinschneider, *Die hebraeischen Übersetzungen des Mittelalters und die Juden als Dolmetscher* (rpt. Graz, 1956), 762; Baer, *History of the Jews* 2:139 (Baer thought that Benvenist de la Cavalleria [Ibn Labi] lived in a "small community"—Zaragoza!—and that he was its "father and patron," which is incorrect). See *Libro verde de Aragón*, 45. (Nevertheless, Joshua was also a physician, and once received payment from the pope in that connection.)

76. Landau, *Das apologetische Schreiben*, vi. Only one of the manuscripts has "my master and teacher" (4), and this is either an interpolation or a mere metaphor.

77. See on this my review of *The Hebrew Letters of Prester John*, ed. and trans. Edward Ullendorf and C. F. Beckingham (Oxford, 1982), in *Hebrew Studies* 25 (1984): 192–95 (the assumptions and conclusions of the editors-translators are full of errors). See also M. Bar-Ilan in *History of European Ideas* 20 (1995): 291–98.

78. Joshua's letter in Landau, *Das apologetische Schreiben*, 1–4, Hebrew section. This Joseph Orabuena was chief rabbi of Navarre and physician of Carlos III (not, however, tutor of his son); see Meyer Kayserling, *Die Juden in Navarra . . .* (Berlin, 1861), 88–89, and various documents in Baer, *Die Juden* 1:980ff., and new ones in Mercedes García-Arenal and Béatrice Leroy, *Moros y judíos en Navarra en la Baja Edad Media* (Madrid, 1984), 254 (index).

79. Text of Pablo's Hebrew reply in Landau, *Das apologetische Schreiben*, 20–21; earlier ed. by Abraham Geiger in the Hebrew journal *Oṣar neḥmad* 2 (1857): 5–6; see Nehemiah Brüll on the meaning of the closing, in *Jahrbücher für jüdische Geschichte und Literatur* 4 (1879): 54.

80. Profiat Duran, "Al tehiy ke-avotekha," conveniently available in Frank Talmage, ed., *Kitvey polmos le-Profiat Duran* (Jerusalem, 1981), 81–82; cf. Baer, *History of the Jews* 2:154–55 and 475 n. 42.

81. Duran, "Al tehiy ke-avotekha," 82; Netanyahu, *Marranos*, 90 and 224–26.

82. Baer, *Die Juden* 2:520–21. The Talmud, *B.Q.* 113a, bottom, states that in a case between a Jew and a "Cushite" (Samaritan, or Roman according to some) this is to be done. The citation of Pablo's *Additiones ad postillam* is correct (Pablo's writings will be discussed below).

83. Amador de los Ríos, *Historia . . . de los judíos* 1:13–14 n. 1.

84. Madrid, B.N. MS. 9927, fols. 60r–65v. The previously cited Pérez de Guzmán twice called him "a great preacher," but gave no indication that he personally converted Jews or Muslims.

85. For the details of his life, see the introduction of Manuel Alonso to his previously cited edition of Alonso's *Defensorium*, and also Serrano, *Los conversos*, 121ff., which is more ample than Manuel Alonso.

86. Tate claimed that "purity here has a meaning distinct from that contained in the expression 'limpieza de sangre'" (Pulgar, *Claros varones*, 104 n. 189). However, in Spanish as well as English "purity" means "purity." It is, in fact, obvious what Pulgar's intention was.

87. Diego de Valera, *Memorial de diversas hazañas*, chap. 15, p. 18.

88. See the letter concerning the San Ildefonso Monastery in Julian García Sáinz de Baranda, *La ciudad de Burgos y su concejo en la edad media* (Burgos, 1967), 1:251, and on 247 the interesting story concerning the Monasterio de la Anunciación; cf. also *Burgos en la edad media* (Valladolid, 1984), 445 (incomplete, however).

89. See Amador de los Ríos, *Historia de la literatura española* 6:34, and Birken-maier's article cited by Tate, in Pulgar, *Claros varones*, 105 n. 193 (see also Andrés Soria, *Los humanistas de la corte de Alfonso el magnánimo* [Granada, 1956], 75–76).

90. Torres Fontes, "Los judíos murcianos," 114–15, Doc. 8.

91. Julio Puyol, "Los cronistas de Enrique IV," *B.A.H.* 79 (1921): 12.

92. Edited in *Ciudad de Dios* 35 (1894): 124–29, 211–17, 523–42, and cf. Serrano, *Los conversos*, 140–43, and the important observations in Soria, *Los humanistas*, 69–74, and cf. also Castro, *España en su historia*, 26–28.

93. See generally Amador de los Ríos, *Estudios*, 361ff. (see Works Frequently Cited). It is worth noting his contention that many "Hebraisms" are to be found in Alonso's Spanish style, particularly in his translations of classical works (366). More research is needed on that possibility.

94. See Edward A. Synan, *The Popes and the Jews in the Middle Ages* (New York, 1965), 135–38 and notes; for the pope's physician, see Cecil Roth, *The Jews in the Renaissance* (Philadelphia, 1959), 215, and Henry Friedenwald, *The Jews and Medicine* (Baltimore, 1944), 2:566, 570, and frontispiece to Vol. 1. The text of Eugenius' ignored bull of 1433 was edited by Adolph Neubauer in *J.Q.R.*, o.s. 2 (1890): 530–31.

95. Cantera Burgos, *Alvar García*, 237.

96. Ibid., 29–30, 240–41. In 1417 we hear of his agent in Toledo taking possession of some houses in the *judería* which belonged to his father-in-law, Luis Méndez of Toledo (León Tello, *Judíos de Toledo* 2:218, no. 733). Pérez de Guzmán's "Tratado de vicios y virtudes" has been partially edited several times, following the complete ed. under the title of *Las setecientas* which appeared frequently from 1497 to 1564. Modern complete eds. in R. Foulché-Delbosc, *Cancionero castellano del siglo XV*, Vol. 1, N.B.A.E. 19 (Madrid, 1912), 575–626, but with no mention there of Alvar García; and in *Cancionero de Juan Fernández de Ixar* (Madrid, 1956), 1:3–101 and Vol. 2, appendix I. The eulogy on Alonso de Cartagena also in these eds.

97. Cantera Burgos, *Alvar García*, 172, 241; cf. 379–80. His confusion is all the more puzzling in light of the fact that the *Libro verde* already mentions Gonzalo, and Serrano (whose work was published long before Cantera's) also discussed him.

98. Cantera Burgos, *Alvar García*, 411, 413. See also Carillo, *Crónica del halconero*, 154. The standard work on the Council of Constance is a book by that title by Louise R. Loomis (New York, 1961), cf. Netanyahu, *Origins*, 1306 n. 39! For the concept of medieval ecumenical councils in general, E. I. Watkin, *The Church in Council* (London and New York, 1960), though very basic, is a simple introduction. An important review essay on the history and theory of "Conciliarism" is Heiko Oberman, "'Et tibi dabo claves regni caelorum': Kirche und Konzil von Augustin bis Luther," *Nederlands theologisch Tijdschrift* 29 (1975): 97–118.

99. R. B. Tate, "Four Notes on Gonzalo García de Santa María," *Romance Philology* 17 (1963–64): 364, 366–72.

100. Cantera Burgos, *Alvar García*, 280, 536ff., 559ff. Cantera proved quite conclusively that all the doubts as to Teresa's origin are without foundation, but it is surprising that he did not recall that his "master" (the term is his) Américo Castro

had already made this suggestion in his *España en su historia,* 324 n. 2 (Cantera's criticism of Castro [64, 308] is quite correct, however).

101. See Carrillo, *Crónica del halconero,* 343, on Pablo's political activities. The whole career of Alvar García, his involvement with Fernando I of Aragón (whom he followed from Castile), etc., has been well detailed by Cantera and need not be repeated here. Above, we have mentioned his connection with the Pedro Sarmiento affair, and have cited his *Crónica* of Juan II.

102. Cantera Burgos, *Alvar García,* 416ff. (where he is incorrectly called Alonso García de Santa María); see also Carillo, *Crónica del halconero,* 366, 378, 386, 409, 410, 415, 417.

103. Cantera Burgos, *Alvar García,* 365ff.

104. Not all of Cantera's publication information is complete. Thus, the "Proposición sobre la prehemcia que el rey nuestro señor ha sobre el rey de Inglaterra," etc. (*Alvar García,* 451 no. 3) is also found in B.A.E. 116:205–32; the *Alegato contra los portugueses* (no. 4) was published in 1912. The translation of *Libros de Seneca* (Cantera, 458–59) was published in Seville, 1491; Toledo, 1510; Alcalá, 1530; Antwerp, 1548, 1551; and Madrid, 1627. Similarly, the translation of Cicero, *De officiis,* was published in Seville, 1501; also the translation of Boccaccio was published in Seville, 1495; Toledo, 1511; Alcalá, 1552.

105. Numerous other published and unpublished works; see Cantera Burgos, *Alvar García,* 450ff., and on his poetic works, Amador de los Ríos, *Estudios,* 369ff. Generally ignored is the letter of Fernán Pérez de Guzmán to Alonso, with his reply; see *Generaciones y semblanzas,* ed. Domínguez Bordona, 217–21.

106. He also "revised" Gauberto Fabricio de Vagad's chronicle of the kings of Aragón-Catalonia, published in 1499, but actually he merely translated it from Latin into Castilian (see Sánchez Alonso, *Historia de la historiografía,* 387 [see Works Frequently Cited]).

107. *Libro verde de Aragón,* 14–16.

108. Isaac b. Abraham Ibn Faraj, *Memoir,* ed. and trans. in Marx, *Studies,* 100–103.

109. Capsali, *Seder Eliyahu* 1:182–84.

110. See Chapter 4, n. 23.

111. See Tarsicio de Azcona, "El tipo ideal de obispo en la iglesia española antes de la rebelión luterana," *Hispania sacra* 11 (1958): 12–64, especially 41ff.; Pulgar, *Crónica de don Fernando é doña Isabel,* 549; Francisco Márquez Villanueva's introduction to Hernando de Talavera, *Católica impugnación,* 9 (this work was first published as *Confesión general* in Salamanca [?], 1498). Other works of importance by Talavera are: *Tratados de la doctrina cristiana* (Granada, [1496?]; *Cartas,* ed. E. de Ochoa, B.A.E. 13 (Madrid, 1913): *Reforma de trages* (Baeza, 1638); *Tratados* (above), rpt. as "Breve y muy provechosa doctrina de lo que debe saber todo cristiano con otros trados muy provechosos" in N.B.A.E. 16 (Madrid, 1911), including also a sermon (first published in José Amador de los Ríos, *Historia de la literatura española* 7:541–61); "Suma y breve compilación de cómo han de vivir y conversar las religiosas de San Bernardo que viven en los monasterios de la ciudad de Ávila," ed. O. González Hernández in *Hispania sacra* 13 (1960): 149–74; "Instrucción que ordenó el Rvmo. Sr. Don Fray Hernando de Talavera . . . por do se rigiesen los

oficiales, oficios y otras personas de su casa" (very interesting and important), ed. J. Domínguez Bordona in *B.A.H.* 96 (1930): 787–835; "Glosa sobre el Ave María," in José de Sigüenza, *Historia de la Orden de San Jerónimo,* 2d. ed., N.B.A.E. 8 and 12 (Madrid, 1907–9), 423–26, and rpt., together with another verse work, "Obra . . . sobre la salutación angélica," in M. Menéndez y Pelayo, *Antología de poetas líricas castellanos,* Vol. 5 (Vol. 21 of the National Edition) (Santander, 1946–), 368–71. Hernando also corrected and annotated Francisco (Francesc) Eximinis, *Vita Christi* (Granada, 1496). Very interesting is his "Instrucción en respuesta a cierta petición que hicieron los vecinos de Albarracín sobre lo que debían hacer y las prácticas cristianas que debían observar," ed. Tarsicio de Azcona, *Isabel la católica* (Madrid, 1964), 761–63. While nothing proves this, the fact that most of the Jews of that small village converted at the time of the Tortosa disputation might suggest that conversos (their descendants) were the originators of that petition.

112. Hernando de Talavera, *Católica impugnación,* 82–83; dedicatory letter (68).

113. See Carriazo's introduction to his ed. of Pulgar, *Crónica de los reyes católicos* 1:xl–xli; cf. A. Paz y Mélia, *El crónista Alonso de Palencia* (Madrid, 1914), vii n. 1.

114. Manuel Serrano y Sanz, *Orígenes de la dominación española,* xlv.

115. Sigüenza, *Historia de la Orden de San Jerónimo* 2:288–307.

116. See Azcona, "El tipo ideal," 54ff., and the text of Hernando's defense there (62–64); cf. Herrero de Colado, "El proceso inquisitorial por delito de herejía contra Hernando de Talavera," *Anuario de historia del derecho español* 39 (1969): 671–706.

117. Gracia Boix, *Colección de documentos,* 89 (see Works Frequently Cited).

118. "Del origen de los villanos, que llaman christianos viejos," anonymously edited in *Revista mensual de filosofía* (Seville) 6 (1875): 518–28. This journal apparently exists in this country only at the Hispanic Society in New York (whose "cooperation" in making materials available to scholars is well known!). The only copy I was able to find in Spain was one at the library of the Consejo Superior de Investigaciones Científicas in Madrid, where a staff member graciously rescued it from a pile on the floor of a storeroom. I do not recall who attributed it to Hernando; I am inclined to think Márquez Villanueva, but I no longer have a copy of his edition of *Católica impugnación* with me. According to a note of the anonymous editor, the catalogue of manuscripts at Seville attributed the work to a Dominican, fray Agustín Salucio (1523–1601), but this also seems highly unlikely. I have a photocopy of the treatise which interested scholars are welcome to examine.

119. See Amalia Prieto Cantero, *Casa y descargos de los reyes católicos* (Valladolid, 1969), e.g., 218 (fol. 735), 360 (fols. 881–82 and 919), 421 (fol. 177), 447 (fol. 50), 511 (fol. 442), 369 (fols. 1025–26) and also pp. 391 (fol. 207) and 403 (fols. 346–49); from these latter documents, it would appear that Fernand Núñez Coronel was dead by 1500.

120. Ibid., e.g., 500 (fol. 331): Ruy and Gonzalo López of Soria (ca. 1505), payment for money that they had contributed to the taxes of the Jewish *aljama* in 1489 and 1490, when they were Jews (Alasar and Abraham Romi). Conversos were reimbursed for such tax payments, made in the year they converted; 55 (fol. 203) to

converts in Aranda and Talavera (1502); 197 (fols. 375–80); 282 (fols. 166–68) for work done for the friars of Santa María de Jesús in Zaragoza, authored by María de Lucena of Granada, daughter of Juan de Lucena (possibly the famous converso poet, who did, in fact, have ties to Granada); and 286–87 (fols. 214–15) concerning the tithes to be used for the churches of the *abadía* de Baza.

121. Baer, *Die Juden* 1:910–11, no. 560.

Chapter 6. Converso Authors, Chroniclers, and Polemicists

1. Américo Castro was the one who, by uncanny guesses which most often turned out to be correct, began uncovering the extent of converso literary activity (although Amador de los Ríos and others already made some contributions), and virtually all of his works deal with this. For other aspects of converso cultural activity, see, e.g., Eugenio Asensio, "El Erasmismo y las corrientes espirituales a fines. Conversos, franciscanos, italianizantes," *Revista de filología española* 36 (1952): 31–99, a somewhat controversial article (H. R. Trevors-Roper, in chaps. 6 and 7 of his famous *Historical Essays*, already argued the influence of Erasmus through the conversos; the subsequent bibliography on this issue is vast and, fortunately, beyond the scope of the present book). See also, for yet another important area of contribution, Carlos Carrete Parrondo, *Hebraístas judeoconversos en la universidad de Salamanca (siglos XV–XVI)* Salamanca, 1983).

Since the present study is limited to the period up to the Expulsion, we shall unfortunately have to ignore discussion of such major figures as Saint Teresa and her companions; Alfonso de Zamora; Benito Arias Montano; Luis de León; Luis Vives; and others of the sixteenth and seventeenth centuries. While much has been written on each of these, there is still no general treatment of the cultural influence of conversos and descendants of conversos in the later Spanish period.

For Saint Teresa, on whom there is a substantial literature, see especially Francisco Márquez Villanueva, *Espiritualidad y literatura en el siglo XVI* (Madrid, 1968), 139–205, and José Gómez-Menor, *El linaje familiar de Santa Teresa y de San Juan de la Cruz* (Toledo, 1970). Victoria Lincoln, *Teresa: A Woman* (1985), claims to find "Jewish influences" in her writing, but it is easy to confuse biblical influence with Jewish (see briefly what I wrote about Juan de la Cruz in my "'My Beloved Is Like a Gazelle': Imagery of the Beloved Boy in Religious Hebrew Poetry," *Hebrew Annual Review* 8 (1984): 144–45). Efren (Vol. 1 of Saint Teresa's *Obras completas* [Madrid, 1951] erroneously claimed that her father converted *to* Judaism and then back to Christianity. On Saint Teresa and the Inquisition, see Enrique Llamas Martínez, *Santa Teresa de Jésus y la inquisición española* (Madrid, 1972). For Juan de Ávila, see his *Obras completas* (Madrid, 1952–53), 1:46–73 on the converso background (there is a critical edition, in six volumes, of his *Obras* [Madrid, 1970]). Fray Íñigo de Mendoza will be discussed below.

2. Juan del Encina will be discussed in more detail below; for his musical composition, see Leslie U. Brewer, "The Life and Works of Juan del Encina with Sixty-eight of his musical compositions transcribed into modern notation and annotated," Thesis, Univ. of Arizona, Tucson, 1933, and Gilbert Chase, "Juan del Encina, poet and musician," *Music and Letters* 20 (1939): 420–30. Some of his songs have been recorded: Victoria de los Angeles, "Spanish Songs of the Renaissance" (Angel rec-

ords; reissued on Seraphim); "Music of the Spanish Renaissance" (Montreal Bach Choir, etc., on Turnabout); and Teresa Berganza, "Canciones Españoles" (Deutsche Grammmophon). The last recording also has music of the other possible *converso*, Francisco de la Torre.

3. See M. Serrano y Sanz, "Documentos relativos a la pintura en Aragón," *R.A.B.M.*, 3a. ép., 32 (1915): 147–53; 33 (1915): 413; 34 (1916): 464–66, 480; 35 (1916): 415; 36 (1917): 434–36 on these *conversos*.

4. According to A. Domínguez Ortiz, the first to suggest the "converso mentality" theory was the famous literary scholar G. Díaz Plaja, followed by Castro, Bataillon, and others. Domínguez himself rejected the idea ("Historical Research on Spanish Conversos in the Last 15 Years," in Hornik, *Collected Studies*, 78–79 [see Works Frequently Cited]). Current proponents of the theory include, especially, Stephen Gilman (see, e.g., in the same volume his "The 'Conversos' and the fall of fortune," 127–36). While the possibility of "Hebrew" influences on syntax, etc., in converso writing, particularly of poets, may be worth examining, caution must also be used in accepting Amador's overly enthusiastic views; cf. Cantera Burgos' correct criticism in relation to the writings of Alvar García de Santa María and of Alfonso de Cartagena (*Alvar García*, 230 and 492 n. 62); note also his criticism of Castro's statement about Juan de Mena's "desperate" *converso* "mentality" (ibid., 492 n. 59).

5. No monographic survey of converso historiography has been attempted since the beginning of the century; see Georges Cirot, *Les histoires générales d'Espagne entre Alphonse X et Philippe II* (Paris, 1904), especially 52–54; M. Gaspar Remiro, *Los cronistas hispanojudíos* (Granada, 1920), originally in *Revista centro de estudios históricos de Granada* 10 (1920): 30–107. However, there is a very considerable literature on individual converso historians; e.g., Tomás Rodríguez, "El cronista Alfonso de Palencia," *Ciudad de Dios* 15 (1888): 17–26, 77–87, 149–56, 224–29, 298–303, generally supplanted by A. Paz y Mélia, *El cronista Alonso de Palencia* (Madrid, 1914); consult also G. Cirot, "Les decades d'Alfonso de Palencia," *Bulletin hispanique* 11 (1909): 425–42. Alonso's *Gesta hispaniensa*, a Latin compendium, exists only in an incomplete version (Madrid, 1834). There are manuscripts of this work extant, and it should have a complete critical edition.

For Diego de Valera, Juan de Mata Carriazo's introductory study of his edition of *Memorial de diversas hazañas* (1941) is important. See also Lucas de Torre y Franco Romero, *Mosén Diego de Valera* (Madrid, 1914; originally in *B.A.H.* 44 [1914]); H. Sancho de Sopranis, "Sobre mosén Diego de Valera," *Hispania* 24 (1947): 531–53; C. Real de la Riva, "Un mentor del siglo XV: Diego de Valera y sus epistolas," *Revista de literatura* 20 (1961): 271–306; and other studies dealing mostly with his political writings and views.

For Alvar García de Santa María, see also Juan de Mata Carriazo, "Notas para una edición de la 'Crónica' de Alvar García," *Estudios dedicados a Menéndez Pidal* (Madrid, 1950–57), 3:489–505, and his "Sumario de la crónica de Juan II, glosado por un converso en 1544," *Anales de la universidad hispalense* 12 (1951): 11–71; also F. Cantera Burgos, *Alvar García de Santa María, cronista de Juan II de Castilla* (Madrid, 1951), largely replaced by his more detailed study of the entire family in *Alvar García*.

6. See Juan de Lucena, *Vida beata*, ed. A. Paz y Mélia, *Opúsculos literarios de*

los siglos XIV a XV (Madrid, 1892), 108, and the reference cited in the introduction concerning Lucena himself as a chronicler (xi).

7. See Cantera Burgos, *Alvar García,* 344–45; Sánchez Alonso, *Fuentes,* no. 69 and apéndices, and his *Historia de la historiografía española* 1:3121 (see Works Frequently Cited for these).

8. Also in Andrew Schott (not "Schottus," as often spelled), *Hispania illustrata* (Frankfurt, 1605), Vol. 1.

9. Sánchez Alonso, *Historia de la historiografía,* 387.

10. See examples in the citations by Paz y Mélia, in his translation of Palencia's *Crónica de Enrique IV* 3:302–4.

11. Modern eds. of his chronicles are cited elsewhere here. His *Doctrinal de principes* has been edited by Mario Penna, *Prosistas castellanos del siglo XV* (Madrid, 1959), with the *Epistolas* and other treatises. For the lost (?) chronicles of Enrique by Diego de Valera, see José López de Toro's introductory study to Alonso de Palencia, *Cuarta década* (Madrid, 1970), 1, 192, no. 100.

12. Brian Tate, "The *Anacephaleosis* of Alfonso García de Santa María," in Frank Pierce, ed., *Hispanic Studies in Honour of I. González Llubera* (Oxford, 1959), 387.

13. Indeed, in the fifteenth century we find an outstanding example of this in Fernán Pérez de Guzmán (whose *Generaciones y semblanzas* was cited by Tate!). That author knew no Latin at all; see José Luis Romero, "Fernán Pérez de Guzmán y su actitud histórica," *Cuadernos de historia de España* 3 (1945): 117–51. Another example, possibly a converso, is Gonzalo Chacón in his *Crónica de don Alvaro de Luna* (see index, s.v. "España").

14. Tate discussed Alfonso García's role at Basel, but nowhere mentioned that of Alonso de Cartagena, which was far more important. In spite of our criticism, Tate's article nevertheless provides some valuable insights into the "nationalistic" character of Alfonso García's work.

15. Pulgar, *Crónica de los reyes católicos* 2:314; cf. also his *Crónica de don Fernando é doña Isabel,* 465.

16. Torquemada (not the Inquisitor) wrote *Contra Madianitas et Ismaelitas,* ed. Nicolás López Martínez and V. Pruaño Gil (Burgos, 1957), in defense of the conversos. Pulgar mentions his converso origin (*Claros varones,* tit. 17), and he is called a descendant of conversos (together with San Pedro Regalado and the Franciscan reformer Francisco de Soria) by the anonymous glossator of Pablo de Santa María's *Scrutinium scriptuarum;* cf. Beltrán de Heredia, "Las bulas de Nicolás V," 26 n. 6.

17. Fernán Pérez de Guzmán, *Generaciones y semblanzas,* ed. Tate, 29–31.

18. See the list of his library in Tate's edition (99–100).

19. Diego de Valera, *Espejo de verdadera nobleza,* ed. Mario Penna, *Prosistas castellanos del siglo XV,* B.A.E. 116:102–4.

20. See his *Discurso* at the Council of Basel, ibid., 225–26.

21. J. Lucio d'Azevedo, *Historia dos cristaõs novos portugueses* (Lisbon, 1921), 11.

22. H. Pflaum [Peri], "Une ancienne satire espagnole contre les Marranes," *R.E.J.* 86 (1928): 131–50; Netanyahu, *Origins,*1259 n. 2.

23. See the interesting paper of Cristina Arbos, "Los cancioneros castellanos del siglo XV como fuente para la historia de los judíos [sic] españoles," World Congress

of Jewish Studies, 8th *Proceedings* (Division B: History of the Jewish People) (Jerusalem, 1982), 35–42. Nevertheless, she there deals with only a few of the actual sources.

24. Manuel Ferrer-Chivite, "Los *Coplas del Provincial:* sus conversos y algunos que no lo son," *La Corónica* 10 (1982): 156–85 and 169 (Table 2).

25. *Cancionero de Juan Alfonso de Baena,* ed. José María Azáceta (Madrid, 1966), 3 vols. References will be to this edition, by number of the poem, as is traditional. There have been numerous articles and studies of the *Cancionero,* few of which are relevant to our concerns. However, very important are the articles of Manuel Nieto Cumplido, "Aportación histórica al Cancionero de Baena," *Historia, instituciones, documentos* 6 (1979): 197–218, and "Juan Alfonso de Baena y su Cancionero," *Boletín de la Real Academia de Córdoba* 52 (1982): 35–57, which refer, *inter alia,* to an order by the king to the previously mentioned converso Pedro Ortiz, a collector of taxes in Seville, in 1408 to pay Baena 2,000 *mrs.* Other documents locate him in Seville and Córdoba, and, most important, show that he died prior to 1435.

26. *Dezir que fizo Juan Alfonso de Baena,* ed. and trans. Nancy F. Marino (Jávea [Valencia], 1978).

27. Francisco Cantera Burgos, "El Cancionero de Baena," *Sefarad* 27 (1967): 82 (this article [71–111] is by far the most important ever written on the *Cancionero,* yet is not generally known by literary scholars).

28. Charles Fraker, Jr., *Studies on the Cancionero de Baena* (Chapel Hill, N.C., 1966), 61. Fraker's work, interesting as it is, shows little awareness of the converso background of the *Cancionero,* and is itself marred by something of an anti-Jewish perspective.

29. Although Cantera at least realized that this is a biblical name, he did not consider the biblical references or make any effort to explain it. Amador de los Ríos conjectured that it was the name of a demon! (See Cantera, "El Cancionero de Baena," 98 n. 79.)

30. No. 501; see the valuable notes in Cantera, who also reproduced the text ("El Cancionero de Baena," 97–101). Other transliterated Hebrew words in verses 30–36 are given tentative, if not totally convincing, explanations by Cantera. Much of the explanation here is my own. See also Josep M. Sola-Solé and Stanley E. Rose, "Judíos y conversos en la poesía cortesana del siglo XV," *Hispanic Review* 44 (1976): 371–85, devoted entirely to this poem. Their suggested interpretations add nothing to what Cantera already wrote, and those in which they differ from him are not convincing.

31. Nos. 517–26. On one of the respondents, also possibly a converso, García Alvarez de Alarcón (no. 523), see Cantera, "El Cancionero de Baena," 104, as against the incorrect identification of Amador, followed by Fraker, *Studies on the Cancionero de Baena,* 58.

32. See on this line the remarks of Lucien Dollfus, "Garci Ferrans de Jerena et le juif [!] Baena," *Revue de l'histoire des religions* 13 (1892): 316–30, especially 318; remarks not only anti-Semitic in tone but anti-Spanish (Enrique IV was an "imbecile" 319]). Equally injudicious are the surmises of Claudine Potvin, *Illusion et pouvoir: La poétique du Cancionero de Baena* (Montreal and Paris, 1989), 21–22.

In general, "literary scholars" have shown little awareness of or interest in the converso background of fifteenth-century Spanish writers (with the exception, of course, of Américo Castro). For this reason, the vast majority of the numerous studies on individual authors and their work are not cited in the present chapter, as these contain little of value for our perspective.

33. In Hernando del Castillo, *Cancionero general* (Valencia, 1511 ed. facs. rpt. Madrid, 1958), fols. 232v–233v; also in Brian Dutton, ed., *El cancionero del siglo XV* (Salamanca, 1990–91), s.v. ID 6787 R 1865, V, 534–37 (ID 6787 R 1865).

34. First edited from MS by Francisca Vendrell de Millás, the wife of the renowned José Ma. Millás Vallicrosa and herself a distinguished historian, "Retrato irónico de un funcionario converso," *Sefarad* 28 (1968): 40–44, and also in Dutton, *op. cit.* I, 530 (ID 0517 R 0141), with the addition of a closing stanza not found in Vendrell's MS.

35. The best introductory study dealing with Montoro is that of Carrete in Antón de Montoro, *Cancionero*, ed. Francisco Cantera Burgos and Carlos Carrete Parrondo (Madrid, 1984). An idea of Montoro's wealth may be obtained from his will; see R. Rámirez de Arellano, "Antón de Montoro y su testamento," *R.A.B.M.* 4 (1900): 489.

36. Montoro, *Cancionero*, 269; Montoro, *Poesía completa*, ed. Marithelma Costa (Cleveland, 1990), 16 (*parientes* here has the common meaning of "ancestors" and is not a reference to "non-converted Jewish members of his family," nor is "holy Temple" a reference to "synagogue," as Costa assumed). On his family, see *Cancionero de obras de burlas provocantes a risa*, ed. Frank Domínguez (Valencia, 1978), 105.

37. *Cancionero*, 189; *Poesía*, 205.

38. *Cancionero*, 211, 368; *Poesía*, 166, 15.

39. *Cancionero*, 119, 133–35; *Poesía*, 29 (stanza 19), 202–3 (stanza 4).

40. *Cancionero*, 128ff.; *Poesía*, 141ff. (cf. 333, etc.). Even more absurd in its flattery was his lengthy (34 stanzas) praise of Enrique IV (*Poesía*, 296ff.; not in *Cancionero*).

41. *Cancionero*, 301ff.; *Poesía*, 63ff.

42. *Cancionero*, 327; *Poesía*, 82 (for the variant, I thank Brian Dutton; my understanding of this word is that it probably represents Heb. ṣom qipur, the fast of atonement).

43. *Cancionero*, 310; *Poesía*, 72.

44. In the *Cancionero de burlas*, cited by Marcelino Menéndez y Pelayo, *Antológia de poeticas líricas castellanos* (Vol. 18 of the National Edition) (Santander, 1946–), 306–7; text in *Cancionero de obras de burlas provocantes a risa*, ed. Frank Domínguez (Valencia, 1978), 98–100.

45. Montoro, *Cancionero*, 337–51; *Poesía*, 100–106 (cf. also 130, 238–29, 242ff.).

46. *Cancionero*, 63, 285, 73, 93, 71; *Poesía*, 107, 271, 274, 286, 293.

47. Hernando del Castillo, *Cancionero general* (Toledo, 1520; facs. rpt. New York, 1967), fol. ccii; cf. also another anonymous poem there, *verso* of the same folio, bottom.

48. *Cancionero de obras de burlas*, 76–79 (further references in parentheses in

the text; these and other poems cited in this chapter will be found also in Dutton, *El cancionero del siglo XV*. Meanwhile, this poem appears in numerous collections; e.g., Hernando del Castillo, *Cancionero general*, ed. of 1911 (rpt. Madrid, 1882), 2:234–35; Jorge Manrique, *Cancionero*, ed. Augusto Cortina [Madrid, 1929], 246–52; Juan Fernández de Ixar, *Cancionero*, ed. José María Azáceta [Madrid, 1956], 2:773; etc.).

49. *Cancionero de obras de burlas*, 87–94, and in Dutton, *op. cit.* V (ID 6756).

50. The poems of Gómez Manrique mentioned may be found in his *Cancionero*, ed. Antonio Paz y Mélia (Madrid, 1885), 2:116, 117–18, 119–20, 159, 227 (and see his verses in the name of "el Ropero," Montoro, against Juan [155–58]), or in *Cancionero castellano del siglo XV*, ed. R. Foulché-Delbosc, Vol. 2, N.B.A.E. 22 (Madrid, 1916), 98, 106, 109, 110. His poem against the converso jester is in his *Cancionero* 2:114–15; ed. Foulché, 2:97. The sharp exchange between Juan and Gómez is in Dutton, *op. cit.* II, 108–9 (ID 2940 and 2941). See also the citations in José Gómez-Menor, *Cristianos nuevos y mercaderes de Toledo* (Toledo, 1970), xxiii.

51. Hernando del Castillo, *Cancionero general* (n. 47 above), fol. ccii *verso*, col. a.

52. *Cancionero de obras de burlas*, 133.

53. Dutton, *op. cit.* I, 180–81 (ID 0836). See there also his rebuke of a secretary of the duchess of Medina Sidonia who called him a Marrano. ID 0838.

54. Francisco Márquez Villanueva, *Investigaciones sobre Juan Alvarez Gato* (Madrid, 1960), 31, 84 n. 5. This book contains much useful information, but many of its conclusions must be treated with caution; cf. the critical remarks of Francisco Cantera Burgos in his review in *Sefarad* 21 (1961): 399–402.

55. Juan Alvarez Gato, *Obras completas*, ed. Jenaro Artiles Rodríguez (Madrid, 1928), x (there is a MS of his poetry in the Ticknor Collection of the Boston Public Library which should be consulted).

56. Márquez, *Investigaciones sobre Juan Alvarez Gato*, 33, 143; cf. Cantera, review (400–401).

57. Gato, *Obras*, xxiii; Márquez, *Investigaciones sobre Juan Alvarez Gato*, 36.

58. Foulché-Delbosc, *Cancionero Castellano del siglo XV*, ed. R. Foulché-Delbosc, Vol. 1, N.B.A.E. 19 (Madrid, 1912), 242–43, 246; Gato, *Obras*, 96–97, 106.

59. The most comprehensive study of the poet and his family is Francisco Cantera Burgos, *El poeta Rodrigo Cota y su familia de judíos conversos* (Madrid, 1970). However, much additional information may be gleaned on the family from León Tello, *Judíos de Toledo* (Index, s.v. "Aben Cota," "Cota," "Sancho Fernández Cota"). The name "Cota" is not, as Cantera thought, found in the Mozarabic documents concerning Jews of Toledo; rather, it is Ibn Quṭa, which may or may not be the origin of the Spanish form. Most of the converso Cota family discussed by Cantera appears in León Tello. For instance, no. 978 there is Rodrigo, the *jurado*, son of Sancho Cota "I," while no. 1207 is Rodrigo Cota—not "Rodrigo Alfon" as in Cantera—the son of Alfonso Martínez Cota the merchant. He is also probably the Rodrigo who was a jeweller (563, no. 1565) (see index to Cantera, s.v. "Rodrigo," *joyero*").

60. Published by Agustín Millares Carlo, "Indice y extractos de los libros de cédulas y provisiones del archivo y museo de Madrid," *Revista de la biblioteca archivo y museo* (Ayuntamiento de Madrid) 6 (1929): 292–93. On Alonso, see above concerning Sarmiento and the Toledo riots.

61. León Tello, *Judíos de Toledo* 2:580, no. 4624, 601 no. 1710, 605 no. 1725. Not one of these people is mentioned in Cantera, *El poeta Rodrigo Cota.*

62. Ibid., 392 no. 1094, 432 no. 1193, 518, no. 1506.

63. Ibid., 344–45 no. 978. All of these people, but not this incident, are discussed in Cantera, *El poeta Rodrigo Cota.* León Tello gave no indication of any awareness that this was the family of the famous poet.

64. *Memorias de Sancho Cota,* ed. Hayward Keniston (Cambridge, Mass., 1964), cf. Cantera, *El poeta Rodrigo Cota,* 53ff., for a detailed discussion of this.

65. Cantera, *El poeta Rodrigo Cota,* 22ff. (with the error of making "Pedrarias," i.e., Pedro Arias, the *contador mayor* both of Enrique IV and of the Catholic Monarchs; he died in 1476). Critical ed. of the *Epitalamio,* first published by Foulché-Delbosc, *Cancionero castellano del siglo XV* 2:580ff., from a newly found MS, in Cantera, (111ff). Another version, based on the same MSS, is offered by José Gómez-Menor, *Cristianos nuevos,* 101ff., with some interesting notes (it should perhaps be mentioned that "Anton de Faro" [106, 124] is certainly intended to refer to the Faro family of conversos; cf. index to Gómez-Menor and also to León Tello).

66. See Baer, *Die Juden* 2:211, 235, 236, 334, 388 (bottom of the page), 424, 304, and see index (550) on the aben Atabe family of Seville.

67. Text in Cantera, *El poeta Rodrigo Cota,* 132ff., and in Antón de Montoro, *Poesía,* 210ff. On the probable meaning of the appellative "Maguaque" for Cota, see Cantera, "Maguaque, remoquete de Rodrigo Cota y otros detalles acerca de éste," *Sefarad* 30 (1970): 339–47.

68. See briefly Cantera, *El poeta Rodrigo Cota,* 69ff. The literature on *La Celestina* is vast, almost equaling that on Chaucer. Works attributed to Cota also include *Coplas de Mingo Revulgo* and *Coplas del Provincial* (doubtful). His *Dialogo entre el amor y un viejo,* his most famous work, was first published in *Cancionero general* (Palencia, 1511), but in none of the subsequent editions until the Madrid 1958 facsimile; however, it appeared separately in numerous eds. after 1569, and finally in a critical edition by A. Cortina (Buenos Aires, 1929; rpt. in *Boletín de la academia argentina de letras* 4 (1936): 219–47). The *Epitalamio burlesca* appeared in various eds. from 1894, as noted above, n. 65. Some additional poems in Foulché-Delbosc, *Cancionero castellano del siglo XV.*

69. These are found in Hernando del Castillo, *Cancionero general.* I have used the Toledo 1520 ed. (facs. rpt. New York, 1967), fols. xxii–xxvii. The largest collection of his poetry, however, is to be found in Foulché-Delbosc, *Cancionero castellano del siglo XV* 1, N.B.A.E. 19 (Madrid, 1912), 120–221. The *Laberinto* is also there (152–82). The most important study of the *Laberinto,* still not superseded, is C. R. Post, "The Sources of Juan de Mena," *Romantic Review* 3 (1912): 223–79. Many individual topics in this and other poems, e.g., the *Coronación,* such as the order of the kings of Spain, etc., have been dealt with (e.g., Inez MacDonald, "The Coronación of Juan de Mena: Poem and Commentary," *Hispanic Review* 7 (1939)). Important, too, is María Rosa Lida de Malkiel, *Juan de Mena, poeta del prerenacimiento español* (Mexico, 1950). Otis Green has noted that "the hope of a monar-

chial unity (soon to be realized) is an essential part" of the *Laberinto*, a Spanish (united) monarchy to rule "not only over Spain, but over the whole world" (*Spain and the Western Tradition* [Madison, Wis., 1969], 3:7).

70. Foulché-Delbosc, *Cancionero castellano del siglo XV* 1:122:

> Primero seyendo cortadas
> las uñas y los cabellos,
> podian casar entre ellos
> sus cativas aforradas
> los judíos; y linpiadas,
> fazer las ysraelitas
> puras, linpias y benditas,
> al su-ley consagradas

71. Ibid., 201, stanza 18. Bartolomé José Gallardo, *Ensayo de una biblioteca española de libros raros y curiosos* (Madrid, 1863), 1:613–17, and Miguel Artigas, "Nueva redacción de las 'Coplas de Ay Panadera' según un manuscrito . . . ," *Estudios in memoriam de A. Bonilla y San Martín* (Madrid, 1927), 1:75–89.

72. See Juan Carlos Temprano, *Moviles y metas en la poesía pastoril de Juan del Encina* (Oviedo, 1975), 17–18. It is interesting that while Green, *Spain and the Western Tradition*, 3:14, points to the significance of the first performance of Encina's work in 1492, the year of the conquest of Granada and of Columbus, he neglects to mention the Expulsion of the Jews. It is also amazing that as recently as 1976 an author could hesitantly raise the *possibility* that Encina was a converso (Henry V. Sullivan, *Juan del Encina* [Boston, 1976], 45ff.).

73. Maxim Newmark, *Dictionary of Spanish Literature* (Totowa, N.J., 1970), 105.

74. Text, from the 1496 edition, in Temprano, *Moviles y metas*, 164.

75. *Eglogas completas de Juan del Enzina* [*sic*], ed. Humberto López-Moralez (Madrid, 1968), 98–102. In addition to the previous references to his musical works (see n. 2 above), see *Cancionero musical de los siglos XV y XVI*, ed. F. Asenjo Barbieri (Madrid, 1890), and *Cancionero musical de Palacio* (Madrid, 1946). Numerous eds. of his poetry and theatrical works have appeared, including his translation of Virgil, *Bucólicas*, in Menéndez y Pelayo, *Antológia* 21:232–314.

76. Julio Rodríguez Puértolas, "Sobre Iñigo de Mendoza," *Boletín de Menéndez Pelayo* 14 (1969): 331–47 (see 336); cf. his earlier "Sobre el autor de las *Coplas de Mingo Revulgo*," *Homenaje a Rodríguez-Moñino* (1966) 2:131–42. See generally Cantera Burgos, *Alvar García*, 559–70.

77. Text conveniently available in Foulché-Delbosc, *Cancionero castellano del siglo XV* 1:23. The work was first published as a separate book in Zamora in 1482 (facs. rpt. N.B.A.E. 19 [Madrid, 1953] 97–104, and in Julio Rodríguez-Puértolas, *Fray Iñigo de Mendoza y sus "Coplas de vita Christi"* [Madrid, 1968], 84–117, and also in his ed. of the *Cancionero* of Mendoza [Madrid, 1969]).

78. Foulché-Delbosc, *Cancionero castellano del siglo XV* 1:108–9, and in the other sources cited above. Cantera, *Alvar García*, made no mention of these anti-Jewish verses.

79. Cantera Burgos, *Alvar García*, 571–79. Cantera returned to this subject in

a lengthy article endeavoring to prove, perhaps successfully, that the poet was indeed Pedro, son of Garci Franco ("El poeta Cartagena del 'Cancionero general' y sus ascendientes los Franco," *Sefarad* 28 [1968]: 3–39). If so, he was at least a fourth-generation Christian! See also Netanyahu, *Origins*, 1259 n. 2.

80. Complete texts of his poetry in Hernando del Castillo, *Cancionero general,* fols. lix–xvi verso; some also in Foulché-Delbosc, *Cancionero castellano del siglo XV* 2:509–35.

81. See León Tello, *Judíos de Toledo,* index. A genealogical table of his descendants is found in Gómez-Menor, *Cristianos nuevos,* LX–LXI (see n. 18 above).

82. Hernando del Castillo, *Cancionero general,* fols. lxxvi–ix and cxcvii, verso.

83. See, e.g., the previously cited *Cancionero de obras de burlas,* 97–98. Diego's *Obras completas* have been edited by Keith Whinnon (Madrid, 1971–73), whose doubts as to Diego's converso origin need not be taken seriously.

84. Chaim B. Friedberg and Baruch Friedberg, *Toldot ha-defus ha-'ivry be-medinat Italiah, Ispamiah-Portugaliah ve-Togramah* (Tel Aviv, 1956), 95–96 (on the Yom Kippur *maḥzor,* Montalbán, ca. 1475, see *Soncino Blätter* 3 (1930): 173–82; *J.Q.R.* 30 (1939): 51–57), but cf. Alexander Marx, *Studies in Jewish History and Booklore* (New York, 1944), 295 n. 62. Stephen Gilman, *The Spain of Fernando de Rojas* (Princeton, 1972), 129, gives the incorrect information that Juan "in the 1480's set up a printing shop" in Montalbán, information which he apparently obtained from a verbal translation of a passage in an older and unreliable book on Hebrew printing (see 233 n. 55). In fact, as stated, Juan de Lucena fled Spain in 1481, and the Hebrew presses were established at least in 1476 or earlier.

85. This "discovery," that Juan de Lucena the printer and the author were one and the same, was made *not* by Angel Alcalá (Galve), "Juan de Lucena y el pre-erasmismo española," *Revista hispánica moderna* 34 (1968): 108–31, but earlier by Richard Kukula (*Centralblatt für Bibliothekswesen* 13 [1896]: 174), and was of course known to scholars such as the Friedbergs (above, n. 84).

86. Details in the introduction of Pas y Mélia to the *Vita beata* (*Opúsculos literarios de los siglos XIV a XV* [Madrid, 1892], xi); see also Chapter 7, below. Paz y Mélia was inclined to identify him also with Juan Ramirez de Lucena, or the chronicler of the Monarchs (see 159 above). However, the identity of the Lucena who was a chronicler is in doubt.

87. León Tello, *Judíos de Toledo* 2:556, 579, 597.

88. See on Lucena, e.g., M. Morreale, "El tratado de Lucena, 'De Vita beata,'" *Nueva revista de filología hispánica* 9 (1955): 1–21; "Carta consolatoria a Gómez Manrique," in Juan de Flores, *Triunfo de amor* (Pisa, 1981), 13–14; B. Manulka *An Anti-Feminist Treatise* (1931); etc. Juan's observations on Latin prayers cited by Gilman, *Spain of Fernando de Rojas,* 344.

89. Gilman, *Spain of Fernando de Rojas,* 125, 129, and the reference to Serrano y Sanz in n. 40 there.

90. Ibn Verga, *Shevet Yehudah,* ed. Shochet, 118 (end of chap. 44).

91. Very important information on him, with some excerpts from his writings, may be found in Harry Friedenwald, *The Jews and Medicine* (Baltimore, 1944), 1:280–89. See also Antonio Fabie, *Vida y escritos de Francisco de Villalobos* (Madrid, 1886); George Gaskoin, trans., *The Medical Works of Francisco Lopez de*

Villalobos (London, 1870); Villalobos, *Sumario de la medecina* (Salamanca, 1498; rpt. Madrid, 1948); *Dialogo,* ed. A. Paz y Mélia, *Sales españolas* (Madrid, 1902); *Algunas obras* (Madrid, 1886); and (probably his) "Carta de amores," ed. Alfonso de Marítegui y Pérez de Barradas, *Tratado de monteria del siglo XV* (Madrid, 1936), 125–26. (Márquez Villanueva thought that almost all of the physicians of Isabel and Fernando were *conversos,* but without sufficient evidence; *Investigaciones sobre Juan Alvarez Gato,* 101.) See now especially Carlos Calamita, *Francisco López de Villalobos, médico de reyes y principe de literatura* (Madrid, 1952).

92. Gilman, *Spain of Fernando de Rojas,* 100, 106, 340.

93. Gilman, *Spain of Fernando de Rojas,* and see also his earlier *The Art of La Celestina* (Madison, Wis., 1956). The *Celestina,* whose actual title is *Comedia de Calisto y Melibea,* was given a modern edition by R. Foulché-Delbosc, 2 vols. (Madrid, 1900, 1902), and there is a facsimile rpt. of the 1492 ed. (New York, 1909). There are numerous other eds. and translations of the play. See the interesting article of D. W. McPheeters on a Hebrew translation, "Una traducción hebrea de 'La Celestina' en el siglo XVI," *Homenaje a* [Antonio] *Rodríguez-Moñino* (1966), 1: 399–411.

94. Gilman, *Spain of Fernando de Rojas,* 100. A different understanding entirely from mine, and I believe Gilman's, is represented in the thesis of Orlando Martínez-Miller, *La ética judía y La Celestina como alegoría* (Miami, 1978). The literature on the *Celestina* continues to grow, but as usual there is little consideration of the converso background. In spite of criticism, Gilman's book is likely to remain the most important contribution in this regard.

95. J. Rodríguez de Castro, *Biblioteca española* (Madrid, 1781), 1:258; reproduced in *Memorial histórico español* 2 (1852): 154–55; cf. 156–57, 166. Jacobo de Uclés, also mentioned there (author of *Libro de dichos de sabios*), was also not a *converso* but a Jew.

96. Raphael de Ureña y Smenjaud and Adolfo Bonilla y San Martín, *Obras de maestro Jacobo de las leyes* (Madrid, 1924) must be used with caution; cf. the revisions of Alfonso García-Gallo, "El 'Libro de las leyes' de Alfonso el sabio," *Anuario de historia del derecho español* 21–22(1951–52): 344–528.

97. Amador de los Ríos, *Estudios,* 412.

98. See Benzion Netanyahu, "Alonso de [*sic*] Espina: Was He a New Christian?" *P.A.A.J.R.* 43 (1976): 109–10 for the origin of the oft-repeated claim.

99. Lluís Marcó i Dachs, *Los judíos en Cataluña,* 192–93. Against this hypothesis are the studies of the family cited by Martín de Riquer, *Història de la literatura catalana* (Barcelona, 1964), 2:472, to which add Ricardo Carreras i Valls, "Noves notes genealògiques dels poetes . . . March," *Estudis universitaris catalans* 18 (1933): 310–32, and offprint. To add to the confusion, there was in fact a Pere March and his wife who converted in Tortosa in 1391 and who were apparently from Valencia, just as was Pere March the father of Ausias at precisely the same time; cf. Francesch Carreras i Candi, *L'aljama de juhéus de Tortosa,* 153ff.

100. Gilman, *Spain of Fernando de Rojas,* 154.

101. Julio Cejador y Frauca, *Historia de la lengua y literatura castellana* (Madrid, 1915), 1:53ff.; F. Vendrell, *La corte literaria de Alfonso V de Aragón* (Madrid, 1953); but especially Andrés Soria, *Los humanistas de la corte de Alfonso el magnánimo* (Granada, 1956).

102. Juan Mario Penna, introduction to his ed. of *Prosistas castellanos del siglo XV*, B.A.E. 116:cxxxix.

103. Denys Hay, *The Italian Renaissance in Its Historical Background* (Cambridge, 1970), 81–82.

104. See the very suggestive remarks and informative background on the University of Salamanca in Gilman, *Spain of Fernando de Rojas*, chap. 6 (and cf. 209), although there are errors in identifying as "conversos" those definitely not (274, Alonso del Espina) or probably not (275 n. 13).

105. His library became the foundation of that of the modern Vatican; see Ferdinand Schevill, *Medieval and Renaissance Florence*, Harper ed. (New York, 1963), 2:324.

106. Ibid., and cf. 411. He, of course, erred completely in stating that the Inquisition "lost its teeth" in the fifteenth century and could not affect this dissent. Not only is that obviously false for Spain, it ignores the case of Pico della Mirandola in Italy itself.

107. *Mar de historias*, found only in Fernán Pérez de Guzmán, *Generaciones y semblanzas*, ed. Domínguez Bordona, 161. (See generally my "The 'Theft of Philosophy' by the Greeks from the Jews," *Classical Folia* 32 [1978]: 52–67.)

108. [Cicero], *Tulio de officiis y de senectute* (Seville, 1501), and *La rhetorica*, ed. Rosalba Mascagna (Naples, 1968); [Seneca], *Cinco libros* (Seville, 1491, etc. [cf. chap. 5, n. 106]), "Libro que hizo Seneca a su amigo Galión contra las adversidades de la fortuna," ed. R. F. Pousa in *Escorial* 10 (1943): 73–82; [Boccaccio], *Cayda de principes* (Seville, 1495; Toledo, 1511; Alcalá, 1552).

109. Alonso de Cartagena, *Un tratado sobre la educacción y los estudios literarios*, ed. Jeremy N. H. Lawrance (Barcelona, 1979).

110. Library of Congress catalogues him as "Palencia, Alfonso [sic] Fernández [sic] de." The best general study is A. Paz y Mélia, *El cronista Alonso de Palencia* (Madrid, 1914), which, of course, must be augmented by his introduction to his translation of *Crónica de Enrique IV* (Vol. 1). References to earlier authors will be found in those two studies. J. López Toro, "La cuarta década de Alfonso [sic] de Palencia," *B.A.H.* 159 (1966): 89–100, is replaced by his edition of that Latin text.

111. Paz y Mélia in the two above-cited studies (though hardly doing justice to the question of classical influences); Robert B. Tate and A. Mundo, "The *Compendium* of Alfonso [sic] de Palencia: A Humanist Treatise on the Geography of the Iberian Peninsula," *Journal of Medieval and Renaissance Studies* 5 (1975): 253–78, with an edition of that tiny treatise (264ff.). Alonso's dictionary (Latin-Spanish) of certain terms has a modern edition, *Universal vocabulario*, ed. John M. Hill (Madrid, 1957), and also a facsimile rpt. of the Seville 1490 ed. (Madrid, 1967).

112. [Plutarch], *Vitae parallelae*, 2 vols. (Seville, 1491; Madrid, 1792); [Domenico Cavalca], *Espejo de la cruz* (Seville, 1486, 1492); [Josephus], *De bello judaico* (Seville, 1492, 1532, 1536). *Guerra e batalla campal de los perros y lobos* and *Perfección del triunfo militar* were reedited by A. M. Fabié, *Dos tratados de Alfonso [sic] de Palencia* (Madrid, 1876), and again by M. Penna, B.A.E. 116. Robert Tate, "Political Allegory in Fifteenth-Century Spain: A Study of the *Batalla campal* . . . ," *Journal of Hispanic Philology* 1 (no date): 169–86, adds nothing that was not already said by Paz y Mélia in his introduction to *Crónica*.

113. The importance of Homer's work as reflecting the virtues necessary in a

warrior society, as well as Virgil and the motif of "wisdom and fortune," which especially in Spain became transformed into the "arms and letters" *topos,* is discussed by Ernst Robert Curtius, *European Literature and the Latin Middle Ages* (Princeton, 1973), 171, 174, 178. The glorification of "warrior" Spain in its campaign against Muslim Granada was, of course, another major element in converso writing.

114. Juan de Lucena, "Epistola exhortatoria á las letras," ed. A. Paz y Mélia, *Opúsculos literarios de los siglos XIV a XV* (Madrid, 1892), 209–17; see 215, 216.

115. Manuel Serrano y Sanz, *Origenes de la dominación española en América,* N.B.A.E. 25 (Madrid, 1918), clxxxviii–clxxxix.

116. Soria, *Los humanistas,* 25.

117. *Visión delectable de la filosofía y artes liberales,* first ed. s.l.s.a. (Barcelona, 1484; facs. rpt. Barcelona, 1911) with several subsequent eds. An Italian translation (Venice, 1556) was *retranslated* into Spanish by a Jew, Francisco de Cáceres (Frankfurt, 1623; Amsterdam, 1663). Modern eds. include a B.A.E. 36:339–402; one by Caspar Joseph Morsello (diss., Univ. of Wisconsin, Madison, 1965); and one by Jorge García López (Salamanca, 1989). For the influence on Maimonides and studies concerning that, see my *Maimonides: Essays and Texts* (Madison, Wis., 1985), 138. See also Afterword here.

118. Diego de Valera, *Epístolas* (Madrid, 1878), 31, 35, 86, 88; Juan de Lucena, "Epistola exhortatora á las letras," ed. Paz y Mélia, *Opúsculos literarios* (Madrid, 1892), 215–16. Some of the converso poems praising Isabel have been mentioned earlier. On the general theme of praise of the queen, see R. O. Jones, "Isabel la Católica y el amor cortés," *Revista de literatura* 21 (1962): 55–64; María Rosa Lida de Malkiel, "La hiperbole," *Revista de filología hispánica* (Buenos Aires) 8 (1946): 125–30. Roger Boase, *The Troubadour Revival* (London, 1978), 117, claimed that the "messianic zeal" and "self-mockery" in these poems can be explained only in the converso context (once again, the "converso mentality"). Juan Alvárez Gato also wrote a lengthy hymn of praise to Isabel (*Obras,* 126–31).

119. In addition to Lida de Malkiel, Márquez Villanueva has sought to revive Castro's theories about supposed "Arabic" and Hebrew influences on fifteenth-century converso writers. According to Márquez, this phenomenon, e.g., hymns in the vernacular and Castilian-language religious poetry, was the product of converso "interior religiosity," which in turn was the result of literary biblical influence and the "Semitic mentality" in its conception of religion (!), which occasionally permitted an "authentic return to the divine" in such popular expressions of religious sentiment. Nevertheless, these were phrased in the vulgar style of "tavern songs," according to him, which characterized Arabic poetry (of several centuries earlier).

120. Netanyahu, *Marranos,* 131–32; Hayim Ibn Musa, *Sefer magen ve-ramaḥ,* facs. ed. of the Poznánzki MS (Jerusalem, Hebrew National Library 787) (Jerusalem, 1970), 1.

121. Isaac Iudaeus, *Expositio fidei catholicae,* ed. A. Hoste, in *Corpus christianorum, Series latina* 9 (Turnholt, 1962).

122. Petrus Alfonsus, *Dialogi contra Iudaeos,* in Migné, *Patrologiae series latina* 157:535–672; modern ed. and analysis, Klaus-Peter Mieth, "Der Dialog des Petrus Alfonsi," diss., Berlin, 1982. The most important study of the work, and of Pedro generally, is John V. Tolan, *Petrus Alfonsi and His Medieval Readers* (Gainesville,

Florida, 1993). See also Ch. Merchavia, *ha-Talmud be-re'iy ha-noṣrut* (Jerusalem, 1970), especially chap. 3. Tolan's work is solid and accurate, replacing everything hitherto done.

123. See Tolan, *Petrus Alfonsi*, 115ff., and his important discussion of the Catalan MS (126ff.). To his list of works influenced by the Dialogue may be added "Pseudo-Grosseteste," *Summa philosophiae*, ed. L. Baur, in *Beiträge zur Geschichte der Philosophie des Mittelalters* 9 [1912]: 280; the Dominican (ca. 1330) Berthold von Moosburg (see M. Grabmann, "Die Neuplatonismus in der deutschen Hochscholastik," *Philosophische Jahrbuch* 23 [1910]: 54, but corrected by Wolfgang Kluxen, "Literargeschichtliches zum lateinische Moses Maimonides," *Recherches de théologie ancienne et médiévale* 21 [1954]: 50); and an anonymous fifteenth-century French poem of a "disputation" between the Church and the Synagogue (ed. in *Zeitschrift für romanische Philologie* 17:404–8, and again by H. Pflaum, "Der allegorische Streit zwischen Synagoge und Kirche in der europäischen Dichtung des Mittelalters," *Archivum romanicum* 18 [1934]: 243–340; there are, however, two other MSS, one thirteenth-century [B.N. MS. fr. 837] and the other fourteenth-century [Tours, Bibl. municipale MS. 948]).

124. The bibliography on Abner is extensive. Important studies include Yiṣḥaq Baer, "Sefer minḥat qenaot shel Avner mi-Burgos ve-haspha'ato 'al Ḥasdai Crescas," *Tarbiz* 11 (1940): 188–206 (his earlier "Abner aus Burgos," *Verein zur Gründung und Erhaltung einer Akademis für die Wissenschaft des Judentums* [Berlin, 1929], 20–37, is of little value); his "Torat ha-qabalah be-mishnato ha-Keristologit shel Avner," *Tarbiz* 27 (1958): 152–63 (*Sefer ha-yovel le-Ḥayim Schirmann*); Baron, *Social and Religious History* 9:108–9, 121, 127, 305 n. 32, 307 n. 39; Judah Rosenthal, *Meḥqarim ve-meqorot* (Jerusalem, 1967); and Robert Chazan, "Alfonso of Valladolid and the New Missionizing," *R.E.J.* 143 (1984): 83–94. (See now Jonathan L. Hecht, "The Polemical Exchange between Isaac Pollegar [*sic*] and Abner of Burgos . . ." (dissertation, New York University, 1993).

125. The document mentioning Abner as scribe and bookbinder: Vicente Castañeda, "Ensayo de un diccionario de encuadernadores españoles," *B.A.H.* 141 (1957): 474–75. On Abner and Moses Narboni in Valladolid, see Alfonso Carlos Merchán Fernández, *Los judíos de Valladolid* (Valladolid, 1976), 129 (he had no idea, of course, who they were); this should read "fourteenth" century, and Narboni was there certainly after Abner had died.

126. José Amador de los Ríos, *Historia de la literatura española* 4:85ff. On the *infanta* Blanca and the translation of "Wars," see Mercedes Gaibrois de Ballesteros, *Historia del reinado de Sancho IV de Castilla* (Madrid, 1922–28), 2:393.

127. Baer, *History of the Jews* 1:328ff.; *however*, it needs to be mentioned that this entire section has been significantly abridged in the English translation, and in addition important passages of citations of Abner have been incorrectly translated from the Hebrew; cf. Baer, *Toldot ha-yehudim bi-Sefarad ha-noṣrit*, 2d ed. (Tel Aviv, 1965), 192ff. Baer's important summary of Abner's charges there (207), has in particular been severely abridged and even "censored" by the English translator. José Luis Lacave, again, has made a complete and accurate translation of the entire section, in his translation of Baer, *Historia de los judíos en la España cristiana* (Madrid, 1981), 1:278–29.

Important new information on the relationship between the thought of Alfonso and of Ḥasdai Crescas may be found now in Aviezer Ravitzky, *Derashat ha-Pesaḥ le-R' Ḥasdai Crescas* (Jerusalem, 1988), especially 40–41, 61 (on 41 n. 20, it is not entirely correct that Abner [Alfonso] took his interpretation of reward and punishment from Abraham b. Ḥaya; he borrowed only the illustration of fire from that book, but Abraham certainly did not there say anything at all like what Alfonso wrote). In connection with what Baer wrote (Hebrew, 207; Spanish trans., 278–29; not at all in the English version) about Alfonso's claim as to the superiority of Christian law in certain matters, see the important observations of Ravitzky (44 n. 26).

128. Baer, *History* 1:330ff. discusses the *Moreh ṣedeq* in some detail, and there is now an edition of *Mostrador de justicia,* ed. Walter Mettmann (Opladen, 1994–96), 2 vols., and an ed. of *Teshuvot lamearef* (Sp.) by Mettmann. The Hebrew title may refer to Isaiah 3.9–10 (cf. the LXX), i.e., Jesus in Christian interpretation. On the other hand, Maimonides was called *moreh ṣedeq* ("teacher of righteousness"); e.g., by Isaac Ibn Laṭif, "Igeret teshuvah," *Qovets al-yad* (1885): 56, which may mean that Alfonso was contrasting his work with that of Maimonides (on the term generally, see the instructive article of J. Weingreen, "The Title Moreh Sedek," *Journal of Semitic Studies* 6 [1961]: 162–74). Mettmann (1 n. 1) demonstrates that the *Libro declarante* is not Alfonso's.

129. Matias Sangrador Vitores, *Historia de la muy noble y leal ciudad de Valladolid* (Valladolid, 1851), 1:237; see also Amador de los Ríos, *Estudios,* 281–86, with excerpts from MSS. A complete edition of these is very much needed.

130. Judah Rosenthal, "Mi-sefer Alfonso," with the reply of Joseph Shalom to all of Abner's letters, in *Studies and Essays in honor of Abraham A. Neuman* (Leiden, 1962), 588–621; "The second letter . . ." (Heb.), *Abraham Weiss Jubilee Volume* (New York, 1964), 483–510; and "The third letter . . ." (Heb.), *Studies in Bibliography and Booklore* 5 (1961): 42–51 (Heb. section). (See generally on extant MSS of Alfonso's works Klaus Reinhardt and Horacio Santiago-Otero, *Biblioteca bíblica ibérica medieval* [Madrid, 1986], 84–89). The Spanish translations of Alfonso's *Minḥat qenaot* and *Teshuvot la-meḥaref* (MS Vat. 6423) have been edited and discussed in a dissertation by Carlos Sainz de la Masa (Madrid, Universidad Complutense, 1989). See also his "El converso y judío Alfonso de Valladolid y su *Libro de zelo de Dios*" in *Las tres culturas en la corona de Castilla y los Sefardíes* (Salamanca, 1990), 71–85. See also Carlos del Valle, "El libro de las Batallas de Dios de Abner de Burgos," in del Valle, ed., *Polémica judeo-cristiana. Estudios* (Madrid, 1992).

131. Samuel Ibn Sason, *Sefer avney shoham,* ed. Ḥaim Chamiel (Jerusalem, 1962), 10 (the editor's interpretation of the historical aspects of the work are often erroneous).

132. Baer, *History* 1:331; Robert Chazan, "Alfonso and the New Missionizing" (see n. 124 above), 86. The German Jewish pietist Judah ha-ḥasid wrote that "if a Jew converts he is called by an evil name . . . just as idolatrous things should be given a name of contempt" (*Sefer ḥasidim,* ed. Jehuda Wistinetzki [Berlin, 1891], 74, no. 193).

133. The form of the name "Polgar" is provided in the MS of his extant Spanish work. However, as is known, Jews were not always precise in the correct spelling of their Romance names. As variant forms, we find Salomon Enpollegar in Burgos,

1207; Abraham Pulligar (also Poligar and Aben Poligén) in Jerez, ca. 1266. Note also the town of Pulgar, near Toledo. Isaac was praised by Samuel Ibn Sason, *Sefer avney shoham,* 100–101. His work, *'Ezer ha-dat,* exists in a poor edition by George Belasco (London, 1906; photo rpt., Israel [s.l.], 1970), with English introduction, and a critical edition by Jacob Levinger (who seems entirely unaware of Belasco's previous ed.) (Tel Aviv, 1984).

134. Isaac Ibn Polgar, *'Ezer ha-dat,* ed. Levinger, 29–30, 60, 64. See my "Isaac Polgar y su libro contra un converso," in Carlos del Valle, *Polémica judeo-cristiana. Estudios,* 67–73 (n. 130 above).

135. See Baer's important article, "Sefer minḥat qenaot" and Ravitsky, *Derashat ha-Pesaḥ.* It is also possible that Judah b. Asher of Toledo refers to this work of Abner, or at least his ideas, in his strongly worded attack on belief in astrology and determinism (end of his *Zikhron Yehudah* [Berlin, 1846]), and note also that Judah corresponded with Moses Ibn Zaradiel (or Abzaradiel), who was the scribe of Alfonso XI (ibid., no. 77, end), who was involved with Abner in the controversy over the Jewish prayers. Cf. Baer, *History of the Jews* 1:358; what Baer wrote there (444 n. 10) is a total misinterpretation of the text. The dates involved make this relation between Abner and Judah at least a possibility, as Abner converted ca. 1320 and the translation of *Moreh ṣedeq* was before 1331 (cf. Baer [329]), and Judah died in 1328.

136. Duran's main polemical works are now conveniently available in *Kitvey polmos le-Profiat Duran,* ed. Frank Talmage (Jerusalem, 1981), including *Kelimat ha-goyim* and the letter. The complete ed. of the latter, however, with additional letters and the commentary of Joseph Ibn Shem Ṭov, with notes (Abraham Geiger?), was published as *Igeret ogeret* (Breslau, 1844). Geiger also wrote some notes on this in his *Melo ḥofnayim* (Berlin, 1840), 101–2 (German), and see there the Hebrew text (42–50). Netanyahu, *Marranos,* 223 (rejected, for no reason, by Talmage [14 n. 23]).

137. Netanyahu, *Marranos,* 84 n. 6 (Emery already made similar observations in *J.Q.R.* 58:329). It was the same Isaac 'Aqrish who discovered and first published the famous letter of Ḥasdai Ibn Shaprut to the Khazar king, as well as other important publications. D. M. Dunlop, *The History of the Jewish Khazars* (Princeton, 1954), 128ff., calls 'Aqrish "an otherwise unknown Jew."

138. See the text of Joseph Ibn Shem Ṭov's introduction to the letter, from a Breslau MS, cited by S. Poznánski in his notes to his ed. of *Kelimat ha-goyim* in *ha-Ṣofeh le-ḥokhmat Yisrael* 4 (1915): 126, and see also Geiger's previously cited notes and text. Apparently the MS of that introduction is no longer extant; at least it is not mentioned by Talmage in his list of MSS of the letter (*Kitvey,* 29–30; however, he does cite it [13], but claims it was a fictitious introduction by Duran). See Baer, *History of the Jews* 2:150ff., and *Die Juden* 1:259.

139. Strassburg, 1469; Rome, 1470 (supposedly at Universidad de Salamanca, but they currently cannot find it), 1471, 1472, 1475, 1478; also Burgos, 1591. See Reinhardt and Santiago-Otero, *Biblioteca bíblica,* 240–49 on Pablo (by no means complete, however, on the eds. of *Scrutinium*). See also Amador de los Ríos, *Historia de la literatura española* 5:333–37.

140. See the useful summary of *Scrutinium* in A. Lukyn Williams (a missionary to the Jews), *Adversus Judaeos* (Cambridge, 1935), 267–76 (275 on the section

discussed here). On the messianic calculations mentioned, see Abba Hillel Silver, *A History of Messianic Speculation in Israel* (New York, 1927), 84, 94. Baer's discussion of the "miracle of Ávila" (*History of the Jews* 1:277–81) is essentially correct, although his bibliographical references are incomplete.

141. Alonso de Cartagena, *Defensorium unitatis christianae*, 158, 161, etc.

142. Ibid., 169–70, 173–75; the editor's incorrect observation is in his introduction (48).

143. See the synopsis of the work by S. Poznánski, "Le colloque de Tortose et de San Mateo," *R.E.J.* 74 (1922): 19–22, 33, 34–39, 160–64. On the manuscripts and editions, see Reinhardt and Santiago-Otero, *Biblioteca bíblica*, 182–83 (with no reference to Poznánski, however; hence the error on 182 that the Hebrew version was written "by" Alonso). There is also an Augsburg ca. 1468 ed., not noted there, but the second, Zurich 1552, ed. is the only complete one.

144. Vidal Benvenist, *Qodesh ha-qodashim* (MS no. 800 in Jerusalem, Hebrew University and National Library); cf. Netanyahu, *Marranos*, 89 n. 14).

145. Solomon b. Simon b. Ṣemaḥ Duran, *Milḥmet miṣvah*, printed with Simon b. Ṣemaḥ Duran, *Qeshet ve-magen* (Livorno, 1785; photo rpt. Jerusalem, 1970), a faulty text; and again with Saʿadya *Gaon, Emunot ve-deʿot* (Leipzig, 1860); and in a less reliable text by J. D. Eisenstein, *Oṣar viquḥim* (New York, 1928), 134–43. The introduction, only, is translated (Spanish) by Orfali (see n. 146 below) from Eisenstein's ed. (he apparently did not know of the Leipzig ed.), 200–208.

146. Moises Orfali, *El tratado "De Iudaicis erroribus ex Talmut" de Jerónimo de Santa Fe* (Madrid, 1987), with references also to some of the Jewish responses.

147. Ibid., 47 (*Sanhedrin* 85b), 51 (*Sanhedrin* 61b).

148. Francisca Vendrell, "La política proselitista del rey d. Fernando I de Aragón," *Sefarad* 10 (1950): 350 n. 6; there is no reference at all to Pedro in her earlier "Aportaciones documentales para el estudio de la familia Caballería," ibid. 3 (1943): 115–54.

149. *Libro verde de Aragón*, 33, 35. M. Serrano y Sanz, *Origenes de la dominación española en America*, N.B.A.E. 25 (Madrid, 1918), lxxvi, apparently misunderstood the *Libro verde* to say that Pedro *himself* was Bonafos.

150. Serrano y Sanz, *Origenes de la dominación española*, cxc–iii. Castro, *España en su historia*, 585–86, merely copies information from this book.

151. See Reinhardt and Santiago-Otero, *Biblioteca bíblica*, 260–61 (however, with the erroneous information that Pedro was born ca. 1415, and citing the wrong article of Vendrell, and citing Castro but not Serrano).

152. See also the brief description of the work, ibid., 237–38, mentioning a Florence 1482 (?) ed., unknown to me, and giving the date of the Rome ed. as "ca. 1488"; nevertheless, the catalogues say ca. 1480, which is the date I have used. I consulted the Madrid copy.

153. See ibid., 239, no. 2, on this work, which is still in MS. See, however, Francois Secret, "L'*Ensis Pauli* de Paulus de Heredia," *Sefarad* 26 (1966), 79–102 and 253–71, which contains excerpts of the work (not noticed by Reinhardt and Santiago).

154. Both works are extant in various MSS; cf. ibid., 220–22. They deserve publication, or at least a careful study. Meanwhile, see the excerpts in Amador de

los Ríos, *Estudios*, 403–6, and the discussion in Baer, *History of the Jews* 2: 159–60 and 476 n. 45.

155. On Alfonso de Zamora see, *inter alia*, José Llamas in *Sefarad* 6 (1946): 289–311 (and other articles by him); Federico Pérez Castro, ed. and trans., *El manuscrito apologético de Alfonso de Zamora* (Madrid-Barcelona, 1950); his *Targum de Salmos*, ed. Luis Diez Merino (Madrid, 1982); *Targum de Job*, ed. idem (Madrid, 1984), and *Targum de Proverbios* (Madrid, 1984); and Moshé Lazar, "Alfonso de Zamora, copiste," *Sefarad* 18 (1958): 314–27. On the Complutensian itself, much has been written (e.g., M. Revilla Rico, *La Poliglot de Alcalá* [Madrid, 1917]), but new studies are needed. On Pablo Coronel (certainly a member of that important converso family) see Reinhardt and Santiago-Otero, *Biblioteca bíblica*, 12, 13 (the MS should be edited).

156. For Buxtorf's list, see P. T. van Rooden and J. W. Wesselius, "The Early Enlightenment and Judaism: The 'Civil Dispute' between Philippus van Limborch and Isaac Orobio de Castro (1687)," *Studia Rosenthaliana* 21 (1987): 144. Another work cited by Buxtorf, "Porchetus," is, of course, Porchetus Salvaticus, cited also in an anonymous Spanish manuscript written in connection with the sixteenth-century debate over *limpieza de sangre* (Madrid, B.N. MS 13043, fols. 52–53). That author, not Spanish, died ca. 1320, and utilized the work of Ramón Martí. The last work mentioned by Buxtorf, *Stella Messiae*, is unknown to me.

157. Pedro de Caballería, *Tractatus zelus Christi*, fol. 94v; cf. Amador de los Ríos, *Historia . . . de los judíos* 1:16–17 n. 1.

158. Pablo de Santa María, "Las edades del mundo," conveniently available in R. Foulché-Delbosc, *Cancionero castellano del siglo XV* 2:155ff.

159. Alonso de Palencia, *Crónica de Enrique IV* 2:88, 94.

160. See Francisco Márquez Villanueva, *Investigaciones sobre Juan Álvarez Gato* (Madrid, 1960), 123 n. 76, citing Marcel Bataillon, "Jean d'Avila retrouvé," *Bulletin hispanique* 57 (1955): 42, and adding the reference to Fernando Díaz de Toledo, "Diálogo e razonamiento en la muerte del marqués de Santillana," in *Opúsculos literarios*, ed. A. Paz y Méliz, 342. Coincidentally, perhaps, both the seventeenth-century anti-Jewish author Francisco de Torrejoncillo and the descendant of conversos Isaac Cardoso (a Jew) used almost the identical expression to refer to Jews (not conversos), each responsible for the other, like a "mystic body" (Torrejoncillo, *Centinela contra judíos* [Pamplona, 1691], 113: "Como los Judíos, donde quiere que estan, son unos para otros, como un cuerpo místico"; Cardozo, *Excelencias de los hebreos* [Amsterdam, 1679], 26: "y desta union y conformidad [of Sinai] nasció el ser los hijos de Ysrael fiadores unos de otros, todos hazen un cuerpo místico"), both cited by Yosef Hayim Yerushalmi, *From Spanish Court to Italian Ghetto* (New York, 1971), 384 n. 77. Yerushalmi, however, noted neither Bataillon's nor Márquez' discussion of previous sources, nor did he comment on the obvious relationship to the Talmudic concepts I have mentioned (cf., e.g., *Shavu'ot* 39a; *Lev. R.* "Vayiqra" 4.6; etc.). The Portuguese Jewish author Samuel Usque also wrote of his conceptualization of the patriarch Jacob "often standing for the entire body of Israel" (which, of course, is also derived from rabbinical traditions of the "grandfather Jacob"); *Consolations for the Tribulations of Israel*, trans. Martin A. Cohen (Philadelphia, 1965), 39, and cf. 206, "one body" (also not noted by Yerushalmi).

161. José Gómez-Menor, *Cristianos nuevos y mercaderes de Toledo* (Toledo, 1970), li–liii; "Documentos" (appendix there), [9]–[14], no. 3. A list of those who joined in 1493 is on [14]–[15], and see the text (37).

162. Simon Marcus, "A-t-il existé en Espagne une dialecte judéo-espagnol?" *Sefarad* 22 (1962): 139–40.

163. Luis Rubio, "¿Tolerancia o intolerancia?" *Anales de la Universidad de Murcia: Filosofía y letras* 18 (1959–60): 162 n. 4.

164. *Poema de Yosef,* ed. Moshé Lazar, *Joseph and His Brethren: Three Ladino Versions* (Culver City, Calif., 1990), 1, 16, 26, 32, etc. The problem is that the only complete MS of this undoubtedly medieval Spanish Jewish work is a sixteenth-century Turkish one, and obviously the possibility of corruption of the text exists. The Spanish (not "Ladino") translation of *Book of the Kuzari,* ed. Lazar (Culver City, Calif., 1990), has even more problems. The editor writes that it "might" have been done "before or about" the mid-fifteenth century, on somewhat questionable grounds (xviii), and it may well be later than that.

165. Baer, *Die Juden* 2:474–75.

166. Ibid., 477, no. 405.

167. Ibid., 497, 498, 511 (no. 413), 527.

168. Eduardo García de Diego, *Glosarios latinos del monasterio de Silos* (Murcia, 1933), 205.

Chapter 7. The Inquisition

1. Nicholas Eimeric, *Manuel des inquisiteurs,* trans. Louis Sala-Molins (Paris, 1973), 25.

2. Alfonso II's decree ed. Jaime Marqués Casanovas, "Alfonso II el Cast y la seo de Gerona," *VII Congrès d'historia de la corona d'Aragó: Crónica, ponencias y comunicacions* (1962), 2:218–19. The confirmation of Pedro II: Pierre de Marca, *Marca hispanica* (Paris, 1688; rpt. Barcelona, 1972), 1384.

3. On the Albigensians in Spain, see my "Jews and Albigensians in the Middle Ages," with complete bibliography in the notes there. On the events here related, see Lea, *History of the Inquisition* 1:141–42, 154 (see Works Frequently Cited for these).

4. For Innocent III, see Solomon Grayzel, *The Church and the Jews in the XIIIth Century* (Philadelphia, 1933), 90–91, 101–3. Nicholas III, "Vineath soreth vehut," *Les registres de Nicholas III,* ed. J. Gray (Paris, 1898–1938), 5:408–11.

5. Menéndez Pelayo, *Historia de los heterodoxos* (1947 ed.), 2:460. See Alfonso X of Castile (attributed; not actually by him), *El fuero real de España* (Madrid, 1781), 2:322 (IV.i.1), or in *Los códigos españoles* 1:405 (see Works Frequently Cited). The *Fuero juzgo* is also in the latter work (1:189), giving this law in the name of Egica, but there is no such law in the Latin text of the authentic *Lex Visigothorum.* As previously mentioned, the fifteenth-century jurist Alonso Días de Montalvo, in his lengthy gloss dealing with the converso problem (discussed elsewhere), stated that such laws in the *Fuero juzgo* are "not authentic" (*Fuero real de España* 2:349). See also *Siete partidas* (Madrid, 1807), VII.xxiv.7, and cf. *Fuero real* IV.i.2.

6. Llorente, *Historia* 1:77–78; the above-cited *Marca hispanica,* col. 1408 (not

1406) and 1414 (not 1412, as incorrectly cited by Llorente). The church council of Tarragona, ibid., cols. 1425–27.

7. Joaquim Miret i Sans, ed., *Itinerari de Jaume I "el conqueridor"* (Barcelona, 1918), 261, 262, 264, 268, 337, 376.

8. Baer, *History of the Jews*, 1:154; see Edward A. Synan, *Popes and the Jews in the Middle Ages* (New York and London, 1965), 117 for the documents on the pope. Peter Linehan, *The Spanish Church and the Papacy in the Thirteenth Century* (Cambridge, 1971), 38. Although generally good, Linehan's book sheds little light either on the relations of Jaime I with the papacy, an extremely important issue, or on the question of heresy, much less the Inquisition.

9. J. D. Mansi, ed., *Sacrorum conciliorum nova et amplissima collectio* (Florence, etc., 1759–1927), 23:553–58; not in *Marca hispanica*.

10. Augustus Potthast, ed., *Regesta pontificium romanorum* (Berlin, 1875), no. 20095; the translation is that of Solomon Grayzel, "Popes, Jews, and Inquisition," in Abraham I. Katsch and Leon Nemoy, eds., *Essays on the Occasion of the Seventieth Anniversary of Dropsie College* (Philadelphia, 1979), 173–74, with corrections and additions in brackets; cf. also the Latin text in Synan, *Popes and the Jews*, 241. The bull was confirmed by Gregory X in 1274, Nicholas IV in 1288, and by other popes.

11. Synan, *Popes and the Jews*, 118. See William Popper, *The Censorship of Hebrew Books*, revised ed. (New York, 1969), 13–15. Some details may also be found in Baer, and in Grayzel.

12. Salvador Carrasco, "Herejes e infieles en la ciudad medieval," *Escritos del Vedat* 4 (1974): 703, 707 (article 699–708).

13. The best brief discussion of Ramón Martí is in Robert Chazan, *Daggers of Faith* (Berkeley, 1989), 115ff. Chazan does not consider Thomas Aquinas at all, however. Jeremy Cohen, *The Friars and the Jews* (Ithaca, N.Y., 1982) does, but his conclusions must be treated with extreme caution; see my review of that book in *J.Q.R.* 74 (1985): 321–25.

14. See Grayzel, "Popes, Jews, and Inquisition" 179. I do not agree with his interpretation there that this was some peculiar definition of "force"; nor, indeed, do I agree with most of what he says in that article, although the sources cited are valuable.

15. F. Donald Logan, "Thirteen London Jews and Conversion to Christianity," (Univ. of London) *Bulletin of the Institute of Historical Research* 14 (1972): 214–29.

16. Potthast, *Regesta*, no. 22290-1.

17. Régné, no. 1206; cf. Baer, *History of the Jews* 1:175.

18. Pedro Miguel Carbonell, *Opúsculos inéditos* (CODOINA 28:76–77); we shall return to this important source.

19. Régné, no. 2926.

20. Victor Balaguer, *Historia de Cataluña* (Madrid, 1885), 5:6–12.

21. Heinrich Finke, *Acta aragonensia* (Berlin and Leipzig, 1907–22), 2:859.

22. The only reliable work so far on the history of the Inquisition in Catalonia (with little or nothing, of course, on Aragón or Valencia) is Fort i Cogul, *Catalunya i la Inquisició*, see especially 67–90 (see Works Frequently Cited).

23. Ibid., 107–8. See also his more popular *La Inquisició i Ramon Llull* (Bar-

celona, 1972), which adds little to what he already said. On the last years of Llull's career and the schools established by the king, see *Catalunya i la Inquisició*, 91–96.

24. Menéndez Pelayo, *Historia de los heterodoxos* (1956), 1:521–25: "Quod tempus aderat, iuxta sanctorum vaticinia, in quo omnes iudaei debebant interfici, ut nullus iudaeus in mundo deinceps remaneret"; "Quod tempus adesset quo lex christianourm, lex iudaeorum, et lex sarracenorum converterentur in unam legem, scil. quod esset illa lex quae omnium generaliter esset una, nesciebatur si esset lex christianorum, iudaeorum vel sarracenorum sed solus Deus noverat quae esset lex illa et nullus alius." See also Fort i Cogul, *Catalunya i Inquisició*, 106.

25. Nicolás Eimeric *Directorium inquisitorum* (Venice, 1607), 2:46, fol. 353ff.; the English translation here is that of Baron, *Social and Religious History* 13:4 (see Works Frequently Cited). The aforementioned French translation (see n. 1 above) is severely abridged, lacking all of part 1 and containing only the last chapter of part 2. It has neither bibliography nor index.

26. Baer, *Die Juden*, Vol. 1, no. 249, and p. 344.

27. Roth, "Jews and Albigensians in the Middle Ages," 87ff (see n. 3 above); A. Dondaine, "Le Manuel de l'Inquisiteur (1230–1330)," *Archivum fratrum praedicatorum* 16 (1946): 85–194 (the quotation is from 96). Douais published it ("Saint Raymond de Pennafort et les hérétiques") in *Le moyen âge* 3 (1899): 315–25; cf. also Baron, *Social and Religious History*, 41–42.

28. See the texts edited by Ambrosio de Saldes, "La orden franciscana en el antiguo reino de Aragón," *Revista de estudios franciscanas* (now *Estudis franciscans*) 2 (1908): 26–30.

29. Baer, *Die Juden* 1:350.

30. Menéndez y Pelayo, *Historia de los heterodoxos* (1956), 1:520; Fort i Cogul, *Catalunya i la Inquisició*, 98–99. He is, in fact, mentioned by Eimeric, *Directorium*, pars 2, p. 314. (I have not been able to see the little pamphlet of J. M. Coll, *¿Ramón de Tárrega fue formalmente hereje?* [Lérida, 1949].) The *Ars operativa medica* attributed to him is perhaps actually by Ramón Lull (the *De secretis naturae* and *De alquimia* are, in fact, the same as that work; cf. *Repertorio de historia de las ciencias eclesiásticas en España* 3:101–02). The very important authority Manuel Díaz y Díaz, *Index scriptorum latinorum medii aevi hispanorum* (Madrid, 1959), no. 1461, nevertheless considers it to be Tárrega's work. Antoni Cardoner i Planas, *Història de la medecina a la corona d'Aragó (1162–1479)* (Barcelona, 1973), mentions neither Ramón de Tárrega nor the *Ars operativa*.

31. Baer, *Die Juden*, Vol. 1, no. 257 (P. Cancellarius is Pedro Amáriz Glascario, archbishop of Tarragona); Carreras y Candi, "L'Inquisició barcelonina" 131.

32. A copy of this letter was made by Pedro Miguel Carbonell, royal archivist of Juan II and Fernando I, for Alfonso del Espina (CODOINA 27:378–84), followed by his own notes on canonical sources on heresy. See also the order for an annual salary of the Inquisitors, ibid. 28:7–8 (these sources have been ignored by scholars).

33. Carreras, "L'Inquisició," 148–49, Docs. I and II.

34. Lea, *History of the Inquisition* 1:130.

35. Baer, *Die Juden*, Vol. 1, no. 133 (there is no mention of this important document in his *History*).

36. M. Serrano y Sanz, "Notas acerca de los judíos aragoneses," *R.A.B.M.*, 3a. ép., t. 37 (1917): 325.

37. Baer, *Die Juden*, Vol. 1, no. 166; Régné, nos. 2952 and 2971 (the latter not in Baer).

38. Régné, nos. 2954, 2966, and cf. Gabriel Secall i Güell, *Les jueries medieval tarragonines* (Valls, 1983), 265–66, and the photograph of Jaime's letter (267). Baer somewhat distorted these incidents in *History of the Jews* 2:11.

39. Baer, *Die Juden*, Vol. 1, no. 180; Régné, no. 3256; Baer, *History of the Jews* 2:11–12. The text to which Baer refers, in which Kalonymos B. Kalonymos praised one of these Jews, Astrug Crespi (or Crespin), is his *Even boḥan*, ed. M. Wolf (Lemberg, 1865), 107. Baer did not notice that yet another of the Jews involved, magister Bonetus, was similarly praised there. See briefly on these incidents Secall i Güell, *Les jueries medieval*, 508–9 and his *Els jueus de Valls i la seva època* (Valls, 1980), 322–23.

40. Rubió y Lluch, *Documents* 2:50, no. 52 (see Works Frequently Cited).

41. J. Ernest Martínez Ferrando, *Jaime II de Aragón, su vida familiar* (Barcelona, 1948), 2:307, no. 425.

42. Baer, *Die Juden* 1:476–77. On Alfonso IV, and Pope Martin V, see Pierre Vidal, "Les juifs des anciens comtés de Roussillon et de Cerdagne," *R.E.J.* 16 (1888): 14–17.

43. Baer, *Die Juden*, Vol. 1, no. 561. The cities to which this was addressed were Zaragoza, Calatayud, Tarazona, Huesca, Daroca, "and many others." The sacristan, often the Hebrew term *shamash* being transliterated as *samas*, was a minor official responsible for maintaining the synagogue, oil in the lamps, etc., and sometimes for reading the Torah.

44. Elijah Capsali, *Seder Eliyahu* 1:189 (see Works Frequently Cited).

45. Solomon Ibn Verga *Shevet Yehudah*, ed. Shochet, 127, no. 62.

46. Marx, *Studies*, 87 (text), 96 (trans.).

47. León Tello, *Judiós de Toledo*, Vol. 2, nos. 1455–58, 1461, 1463, 1484–86, 1504, 1506, 1508, 1533, etc.

48. Fernando de Pulgar, *Crónica de don Fernando é doña Isabel*, 432.

49. Baer, *Die Juden* 2:509–10 and 512.

50. Heinrich Brody, *Beiträge zu Salomo da-Piera's Leben und Werken* (Berlin, 1893), 29–30 (Hebrew); text is also in Baer, *Die Juden*, Vol. 1, no. 470, yet he ignored it in his *History of the Jews*.

51. Carlos Carreta Parrondo in *Sefarad* 32 (1972): 145 n. 15.

52. Isidore Loeb, "Polémistes chrétiens et juifs," 235–36, etc. (see Works Frequently Cited). (Rpt. in *B.A.H.* 23 [1893]: 374–75.)

53. Jaume Riera i Sans, "Un recull d'oracions en català dels conversos jueus (segle XV)," *Estudis romànics* 16 (1971–75): 49–97, especially 54 n. 16, and text (67ff. and 85ff.).

54. Jaume Riera i Sans, "Oracions en català dels conversos jueus. Notes bibliogràfiques i textos," *Anuario de filología* (1975): 347–67, see 349–52. Riera did not, understandably, recognize the Passover song.

55. Pilar León Tello, "Costumbres, fiestas y ritos de los judíos [*sic*] toledanos a fines del siglo XV," *Simposio Toledo judaico* (Toledo, 1972), Vol. 2, especially 82ff.

56. Ibid., 70–71 (extremely important, as it is the only actual listing of ingredients). The count's verses are in *Cancionero de obras de burlas*, ed. Frank Dominguez (Valencia, 1978), 77; see Juan Alfonso de Baena's previously cited *Cancionero*, no.

404 and p. 846, line 49; Juan Ruiz, *Libro de buen amor*, stanza 781 c. See also the satirical attack of the *comendador* of the duque de Alba against the converso poet Antón de Montoro in which he says he will give him "*adafina*, cooked all night without pork"; in Antón de Montoro's previously cited *Poesía*, 73. One of the earliest references is the anti-converso satire by a supporter of Pedro Sarmiento, discussed above, Chap. 6.

57. See my "La lengua hebrea entre los cristianos españoles medievales: voces hebreas en Español," *Revista de filología española* 71 (1991): 143. On the trial of the Arias Dávilas, see Gutwirth, "Elementos étnicos," 88, (see Chap. 5 n. 18), and especially Carlos Carrete Parrondo, *Proceso inquisitorial contra los Arias Dávila segovianos, Fontes iudaeorum regni Castellae*, [no.] 3, (Salamanca, 1986), 22–23, nos. 9 and 10.

58. Baer, *Die Juden* 2:500–509.

59. See Amador de los Ríos, *Historia . . . de los judíos* 1:24 n. 1, and the various Spanish dictionaries, on *sambenito*. *None* of the standard reference works on Christian theology, the Christian encyclopedias, etc., mentions the *sambenito*. Authorities on the Inquisition also have not noticed the synonymous term *garnaxia*, which appears in an essential source mostly ignored: Pedro Miguel Carbonell, archivist of the Inquisition in our period (CODOINA 28:50–51, 63). Fidel Fita, at the end of his "La Inquisición de Jerez de la Frontera," *B.A.H.* 15 (1889): 333ff., gives some information from the eighteenth century on *sambenitos* in a church in Ávila.

60. Lea, *History of the Inquisition* 1:147–48 (on the loss of many, or most, of the early documents of the Inquisition, including those burned and stolen by Llorente, see 159 n. 1). Alonso del Espina's "record" of a supposed 1449 Inquisition, in his anti-Jewish polemic *Fortalium fidei*, is certainly a forgery probably based on something like the much later document analyzed by León Tello, "Costumbres, fiestas y ritos."

61. Letter ed. Fidel Fita in *B.A.H.* 15 (1889): 450ff.; Baer, *Die Juden* 2:333; cf. Lea, *History of the Inquisition* 1:158. See also Baer, *History of the Jews* 2:325. On the establishment of the Inquisition in Sicily, see Luis Suárez Fernández, ed., *Política internacional de Isabel la católica* (Valladolid, 1965), 1:437, a document which also has been overlooked by historians of the Inquisition. See also the important documents edited by Fita in *B.A.H.* 16 (1890): 564–70, concerning Filippo de Barbaraj and the supposed decree of Frederick. Lea rightly guessed this decree was a forgery (*History of the Inquisition* 1:155), but the confirmation by Isabel in 1477 is real enough (text in Fita).

62. Enrique Flórez, *Memoria de las reynas cathólicas* [*sic*] (Madrid, 1761), 813–14; cited in Vicente Rodríguez Valencia, *Isabel la católica en la opinion de españoles y extranjeros* (Valladolid, 1970), 2:69. Flórez quotes Zurita, *Anales* 4.20.49, fol. 323v.

63. Text of 27 December letter in Joaquin Guichot y Parody, *Historia de la muy noble, muy leal, muy heróica é invicta ciudad de Sevilla* (Seville, 1896), 1:183; cf. also Mario Méndez Bejarano, *Histoire de la juiverie de Seville* (Madrid, 1922), 160–61. Also in November the pope had repeated his instruction that "three bishops" as well as "others," priests or friars, be appointed. In fact, these instructions were ignored (text ed. Fita, "La Inquisición de Torquemada" *B.A.H.* 23 [1893]: 405 n. 1).

64. Text, Guichot, *Historia de . . . Sevilla,* 184.

65. Lea, *History of the Inquisition* 1:166 n. 1. (For Rodrigo de Orense, see below on the Jerónimite Order.) On the trial of Pedro de Aranda, see C. Baronius—O. Raynaldus, *Annales ecclesiastici* (Lucca, 1738–56), 30:285–86.

66. Pulgar, *Claros varones,* ed. Tate, 57; ed. Domínguez Bordona, 168 n. 6. Tate's observations about Torquemada's arguments in favor of the "chosen race" (i.e., conversos) sheds light on nothing but Tate's own bias (100 n. 162). For the appointment of Tomás de Torquemada, see the text in Carlos Carrete Parrondo, ed., *Fontes iudaeorum regni Castellae,* [no.] 1: *Provincia de Salamanca* (Salamanca, 1981), 131–32, no. 377. Among the numerous erroneous discussions of the establishment of the Inquisition in Castile, that of José Martínez Millán, *La hacienda de la Inquisición* (Madrid, 1984), 6, is one of the most inaccurate, including the claim that Torquemada became Inquisitor General in 1482.

67. Alonso de Palencia, *Crónica de Enrique IV (Décadas),* trans. A. Paz y Mélia, B.A.E. 267 (rpt. Madrid, 1975), 3:87, 119.

68. Diego de Valera, *Crónica de los reyes católicos,* ed. Juan de Mata Carriazo (Madrid, 1927), 123–24. (Again, these important sources have been ignored by modern historians of the Inquisition.)

69. The two versions are Fernando de Pulgar (as already noted *not* "Hernando del Pulgar," an altogether different person), *Crónica de los reyes católicos* and *Crónica de don Fernando é doña Isabel* (see Works Frequently Cited). See Francisco Cantera Burgos, "Fernando de Pulgar y los conversos," *Sefarad* 4 (1944): 295–348, particularly 337–42. In spite of the obvious importance of Pulgar's chronicle, and in spite of Cantera's masterful article, not only recent historians but even Baer ignored these in his account of the Inquisition in his *History.*

70. Pulgar, *Crónica de don Fernando é doña Isabel,* 518–19. This addition was no doubt the work of an "old Christian."

71. Andrés Bernáldez, *Historia de los reyes católicos,* 598–600 (see Works Frequently Cited).

72. Antonio Domínguez Ortiz, *Los conversos de origen judío después de la expulsión* (Madrid, [1959?]), 57 (not in Carrete Parrondo, *Provincia de Salamanca*).

73. Gloria Lora Serrano, "Belmez: un intento fallido de señorialización en el siglo XV," *Andalucía medieval. Actas I coloquio histórico de Andalucía* (Córdoba, 1982), 97 and n. 36. For the Order of Santiago, see León Tello, *Judíos de Toledo* 1:501–2, Doc. 67, Tit. VII. Albert Sicroff's frequently cited book, *Les controverses des statuts de "pureté de sang" en Espagne du XVe au XVIIe siècle* (Paris, 1960), is of no value for the medieval period (fifteenth century), based entirely on readily available and widely known published sources and secondary literature. He introduced some new material only for the seventeenth century.

74. This appears to be related to the argument of Alonso de Oropesa, former general of the order, based on Isaiah 28.19 (the Vulgate: "et tantummodo sola vexatio intellectum dabit auditui," which should be the correct reading), which he apparently understood to refer to the exile of the Jews so that they could be converted; cf. Luis Alfredo Díaz y Díaz, "Alonso de Oropesa y su obra," *Studia Hieronymiana* (Madrid, 1973), 1:286.

75. José de Sigüenza, *Historia de la Orden de San Jerónimo,* 2d ed., N.B.A.E. 8 and 12 (Madrid, 1907–9), 2:26, 31–33. See the text of the directive to the prior of

Guadalupe, cited by Tarsicio de Ascona, "Dictamen en defensa de los judíos conversos de la Orden de San Jerónimo a principios del siglo XVI," *Studia Hieronymiana* 2:350 n. 6.

76. Text ed. V. Beltrán de Heredia, "Las bulas de Nicolás V acerca de los judíos" (*sic*) *Sefarad* 21 (1961): 45–47. This letter, as well as some of the other sources here mentioned, has been ignored by those who subsequently have written on the Jeronimite issue.

77. He was *not* a converso, as suggested, e.g., by Baron, *Social and Religious History* 13:316 n. 25, following Lea and others. Practically the only source for his career is Sigüenza, *Historia de la Orden de San Jerónimo* 1:361–88, with some additional material in Vol. 2. See also *Memorias de don Enrique IV de Castilla* 2:343–44, 347, 351, and especially 356ff.

78. The work has been analyzed in detail by Díaz y Díaz, "Alonso de Oropesa," and finally edited (translated into Castilian) by him, *Luz para conocimiento de los gentiles* (see Works Frequently Cited; further references in parentheses in the text), of which the introduction is the cited article. The second part of the title, "and the glory of Israel, the people of God," of which Alonso made much in his introduction (77), was entirely omitted by Díaz. The work is a strange mixture of favorable and negative attitudes toward Jews; the polemics I shall discuss in my book on Jews and Christians in Spain.

79. See especially Oropesa, *Luz*, 761–62. Díaz correctly observed that the first part of the work is hardly "pro-converso," but only an argument for equality between "old" and "new" Christians ("Alonso de Oropesa" 277). Nevertheless, the argument of the author in his preface is specifically that "old Christians" must abandon their hatred of "those faithful who come from Judaism to Christ, and who prior to their coming were alone called in scripture 'Israel the people of God'; which certainly indicates their honor, favor and glory, and which is also seen in consequence of the fact that Christ, our legislator, came according to the flesh from their race, i.e., of the line of David; and that, as John attests, salvation comes from the Jews (John 4.22; cf. Romans 1.3)" (*Luz*, 77).

80. Díaz y Díaz, "Alonso de Oropesa," 264.

81. This bull, *Percepimus quosdam* (1449), has been frequently published, at least in part. It is also discussed by Ascona, "Dictamen en defensa de los judíos conversos," 356. The entire text is included in Alonso de Oropesa, *Luz*, chap. 63.

82. Sigüenza, *Historia de la Orden de San Jerónimo*, 33–38. This is all mentioned, briefly and inadequately, by Haim Beinart, "The Judaizing Movement in the Order of San Jeronimo in Castile," *Scripta Hierosolymitana* 7 (1961): 167–92.

83. Beinart, "Judaizing Movement," 188.

84. Ibid., 169–70; Albert A. Sicroff, "Clandestine Judaism in the Hieronymite Monastery of Nuesta Señora de Guadalupe," *Studies in Honor of M. J. Benardete* (New York, 1965), 95, and more completely his subsequent detailed study "El caso del judaizante jerónimo fray Diego de Marchena," *Homenaje a Rodríguez-Moñino* (Madrid, 1966), 2:227–33. For the "old Christian" who said that most of the converso monks were good Christians, see Sicroff's first-cited article (115).

85. Beinart, "Judaizing Movement," 176–77; cf. Baer, *Die Juden* 2:474–76, for the text of the process against Alfonso de Toledo, and cf. 375–76 and his *History of the Jews* 2:342 on Rabbi Samuel Valanci and the brother of Abraham Saba.

León Tello, *Judíos de Toledo* 2:524, no. 1455, cites the Alfonso de Toledo process without having noted Baer's publication of it. Is this Samuel Valenci the same as "Symuel Valenty" mentioned in a tax record of 1463 there? (315). (See also above, Chapter 3.)

86. Sigüenza, *Historia de la Orden de San Jerónimo,* 60–61; Azcona, "Dictamen en defensa de los judíos conversos," 357–58, 359–60.

87. Sicroff, "Clandestine Judaism," 91. Further references in parentheses in text.

88. Madrid, B.N. MS. 18183, fol. 130; cited by Antonio Domínguez Ortiz, *Los conversos de origen judío,* 17–18 n. On the other hand, the growing tendency to limit membership in religious orders and *cofradías* to those of more or less noble, or at least "old Christian," families may not necessarily reflect anti-converso hostility but may sometimes be related to the general European tendency at that time; cf. Marc Bloch, *Feudal Society* (Chicago, 1968), 328.

89. Ed. Fidel Fita in *B.A.H.* 11 (1887): 429–30.

90. *Algunas obras del Doctor Francisco López de Villalobos* (Madrid, 1886), 165–77, section "Cartas castellanas."

91. Eusebio Rey, "San Ignacio y el problema de los cristianos nuevos," *Razon y fe* 153 (1956): 173–204.

92. See John Edwards, *Christian Córdoba* (Cambridge, 1982), 184–85; Baer, *Die Juden* 2:472, and his *History of the Jews* 2:299.

93. "Chronicon de Valladolid," CODOIN 13:187; not mentioned by Edwards, or historians in general.

94. Gracia Boix, *Colección de documentos,* 86, 96ff., 103, and see 28–31 for the protest movement against Pedro Guiral (see Works Frequently Cited).

95. Ibid., 97.

96. Coronas Tejada, *Conversos and Inquisition in Jaén,* 50–51.

97. Gracia Boix, *Colección de documentos,* 31–79.

98. Ibid., 85; that case was discussed also by Haim Beinart, "Agudo asher be-La Mancha ve-anuseyah," *Tarbiz* 50 (1981): 423–49.

99. Gracia Boix, *Colección de documentos,* 246 and plates.

100. Luis Coronas Tejada, "Judíos en Jaén en los años inmediatos a la expulsión," World Congress of Jewish Studies, 8th *Proceedings,* Division B: History of the Jewish People (Jerusalem, 1982), 29–34, and his *Conversos and Inquisition in Jaén,* 20.

101. Fernando de Pulgar, *Crónica de los reyes católicos* 2:210.

102. Ibid., 211. It is unfortunate that *none* of the people who has written on the Inquisition has seen this statement. (*Raezes,* vile men, is a variant of *rafez, rahez,* etc.)

103. Alonso de Palencia, *Crónica de Enrique IV* 3:120.

104. Fidel Fita, "La inquisición toledana" 289–322; see 311–19 for the names of those from other cities.

105. León Tello, *Judíos de Toledo,* Vol. 2, e.g., nos. 1412–15, 1418, 1420, 1454, 1455–58, etc.

106. Ibid. 1:516–18, Doc. 74.

107. Baer, *Die Juden* 2:480–83.

108. Ibid., 478.

109. Ibid., 468–72.

110. León Tello, *Judíos de Toledo* 1:512–14, Doc. 72.

111. Rafael Lapesa, "Sobre Juan de Lucena," in Hornik, *Collected Studies,* especially 279, 288 (see Works Frequently Cited).

112. Teófilo López Mata, *La provincia de Burgos en la geografía y en la historia* (Burgos, 1963), 115–16.

113. Bernáldez, *Memorias del reinado,* 96–101 (see Works Frequently Cited).

114. Amador de los Ríos, *Historia . . . de los judíos* 3:249; Lea, *History of the Inquisition* 1:163. A recent popularized account, Antonio Cascales Ramos, *La inquisición en Andalucía* (Seville, 1986), refers to him as "Suson" and to his daughter as "Sara" (!), although the two documents referring to him spell the name correctly as Susan (113, 116). The anonymous source was edited by Fidel Fita, "Los conjurados de Seville en 1480," *B.A.H.* 16 (1890): 450–56 (cited here), an older MS than the one consulted by Amador (Cascales made no mention of either of these). Further on, Fita edited also another account of the legend, from a seventeenth-century source (556–60).

115. There was a Jacob Aben Xuxen who was *arrendador* of taxes and *almoxarife* of Seville in 1309; and also Mayor Aben Xuxen (1368–88).

116. In addition to the documents relating to Jews of Seville in Baer, Collantes de Terán, etc., see Isabel Montes Romero-Camacho, "Notas para el estudio de la judería sevillana en la baja edad media (1248–1391)," *La ciudad hispánica durante los siglos XIII al XVI, En la España medieval* 10 (1987), especially the table of names (360–65), a very important study.

117. Wagner, *Regesto de documentos,* 22–23 (see Works Frequently Cited). These are reprinted in Cascales Ramos, *La inquisición en Andalucía,* 113–18, nos. 9, 10, 11, who also edited there the text of the 1479 document.

118. Collantes de Terán, *Sevilla,* 447.

119. Joseph Ibn Ṣadiq of Arévalo, *Qiṣur zekher la-ṣadiq,* ed. Adolph Neubauer, *Medieval Jewish Chronicles* (Oxford, 1887), 1:99.

120. The index to Baer, *History of the Jews,* has precisely this confusion. To further add to the confusion, another Juan de Sevilla, or Juan Fernández, *contador* of don Enrique de Guzmán, the powerful duque de Medina Sidonia, was also condemned *in absentia,* having fled the city in 1483; cf. Cascales Ramos, *La inquisición en Andalucía,* 60–62; and yet another Juan Sánchez de Sevilla who also lived in Toledo and abandoned a store there in 1460 (probably owing to the massacre of the conversos); cf. León Tello, *Judíos de Toledo* 2:357, 472. The case of our Juan de Sevilla is in Baer, *Die Juden* 2:444–47, and cf. *History of the Jews* 2:354–56 for more or less accurate details of the case. León Tello (2:510, no. 1418) cites the document, but only for the names of the Jews mentioned.

121. Could it be that this is the same as Johan de Cuenca, *toquero,* with whom a Jewish boy was apprenticed in 1465? (Wagner, *Regesto de documentos,* 19–20, Doc. 28).

122. Those cities which have received study so far include Cuenca, Ciudad Real (in addition to Haim Beinart, *Records of the Trials of the Spanish Inquisition in Ciudad Real,* 4 vols. [Jerusalem, 1981], see Juan Blázquez Miguel, *Ciudad Real y la Inquisición* [Ciudad Real, 1986]; few cases in either of these are relevant to our period); Jerez (H. Sancho de Sopranis, "Los conversos y la Inquisición primitiva en

Jerez," *Archivo Iberoamericano* 4 [1944]: 196–610); Toledo (many more studies, mostly articles, than what has been cited here); Seville; Burgos; and Granada. A partial bibliography of these, by no means complete, may be found in Juan Blázquez Miguel, *Inquisición y criptojudaísmo* (Madrid, 1988), a good if somewhat basic and too broad general survey. Fita has also published numerous documents, largely ignored (e.g., for Guadalupe, *B.A.H.* 23 [1893]: 283–343).

123. Carlos Carrete Parrondo, "Talavera de la Reina y su comunidad judía," *En la España medieval. Estudios dedicados al profesor Dr. Julio González González* (Madrid, 1980), 50 and n. 41. "Chronicon de Vallvadolid," CODOIN 13:179–80.

124. Carlos Carrete Parrondo, ed., *Fontes iudaeorum regni Castellae*, [no.] 2: *El tribunal de la Inquisición en el obispado de Soria (1486–1502)* (Salamanca, 1985), nos. 5–9, 11, 27, etc.

125. Ibid. nos. 6, 8, 13, 78, 80, 111, 113, 140 (for Hebrew); reasons for converting: nos. 34, 111, 231, 305; husband and wife, no. 113; going to Israel: nos. 9, 114, 136.

126. Text ed. Fidel Fita, "La inquisición de Torquemada," *B.A.H.* 23 (1893): 393–402. As is unfortunately the case with *most* of the invaluable work of this important scholar and accomplished Hebraist, this has been ignored by all subsequent writers on the Jews and on the Inquisition, including even Carrete Parrondo, *Fontes iudaeorum regni castellae*, [no.] 1: *Provincia de Salamanca* (Salamanca, 1981). On Gonzalo de Cuéllar and the queen, see Fita, op. cit. (403 n. 1). Mosé de Cuéllar (but not his son or brother) is named among those Jews who left property in Buitrago as a result of the Expulsion; Baer, *Die Juden* 2:386 and cf. also no. 385 (houses in Hita). He also owned farms and houses in Gargantilla (one of the *barrios* of Buitrago) and a *lavadero de lana* (place for washing wool) there; see F. Cantera Burgos, "Los judíos expulsados de San Martín de Valdeiglesias," *Actas del primero simposio de estudios sefardíes* (Madrid, 1970), 31–32 (see the introduction to the document there [29–30]).

127. Gracia Boix, *Colección de documentos*, 80, nos. 221, 222. Carrete, *Provincia de Salamanca*, contains no information at all on the Inquisition in the province of Salamanca.

128. Baer, *History of the Jews* 2:399–423. The errors here mentioned are on 401.

129. It should incidentally be pointed out, in light of some absurd claims by an American writer, Henry May, that the late head of state of Spain supposedly was of Jewish descent, that while the name of Franco was fairly common among conversos, it was equally common among "old Christians." There is no evidence to support the theory of Franco's Jewish origin.

130. Fidel Fita, "La Inquisición de Torquemada" 415–19; which if Baer had seen would have dispelled his doubts as to the very existence of Moses Abenamías (*History of the Jews* 2:503 n. 79). The Hebrew term *oto ha-ish* for Jesus is found in Luke 23.4, Acts 5.28; yet nevertheless it is also found in such Jewish sources as the infamous *Toldot Yeshu*, etc. It is a term of contempt.

131. Fidel Fita, "La Inquisición y el santo niño de La Guardia," *B.A.H.* 11 (1887): 7–160; see especially 22–52. For Rabbi Peres and the 1485 case, see León Tello, *Judíos de Toledo* 2:506, no. 1414.

132. Fita, "La Inquisición y el santo niño," 420–23; also in Pilar León Tello, *Los Judíos de Ávila* (Ávila, 1963), 89–90. Baer overlooked this important document; probably deliberately, since it is mentioned in *Die Juden* 2:404 no. 377.
133. Fita, "La Inquisición y el santo niño," 22–24, 69–70, 100–108. (Additional bibliography on the case in Baer, *History of the Jews* 2:502 n. 75; better, and with additions, in the Spanish translation, *Historia de los judíos* 2:784 n. 83.)
134. Lea, *History of the Inquisition* 1:134.
135. Pedro Miguel Carbonell, *Opúsculos inéditos* (CODOINA 28:68–75); cf. also Alfonso de la Torre, "Un incunable," *Butlletí de la Biblioteca de Catalunya* 7 (1932): 333–36, after Carbonell's important source (which he like others ignored) was published. Lope de Vega, of converso origin, also wrote a play, *El niño de La Guardia* (critical ed. Anthony J. Farrel [London, 1985]).
136. Fita, "La Inquisición y el santo niño," 84.
137. See, e.g., Coronas Tejada, *Conversos and Inquisition in Jaén*, 24, 35, 36.
138. See Pico della Mirandola, *Oration on the Dignity of Man*, trans. A. Robert Capognigri, 5th ed. (Chicago, 1970), 9, 23ff., 45, 59. Pico's older contemporary, Marsilio Ficino, already in 1474 had cited Jewish sources, including the Talmud.
139. Papal letter, edited (and as usual since ignored) by Fidel Fita in *B.A.H.* 16 (1890): 314–16, and the bull on the Inquisition in general, (367ff.). See E. Rosenthal's interesting study of the important manuscript of Alemano's commentary, "Some Observations on Yoḥanan Alemano's Political Ideas," *Studies in Jewish Intellectual and Religious History Presented to Alexander Altmann* (University of Alabama, 1979), 248. There have been several studies on Pico's relationship to *qabalah*.
140. Carreras y Candi, "L'inquisició barcelonina," one of the most important studies ever done; cf. generally Lea, *History of the Inquisition* 1:239. Both Carreras and Lea cited different sources, unknown to each other. (Lea probably did not read Catalan, and in any case did not know Carreras' article.)
141. Carreras, "L'inquisició barcelonina," 146–48 and the documents (167–77); cf. Lea, *History of the Inquisition* 1:263. The text of the oath is in Pedro Miguel Carbonell, *Opúsculos inéditos* (CODOINA 28:5–6).
142. Secall i Güell, *Jueries medievals tarragonines* (Valls, 1983), 515–16.
143. Carreras, "L'inquisició barcelonina," 142–43; documents (162–64).
144. Ibid., 167–68, Doc. 17.
145. The processions and the *auto* are described, with the names of those involved, by Carbonell, *Opúsculos inéditos*, 9–13.
146. Ibid., 14–19, 27–28, 20–26, 29–35, 41–49, 53–61, 63–65.
147. Francesch Carreras y Candi, "Evolució històrica dels juheus y juheissants barcelonins," *Estudis universitaris catalans* 4 (1910): 52, 57–58. See Carbonell, *Opúsculos inéditos*, 54. According to Antoni Cardoner i Planas, *Historia de la medecina a la corona d'Aragó* (Barcelona, 1973), 210, Sant Jordi was also an astrologer (he was not "probably" a converso, however, but definitely).
148. Carbonell, *Opúsculos ineditos*, 40–41, 52–53.
149. Pulgar, *Crónica de los reyes católicos*, 2:337–38.
150. Baer, *Die Juden* 2:449–66 (he distorted the simple facts of the case in his discussion in *History of the Jews* 2:372). On the suspension and reinstitution of the

Inquisition, see José Cabezudo Astrain, "Los conversos aragoneses según los procesos de la Inquisición," *Sefarad* 18 (1958): 272.

151. Cabezudo, "Los conversos aragoneses," 281–82 (the article was never completed).

152. Lea, *History of the Inquisition* 1:587–90, Doc. 10; cf. 233–34. Carreras y Candi, "L'Inquisició barcelonina," for instance, neglected it entirely; Fort i Cogull, *Catalunya i la Inquisició* makes only a brief reference to it (129), ignoring Lea's publication of the document (the fact that Lea's book was not translated into Spanish until recently does not excuse Spanish scholars having ignored it.

153. Lea, *History of the Inquisition* 1:234–35, 590–92, Doc. 11.

154. León Tello, *Judíos de Toledo* 1:512–14, Doc. 72.

155. Lea, *History of the Inquisition* 1:246; see also Cabezudo, "Los conversos aragoneses," 273.

156. For the commission granted by Torquemada to Juan Colivera as Inquisitor for Aragón, including Teruel, see Manuel Sánchez Moya, "Aportaciones a la historia de la Inquisición," *Sefarad* 18 (1958): 283–90.

157. Manuel Sánchez Moya and Jasone Monasterio Aspiri, "Los judaizantes turolenses en el siglo XV," *Sefarad* 32 (1972): 105–40, 307–40. See also Baer, *Die Juden* 2:467–68: Rabbi Samuel of Teruel testified in 1486 against several conversos, as did other Jews (the Inquisition of Teruel was under the jurisdiction of that of Valencia, from concerns about the corruption of converted Muslims in Teruel).

158. Pulgar, *Crónica de los reyes católicos* 2:339–40 (the later version remains unchanged; *Crónica de don Fernando é doña Isabel*, 473–74).

159. Baer, *History of the Jews* 2:367, 270–71 (again, he did not see Pulgar, nor did Netanyahu, *Origins*.) See generally, Lea, *History of the Inquisition* 1:244ff.

160. See Angel Alcalá Galve, *Los orígenes de la Inquisición en Aragón. S. Pedro Arbués, mártir de la autonomía aragonesa* ([Huesca?], [1984?]), an extremely popularized work whose apologetic bias is obvious from the title, yet it is the only modern study of the subject. Among other things, the author ignored the important documents in *Libro verde de Aragón*, 77–103. See also Lea, *History of the Inquisition* 1:256–57, which is better in some respects than Alcalá's pamphlet. See also M. P. Hornik, "Death of an Inquisitor" in Hornik, *Collected Studies*, 233–57. The *Libro verde* calls Francisco the "son" of Jerónimo, but that is chronologically impossible. Llorente stated that in 1813 he saw the records in Zaragoza of over three hundred persons punished as a result of the assassination (*Historia* 1:178).

161. Baer, *Die Juden* 2:484 n. 4, misread the sources he cited. Rosanses, *Divrey yemey Yisrael be-Togremah*, whom Baer copied in his *History*, simply copied verbatim from David Conforte (a seventeenth-century chronicler), *Qore ha-dorot* (Berlin, 1846), fol. 40b, who wrote that Abraham (not Açach) Cocumbriel and Simon (not Abraham) Almosnino were martyred in Aragón. Conforte, it should be noted, was a great-grandson of Abraham Cocumbriel. We do not know who Simon Almosnino was, but he undoubtedly had nothing to do with this case.

162. Baer, *Die Juden* 2:484–509; cf. *History of the Jews* 2:384ff. The citation of the *Tur*, code of Jewish law, is another indication of the danger which conversos posed to the Jewish community in such matters.

163. Baer, *Die Juden*, Vol. 2, no. 392; cf. *History of the Jews* 2:292 for similar

statements about such "letters" in Alonso del Espina. The earliest (?) process in Valencia was 1461, accusations against the Colom family for having performed Jewish burial rites (*Die Juden* 2:444, note at the end of no. 392).

164. Lea, *History of the Inquisition* 1:230ff.

165. Baer, *Die Juden* 2:483–84.

166. Lea, *History of the Inquisition* 1:243.

167. Alvaro Santamaría Arández, "En torno a la situación de los judíos conversos de Mallorca en el siglo XV," *Boletín de la sociedad arqueológica luliana* 31 (1953–60): 187.

168. Ibid., 189 (or 1404—see E. Fajarnes y Tur, "Cofradía de los conversos de judaísmo fundada en Mallorca en 1404," in the same journal, 7 [1897]: 365ff.).

169. Santamaría, "En torno a la situación de los judíos conversos," 195.

170. Jordi Ventura Subirats, "Els inicis de la inquisició espanyola a Mallorca," *Randa* 5 (1977): 74 (article, 67–116). The article deals chiefly with the salaries of Inquisition officials, primarily in the sixteenth century.

171. Pulgar, *Crónica de los reyes católicos,* 2:353–54; unchanged in the later redaction, *Crónica de don Fernando é doña Isabel,* 478.

172. See Baer, *History of the Jews* 2:363–64; Manuel Serrano y Sanz, *Origenes de la dominación española en América,* N.B.A.E. 25 (Madrid, 1918), 159ff.

173. Baer, *Die Juden* 2:402.

174. Fidel Fita, "Los judaizantes en el reinado de Carlos I," *B.A.H.* 33 (1898): 334.

175. Miguel Ángel Ladero Quesada, *La hacienda real,* 237 n. 31; see also his "Judeoconversos andaluces en el siglo XV," *Actas del III coloquio de historia medieval andaluza* (Jaén, 1982), 38–39.

176. Coronas Tejada, *Conversos and Inquisition in Jaén,* 42, 45. Some interesting documentation for Seville (1485) was published by Juan de Mata Carriazo, "La inquisición y las rentas de Sevilla," *Homenaje a don Ramón Carande* (Madrid, 1963), 2:95–112.

177. Amalia Prieto Cantero, *Casa y descargos de los reyes católicos* (Valladolid, 1969), 383 (fols. 109–11).

178. Haim Beinart, "Two Documents concerning Confiscated Converso Property," *Sefarad* 17 (1957): 280–313. In 1489 there were various grants by the Inquisition to individuals, charitable institutions, etc. (Prieto, *Casa y descargos,* 518, fol. 536; cf. p. 501).

179. León Tello, *Judíos de Toledo* 2:544, no. 1513. The marriage of Arbués' sister has been previously mentioned; see also José Cabezudo Astrain, "La judería de Épila," *Sefarad* 17 (1957): 116–17.

180. León Tello, *Judíos de Toledo* 2:553, no. 1550.

181. Gracia Boix, *Colección de documentos,* 93–94.

182. Diego de Valera, *Crónica de los reyes católicos,* 124.

183. "Illustraciones de la casa de Niebla," *Memorial histórico español* 10 (1857): 299. His account of the establishment of the Inquisition (298) is not exact.

184. [J. M. Montero de Espinosa], *Relación histórica de la judería de Sevilla* (Seville, 1849), 229–34.

185. Henry Kamen, *La Inquisición española* (Barcelona, 1985), 64, 75.

186. Llorente, *Historia* 4:186–88; cited also by Coronoas Tejada, *Conversos*

and Inquisition in Jaén, 38 (see Works Frequently Cited). For Cuenca, see details in Sebastián Cirac Estopaña, ed., *Registros de los documentos del santo oficio de Cuenca y Sigüenza* (Cuenca-Barcelona, 1965) (the editor has expressed strong anti-Jewish bias).

187. Jacques Lafaye, "Le messie dans le monde ibérique: aperçu," *Mélanges de la Casa de Velázquez* 7 (1971): 163; an article of interest chiefly for the seventeenth century, but of little importance for Jewish messianic ideology, about which the author was ill-informed. For the "*Chuetas*," the most popular studies are Lionel Isaac, *The Jews of Majorca* (London, 1936), and Baruch Braunstein, *The Chuetas of Majorca* (New York, 1936), and, more recently, Kenneth Moore, *Those of the Street: The Catholic Jews of Mallorca* (New York, 1976). Of an entirely different category is Angela Selke, *Los chuetas y la inquisición* (Madrid, 1972), based on careful research of the archives, chiefly of the seventeenth century.

188. Gracia Boix, *Colección de documentos*, 255–57, 284–85; Juan Bautista Vilar (Ramírez), *Fernando VII, la inquisición y los judíos en Gibraltar* (Caracas, 1973; photo offprint from *Maguea-escudo*, nos. 33–34 [1973]).

189. Isaac ʿArama, *ʿAqedat Yiṣḥaq*, as cited by Netanyahu, *Marranos*, 154, and cf. n. 51a there. As Netanyahu observed, these words could not have been written earlier than 1489, and perhaps even after the Expulsion.

190. Carlos Carrete Parrondo, "Las judaizantes de Cuenca procesadas por la inquisición en 1490," *Actas del II congreso international, Encuentro de las tres culturas* (Toledo, 1985), 97–104.

Chapter 8. Expulsions of the Jews

1. Teodoro González García, "El judaismo," in Ricardo García Villoslada, ed., *Historia de la iglesia en España* (Madrid, 1979), 1:672.

2. Baer, *History of the Jews* 2:321, 333.

3. Capsali, *Seder Eliyahu* 1:188. (This chapter already was published by Meir Lattes, ed., *Liquṭim shonim mi-s[efer] devey Eliyahu* [Padua, 1869; rpt. Jerusalem, 1968], 63–64, which Baer should have seen.)

4. José Faur, *In the Shadow of History: Jews and Conversos at the Dawn of Modernity* (Albany, 1992), 39 (see my review in *Sefarad* 54 [1994], 201–3). Benzion Netanyahu, *Don Isaac Abravanel* (Philadelphia, 1972), 46–47 (further references in parentheses in the text). For the title "Catholic Monarchs," see Vicente Rodríguez Valencia, *Isabel la católica en la opinión de españoles y extranjeros* (Valladolid, 1970), 1:48.

5. Francisco Cantera Burgos, "Fernando de Pulgar y los conversos," *Sefarad* 4 (1944): 307.

6. Pulgar, *Crónica de los reyes católicos*, 1:77 (unchanged in the later redaction, 257).

7. See the letter of Hernando in *Espistolario español*, B.A.E. 62:19. For the dancing in Córdoba, see Diego de Valera, *Crónica de los reyes católicos*, ed. Juan de Mata Carriazo (Madrid, 1927), 170–71. The extremes to which romanticizers of Isabel would go in the last century in praise of the "glorious queen" may be seen in the unpublished work of Modeste Lafuente (not to be confused with the ecclesiastical historian Vicente Lafuente), one of those who supported the move for her

canonization. He was not above deliberate distortion and lying about Isabel's "despising" luxury and *not* participating in the celebrations at Barcelona, hating bullfighting (she was criticized for the *opposite*), etc. (see Rodríguez Valencia, *Isabel la católica* 2:128–29). As recently as 1964 the archbishop of Valladolid still seriously pressed the case for canonization of Isabel (see *Isabel la católica*, 641–42), and the issue is still not dead. (The criticism of that volume is that not a single negative statement about Isabel appears, and only very selective opinions are included.) While Isabel was certainly no "saint," neither does she deserve the bad reputation she has among many.

8. *Poema de Alfonso XI*, in B.A.E. 57:515, stanza 1265. Alonso de Palencia attests to the Christian insults against Fernando (*Crónica de Enrique IV*, trans. A. Paz y Mélia, B.A.E. 267 [rpt. Madrid, 1977] 2:51, 60). For Ávila, see Pilar León Tello, "La judería de Ávila durante el reinado de los reyes católicos," *Sefarad* 23 (1963): 39.

9. Suárez Fernández, *Documentos* (see Works Frequently Cited).

10. *Ordenanzas reales* VII.viii.4, in *Colección de códigos* 6:530, and *Códigos españoles*, 519 (see Works Frequently Cited).

11. Ibid. (*Colección*, 6:520–21; *Códigos*, 510–11). Alonso de Palencia, *Cuarta década*, ed. and trans. José López de Toro (Madrid, 1970), 1:171 (Latin text), 2:201 (trans.). Netanyahu, *Origins* ignored this.

12. Suárez Fernández, *Documentos*, 344–46.

13. Ibid., 348–50.

14. Ibid., 372–73.

15. León Tello, *Judíos de Toledo;* the documents in support of this are too many to enumerate fully, cf. Vol. 2, nos. 1281, 1465, 1474, 1495, 1498, 1534, 1539. Santa Ollala, nos. 1522, 1524; and see, e.g., no. 1565 for the situation in 1492.

16. Ibid., no. 1561.

17. Suárez Fernández, *Documentos*, 362–66.

18. Ibid., 373–77.

19. Pedro-Antonio Muñoz Casayús, "Los capítulos de la Santa Hermandad de Aragón," *Universidad* (Zaragoza) 4 (1927): 945–46.

20. Suárez Fernández, *Documentos*, 162–63, no. 39.

21. Francesch Carreras i Candi, *L'aljama de juhéus de Tortosa* (Barcelona, 1928), 163–65 (text of documents is Catalan).

22. Alvar García de Santa María, *Crónica de Juan II*, ed. Juan de Mata Carriazo, B.A.E. 68:305–6.

23. There is still no satisfactory history of the entire subject of relations between the Christian kingdoms and the Muslim kingdom of Granada, nor even a thorough treatment of the conquest. Some worth consulting are Cristóbal Torres Delgado, *El antiguo reino nazarí de Granada (1232–1340)* (Granada, 1974), and, particularly, Rachel Arié, *L'Espagne musulmane au temps des Naṣrides (1232–1492)* (Paris, 1973); Luis Seco de Lucena's various articles, and his *Muhammad IX de Granada* (Granada, 1978); Antonio de la Torre, *Los reyes católicos y Granada* (Madrid, 1946); Armando Saitta, *Dalla Granada mora alla Granada cattolica* (Rome, 1984), a convenient summary but based only on secondary material; and Miguel Ángel Ladero Quesada, *Castilla y la conquista del reino de Granada* (Granada, 1987), primarily a statistical study, but solidly researched.

24. Alvar García de Santa María, *Crónica de Juan II de Castilla*, 242. On the term *alfaqueque*, see Fita in *B.A.H.* 48:302. Originally the *fakkāk* (emancipators) were private individuals who offered their services for a fee to redeem captives held by the Christians. From this originally Muslim function the term entered into Castilian, and is mentioned in *Siete partidas* II.xxx.i as one who ransoms captives (in this case, from Muslims), and the duties and qualifications are set forth there in *leyes* ii and iii. The use of Christian *alfaqueques* in Murcia is attested in 1371 (see generally Arié, *L'Espagne musulmane*, 326–28).

25. Suárez Fernández, *Documentos*, 18. However, Ladero Quesada states that Jews were automatically exempt from military obligation, which seems likely (*Castilla y la conquista del reino de Granada* [Granada, 1987], 132). No source so far reveals the presence of Jewish soldiers.

26. León Tello, *Judíos de Toledo* 2:494, no. 1370.

27. Suárez Fernández, *Documentos*, 243–45.

28. Fita in *B.A.H.* 15 (1889): 319.

29. Suárez Fernández, *Documentos*, 246–47, 272–73. For Burgos, see the letter in Javier Ortiz Real, *Los judíos de Cantabria en la baja edad media* (Torrelavega, 1985), 62–63. Many more details concerning the Jewish taxes for the war are reserved for future treatment.

30. Florentino Zamora, "Los judíos en Soria," *Celtiberia* 14 (1964): 123.

31. Ladero Quesada, *Castilla y la conquista*, 299–301. On the role of Santángel and the *Mesta*, see 217.

32. Pulgar, *Crónica de los reyes católicos* 2:25–26.

33. Ibid., 314; *Crónica de don Fernando é doña Isabel*, 465.

34. Joseph Ibn Ṣadiq of Arévalo, *Qiṣur zekher la-ṣadiq*," ed. Adolph Neubauer, *Mediaeval Jewish Chronicles* (Oxford, 1887), 1:99–100. The towns as I have identified them are all in the region between Marbella and Ronda. Cartajima does not appear on most maps, but is south of Ronda (it cannot, of course, be Cartagena, as the Hebrew would suggest, which was already Christian).

35. Abraham b. Solomon Ibn Ardutiel, *Sefer ha-qabalah*, ed. Neubauer, *Mediaeval Jewish Chronicles* 111. Zacut, *Sefer yuḥasin ha-shalem*, fol. 227a (see Works Frequently Cited). Capsali, *Seder Eliyahu* 1:201.

36. Text in Miguel Ángel Ladero Quesada, *Granada después de la conquista* (Granada, 1988), 350 (Almería); for the former conversos of Granada see 250 (text in n. 11).

37. Carlos Carrete Parrondo, "Fraternization between Jews and Christians in Spain before 1492," *American Sephardi* 9 (1978): 17–18.

38. Text published frequently; e.g., Fita in *B.A.H.* 23 (1893): 431; Suárez Fernández, *Documentos*, 391; León Tello, *Los judíos de Ávila* (Ávila, 1963), 92; etc. This expulsion is discussed generally by Haim Beinart, "La inquisición española y la expulsión de los judíos de Andalucía," in Yosef Kaplan, ed., *Jews and Conversos: Studies in society and the Inquisition* (Jerusalem, 1985), 103–23; but the sources cited here were not used in that article.

39. "Christopher Columbus" (Cristóbal Colón), *Diario del descubrimiento*, ed. Manuel Alvar (Madrid, 1976), 2:17; *Diario de navegación y otros escritos*, ed. Joaquín Balaguer, Ramón Menéndez Pidal, Carlos Esteban Deive (Santo Domingo, 1988), 92.

40. Baer, *Die Juden*, Vol. 2, no. 337; his surmise there that "Ysaque" (Abense-merro) should be read instead of "Yuda" is confirmed by the document in Wagner, *Regesto*, no. 188.

41. Suárez Fernández, *Documentos*, 267–68.

42. See the documents edited by Fidel Fita, "Nuevos datos para escribir la historia de los judíos españoles," *B.A.H.* 15 (1889): 323–25, 327–28, and his observations on 330.

43. Suárez Fernández, *Documentos*, 224–26, 238–40 (also in Baer, *Die Juden* 2:344).

44. Suárez Fernández, *Documentos*, 35–36; cf. 256–58 for the communities of Córdoba in 1485. See also 361 for property in Seville. In 1485 the Monarchs expelled a Jew and his wife from Andalucía because of their alleged inducement of conversos to observe Jewish rites, and in their defense they mentioned that the Jews had been punished enough when the Inquisitors ordered them expelled from Córdoba and Seville. After consultation, they were banned from ever entering Andalucía and had to pay a fine of 300,000 *mrs.* for redemption of captives in Granada (267–68).

45. Baer, *Die Juden* 2:387, 424.

46. Pedro Barrantes Maldonado, "Ilustraciones de la casa de Niebla," *Memorial histórico español* 10 (1857): 299.

47. Manuel Serrano y Sanz, *Origenes de la dominación española en América* N.B.A.E. 25 (Madrid, 1918), clvii n. 1.

48. Baer, *Die Juden* 1:562.

49. Cited by Lea, *History of the Inquisition* 1:132 n. 1; cf. Baer, *Die Juden* 1:563.

50. León Tello, *Judíos de Toledo*, Vol. 2, nos. 1573, 1574, 1575, 1576.

51. "Chronicon de Valladolid," CODOIN 13:192.

52. Antonio de la Torre, ed., *Documentos sobre relaciones internacionales de los reyes católicos* (Barcelona, 1962), 31; León Tello, *Judíos de Toledo* 1:535–36. A similar letter of the same date was sent to Aragón, to the conde de Belchite; see Motis Dolader, *Expulsión de los judíos* 1:36 (see Works Frequently Cited). Other letters cited there (37) conclusively prove that it was Torquemada, and not the Inquisition in general, who was responsible for the idea of expelling the Jews.

53. Bernáldez, *Historia de los reyes católicos*, 651; the remainder of the account will be discussed below. Bernáldez apparently was the source for the previously mentioned sixteenth-century writer Pedro Barrantes Maldonado, "Ilustraciones de la casa de Niebla" 395–96.

54. Pedro Miguel Carbonell, *Opúsculos inéditos*, CODOINA 27:370.

55. Text ed. Ricardo del Arco, "Las juderías de Jaca y Zaragoza," *Sefarad* 14 (1954): 82–83; similarly, the former *judería* of Zaragoza was given to the city by the king (88ff., and see Motis, *Expulsión de los judíos*).

56. Amalia Prieto Cantero, *Casa y descargos de los reyes católicos* (Valladolid, 1969), 445 (fol. 32), and 472.

57. Pulgar, *Crónica de don Fernando é doña Isabel*, 520.

58. Joseph Hacker, ed., "Keroniqot ḥadashot ʿal geirush ha-yehudim mi-Sefarad," in Salo W. Baron et al., eds., *Sefer zikaron le-Yiṣḥaq Baer* (Jerusalem 1979–81), 227, line 35.

59. *Sefer ʿezrat nashim,* ed. S. Z. H. Halberstamm in *Jeschurun* 7 (1871): 39.

60. Elijah Capsali, *Seder Eliyahu* 1:141–42.

61. Ibid., 206–7, 209.

62. Heinrich Graetz, *Geschichte der Juden* (Leipzig, 1896–1902), 8:349; Rosanes, *Divrey yemey Yisrael be-Togremah* (Tel Aviv, 1930), 1:58.

63. Abraham Ibn Ardutiel, *Sefer ha-qabalah,* 111, and cf. Capsali, *Seder Eliyahu,* 208.

64. Abraham Zacut, *Sefer yuḥasin,* fols. 223a, 227a.

65. Ibid., fol. 227a.

66. Marx, *Studies,* 84–85 (text), 88 (trans.); cf. Zacut, *Sefer yuḥasin,* fol. 227a.

67. Ibn Verga, *Sheveṭ Yehudah,* ed. Shochet, 122.

68. Capsali, *Seder Eliyahu* 1:211.

69. Marx, *Studies,* 86 (text), 95 (trans.). There was a famous pirate named Columbus. The real name of the discoverer of America was Juan ("Cristóbal") Colon.

70. Capsali, *Seder Eliyahu,* 210.

71. Yosef Hayim Yerushalmi, *The Lisbon Massacre of 1506 and the Royal Image in the Shebet Yehudah* (Cincinnati, 1976), 49.

72. Ibn Verga, *Sheveṭ Yehudah,* ed. Shochet, 117–18.

73. Ibid., 127–28.

74. Abravanel, *Mirkhevet ha-mishnah,* commentary on Deut. (Sabbioneta, 1551), fol. 2a; deleted in all subsequent eds. Neither Netanyahu, *Don Isaac Abravanel,* nor Ephraim Shmueli, *Don Yiṣḥaq Abravanel ve-geirush Sefarad* (Jerusalem, 1963), saw this important text. Shmueli's book is generally of little value.

75. Netanyahu, *Don Isaac Abravanel,* 280 n. 61, cites *only* this last sentence about the queen.

76. Ḥayim Gagin, MS of ʿEṣ ḥayim (J.T.S. Benaim 336), f. 2a; cited by Hacker, "Keroniqot" 212 n. 57.

77. MS, cited by Ephraim Kupfer, "Ḥazionatav shel R. Asher bar Meir ha-mekhunah Lemliyn Reutlingen," *Qoveṣ ʿal-yad,* n.s. 8 (1976): 387 n. 2. On other qabalists of Safed, Italy, etc., who held similar views, see nn. 5–6. See also Baer, *History of the Jews* 2:500–501 n. 66. Some of the things mentioned there, and other aspects of this question, will be discussed in more detail in my future book.

78. Abravanel, *Maʿayney ha-yeshuʿah* (Stettin, 1860), fol. 57; cf. Abraham b. Ḥaya, *Megilat ha-megaleh,* ed. Adolf Poznanski (Berlin, 1924; photo rpt. Jerusalem, 1967), 152; the excellent Catalan trans., *Llibre revelador,* trans. José M. Millás Vallicrosa (Barcelona, 1929), 248, and cf. Guttmann's introduction, xxvii of the Hebrew edition (also in the Catalan trans.). Netanyahu, *Don Isaac Abravanel,* says nothing of this, but see generally his remarks (195ff.). See further on Abravanel's messianic notions Isaiah Tishby, *Meshiḥiyot be-dor geirushey Sefarad ve-Portugal* (Jerusalem, 1985), 80 n. 249 (this book deals more with Portugal than with Spain).

79. Abravanel, *Maʿayney ha-yeshuʿah,* fol. 60.

80. Ibn Verga, *Sheveṭ Yehudah,* ed. Weiner, 33; ed. Shochet, 56. Henri Gross, *Gallia judaica* (Paris, 1897; photo rpt., with additions, Amsterdam, 1969), 437, was completely wrong in his conjectures on this. See on the expulsion from Lithuania Abraham Harkavy, *Hadashiym gam yeshaniym* (Jerusalem, 1970 rpt. from the journal *Miṣpah,* 1886), 6–11, 25–29.

81. Isaac Ṣarfaty, Letter, ed. Adoph Jellinek, *Quntres gezeirot TaTN"U (Zur*

Geschichte der Kreuzzüge) (Leipzig, 1854), 21. As Graetz correctly realized, this letter relates not to the Crusade but to the events of 1475. Isaac is very probably the same mentioned in the responsa of a great sage of that period; cf. David Conforte, *Qore ha-dorot,* ed. David Cassel (Berlin, 1846; photo rpt., Jerusalem, 1969), fol. 37a.

82. Luis Suárez Fernández, ed., *Política internacional de Isabel la católica* (Valladolid, 1965), 1:253, 491, 497. Pulgar, *Crónica de don Fernando é doña Isabel,* 378; slightly different version in *Crónica de los reyes católicos* 2:48.

83. See Baer, *History of the Jews* 2:292. Pérez de Guzmán, "Requesta fecha al magnífico marqués de Santyllana por los gloriosos emperadores Costantyno, Theodosio, Justyniano sobre estruyción de Constantynopla," in *Cancionero castellano del siglo XV,* ed. R. Foulché-Delbosc, N.B.A.E. 19 (Madrid, 1912), 1:677–82. See Isaac Abravanel, *Yeshuʿot meshiho* (Königsberg, 1860), 1:15a; and cf. Ibn Shem Ṭov, *Sefer ha-emunot* (Ferrara, 1556; photo rpt. Farnborough, England, 1969), fols. 55b–56b. See also Tishby, *ha-Meshihiyot,* 76 n. 237 (Tishby was absolutely correct in his criticisms of Netanyahu and Shmueli [321 n. 161 and 144–45], who erroneously assumed that Abravanel meant that the sultan would be the messiah). See also Joseph Hacker, "ʿAliyat yehudey Sefarad le-Ereṣ Yisrael . . ." *Shalem* 1 (1974), especially 117–21 and the appendices on the "conjunction." Hacker referred to, but neglected to cite, the text of Abravanel.

84. Carlos Carrete Parrondo, *Fontes iudaeorum regni Castellae,* [no.] 2: *El tribunal de la inquisición en el obispado de Soria (1486–1502)* (Salamanca, 1985), 40–41, nos. 58, 59. On Alonso del Espina see Baer, *History of the Jews.* I was able to discover the Aramaic translation, not commentary, to which Espina referred (*Fortalitium fidei* 3.4.21, cited in full by Baer, "ha-Tenuʿah ha-meshihit bi-Sefarad bitequfot ha-geirush," *Meʾasef Ẓion* 5 [1931–32]: 62 [note: this is not the journal *Ẓion* but a separate publication, recently reprinted]; however, he made no attempt to identify the source. It is in Paul de Lagarde, ed., *Hagiographa chaldaice* (Leipzig, 1873), 178, the *Targum* to Lamentations 4.21 (censored in printed eds. of the Bible). See Abravanel, *Yeshuʿot meshiho,* fol. 52b, cited also by Baer, "ha-Tenuʿah" 73–74, but he did not remark that this does not appear in the text as printed in standard Bible eds. Abravanel there erroneously cited Psalm 108.7, when the *Targum* which refers to Rome and Constantinople is, in fact, on verse 11, only in Lagarde (66). (But Abravanel's version has important variants according to which Lagarde's text must be corrected. Any future critical edition of the *Targum* must take these into account.) Abravanel adds that in the *Targum* to Lamentations 4.22 it is said that the Persians will destroy Constantinople, adding: "Know that the Gentiles called today Turks originate from Persia."

85. Baer, *Die Juden* 2:443. Baer discussed this ("ha-Tenuʿah," 63) but was unable to translate many of the words (the language is Catalan). See also *Die Juden* 2:470.

86. Ibid., 514–15. See correction by Lacave in his translation of Baer, *Historia* 2:778, n. 29.

87. Attention was called to these letters by Arséne Darmester in *R.E.J.* 1 (1880): 119, see the response by the Spanish scholar Alfred Morel-Fatio (301–4), with the text of the supposed inquiry from Spain, but not the reply. A somewhat different

version of the complete text was published, without comment, by one "S. M." in *R.A.B.M.* 2 (1872): 254–55, and the letters were discussed by Amador de los Ríos, *Estudios*, 193. Finally, Graetz dealt at length with them, "But réel de la correspondance . . . ," *R.E.J.* 19 (1889): 106–14, publishing the text from a MS of the *Libro verde de Aragón.* Mario Méndez Bejarano, *Histoire de la juiverie de Seville* (Madrid, 1922), 266–67, unaware of any of the previously mentioned publications, edited the text from a MS of the Real Academia de la Historia. (Graetz, peculiarly, did not refer at all to Morel-Fatio's earlier article.) Baer ignored all of this; also Netanyahu, *Origins*, 1311 n. 2 (and letters cited in n. 85 above).

88. Bernáldez, *Historia de los reyes católicos*, 644–45; reported less hysterically also by Pulgar, *Crónica de don Fernando é doña Isabel*, 511. The 1484 discovery is also in Bernáldez (617).

89. Fita in *B.A.H.* 11 (1887): 424. The story of the king's physician in *Libro verde de Aragón*, 105–6 (see Works Frequently Cited), but without the name of the physician, and in Lea, *History of the Inquisition* 1:610, and cf. 133.

90. Julius Klein, *The Mesta* (Cambridge, Mass., 1920), 217, and cf. 399, *judíos portadgueros*, tax collectors of Medellin. Klein repeated his unsubstantiated charges that the *Mesta* was "a party" to the Expulsion again on 351. For Zag de la Maleha, see my "Two Jewish Courtiers of Alfonso X Called Zag (Isaac)," *Sefarad* 43 (1983): 75–85; Abraham Barchilūnī's career will be detailed in my future work. See Baer, *Die Juden* 2:422–23 for Abayud.

91, Abraham Ibn Ardutiel, *Sefer ha-qabalah*, 112. On Seneor's son Solomon, see Baer, *Die Juden* 2:334, bottom.

92. Eliyahu Capsali, *Seder Eliyahu*, 1:208–9.

93. Marx, *Studies*, 85 (text), 93 (trans.). All of the other details mentioned, the conversion of Seneor and Meir *Melamed* and Seneor's "arrangement of the nuptials" of Fernando and Isabel, are certainly taken from Capsali.

94. Netanyahu, *Don Isaac Abravanel*, 54.

95. Cf. ibid., 54–55 and notes; the complete text of Abravanel is cited by Ibn Verga, *Shevet Yehudah*, ed. Shochet, 121. The rest of Netanyahu's account there is romantic fantasy; nor is there the slightest basis for his claim that by 1492 Abravanel was recognized as the "unofficial leader of Spain's Jewry" (53). He was nothing of the sort.

96. Abravanel, *She'elot u-teshuvot* to Saul ha-Kohen (Venice, 1574), fol. 8b (photo rpt. in Abravanel, *Opera minora* [London, 1971]); cf. Netanyahu, *Don Isaac Abravanel*, 86–87 and 284 n. 28 (Netanyahu repeatedly erred in citing page references).

97. Suárez Fernández, *Documentos*, 403–8; Baer, *Die Juden* 2:380.

98. Baer, *Die Juden*, 411 (31 May). Suárez Fernández, *Documentos*, 435–36; cf. also 436–37. Additional details on Yuçe and Jacob are from Baer (no. 384). All these were ignored by Netanyahu.

99. Suárez Fernández, *Documentos*, 456–58, 472–73.

100. Ibid., 420–22, 438–39.

101. The Spanish (Castilian) text of the letter was edited, with a somewhat incorrect Hebrew translation, by Haim Beinart, in *Zion jubilee volume* (*Zion* 50 [1985]: 272–74). The words translated here are: "asi por actos por el fechos con-

cernientes nuestro servicio y beneficio deste reyno como por la expulsion de los judios, en la cual se dize les han dado a entender que el ha entretendido." See the Inquisition testimony of the converso Pedro de San Miguel in Baer, *Die Juden* 2 : 397; erroneously cited by Beinart as being in Baer, *Toldot (History)* and cf. p. 256 above. The remainder of Beinart's article (265–71) is a rehash of documents already published by Baer. It should also be noted that Beinart published this article *after* Hacker's important source (see below), with no reference to it.

102. Hacker, "Keroniqot," especially 221–22, and see 207 and notes where Hacker attempts, largely without success, to identify which Vidal it was who did not convert. Note also Hacker's important observations on another matter (214–15). The famous statement about Moses is found in *Midrash Tanḥuma*, "Vayigash" 7, and is cited by Rashi on Exodus 18.7.

103. See Baer, *History of the Jews* 2:371–79; however, since Baer never read the chronicle of Fernando de Pulgar, one of the most important sources for the period, he overlooked the information about Alfonso and the Inquisition of Aragón. Beinart presumably has seen Pulgar, and certainly read his master's *History*.

104, León Tello, *Judíos de Toledo*, e.g., 2:562–63, 565 (no. 1576), 567–74, etc. Jews were permitted to collect debts outstanding from Christians or Muslims (571, no. 1597). See generally also Baer, *Die Juden* 2:412 (synagogue of Maqueda), 425–28.

105. Serrano, *Origenes de la dominación española*, lxii n. 3 (text). See Motis Dolader, *Expulsión de los judíos* 2 : 147ff., 156, 158.

106. Serrano, *Origenes de la dominación española*, lix–lx, and n. 1.

107. See Carlos Carrete Parrondo, *Fontes iudaeorum regni Castellae*, [no.] 1: *Provincia de Salamanca* (Salamanca, 1981), 47–48. For Ávila, see Pilar León Tello, "La judería de Ávila . . . ," *Sefarad* 23 (1963): 45, and documents in her *Judíos de Ávila* (Ávila, 1963), 98ff. Special permission was given by the Monarchs, for example, for the Jews to collect debts and receive payment for property sold before they were to leave in July.

108. León Tello, *Judíos de Toledo* 1:540–41, Doc. 86 (copy also in Madrid, B.N. MS Burriell 13089, fols. 126r–128v); see also Baer, *Die Juden* 2:412, for debts to Jews of Maqueda.

109. Amalia Prieto Cantero, *Casa y descargos*, 230 (fols. 192–93).

110. León Tello, *Judíos de Toledo* 1:542–43, Doc. 87; cf. Carrete Parrondo, *Fontes iudaeorum regni Castellae*, [no.] 1:133, no. 381 (to Salamanca) and 134, no. 384 (Medina del Campo); Motis Dolader, *Expulsión de los judíos* 2:10–11.

111. Prieto Cantero, *Casa y descargos*, 211 (fol. 624), 217 (fols. 722–25), 239 (fols. 358–60), 507 (fol. 398).

112. The story is told in Jacob Ibn Ḥabib's introduction to his famous *'Ein Ya'aqov* (numerous eds. and translations).

113. León Tello, *Judíos de Toledo* 1:542–43 (Doc. 87; copy also in Madrid, B.N. MS. Burriell 13089, fols. 129r–130v), 548, 609–10 (Doc. 93), and cf. 615–16 (Doc. 96); "La judería de Ávila," 45; Serrano, *Origenes de la dominación española*, lx; Motis, *Expulsión de los judíos*, 2:79ff., 105 (the cemetery of Tauste).

114. Ed. Fita in *B.A.H.* 11 (1887): 425–27; Amador de los Ríos, *Historia . . . de los judíos* 3:608–9; León Tello, *Judíos de Ávila*, 95–98. Baer made no men-

tion of this document, either in *Die Juden* or in *History of the Jews*. The letters extending protection to the Jews for forty days are discussed by Motis, *Expulsión de los judíos* 1:92.

115. León Tello, *Judíos de Toledo* 1:539–41, Doc. 86; Carrete Parrondo, *Fontes iudaeorum regni Castellae*, [no.] 1:49–54.

116. Javier Ortiz Real, *Los judíos de Cantabria* (Torrelavega, 1985), 65–66.

117. Baer, *Die Juden* 2:381.

118. Juan A. Balbas, *El libro de la provincia de Castellón* (Castellón, 1892), 147–49; on Abraham Legem, see the index to the documents in José Ramón Magdalena Nom de Déu, *Judíos y cristianos ante la "Cort del justícia" de Castellón* (Castellón, 1988).

119. Antonio González Gómez, "La población de Jerez de la Frontera en el siglo XV," *Andalucía medieval. Actas [del] I coloquio [de] historia de Andalucía* (Córdoba, 1982), 43.

120. Miguel Ángel Ladero Quesada, *Granada después de la conquista* (Granada, 1988), 249, 251–53.

121. Text, ibid., 253–54 (excerpt in Baer, *Die Juden* 2:382); tables, ibid., 255–60.

122. Alonso Fernández de Plasencia, *Historia de Plasencia* (Madrid, 1627), Vol. 2, chap. 14; cf. also Alejandro Matías Gil, *Las siete centurias de la ciudad de Alfonso VIII* (Plasencia, 1877), 135–37.

123. Diego de Colmenares, *Historia de . . . Segovia* (rpt. Segovia, 1921), 357 (chap. 35).

124. Gabriel Secall i. Güell, *Les jueries medievals tarragonines* (Valls, 1983), 56, 532. Ampolla is too tiny to appear on most maps; however, it is found in the invaluable *Diccionari nomenclator de pobles i poblats de Catalunya*, 2d ed. (Barcelona, 1964), 543, section 3c. There is a photograph of the port in Secall (57).

125. Miguel Ángel Motis Dolader, *Los judíos aragoneses en la época de descubrimiento de América* (Zaragoza, 1989), 86ff., with maps of the routes to Navarre and the maritime embarkation (91, 93); cf. also his *Expulsión de los judíos . . . Aragón* 2:181ff. and map (187) (see the general remarks on Jews expelled from Spain and Navarre in Benjamin R. Gampel, *The Last Jews on Iberian Soil* [Berkeley and Los Angeles, 1989], 89ff.).

126. Secall, *Les jueries*, 308–13.

127. Antonio Chabret, *Sagunto, su historia y sus monumentos* (Barcelona, 1888), 2:351 and 463–67 (appendix XXVI). The names of several Jews of Jérica are given in the text. Chabret added Zaragoza to the list, but there is no mention of this in the document; cf., however, Motis, *Los judíos aragoneses*, 99–100 (it would seem that the text to which he refers there [100, no. 2] is the same as the one in Chabret, however). The witnesses on the Valencia contracts were the Christian *corredor* of Valencia and Mosses Abengan, a Jew of "Bexis" (Bejis, or Begis, near Jérica).

128. Giovannia de Giovanni, *L'ebraismo della Sicilia* (Palermo, 1748), 204–6. Naples, although part of Sicily, was not then under Spanish domination, and is therefore a separate issue. When Spain regained it, an order for the expulsion of the Jews was also issued there, in November of 1510 (see Capsali, *Seder Eliyahu* 1:221).

129. Cecil Roth, "Le-toldot goley Siṣiliah," *Eretz-Israel* 3 (1954): 230–34.

130. Text in León Tello, *Judíos de Ávila*, 107–9, Doc. 38.

131. Bernáldez, *Historia de los reyes católicos*, 652–53.

132. Carlos Carrete Parrondo in *Sefarad* 32 (1972): 142 n. 3, 145 n. 15, and 147.

133. *El fuero, privilegios, franquezas y libertados del . . . señorio de Vizcaya* (Bilbao, 1950), 8; Tit. 1, ley 12. Ley 14 contains the text of a letter of Queen Juana confirming this privilege. We recall that in 1486, however, the Catholic Monarchs had expressly forbidden the officials of Valmaseda, Viscaya, etc., to prohibit Jews from living there, which was repeated in 1490 with respect to Bilbao, so that the prohibition technically applied only to conversos.

134. Klein, *The Mesta*, 38. Klein's book was quickly translated into Spanish, and is still considered a "classic." In fact, the entire subject needs a thoroughly new treatment.

135. Stephen Haliczer, "The Expulsion of the Jews and the Economic Development of Castile," in Josep M. Solà-Solé et al., *Hispania Judaica* (Barcelona, 1984), 1:39–47. More recent, and even earlier, studies of Ladero Quesada and other specialists need to be consulted.

136. Motis, *Expulsión* 1:59.

Afterword

1. Baron, *A Social and Religious History of the Jews,* 9: 119.

2. No. 25 in the edition by Leon Feldman, *She'elot u-teshuvot* (Jerusalem, 1984); it is not in the Rome, 1545 edition which I used when writing the book.

3. *The Refutation of the Christian Principles,* tr. Daniel J. Lasker (Albany, 1992), 20.

4. *Kevod ḥakhamim,* ed. S. Bernfeld (Berlin, 1899), 64; that it certainly did not refer to Solomon ha-Levy of Burgos (Pablo de Santa María), as Bernfeld thought, was correctly noted by Alexander Marx, *Studies in Jewish History and Booklore,* 92.

5. Baer, *Die Juden* 2:375–76.

6. Netanyahu, *The Origins of the Inquisition in Fifteenth-century Spain,* (New York: Random House, 1995), 421–86.

7. Thomas M. Izbicki, "Juan de Torquemada's Defense of the *Conversos,*" *Catholic Historical Review* 85 (1999): 195–207.

8. "¿Ascendencia judía de Fernando el Católico?" *Sefarad* 55 [1995]: 163–72. See 169 for the Barrientos statement; cf. 94 here.

9. Eliezer Gutwirth, "Conversions to Christianity amongst Fifteenth-century Spanish Jews: An Alternative Explanation," in *Shlomo Simonsohn Jubilee Volume* (Tel Aviv, 1993), 109, 113. I had not seen this article when I wrote my book.

10. *Derekh emunah,* ed. Chava Fraenkel-Goldschmidt (Jerusalem, 1978), 188.

11. Ram Ben-Shalom, "The Converso as Subversive: Jewish Traditions or Christian Libel?" *Journal of Jewish Studies* 50 (1999): 260.

12. Ibid., 261 n. 11; cf. Netanyahu, *Marranos,* 195–96, not acknowledged as the source.

13. The majority of Ben-Shalom's article (259–83) is worthless; aside from the erroneous belief that Abravanel was discussing "Averroists," the rest of the article con-

sists of digressions on various Jewish legends concerning Christianity and Islam, of no relevance at all to the converso question. The author also ignored what Netanyahu and others have written about Abravanel and these issues.

14. See Israel Tishby, *Meshihiyut be-dor geirushei Sefarad u-Portugal* (Jerusalem, 1985), 80 and n. 249.

15. Regev, "The Attitude Towards the *Conversos* in 15th–16th Century Jewish Thought," *R. E. J.* 156 (1997): 117–34.

16. Caro, *Toldot Yishaq,* (Warsaw, 1887; Jerusalem, 1978), f. 78b. Netanyahu, from whom Regev apparently derived this reference (*Marranos,* 159) used the first edition.

17. Netanyahu, *Marranos,* 169 and 170 n. 74. Abraham Gross, *Iberian Jewry from Twilight to Dawn: The World of Rabbi Abraham Saba* (Leiden, 1995), 105 is again a distortion of what Netanyahu actually wrote and is completely wrong; see generally my review of the book in *J. Q. R.* 88 (1998): 344–47.

18. Worthless, incidentally, is Colbert I. Nepaulsingh, *Apples of Gold in Filigrees of Silver: Jewish Writing in the Eye of the Spanish Inquisition* (New York, 1995), dealing with some alleged "converso" (or are they "Jewish"?) sixteenth-century works. See Kamen's review in *Hispanic Review* 64 (1996): 534.

19. Kaplan, "In Search of Salvation: The Deification of Isabel La Católica in Converso Poetry," *Hispanic Review* 66 (1998): 289–308.

20. Cumplido, "La revuleta contra los conversos de Córdoba en 1473," *Homenaje a Antón de Montoro en el V centenario de su muerte* (Montoro, 1977), 29–49 (which book, of course, has some additional information about that converso poet). Ladero Quesada, "Los conversos de Córdoba en 1497," *El Olivo* 13 (1989): 187–205.

21. Anna Foa, "Un vescovo marrano: Il processo a Pedro de Aranda (Roma 1498)," *Quaderni storici* [Italy] 33(1998): 533–551.

22. See also Henry Charles Lea, *A History of the Inquisition in the Middle Ages* (New York, 1906), 1:123.

23. On the Albigensians and the Jews, see my article "Jews and Albigensians in the Middle Ages: Lucas of Tuy on Heretics in León," *Sefarad* 41 (1981): 71–93.

24. J. Angel Sesma Muñoz, ed., *El establicimiento de la inquisición en Aragón (1484–1486). Documentos para su estudio* (Zaragoza, 1987), 80, No. 43; see further on resistance to the Inquisition in my book, 252–53.

25. Diogo, "El protonotario Lucena en su entorno sociopolítico," *Sefarad* 53 [1993]:249–71.

26. Edwards, "Jewish Testimony to the Spanish Inquisition—Teruel, 1484–87," *R. E. J.* 143 (1984): 333–50.

27. Henry Kamen, "Limpieza and the Ghost of Américo Castro: Racism as a Tool of Literary Analysis," *Hispanic Review* 64 (1996): 19–29.

28. Shlomo Simonsohn, ed., *The Papacy and the Jews. Documents: 1394–1464* (Toronto, 1990), 1254–56.

29. Edwards, "The Beginnings of a Scientific Theory of Race? Spain, 1450–1600," in Yedida A. Stillman and Norman K. Stillman, eds., *From Iberia to Diaspora: Studies in Sephardic* [sic] *History and Culture* (Leiden, 1999), 179–96. This article was written *after* Edwards had read my book, however hastily.

30. Marvin Lunenfeld, "Facing Crisis: The Catholic Sovereigns, the Expulsion, and the Columbian Expedition," in Moshé Lazar and Stephen Haliczer, eds., *The Jews of Spain and the Expulsion of 1492* (Lancaster, Calif., 1997), 256–57; there are some minor corrections to be made to this otherwise excellent article: that after the so-called "pogroms" in 1391 Jews scattered to small communities was only true in León, but not generally, and of course there was no "proffered bribe" by the Jews to avert the decree of expulsion (258), this is an old myth. Similarly, Haliczer's article in the same volume incorrectly claims that Jews lived mostly in smaller villages in the fifteenth century, yet on the same page he observes that the towns and cities were "dominated by a hereditary urban oligarchy which had been heavily penetrated by converted Jews" (248)—but where did they come from?

31. León Tello, *Judíos de Toledo*, 1:347 (see Works Frequently Cited). The publication that she cited in the footnote apparently exists in no library, including those in Spain; at least it is not to be found in any "online" catalogue, here or in Spain.

32. Needless to say, Stephen Haliczer, "The Expulsion of the Jews as Social Process," in the aforementioned collection *Jews of Spain and the Expulsion of 1492*, is completely wrong in his skepticism about the Inquisition's influence and his criticism of Maurice Kriegel (245).

33. I had forgotten the important article of Dov Weinryb, "The Myth of Samuel of Russia," in Abraham Neuman and Solomon Zeitlin, eds., *The Seventy-Fifth Anniversary Volume of The Jewish Quarterly Review* (Philadelphia, 1967), 540–41.

34. See Henri Gross, *Gallia judaica* (Paris, 1897; Amsterdam, 1969), 437.

35. Cited by Haliczer in Lazar and Haliczer, *Jews of Spain and the Expulsion of 1492*, 249 n. 9. On Jews who returned to Spain after the Expulsion (here, 311–12), see now also Yolanda Moreno Koch, "De la diáspora hacia Sefarad ¿La primera carta de regreso de un judío convertido?" *Michael* 11 (1989): 257–65.

36. Motis Dolader, *La expulsión de los judíos de Zaragoza* (Zaragoza, 1985) and "La conversión de judíos aragoneses a raiz del edicto de expulsión," in *Encuentros en Sefarad: Actas del Congreso Internacional "Los Judios en la historia de España"* (Ciudad Real, 1987), 217–52.

37. Antonio Rumeu de Armas, "El decreto de 1492 expulsando a los judíos de Castilla. Anomalías cancillerescas," *B. A. H.* 195 (1998): 1–17; for those who have never seen a photograph of the edict in one of the many publications in which it has appeared, there are photographs appended.

38. The most severe critique, perhaps, and certainly the longest, is by the eminent legal historian José Antonio Escudero in *Revista de la inquisición* 7 (1998): 9–46.

39. Gutwirth, "The Jews in 15th Century Castilian Chronicles," *J. Q. R.* 74 (1984): 379–96.

40. See generally the excellent statement by the renowned authority Bertrand de Jouvenel, *On Power* (Boston, 1962), 28 ff. on the lack of a medieval divine right of kings.

41. Incidentally, both Pacheco and Pedro Girón "were known" to be descendants of Moors and of Jewish converts, according to Netanyahu (416); "known" by whom, he does not say; as for Pacheco this is hardly likely—see my book, 106—and Girón probably also had no such romantic ancestry; see here, 165, and see the doubts expressed by A. Domínguez Ortiz, *La clase social de los conversos* (Madrid, 1955), 12 n. 7.

42. Alonso Fernández de Madrid (ca. 1475–1559), *Vida de fray Fernando de Talavera, primer Arzobispo de Granada*, ed. Félix G. Olmedo, with introductory study by Francisco Javier Martínez Medina (Granada, 1992); Luis Resines Llorente, *Hernando de Talavera, prior del Monasterio de Prado* (Valladolid, 1993); Jesús Suberbiola Martínez, *Real Patronato de Granada: El arzobispo Talavera, la Iglesia y el estado moderno, 1486–1516* (Granada, [1985?]). I regret that space does not permit additional discussion of Talavera, particularly in light of these new works. There is a need for a complete treatment of his attitude to Jews and conversos.

43. Kaplan, "In Search of Salvation: The Deification of Isabel La Católica in Converso Poetry," *Hispanic Review* 66 (1998): 291; unfortunately, he does not cite the number or page of the letter, and I do not have the edition that he used.

44. See the important review by John Edwards in *Journal of Ecclesiastical History* 50 (1999): 336–39.

45. Meyuhas Ginio, "Self-Perception and Images of the Judeoconversos in Fifteenth-century Spain and Portugal," *Tel Aviver Jahrbuch für deutsche Geschichte* 22 (1993): 127–52; the quoted statement is on 130.

46. See the previously cited article of Marvin Lunenfeld, "Facing Crisis," in *The Jews of Spain and the Expulsion of 1492*, especially 254–58.

47. Kamen, "Una crisis de conciencia en la Edad de Oro en España: Inquisición contra 'limpieza de sangre,'" *Bulletin Hispanique* 88 (1986):321–56; quotations from 323; the remainder of the article discusses the early modern period.

48. Kamen, "Limpieza and the Ghost of Américo Castro: Racism as a Tool of Literary Analysis," *Hispanic Review* 64 (1996): 22.

49. Yerushalmi, "L'antiémitisme racial est-il apparu au XXe sie`cle? De la *limpieza de sangre* espagnole au nazisme: continuités et ruptures," translated in *Esprit*, n.s., 190 (1993): 5–35; quotations from 22–23, 29. Yerushalmi had already written a booklet on the subject, *Assimilation and Racial Anti-Semitism: The Iberian and the German Models*, Leo Baeck Memorial Lecture (New York, 1982).

50. Schweid, "The Spanish Exile and the Holocaust: A Study in Jewish Spiritual Response to Catastrophe," first published in Hebrew and also in Spanish translation in Buenos Aires in *Indice* 6 (1993): 1–17. It was finally reprinted in English in the his *Wrestling Until Daybreak: Searching for Meaning in the Thinking on the Holocaust* (Lanham, Md., 1994), 299–329.

51. See the interesting article by Na'ama Sheffi, "The Jewish Expulsion from Spain and the Rise of National Socialism on the Hebrew Stage," *Jewish Social Studies* 5 (1999): 82–103; the author herself appears ready to accept the validity of much of the comparison (90).

52. There are sounder approaches to understanding racism in Nazi Germany, even among Israeli scholars; for a very thorough and excellent survey of theories, see Yisrael Gutman, "On the Character of Nazi Antisemitism," in Shmuel Almog, ed., *Antisemitism Through the Ages* (Oxford, 1988), 349–80; see especially on "Hitler's Racist Ideology," 362 ff., as a corrective to the exaggerated theories of "racism" in medieval Spain. Few of the other articles in that collection are of value with respect to the medieval period, but important is Kenneth Stow, "Hatred of the Jews or Love of the Church: Papal Policy Toward the Jews in the Middle Ages," 71–90.

53. Meyerson, *American Historical Review* 102 (1997): 97–98.

54. Hillgarth, *The Catholic Historical Review* 83 (1997): 97–99.
55. Edwards, *Jewish Quarterly Review* 87 (1997): 66.
56. See, incidentally, my review of his life and work, "Salo Wittmayer Baron," in Helen Damico and Joseph B. Zavadil, eds., *Medieval Scholarship* (New York, 1995), 1:277–87.
57. Cohen, "Between Judaism and Christianity: The Semicircumcision of Christians according to Bernard Gui, His Sources and R. Eliezer of Metz," *Harvard Theological Review* 94 (2001): 285–321; Cohen carefully and correctly analyzes a text concerning the "semi-circumcision" of converts to Judaism. All of the papal bulls cited there are also found in my book. For a similar article, much less accurate and thorough, see the next note.
58. Kristine T. Utterbkck, "'Conversi' Revert: Voluntary and Forced Return to Judaism in the Early Fourteenth Century," *Church History* 64 (1995): 16–28. The author cites two responsa of Ibn Adret concerning immersion of repentant apostate Jews; the first of which (23) is not by Ibn Adret, in fact (see here, 34). The fault, however, is not the author's but Joseph Shatzmiller, on whose translation she relied ("Converts and Judaizers in the Early Fourteenth Century," *Harvard Theological Review* 74 [1981]: 65). The second responsum (see my book 7 and 24 and notes) is the one upon which she built an entirely unfounded hypothesis, distorting Shatzmiller's (correct) translation to read instead that such a repentant apostate "deserved stripes as he transgressed in several positive and negative precepts and *thus deserved premature death by divine visitation (Karet) as well as capital punishment by (regular) courts*" (my emphasis). Shatzmiller's translation, quoted in her note 36, reads: "we saw that he deserved stripes as he transgressed in several positive and negative precepts *and those deserving premature death* by divine visitation (Karet) as well as capital punishment by (regular) courts." In other words, of course, Ibn Adret said that even though such an apostate had transgressed laws which *were* deserving of death, he is now to be accepted as a complete Jew because of his repentance, and his *only* punishment is that he receives "stripes" (lashes) for his past transgressions. (The Lérida case and others relating to Spain mentioned in the article are dealt with in my book.)
59. Kamen, *Journal of Ecclesiastical History* 47 (1996): 734–36.
60. Seidenspinner-Núñez, "Inflecting the Converso Voice: A Commentary on Recent Theories," *La Córonica* 25 (1996): 6–17.
61. Motis Dolader, in the prestigious *Anuario de estudios medievales* 26 (1996): 1104–11.

Appendix A. Critical Survey of the Literature

1. Baer, *History of the Jews* 2:424–25 and 274.
2. Haim Beinart, "The Records of the Inquisition, a Source of Jewish and Converso History," *P.A.A.J.R.* 2 (1968): 215.
3. Benzion Netanyahu, *Marranos,* 3. On the other hand, as already pointed out in Chapter 8, his earlier study of Abravanel contains many errors and omissions.
4. Norman Roth, "Jewish Conversos in Medieval Spain: Some Misconceptions and New Information," in William D. Phillips, Jr., and Carla Rahn Phillips,

eds., *Marginated Groups in Spanish and Portuguese History* (Minneapolis, 1989), 23–52.

5. Baron, *Social and Religious History* 13:349–50 n. 19; Yosef H. Yerushalmi, *From Spanish Court to Italian Ghetto* (N.Y., 1971), 21–22 (the book as a whole, a study of the seventeenth-century Isaac Cardoso, certainly is not hereby condemned; only the author's competence to pronounce on the medieval Spanish Jewish situation.)

6. Benedict de Spinoza, *Theologico-Political Treatise,* trans. R. H. M. Elwes (New York, 1951), 56.

7. Antonio Domínguez Ortiz, "Historical Research on Spanish Conversos in the Last 15 Years," in Hornick, *Collected Studies,* especially 17–19 (see Works Frequently Cited). Most of the work on conversos in recent years is actually on their postmedieval descendants and thus not relevant to the present study.

8. Américo Castro, *España en su historia* (see Works Frequently Cited), and other works.

9. Nicolas López Martínez, *Los judaizantes castellanos y la Inquisición en tiempo de Isabel la católica* (Burgos, 1954).

10. Castro, *España en su historia,* 544, 547; Claudio Sánchez Albornoz, *España, un enigma histórico* (Buenos Aires, 1956), 2:255, 292.

11. López Martínez, *Los judaizantes castellanos;* Gabriel, duque de Maura, "Nueva luz sobre la expulsión de los judíos en 1492," *B.A.H.* 137 (1955): 187–201 (an article prompted by the book of López). Cirac Estopañan, *Registros de los documentos del Santo Oficio de Cuenca y Sigüenza* (Cuenca-Barcelona, 1965), e.g., 47ff. Ramon d'Abadal, *Dels visigots als catalans* (Barcelona, 1969–70), 82. See also the curious letter of Menéndez Pelayo (1887) cited by José Ma. Millás Vallicrosa, "Menéndez Pelayo y la literature hebraicoespañola," *Sefarad* 16 (1956): 255–56, and note Millás' own noble effort to condemn such attitudes. That single letter did not make Menéndez an anti-Semite, of course, as José Faur has claimed (*In the Shadow of History* [Albany, 1992], 50.)

12. Juan Antonio Llorente, *Historia,* and his earlier *Memoria histórica sobre qual ha sido la opinión nacional de España acerca de la Inquisición* (Madrid, 1812). These, and von Ranke and Hefele's views, are well summarized and criticized, but from a different perspective from that presented here, by Benzion Netanyahu, "¿Motivos o pretextos? La razón de la inquisición," translated in (by?) Angel Alcalá, ed., *Inquisición española y mentalidad inquisitorial* (Barcelona, 1984), 24–26.

13. Lea, *History of the Inquisition* 1:172, 154–55; the bull of Sixtus was published by Lea in *American Historical Review* 1 (1896): 46. Llorente, *Historia* 1: 125–26.

14. Pinta Llorente, *La Inquisición española y los problemas de la cultura y de la intolerancia* (Madrid, 1953). Plaidy, *The Growth of the Spanish Inquisition* (London, 1960). Ortí y Lara, *La Inquisición* (Madrid, 1877). Hauben, *The Spanish Inquisition* (New York, 1969). Cecil Roth, *The Spanish Inquisition* (rpt. New York, 1964; etc.).

15. Henry Kamen, *La Inquisición española* (Barcelona, 1979), translated by Gabriela Zayas from Kamen, *Inquisition and Society in Spain,* apparently with some revisions by the author.

16. Juan Blázquez Miguel, *Inquisición y criptojudaísmo* (Madrid, 1988). Statements cited are pp. 50 and 85.

17. Angel Alcalá Galve, *Los origenes de la Inquisición en Aragón* [Huesca? 1984?]. In contrast to these apologetic claims, see Coronas Téjada, *Conversos*, 24, 36. Another apologist for the Inquisition, Benassar, has claimed that it did not use torture at all in the "early period," but Coronas again proves that torture was a *regular* part of the Inquisition (35).

18. Eufemià Fort i Cogul, *Catalunya i la Inquisició* (Barcelona, 1973). Far better is the crucially important, and equally ignored, article of Carreras (see Works Frequently Cited).

19. Juan Blázquez Miguel, *La Inquisición en Cataluña, el tribunal del Santo Oficio de Barcelona (1487–1820)* (Toledo, 1989).

20. Manuel Ardit, *La Inquisició al país Valencià* (Valencia, 1970). Statement cited is on p. 11.

21. Stephen Haliczer, *Inquisition and Society in the Kingdom of Valencia, 1478–1834* (Berkeley, 1990).

22. Juan Blázquez Miguel, *El tribunal de la Inquisición en Murcia* (Murcia, 1986).

23. José Martínez Millán, *La hacienda de la Inquisición* (Madrid, 1984); *Autos de fe y causas de la Inquisición de Córdoba* (Córdoba, 1983).

24. Benzion Netanyahu, "Américo Castro and His View on the Origins of the *Pureza de Sangre*," *P.A.A.J.R.* 46–47 (1979–80): 397–457 (what caused Netanyahu to use the incorrect terminology *"pureza" de sangre* in an otherwise excellent article is unclear).

Appendix B. Jewish and Converso Population in Fifteenth-Century Spain

1. Netanyahu, *Marranos*, 239–40. Crescas' letter in Ibn Verga, *Shevet Yehudah*, ed. Wiener, 128 (only in that edition).

2. Miguel Ángel Ladero Quesada, *Historia de Sevilla*, [no.] 2: *La ciudad medieval (1248–1492)* (Seville, 1976), 124; Collantes de Terán, *Sevilla*, 207 (Netanyahu consulted neither of these).

3. Baer, *Die Juden* 2:262 (top).

4. Netanyahu, *Marranos*, 242.

5. Letter discussed by Marx, *Studies*, 82–83, with the complete text in Baer, *Die Juden*, Vol. 2, no. 360. Tax list in Suárez Fernández, *Documentos*, 342–44 (and compare this with a list from 1485 in Baer [no. 350]).

6. Joseph Hacker, ed., "Keroniqot ḥadashot 'al geirush ha-yehudim mi-Sefarad," in Salo W. Baron et al., eds., *Sefer zikaron le-Yiṣḥaq Baer* (Jerusalem, 1979–81), 225 (lines 19–20), 226 (line 22b).

7. Isidore Loeb, important review of Graetz, in *R.E.J.* 21 (1890): 155 (this has been overlooked by Baer, Netanyahu, etc.).

8. Marx, *Studies*, 85–86 (text); 93–94 (trans.), and 85, 88.

9. Motis Dolader, *Expulsión de los judíos* (see Works Frequently Cited) 2: 153–54, 309–14.

10. Joseph Ya'aveṣ, *Or ha-ḥayim* (Lublin, 1912; rpt. [Jerusalem], s.a. in *Sifrey Ya'aves*, and again in Israel, s.a., in *Kol sifrey R' Yosef Ya'aveṣ*, Vol. 1), introduction, 7–8.

Works Frequently Cited

Amador de los Ríos, José. *Estudios históricos, políticos y literarios sobre los judíos de España.* 2d ed. Buenos Aires, 1942.

Amador de los Ríos, José. *Historia social, política y religiosa de los judíos de España y Portugal.* 3 vols. Madrid, 1875–76.

[Anchias, Juan de]. See *Libro verde de Aragón.*

Baer, Fritz (Yitzhak), ed. *Die Juden im christlichen Spanien.* 2 vols. Berlin, 1929–36.

Baer, Yitzhak. *History of the Jews in Christian Spain.* 2 vols. Philadelphia, 1966.

Baer, Yitzhak. *Historia de los judíos en la España cristiana.* Trans. (from Hebrew) José Luis Lacava. 2 vols. Madrid, 1981.

Baron, Salo W. *A Social and Religious History of the Jews.* New York, 1952–83.

Beltrán de Heredia, V. "Las bulas de Nicolás V acerca de los judíos." *Sefarad* 21 (1961): 22–47.

Bernáldez, Andrés. *Historia de los reyes católicos.* B.A.E. 70:567–773.

Bernáldez, Andrés. *Memorias del reinado de los reyes católicos.* Madrid, 1962.

Capsali, Elijah. *Seder Eliyahu zuṭa.* Ed. Aryeh Shmuelevitz, Shlomo Simonsohn, and Meyer Benayahu. 3 vols. Jerusalem, 1975–83.

Carreras y Candi, Francesch. "L'Inquisició barcelonina substituida per l'Inquisició castellana." *Anuari de l'institut d'estudis catalans* 3 (1909–10): 130–77.

Carrillo de Huete, Pedro. *Crónica del halconero de Juan II.* Ed. Juan de Mata Carriaso. Madrid, 1946.

Castro, Américo. *Españo en su historia.* Buenos Aires, 1948.

Los Códigos españoles. Madrid, 1872–.

Colección de códigos españoles. Madrid, 1847–49.

Collantes de Terán Sánchez, Antonio. *Sevilla en la baja edad media. La ciudad y sus hombres.* Seville, 1977.

Coronas Tejada, Luis. *Conversos and Inquisition in Jaén.* Jerusalem, 1988.

(Spain. Leon and Castile, Laws). *Cortes de los antiguos reinos de León y Castilla.* Madrid, 1861–.

Fort i Cogul, Eufemià. *Catalunya i la Inquisició.* Barcelona, 1973.

Gracia Boix, Rafael. *Colección de documentos para la historia de la Inquisición de Córdoba.* Córdoba, 1982.

Ḥemdah genuzah. Jerusalem, 1863.

Hershman, Abraham M. *Rabbi Isaac Ben Sheshet Perfet and His Times.* New York, 1943.

Hornik, M. P., ed. *Collected Studies in honour of Américo Castro's Eightieth Year.* Oxford, 1965.

Ibn Verga, Solomon b. Judah. *Sheveṭ Yehudah.* Ed. Meir Wiener. Hanover, 1924.

Ibn Verga, Solomon b. Judah. *Sheveṭ Yehudah.* Ed. Ezriel Shochet. Jerusalem, 1946.

Isaac b. Sheshet. *She'elot u-teshuvot.* Vilna, 1878; photo rpt., Jerusalem [1968].

Lea, Henry Charles. *A History of the Inquisition of Spain.* Vol. 1. New York, 1906–7; rpt. 1988.

León Tello, Pilar. *Judíos de Toledo.* 2 vols. Madrid, 1979.

Libro verde de Aragón. (Juan de Anchias, presumed author). Ed. Isidro de las Cagigas. Madrid, 1929.

Llorente, José Antonio. *Historia crítica de la Inquisición en España.* Madrid, 1981. Trans. of his *Histoire critique de l'Inquisition d'Espagne,* 4 vols. in 2 (Paris, 1817).

Loeb, Isidore. "Polémistes chrétiens et juifs en France et en Espagne." *R.E.J.* 18 (1890): 43–70, 219–42.

Marx, Alexander. *Studies in Jewish History and Booklore.* New York, 1944.

Moses b. Maimon. *Mishneh Torah.* Numerous editions.

Motis Dolader, Miguel Ángel. *La expulsión de los judíos del reino de Aragón.* 2 vols. Zaragoza, 1990.

Netanyahu, Benzion. *The Marranos of Spain.* 2d ed. Millwood, N.Y., 1973.

Netanyahu, Benzion. *The Origins of the Inquisition in Fifteenth-Century Spain.* New York, 1991.

Oropesa, Alonso de. *Luz para conocimiento de los gentiles.* Trans. Luis Díaz y Díaz. Madrid, 1979.

Pérez de Guzmán, Fernán [Fernando]. *Generaciones y semblanzas.* Ed. J. Domínguez Bordona. Madrid, 1941.

Pérez de Guzmán, Fernán. *Gerneraciones y semblanzas.* Ed. R. Brian Tate. London, 1965.

Pulgar, Fernando de. *Crónica de los reyes católicos, version inédita.* Ed. Juan de Mata Carriazo. 2 vols. Madrid, 1943.

Pulgar, Fernando de. *Crónica de don Fernando é doña Isabel* (later redaction). *B.A.E.* 70:229–411.

Régné, Jean. *History of the Jews in Aragon. Regesta and documents, 1213–1327.* Ed. Yom Tov Assis. Jerusalem, 1978.

Reinhardt, Klaus, and Horacio Santiago-Otero. *Biblioteca bíblica Ibérica medieval.* Madrid, 1986.

Rubió y Lluch, Antoni, ed. *Documents per l'historia de la cultura catalana mig-eval.* 2 vols. Barcelona, 1918–21.

Sánchez Alonso, Benito. *Fuentes de la historia española e hispanoamericana.* Madrid, 1919.

Sánchez Alonso, Benito. *Historia de la historiografía española.* Madrid, 1947.

Sha'arey ṣedeq. Salonica, 1792.

She'elot u-teshuvot ha-geonim "ha-yashan." Jerusalem, 1960.

Suárez Fernández, Luis. *Documentos acerca de la expulsión de los judíos.* Valladolid, 1964. (L.C. lists s.v. "Spain, Sovereigns, etc. 1479–1504, Ferdinand V and Isabella I.")

Teshuvot ha-geonim. Lyck, 1864.

Torres Fontes, Juan. "Los judíos murcianos a fines del siglo XIV y comienzos del XV." *Miscelánea medieval murciana* 8 (1981): 57–117.

Ṭur. Jacob b. Asher, *Arba 'a ṭurim* (many editions).

Wagner, Klaus. *Regesto de documentos del Archivo de Protocolos de Sevilla referentes a judíos y moros.* Seville, 1978.
Zacut, Abraham. *Sefer yuḥasin ha-shalem.* Ed. Herschell Filipowski. London, 1857; photo rpt. Jerusalem, 1963.

Manuscripts Utilized

Alfonso González de Toledo, "Judios y cargas publicas," Madrid B.N. MS. 1181.
Juan de Vergara, "Contradiccion del Estatuto de Toledo," Universidad de Salamanca, MS 455.
"Memorial de su [Pablo de Santa María] lineaje," Madrid B.N. MS. 9927.
Madrid B.N. MS. 13043.
Madrid B.N. MS. 18183.
Madrid B.N. MS. Burriell 13089.

Glossary

adafina	(see Index)
alfaqueque	(see Index)
aljama	community, either Jewish or Muslim
arrendador	see tax-farmer
baile	administrative official of town or district
caballero	knight, aristocrat
call	Catalan term for a Jewish community
cofradía	society organized for religious-charitable goals
condestable	head of the royal army; "constable"
contador mayor	supervisor of tax assessments and royal accounts
corregidor	chief administrative official of city
cortes (Cat. corts)	parliament
gaon (pl. geonim)	Heb., head of academies in Iraq; authorities of Jewish law
hidalgo	aristocrat
infante (Cat. infant)	member of the royal family, including the heir
judería	Jewish quarter, separated from Christians
mayordomo	superintendent, steward of household or property
meshumad	(see Index)
midrash	homiletic interpretation of scripture (book)
Mozarab	Christian living in Muslim territory and adapting certain Muslim customs
Mudéjar	Muslim living in predominantly Christian area
mumar	(see Index)
procurador	representative of community (e.g., for tax assessments; also delegate to *Cortes*)
qabalah	mystical (Jewish) teaching
qidushin	marriage contract
recaudador mayor	chief official in charge of receipts of taxes
reconciliado	"repentant heretic" who is pardoned ("reconciled" to the Church)
relajado	"unrepentant heretic" who is condemned
romancero	ballad in Spanish (or by Sefardic Jews, Spanish in Hebrew characters)
Shema'	"Hear, O Israel" (Deut. 6.4 ff.), so-called "Jewish creed," recited at prayers
sukkah	booth built for holiday of Tabernacles, to eat and sometimes sleep in

tax-farmer   one who rents privilege of collecting taxes; advances agreed-
                      upon sum and collects the amount, more or less, over a pe-
                      riod of time
yeshivah   Jewish academy for study of Talmud
zarzuela   form of drama combining dialogue, dance and singing

Bibliography of Norman Roth's Writings Exclusive of Reviews and Occasional Papers

Books

1. *Maimonides: Essays and Texts, 850th Anniversary.* Madison: Hispanic Seminary of Medieval Studies, 1986.
2. *Jews, Visigoths & Muslims in Medieval Spain: Cooperation & Conflict.* Leiden: E. J. Brill, 1994.
3. *Conversos, Inquisition, and the Expulsion of the Jews from Spain.* Madison: University of Wisconsin Press, 1995; revised paper back edition, 2002.
4. Editor (and author of several articles), *Encyclopedia of Medieval Jewish Civilization.* New York: Routledge, Taylor and Francis, 2002.

Articles

I. Philosophy

1. "The 'Theft of Philosophy' by the Greeks from the Jews." *Classical Folia* 32 (1978): 52–67.
2. "Attaining 'Happiness' (*Eudaimonia*) in Medieval Muslim and Jewish Philosophy." *Centerpoint* 4 (1981): 21–32.
3. various chapters in *Maimonides* book.

II. Science, Medicine

1. "Jewish Translators at the Court of Alfonso X." *Thought* 60 (1985): 439–55.
2. "Jewish Collaborators in Alfonso's Scientific Work." In *Emperor of Culture: Alfonso X the Learned of Castile and His Thirteenth-century Renaissance.* Edited by Robert I. Burns, 59–71, 223–30. Philadelphia: University of Pennsylvania Press, 1990. Translated as "Les collaborateurs juifs à l'oeuvre scientifique d'Alphonse X." In *Chrétiens, musulmans et juifs dans l'Espagne médiévale: De la convergence à l'expulsion.* Edited by Ron Barkaï, 203–25. Paris: Editions du Cerf, 1994.
3. "Relojes de agua en la Toledo islámica" (Water-clocks in Muslim Toledo). *Miscelanea de estudios árabes y hebraicos* 51 (1992): 151–52.
4. "Jewish and Muslim Physicians of ʿAlī Ibn Tashufīn." *Korot. The Israel Journal of the History of Medicine and Science* 10 (1993–94): 83–91.

5. (Translation) José Ma. Millás Vallicrosa. "The Beginning of Science among the Jews of Spain." *BINAH* 3 (1994): 35–46, with new notes added.

III. History

1. "The Jews and the Muslim Conquest of Spain." *Jewish Social Studies* 37 (1976): 145–58.
2. "Jews and Albigensians in the Middle Ages: Lucas of Tuy on Heretics in León." *Sefarad* 41 (1981): 71–93.
3. "The Kahina: Legendary Material in the Accounts of the 'Jewish Berber Queen'." *Maghreb Review* 7 (1982): 122–25.
4. "Again Alfonso VI, 'Imbaratur dhu'l-Millatayn,' and Some New Data." *Bulletin of Hispanic Studies* 51 (1984): 165–69.
5. "Some Aspects of Muslim-Jewish Relations in Spain." *Estudios en Homenaje a Don Claudio Sánchez Albornoz* (Buenos Aires, 1983) II, 179–214.
6. "Two Jewish Courtiers of Alfonso X called Zag (Isaac)." *Sefarad* 43 (1983): 75–85.
7. "Alfonso VI: An Answer to MacKay and Benaboud's Reply." *Bulletin of Hispanic Studies* 62 (1985): 179–81.
8. "'Seis edades durará el mundo,' temas de la polémica judía española" ("For six ages shall the world endure": Themes of Spanish Jewish polemic). *Ciudad de Dios* 199 (1986): 45–65.
9. "Dar 'una voz' a los judíos: representación en la España medieval" (Giving a "voice" to the Jews: Legal representation in medieval Spain). *Anuario de Historia del Derecho Español* (1986): 943–52.
10. "New Light on the Jews of Mozarabic Toledo." *Association for Jewish Studies Review* 11 (1986): 189–220.
11. "José Antonio Maravall: A Critical Appreciation." *Bulletin of the Society for Spanish and Portuguese Historical Studies* 11 (1987): 16–20.
12. "Forgery and Abrogation of the Torah: A Theme in Muslim and Christian Polemic in Spain." *Proceedings of the American Academy for Jewish Research* 24 (1987): 203–36.
13. "The Arrest of the Catalan Rabbis: An Unexplained Incident in Jewish History." *Sefarad* 47 (1987): 163–72.
14. "Rodrigo Jiménez de Rada y los Judíos: La 'Divisa' y los Diezmos de los Judíos" (Rodrigo Jiménez de Rada and the Jews: The "Badge" and Jewish Tithes). *Anthologica Annua* 35 (1988): 369–481.
15. "The Jews in Spain at the Time of Maimonides." In *Moses Maimonides and His Time*. Edited by Eric L. Ormsby, 1–20. Washington, D.C.: Catholic University of America Press, 1989.
16. "Jewish Conversos in Medieval Spain: Some Misconceptions and New Information." In *Marginated Groups in Spanish and Portuguese History*. Edited by William D. Phillips Jr. and Carla Rahn Phillips, 23–52. Minneapolis: Society for Spanish and Portuguese Historical Studies, 1989.
17. "Los Judíos Murcianos desde el Reinado de Alfonso X al de Enrique II" (Jews of Murcia from the reign of Alfonso X to that of Enrique II). *Miscelánea Medieval Murciana* 15 (1989): 25–51.

18. "The Jews of Spain and the Expulsion of 1492." *The Historian* 55 (1992): 17–30. Reprinted (without the notes) in *Social History of Western Civilization.* Edited by Richard Golden. New York: St. Martin's Press, 1996.
19. "Isaac Polgar y su Libro contra un Converso" (Isaac Polgar and his book against a converso). In *Polémica judeo-cristiana: Estudios.* Edited by Carlos del Valle, 67–73. Madrid: Aben Ezra Ediciones, 1992.
20. "Anti-Converso Riots of the Fifteenth Century, Pulgar, and the Inquisition." *En la España Medieval* 15 (1992): 367–94.
21. "Bishops and Jews in the Middle Ages." *Catholic Historical Review* 70 (1994): 1–17.
22. "Salo Wittmayer Baron." In *Medieval Scholarship,* 277–87. Edited by Helen Damico and Joseph B. Zavadil, I:277–87. New York and London: Garland, 1995.
23. "The Civic Status of the Jew in Medieval Spain." In *Iberia and the Mediterranean World of the Middle Ages: Essays in Honor of Robert I. Burns, S. J.* Edited by P. E. Chevedden, D. J. Kagay, and P. G. Padilla, 2:139–61. Leiden: E. J. Brill, 1996.
24. "Coexistence and Confrontation: Jews and Christians in Medieval Spain." Symposium paper from a conference at the University of Southern California in 1992. In *The Jews of Spain and the Expulsion of 1492.* Edited by Moshe Lazar and Stephen Haliczer. Lancaster, Calif.: Labyrintos,1997.
25. "*Dhimma:* Jews and Muslims in the Early Medieval Period." In *Studies in Honour of Clifford Edmund Bosworth.* Edited by Ian Richard Netton, 1:267–79. Leiden: Brill, 2000.
26. "Coexistencia y confrontación de judíos y cristianos españoles." In *Judíos entre árabes y cristianos: Luces y sombras de una convivencia.* Edited by Ángel Sáenz-Badillos. Córdoba: Ediciones El Almendro, 2000.

IV. *Language*

1. "Seeing the Bible Through a Poet's Eyes: Some Difficult Biblical Words Interpreted by Moses Ibn _Ezra." *Hebrew Studies* 23 (1982):111–14.
2. "Jewish Reactions to the _Arabiyya and the Renaissance of Hebrew in Spain." *Journal of Semitic Studies* 28 (1983): 63–84.
3. "Maimonides on the Hebrew Language and Poetry." *Hebrew Studies* 26 (1985):93–101.
4. "La Lengua Hebrea entre los Cristianos Españoles Medievales: Voces Hebreas en Español" (The Hebrew language among medieval Spanish Christians: Hebrew words in Spanish). *Revista de filología española* 71 (1991):138–43.
5. "Algunos de los Primeras Hebraistas de España y su Influencias." *Miscelánea de estudios árabes y hebraicos* 37–38 (1991): 317–23.

V. *Literature*

1. "The 'Wiles of Women' Motif in Medieval Hebrew Literature of Spain." *Hebrew Annual Review* 2 (1978): 145–65.

2. "The 'Ubi Sunt' Theme in Medieval Herbew Poetry." *Hebrew Studies* 19 (1978):56–62.
3. "Satire and Debate in Two Famous Medieval Hebrew Poems: Love of Boys vs. Girls, the Pen, and Other Themes." *Maghreb Review* 4 (1980): 105–13.
4. "'Sacred' and 'Secular" in the Poetry of Ibn Gabirol." *Hebrew Studies* 20–21 (1979–80): 75–79.
5. "The Lyric Tradition in Hebrew Secular Poetry in Medieval Spain." *Hispanic Journal* 2 (1981): 7–26.
6. "'Deal Gently with the Young Man': Love of Boys in Medieval Hebrew Poetry of Spain." *Speculum* 57 (1982): 20–51. Reprinted in *Homosexual Themes in Literary Studies*. Edited by Wayne R. Dynes and Stephen Donaldson, 8:268–99. New York: Garland, 1992.
7. "The 'Ages of Man' in Two Medieval Hebrew Poems." *Hebrew Studies* 24 (1983): 41–44.
8. "Judah Ha-Levi." In *Critical Survey of Poetry: Foreign Language Series*. Edited by Frank N. Magill, 2:776–82. Englewood Cliffs, N.J.: Salem Press, 1984.
9. "Panegyric Poetry of Ibn Gabirol: Translations and Analysis." *Hebrew Studies* 25 (1984): 62–81.
10. "My Beloved Is Like a Gazelle: Imagery of the Beloved Boy in Hebrew Religious Poetry." *Hebrew Annual Review* 8 (1984): 143–65. Reprinted in *Homosexuality and Religion and Philosophy*. Edited by Wayne R. Dynes and Stephen Donaldson. New York: Garland, 1992.
11. "The Care and Feeding of Gazelles: Medieval Arabic and Hebrew Love Poetry." In *Poetics of Love in the Middle Ages*. Edited by Moshé Lazar and Norris Lacy, 95–118. Fairfax, Va.: George Mason University Press, 1989.
12. "Polemic in the Hebrew Religious Poetry of Medieval Spain." *Journal of Semitic Studies* 34 (1989): 153–77.
13. "Fawn of My Delights: Boy-Love in Hebrew and Arabic Verse." In *Sex in the Middle Ages*. Edited by Joyce Salisbury, 157–72. New York: Garland, 1991.
14. "Jewish Literature in Medieval Spain." *Jewish Book Annual* 50 (1992–93): 99–113.
15. "Boy-Love in Medieval Arabic Verse." *Paidika* 3 (1994): 12–16.
16. "Religious Constraints on Erotic Poetry among Muslims and Jews in Al-Andalus." *The Maghreb Review* 19 (1994): 194–205.
17. "Hebrew Poetry" (translations). In *Gay and Lesbian Poetry*. Edited by James Wilhelm, 235–60. New York: Garland, 1995.
18. "What Constitutes Sefardic Literature?" In *From Iberia to Diaspora*. Edited by Yedida K. Stillman and Norman A. Stillman, 247–63. Leiden: E. J. Brill, 1999.

VI. Miscellaneous

1. *Treasures of Judaica*. Descriptive catalogue of some rare books in the Hebraica-Judaica collection, University of Denver Libraries, 1971

2. "We Need Love and Objectivity" (contribution to a symposium). *Judaism* 23 (1974): 459–61.
3. "The Needs of Jewish Scholarship in America." *Judaism* 27 (1978): 72–79.
4. "Jewish Studies in America: Present Problems and Future Prospects." *Judaism* 35 (1986): 162–69. Reprinted in *The Academy and Traditions of Jewish Learning*. Edited by Jacob Neusner. Judaism in Cold War America, 1945–1990, vol. 9. New York: Garland, 1993.
5. "*Am Yisrael:* Jews or Judaism?" *Judaism* 37 (1988): 199–209.
6. "1992 and Its Mythology: A Warning." *Jewish Spectator* 55 (1991): 26–30. Partial reprint in *Wexner Heritage Foundation Review* 3 (1991): 29–31.
7. "A Note on Research into Jewish Sexuality in the Medieval Period." In *Handbook of Medieval Sexuality*. Edited by Vern L. Bulluough and James A. Brundage, 309–17. New York: Garland, 1996.
8. "A Research Note on Sexuality and Muslim Civilization." In *Handbook of Medieval Sexuality*. Edited by Vern L. Bulluough and James A. Brundage, 319–27. New York: Garland, 1996.

Index

Only the most important towns and names are included. Not every citation of a modern author from the notes is indexed, but only the most important, or those discussed. Asterisks before names indicate conversos; names with asterisks and question marks indicate uncertainty.